The Books That Made the European Enlightenment

Cultures of Early Modern Europe

Series Editors: Beat Kümin, Professor of Early Modern European History, University of Warwick, UK, and Brian Cowan, Associate Professor and Canada Research Chair in Early Modern British History, McGill University, Canada

Editorial Board: Adam Fox, University of Edinburgh, UK
Robert Frost, University of Aberdeen, UK
Molly Greene, University of Princeton, USA
Ben Schmidt, University of Washington, USA
Gerd Schwerhoff, University of Dresden, Germany
Francsesca Trivellato, University of Yale, USA
Francisca Loetz, University of Zurich, Switzerland

The "cultural turn" in the humanities has generated a wealth of new research topics and approaches. Focusing on the ways in which representations, perceptions, and negotiations shaped people's lived experiences, the books in this series provide fascinating insights into the past. The series covers early modern culture in its broadest sense, inclusive of (but not restricted to) themes such as gender, identity, communities, mentalities, emotions, communication, ritual, space, food and drink, and material culture.

Published:
Food and Identity in England, 1540-1640, Paul S. Lloyd
The Birth of the English Kitchen, 1600-1850, Sara Pennell
Vagrancy in English Culture and Society, 1650-1750, David Hitchcock
Angelica's Book and the World of Reading in Late Renaissance Italy, Brendan Dooley
Gender, Culture and Politics in England, 1560-1640, Susan D. Amussen and David E. Underdown
Food, Religion, and Communities in Early Modern Europe, Christopher Kissane
Religion and Society at the Dawn of Modern Europe, Rudolf Schlögl
Power and Ceremony in European History: Rituals, Practices and Representative Bodies since the Late Middle Ages, Anna Kalinowska and Jonathan Spangler (eds.) with Pawel Tyszka
Private/Public in 18th-Century Scandinavia, Sari Nauman and Helle Vogt (eds.)
Catherine the Great and Celebrity Culture in the Eighteenth Century, Ruth Pritchard Dawson
The Books That Made the European Enlightenment: A History in 12 Case Studies, Gary Kates

The Books That Made the European Enlightenment

A History in 12 Case Studies

Gary Kates

BLOOMSBURY ACADEMIC
LONDON • NEW YORK • OXFORD • NEW DELHI • SYDNEY

BLOOMSBURY ACADEMIC
Bloomsbury Publishing Plc
50 Bedford Square, London, WC1B 3DP, UK
1385 Broadway, New York, NY 10018, USA
29 Earlsfort Terrace, Dublin 2, Ireland

BLOOMSBURY, BLOOMSBURY ACADEMIC and the Diana logo are trademarks of Bloomsbury Publishing Plc

First published in Great Britain 2022

Copyright © Gary Kates, 2022

Gary Kates has asserted their right under the Copyright, Designs and Patents Act, 1988, to be identified as Author of this work.

Cover image: Madame Francois Buron, 1769, by Jacques-Lous David
(© Art Institute of Chicago / Wikipedia)

All rights reserved. No part of this publication may be reproduced or transmitted in any form or by any means, electronic or mechanical, including photocopying, recording, or any information storage or retrieval system, without prior permission in writing from the publishers.

Bloomsbury Publishing Plc does not have any control over, or responsibility for, any third-party websites referred to or in this book. All internet addresses given in this book were correct at the time of going to press. The author and publisher regret any inconvenience caused if addresses have changed or sites have ceased to exist, but can accept no responsibility for any such changes.

Every effort has been made to trace copyright holders and to obtain their permissions for the use of copyright material. The publisher apologizes for any errors or omissions and would be grateful if notified of any corrections that should be incorporated in future reprints or editions of this book.

A catalogue record for this book is available from the British Library.

A catalog record for this book is available from the Library of Congress.

ISBN: HB: 978-1-3502-7764-9
PB: 978-1-3502-7765-6
ePDF: 978-1-3502-7766-3
eBook: 978-1-3502-7767-0

Typeset by Deanta Global Publishing Services, Chennai, India

To find out more about our authors and books visit www.bloomsbury.com and sign up for our newsletters.

Contents

List of Illustrations	vi
Acknowledgments	viii
Introduction	1
1 The Enlightenment Reading Public	7
2 Fénelon's *The Adventures of Telemachus* (1699)	41
3 Montesquieu's *Persian Letters* (1721)	75
4 Voltaire's *History of Charles XII* (1731) and Montesquieu's *Considerations on the Causes of the Greatness of the Romans and Their Decline* (1734)	97
5 Voltaire's *Philosophical Letters* (1733–4)	131
6 Richardson's *Pamela* (1740)	155
7 Hume's *Essays, Moral and Political* (1741–2)	177
8 Graffigny's *Letters of a Peruvian Woman* (1747)	201
9 Montesquieu's *The Spirit of the Laws* (1748)	219
10 Rousseau's *Emile* (1762)	255
11 Smith's *Wealth of Nations* (1776)	277
12 Raynal's *History of the Two Indies* (1770–80)	299
Notes	327
Bibliography of Works Cited	394
Index	427

Illustrations

Figures

1.1	Painting by Jacques Louis David of Madame Duron (1769)	7
2.1	First edition title page from Fénelon's *The Adventures of Telemachus*	41
2.2	First edition title page from the complete *The Adventures of Telemachus*	47
2.3	Mirabeau arrives at Elysian Fields	71
3.1	First edition title page Montesquieu's *Persian Letters*	75
4.1	First edition title page Voltaire's *History of Charles XII*	97
4.2	First edition title page Montesquieu's *Considerations on the Causes of the Greatness of the Romans and Their Decline*	97
4.3	Title page of the 1733 edition of *Charles XII* with Motraye's critical remarks and Voltaire's responses	108
4.4	Page 130 uncensored version of Montesquieu's *Considerations*	124
4.5	Page 130 censored version Montesquieu's *Considerations*	125
4.6	Page 131 of the uncensored Montesquieu's *Considerations*	126
4.7	Page 131 of the censored Montesquieu's *Considerations*	127
5.1	First edition title page Voltaire's *Philosophical Letters*	131
5.2	Title page English version *Voltaire's Letters Concerning an English Nation*	143
5.3	Title page from *Lettre philosophique de M. de V***...*	151
6.1	First edition title page Richardson's *Pamela*	155
7.1	First edition title page Hume's *Essays, Moral and Political*	177
8.1	First edition title page Graffigny's *Letters of a Peruvian Woman*	201
8.2	Second edition title page Graffigny's *Letters of a Peruvian Woman*, along with a frontispiece designed by Charles Eisen	213
9.1	First edition title page Montesquieu's *The Spirit of the Laws*	219
10.1	First edition title page Rousseau's *Emile*	255
11.1	First edition title page Smith's *Wealth of Nations*	277
12.1	1780 edition title page Raynal's *History of the Two Indies*	299
12.2	Frontispiece of 1780 edition showing the author's portrait	317
12.3	Painting: *Citizen Jean-Baptiste Belley, Ex-Representative of the Colonies* by Anne Louis Girodet	321
12.4	Toussaint Reading the Abbé Raynal's Work	324

Tables

2.1	Eighteenth-Century Editions of *The Telemachus*	43
3.1	Eighteenth-Century Editions of *Persian Letters*	77
4.1	Eighteenth-Century Editions of *Charles XII* and *Considerations*	99
4.2	Essays Voltaire Attached to His *History of Charles XII*	119
5.1	Eighteenth-Century Editions of *Philosophical Letters* in Various Versions	133
6.1	Eighteenth-Century Editions of *Pamela, Clarissa*, and *Sir Charles Grandison*	157
7.1	Eighteenth-Century Editions of *Essays: Moral and Political*	179
8.1	Eighteenth-Century Editions of *Letters of a Peruvian Woman*	203
9.1	Eighteenth-Century Editions of *The Spirit of the Laws*	221
9.2	Eighteenth-Century Editions for Montesquieu's Five Most Popular Books by Decade	226
9.3	Most Citations Referenced from *The Documentary History of the Ratification of the Constitution*	247
9.4	Most Cited Thinkers by Anti-Federalists	248
10.1	Eighteenth-Century Editions of *The New Heloise, Social Contract,* and *Emile*	257
11.1	Eighteenth-Century Editions of *Wealth of Nations*	279
11.2	Eighteenth-Century Editions of *Wealth of Nations* Published by Strahan and Cadell	284
12.1	Eighteenth-Century Editions of *History of the Two Indies*	301
12.2	The Three Versions of *History of the Two Indies*	301

Acknowledgments

Historians are obligated first and foremost to librarians, and those at the Honnold Library of the Claremont Colleges have guided and helped me, especially during these Covid years, when print collections were shut down and sharing books among libraries became especially difficult. The dogged dedication of the Honnold library staff is one key reason why you are able to read this book.

This book's origins lay in the dialog I've sustained with students in my annual fall first-year seminar on the Enlightenment, as well as in my upper-level class, Enlightenment and Capitalism. My debt is infinite to those students at Pomona College willing to engage in close reading of eighteenth-century texts. Brett Reilly is one student who made several important interventions that improved both the gist of the argument and the text's readability.

Jack Censer was there at the start of this project and I am eternally grateful for his support. Later, he read every page, making comments on paper and phone. Dena Goodman not only read every word of the manuscript, but her critical comments often caused me much rewriting, and while she is not responsible for the book's faults, her mark is apparent everywhere.

Early on, a lunch with Keith Baker proved instrumental. Another lunch with Nina Gelbart, who later read parts of the manuscript, was critically important to the way the book turned out. Charly Coleman helped me revise my understanding of the role Fénelon played in the Enlightenment. I appreciate his invitation to workshop the Fénelon chapter at a gathering of colleagues at Columbia University. I'm grateful to J. B. Shank for inviting me to speak to graduate students at the University of Minnesota about parts of the book and the database upon which it is based. Without Eileen Hunt Botting's critical help, I would not have been able to appreciate Louise Dupin's reading of Montesquieu.

My Pomona colleague Helena Wall read every page of the manuscript and her comments improved it immensely. I'm also grateful to Simon Burrows and Ken Loiselle for their careful reading of the manuscript.

Judith Lipsett has edited my books since the early 1980s and remains an ideal critic and reader.

Claremont California
March 9, 2022

Introduction

Scholarship by historians on the Enlightenment is not very old. Until the Second World War, the most important work was done by philosophers such as Ernst Cassirer and literary scholars such as Daniel Mornet and Paul Hazard. Occasionally there was an interesting book by an historian—for example, Carl Becker's 1932 classic, *The Heavenly City of the Eighteenth-Century Philosophers*—but these were usually idiosyncratic essays that did not inspire research by aspiring colleagues.[1] One important exception was the British historian Alfred Cobban, whose books and articles on the Enlightenment influenced many readers. But Cobban was criticized for writing too much like a political theorist. None of the techniques he later developed as a social historian were applied to the Enlightenment; he kept these two research interests far apart. And notably, few of his doctoral students trained to study the Enlightenment; most went on to specialize in empirically based social history.[2]

When Peter Gay, a Columbia-trained political scientist who taught European history at Yale University, began to publish Enlightenment history in the 1950s that culminated in the prize-winning two-volume *The Enlightenment* (1966 and 1969), he too privileged literary and philosophical questions because these had been the focus of scholarship. Influenced heavily by Cassirer, Gay accepted that the heart of the Enlightenment lay in its invention of new ideas—"Modern Paganism" provided his fundamental category. He credited the small group of writers around Voltaire, the philosophes who contributed to the *Encyclopédie*, whom Gay coined the Party of Humanity, as the main drivers of the movement. Gay portrayed the social and political context that made the philosophes such an effective group of authors. Influenced by the sociology of knowledge, Gay viewed the philosophes through a lens that contextualized their ideas through the struggles encountered by these upstarts. For this reason, he sometimes referred to his method as a social history of ideas, distinguishing it from the more textual pursuits of Mornet, Hazard, and Cassirer.[3]

Gay's approach still influences today's historians. We see it sparkle, for example, in Anthony Pagden's *The Enlightenment: And Why It Still Matters*. Its title reveals a focused agenda. In addition to establishing the context for Enlightenment ideas, Gay and Pagden are concerned with the legacy of the Enlightenment in today's world. For Gay, writing from the perspective of a Jewish refugee fleeing Nazi Europe, the Enlightenment served as the bedrock of a liberal democratic Western framework that formed the foundation of the European Union and NATO alliance.[4] Writing forty years later, Pagden defends Enlightenment values against attacks from both Left and Right, whose advocates see "the Enlightenment project" as either so skeptical and disrespectful of religion that it cannot serve as any sort of bedrock for Western culture, or so full of arrogance from its supposed universalism that it abets Western imperialism and colonialism, as well as male hegemony. For Pagden, the Enlightenment "was about creating a field of values, political, social, and moral, based upon a detached and scrupulous understanding of what it means to be human. And today most educated people, at least in the West, broadly accept the conclusion to which it led."[5] Like Gay, Pagden champions the philosophes as the founders of modern liberalism.

Nonetheless, Gay's and Pagden's arguments carry excessive literary and philosophical baggage. By focusing attention on the Enlightenment's trajectory toward modernity, Gay and Pagden misconstrue the place of the Enlightenment within eighteenth-century Europe. Borrowing from philosophers and literary critics, they play down the historical quality of the Enlightenment as a set of events that developed over time, instead conceiving its ideas as a timeless and philosophical advance. Ignoring readers and publishers, they focus almost exclusively on authors, as if their ideas are humanity's software that can be activated in any century. Pagden replaces contemporary "educated people" for the reactions of readers during the eighteenth century. However, while twenty-first-century readers may reinterpret Enlightenment ideas, they are no longer making the Enlightenment. Nor were Enlightenment books produced solely by the philosophes. The making of the Enlightenment canon was an intensely collaborative process among readers, bookseller/publishers, and authors that occurred only during the eighteenth century. When some today call for "Enlightenment Now," they may be suggesting good ideas for addressing contemporary problems, but they explain little about how those ideas were produced 300 years ago, and the significance they held for the active readers living at that time.[6] While literary specialists, philosophers, and political theorists may find much nourishment in the Enlightenment's liberal values, historians—bound by the principle of periodization—must acknowledge that the Enlightenment was a thoroughly eighteenth-century phenomenon, well over by 1815, if not by 1789. When historians approach the Enlightenment as an historical event involving readers, authors, and publishers, it becomes clearer that it was produced by a developing critical reading public that emerged in Europe and its overseas colonies.

At least that was the conclusion of a young Robert Darnton, who, in a 1971 manifesto in the guise of a review article about Gay's work, set the course for a cultural history of the Enlightenment that was independent of the modernizing concerns of literature, philosophy, and political theory. Along with French colleagues Roger Chartier and Daniel Roche, Darnton insisted that a social history of ideas should start not with notions in the heads of authors, but with an understanding of how ideas became social in the first place; that is, how organized systems of thought were transmitted throughout complex societies, such as those that existed during the eighteenth century. This meant, first and foremost, an understanding of the book trade in all its aspects, since the distribution of books and periodicals determined the spread of ideas in eighteenth-century Europe. In that sense, Darnton, Roche, and Chartier may have been the first historians of the eighteenth-century Enlightenment to place historical questions at the center of their enterprise, rather than concerns borrowed from literature, philosophy, and political theory.[7]

Darnton set his sights on writing the history of the greatest Enlightenment publishing project, Diderot and d'Alembert's twenty-eight volume *Encyclopédie* and its successors. In what is still among the best monographs in the nascent field of early modern book history, Darnton's *Business of Enlightenment* (1979) focused not on the authors of its many influential articles, nor on its values or progressive ideas, but rather on how this French work became so popular despite its legal suppression in 1759. Darnton meticulously showed the complicity among booksellers, printers, government censors, police spies, and even church officials that operated in France and among its neighbors. Perhaps for the first time, students of the Enlightenment began to see that its significance lay not only in its bold ideas, but also in the novel institutions surrounding the book trade that made such ideas available across Europe and, indeed, throughout the European colonial world.[8]

After *Business of Enlightenment*, Darnton investigated the relationship of the Enlightenment to the overall book trade during the late eighteenth century. How did ideas penetrate into society two centuries ago? What was the connection between the Enlightenment and the French Revolution? Although these questions had once preoccupied literary historian Daniel Mornet,[9] they were addressed very differently by Darnton, whose research culminated in the twin volumes *The Corpus of Clandestine Literature in France 1769–1789* and *The Forbidden Best-Sellers of Pre-Revolutionary France*, both published in 1995.[10] In these studies, Darnton argued that while the philosophes were represented among the best-selling authors in eighteenth-century France, they were eclipsed by the popularity of more salacious, lowbrow literature that mixed libertine erotica and atheism. During the 1770s and 1780s, if not well before, "the seemingly self-evident distinction between pornography and philosophy begins to break down."[11] While the more libertine work of the philosophes was still present in Darnton's list of bestsellers, the more formal works of political theory were gone—Hume's *Essays*, Montesquieu's *The Spirit of the Laws*, Rousseau's *Social Contract*, and Smith's *The Wealth of Nations* made, according to Darnton, little direct impact on the pre-revolutionary European public. Cultural historians such as Peter Gay had overvalued their importance for the eighteenth-century reader. The French Revolutionaries had grown up reading libels of royal mistresses instead of more theoretical criticisms of France's monarchical constitution.

The way in which Darnton uses book history, the history of reading, and reception studies as vehicles for a larger social and cultural history is a model that inspires imitation. The debt historians owe him is deep and abiding. However, there are three criticisms that I have with Darnton's work, at least as represented first in *Forbidden Best-Sellers of Pre-Revolutionary France*, and more recently in *A Literary Tour de France*.[12] First, Darnton's central archival repository, the Société typographique de Neuchâtel (StN) archive, covers only a twenty-year period between 1769 and 1789, that is, well after much of the Enlightenment had already developed. The work of Hume, Richardson, Graffigny, Voltaire, Montesquieu, and much of Rousseau had been first published before the StN was established. At best, the records of the StN highlight the

Enlightenment's sunset years, but they inform us less about how the Enlightenment was actually made. Second, Darnton's work is concerned primarily with the Enlightenment in France, because his overall aim is to investigate the relationship of the Enlightenment with the outbreak of the French Revolution. Viewing the Enlightenment as a precursor to revolution, however, obscures its European and cosmopolitan nature. After all, most Enlightenment books were produced and consumed outside France. Third, by no means is it clear that the StN was representative of other bookseller/publishers at the time. The StN may have found a niche in certain areas of publishing, and its customers may have ordered different books from other more competitive publishers.[13] Ironically, Darnton followed Alfred Cobban in separating his innovative social history of eighteenth-century books from a more traditional view of Enlightenment culture.[14]

The StN lens may also obscure the vital role played by women in the Enlightenment's making. As this study will make clear, women participated fully in the European Enlightenment as authors, publishers, and especially readers. Graffigny's *Letters of a Peruvian Woman* went through ninety-five eighteenth-century editions, making it among the century's top bestsellers, even though only thirty-four copies were sold by the StN. Likewise, women sometimes took over publishing firms following the deaths of their husbands, which is how Fénelon's *Telemachus* and Montesquieu's *Persian Letters* were originally published. As for women readers, this study leans on the work of Dena Goodman regarding the contributions of Enlightenment women.[15]

Alongside the work of Darnton and Goodman have been two huge scholarly projects by historians Franco Venturi and Jonathan Israel, involving many volumes and thousands of pages on the Enlightenment that have made an oversized impact on the field. Venturi (1914–94) published the first volume of *Settecento Riformatore* in 1969, and by 1990, he had produced almost 4,000 pages in 6 volumes. Where Darnton and Goodman write from a French perspective, Venturi's work demonstrates how closely the Enlightenment in Italy mirrored issues at the heart of the Enlightenment in other countries. Where the early volumes focused on Naples and Tuscany, the central volumes cover Europe as a whole. For Venturi, the Enlightenment was a European response to the crisis in the framework of modern monarchies. Calcified with remnants of feudalism, burdened with impoverished peasantries, obligated to fight expensive wars, and thrown into competition for global commerce, Enlightenment writers suggested ways for monarchies to reform themselves. The limits, failures, and some successes of these efforts form the basis of Venturi's narratives. Montesquieu is a key figure for Venturi, precisely because his work seemed to brilliantly elucidate the strengths and weaknesses of eighteenth-century European monarchies. "He was the real arbiter and lord of political thought of his time," Venturi said in a well-known 1971 lecture. As Venturi's younger colleagues have demonstrated, the view that Montesquieu was a practical reformer of monarchy is why the key political economists of the 1750s and 1760s, such as François Véron de Forbonnais and Antonio Genovesi, became so tied to him.[16]

My definition of the Enlightenment closely follows the work of Venturi acolyte John Robertson, who makes four broad claims: first, the Enlightenment was a "movement" that expanded well beyond small groups of elite writers. Second, this movement was dedicated to the social improvement of humanity and public happiness. Third, that while each country contributed distinctive aspects to the movement, there was nonetheless a cosmopolitan unity from Philadelphia to St. Petersburg that gave it a broadly European perspective. Finally, Robertson argues that the rise of eighteenth-century political economy, both as a theoretical discipline and especially as policy options for governments, best illustrates the Enlightenment's success upon reforming eighteenth-century European society.[17]

Like Venturi, Israel's multivolume Enlightenment history is told from a genuinely European perspective. With considerable erudition, across a range of languages, Israel documents the close circuits among authors, including many subversive ones. The result highlights the followers of the Dutch-Jewish philosopher Spinoza and traces a cleavage between what Israel insists are Moderate and Radical strands of the Enlightenment. Unfortunately, Israel ignores the social history of reading. He seems uninterested in the institutions surrounding the book trade—printers, booksellers, circulating libraries, the reading patterns, and buying habits of middling people—that made the Enlightenment particularly widespread. Often Israel gives equal weight to a best-selling political treatise and an underground manuscript, even though the later may have been read by fewer than fifty people. Israel's formulation, however innovative, rests upon a traditional history of ideas in the mold of Gay, Cassirer, Mornet, and Hazard.[18]

Israel argues that writers such as Spinoza and Diderot were far more radical than Voltaire or Montesquieu because of their atheism and commitment to democracy. But here perhaps Israel misunderstands the radical quality of these so-called Moderates. In this book, I argue that what made Voltaire, Montesquieu, and others radical was the ways in which their books helped to give agency to an expanding critical reading public. As I narrate especially in Chapters 9–12, the works of Montesquieu, Rousseau, Smith, and Raynal/Diderot together initiated a radical transformation of the European book trade that popularized books about politics and political economy.

This book is based on an original online database of 7,500 records developed at Pomona College, divided into bibliographical checklists of editions for some 250 titles published between 1700 and 1800.[19] The list builds on Richard Sher's method of determining book popularity by counting up a title's number of editions. For Sher, ten or more eighteenth-century editions qualify as a bestseller.[20] Where Sher's study concerns only Scottish authors published within the UK (and its colonies), my database includes titles produced in any language. Likewise, I decided that for the bestseller category, a book must have been produced in at least three languages. In the database, each of the top fifty titles went through at least thirty editions and all but four were published in three or more languages. In the following chapters, I sample twelve bestsellers from this group based on the following criteria: (1) enough documentary evidence to narrate the book's history; (2) representation across the century from the 1720s to the 1780s, so that we can study how the Enlightenment developed over time; and (3) books from different viewpoints and sectors of Enlightenment book publishing, so that repetition is minimized.

The result is a list of bestsellers that differs markedly from Darnton's in minimizing the role of hack writers and obscene literature, restoring well-known books traditionally considered hallmarks of Enlightenment political thought. For example, if we compare Darnton's bestsellers with mine, juxtaposing editions produced solely in those years studied by Darnton (1769–89), we find that Rousseau's *Social Contract* went through twenty-three editions and *Emile* thirty-two, while Pidansat de Mairobert's gossipy biography of Madame de Barry went through only thirteen; likewise where Montesquieu's Roman history garnered fifty editions, the obscene novel *Thérèse Philosophe* went through only eight. Enlightenment political theory held its own against political pornography.[21]

The Books That Made the European Enlightenment narrates the histories of some of the most popular Enlightenment books. Chapter 1 introduces the different roles played by readers, publishers, and authors in making the Enlightenment. From there, Chapters 2–12 are case studies in the composition, distribution, and reception of canonic Enlightenment bestsellers. Presenting these books chronologically allows us to see the Enlightenment's internal development. For example, readers in the 1770s, such as the Portuguese university students featured at the beginning of Chapter 3, read *Persian Letters* quite differently than their counterparts in the 1720s. A book such as Fénelon's *Telemachus* remained popular through the century, but its meaning shifted from one generation to another. In this sense the production of an Enlightenment canon was itself a series of dynamic events.

Such a case-study approach allows us to see up close the extent to which books and the book trade were central to making the Enlightenment a pervasive and impactful phenomenon across eighteenth-century Europe. Of course, there is a difference between the most popular Enlightenment books and the books most popular in eighteenth-century society at large. The books discussed in this study are not meant to identify the titles most in demand throughout society; such works, as Chartier argued decades ago, included the Bible, devotional works, chapbooks, and almanacs.[22] The importance of Enlightenment books is not that they were among the most popular in the overall book trade, but rather, that for the first time in European history, such books became widely read at all. If we already knew that Montesquieu and Rousseau were among the eighteenth century's most important political philosophers, this cliché has allowed scholars to obscure the insight that Montesquieu, Rousseau, Smith, and Raynal/Diderot[23] may also have been the first political theorists in European history whose books were read by a wide audience. Before this period there were few philosophers whose books made their authors famous during their own lifetime. Machiavelli, Hobbes, Pufendorf, Leibniz, and Grotius were arguably better known among readers in the second half of the eighteenth century than in their own day. Only during the eighteenth century did political theorists gain traction in the European book trade. In this sense, the heart of Enlightenment culture, and perhaps its defining historical significance, is precisely the popularization of political thought through books made possible through the development of a European reading public.

Chapter 1

Figure 1.1 Painting by Jacques Louis David of Madame Duron (1769). Madame Duron was the aunt of the artist, who lived in her home for a period of his youth. Here she is portrayed as an avid reader at home, perhaps annoyed at the interruption.

Chapter 1
The Enlightenment Reading Public

Readers and Their Libraries

In 1783, the German-Jewish philosopher and venerated sage of the European Enlightenment Moses Mendelssohn went on a tirade about reading and writing. His complaint was not that there was too little reading in Europe, but that there was too much. Instead of walking to each other's homes and conversing in person, he argued, Europeans read books and wrote letters about one another. Rather than learn from a mentor face to face, they preferred to remain in their libraries with their faces stuck in books:

> We teach and instruct one another only through writings. We learn to know nature and man only from writings. We work and relax, edify and amuse ourselves through too much writing. The preacher does not converse with his congregation. He reads or declaims to it a written treatise. The professor reads his written lectures from the chair. Everything is a dead letter. The spirit of living conversation has vanished.[1]

For Mendelssohn, too much reading and writing had "many evil consequences." We don't know one another as well as we did before, he claimed. The enlightened community of scholars—the Republic of Letters—was less hospitable than it used to be. It was far easier, Mendelssohn despaired, for scholars to fight one another through correspondence and publication than to work out their differences in person. For him, the development of the printed book had created an impersonal world of strangers, who no longer cared to speak with each other. To put it plainly, scholars had become unsociable nerds who preferred print to people. "We are literati, men of letters. Our whole being depends on letters, and we can scarcely comprehend how a moral man can educate and perfect himself without a *book*."

The source of Mendelssohn's jeremiad, *Jerusalem*, is usually considered a landmark text for endorsing religious toleration. But it also represents a peculiar moment in the history of the Enlightenment, in which one of its deans laments the movement's addiction to books. For Mendelssohn, even relationships with friends and family were affected by a reliance on reading and writing instead of intimate conversation. "We express our love and anger in letters, quarrel and become reconciled in letters. All our personal relations are by correspondence, and when we get together, we know of no other entertainment than playing or *reading aloud*." By cutting ourselves off from other people, even immediate family, he believed, our learning comes at the expense of our humanity. What some today see as dangers inherent in social media, Mendelssohn presciently understood as a consequence of Gutenberg's printing press.

Mendelssohn's lament was idiosyncratic, but his basic observation regarding the ubiquity of reading became commonplace during the eighteenth century. Another German, while visiting Paris, noticed how "everyone, especially the women, has a book in his pocket. Women, children, workmen, apprentices read in the shops. On Sundays the people who sit on their doorsteps read. Lackeys read behind coaches, coachmen up on their seats, soldiers at their quarters and commissionnaires at their posts."[2] When Françoise de Graffigny's fictional Inca princess, Zelia, arrives in Europe, she is most impressed with the prevalence of books all around her. "I can see that they are to the soul what the Sun is to the earth."[3] Lady Mary Wortley Montagu surely would have understood Mendelssohn's critique but would have strongly disagreed with it: "No entertainment is so cheap as reading, nor any pleasure so lasting," she remarked. "There is no remedy so easy as books, which if they do not give cheerfulness at least restore quiet to the most troubled mind."[4] During the eighteenth century, witnesses attest reading's ubiquity: "We are no longer in an era where journals are made only for savants. Now everyone reads and wants to read about everything."[5]

Two hundred years after Mendelssohn, the notion of an emerging reading public became the cornerstone of another German philosopher. Jürgen Habermas's influential book, *The Structural Transformation of the Public Sphere* (1962), transmuted Mendelssohn's insight into a fully forged analysis of European cultural history, albeit one shorn of any regret over the invention of the printing press. During the Middle Ages, Habermas argued, there was no distinction between the public authority of the state and the private sphere of individual subjects. As governments slowly centralized around the notion of sovereignty, early modern states began to recognize a private sphere that lay outside but was ultimately obedient to state authority. Here was the start of the modern idea of "civil society." Habermas gave Mendelssohn's insight a Marxist spin, focusing on the role of capitalist markets, international commerce, and notions of private property. Yet he also recognized a cultural sphere in which the middle and upper classes networked through reading clubs, public libraries, Masonic lodges, urban salons, academies, coffeehouses, provincial academies, and other types of civic institutions that usually lay outside church or state. Together these novel institutions made up the "public sphere," which was characterized by three essential elements: a commitment to openness and publicity that implied hostility to secrecy; an acceptance that no topic was immune from criticism; and, finally, an understanding that reason (rather than personal status or identity) was the sole standard for judging debate.[6]

More specifically, the public sphere recognized by Habermas (and Mendelssohn) was a literary culture governed by a reading public, where the broad circulation of printed works galvanized a new virtual community. The epistolary novel, which emerged as a popular form of fiction during the early eighteenth century, best reflected for Habermas the new values of this literary public sphere. Here was a genre that took the intimate details of private letters and, through publication, offered them for scrutiny to a critical public. Habermas gave much credit to Samuel Richardson's *Pamela* for awakening the European public during the 1740s, and for significantly altering the roles among readers and authors. "The relations between author, work, and public changed," noted Habermas. "They became intimate mutual relationships between privatized individuals who were psychologically interested in what was 'human,' in self-knowledge, and in empathy. Richardson wept over the characters in his novels as much as his readers did; author and reader themselves became actors who 'talked heart to heart.'" Habermas also credited Montesquieu's *The Spirit of the Laws* as the text most responsible for aligning political theory with this new expression of public opinion.[7]

Habermas's claim was not simply that epistolary novels and political treatises became popular, but, rather, that institutions were developed around them that made participants more active and known to one another. "The privatized individuals coming together to form a public also reflected critically and in public on what they had read, thus contributing to the process of enlightenment which they together promoted. Two years after *Pamela* appeared on the literary scene the first public library was founded; book clubs, reading circles, and subscription libraries shot up."[8] Both Mendelssohn and Habermas claimed, then, that more people were reading more books during the eighteenth century than ever before, and that consequently these books became more culturally significant than ever. Printed books may have been around since Gutenberg invented moveable type in the fifteenth century, and to be sure, it was not unusual for ordinary Europeans of the early modern period to own copies of the Bible, chapbooks, and almanacs. However, novels and poetry, as well as books about history, ethics, science, and politics, were generally unavailable to most of the population before 1700. What Mendelssohn decried and what Habermas embraced was that eighteenth-century elites acquired new hunger for books, sometimes going to great expense and traveling distances to obtain them. While universal reading must wait until the nineteenth century, its foundations were laid during the eighteenth when reading became a popular social practice.[9]

The core of Habermas's notion of a reading public, in fact, is found in the writing of the Enlightenment's most famous philosopher, Immanuel Kant. In his answer to the question, "What is Enlightenment?" posed in 1783 by the Berlin periodical *Berlinische Monatsschrift*, Kant distinguished between the enlightenment of an individual and the emergence of an enlightened public. "But that a public [*Publikum*] should enlighten itself is more likely [than an individual]; indeed it is nearly inevitable, if only it is granted freedom." In this context, what Kant meant by freedom was the ability to criticize; that is, to disagree with and contest both ideas and government policies. According to Kant, an enlightened public was first and foremost a community that discouraged blind obedience and conformity.

For this enlightenment, however, nothing more is required than *freedom*; and indeed the most harmless form of all the things that may be called freedom: namely, the freedom to make a *public use* of one's reason in all matters. But I hear from all sides the cry: *don't argue*! The officer says: "Don't argue, but rather march!" The tax collector says: "Don't argue, but rather pay!" The clergyman says: "Don't argue, but rather believe!" (Only one ruler [Prussian King Frederick the Great] in the world says: "*Argue*, as much as you want and about whatever you want, *but obey*!") . . . .I understand, however, under the public use of his own reason, that use which anyone makes of it *as a scholar* before the entire public of the *reading world*.

Kant went on to say that a civil servant cannot speak out against the orders of a superior, but no one has the right to prevent him from publishing an article in a periodical that advocates a new policy or set of actions. Likewise, the taxpayer must pay his taxes, but he nonetheless has a right to "express his thoughts publicly on the inappropriateness or even the injustice of such taxes." Citizens who obeyed the state had every right to subject its policies to criticism; indeed, they had the obligation to do so.[10]

Reading books that challenged government policies became a preoccupation for this emerging public during the eighteenth century. Indeed, such books contributed to the invention of the modern notion of civil society itself.[11] Often the first books one learned to read were religious and devotional works that never went out of fashion. But over the years the percentage of secular titles began to outpace religious books. One study of 500 catalogs of private libraries in France between 1750 and 1780 suggests a sharp rise in the number of books devoted to literature, science, arts, and especially history at the expense of theology. At the Leipzig Book Fair, religious books declined from 38.5 percent in 1740 to 13.5 percent in 1800. The same trend can be seen at the Gray Library in the small town of Haddington, Scotland, where theological borrowings plummeted during the eighteenth century and were replaced by dramatically rising interest in history and biography. Meanwhile, a similar development occurred in Naples, where after rising in the first half of the century, the sale of religious books fell moderately in the second half. While European culture remained intensely religious, the publication of Enlightenment books reflected growing secularization within the book trade.[12]

Kant's abstraction of the new reading public as embodying the "public use of his own reason" may be somewhat idealistic, but it at least partially reflects the critical manner in which European readers approached their books. It was not until much later in the century—the 1770s and 1780s—that authors emerged as celebrities and readers became literary fans. Until then, readers were often genuinely critical of one another when discussing their books. Indeed, it was quite common for readers to recommend a book to a friend, even though they had profound disagreements with the author. The most important reason for praising an author was not whether one agreed with their positions, but whether their arguments were engaging and their writing style elegant. "It's really quite shocking, my dear sister, that such an old wretch, loaded with infirmities, just going out of the world, should take the trouble to disturb those who are so happy as to enjoy the only thing that makes life comfortable in it," wrote Caroline Fox, 1st Baronness Holland, about Voltaire's *Philosophical Dictionary*. "I have quite a horror for him; but

I comfort myself he is little qualified to convince people's understanding, tho' he has in my opinion more talents to divert their fancy than any author I ever read."[13] Clearly Lady Holland found Voltaire's book despicable and viewed its author as hostile to her most cherished values. Yet, it is also clear that she found his book worth reading, and obviously very much worth discussing with friends and relatives. Nowhere in her vast correspondence did she call for any type of censorship or legal campaign against those in her own country who published Voltaire's works. While she found his ideas abhorrent, she was not inclined to use her aristocratic influence to silence them. Likewise, while the Surinamese Jewish writer David Nassy strongly regretted Voltaire's anti-Semitism, he nonetheless appreciated his overall commitment to religious toleration. A similar critical attitude toward Montesquieu is found in the reaction of the Finnish Protestant minister Anders Chydenius, who was able to read the philosophe in Swedish translation. Likewise, Elizabeth Vesey continued to read Raynal's *History of the Two Indies*, even though she acknowledged him to be a "licentious profligate infidel." Her friend pleaded with her to put down the book. "You well know that from sources such as these no solid comfort can be derived, why then will you idly spend your time in reading what ought never to have been written? But you do it, you say, merely for amusement: 'tis dangerous amusement to a mind like yours, indeed to any mind."[14]

The emergence of a critical reading public was not limited to France, Holland, Prussia, and England, but extended, if more sparsely, throughout Europe. In Romania, Moldova, and Hungary, Enlightenment works became well known, at least by scholarly elites. The Transylvanian Count Ignatius Battyani, for example, established a large library in Alba Iulia (then in Hungary, today Romania), which stocked many Enlightenment books, including one of the earliest editions of Voltaire's *History of Charles XII*.[15] In Italy, commentators noted in particular how vibrant the book industry there had become. In his journal, *Il Caffè*, meant to be distributed to Milan coffeehouses, Pietro Verri noted that reading books had become a ubiquitous feature of elite culture there. "The public reads more than it ever has, perhaps even since the invention of writing." The result was not only a boon to writers but also represented a considerable elevation of standards that set a high bar for new authors. This public, Verri claimed, no longer tolerated poorly written books. Authors were on notice that their books must now exhibit "order, clarity, and grace," or they would rot on bookstalls. Verri remarked that the Republic of Letters, which had in previous times been insular and driven by patronage, was now beholden to an emerging reading public.

> A book is not something reserved only for those in isolated study, used under the pale light of an old lamp, as in centuries long ago, by an unkept scholar looking like some kind of human monster. A book is found in the most elegantly decorated rooms; a book is found on the vanities of the most lovable ladies; a book is read so long as the author has the talent to write.[16]

This Habermasian public sphere expanded into communities where no Parisian philosophe dared venture. From Halifax, Nova Scotia, we find reader "Atticus" responded virtually to Mendelssohn in the pages of the *Nova Scotia Gazette*: "To read for delight and profit is a most rational way of employing a part of our time, and is what in this happy age and country, people of all classes, that can read at all, may do, in greater or less variety." Even near the world's edge in northeastern Canada (the entire population of Nova Scotia in 1762 was 8,000), reading books had become commonplace, and readers were pulled together by clubs and libraries. "The institution of library companies, in neighborhoods, both in town and country," noted Atticus, "have [sic] contributed greatly to the love of reading, as well as furnished opportunities to gratify it." It is notable that Atticus made no mention of devotional works, instead highlighting how novels entertained and delighted their readers while also improving their character. He urged his countrymen to return again and again to "Fénelon, Fielding, and Richardson [who] ought unquestionably to be considered as excellent in their kind, and cannot be read to any bad purpose." For Atticus, unlike Mendelssohn, there was no such thing as too much reading. All reading, of any kind, done anywhere, was a vehicle for self-improvement. "I will venture to say, that I do not believe a very wicked man can delight much in reading of any kind," he wrote, because reading will invariably make a wicked man virtuous.[17]

The more people read books, the more they needed places to store them. In fact, everywhere we look we see libraries proliferating during the eighteenth century. Tremendous growth in the private libraries of wealthy noblemen and book collectors is evident across Europe. Libraries became important rooms in grand houses, not simply as storerooms for books, but as venues for social activity in the midst of books, where learning could be visually displayed, if not demonstrated. In eighteenth-century Ireland and Scotland, a room showing off books became a necessary element of any grand home. The Duke of Argyll's extraordinary collection of over 12,100 volumes was housed mostly in his London mansion that friends came to refer to as "the library." In Lyon, Pierre Adamoli assembled an army of 6,000 volumes, while in London the exiled transgender diplomat the Chevalière d'Eon amassed a similar-sized library, which included what may have been the world's largest collection of Horace. Early in his career, Adam Smith helped spread Enlightenment ideas when, as Librarian for the University of Glasgow, he ordered a partial set of Diderot and d'Alembert's *Encyclopédie* for its library. In Hanover, a sister to Frederick the Great collected a library of 4,000 volumes focused on Enlightenment classics by David Hume, Jean-Jacques Rousseau, Voltaire, and others. A growing number of noblemen across Europe made their libraries available to the public. These large noble libraries were often staffed by a librarian, who sometimes retrieved books for borrowers to keep them from coming into the house.[18]

In Paris before 1750, at least fifteen wealthy bibliophiles had established libraries of more than 10,000 titles. The rise of such libraries was publicly recognized in 1709 when the annual *Almanach Royal* began listing the most prominent ones. At the same time, there was strong growth in the number of more modest libraries of 100–500 books. These libraries were not necessarily owned by men: According to Anne Beroujon, the number of books in female-run estates was no different than in male estates.[19] As David

Allan argues, the Enlightenment's most vibrant location was "surely in the library."[20] As the value of libraries increases, we find heightened anxiety over fire danger.[21]

The private libraries of wealthy collectors were magnets of social networking, especially in the countryside, where booksellers were few and far between. Often visits were planned with reading books in mind. When the Brodie or Russell sisters visited their friend, Elizabeth Rose, Lady of Kilravock, at her estate near Inverness in Northwest Scotland during the 1780s and 1790s, they were enchanted by her collection of some 2,000 books, and passed warm summer afternoons "agreeably in reading, walking, music and conversation." Despite her already enormous collection, Rose carefully plotted to obtain even more books through her friends. "Try if you can get the 3rd vol: of Raynal [*History of the Two Indies*] from Altyre [an estate seventeen miles away]," she wrote to one friend, "for I'm near done the 2nd . . . Will you try?"[22]

Middle-class families took great pride in the modest libraries they amassed. One British family owned around sixty books, sharing such classics as Locke, Montesquieu, and Mandeville among relatives and friends.[23] Books were often in such demand that they became objects of theft. In 1743, Thomas Thompson had over 100 books in the library of his modest summer cottage in Weybridge, a small Surrey town southwest of London. One day he came home to find that a burglar had bored a hole through an outside wall and taken off with all of his books. Soon after a Miss Hannah White was caught attempting to sell Thompson's books. She was promptly arrested and tried for grand larceny.[24] A few years after this incident, University of St Andrews professor Robert Watson allowed investigators to break into the personal closet of student David Ramsay. There they found sixty-two books that Ramsay had stolen from the university library, including works by Voltaire, Addison, and Adam Smith.[25]

As libraries grew in early modern Europe, so did a self-conscious culture of bibliophiles. An early example was Pierre Le Gallois' *Traité des plus belles bibliothèques de l'Europe* [Treatise on the Most Beautiful European Libraries] (1680), which introduced readers to the great libraries of France at the time of Louis XIV. Soon there even emerged a kind of library tourism, in which adventurers journeyed hundreds of miles to visit book collections. Friedrich Karl Gottlob Hirsching (1762–1800) and Adalbert Blumenschein (1720–81) were two striking examples. Hirsching, a professor at the University of Erlangen, visited over 300 libraries mainly in German-speaking Europe. Blumenschein, who was a priest and the librarian of an Austrian church and pilgrimage site, visited almost 400 libraries and researched over 2,400 others, making his compendium the largest known inventory of libraries in eighteenth-century Europe. They described or visited all sorts of libraries—public and private, personal and institutional. Once, when Blumenschein was making the rounds of the libraries in Verona (Italy), he was rudely refused entry into the Franciscan monastery library. Blumenschein asked for help from the monk in charge. "He remained sitting, leaned on his right hand, and looked at me for a good while without uttering a word. Finally, he said with a scornful look that the books were for them and not for strangers, since it really wasn't advisable to allow just anybody to look in them." Needless to say, such behavior was rare; most libraries welcomed him and he took copious notes on all of them.[26]

In cities and towns throughout Europe, the new demand for book reading was often met through the establishment of circulating and subscription libraries. Circulating libraries were usually begun by booksellers as a way of extending profits to a rental market. For a set fee (weekly, monthly, or annually), customers could rent, rather than purchase, the books they desired. In Weymouth during the 1780s, the bookseller James Love named his library "The Pantheon of Taste." It was open from 6:00 a.m. to 10:00 p.m. and included over 100 newspapers and journals. Many readers got their start in literature at circulating libraries like this one. "After the trials of the day were past, the little I could snatch from sleep was devoted to the perusal of such books as the library could supply," wrote one working-class teenager at the turn of the nineteenth century:

> Often have I trudged, in the dark winter nights, a distance of several miles, through wind and rain, to get my books exchanged. I read much of History, Biography, Voyages, Travels, almost all the old Dramatic Poets, of whom I was passionately fond, and the majority of the English Classics. In this way I laid in a considerable stock of miscellaneous knowledge while yet very young.[27]

The future economist David Ricardo first encountered Smith's *Wealth of Nations* when the twenty-seven-year-old banker was browsing in a circulating library in Bath.[28] Women supposedly used circulating libraries to find new novels. The *Annual Register* noted derisively that "the reading female hires her novels from some country circulating library."[29] Meanwhile *The Lady's Magazine* offered a more sympathetic observation: "Look at the popular books of a circulating library and you will find the binding cracked by quantities of [hair] powder and pomatum between the leaves."[30]

French circulating libraries also developed during the eighteenth century. In Paris one promised a heated reading room without any literature that might anger church or state. In Montpellier, readers could easily obtain works of Voltaire or Rousseau in the circulating library operated by bookseller Abraham Fontanel. In Lyon, France's second-most-populous city, the bookseller Claude Morlet started a circulation library adjacent to his store in 1769. For an annual fee of twenty-four livres, customers could have access to a large reading room or check out books for a few days. By 1772, Morlet advertised almost 2,000 titles in his library. Yet Morlet's was not as extensive as Pierre Cellier's nearby library with almost 4,000 titles, run more or less in the same fashion. What Louis Sebastian Mercier wrote in his *Tableau de Paris* in 1782 is probably an exaggeration but may nonetheless contain a kernel of truth: "There are works that incite such ferment that the bookseller is obliged to cut the volume in three parts in order to be able to satisfy the pressing demands of many readers; in this case you pay not by the day but by the hour."[31]

Circulating libraries made Enlightenment bestsellers available to a set of readers who would otherwise have had little access to expensive books. For example, despite its illegal status, Raynal's *History of the Two Indies* was available in the Poitiers circulating library established by the bookseller Jean François Chevrier.[32] Sometimes circulating library operators saw themselves as doing much more than simply running a rental business; they viewed themselves as de facto educators. "I can say that I have contributed to increasing the mass of knowledge by means of this establishment," a Grenoble bookseller wrote of his circulating library. "Because of me," he insisted, powerful people are more learned, women and businessmen have made reading a habit. "There has been a general revolution and my circulating library has affected all classes." Young people had learned to think earlier about how to develop their ideas, the bookseller claimed; even soldiers had improved their manners because they were better educated. "In a nutshell, I have helped to train men of letters."[33]

If circulation libraries provided a way for booksellers to become secular ministers, subscription libraries were sites of self-improvement. Subscription libraries were not-for-profit associations of like-minded people who formed a committee to select books, and paid dues to purchase them. They set rules for borrowing and arranged for the books to be housed somewhere. Some subscription libraries allowed their collections to grow over time, while others quickly sold off volumes that were no longer of interest. These libraries extended beyond Europe to the colonies—Benjamin Franklin's Library Company, established in Philadelphia in 1731, was the earliest known subscription library in the Americas. Many readers encountered Enlightenment books for the first time in these libraries, and these books were often among a library's most popular offerings. While *The Spirit of the Laws* was checked out from the Bristol Library only fifteen times between 1773 and 1784, works by Hume, Voltaire, and Rousseau were well worn, and the Abbé Raynal's *History of the Two Indies* was borrowed 173 times, making it the fifth-most-popular work in that library.[34] Likewise, Raynal was checked out twenty-one times between 1796 and 1799 from the Wigtown library, and sixty-five times between 1774 and 1789 from Gray Library in Haddington, both remote areas in rural Scotland. The Enlightenment was not only represented in subscription libraries, but it was a magnet that attracted patrons.[35]

The Liverpool subscription library was typical in its organization. Begun in mid-century largely by successful professionals, teachers, and ministers, this library had 140 members around 1750, 300 in 1760, and 400 in 1770. Strict rules agreed upon by all members through voting by ballot governed the library. In addition to an annual membership payment of five shillings, its leadership set the entrance fee of one guinea, raising it to five by the end of the century. The membership at large annually elected a sixteen-member board that effectively supervised the operation. Every second Tuesday of each month they gathered to decide on books to be ordered from London booksellers. This board also hired the librarian. The number of titles rose during the century from 304 in 1760 to over 8,000 by 1800. Members checked out one book at a time and could suggest titles for purchase. Between November 1777 and December 1778, members suggested 267 titles, of which 172 were ordered, 29 deferred, and 66 rejected. Discussions among board members over book selection could be contentious, prompting protests from the membership. In 1793, for example, objections were suddenly raised over Hume's *Essays* (first published in 1741), perhaps reflecting how the skeptic's reputation had become tarnished by French radical Jacobinism.[36]

The example of the Liverpool Library Selection Committee shows that libraries were not simply, or even primarily, mere repositories for books; rather, they were places where books were integrated into society and made the focal point for critical discussion. In this way, libraries often overlapped in role and function with reading clubs and debating societies. The Powder Literary Society, a group of thirteen women who agreed to read history, politics, biography, and travel literature under the direction of their minister, was a case in point. They came together annually for a special dinner at the Queen's Head in Tregony, a hamlet in England's southwest corner. At about the same time in Scotland, a fifteen-year-old boy, George Sandy, formed a club with a few other friends. They established a small gallery and museum, presumably to exhibit insects and small animals collected in the woods, and, pooling their resources, managed to build a library of thirty-four books that emphasized travel literature.[37] In Norwich the wool merchant James Smith recorded reading 650 books between 1762 and 1795, of which 250 were obtained from his local subscription library.[38] Enlightenment history has focused on Paris writers at the expense of these small, obscure, communities of everyday readers. And yet they constituted the public that Voltaire, Montesquieu, Hume, Richardson, Graffigny, Rousseau, Raynal, Diderot, and Smith hoped to reach.[39]

Circulation and subscription libraries appealed mostly to the middling professional classes and accordingly dominated by ministers, schoolteachers, merchants, and lawyers. There are, however, several known instances of libraries that attracted a working-class clientele. The Ayr Library Society, established in 1762 on Scotland's western coast, boasted a membership of 103 that included a baker, a cabinet maker, a tanner, and a watchmaker.[40] Likewise, "brewers, shoemakers, watchmakers, and glovers" borrowed books from Gray Library in Haddington, Scotland, which allowed free access to all the town's residents.[41] The earliest examples of working-class subscription libraries come from rural Scotland in the mid-1740s. There the Leadhills Mining Society was begun with twenty-three members who pledged "to purchase a collection of books for our mutual improvement." As in neighboring Wanlockhead, which established a similar library for miners in 1756, rules outlawed the purchase of plays and novels, signaling fears among some authorities that such genres might not lead to moral improvement. By the end of the century, such working-class libraries and reading clubs had spread throughout Scotland.[42]

John Millar, the Scottish law professor, social theorist, and author of *Observations on the Distinction of Ranks* (1771), was deeply impressed by one of these relatively new working-class subscription libraries. When his carriage broke down in 1796, he was forced to seek refuge overnight with a quarry laborer. Fortunately, this worker had been a member of his company's reading society, and he was currently at home engaged in reading a long sentimental novel.[43] The laborer and his guest discussed the reading society, its rules and benefits, and the other books he had previously checked out. Millar was deeply impressed with the man's dedication to learning, and in a series of newspaper articles, he tied it directly to political reform:

> Nine-tenths of a people really form that part which may be called the Nation. This new order of things has led to consider less the glory of the State than the happiness of the multitude of individuals of which it is composed. To enlighten the minds of this mass, then, while it extends the circle of individual happiness is to perform an important duty to Society at large.[44]

Subscription libraries, while a powerful force for educating the public, did not always work out for the best. When one prominent Lanarkshire landowner, Robert Riddell, convinced his tenants and rural neighbors to form a reading club, it was so well funded that its librarian bragged that it would soon provide working men and women "a source of innocent and laudable amusement," which might even "raise them to a more dignified degree in the scale of rationality." Unfortunately, the group soon fell apart over disagreements whether the books procured from Edinburgh should be religious works or secular novels.[45]

Reading groups were also influential on the continent. Even in Spain, where literacy rates were low and the Inquisition still active, over thirty reading groups operated in Madrid and throughout its empire. There they read newspapers edited by leaders with reforming ideals. During the 1770s, the *Real Sociedad Economica* became a model for the Spanish world. Civil servants and university professors cautiously endorsed the works of Voltaire, Montesquieu, and Raynal.[46]

Throughout the German states, lending libraries and reading clubs grew during the second half of the century, numbering close to 200 by 1790. In Bonn, for example, one reading group had 172 members between 1787 and 1799, and this membership included a wide range of occupations. One member declared that its aim was "exerting our joint strength to promote the spread and acceptance of the Enlightenment."[47] Specialized studies confirm that these German clubs routinely read the works of Montesquieu, Hume, Rousseau, Smith, and Raynal, confirming Dan Edelstein's reflection that "more than anything, the Enlightenment seems to have been the period when people thought they were living in an age of Enlightenment."[48]

Five Vignettes

Mendelssohn's lament that books had supplanted conversation was a personal response to the emergence of a new reading public. How much of an outlier was he? How did others experience and think about reading during the Enlightenment? Whether there are typical and representative readers today or during the eighteenth century is anyone's guess. Reading and writing habits are as difficult to pin down as conversation and eating habits—they beg for a sociological analysis but are highly elusive. During the eighteenth century, even sticking mainly to Western Europe, reading and literacy were complicated by wide geographical variation. Nonetheless, a sampling of five readers can indicate the extent of interest in Enlightenment books, especially during the third quarter of the eighteenth century, when readers became increasingly aware of the Enlightenment as a movement.[49]

Geneviève Randon de Malboissière (1746–66) was an aristocratic Parisian teenager who obsessively wrote letters to her close friend, Adélaïde Méliand, from 1761 to 1766, when she died of measles at age twenty. These letters were first published in 1866 and again in 1925. They constitute an extraordinarily detailed record of Geneviève's daily life: her walks in the promenades of Paris; her frequent trips to the theatre and opera; her own efforts at writing, translating, acting, and directing; and, above all, her reading. "Yesterday," she wrote Adélaïde on April 16, 1764, "I worked hard all day. I finished my German lesson, then did a bit of Italian and Spanish. I read the first book of *Roman Revolutions*, finished the first volume of [historian William] Robertson, and read twenty-two pages of Buffon's *Natural History*."[50] On another day, she polished her foreign languages by translating various plays into English, Italian, and Spanish, including Diderot's *Natural Son*. She did the same for one of Horace's odes, read a bit of Herodotus, and worked on her mathematics. She had many days like those, and virtually none where she did no reading at all. "I'm constantly working," she told her young friend in a cheerful tone.[51]

Geneviève mentioned around fifty books in her correspondence with Adélaïde. A few of them, such as Valmont de Bromare's *Dictionnaire raisonné universel d'histoire naturelle*, may have been textbooks assigned by tutors. Most, however, came from her mother or friends and were books that Geneviève chose to read. She often recommended these books to Adélaïde. Geneviève's teenage life appears to have been centered around books. As a young aristocrat, her family connection sometimes afforded her special access to well-known writers. For example, she befriended the already famous David Hume when he became the private secretary to England's ambassador to Paris during the early 1760s (Geneviève improved her English by translating his famous essay, "Of the Rise and Progress of the Arts and Sciences"). In this way, Geneviève was one of a kind. However, while she was special, her intense interest in reading was mirrored to some degree by her friend. The fact that she would nonchalantly tell Adélaïde so much about her reading (unfortunately Adélaïde's letters have not survived) suggests that she was in a web of friendships and family relationships in which everyone discussed books with each other. Contrary to Mendelssohn's fears, Geneviève's reading did not cut her off from her peers or family but formed a centerpiece of her friendships and social networks.

Geneviève's fifty books tell us a lot about her reading choices during the Enlightenment. Perhaps the list's most interesting feature is the absence of religious books. There is no theology, no sermons, or other types of religious primers, or, for that matter, no anti-Christian books such as those by d'Holbach that were popular at the time. This is a completely secular library, much of it devoted to the *belles lettres*, that is, to poetry, novels, history, and theatre. There was a bit of science, such as Buffon's *Natural History*, but very little about art or music.

Geneviève focused on contemporary books written by living writers whose new works had recently arrived in the bookseller's shop. Aside from five ancient Greek and Roman authors, there are no authors represented from the medieval, Renaissance, or Reformation eras. For Geneviève, books were items of fashion; like a dress or hairstyle, they were in vogue for that season, and she very much wanted to be part of the crowd that talked them up or down. One has the sense, for example, that she read the *Histoire de la maison de Montmorenci*, not because of its great historical or literary value, but rather because it was about a noteworthy family and was newly published that year—it may have been "in" for a time, although it never went through any other edition.[52]

Despite Geneviève's Parisian origins, she was clearly fascinated by other parts of the world, especially England. Her interest in foreign languages and cultures was no doubt fed by her parents, who welcomed visitors from afar. Guests would bring her things to read, such as an English copy of *Robinson Crusoe*.[53] When Lady Mary Wortley Montagu's letters were posthumously published in 1763, Adélaïde obtained the book first, and Geneviève borrowed it from her.[54]

A distinct feature of Geneviève's list is the prevalence of Enlightenment philosophy. Geneviève worked her way through Locke, Descartes, and even the supposed atheist Spinoza. From there she moved on to Montesquieu's *The Spirit of the Laws* and Hume's *Essays*. Notably, Rousseau's *Emile* is the only work Geneviève specifically mentions not reading: "I have not read Jean Jacques, nor [has] my mother either; it is said that there are childish things there, but also singular things and well written."[55] She especially relished the Swiss political theorist Jean Jacques Burlamaqui, whose treatise, *The Principles of Natural and Politic Law*, found its way onto her bedside table. "*Adieu, mon enfant*, I'm going to read my dear Burlamaqui; it is more honest and virtuous than any man."[56] Indeed, Geneviève received essentially the kind of education that Denis Diderot recommended for his own daughter: "Grammar, mythology, history, geography, a little drawing and a great deal of ethics." Even Diderot, a notorious atheist, had his daughter Angélique raised on the Bible—a work conspicuously missing from Geneviève's correspondence.[57]

Also in Paris was another girl, Manon Phlipon (1754–93), who kept a meticulous record of her reading habits in her correspondence with her friends, most notably with pen pal Sophie Cannet. Although from a lower social rank than Geneviève—her family were merchants—Manon was still well-off enough to afford a convent education and tutors. Her letters, like Geneviève's, are full of references to the books she read. Despite the differences between them, Manon and Geneviève had remarkably similar reading habits and work schedules. Manon didn't only read in a serious way, she often extracted long quotations into a notebook. "One never learns anything when one simply reads," Manon explained. "One must extract and transform, as it were, into one's own substance those things that one wishes to preserve, in penetrating their essence."[58] Manon was proud of her studious nature.

The books mentioned by Manon in her letters between 1767 and 1787 offer an accurate picture of her intellectual life, starting as a teenager through her early thirties. Like Geneviève, Manon's books were thoroughly secular, despite her convent training. Only six of the eighty-five books she recorded can be classified as religious in nature. The vast majority were in the humanities (classics, literature, history, philosophy, political thought)—again, exactly the type of education recommended by Diderot for his own daughter. Her reading habits were also like Geneviève's in that most of her books were written by living authors. Very few were novels, although Richardson's *Clarissa* was represented.[59]

There are two aspects of Manon's selection that distinguish it from Geneviève's: first was her interest in classical literature, especially Roman literature and philosophy; and second was her particular devotion to the Encyclopedists. No fewer than eight works of Voltaire are mentioned in her correspondence, as well as seven by Rousseau, who became her favorite author. Manon repeatedly returned to the *Encyclopédie*, read the philosophical works of d'Alembert and Diderot's literary works, and digested Fénelon, d'Holbach, Morelly, and Raynal's *History of the Two Indies*. Except for books from ancient Greece and Rome, most of her books were written by French or British authors. Like Geneviève, then, Manon was a child of the Enlightenment; and, like Geneviève, books dominated her daily life.

The Enlightenment held a looser grip on the Scottish Presbyterian minister George Ridpath (1717?–72), whose diary records some 150 titles between 1755 and 1761. Despite being an ordained minister for the village of Stitchel, he mentioned very few theological books in his diary. Although George delivered sermons on Sundays, he chose to read about more secular topics during the week. History and literature, especially regarding ancient Greece and Rome, preoccupied him. For example, one ordinary Monday evening found him at home reading Plato's *Laws*. In general, he found Plato's reasoning "excellent and invariable, but a great number of the particulars do not [suit] the constitution or manners of any modern state."[60] He read many works in the Enlightenment canon, but not as intensively as Manon's. He knew Hume's *History of England*, and he also enjoyed his *Essays* as well as Adam Smith's *Theory of Moral Sentiments*. He seems to have had no contact with the *Encyclopédie*, and none with radical authors such as Diderot, d'Holbach, or Helvétius. Rousseau is never mentioned. On the other hand, he did read Montesquieu's *Persian Letters* and Voltaire's *Candide* and *History of Peter the Great*. While George was certainly not—like Manon and Geneviève—an acolyte of the philosophes, the Enlightenment still affected his reading choices.

The feature that most distinguished George from Geneviève and Manon was not the books he chose to read, but rather how he obtained them. Where the Parisian girls' families were wealthy enough to purchase their books from local booksellers, George could not afford to do so on the modest income of a village minister. Instead, he depended on the nearby subscription library in Kelso. On a typical day, after making the rounds to his bedridden parishioners, Ridpath would make the hour walk, or sometimes ride, to Kelso, where he would get together with friends and choose the books he wanted to borrow. He eventually became an important officer in the library itself, helping to choose a librarian, and spending endless hours preparing an alphabetical index for a printed catalog.[61]

A fourth lover of books during the Enlightenment was the Italian Canon of Casale Monferrato, Father Ignazio di Giovanni (1729–1801), who during 1760–1 alone ordered 114 books from the Swiss bookseller brothers Henri-Albert and Jean Gosse. The Gosse brothers were French Protestants from Strasbourg who fled to The Hague after Louis XIV's 1685 Revocation of the Edict of Nantes. There, they built a large publishing firm and bookshop. During the 1740s, parts of the family expanded the enterprise to Geneva, some 300 kilometers northwest of Giovanni's home.

The Italian historian Lodovica Braid discovered the Gosses' correspondence in the Genevan State Archives and reconstructed the list of book orders, based upon the most likely editions. Despite Giovanni's clerical position, only 10 percent of the books he ordered were religious books. About 20 percent were history, philosophy, and political economy, including a life of the materialist La Mettrie, Frederick the Great's philosophical works, Mirabeau's *Théorie des impôts*, Diderot's *Pensées sur l'interpretation de la nature*, and Helvétius's *De l'esprit*. However, by far the largest single genre that attracted Giovanni was literature, constituting about half of the orders for this brief period. Here he ordered the latest bestsellers, including several works by Voltaire, French translations of Richardson's *Clarissa* and Daniel Defoe's *Moll Flanders*, and Rousseau's *New Héloïse*. Most surprising is the presence of several pornographic novels in this list, including the notorious *Histoire du dom B . . ., portier des Chartreux*, which, while banned everywhere, may have gone through as many as nineteen underground editions. This book, like *Canapé couleur de feu*, the *Vie voluptueuses des capuchi, Intrigues Monastiques*, and *Galanteries d'une religieuse*, were hard-core works of erotica. Giovanni also made several orders from a mixed genre of books that presented themselves as philosophy but were libertine in spirit. Voltaire's epic poem on Joan of Arc, *La Pucelle*, fits this description, as does a French translation of Bernard Mandeville's *Modest Defense of Publick Stews*, which slyly advocated for government-run brothels. Such books were, of course, outlawed in Italy, and were regularly confiscated by the police. Still, Ignazio was apparently able to import these books with impunity. His reading habits, mixing highbrow philosophy with gutter-level erotica, confirms Robert Darnton's claim that Enlightenment reading included much more than Montesquieu, Voltaire, and Rousseau.[62]

The last of our vignettes, Thomas Thistlewood (1721–86), is the most surprising and enigmatic reader of the lot. The son of a tenant farmer from Lincolnshire, Thistlewood was well educated by his step-uncle following the early death of his father. Failing to establish himself as farmer, and after a sojourn to India, he emigrated to Jamaica. At age twenty-nine in 1750, he found himself reading Enlightenment books in one of the most unequal societies in human history. For his first fifteen years in Jamaica, he worked for others, saving money for himself, and in 1766, he became a landowner. Thistlewood spent the last twenty years of his life raising livestock and growing vegetables, and eventually owned thirty slaves. He died rich and unmarried in 1786.[63]

Because of his diary, in which he recorded virtually every book he read from when he was twenty until he died at age sixty-five, we know that Thistlewood was an intense reader well before he moved to Jamaica. He was in particular a voracious consumer of Enlightenment canonical works, often copying long transcriptions into his commonplace books. He pored over the works of Montesquieu and Rousseau; he owned an expensive set of Voltaire's writings; he read Smith's *Wealth of Nations* and Hume's *Essays* and *History of England*; he knew Fénelon's *Telemachus* as well as any reader; and he read about Jamaica in Raynal's *History of the Two Indies* and Robertson's *History of America*. Following his first son's birth (by one of his slaves), he read Locke's *Some Thoughts on Education* and, a bit later, Rousseau's educational treatise *Emile*. He read daily, often reading more than one book at the same time.

Contrary to Mendelssohn's fears, Thistlewood's books facilitated a vibrant social life. Because books were hard to come by in Jamaica, he constantly exchanged them with his friends using social occasions and special library visits. During 1770–3, he traded books with twenty-three people, including two women, and generally borrowed more books than he lent. In 1770, for example, he borrowed a 1764 two-volume English translation of Montesquieu's *The Spirit of the Laws* from Captain Benjamin Black. He kept it for three months, taking copious notes and transcribing many passages, before returning it. Thistlewood lent many of his books to his circle of acquaintances, but never allowed anyone to borrow his precious volumes of Voltaire, which was among the most expensive collections he owned.[64]

Thistlewood not only read these books but also loved owning them. With one of his slaves, he would spend many afternoons rearranging the books on his library shelves and preparing catalogs. A good deal of his money was spent on importing books from London and building a personal library. Every year, Thistlewood's agent in London sent him a chest of books. In 1758, the shipment numbered seventeen books, including Josiah Child's treatise on political economy and Joshua Gee writings on trade, as well as works in history, science, math, and gardening. In this way, Thistlewood amassed a library of some 1,000 volumes. Sadly, most of them were destroyed in the great 1780 hurricane, and by the time of his death six years later, his rebuilt library included only 216 titles.

Thistlewood's reading is of particular interest because it contradicts a key idea among eighteenth-century philosophes: that reading and education necessarily lead to an improvement in moral behavior. "Enlightenment renders virtue easy," Condorcet told the French Academy in 1782. "The love of the general good and the courage to devote oneself to it, is the habitual state of the enlightened man."[65] However much the philosophes and readers such as Halifax's Atticus believed that Enlightenment reading sparked virtuous behavior, this was decidedly not the case with Thistlewood. From his first year in Jamaica, Thistlewood acted brutally toward his slaves. As Trevor Burnard has described, Thistlewood "demonstrated his power and toughness daily through acts of violence intended to humiliate as much as to punish . . . In 1756, he gave slaves

57 whippings, gagged 4 slaves without whipping them, and put 11 slaves in stocks overnight." Burnard also describes Thistlewood as a serial rapist. Of the 3,852 sex acts with 138 women noted in his diaries, the vast majority were with Black female slaves, usually his own, and some as young as 14.[66]

In his brilliant study of Thistlewood, Burnard asks: "How could an Enlightenment man also be a cruel tyrant?"[67] Whatever the answer may be, it is not because Thistlewood ignored the overtly political passages of Enlightenment literature regarding slavery. From *The Spirit of the Laws*, he carefully transcribed the relevant portions of Book 15, Chapter 5, in which Montesquieu specifically attacked slavery by satirizing the excuses commonly made for it. Likewise, when Thistlewood read Rousseau's "Profession of Faith of the Savoyard Vicar" from *Emile*, he jotted down "excellent" into his notebook under its title. How could he justify his own actions while also subscribing to the Vicar's theory of virtue? A few years later when Thistlewood read Rousseau's political masterpiece, *Social Contract*, he transcribed passages from its fourth chapter, "On Slavery," and specifically jotted down its dramatic final sentence: "I make an agreement with you that is wholly at your expense and wholly to my advantage; for as long as it pleases me, I will observe it and so will you." How could a man spend so much time reading and thinking about these ideas without them having the least effect on his cruel behavior?[68]

One answer was suggested by none other than Montesquieu in 1721, in a book likely encountered by Thistlewood. The plot of *Persian Letters*, Montesquieu's best-selling epistolary novel, revolves around the actions of the protagonist, Usbek. He occupies three separate roles that are represented in his correspondence: First, he is a Muslim traveler to France; second, he is a moral philosopher; and third, he is husband to several wives, who are all thousands of miles away from him. In this last role, Usbek acts cruelly and despotically, using violence and coercion through his eunuchs to force his wives and other slaves to bend to his will. In one letter, for example, he recalls raping his favorite wife, Roxana, carefully described by Montesquieu in such a way that readers know Usbek is blind to the moral implications of his actions. Like Thistlewood, Usbek is a serial sexual predator whose erudite and humanistic philosophy has no impact on his behavior toward his wives and slaves. He psychologically compartmentalizes his different roles, and, like Thistlewood, he never allows one to engage the other. What Usbek learns from traveling in France is not applied to his moral theory, and, more importantly, his philosophical ideas regarding virtue have nothing whatsoever to do with his own moral behavior.

Through Usbek, Montesquieu seems to be suggesting at least three points: First, that in a despotic society such as the one Montesquieu imagines in Persia (or the very real Jamaican slave society), evil acts are routinized such that a Usbek or Thistlewood are seen by peers as decent men; second, that radical compartmentalizing is one mechanism by which such men in despotic societies continue to live their lives; and third, through the novel's rebellious ending, Montesquieu warned that such a perverse way of living is bound to be unsustainable and will inevitably collapse into revolution. While Thistlewood's diaries never acknowledge the type of anxiety we see in Usbek, it is striking that within a decade of his death, the French plantation colony, Saint-Domingue, was in full revolt, and the British abolitionist movement was active throughout the empire, resulting first in the suppression of the Atlantic slave trade in 1807 and finally in the end of slavery altogether in Jamaica in 1834.[69]

Recent histories of the Enlightenment have emphasized the role of conversation in its development, wherein elite men and women discussed issues over private meals in salons, Masonic lodges, academies, and the like.[70] Geneviève Malboissière, Manon Phlipon, George Ridpath, Ignazio di Giovanni, and Thomas Thistlewood, however, all experienced the Enlightenment through book reading. For them, as well as for most readers, this "Age of Conversation" often revolved around books. They would discuss books with their friends and write about them in their letters and diaries. The book made the Enlightenment accessible to readers who were either unqualified for academies, lodges, and salons, or who lived too far from them. Very few Europeans were in a position, like the Parisian playwright Bernard Joseph Saurin, to write to Voltaire for his opinion of Rousseau, but virtually all readers could discuss *Emile* with their friends or acquaintances they met at a library or reading club.

Booksellers, Printers, and Publishers

The book was the Enlightenment's key building block, and the making of an edition its central event. Every book is the result of three fundamentally different activities: an author produces a manuscript, a printer/publisher converts the manuscript into a book and makes it available for sale in a marketplace, and, finally, readers encounter the book. Any history of the Enlightenment should address these discrete activities with balanced attention.

During the mid-eighteenth century, a tipping point was reached in book publication. According to estimates made by Eltjo Buringh and Jan Luiten Van Zanden, there was a surge in book buying during the eighteenth century. For the 250-year period between 1454 and 1700, booksellers sold approximately 762 million books in Europe, whereas between 1700 and 1800, just under one billion were produced, with particular intensity during the second half of the century.[71] During the sixteenth and seventeenth centuries, books were luxuries coveted by mostly religious readers in particular communities: scholarly, religious, and literary. During the decade from 1500 to 1510, Britain produced some 400 different book titles; 200 years later, between 1710 and 1720, that number had soared to 22,000.[72] Only during the eighteenth century can one begin to speak of a popular market for fashionable books.

Of course, the distribution of book production and consumption remained highly uneven across Europe and the European world. According to Buringh and Van Zanden, France, Great Britain, the Netherlands, Italy, and the German states accounted for 87.5 percent of the production of the book trade, while the rest of Europe (Austrian Empire,

Switzerland, Spain, Ireland, Sweden, Poland, Russia, Norway, Finland, Portugal, and Europe's global colonies) constituted the remainder. By the 1770s even relatively remote countries like Sweden and Russia produced respectively as many as 900 and 250 book titles per year. Consumption was less uneven than production, reflecting the fact that the dominant countries had many publishers that specialized in the export market. Sweden and North America, for example, imported most of the books consumed in those countries during the eighteenth century.[73]

Eighteenth-century Ireland presents a representative example of the Western European book trade. According to Mary Pollard, production of Irish books doubled between 1760 and 1790, dominated by a surge in the growth of Dublin printers, publishers, and booksellers. Most books were printed from Irish manuscripts, but a sizable portion (perhaps a third to a half) reprinted London imprints. Because production costs were less in Ireland than in England (in part because of a heavy English paper tax), Irish publishers charged less for books, and some reprints were smuggled across the border into England. However, smuggling was never as large a problem as English publishers made it out to be. Until 1780, Irish booksellers were not allowed to export to the British colonies. The vast majority of Irish books were produced for the home market. Analyzing both publisher stock and large libraries, Pollard shows how the percentage of religious books declined throughout the century, overtaken by books about politics, history, and literature.[74]

The Irish case also demonstrates that growth in the general book trade involved strong demand for Enlightenment books. It is hardly surprising, of course, that Dublin publishers reprinted Hume and Smith several times. But Graham Gargett and his colleagues have noted the intense demand in Ireland for works by French Enlightenment authors as well. Fénelon and Voltaire vied for the title of Ireland's most popular European writer, while editions of Montesquieu, Rousseau, and Raynal abounded. Graffigny's *Letters of a Peruvian Woman* was reproduced in Dublin within a year of its initial publication in France, while *The Spirit of the Laws* was reprinted as an unabridged two-volume set on four separate occasions. Altogether Gargett lists almost 300 French Enlightenment books published in Dublin between 1700 and 1800.[75]

This expansion of the book trade followed the uneven growth of literacy. The efforts of many eighteenth-century states to increase literacy bore some success, despite wide variation. The ability to sign one's name to a marriage contract was much higher in Northwest Europe than in Southern or Eastern Europe, and higher in towns and cities than in the countryside. Likewise, a significant gender gap existed throughout Europe that was more pronounced in Southern than Northern Europe. For example, some 80 percent of women were literate in Paris against 90 percent of men, but in Madrid during the 1790s, only 36 percent of women were literate compared with 83 percent of men. In Protestant countries, literacy grew dramatically during the early modern period. In England, for example, male literacy doubled between 1640 and 1750. In Scotland, two-thirds of men were literate by 1765, whereas only one-quarter could sign their names in 1643. Catholic France was lower but in the same direction: 30 percent in 1690 and 48 percent in 1790. Literacy figures were much lower in Eastern Europe but nonetheless grew: In East Prussia, literacy went from 10 percent in 1750 to 25 percent in 1765, and to 40 percent in 1800. There female literacy was roughly half that of males. Suggesting that the popularity of Enlightenment books implies growing secularization certainly does not mean that the Enlightenment reached everywhere. In rural Jutland between 1760 and 1780, about 20 percent of the households included books, almost all of them religious.[76]

The fortunes of the publishing industry depended, of course, on the growth of literacy. During the eighteenth century the roles of printers, booksellers, and publishers were distinct even as they overlapped. Printing was a craft, and printers normally belonged to a guild regulated by local traditions and royal statutes. Printers manufactured several products besides books, including business and invitation cards, public announcements, political broadsides, government decrees, and the like. Publishers were businessmen and women who raised capital to hire printers to manufacture their books, paid for advertisements in the press, and distributed the books to booksellers. Once in a while, as in the famous cases of Samuel Richardson or Benjamin Franklin, a successful printer might fund his own work and expand into publishing, using booksellers as retailers. More commonly booksellers joined together in publishing schemes. Authors rarely printed their own material, although they could serve as their own publishers, using personal funds as capital.[77]

Although William Smellie was among the Enlightenment's most extraordinary printers, he represents features common to the group. Printers had to be literate, and many were avid readers themselves. Born in 1740, Smellie spent his entire life in Edinburgh. At twelve years old he was apprenticed to a large printing firm where his employers recognized his impressive intellectual talents. With their encouragement, each day he would be permitted to leave work to spend two hours at the University of Edinburgh, where he audited courses in medicine, moral philosophy, and literature. After five or six years as a journeyman printer, he was invited to edit *The Scots Magazine* at the age of twenty-five. He returned to printing five years later. As a master printer, he worked on books by Hume, Smith, and other Scottish Enlightenment writers. He taught himself French and Hebrew in order to work properly on translations. Although his intellectual gifts made him an outlier, his ability to move back and forth between printing and other intellectual endeavors shows the high social respect possible for successful printers.[78]

For the most part, publishing remained in the hands of private business. Rare was it for an Enlightenment philosophe, such as the naturalist Buffon, to be published almost exclusively by the government. The original publication of Rousseau's "Discourse on the Arts and Sciences" was far more typical: after winning first prize in an essay contest sponsored by the Academy of Dijon, it was published not by that academy, but in a for-profit arrangement by the Swiss firm Barrillot & Fils, the same outfit that had recently published Montesquieu's *The Spirit of the Laws*.

Although publishers were businessmen who constantly focused on the bottom line, they often identified with their authors and saw themselves as conduits between the public and the Republic of Letters. They expected to be treated by their authors as more than simply business associates and sometimes aspired to become friends. William Strahan and Thomas Cadell felt they had special relationships with Edward Gibbon, William Robertson, David Hume, and Adam Smith. Likewise, when booksellers in France learned that the Abbé Raynal had been exiled for his 1780 edition of the *History of the Two Indies*, at least one of them exclaimed, "You must understand that everyone in general and booksellers in particular have to be interested in the fate of such a famous man."[79]

During the eighteenth century, a book belonged more to the publisher than to the author, and as notions of copyright and intellectual property developed, the rights of publishers versus authors became contested and more ambiguous. For the most part, when an author delivered a manuscript to a publisher, the latter paid him or her a fee there and then, or at least contracted to do so later. Rousseau, for example, praised his publisher, Marc Michel Rey, for paying him "on the spot."[80] This usually was the last remuneration an author could count on, unless new material was offered to the public through corrected or expanded editions. Earnings from mere reprintings were generally not shared with the author, nor was the author further compensated if the publisher resold the manuscript to another publisher, as Suzanne de Caux did with *Persian Letters*. To my knowledge, no author during the eighteenth century was ever paid for a translation published in a country outside the author's own. After all, in most of Europe it was the publisher, not the author, who took most of the financial and legal risks, and, thus, owned whatever copyright existed in the country. By law and custom, the author's name on the title page was optional, and often discouraged, while the publisher's name and location were required. If a publication offended church or state, authorities usually went after the publisher and booksellers more vigilantly than the author.

As Roger Chartier notes, following the exchange or promise of payment for a completed manuscript, publishers made a series of decisions about the impending book regarding the quality of its paper, format (folio, quarto, octavo, or duodecimo), design elements, extent of the print run, and the steps involving compositors and copy editors in the printing process. Publishers were also responsible for choosing the paratexts—that is, deciding on prefaces, introductions, table of contents, marginal commentary, and footnotes that might frame the author's work for the reader. Paratexts contextualized the book for a specific readership. Publishers also signaled a books' significance by including an index, or hiring artists to produce illustrations.[81]

An important new publishing vehicle in guiding the reading public was the appearance of review journals that mainly reviewed and advertised newly published books. The *Monthly Review* and the *Critical Review*, begun respectively in 1749 and 1765, helped members of subscription libraries decide on which new books to purchase.[82] With their enormous success—the *Monthly Review*'s circulation rose to 3,500 by 1776—journals built around book reviews mushroomed across Europe. In France, the *Mercure de France* became the leading literary review, expanding to 756 subscribers by the mid-1750s.[83] Already in 1718 there emerged over 100 such magazines operating in the German states, albeit with lower circulation figures. In Scotland, Adam Smith's first publication was a review of Rousseau's *Discourse on the Origins of Inequality* in the *Edinburgh Review*, while in England Mary Wollstonecraft began her own writing career at the *Analytical Review*. These review journals mediated the gap between reader and writer. At the same time, magazines sometimes serialized portions of Enlightenment books. For example, the *Dublin Magazine* in February and March 1764 translated and reproduced Rousseau's "Savoyard Vicar" section from *Emile*, only two years after its initial publication.[84]

Among the most important review journals of the century's middle decades was the *Journal encyclopédique*, published with striking success for many decades by Pierre Rousseau. Printed and distributed across the French border in an independent principality whose sovereign blessed the project, Rousseau's journal followed its eponymous series as the volumes of Diderot and d'Alembert's *Encyclopédie* appeared, and thus, its stock rose as the reputation of the *Encyclopédie* soared. As the Enlightenment became seen more and more as an intellectual movement, the *Journal encyclopédique* quickly became its standard witness. Notable recognition of its status came early in its development when an Italian version of the journal was made from 1756 to 1760 by intellectuals in Lucca, Tuscany.[85]

Literary piracy deeply affected eighteenth-century publishing. Often historians of the book treat literary piracy as but one among many factors that affected publishers. But literary piracy—at least as we understand the term today—must be considered among the fundamental elements that structured eighteenth-century publishing. Technically, literary piracy is the reproduction of print materials without permission or remuneration of its owners. And yet, during the eighteenth century, this was a common, usually legal, practice throughout the European world, and few objected to it. Sovereignty gave every state in Europe the right to authorize whatever printing matter it wished. Today when we use the word "pirated" regarding intellectual property, we assume that it refers to criminality. But during the eighteenth century, the production of unauthorized editions was normal in every country. In the eighteenth century often states awarded monopolies to publishers who had their book manuscripts approved through the government. However, this system of awarding privileges, patents, or copyright to publishers was often unenforceable within individual borders, and no state intended for its own literary privileges to be respected elsewhere in Europe.[86]

It is common now to believe that authors have rights to their intellectual property that extend beyond national borders. Historically, however, such a notion derives only from the Berne Convention signed in 1886 by a dozen countries, and gradually enlarged during the twentieth century. Today virtually all countries have accepted the Berne agreement, and it has been adopted into core features of the World Trade Organization. However, an international legal system recognizing intellectual property rights is far more recent than other rights, such as freedom of the press or religious expression. The Berne Convention was established when Europe was composed of the fewest number of sovereign borders in its long history.[87]

What became possible during the late nineteenth century was unthinkable 100 years earlier, when Europe comprised hundreds of sovereign principalities, republics, and kingdoms. Each state—no matter how small—offered its own monopolies to publishers. There was neither the expectation nor even the vision to internationalize this system, except by very few eccentric voices, such as Daniel Defoe.[88] When near the end of the century, Immanuel Kant suggested something like an international system of copyright protection that was based on the moral rights of authors, his idealism was buried in obscurity for a century.[89] Consequently, for government-approved books published in eighteenth-century Paris, it was neither illegal nor considered unethical for publishers in Geneva, Amsterdam, Liège, London, and Leipzig to produce unauthorized editions (*contrefaçons*). Thus, the pejorative term "piracy" applies only to such books when they were smuggled into the home country and sold there, violating its own laws. Not surprisingly, vibrant publishing centers specializing in unauthorized editions sprouted up in microstates that neighbored major states. For example, Avignon—located in the middle of the southern French region of Provence, but politically part of the Papal States until the French Revolution—became notorious for reprinting French books, often at prices 25–50 percent below Paris's. What was true of France was even more apparent on the Italian peninsula, where each city—Turin, Rome, Venice, Livorno, Naples, Florence, Milan—determined its own policies regarding book publishing and local copyright.[90]

Although France was the most important literary market in Europe, granting "privileges" for approved books, it did not try to prevent its neighbors from issuing unauthorized reprints. When we find a publisher/bookseller such as French Huguenot refugee Elie Luzac producing over 1,400 French-language titles in Leiden, we need to consider this operation not so much as Dutch, but as a French business operating across the border in Holland, in accordance with the laws of the Dutch republic. Even in London, it became commonplace to reproduce quick facsimiles of French works until there was time and capital to produce an English translation. Within months of the first edition of *The Spirit of the Laws* printed in Geneva, for example, John Nourse published a copycat edition, matching the Geneva edition in virtually every way, including the expensive price of eighteen livres for the quarto. A few months later, Nourse put out a duodecimo edition that sold for less than half that amount, and in 1751, he published an English translation by Thomas Nugent. Montesquieu himself was well aware of Nourse's activities and was not bothered by them, as they were a normal and accepted part of international publishing.[91] While authorities might ban the commercial importation of such material, the advantage was with the smugglers. Pierre Rousseau, for example, produced many *contrefaçons* from his base just across the French border in the independent, if tiny, principality of Liège. In 1759, Rousseau was able to undercut the competition for Voltaire's *Candide* by squeezing twice the number of lines per page as anyone else.[92] Besides, although it may have been illegal to buy and sell some unauthorized foreign imports within France's borders, it was perfectly legal for an individual to possess them and show them off in one's library. There was nothing prohibiting, after all, a Parisian from traveling to Amsterdam or London, purchasing an edition there, and bringing it back home.[93]

Translations made up a profitable area for eighteenth-century publishers, since they did not need to share revenue with the original authors. But translations were highly asymmetrical among European states. Many more books were translated from French into other vernacular languages than vice versa. While France and England translated one another's fiction with mutual interest, publishers less often translated German, Italian, or Spanish works into French. On the other hand, German publishers routinely translated new English fiction and works of the Scottish Enlightenment. Cesare Beccaria's influential short treatise, *On Crimes and Punishments*, first published in Italian in 1764, and which sparked a European-wide campaign against torture and the death penalty, became a bestseller only after André Morellet translated it into French. The French text provided the basis of the English, Danish, German, and Swedish translations. By the 1760s, as one Irish commentator described, French had become "almost the universal language of Europe."[94]

The prevalence of translations in the European book trade demonstrates the limitations of focusing only on national literatures within what are sometimes perceived to be secure linguistic borders. In his otherwise masterful *The Enlightenment and the Book*, Richard Sher concentrates on Scottish authors, as though Scottish readers read only their own writers. While they may have favored home-grown writers, they also read widely. As Alissa Johns and Mary Helen McMurran have shown, between 1700 and 1740 the four best-selling works of literature in Britain were translations (*Telemachus, Don Quixote, Arabian Nights, Guy of Warwick*) and even during the next twenty years, when the British invented the modern novel, foreign authors were well represented among the bestsellers. Indeed, the significance of translations, as well as the presence of French works outside of France, highlights the cosmopolitan aspect of the European Enlightenment.[95]

Abraham and Anna Vandenhoeck exemplify the international features of eighteenth-century European publishing. Born in Holland, Abraham met Anna when he became a bookseller in London. After several successful years, they decided to move their operation to Germany, where, during the 1740s, the University of Göttingen invited them to become the university's official printer. Soon after taking up this new position, Abraham died, leaving Anna to run the business for almost forty years. Anna early on printed and sold books by several of Göttingen's professors, slowly branching out into other areas of literature. Between 1748 and 1753 she produced a German translation of Richardson's *Clarissa*. Indeed, her bookstore became a center in Germany for English-language books, and a circulation library associated with her shop became a cultural center in its own right.[96]

The ease of smuggling foreign imports into France and other countries helped give rise to domestic literary piracy. A French publisher, typically in the provinces, would produce a knockoff of a legitimate Paris publication, often employing a false imprint, making the book look like it had been produced outside of France. For French authorities, always two steps behind clever publishers, the line separating an unauthorized foreign import from domestic fakes all but disappeared. All these factors—unauthorized international editions, domestic piracy, censorship, arbitrary police seizures, and lack of copyright protection—combined to make the European book trade highly unstable, inducing publishers to hold small amounts of inventory as a hedge against unauthorized international editions and domestic piracy. Publishers realized that if a book were successful, it might take only six to eight weeks for another firm to produce an unauthorized or pirated copy at a cheaper price, placing the original edition in some financial jeopardy. Therefore, it became standard practice for a publisher to produce enough copies to sell out in one or two months, and then, if the market warranted, produce a second reprint or new edition shortly thereafter. This meant that the average print run per edition was constrained, usually between 500 and 2,000 copies. The Marseille bookseller Jean Mossy made this strategy clear when he reported that "the science of our trade is not to acquire too much inventory and to get rid of it quickly."[97]

Government censorship was pervasive, of course, in most European countries during the eighteenth century, and France was especially notorious for persecuting writers. Montesquieu, Graffigny, Voltaire, Rousseau, Raynal, and many others faced legal intimidation. The French philosophes worried not only about book censorship but about arrest as well. So long as a writer did not seek publication, or at least publication inside France, he or she was safe from harm. Arrests for unpublished manuscripts—that is, for writing down one's thoughts without publishing them—were extremely rare. However, those who sought publication without government approval placed themselves in jeopardy, as Denis Diderot discovered in 1749 and Rousseau a decade later. Overall, between 1659 and 1789, 942 authors in France were imprisoned in the Bastille for book-related offenses.[98]

Various institutions sometimes rivaled one another in censoring Enlightenment works. In France, the director of the book trade had a staff of over 100 part-time censors to monitor a haphazard approval process, whose decisions could be overturned by the Conseil d'Etat (Royal Council). The Paris Parlement also had the authority to suppress books by taking action against publishers and authors. Likewise, the Catholic Church, independently acting through the Sorbonne faculty (or more distantly from the Vatican), could advise the king to suppress a book. Meanwhile bookseller and printer guilds also had the authority to exercise censorship. This balkanized nature of censorship in France and elsewhere made the system for book approval complex. To be sure, publishers producing almanacs, reference works, devotional tracts, bibles, classical literature, and the like had few worries in this regard; they could focus their concern on the counterfeit publishers out to undercut them. But those publishing Enlightenment literature constantly worried that approval at one stage might be later undone by one of these rival institutions or their counterparts in other European countries. The reversal of fortune for Helvétius's *De l'Esprit* in 1759 is a famous case of such upheaval. Thus, the apparatus of government censorship rendered the literary marketplace ever more unstable, forcing publishers to act more cautiously by restraining print runs.[99]

Another strategy publishers used to combat such market instability was to exchange inventory with one another, serving as much as wholesalers as producers, effectively hedging their overall accounts. As Robert Darnton has shown, this made for a complex, if sometimes effective, international commercial network in which rivals were simultaneously acting as partners, and in which retailing booksellers could secure the same book from a variety of suppliers.[100] Given that most publishers doubled up as wholesalers or retailers, it benefited them to have foreign editions of books desired by their clientele. In this sense, many booksellers and publishers engaged in commerce involving unauthorized editions. "Instead of being produced in huge numbers by a single publisher, who might auction rights to a paperback house," notes Darnton, unauthorized books "appeared in many small editions put out simultaneously by competing firms, which tumbled over one another in the general rush to get to the market first."[101] Depending on the circumstances, then, the same publisher who complained to government officials regarding what he or she considered a pirated import of a legitimate book might turn around the next week and indulge customers in that very work. Defending one's own privileges while harming the legal property of others was a necessary game of survival in the topsy-turvy publishing world of Enlightenment Europe.

The successful Paris publisher Laurent Durant (1712–63) reflected these complexities. His firm won coveted privileges to sell books printed by the French government's Imprimerie Royale, such as the scientific works of Buffon and René Antoine Ferchault de Réaumur, and distributed as well the proceedings of some of France's most important academies.[102] But Durant also trafficked in *contrafaçons* and other suspicious imports. His relations with the censors were complicated. For example, Durant used Malesherbes, director of the book trade, to mediate between him and Marc Michel Rey, Jean Jacques Rousseau's publisher in Amsterdam, to import copies of Rousseau's *Discourse on the Origin of Inequality*, in exchange for inventory. Durant also produced his own illegal editions, using false imprints on the title page to mask his activities. When he died in 1763, Durant had hundreds of such books in his inventory, including works by Montesquieu and Voltaire.[103]

No one was more upset by the contradictions and hypocrisies of the French book trade than Denis Diderot. In a 1763 letter written on behalf of Paris booksellers and authors to the new director of the book trade, Antoine de Sartine, Diderot explained that even for the government's own interest, current French censorship policy had been a disaster. Unauthorized books were flooding into France, with revenue from sales going to foreign publishers. Any policy of keeping such books out of France was futile. "Line all your borders with soldiers, sir, arm them with bayonets to repel any dangerous book that may appear, and those books will—pardon the expression—pass between their legs or jump over their heads to reach us." Focusing on one prime example, Diderot chose Montesquieu's *Persian Letters*:

> What book is more contrary to good morals, to religion, to conventional ideas of philosophy and administration, in a word, to all vulgar prejudices, and, consequently, more dangerous, than *Persian Letters*? Is there anything worse? Yet there are a hundred

editions of *Persian Letters*, and there is not a single student of the Quatre Nations [part of the Sorbonne seminary] who can't find a copy on the quay for twelve sous.

While consumers benefited from buying *Persian Letters* cheaply, French authors, printers, and booksellers were losing revenue. After all, Diderot insisted, not everyone was a Montesquieu, already wealthy and well known before becoming an author. "Suppose that *The Spirit of the Laws* was the first work by an unknown author relegated by misery to a fifth-floor apartment; despite the excellence of the work, I doubt that it would have made three editions, and there are now perhaps twenty." For every Montesquieu, there were a hundred less fortunate authors, who—like Diderot himself, who was then living in a fifth-floor flat—were on the edge of poverty.[104]

The combination of pervasive literary piracy and confusing and complex overlapping systems of censorship created major difficulties for publishers and authors. Few authors in continental Europe were able to make a living from writing books, and, as Mark Curran has documented, even large publishers such as the Société typographique de Neuchâtel were never far from bankruptcy. Indeed, Voltaire's masterful manipulation of the book trade succeeded only because he was far more interested in getting his many works in front of the public than in making a living from them. "It is hereby permitted to any bookseller to print my silliness, be it true or false, at his risk, peril, and profit," he announced in 1771.[105] Only in England during the second half of the century do we see Enlightenment authors like Hume or Smith become wealthy from their book royalties because publishers had enough confidence to allow their print runs to sell out without regard for any government censor or the prevalence of unauthorized editions. But even Hume and Smith did not earn a cent from any edition produced outside of England or Scotland.

However, what may have been a sharp disadvantage for publishers and authors was a boon for readers. The pervasiveness of unauthorized editions and translations across European borders raised the overall supply of Enlightenment books available. This vibrant "grey press," as François Moureau has coined it, meant that European markets were flooded with cheap duodecimo reprints months after an octavo or expensive quarto was selling well. Voltaire well understood this phenomenon: "I'd really like to know what harm a book costing a hundred écus can do. Twenty folio volumes will never cause a revolution; it's the small portable books that cost thirty sous that are to be feared. If the gospels had cost 1,200 sesterces, the Christian religion would never have become established."[106] If eighteenth-century Europe had had a more stable marketplace for Enlightenment books, featuring press freedom and secure copyright, it is possible that book prices may have been higher and available only in relatively expensive editions. Supply might have been reduced, and accessibility less ubiquitous. After all, in contrast to the publishing history of *Wealth of Nations*, in which its legal status and careful coordination between author and publisher helped to keep its price initially quite high, Montesquieu's *The Spirit of the Laws* was pirated with cheap editions from the start, allowing readers from Boston to St. Petersburg to purchase what began as a very expensive book. A similar story was, of course, the case with the *Encyclopédie*, which became available in a series of unauthorized editions that Darnton dubbed the "Encyclopédie wars."[107]

Only by placing readers, publishers, and authors together in this zone of cheap largely unauthorized reprints can we see how eighteenth-century books about political and economic ideas influenced general readers for the first time in European history. Until the eighteenth century, such books were generally the province of male scholars; it was only during the Enlightenment that a more general and mixed-gender readership developed for books such as *The Spirit of the Laws, Emile, The Wealth of Nations*, and *History of the Two Indies*. The marketplace for political ideas was vastly different during the age of Hume, Voltaire, and Rousseau than it had been during the age of Hobbes, Filmer, and Grotius. "The present age is not, we believe, distinguished from those that are past by any peculiarity more than by that liberality of sentiment arising from a free discussion of political questions," noted *The Scots Magazine* in 1788, "which our forefathers had thought so decided as to admit no sort of doubt; and which, therefore, it was our duty to admit as infallible truths, without difficulty or hesitation."[108]

Authors

During the seventeenth century, the dominant mode for authorship was the gentleman scholar, who was an amateur. To be sure, there were female savants before the eighteenth century, but their struggle for recognition was difficult. Writing was less a profession than a hobby, even if an obsessive one. Many writers and scholars who wrote manuscripts gave no thought to achieving fame or wealth through publication. Often the writer's key identity was as a member in the Republic of Letters, a virtual community usually exclusive to men across Europe who communicated often in Latin through correspondence and irregular publication. As Anne Goldgar and April Shelford have shown, members of this community practiced protocols of civility that allowed for the free exchange of ideas. The goal of producing bestsellers was not on anyone's agenda.[109]

This Republic of Letters did not disappear but was superseded during the early eighteenth century by writers who sought to establish a more direct connection with the new Habermasian public. Literate elites such as noblemen, merchants, civil servants, lawyers, and clergy wanted more sustained understanding of new innovations in the sciences, arts, and literature. Responding to this marketplace of ideas was a new type of writer-journalist popularizing ideas that originated in the Republic of Letters. These middlemen between the Republic of Letters and a newly emerging public could make the work of the erudite attractive to those who had fewer intellectual pretentions. Pierre Bayle's *Nouvelles de la République des Lettres*, a literary review journal published in Amsterdam intermittently between 1684 and 1718, became a model of this genre and was imitated by many others. More successful, if less long-lasting, was Joseph Addison and Richard Steele's *Spectator*, published between 1711 and 1714 and reprinted in book form throughout the century. Teaching moral philosophy and ethics through short essays written in an elegant and novelistic style, its goal was to "enliven morality with wit and temper wit with morality."[110]

The type of middleman that Bayle, Addison, and Steele invented appealed to a younger group of scholars, such as Montesquieu, Hume, and Voltaire. During his twenties, Montesquieu pursued a fairly traditional career in the Republic of Letters. He wrote several essays, reports, and literary pieces but hardly gave thought to publication. He certainly cut a figure in the new Bordeaux Academy, where he read papers ranging from the relationship of politics and religion in ancient Rome to renal physiology. Given his intellectual gifts and social standing as a scion of an ancient noble family, Montesquieu could look forward to a successful career as an academician that might even translate one day into a political or diplomatic career. One might have expected, then, that his first publication would have been a treatise on a philosophical topic related to nature or the law, geared for a scholarly readership, and perhaps like Hobbes, Locke, Leibniz, or Spinoza, written in Latin.

Surprisingly, the thirty-two-year-old Montesquieu published anonymously (but hardly secretly) *Persian Letters*, which he later described as a novel. Mixing erotic themes with religious and political satire, its publication was an unusual and risky move for the young noble academician. What motivated Montesquieu to move outside of his scholarly and elite community and establish himself as an author of fiction among a much wider public? Certainly his ambition had nothing to do with money. Not only did Montesquieu's Bordeaux vineyards make him wealthy enough, but given that his identity was initially kept from even his publisher, he likely made little money from the book's publication. Rather, influenced by Bayle, Addison, and Steele, and especially by the success of Fénelon's *The Adventures of Telemachus*, Montesquieu perceived that serious political ideas might be conveyed to the public in new and lighter formats. This discovery is what separates the early Enlightenment of Montesquieu from the older Republic of Letters.

A comparison between Montesquieu and John Locke reveals this change. Locke (1632–1704) was born a half-century before Montesquieu (1689–1755), and both had written substantial works by the time they were fifty years old. The difference between them was that by that age Locke had published none of his manuscripts, while Montesquieu was already very well known for *Persian Letters* (1721) and *Considerations on the Causes of the Greatness of the Romans and Their Decline* (1734). Locke composed his *Two Treatises of Government* around 1683 in the wake of a succession crisis. Like his other essays written up to that point, he showed the manuscript only to a small group of influential leaders.

It is likely that originally Locke did not envision publishing what would become, of course, his political masterpiece. However, when he spent the bulk of the 1680s in self-imposed exile in the Netherlands, he saw firsthand how intellectuals could be affected by the emergence of a wider reading public. He familiarized himself with

Bayle's *Nouvelles de la Republique des Lettres* and was introduced to a more vibrant print culture. In rather dramatic form, three of his greatest works (*Essay Concerning Human Understanding, Two Treatises on Government,* and the *Letter on Toleration*) were all first published in 1689, when Locke was already fifty-seven years old. Nonetheless, even then Locke remained nervous about exposing himself to the dangers of publishing books about philosophical and political ideas. He published *Two Treatises* anonymously and at first refused to take credit for it even among friends. Meanwhile, he agreed to publish *Letter on Toleration* only in Latin, and was angered when William Popple put out an unauthorized English translation. Well into the 1690s, then, Locke considered publishing an inherently dangerous activity.[111]

Montesquieu, too, was wary of publishing. He negotiated with publishers indirectly, through third parties, never authorizing his name to be placed on a title page. In 1734 he withdrew at the last moment *Réflexions sur la monarchie universelle en Europe* from publication altogether, fearing controversy.[112] Where Locke avoided literary recognition, however, Montesquieu coveted it, yet still sought to shield himself from state or church rebuke. During the 1720s scribal circulation was in decline. One could no longer achieve a considerable reputation as a writer from manuscripts alone; publication had become a necessity. Montesquieu was eager to publish at a relatively young age, and in 1725 parlayed his authorship of *Persian Letters* to gain entrance into that sacred temple of the Republic of Letters, the French Academy. *Persian Letters* was aimed simultaneously at the Republic of Letters and at general readers untrained and uninterested in reading natural law treatises in Latin.[113]

In Locke's day, much of the conversation within the Republic of Letters was conducted in Latin, in terms of both publication and correspondence. In 1600, only 3 decades before Locke was born, Oxford's Bodleian Library held only 36 titles in English among a collection of 6,000.[114] During Locke's years, the decline of Latin in favor of vernacular publication was apparent, and the trend continued with more intensity following his death in 1704. While Montesquieu was certainly comfortable reading Latin, everything he wrote for publication was in French.

What made Montesquieu's move historically significant was how much his unusual turn toward an emerging reading public became replicated by others in his generation. Until the publication of *Persian Letters*, Voltaire was an aspiring poet, historian, and playwright, all traditionally accepted genres within the Republic of Letters. His own version of *Oedipus* (1718), his honorific poem regarding Henri IV (1723), and his popular history of the Swedish King Charles XII (1731) made him one of France's best-known writers by the time he turned forty. Yet his *Philosophical Letters* (1733/4), modeled directly on *Persian Letters*, caused such an uproar that he was forced to flee France and live abroad for most of his long life. Like Montesquieu, Voltaire made little money from any of his writings (his wealth came mostly from shrewd financial investments); and like Montesquieu, Voltaire's interest in approaching directly this new Habermasian public was not motivated by wealth, but by the desire to connect with new readers who wanted material directly related to government, political economy, and religious toleration.

David Hume was twenty-two years younger than Montesquieu and seventeen years younger than Voltaire. During the 1730s, he decided that this new public was ready for something more substantial than a satirical novel. In 1739–40, he published *A Treatise on Human Nature*, a hefty work of over 800 pages, and was disappointed when sales slowed during the first few months—he had hoped for a blockbuster. Hume realized that he had misunderstood what the emerging public was willing to buy and read, and so, like Montesquieu and Voltaire, he followed Addison, Steele, and Bayle in forging a persona in which he wrote not as a philosopher himself, but as someone who bridged the gap between the scholarly world and the public—an ambassador from the Republic of Letters, as he put it. The result was the best-selling *Essays: Moral, Political, and Literary*, which first appeared in 1741.

Hume's anxious self-consciousness as an author presenting his books to a Habermasian public is nowhere more evident than in his well-known letter to Adam Smith (May 5, 1759) that revealed the immediate success of Smith's first book, *Theory of Moral Sentiments*. Hume's letter is famous precisely because he coyly and humorously plays with Smith's vanity about becoming a famous author, warning Smith that a book's popularity should not be taken as any sort of objective evaluation, since the public is in no position to judge the measured arguments of a philosopher. "My Dear Mr. Smith," wrote Hume tongue in cheek, obviously voicing a caricature of someone inside Locke's Republic of Letters. "Show yourself a philosopher in practice as well as profession: think on the emptiness and rashness and futility of the common judgments of men: how little they are regulated by reason in any subject, much more in philosophical subjects, which so far exceed the comprehension of the vulgar." Indeed, the more popular the book, Hume wrote, the more likely that it was full of nonsense: "Nothing indeed can be a stronger presumption of falsehood than the approbation of the multitude." Only after these warnings did Hume give Smith "the melancholy news that your book has been very unfortunate: for the public seem disposed to applaud it extremely." Indeed, what makes Hume's letter still funny today is precisely its dark humor regarding the obsolescence of an erudite Republic of Letters and the new weight of public opinion.[115]

Hume's playfulness reveals how the eighteenth-century reading public transformed writers into celebrities, and the ambivalence they felt about it. Authors whose fame derived originally from their books now became objects of public interest in their own right. As Frank Donoghue and Antoine Lilti have argued, during the eighteenth century the lives of novelists and poets became almost as widely discussed as their literature. Donoghue suggests that an emerging reading public meant that authors relied much less on aristocratic patrons for sponsorship and protection. This had, of course, many positive benefits for authors, but it also brought about a more chaotic literary world in which authors no longer knew their place. The invention of fame was a response to this condition. Using Google Ngram, Lilti demonstrates how the term "celebrity" gathered steam during the second half of the eighteenth century and was immediately applied to writers. Jean Jacques Rousseau received such public attention that Lilti describes him as "the first modern celebrity." Robert Darnton has likewise described how Rousseau's persona was so real to his public that readers thought of him as their friend Jean Jacques.[116] Rousseau himself expressed regret regarding his new situation. "What is fame?" he wondered aloud in a 1763 preface to his works, in which he complained that his celebrity status had only "brought upon me a harsh penalty."[117] Nonetheless, the public seemed to insist on converting authorship to celebrity status. Josiah Wedgwood's posthumous ceramic medallions of Montesquieu and Voltaire that fans could carry with them or wear on their clothes indicate that Rousseau had rivals for fame. Likewise, not only did frontispiece illustrations of authors become more common in eighteenth-century books, but they were also often sold as separate items in bookshops. Readers desired visual images of their authors.[118]

Paradoxically, then, Enlightenment authors, at least outside the UK, were transformed into celebrities before it was acceptable for them to put their names on the title pages of their books. Neither Montesquieu nor Graffigny dared to allow publishers to print their names, and Voltaire chided Helvétius for doing so. When Rousseau and Raynal did so, they were swiftly run out of France. Voltaire perfected the art of denial, explaining to anyone who would listen that as long as the author officially denied authorship, he could not be held legally culpable, even if a manuscript was discovered in his possession.[119]

Chapter 2

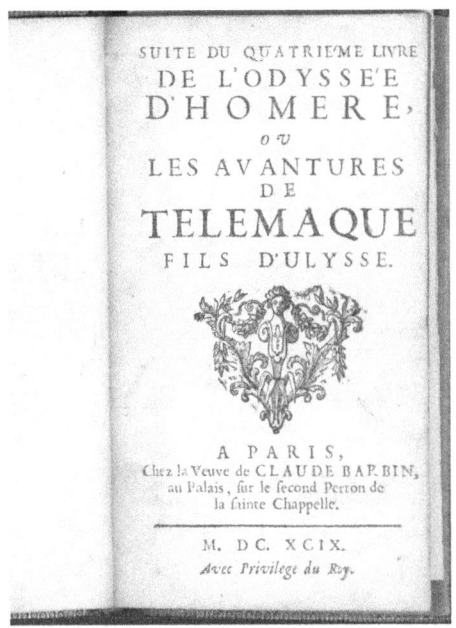

Figure 2.1 First edition title page from Fénelon's *The Adventures of Telemachus*. Only a portion of this edition was published before its suppression by the government, forcing the Paris publisher to sell the entire manuscript to a Dutch colleague.

Chapter 2
Fénelon's *The Adventures of Telemachus* (1699)

Table 2.1 Eighteenth-Century Editions of *The Telemachus*

Decade	1700–09	1710–19	1720–9	1730–9	1740–9	1750–9	1760–9	1770–9	1780–9	1790–1800
Editions	23	23	24	27	37	40	45	51	55	82

Total Editions: 421.
Translations: Danish, Dutch, English, German, Italian, Latin, Polish, Portuguese, Russian, Spanish, Swedish.
Source: https://kates.itg.pomona.edu/books/analytics.php?type=all. Accessed March 9, 2022.

We may say, without romance or exaggeration, that all good and all evil, all that is true, all that is false, all that is real and all that is chimerical, in the great European revolution of opinions and institutions, of which we have been the instruments, the spectators, and the victims, during a century, has flowed from this book, as from the fountain of good and evil. Telemachus is at once the grand revelation and utopia of all classes of society. When we follow the chain attentively, link by link, from the most fanatic tribunes of the Convention to the Girondins, from the Girondins to Mirabeau, from Mirabeau to Bernardin de Saint-Pierre, from Bernardin de Saint-Pierre to J. J. Rousseau, from J. J. Rousseau to Turgot, from Turgot to Vauban, from Vauban to the preceptor to the Duke of Burgundy, we shall discover in Fénelon the first revolutionist, the first tribune of the people, the first reformer of kings, the first apostle of liberty; and in Telemachus we shall acknowledge the evangelist of the truths and errors of modern revolutions.

—Alphonse de Lamartine, *Fénelon* (1876)[1]

The book that gave birth to the eighteenth-century Enlightenment was first published in April 1699. Sometimes it is called a "clandestine" publication, but that is not exactly true.[2] A Parisian bookseller, Claude Barbin's widow, Marie Cochart, had obtained a legal "privilege" to openly publish the book. Midway through its first printing, however, at the point where compositors had completed page 208, the French government suddenly revoked its privilege, effectively banning the book. Cochart improvised by selling only this portion, about 20 percent of the entire manuscript, but at least she could claim that the copies sold before the ban were legal. At any rate, she printed the book in such haste that a typographical error shows up on its title page (Figure 1.1: Chappelle instead of Chapelle). Published anonymously in a cheap duodecimo format with a clumsy title, *Suite du quatrième livre de "l'Odyssée" d'Homère, ou les Avantures de Télémaque, fils d'Ulysse* (*Continuation of the Fourth Book of Homer's Odyssey, or, The Adventures of Telemachus, Son of Ulysses*), this partially produced and soon-banned book didn't seem to have much chance for success.[3]

For years, Claude Barbin had run a successful bookshop in Paris, publishing over 500 titles, including the complete plays of Molière, the fairy tales of Charles Perrault, and new translations of Homer's *Iliad* and *Odyssey*. He died in 1698, leaving his wife in charge of the business, something fairly common in early modern Europe, where wives of artisans sometimes inherited guild privileges from a deceased husband.[4] In fact, *Telemachus* was among her first solo publications. Surely she thought that publishing an adventure tale in the guise of Homer was a safe bet, a work that fit nicely with other books published by her firm—after all, the Barbins had never been involved in a scandalous or illegal publication before. *Telemachus* would present the largest crisis in Marie Cochart's brief solo bookselling career.[5]

When the first run of 600 copies sold out almost instantly, Cochart covertly produced a second printing made to look like it had been completed before the ban.[6] Within a few weeks, however, even this second run was exhausted, but printing more copies seemed too dangerous. Cochart sold the entire manuscript to Adrien Moetjens, an old Dutch business associate of the Barbins's, who managed to publish the first complete edition of *Telemachus* in The Hague in August.[7] Moetjens's publication set off an eruption in the European book market. Before the year was finished, at least nine more unauthorized reprintings were produced in Brussels, Amsterdam, London, and other cities, and five more reprintings followed in 1700. Here was an instant European bestseller that seemed to fly off bookshelves. That all of these 1699 editions were shot through with "many errors" only increased demand for a corrected and definitive edition.[8] One early observer was struck by the immediate success of *Telemachus*: "If we must judge by the burning intensity with which this book is sought, it is the most excellent of all books. Never have so many copies been produced of any work. Never have so many editions been made of the same book. Nothing written has ever been read by so many people."[9] The more authoritative journal *News of the Republic of Letters*, edited by Pierre Bayle, concurred: "It has been a long time since a book has been sought after with such eagerness."[10]

One reason for the instant popularity of *Telemachus* was the pleasure that book buyers found reading it. "This is great writing," Bayle wrote to Earl of Shaftesbury. "The style is lively, happy, and beautiful."[11] The initial drive to popularity was due to its literary qualities. "The story of Telemachus," noted Richard Steele in the *Tatler*, "is formed altogether in the spirit of Homer, and will give an unlearned reader a notion of that great poet's manner of writing, more than any translation of him can possibly do." Steele regarded *Telemachus* as a book easily grasped by juveniles and adults alike. The key term here for Steele was "unlearned reader." One did not need to have read Homer itself to appreciate *Telemachus*—anyone who learned to read could enjoy the book as its own masterpiece, since it was aimed at "the greater part of my readers."[12]

Unlike later eighteenth-century readers, these early consumers did not approach the book as a political satire on Louis XIV. Steele was evidently correct that the book had special appeal for the young reader. "I have read *Telemachus*," wrote the eighteen-year-old Elizabeth James in 1701, "with as much pleasure (lately) as at the first time. I could almost envy the difficulty's [*sic*] of that young man, since it procured him so much wisdom."[13] Another intrepid reader smuggled *Telemachus* into church and read it instead of the prayer book.[14] One marker of the book's instantaneous popularity was the appearance of two major critical works against it that appeared in 1700, only a year following its initial publication. Both complained about the public's "passion" and "furor" to get its hands on the book.[15]

Even had the author's identity been left undiscovered, *Telemachus* would have made its mark as a grand literary success. But once the author's name was associated with it, the weight of his reputation colored every reading of the book. Within days of its first publication, the Abbé Dubos wrote to John Locke identifying the author as François Fénelon, Archbishop of Cambrai, and, more importantly, the former tutor of the Duc de Bourgogne, the eventual heir to Louis XIV.[16] Indeed, as became obvious to all readers, and repeated in one review after another, Fénelon had written *Telemachus* specifically as a tool to teach the preteen dauphin correct moral values. This book, then, provided a window into Europe's most powerful monarchy. In addition to its attractive style, the book's popularity had everything to do with the fame of its author and the specific historical circumstances of his manuscript.

Born in 1651 to an old and established French noble family, François de Salignac de la Mothe-Fénelon was ordained as a priest, committed fully to a religious life, and supported Louis XIV's efforts to purify Catholic France of its Protestant heretics and Spinozist non-believers. He cut an impressive figure with everyone he met. By his mid-thirties, contemporaries regarded him as an ambitious, intelligent, witty courtier with a bright future ahead of him at the apex of church and state. In 1689, his efforts bore fruit when the king appointed him official tutor of the *petit dauphin*, that is, the eldest grandson of Louis XIV. Fénelon oversaw the curriculum of all three grandsons of the king. Already established as an educator with the publication of a book on female education, he took his new task seriously. The young dauphin, only seven years old at Fénelon's appointment, became an unruly preteen who gave all those around him a good deal of trouble. Fénelon was forced to win him over with imaginative pedagogical innovations. *The Adventures of Telemachus*, probably completed between 1692 and 1693, when the dauphin was approximately eleven, was one significant outcome of these efforts.[17]

In 1702, Fénelon outlined the circumstances surrounding the publication of *Telemachus* in a letter to Cardinal Giovanni Maria Gabrielli, the Vatican interlocutor who defended the archbishop to the pope. He explained that he had prepared the book only in his capacity as tutor for the king's grandsons. He never planned to publish it or circulate it beyond a very small circle. Indeed, his great wish was that it never be published. But when a new copy of the manuscript was made, a deceitful valet "greedily" sold it to a bookseller for cash.[18]

There is no reason to doubt's Fénelon's words or intent. Scholars commonly claim that *Telemachus* was outlawed because Louis XIV found it offensive. "Louis XIV banned the book," writes Diane Brown, "which he took to be a *roman à clef* with himself caricatured in the figure of an evil despot."[19] This argument goes back at least to Paul Janet's standard account: "People saw in it a severe and malevolent criticism of the court and government of Louis XIV."[20] Little evidence supports this assertion. As far as is known, Louis XIV admired *Telemachus* and was content to have Fénelon use it in the education of his grandsons. "No one told me that it was forbidden to read *Telemachus* to the royal children," wrote the Duchess d'Orléans in April 1699. "The king gave the entire manuscript to the Duc de Bourgogne."[21] When Fénelon's rival Bishop Bossuet denounced the book, it was on literary grounds, not because of its political principles. Fénelon's enemies thought it undignified for an archbishop to publish light fiction, but nothing suggests they were offended by its political ideas.[22]

More likely, *Telemachus* was banned because it was caught up in the censoring of another book by Fénelon, the *Maxims of the Saints Explained*. A trenchant defense of a Catholic mystical doctrine known as Quietism, this work outraged Bossuet and alarmed the king. Published in 1697, the popular book was banned in March 1699 after a Vatican commission rejected its principles, only weeks prior to the publication of *Telemachus*. At the same time, Fénelon's apartments at Versailles were seized and he was no longer welcomed at court. Quietism split the court into rival factions. Meanwhile, copies of the *Telemachus* manuscript had been circulating around the court, provoking curiosity but no objections.[23] Fénelon's correspondence during the period never mentions *Telemachus*. Clearly, he viewed its publication as a rather minor event compared with the *Maxims of the Saints*, which for him was far more consequential. The government banned *Telemachus* not for its own ideas, but as fallout from the Quietism scandal and the suppression of the *Maxims*.[24]

Above all else, *The Adventures of Telemachus* is an episodic action story, an epic filled with exotic lands, gods and goddesses, and remarkable characters. A tribute to Homer and Virgil, *Telemachus* assumed that its reader is familiar with stories from the *Odyssey*. In the first four books of that great work, Telemachus, the son of Ulysses, leaves home in search of his father. Between Book 4 and Book 20, when he returns home, Telemachus is absent from Homer's narrative. Homer never gives us any information regarding his travels. Fénelon fills in that void. His story begins on Calypso's island, where that Goddess's grotto serves for some reflections on the beauty of natural surroundings. Soon, though, pulled by the hope of finding his father, Telemachus and his all-wise preceptor Mentor (actually the Goddess Minerva in disguise) cross the sea until they are captured and taken to Egypt, where Telemachus becomes a shepherd in the desert. Only books could mollify his despair. "Happy are those who love reading, and are not like me, deprived of books."[25] After endearing himself to the Egyptian king, he departs on a ship for Tyre, represented as a model commercial center where everyone works hard to increase industry. From there he is off to Cyprus, where he gets caught in a sort of love triangle with Venus and Cupid. In Crete, Telemachus encounters the powerful king and military commander, Idomeneus, whose actions give Mentor much fodder for political reflection. At one point, Telemachus and Mentor journey to Bétique, a small rural utopia, where everyone has enough to eat and luxury is disdained. Eventually, Telemachus realizes that Mentor has taught him enough so that he can learn on his own, and soon thereafter, Mentor reveals himself to be the Goddess Minerva, and then disappears. The book concludes with Telemachus finally locating his father.

Moetjens's 1701 Edition

In 1701 Adrian Moetjens published a new one-volume edition (see Figure 2.2), for which the Dutch government awarded him a multiyear "privilege," providing him the exclusive right to produce *Telemachus* in the Netherlands until 1714. Given Dutch hegemony over the European book trade, print runs increased to perhaps 2,000–3,000, making it for several years the standard version of *Telemachus*. Given competition from

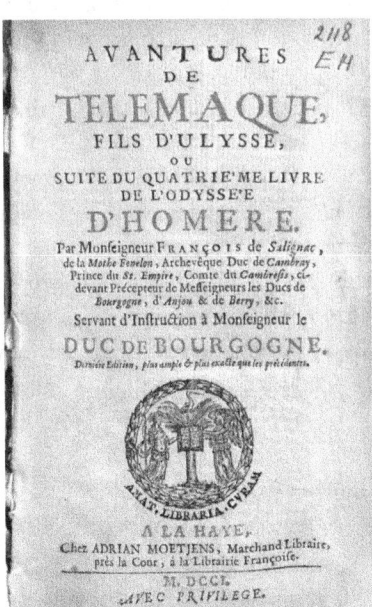

Figure 2.2 First edition title page from the complete *The Adventures of Telemachus*. After the government shut down the Barbin edition, the publisher sold the manuscript to the Dutch publisher Adrian Moetjens.

outside Holland, Moetjens's embellished the editions. The 1701 edition was the first to list Fénelon's name on the title page, albeit without the author's permission, and Moetjens also arbitrarily divided the narrative into ten chapters, adding summaries for each. In 1705, his was the first to feature illustrations. In 1711, he increased the number of illustrations from seven to ten, adding five more for the 1715 edition.[26]

Arguably, Moetjens's most important contribution to these editions was hiring a sympathetic Frenchmen well known to Fénelon, Jean Baptiste de la Landelle, Abbé de Saint-Rémy, to write a long introduction that reframed the work within a narrative that highlighted Quietism and religious dissent. Saint-Rémy retold a story already familiar to many readers: During the 1690s, while Fénelon was tutoring the king's three grandsons, he came under the spell of an inspired mystic, Jeanne-Marie Bouvier de la Motte-Guyon. A wealthy widow who turned her energy to religion, she rooted her ideas in long-standing traditions of Christian mysticism. Like many other theologians, she believed that often the human ego became an obstacle to knowing God's love. If prayer was motivated by an attempt to obtain something from God, whether it be health, long life, redemption, or some other benefit, then prayer was, at the end of the day, worshipping God for selfish ends. What was needed, she argued, was "pure love." This divine love could be experienced only by annihilating the self—that is, by removing any egoistic motivations. Urging Christians to meditate, pray, and rely solely upon God's love and to think of nothing else but God, she promised that with the correct fortitude, such deep reflection would link with God's heart. The result would be an abandonment of the self and a union with the divine. At that point, one could finally experience directly the love of Christ promised in scripture.

Fénelon met Madame Guyon in 1689 and was immediately struck by her insights and seriousness of purpose. In over 125 letters to one another, they became such close friends that enemies hinted that perhaps there was something more carnal to their friendship—a charge without any substantiation. Although Fénelon was ostensibly her supervisor, when it came to Quietist mysticism, he became her student. "God opens [the self] to himself by pushing out the *amour propre* [self-conceit] that once occupied the space," Fénelon wrote. "To be in God is to be entirely dispossessed of one's will and to want only by means of purely divine movement."[27] Soon Guyon's Quietism also captured the imagination of the king's mistress and soon-to-be secret wife, Madame de Maintenon—although unlike Fénelon, her induction into Quietism did not last long.

In his 1701 preface to *Telemachus*, Saint-Rémy placed blame for Fénelon's fall on Bishop Bossuet. Meditation and other forms of pure love, charged Bossuet, prevented a Catholic from fully reflecting upon one's sins in preparation for confession and contrition. Sins, in short, might go unaddressed and even ignored. The danger of such ideas became apparent when Guyon moved into a convent and stories soon leaked out that many of the resident nuns had foregone their regular spiritual duties and daily chores in order to immerse themselves in emotional and solitary meditation. Soon Bossuet and other church elites began to view Guyon's ideas as dangerous.

Nevertheless, Fénelon remained her champion and friend, refusing to break with her. For Saint-Rémy, the conflict between Fénelon and opponents like Bossuet was motivated by fundamentally religious issues rather than political concerns. Fénelon's treatment was evidence of "cruel persecution," in which a man was punished for pursuing a strict Catholicism. For Saint-Rémy, "pure and disinterested love" was no heresy, but a noble calling at the root of Fénelon's inspired Christianity. The more this story was retold, the more "the public condemns [Fénelon's] adversaries and admires his behavior."[28]

According to Saint-Rémy, the circumstances surrounding the publication of *Telemachus* proved inextricable from religious controversies and Fénelon's exile. He explained to readers that Fénelon himself had nothing whatsoever to do with its publication. All responsibility fell on his deceitful valet. Regrettably, Fénelon was still in no position to review or correct this edition: "His modesty and perhaps his fear of reprisal from the powerful" prevents any involvement.[29] Fénelon himself welcomed Saint-Rémy's preface at one level but also complained to friends that it was not sufficiently religious in spirit and purpose.[30]

Saint-Rémy's preface gives *Telemachus* a peculiarly Dutch orientation. Holland and England, after all, had been at war with King Louis XIV for much of the 1690s and the first decade of the eighteenth century. For the Dutch, Louis was a ruthless tyrant who sought to incorporate Holland and all Protestant lands into a universal Catholic monarchy. The preface claims that the king's treatment of Fénelon, whose Christian morals were beyond reproach, demonstrates his bigotry and intolerance. If such a man as Fénelon was unsafe at the court of Louis XIV, everyone outside of France should shudder at the prospect of French expansion. Saint-Rémy's preface was influential, and it was reprinted at least five times during the next decade.

Historian Lionel Rothkrug argues that Fénelon's description in *Telemachus* of the ancient city of Tyre was meant as a veiled tribute to Amsterdam.

> The Tyrians are industrious, patient, laborious, clean sober, and frugal. They have a well-regulated administration; there is no discord among them; never was there a people more firm and steady, more candid, more loyal, more trusty, or more kind to strangers. This, without seeking out other causes, will account for their having the empire of the sea, and such a flourishing commerce in their ports.

Nothing in Saint-Rémy's preface suggested that contemporary readers made this connection explicitly, but it does describe a Dutch ideal of its golden age and may partly explain *Telemachus*'s popularity in Holland. Certainly, Rothkrug is correct to highlight that from the start, *Telemachus* was as admired in Protestant Europe as it was in Catholic France.[31]

Likewise, *Telemachus* had a special resonance in England, which produced more editions of the book than any other Protestant country during the eighteenth century. Many English read *Telemachus* as a call for a more limited monarchy, despite Fénelon's personal commitment to absolutism. Quoting *Telemachus*, one review emphasized "that the king is above the People, but the laws are above the king. He has an absolute power to do good, but his hands are tied so soon as he attempts to do ill." In this monarchical ideal, reflective of Whig principles following the 1689 Glorious Revolution, the monarch's goal is "to sacrifice himself to the public good." The seeds for later viewing Fénelon as a fundamentally political thinker were first planted here.[32]

Saint-Rémy had highlighted Fénelon's religious dissent. With the outbreak of the War of the Spanish Succession (1701–14), however, in which Holland, England, and Austria allied against France over control of the Spanish throne, commentators turned Fénelon from a religious maverick into a political dissident. Despite Fénelon's strict loyalty to the Gallican Church, his Quietism was increasingly presented as a surrogate for dissident political views. "His pretended heresy was only a pretext to turn him off," argued one British writer. "His real crime . . . was in politics and not in divinity." From this perspective, it was not Quietism but writing *Telemachus* that supposedly got Fénelon into trouble; its principles were increasingly perceived contrary to Louis XIV, and readers in this context began to see the book as a covert political act. "A prelate who had the courage to insinuate with so much art and reason to three young Princes, that they ought to take special care not to imitate their Grandfather" was a threat to the court. In this reading, Fénelon was banished from Louis XIV's inner circle less because of his religious mysticism than for the political principles supposedly embedded in *Telemachus*.[33] Fénelon's good friend, the Duc de Saint-Simon, later recalled the situation in similar terms. "*Telemachus*," he wrote, was "the famous work that served most of all to plunge him in disfavor and render him unforgiveable."[34]

The story of Fénelon's *Telemachus* involves not only the reception of the book itself but also the story of the changing context in which it was continually reframed and reintroduced for new purposes. Its most dramatic turning point in the eighteenth century occurred between 1711 and 1717, when the deaths of two dauphins, Fénelon and Louis XIV, allowed for a posthumous reintroduction of *Telemachus* in an entirely new political environment: Louis XV's regency.

In April 1711, Louis, the Grand Dauphin (1661–1711), died, making his eldest son, the Duc de Bourgogne (1682–1712), next in line for the French throne. Fénelon had been the Duc de Bourgogne's tutor, and they had remained close, even during the years of Fénelon's residency in Cambrai. It was clear that Fénelon would play a major role in the government of the new king, alongside other powerful nobles, including the Duc de Saint-Simon; Paul de Beauvilliers, Duc de Saint-Aignan; and Charles Honoré d'Albert de Luynes, Duc de Chevreuse, a group later described as the "Burgundy Circle." But none was as central as Fénelon. "They had one aim," wrote Saint-Simon, "the return to power of Fénelon their leader."[35]

As soon as Bourgogne became next in line, this Burgundy Circle set about making plans for reforming the monarchy. They advocated an immediate end to the long War of the Spanish Succession; they wanted to impose more frugality on the royal court and to tax luxury in general through sumptuary laws; and, most important, they hoped to constrain the monarchy's absolutism through the establishment of local and national advisory councils. Some of these plans circulated among leaders in a manuscript entitled Table de Chaulnes, named for the chateau where Fénelon and friends strategized.[36] Tragically for Fénelon, however, the new dauphin succumbed to measles and died in February 1712, less than a year after his father. Fénelon's political ambitions were now dashed. While continuing to try to press his ideas for political reform, Fénelon found Louis XIV ignoring his recommendations.[37]

Fénelon died in January 1715, and Louis XIV followed him in September. During his first few years as regent, the boy-king's uncle, the Duc d'Orléans, applied some of the Burgundy Circles reforms, specifically adopting the notion of special advisory councils, now called the Polysynody, even stating at one point what Mentor had told Telemachus: "He wished to be obstructed from doing evil, but he wished to be free to do good."[38] Fénelon's political tracts and correspondence circulated among the Paris elite, and sometimes made their way into print. His reputation as a political reformer grew as the Regency tried to modernize the monarchy and gain some distance from Louis XIV. Before 1711, Saint-Rémy and others conveyed a sense that Fénelon was a victim of Louis XIV's absolutism, primarily for the role he played in the Quietist Affair, that is, more for his religious views than for any adverse political dissent. After 1711, a growing sense among commentators emerged that Fénelon was first and foremost a statesman who would have played an important political role, probably at the ministerial level, if only he and his patron/student had lived a little longer. Curiously, readers and commentators projected his would-be future as a minister back to the 1690s when he composed *Telemachus*, as if somehow a mature political program had been embedded in that book.

Ramsay's 1717 "First Edition"

Meanwhile, Fénelon's great-nephew, the Marquis de Fénelon, obtained possession of his uncle's papers and began plans for an edition of *Telemachus* that would be true to the original manuscript. He hired a thirty-year-old Scot, Andrew Michael Ramsay, to oversee the preparation of an entirely new version of *Telemachus*. Already affected by Quietism in England, Ramsay had come to meet Fénelon in 1711, and had lived with him for a few years as one of his closest acolytes. The original manuscript published in 1699 and 1700 had no chapters, and Moetjens's subsequent divisions were arbitrary—a publisher's device. Ramsay discovered that Fénelon himself had divided the story into eighteen chapters in a second manuscript copy. Nevertheless, he and Fénelon's family agreed that it would be best if the text were divided into twenty-four chapters, since that was the case for Homer's *Odyssey*, the book's literary parent. In this new edition, a frontispiece and summary prefaced each chapter. More significant, Ramsay produced a fifty-page essay that now served as the book's introduction, "A Discourse on Epic Poetry and of the Excellence of the Poem of Telemachus." The title page announced that this was no reprint, or new edition, but in fact, the "first edition, conforming to the original manuscript," that rendered all previous editions corrupt and obsolete. Signaling the role that *Telemachus* might play for the new French king (Louis XV was only seven years old in 1717), the title page proclaimed that the Regency government now championed the book ("with the privilege of the king"), allowing it to be openly published in Paris for the first time since 1699. Finally, Fénelon's name was not only printed in large type on the title page, but he was described in the three dimensions most recognized by the public: first, as the late dauphin's preceptor; second, as a religious leader (the Archbishop of Cambrai); and finally as a statesman in his own right, "a prince of the Holy Roman Empire."[39]

With such impressive authority behind it, this 1717 "first edition" instantly became the model for all others during the eighteenth century. All *Telemachus* editions would now be divided into twenty-four chapters, each assuming a uniform title and summary. Not until 1820 would an edition appear that reverted to Fénelon's intended eighteen chapters. Just as important, Fénelon's work remained married to Ramsay's "Discourse on Epic Poetry." It became the most common eighteenth-century introduction to *Telemachus*, pirated by many unauthorized publishers. More than any other single paratext, Ramsay's introduction framed the way readers understood *Telemachus*.

Ramsay's "Discourse" was, of course, principally a literary analysis of *Telemachus* as an epic poem, even though it was written in prose form. And yet it was also among the earliest and most influential essays that made the argument for *Telemachus* as a serious work of political theory. For Ramsay, *Telemachus* was not merely a dramatic adventure story aimed for young people, nor a didactic tale meant to teach adolescents certain moral precepts; it was first and foremost a serious work about the nature of monarchy. He explained that Fénelon was not only a great writer but a philosopher as well. "Sublime in its principles," Fénelon's work "arises from a profound knowledge of man."[40]

Ramsay contended that there were two main features that distinguished *Telemachus* as a work of serious political thought: First, virtue was redefined from a moral characteristic embedded in the personality of the monarch to the ends of political action itself. Above all, virtue meant that the monarch would work toward the interests of the nation, for the welfare of all its people, rather than some other notion of self-satisfying glory. "Virtue not only contributes to prepare Man for a future felicity, but even in this life actually makes society as happy as it is possible for it to be." Second, Ramsey claimed that Fénelon redefined war and conflict among neighboring states as something unnatural. Fénelon conceived "the whole world" as "nothing but a universal Republic. . . . We no longer confine ourselves to the love of our country; our heart enlarges itself, grows immensely capacious, and takes the whole world into an universal friendship."[41]

Ramsay placed *Telemachus* squarely within early modern political theory. "Everybody knows the systems of Machiavelli, Hobbes, and of [the] two authors somewhat more moderate, Pufendorf and Grotius." Although *Telemachus* never mentioned or cited any contemporary thinkers, Ramsay set Fénelon in dialog with these early modern political thinkers. According to Ramsay, Fénelon's theories meant to attack Machiavelli and Hobbes head-on, whose ideas were based on "despotic power, injustice, and irreligion." Having demonstrated the just correspondence between virtue and the public good, *Telemachus* would replace *The Prince* as the leading guidebook for statesmen. With respect to "the more moderate" Pufendorf and Grotius, Fénelon's critique was meant to be subtler. Like *Telemachus*, their work also embraced "the good of society, and referred almost everything to the happiness of man." But their arguments were based on "pagan maxims," largely derivative of Plato and Cicero, and wholly inferior to those ancient authors. Unable to appreciate the central place of virtue, Pufendorf's and Grotius's theories ultimately devolved into sophisticated excuses for egotism and pleasure, a position not so different from that of Machiavelli and Hobbes. Against these four thinkers, argued Ramsay, Fénelon's formulation proved more innovative and significant. "The author of *Telemachus* is Original," Ramsay claimed, "in having joined the most perfect Politics to the ideas of the most consummate virtue."[42]

Affixed to many editions of *Telemachus*, Ramsay's essay helped determine how the book was read during the eighteenth century. Before 1717, *Telemachus* was regarded as a literary masterpiece and moral primer for young adults, but after this "first edition," it became recognized also as a masterpiece of political philosophy. For eighteenth-century readers, *Telemachus* could be read on at least three different levels: First, as a playful adventure story in the style of Homer; second, as a criticism of Louis XIV's court by one of its dissidents; and third, as a work that helped establish the strain of Enlightenment moral and political theory that made virtue central to any legitimate government. Ramsay's preface successfully demonstrated how these different readings could be complementary, feeding off one another.[43]

Of course, throughout the eighteenth century, *Telemachus* also continued to be appreciated for its literary qualities. Many readers used it as a model to improve their own writing. For example, in 1760, a young woman who spent all her years in Pennsylvania, Betsy Fergusson, began an English verse translation when she was twenty-three and finally completed it thirty years later. In her diary, she nicknamed a close friend "Mentor" and hoped that her "Ulysses" (Betsy's traveling husband) would soon come home.[44] And yet, as the book became taken more seriously for its political philosophy, it increasingly became associated with the Enlightenment. One British political commentator noted that while the book has "met with such an universal approbation," it must not be read as merely light fiction. Fénelon's insights are "too amply verified in real life by the histories of all nations, but by none more than those of our own." Increasingly read as a presumptive attack upon despotism, *Telemachus* illustrated what happened when kings amassed too much power. The book taught that a king who rules "the People by force" crossed the line into despotism, the opposite of Fénelon's model of kingship. The despot

> must encourage luxury amongst all degrees of People, in order to reduce them to poverty, and thereby keep them in a constant state of corruption and dependence.

He must discountenance all men of virtue and abilities, in every profession, by preferring only those who are fit tools and instruments for such a design. In short, he must endeavor to quell the spirits, and subvert the liberties of the People, as well as to draw the national wealth into a few coffers by severe and oppressive laws, which cannot be put in execution without military force.[45]

Telemachus was always read as a work about kingship. Ramsey's 1717 edition reframed it as a major work of political thought. Certainly Montesquieu, who set about writing *Persian Letters* in hopes of doing something similar at virtually the same moment, viewed *Telemachus* from this perspective. Readers increasingly recognized Fénelon as a serious philosopher who had chosen a whimsical genre as a vehicle for presenting deep and sustaining ideas, just as Montesquieu, Voltaire, Graffigny, and Hume were soon to imitate. As his philosophical weight increased, his Quietism was minimized. After 1717, for many readers the posthumous Fénelon became a philosophe who had spoken truth at court, who had preached virtue to a vain king, but was banished to Cambrai for his noble actions. Here, too, was a gifted writer whose prose interested not only the narrow band of travelers in the Republic of Letters but all kinds of readers among an emerging public.[46]

As *Telemachus* became read as political thought, its eponymous character was overshadowed by his tutor, Mentor, whom everyone viewed as Fénelon's mouthpiece. In this respect, it is important to note that this 1717 edition was the first—but hardly the last—to include a frontispiece of Archbishop Fénelon himself rather than (as earlier editions had) characters from his story. Like Voltaire and Rousseau, the posthumous Fénelon became an Enlightenment celebrity, and *Telemachus* became absorbed into the Enlightenment. Patrick Riley is not mistaken when he writes that "the two most important pieces of French political theory at the turn of the eighteenth century are Bossuet's *Politics Drawn from the Very Words of Holy Scripture* (completed in 1704) and Fénelon's *Telemachus*," but contemporaries would have begun to agree with this assertion only after 1717.[47] Readers during the Regency of Louis XV—but not before, and certainly not Louis XIV himself—found *Telemachus* a satirical and oppositional political text. In doing so, they reframed *Telemachus* to make it consistent with the emerging Enlightenment. Understandably, enemies of the Enlightenment later blamed Ramsay for kidnapping Fénelon from the church and imprisoning him among the "Sophists [Denis] Diderot and [Jean Le Rond] d'Alembert."[48]

The format of the 1717 edition also helped transform *Telemachus* into a serious philosophical work. Early editions were all mostly duodecimos, that is, fairly small books meant to be inexpensive, as was common for the adventure fiction genre. When Fénelon's reputation as a statesman grew during the period 1711–12, Moetjens produced an octavo edition, claiming on its title page to be "larger and better than earlier editions."[49] The 1717 edition was likewise an octavo, and after 1717, publishers and readers collaborated to make octavo its most common format, raising the stature of *Telemachus* to a more serious book.[50]

One example of its new status and appeal to elite book buyers was the lavish quarto edition published by Parisian Marie-Madeleine Le Gras (widow of Florentin Delaulne) in 1730. A year earlier Le Gras had published a duodecimo edition, so booksellers were offering discriminating consumers a choice by producing the same version in this luxurious format. During the eighteenth century, quartos became more unusual and connoted a book of serious and enduring value. The London quarto edition of Alexander Pope's English translation of Homer's *Iliad*, for example, is noteworthy among book historians because its high price generated much revenue for the publisher.[51] In 1734, the Dutch publishing firm of Wetstein, Smith, and Chatelain went one step further.

> Wetstein, Smith and Chatelain are now distributing their new and noble edition of the Adventures of Telemach, in Folio and in Quarto, which has been so many years preparing. They pretend it is printed, with all the care imaginable, from the original manuscript, communicated to them by the Marquis de Fénelon, the King of France's Ambassador at The Hague, and great nephew of the illustrious author. This volume is embellished with 24 copper-plates, engraven by the best hands, besides the author's picture, and a Frontispiece designed by the late Bernard Picart, and other ornaments at the beginning and end of every chapter.[52]

Not only did Wetstein, Smith, and Chatelain directly compete with the Paris quarto in producing their own, but they specially published 300 copies of a folio edition, intended for readers of "advanced age"[53] who not only loved *Telemachus* but wanted an edition they could cherish and return to again and again.[54] Nonetheless, the publication of these extraordinary editions was not without controversy. Objecting to Wetstein, Smith, and Chatelain's contention that their edition was superior to the 1731 Hamburg octavo edition (because the latter had no illustrations or maps), a British reader claimed "the assertion to be false," criticizing the Dutch publisher for publishing *Telemachus* "at extravagant prices."[55] Regardless of controversy, one mark of a great private library during the eighteenth century was the inclusion of a *Telemachus* quarto, such as the English copy belonging to George Washington at Mount Vernon.[56] Nonetheless, more pedestrian owners of cheaper duodecimos often felt just as strongly about their copies of *Telemachus*. When one American reader inscribed her name boldly—"Sarah Logan Her Book 1723"—into her 1719 Amsterdam duodecimo, no one in Philadelphia or anywhere else was prouder than she.[57]

Another way to observe the remarkable publication history of *Telemachus* during the eighteenth century is to compare it with Fénelon's other writings. After all, he thought of himself fundamentally as a religious thinker, courtier, and spiritual advisor, and regarded his most important work to be the *Maxims of the Saints Explained*. Yet, curiously, no editions in French of the mystical *Maxims* were published during the eighteenth century. Of course, the pontifical decree against the book made it unwise, if not precarious, to publish it in Catholic countries. But surely publishing *Maxims* would have been easy in neighboring Protestant states.[58] England produced only three editions in English, but neither England nor Holland (where it had been published in 1697), nor any Swiss or German publisher, produced the *Maxims* in French. This in contrast to many works of the philosophes—*Candide* and *The Spirit of the Laws* among them—which were printed in French outside of France and easily smuggled into that country. Nothing like that occurred with the *Maxims*. Fénelon's other writings, while certainly available, were much less popular, together totaling around twenty-five editions in all. Even during the French Revolution, when publishers could print virtually anything, the Didot firm excluded the *Maxims* when it published a major collection of Fénelon's works. During the eighteenth century, then, Fénelon's religious writings seem to have been neglected by the public, while *Telemachus* won him status as a proto-philosophe and political theorist. Whatever the reason, compared with the seventeenth, nineteenth, twentieth, and twenty-first centuries, the eighteenth century was unique for embracing only Fénelon's secular works.[59]

Table 2.1 indicates the popularity of *Telemachus* throughout the century. Nearly every decade saw an increased number of editions published, indicating new readers who either did not have access to or were not satisfied with older editions. There were altogether some 421 editions of *Telemachus* published between 1699 and 1800, which is more, in fact, than any of Voltaire's works, more than Richardson's *Clarissa* or any other English novel of the period, and certainly more than Rousseau's works, even when averaging publications per year since first printed. *Telemachus* editions outstripped Montesquieu's *Persian Letters* and Graffigny's *Peruvian Letters* with more than thrice the editions of most other bestsellers. No other book except perhaps the Bible went through as many eighteenth-century editions. The eighteenth-century publication history of *Telemachus* is unique.

Thanks to the ingenuity of Simon Burrows and his team at Western Sydney University, we can map sales of *Telemachus*, at least for one relatively large bookseller/publisher, the Société typographique de Neuchâtel, whose sales records have been digitized for the years 1769–94. From Sweden to Italy, from Ireland and Portugal to Russia and Poland, StN sales of *Telemachus* cover virtually all of Europe. Where the StN did not penetrate—Prussia and the Low Countries—reflects the dominance of Dutch publishers in those markets. Significant are the seventy or so copies sold by the StN to Moscow and St. Petersburg bookstores, given that Neuchâtel is 2,700 kilometers from Moscow! While eastern France led in sales, the cosmopolitan and diverse demand for the book is striking.[60]

Enlightenment Absorption

Enlightenment authors and publishers, including Hume, Montesquieu, Mirabeau, Helvétius, Rousseau, and Raynal, were struck by the influence of *Telemachus*, and wondered if they could produce serious books capable of approaching its popularity. At the same time, they joined many others who recast *Telemachus* as an Enlightenment work. When, for example, a British magazine in 1793 looked back on the century's most celebrated authors of the French Enlightenment, it featured only Fénelon, Voltaire, Rousseau, and Raynal. That a Quietist archbishop could one day seem to belong in a group that included Voltaire, Rousseau, and Raynal is indeed extraordinary. As Colin Jones observed, *Telemachus* is "a classic demonstration of how readers' reception can transcend an author's intentions."[61]

The appropriation of *Telemachus* as a founding text of the European Enlightenment is a complex story involving readers, writers, and publishers, and none was more instrumental than Voltaire. Throughout Voltaire's books and correspondence are references to Fénelon, with whom he engaged over his career. When Voltaire was younger, trying to make his name as a poet, he considered Fénelon primarily as a literary rival.[62] Especially during the 1730s, as both Voltaire and Fénelon began to achieve reputations as literary masters, Voltaire challenged the case being made for Fénelon by Ramsay and others. In the 1737 preface to his best-selling epic poem *La Henriade*, Voltaire dismissed Fénelon for writing *Telemachus* in prose and charged him with lacking the skill to write it in rhymed poetry.[63] To friends, he criticized Fénelon's style as second-rate melodramatic monotone. And yet, he never fully rejected the older writer. Whatever reservations Voltaire may have had, his veneration of Fénelon grew as he himself became more secure. At one point during the Regency, Voltaire urged Cardinal Fleury to read *Telemachus* to the young boy-king, Louis XV, just as Fénelon had done with the Duc de Bourgogne.[64] When the Marquis d'Argenson sent Voltaire a copy of his *Considérations sur le gouvernement ancien et présent de la France* in 1739, Voltaire fondly compared it to *Telemachus*.[65]

Telemachus played an important role in the *Anti-Machiavel*, a collaborative project between Voltaire and the heir to the Prussian throne, Frederick II. "Compare the prince of Fénelon with that of Machiavelli," Voltaire and Frederick wrote, "you will see that one is all about goodness, equity, and virtue," while the other is filled with "villainy, perfidy, and criminality." The contrast is not simply that one author portrayed a good king, while the other indulged a bad one. Rather, the reading process itself becomes a moral exercise. "In reading Fénelon's *Telemachus*," they continued, "it seems like our nature is lifted towards the angels," while "it would seem that our soul nears the devil in Hell when we read Machiavelli's *Prince*." Echoing Ramsay's 1717 "Discourse," Frederick used Fénelon to directly rebuke Machiavelli.[66] However, Voltaire hoped to rein in the Prussian heir's idealism. "The one is principally written for young people, the other for adults," wrote Voltaire. The enjoyable and moral novel, *Telemachus*, is a juvenile "mish-mash of incredible adventures." Voltaire hoped that their *Anti-Machiavel* updated the core message of *Telemachus* for mature readers.[67]

By the 1740s, Voltaire was more admiring of Fénelon as an exemplar and, in particular, praised the "style and morality of *Telemachus*."[68] When he published his play *Oreste* in 1750, Voltaire commented on how Fénelon deserved to be recognized as the "second greatest master of eloquence and the first in making virtue appealing."[69] In order to ready Fénelon for the pantheon of progressive philosophes, an older Voltaire even made excuses for his religious mysticism. "Quietism was a craziness that took over Fénelon's Perigordian head, but an excusable craziness, and even somewhat heroic for him."[70]

Voltaire's most extensive and influential portrait of Fénelon came in *The Age of Louis XIV*, first published in 1751 and among his most popular works. There Voltaire's treatment of Fénelon is highly idiosyncratic. First, contrary to general opinion, Voltaire insisted that *Telemachus* was not written for the Duc de Bourgogne, but completed later in Cambrai, only after Fénelon became archbishop there. This small alteration in *Telemachus*'s genesis was crucial for remapping the book onto an Enlightenment platform. If Fénelon had written *Telemachus* after incurring the wrath of the court, it could more easily be seen as a work of political opposition, and not simply an adventure story written for preteen royal heirs. During the long War of the Spanish Succession, according to Voltaire, Europeans saw in Louis XIV "the character Idomeneus, whose arrogance disgusted his neighbors. . . . Foreigners and even the French themselves, weary of so many wars, saw with malicious relief a satire in a book written for the purpose of inculcating virtue."[71]

In *The Age of Louis XIV*, Voltaire recognized *Telemachus* as "one of the finest monuments of a brilliant age," but he nonetheless could never fully endorse Fénelon's melodramatic writing style. "Its wearisomeness, its details, its too little connected adventures, and its oft-repeated and little-varied descriptions of country life" made *Telemachus* problematic for a writer to emulate. Fénelon invented "a style which could belong to none other than himself."[72] What every writer could hope to imitate, however, was the book's popularity, securing and sustaining a wide readership. "Innumerable editions were brought out. I have myself seen forty in the English language," Voltaire wrote.[73]

As *Telemachus*'s reputation grew as a serious work of social thought, Voltaire published *Le Mondain*, a bold poem published in 1736 that rebuked Fénelon's notion of luxury. The poem specifically called out *Telemachus* for criticism, defending a cosmopolitan and consumerist economy, where individuals spend lavishly on themselves for pleasure.[74] According to Nicholas Cronk's analysis, Voltaire's most famous line from that poem, *Le superflu, chose très nécessaire* (the superfluous, a very necessary thing), was written in direct response to the many times *superflu* is contrasted with *nécessaire* in *Telemachus*. For example, in Book Five, Fénelon contrasts *l'abondance des choses nécessaires, le mépris des superflues* (the abundance of all necessary things, the contempt for superfluities).[75] Voltaire did not deny a monarch's penchant for luxury and extravagance but disagreed that it ruined a nation's economy. Echoing other Enlightenment writers, such as Bernard Mandeville and David Hume, Voltaire insisted that trade in luxuries does not add to the poverty of the poor through worsening inequality, but, rather, that it creates jobs and stimulates wage growth. Voltaire conceded that luxury might ruin an ancient city-state that was already impoverished, but it was necessary for modern monarchies; it "destroys a state that's poor" and "enriches one that's great."[76] Voltaire and Frederick made the same point in their *Anti-Machiavel*: "The luxury which comes from abundance, and which makes riches circulate through all the veins of a state, makes a great kingdom flourish."[77]

As with Voltaire, Montesquieu's engagement with *Telemachus* was enduring. "I have reread *Telemachus* with delight," Montesquieu wrote in an extended undated reflection. For him, *Telemachus* was more than simply advice to a dauphin. Using an inventive format that "rivals the *Odyssey*," Montesquieu found Fénelon constructing a work saturated with profound moral and political truths. Fénelon "knew the heart inside out and he knew the mind inside out."[78]

It is unlikely a coincidence that Montesquieu began writing *Persian Letters* shortly after the "first" edition of *Telemachus* appeared in 1717. "The divine work of this age, *Telemachus*," exclaimed Montesquieu in his notebook.[79] Montesquieu was deeply impressed with how Fénelon had managed to weave adventure, myth, philosophy, and politics into a unified work that navigated the boundaries of various genres, while appealing both to general readers and to more high-minded members of the Republic of Letters. In effect, he read *Telemachus* through Andrew Michael Ramsay's filtered introduction that argued for a work more profound than a juvenile adventure story. Nonetheless, Montesquieu attributed its success more to Fénelon's literary style than its political ideas: "M. [Fénelon] is an enchanter who seduces us by force of charms and spells."[80] Mixing philosophy with a wit and style was what Montesquieu himself set out to do in *Persian Letters*. After all, as Montesquieu recognized, philosophers held very few books in such high regard that were also sought after by servants.[81]

Much of Montesquieu's 1721 novel is modeled on *Telemachus*. Its central character, Usbek, is an amalgam of Telemachus, Mentor, and even Fénelon himself. Usbek finds himself in exile from the Persian royal court because, like Fénelon, he told truth to power. He travels first to Italy and then to France, where, like Fénelon, his friends regarded him an expert in philosophical notions of virtue. Mentor-like, Usbek offers wisdom and advice to his friends on various philosophical subjects. From Fénelon, like *Telemachus*, *Persian Letters* is not governed by an overarching plot as in a modern novel, but is a piece of fictional travel literature, filled with many disparate and episodic tales that provide moral and political reflection. Throughout the eighteenth century, many readers perceived a connection between the two works. Montesquieu "hath adorned his prose with the animated, figurative, and poetic style," wrote one critic, "which the romance of *Telemachus* gave the first example among us."[82] Without *Telemachus*, it is unlikely the youthful Montesquieu would have produced *Persian Letters*.

For decades, scholars have seen in Montesquieu's parable of the Troglodytes (which take up Letters 11-14 of *Persian Letters*) the heavy influence of Fénelon's description of Bétique.[83] And yet, whatever his admiration for *Telemachus*, Montesquieu joined Voltaire in rebuking Fénelon over the role of luxurious consumption in a modern economy. In the Kingdom of Salente, for example, Mentor recommends that monarchs prohibit "all foreign merchandise that might introduce luxury and effeminacy" and regulate "the dress and diet of all different ranks."[84] Montesquieu sharply disagreed with Fénelon. In a modern commercial economy, governments should not restrict a merchant's ability to import and export commodities. Fénelon's ideas "may work in a small Greek town" but "must not be applied to a great monarchy."[85] In *The Spirit of the Laws*, Montesquieu would develop this notion by arguing that while ancient republics were appropriately frugal, modern kingdoms were naturally expansive in terms of both commerce and territory. The British economist Benjamin Vaughn was skeptical that Montesquieu had surpassed Fénelon: "Montesquieu in his writings on this subject of political prosperity has scarcely made nearer approaches to the truth than Fénelon; and he certainly fell short of him in courage in declaring it."[86]

Before Ramsay's 1717 edition that reframed *Telemachus* as a philosophical work, readers appreciated the book mainly for its poetic qualities. Beginning with Voltaire and Montesquieu, political theorists focused most on how Fénelon managed to combine the light and airy vehicle of a clichéd adventure story with innovative and profound reflections on political life. As the book became increasingly known for its political qualities, other writers began to see that one could fruitfully mix entertaining and scholarly genres into a potent new cocktail. By combining some elements of low fiction with deep reflections, Enlightenment writers could bring philosophy to a much larger readership. Such an audience was surely not a mass readership—that would wait for the nineteenth century. Rather, the more moderate goal of these philosophes was to reach the broad swath of middle- and upper-class elites in Europe, who until now had read little political or philosophical literature. Fénelon's "books are made to delight people," wrote the Abbé Raynal. Paraphrasing Mentor's own words in *Telemachus*, Raynal added that Fénelon's "writings are truly inspiring so that people love their kings and are in turn beloved by them."[87]

Montesquieu and Voltaire were typical of their generation who held ambivalent views of Fénelon. Both of them were young adults when Fénelon died, and they were close to people who knew him. They knew that he had been an ambitious religious mystic who never opposed Louis XIV's 1685 Revocation of the Edict of Nantes and who remained a powerful archbishop and royal courtier until his dismissal from the royal court during the 1690s after the publication of the *Maxims of the Saints Explained*. British aristocrat Lord Chesterfield (1694–1773) provided an example of someone from this generation who thought Fénelon was a sincere theologian, but also a two-faced Machiavellian who had hoped to become chief minister one day—someone not so different from Cardinal Richelieu or Bishop Bossuet.[88] Disagreeing with Montesquieu, Voltaire, and Chesterfield was Marie Anne de Vichy Chamroud, Marquise du Deffand (1697–1780), who insisted that "Fénelon was not a hypocrite" but rather a "martyr" who sacrificed himself for his principles.[89] Her view was championed by a mostly younger group of Paris philosophes, including Helvétius, d'Alembert, Mirabeau, Condorcet, and especially Rousseau, who dropped any pretense of critical perspective and identified Fénelon's ideas fully with their own. In their eyes, only a perfect soul was capable of writing *Telemachus*.

The Enlightenment matured during the 1750s and 1760s as these Paris philosophes became recognized throughout Europe for their books and other projects, most notably the twenty-eight-volume *Encyclopédie*, edited by Denis Diderot and Jean Le Rond d'Alembert.[90] According to the ARTFL database, "Télémaque" appears thirty-nine times in the *Encyclopédie* and "Fénelon" thirty-two.[91] Given the size of the

Encyclopédie, this is only a modest appearance, but the placement of these references is instructive. First, Fénelon's participation in Quietism was duly noted, largely through the satirical lens of Voltaire's *Age of Louis XIV*.[92] Second, *Telemachus* was recognized as a literary masterpiece and a treasure of eloquence, noted for its popularity. "The number of editions of *Telemachus* are impossible to count. There are more than thirty in English and more than ten in Dutch."[93] Finally, the *Encyclopédie* used *Telemachus* as a key work of Enlightenment political theory. In the brief, but pithy, article "Revolt," Louis de Jaucourt explained that people rise up only when their leaders become corrupt and oppressive. Jaucourt's model is *Telemachus*, and most of his article is taken up with quoting from Fénelon's book: "The author of *Telemachus* Book XIII [today's Book XI] will explain its causes better than I can," Jaucourt averred.[94] *Telemachus* also is quoted directly in the important article "King": "As for the authority of kings," wrote the article's anonymous author, "it is the role of the author of *Telemachus* to establish its extent and its limits." What follows this proclamation is a direct quote from Book V supporting the monarch who establishes rule of law to "promote the happiness" of "the people." While the king has unlimited authority in political affairs, the laws have unlimited authority over the king.[95] The *Encyclopédie*, then, presents Fénelon less as a major religious thinker and more as a masterful political writer and above all a sharp critic of despotism. He had become, in short, a model of what the other philosophes valued so much in Voltaire and Montesquieu.[96]

The Paris philosophes circulated stories about Fénelon's life. "One day a parish priest working under him outlawed Sunday dancing in his village," noted Helvétius. Fénelon, "being more liberal than anyone else," reinstated peasant dancing, so they had some outlet for their misery. "Fénelon, truly and always virtuous," nonetheless paid for his remarkable behavior by "living part of his life in disgrace."[97] In one imaginary dialog published in the *Journal encyclopédique*, Plato welcomes Fénelon to Elysian Fields, calling him "the most admirable of all disciples produced by modern philosophy."[98]

During the second half of the eighteenth century, Enlightenment commentators merged the fictional character Mentor with the real-life author, erasing much of Fénelon's religious identity. Increasingly, Mentor's personality and not simply his ideas are assumed to be drawn from Fénelon's own spirit, so that readers projected onto the author a model of civic virtue. For example, this short poem served as a caption to a portrait of Fénelon published in the *Journal encyclopédique*:

Qui connaît Fénelon, et le respecte et l'aime
De toutes les vertus son livre est un trésor;
Et de l'heureux génie à qui l'on doit Mentor
Il semble voir Minerve même
[Whoever knows Fénelon, and respects and loves him
Of all the virtues his book is a treasure
And from the happy genius to whom we owe Mentor
He seems to see Minerva herself.][99]

Fénelon's passion, so evident in his Quietism, is cleansed into a pure form of civic virtue. "I dare say," the Abbé Maury remarked, "if Fénelon had not been virtuous, if his writings were not the mirror of his soul, we should all weep over his genius."[100]

This absorption of Fénelon into a founding patriarch of the Enlightenment is seen in the turmoil surrounding the infamous censorship of Helvétius's book, *De l'Esprit*. Like *Telemachus*, the book had first won royal approbation, and it was only after its first publication in 1759 that the government reversed its decision, spurred on by the church's strident opposition.[101] At once, those connected with the affair, including Helvétius himself, could view it only within the lens defined by *Telemachus*. What occurred sixty years earlier to Fénelon was repeating itself: Just like Fénelon, Helvétius explicitly rejected heresy, but was still persecuted for his ideas. The Marquis de Mirabeau wrote to friends that Fénelon's tragic experience must not be allowed to happen again.[102] Helvétius drew upon *Telemachus* to reflect on his own situation. "I like Fénelon," he wrote to a friend. "He was sweet and always humane." No one thinks about his nemesis Bishop Bossuet anymore, he wrote, while "*Telemachus* will subsist so long as there are on this earth honest, tender, and virtuous" supporters like the circle of philosophes surrounding him. Helvétius seems to have gained some solace from his famous predecessor.[103]

Telemachus had always been used by readers for self-improvement, but as the book became increasingly associated with Enlightenment political theory, it began, at least to some readers, to also take on the secular outlook associated with the Encyclopedists. For example, during the early 1750s a Yorkshire teenager named Ralph Jackson would read his copy of *Telemachus* out loud with a friend. But soon Jackson went through a spiritual crisis and began perceiving *Telemachus* as an Enlightenment "bad book." He chose to improve himself by reading pious literature instead, such as *The Whole Duty of Man* or from the Gospels themselves. *Telemachus* had become too secular for Jackson.[104]

The Enlightened Economist

Enlightenment philosophes not only embraced Fénelon as one of their own but also tried to refashion him into an economist. "Much is said of the beauties of Fénelon's *Telemachus* and little of its precepts," wrote Benjamin Vaughan, "which contain the seeds of all the sentiments, if not all the doctrines, of modern political economy."[105] During the 1750s and 1760s, the number of books published on political economy surged to unprecedented levels.[106] Historians of economic thought highlight the French school of Physiocracy (its authors were among the first to refer to themselves as economists), and among the most prominent Physiocrats was Victor de Riqueti, Marquis de Mirabeau. His multivolume *L'Ami des hommes*, first published in 1756, was admired by the founder of Physiocracy, François Quesnay, and other leading philosophes, because it synthesized so well the place of economic policy within the moral and political aims of the early modern state. When, for example, Rousseau went to England in 1766, the only books he brought with him were a few volumes of botany and the works of Mirabeau. "I admire your great and profound genius," he wrote to Mirabeau directly.[107]

L'Ami des hommes was an immensely popular book. Translated into German and Italian, but curiously never into English, it flew from bookshelves, yielding its booksellers some 80,000 livres.[108] Indeed, it may have been the first popular best-selling treatise on political economy in history. In an era supposedly dominated by fiction and poetry, it is noteworthy that this volume on political economy turns up thirteenth on a list of the most prominent books in French private libraries.[109] The great historian of economics Joseph Schumpeter was correct in claiming Mirabeau was the most popular economic writer of the era.[110] After running up perhaps as many as twenty editions during a six-year period, 1756–62, his book clearly led the field until it was superseded in 1776 by Adam Smith's *Wealth of Nations*. No one in 1700 could have predicted that Fénelon's *Telemachus* would have been featured in such a book.

L'Ami des hommes argued that Louis XIV's key finance minister, Jean Baptiste Colbert, had built up an economy based upon luxury, extravagance, and fragile financial schemes of credit. Mirabeau relied on Fénelon to advocate a return to "moderation," meaning a reliance upon basic agriculture that emphasized what the French people needed, not necessarily what they desired. *Telemachus*, argued Mirabeau, was at its core an economic reform program dedicated to "restoring the economy" of a country "exhausted" by the "misery of a long reign in which everything was overdone." Mirabeau recycled the myth that Louis XIV specifically censored *Telemachus* because he opposed economic reforms. "Louis XIV was upset to discover in *Telemachus* principles completely contrary to those he cherished."[111]

Mirabeau used *Telemachus* to oppose a growing sense among writers such as Bernard Mandeville and David Hume, as well as Voltaire and Montesquieu, that individual consumption helped economic growth, and indeed, that it was a hallmark of the modern European economy. Mirabeau argued that Fénelon had clearly shown that such overconsumption led to increased poverty and political instability. Indeed, an economy that looked more like the reformed Kingdom of Salente in *Telemachus* and less like Paris would be more morally virtuous and also sustain long-term prosperity. Mirabeau's condemnation of luxury and financial engineering in favor of a simpler and more austere economic system gave his book popular appeal, and, in turn, made *Telemachus* relevant to mid-century economic debates.[112] Echoing Mirabeau, the *Journal de commerce et d'agriculture* reviewed Fénelon's ideas in 1760, directly quoting from *Telemachus*:

> The true genius who governs the state is he who, doing nothing, makes everything be done—who reflects, who plans, who looks into the future, and resolves past events; who arranges and adjusts, who takes reasonable precautions, and in continual efforts wrestles with fortune; as a swimmer struggles with the stream, employing his attention day and night, so that nothing may be left to accident.[113]

Mirabeau helped start the main French journal promoting political economy, the *Ephemérides du citoyen*, published from 1767 to 1772, that spread new thinking about economics throughout Europe and its colonies.[114] In 1771, the journal covered a French Academy prize contest regarding Fénelon in order to tie *Telemachus* more closely to Physiocratic doctrine. The "energetic plan developed in *Telemachus*," wrote the editors, lay at the basis of the "development and progress of economic science." This new field, economics, "that we cultivate champions the circularity of needs, of work, of rights, of duties, and of the interests of men in this world." Following what they understood to be Fénelon's lessons in *Telemachus*, morality was not something theological or theoretical, but empirical. The key question that mattered to an economist was the effect of public policy "good or bad, which may result on civil society." The principles articulated by Fénelon during the 1690s were "rigorously demonstrated in our own century." Standing on Fénelon's shoulders, the development of political economy constituted, they thought, a remarkable achievement for the Enlightenment. Its insights were "of the greatest significance for humanity, assuring happiness wherever universally adopted." Obviously only a small portion of this new science was revealed in *Telemachus*. Nonetheless, these Physiocratic editors viewed Fénelon "as one of the precursors and founders of economic science."[115]

Of all Enlightenment writers, none embraced *Telemachus* more than Jean Jacques Rousseau. Following Ramsay's death in 1743, Rousseau increasingly became recognized as the Enlightenment's most devoted disciple of Fénelon.[116] Throughout his writings and correspondence, Rousseau made it clear that Fénelon was his model philosophe and *Telemachus* his sacred guidebook. In his 1762 educational treatise, *Emile*, Rousseau "avowedly sought to update *Telemachus*, and the work is crammed with Fénelonian touches."[117] Rousseau wildly disclaims against allowing children to read before the age of ten or eleven—they should be urged instead to experience nature firsthand. Except for *Robinson Crusoe*, the eponymous Emile reads no books until as a young adult his tutor (Rousseau) gives him *Telemachus*. Likewise, *Telemachus* is also the only book Sophie—Emile's future wife—is allowed to read before adulthood. Indeed, *Emile* is itself modeled on *Telemachus* insofar as both are built around the relationship of a young man and his tutor. At one point, Rousseau describes Emile as "the new Telemachus" and himself as Emile's "Mentor."[118]

Rousseau's *Emile* was for both reader and author fused with Fénelon's *Telemachus*. In format and ideology, in playing with the blurry line between a novel and a treatise, and especially in mixing morality and politics, Rousseau aimed to be the new Fénelon. Certainly, Rousseau aspired for the publishing success of the earlier book. Marc Michel Rey, Rousseau's publisher, knew that Rousseau worshiped the author of *Telemachus*. A few months after the publication of Rousseau's epistolary novel, *La Nouvelle Héloïse*, Rey affirmed that "this work will have the same destiny as *Telemachus*."[119] Another friend, the Genevan theologian Antoine Jacques Roustan, told Rousseau that his novel "was worthy of Saint-Pierre, Fénelon, and Montesquieu."[120]

By the 1760s, there was nothing particularly new or innovative in Rousseau's veneration of Fénelon. Like Mirabeau, Rousseau took scattered ideas from *Telemachus* and organized them as a system for regenerating political theory and economics. Rousseau specifically linked Fénelon in a chain of great economic and political thinkers who set the stage for his own innovations: "Bodin and Loysel, Fénelon, Boulainvilliers, the Abbé de Saint Pierre, President Montesquieu, the Marquis de Mirabeau, and the Abbé de Mably, all good Frenchmen and enlightened people."[121] And although he might have expressed himself paradoxically, he believed Fénelon to be, along with Montesquieu and Mirabeau, among the Enlightenment's best political economists whose work nonetheless could not save France from doomed corruption:

> The century in which we live is the most enlightened, even in morals. [But] is it the best? Does all this knowledge benefit society? Books are good for nothing, nor are the academies, nor the literary societies. Nothing useful comes from them but a sterile and fruitless approbation. Were it not for the nation which produced the Fénelons, Montesquieus, and Mirabeaus, would it not be the best and happiest place on earth? Is the nation better since the writings of these great men, and has a single abuse been restored because of their maxims? No, Messieurs, do not hope for more than they have done.[122]

Portraying Fénelon as his mentor, Rousseau challenged Montesquieu in particular, questioning whether any support for the principles underlining modern commerce could lead to moral public policy and effective economic reform. Like Fénelon, Rousseau took a hard line against the consumption of luxury goods—he worried that what appeared to be economic prosperity would create a population dependent upon "effeminate" goods and more easily conquered by despotic neighbors.[123]

Model Philosophe

Rousseau's suggestion that Emile's Sophie read only *Telemachus* seems to have had no small influence upon readers in Western Europe. In the first issue of a new journal, *The Female Mentor*, editors gave an autobiographical justification: "We were accustomed to assemble frequently in the afternoons for our recreation and improvement," the bluestockings noted. Sipping their tea while their young children played in their midst, the ladies soon turned to Fénelon. "*Telemachus* was a favourite book in our society." One day, the group's leader, Amanda, was scolding one of the children, who replied in a sincerely apologetic tone, "Indeed, Madame, I will always follow your advice, for you are our Female Mentor." From that time on, Amanda was known as the Female Mentor, and the tea group became a more organized improvement society; soon the eponymous journal was born.[124]

At least in England, Rousseau's and Fénelon's advice became absorbed in the noisy cultural politics regarding female novel reading. Many Europeans worried about the effect new fiction was having on women's morals. The press noted that many people "despised the idea" of women reading fiction, but noted that everyone could at least agree that "in the delightful pages of Fénelon, the mind stampt [*sic*] with the best gifts of nature may always receive fresh improvement."[125] In *The Lady's Magazine*, a fictional

Charlotte Watson was challenged by a gentleman about her reading: "'May I know the subject of your studies, Miss Watson?' She laid down her book. 'One of the most delightful systems of morality, Sir, I think, that ever was sent into the world'—[The gentleman] took it up, it was the *Telemachus* of Fénelon."[126]

During the 1770s, perhaps even a bit earlier, a previously unknown Fénelon manuscript—a letter that he had supposedly written to King Louis XIV—began to circulate among Paris philosophes. Voltaire mentions it in correspondence with his younger disciple the Marquis de Condorcet. This was no ordinary document. Although short—less than ten pages in the modern Pléiade edition—it was a powerful indictment of Louis XIV's political and economic program. Honest and forthright, although never entirely disrespectful, Fénelon spelled out exactly where he thinks the old king has erred. The discovery of the letter reinforced the view of Fénelon as a model of the enlightened statesman-philosopher. Yet Voltaire was so shocked by the letter that he did not believe Fénelon authored it—it would have been political suicide for him to do so, Voltaire rightly noted. After all, Fénelon had his own political ambitions, and sending such a letter would have meant the end to them. Condorcet and d'Alembert tried in vain to convince the elderly Voltaire that the letter was indeed authentic. Scholars today believe that the letter was authentic, but that it was never sent, hardly circulated, and tucked away, hidden among stacks of papers that later went to Fénelon's family after his death.[127]

D'Alembert himself contributed to the new Fénelon cult by helping the French Academy organize an essay contest devoted to his literary reputation. To a public session of the academy featuring a special guest, the Holy Roman Emperor Joseph II, d'Alembert portrayed Fénelon as model philosophe, exiled by Louis XIV for his *Telemachus*. Virtually ignoring Fénelon's mysticism, political ambitions, and passive support for the persecution of Protestants, d'Alembert nonetheless saw him very much through a kind of Voltairean lens in which even in his religious writings Fénelon "talks less about religion than natural morality." Conceding that all religions share a common and universal morality, d'Alembert claimed that Fénelon's most important goal was to "inspire a horror of tyranny and oppression, but above all else a horror of persecution and fanaticism." D'Alembert helped transform Fénelon into a paragon of religious toleration.[128]

Several writers contributed essays to the French Academy's Fénelon contest. They continued a process of constructing Fénelon into the Enlightenment's founding celebrity. For the Abbé Maury, "Fénelon is among men of letters what Henri IV is among kings."[129] The *Journal encyclopédique* praised Maury for conveying Fénelon's innovative and politically charged definition of civic virtue. In his address, Maury had said: "What is virtue, [Fénelon] asked? It is preferring the general interest over the particular interest." At this point, the *Journal encyclopédique* issued its own footnote commentary: "This definition of virtue is itself exactly right. The preference of the general interest for the particular interest is virtue." In this way, the *Journal encyclopédique* helped to spread Fénelon's reputation as the early Enlightenment's founding political thinker.[130]

By winning the contest's first prize, Jean François de La Harpe became a target of the religious opposition by echoing Fénelon. The archbishop of Paris, Christophe de

Beaumont, complained to King Louis XV that La Harpe's essay contained numerous heresies. Beaumont specifically criticized La Harpe for trashing the reputation of Fénelon's rival, Bishop Bossuet. The government forced La Harpe into a humiliating recantation as he published the essay only after revision. Voltaire sympathized with La Harpe, telling him that all "defenders of *Telemachus* . . . will take his side."[131] In this instance, the church had resisted Fénelon's absorption into the Enlightenment. Ironically, this replay of the Fénelon-Bossuet rivalry seventy-five years later made *Telemachus* even more relevant to the Party of Humanity.[132]

Among the philosophes, there was near unanimity that Fénelon was one of their own. A salon hostess reported that "of all the writers of the last century, the one [Geroges Louis Leclerc, Comte de Buffon] most admired was the author of *Telemachus*." Buffon credited Fénelon with inventing "beautiful images" for ideas that later reappeared in Montesquieu's *The Spirit of the Laws*.[133] The Marquis of Pezay and Denis Diderot marveled at how *Telemachus* was "an immortal work made for the instruction of one child that enlightened everyone."[134] Diderot quipped shortly before his death that he admired Pezay's eulogy on Fénelon more than "all the works of Rousseau."[135] In Fénelon, Pezay and Diderot seem to have found the Enlightenment's founder. "As a statesman," wrote Pezay, Fénelon "enlightened his nation; as a man of letters he was honored by Europe when the Academy inducted him, and he gave back much of the honor to it."[136] Cross-fertilizing ideas among political and intellectual institutions became an Enlightenment goal for which Fénelon served as the progenitor.

Revolutionary Philosophe

A third generation of intellectuals began to inherit the Enlightenment mantle as they came of age during the 1770s and 1780s. Robert Darnton's early work reveals the general divide between younger so-called Grub Street writers and their older more successful counterparts in the academies. However, there was no generational divide when it came to evaluating the place of Fénelon's *Telemachus*.[137] Jacques Pierre Brissot, for example, exemplified his generation when he invoked *Telemachus* upon visiting Boston in 1788: "I thought myself in that Salentum, of which the lively pencil of Fénelon has left us so charming an image."[138] In this respect Jeremy Bentham, born in 1748, was typical. Toward the end of his life, he recalled "when, in the summer of 1754—six years having just passed over my head, *Telemachus* was the delight, not only of my waking but of my sleeping moments, I made a sort of vow, however indistinct, that whenever human beings and human feelings were concerned, the numeration table should be my guide." In this reminiscence, Bentham attributed reading *Telemachus* to his inspiration for later developing utilitarianism.[139]

This younger generation tended to appreciate *Telemachus* through a Rousseauian filter: that is, given Rousseau's debt to Fénelon, and the wide influence of his own writings, it became difficult for Enlightenment readers to view *Telemachus* outside of Rousseau's embrace. Strangely, *Telemachus* often became a book that somehow was made to endorse Rousseau's radical political theories.[140] In a significant change from the 1750s, during the 1770s and 1780s *Telemachus* became a republican handbook for opposing enlightened absolutism and for at least indirectly supporting popular sovereignty. *Telemachus* spoke to the relationship of kings and citizens, and to the problems of reforming European monarchy following the end of the Seven Years War in 1763. The historian and future politician Dominique Joseph Garat saw *Telemachus* as the progenitor of Rousseau's First and Second Discourses.[141] In 1774, the French diplomat Chevalière d'Eon, viewed *Telemachus* as the basis for resisting "arbitrary" taxation.[142] Likewise, the lawyer Michel de Servan considered "*Telemachus* an eternal protest of human reason against political errors." Here was "where poetry becomes wisdom and fiction becomes sublime virtue." For Servan, the book was pleasing to read and immensely influential, but the best thing about it was that readers found themselves "improved after having read it."[143] Of course, not all commentators saw Fénelon as a proto-republican. The *Journal encyclopédique* gave extensive coverage to a book claiming that Fénelon only wished only to improve monarchical sovereignty and make it more stable.[144]

Two well-known younger Rousseau disciples in particular adored Fénelon. The first, Louis Sebastien Mercier, published in 1771 one of the century's most popular novels, *2440*. It posits a utopian society far in the future, featuring a time traveler from Enlightenment Europe. In one chapter, Mercier fantasizes what it would be like to be in the king's library in the year 2440. "In your time," the royal librarian tells him, channeling Rousseau, "men first wrote and then thought. We follow the opposite course ... Nothing leads the mind further astray than bad books." Most books from the Western canon had, in fact, been removed and burned in a massive bonfire. Some treasures, however, remained. Some Greek and Roman classics were there. Milton, Shakespeare, Pope, and Richardson were on an English shelf. When they came to the French books, Mercier noticed Descartes and some other philosophers, but he couldn't locate anything by Fénelon's nemesis, Bishop Bossuet. "We are no friend to Bossuet," the librarian exclaimed. He was a "proud and obdurate man" and a "fawning and ambitious courtier." The librarian continues:

> Behold his rival ... the amiable, the pathetic Fénelon. His *Telemachus* and other works we have carefully preserved, because in them we find a rare and happy agreement between reason and sensibility. To have composed the *Telemachus* at the court of Louis XIV appears to us as an admirable, astonishing virtue. ... Doubtless, that work required a more extensive knowledge, a more profound penetration; but with all its simplicity, what force, what truth, what dignity, is there displayed![145]

While other French writers were mentioned by name—Molière, for example—*Telemachus* was one of only six books the librarian specified by title and the only one he substantively discussed. The other five were Montesquieu's *The Spirit of the Laws*,

Voltaire's *Age of Louis XIV*, Helvétius's *On the Mind*, Rousseau's *New Héloïse*, and Marmontel's novel *Belisarius*. Each of them had close ties with *Telemachus*.[146] Looking back from 2440, Mercier, too, refashioned Fénelon as the first Enlightenment philosophe.

Mercier discussed *Telemachus* in other works, and even wrote a play about Fénelon that was produced during the French Revolution.[147] His fawning attitude toward Fénelon influenced public opinion during the revolutionary decade, as this reaction to one of Mercier's books attests: "What a soul was Fénelon's! The memory of his admirable qualities awakens such flattering and dear feelings!"[148] And yet, even Mercier's hagiographic approach to Fénelon was soon eclipsed by Jacques-Henri Bernardin de Saint-Pierre. All but forgotten today, Bernardin's writings, especially the eclectic and multivolume *Studies of Nature*, were immensely popular during the century's final two decades. The philosophers Bernardin most admired were "Fénelon, Epictetus, Socrates, and Jean Jacques Rousseau."[149] Bernardin believed that the publication of *Telemachus* represented a milestone in moral and political thought equal to the other three thinkers. "*Telemachus* made its appearance, and that book brought Europe back to the harmonies of nature." That is, *Telemachus*—more than Descartes or Locke—set off the spark that would ignite the Enlightenment and even the French Revolution. "It produced a wonderful revolution in Politics."[150]

According to Bernardin, until Fénelon's opposition to Louis XIV, monarchs were expected to look out for their own interests before their people's. Machiavelli's *Prince* was the normative guidebook for early modern rulers, who approached their kingdoms as private fiefdoms, seeking first and foremost to augment their own wealth and power. In Bernardin's eyes—and in the eyes of his contemporary readers, Fénelon wished to make kings understand that their states were actually nations, and it was the nation that every king served. Bernardin's Fénelon wedded a republican sense of civic virtue with an enlightened sense of royal duty. Perhaps someday, Bernardin fantasized, there will be a monument to Fénelon that says how "he made a revolution in Europe by teaching its kings that their glory rests upon the people's happiness."[151]

Bernardin saw in Fénelon the possibility that writing about politics itself could become an effective form of political reform. Bernardin noted that during the War of the Spanish Succession (1702–13), when Louis's forces battled a French-Dutch-Austrian alliance to the north, British troops found themselves in Cambrai, where the front met Fénelon's palace. Noting that *Telemachus* was even a more pronounced bestseller in England, Bernardin related that the troops carried the book in their pockets, and badly wanted to meet its author. On the outskirts of Cambrai, they invited Fénelon to a special celebration in their military camp, "but his modesty declined that triumph" as he "hid himself in his palace." Bernardin remarks that while Louis XIV was earning Europe's fear and loathing, "Fénelon was commanding the adulation of the whole world by a book."[152]

Bernardin's Fénelon was the first to realize that kings were the servants of the sovereign people. Of course, this had been Rousseau's message all along, and it is no wonder that Bernardin became as much a disciple of Rousseau as of Fénelon. Everything for Bernardin, in short, depended upon the correct understanding of Rousseau and

Fénelon. In *Studies in Nature*, Bernardin asks Rousseau for his assessment of Fénelon. "If Fénelon were alive," declares Rousseau to Bernardin, "I would struggle to get into his service as lackey, in hope of meriting the place of his valet de chambre." Bernardin sat at Rousseau's feet just as Rousseau fantasized sitting at Fénelon's.[153]

The remaking of Fénelon into the founding father of French Enlightenment philosophes continued unabated into the revolutionary era throughout much of Europe. As we see in Table 2.1, even though every decade of the century brought more and more editions of *Telemachus*, the jump from the 1780s to the 1790s constituted the largest spike. An astonishing eighty-two editions of Telemachus were published between 1790 and 1800! Disruptions caused by the revolutionary years across Europe seem to stimulate demand for this iconic book rather than turning it into an Old Regime fossil. Despite being 100 years old, *Telemachus* became the standard-bearer for the values of a new revolutionary era.

When readers during the 1790s—both inside and outside of France, both friends and enemies of the Jacobin cause—reflected on the origins of the French Revolution, their first narrative always involved the spread of the Enlightenment. "The ideas that were adopted in that country have since made a sensible progress in Europe," one British observer wrote in 1790, "in defiance of every effort to suppress information, and check the encroachments of reason." Whatever the efforts of the absolutist state and church, the liberal-minded French "literati" outfoxed the hollow Old Regime institutions, and no one could stop the spread of their books. "In liberality and freedom, the ideas of Voltaire, Montesquieu, Fénelon, and Turgot would have done honor to the most glorious periods of Grecian and Roman patriotism."[154] In his well-known speech comparing the French Revolution to the centennial celebration of the Glorious Revolution (a speech that ignited Edmund Burke's famous reply), the British radical thinker Richard Price associated Fénelon and the philosophes with seventeenth-century radical British thinkers: "Such were Milton, Locke, Sidney, Headly, etc. in this country; such were Montesquieu, Fénelon, Turgot, etc. in France. They sowed a seed which has since taken root, and is now growing up to a glorious harvest. To the information they conveyed by their writings we owe those revolutions in which every friend to mankind is now exulting."[155] For Price, as for many others in 1790, Enlightenment books such as *Telemachus* set the course that led to the French Revolution. In 1792, the French Legislative Assembly honored Price himself as being "another Fénelon."[156]

Sometimes careful readers recognized that Fénelon was a product of a different age that did not support popular sovereignty. In 1790, Jean Jacques de Barrett noted that Fénelon went as far as he could go in his own day, but Barrett "will go a step further than the priest" in arguing that it wasn't a question of the monarch's working toward the people's good, but rather, the monarch must be only a tool of the sovereign people.[157] Such distinctions were rare. More likely, readers conflated the desire to improve absolute monarchy with an interest in abolishing it. It is not surprising, then, that the patriot priest Joseph Cérutti saw in Fénelon a leading light of a democratic Enlightenment. After "three centuries of abuse," he explained in a eulogy following the death in 1791 of the famous politician Honoré Mirabeau, the pantheon of Enlightenment thinkers "stamped the French character" with new progressive ideas. "Montesquieu, Voltaire, Mably, Rousseau, Fénelon, and the Encyclopédist school, and the profound school of economists" all led France and Europe toward its revolution.[158] Elsewhere Cérutti was a bit more specific: "The Fénelons, the Montesquieus, the Voltaires, the Rousseaus, and the Mablys" had helped to defeat "ministerial despotism."[159] Little wonder that the most famous image surrounding Mirabeau's untimely death is the great orator reaching the Elysian Fields, where he offers his laws to Rousseau (see Figure 2.3). Crowning him is Benjamin Franklin, with Cicero and Demosthenes in the right background, and with Montesquieu, Voltaire, Mably, and Fénelon (holding what appears to be a folio edition of *Telemachus* and dressed in his ecclesiastical garb) grouped on the left immediately behind Rousseau.[160]

Figure 2.3 Mirabeau arrives at Elysian Fields. Memorializing the 1791 death of the famous French Revolutionary politician, Honoré Gabriel Mirabeau is surrounded by a pantheon of legendary Enlightenment's authors. Holding a folio edition of *Telemachus*, Fénelon watches Ben Franklin crown Mirabeau with a wreath, while Mirabeau hands Rousseau a copy of the Declaration of the Rights of Man and Citizen. Behind Fénelon is Mably, and next to him are Voltaire and Montesquieu. The illustration encapsulates Fénelon's absorption as an Enlightenment philosophe and the high status of *Telemachus* in the French Revolution.

Fénelon, then, was ubiquitous during the French Revolution as a patriarch of the Enlightenment. When the Grenoble librarian Pierre Vincent Chalvet advocated for universal literacy throughout the new nation so that "Telemachus and [Rousseau's] *Social Contract*" could be read by every peasant, his address was placed in the official record of the National Convention.[161] Several theatrical interpretations of *Telemachus* played in revolutionary Paris, and plays about Fénelon were not unusual.[162] The French Constituent Assembly granted a Paris publisher 20,000 livres to finish a nine-volume fancy quarto set of his *Oeuvres*.[163]

As the revolution entered its more radical phases in 1793 and 1794, the stock of Montesquieu and Voltaire fell, but Fénelon rose in stature. During the 1793 debates on a new constitution for a fully democratic and republican France, Fénelon was drafted into service as an expert in popular government. "In *Telemachus*," claimed one pamphlet from 1793, Fénelon "delivered the first basis of a royal republic; some 100 years later, our first Convention in its Declaration of the Rights of Man established the foundations of a popular republic."[164]

The apex of Fénelon's reputation as the Enlightenment's founding philosophe during the 1790s was marked by one of the great books of political theory of that decade, William Godwin's *Enquiry Concerning Political Justice*. Godwin clearly engaged Fénelon as a major political thinker and viewed *Telemachus* as constituting the most vicious attack upon "the evils inseparable from monarchical government" in Enlightenment political theory.[165] However, a more innovative use of *Telemachus* came earlier and more crucially in Godwin's scheme, where he displayed the life and reputation of Fénelon as a model Enlightenment philosophe, that is, as a clichéd example of the century's most accomplished and revered philosophe, in launching an important ethical lesson. If, posited Godwin, Fénelon's "palace" were in flames, and one had to choose between saving the life of Fénelon or "his chambermaid, . . . there are few of us that would hesitate to pronounce . . . which of the two ought to be preserved." Although all people are born equal, Godwin argues, and all deserve "equal attention," people nonetheless have different relative values to society. For Godwin, Fénelon's life meant more to society than that of his chambermaid, and therefore, he deserved to be the first one saved. Besides, argued Godwin, "in saving the life of Fénelon, suppose at the moment when he was conceiving the project of his immortal *Telemachus*, I should be promoting the benefit of thousands, who have been cured by the perusal of it of some error, vice and consequent unhappiness." That is, if the fire had occurred, say, in 1692, the rescuer would be almost as responsible for *Telemachus* as its more illustrious author. "Nay, my benefit would extend farther than this, for every individual thus cured has become a better member of society, and has contributed in his turn to the happiness, the information and improvement of others." Given the importance that *Telemachus* played for eighteenth-century readers, Godwin insisted that everyone should agree with this judgment, even the chambermaid herself. "Supposing I had been myself the chambermaid, I ought to have chosen to die rather than that Fénelon should have died" before writing *Telemachus*. "The life of Fénelon was really preferable to that of the chambermaid." However, asked Godwin, what if the rescuer were the spouse, sibling, or even the mother of the chambermaid? Wouldn't they have a right, indeed, a duty, to save their loved one before rescuing Fénelon? "This would not alter the truth of the proposition," insisted Godwin. Your relationship to the chambermaid does not affect who would be first rescued. "The life of Fénelon would still be more valuable than that of the chambermaid; and justice, pure, unadulterated justice, would still have preferred that which was most valuable. Justice would have taught me to save the life of Fénelon at the expense of the other."[166]

The husband of feminist Mary Wollstonecraft, Godwin nonetheless dismissed the chambermaid's potential—perhaps she might have become a second Joan of Arc, leading amazon armies to victory.[167] Instead, Godwin recognized *Telemachus* for improving the reader's happiness, leading the reader to improve morally and act better toward others—that's quite a tall order for any book. By the end of the century, as Godwin attests, *Telemachus* had become the Enlightenment's Gospel.

That Godwin automatically chose Fénelon for this role reveals that by 1793, Fénelon had become accepted by the public as the Enlightenment's preeminent founder. This choice reflects a remarkable consensus surrounding Louis XIV's archbishop. Never mind that Fénelon himself expected *Telemachus* would never be published; or that he wrote it for a boy who would someday be the kind of king likely despised by the republican Godwin; or that Fénelon's Quietism and his deep evangelical religious faith—arguably his most salient and important quality—were abhorred by Godwin. Indeed, what is most striking is the understated manner in which Godwin presents Fénelon as a secular philosophe. Godwin and his readers had not forgotten that Fénelon was the Archbishop of Cambrai, but like patriotic priests during the French Revolution, Fénelon was dechristianized and assimilated into the secular humanism of late Enlightenment culture.

Telemachus shows how porous political borders were for Enlightenment books. Like other Enlightenment bestsellers, *Telemachus* was in demand throughout Europe and its settlement colonies. Local conditions did not seem to significantly alter its reception. From the perspective of *Telemachus* and its editions, the Enlightenment looks more distinctively cosmopolitan.[168] Moreover, the more we pay attention to readers and booksellers, the less convincing is any analysis of the Enlightenment that posits ideological struggles between moderate and radical philosophes.[169] Once we introduce readers, publishers, and mediating institutions such as academies, journals, and salons into the making of the Enlightenment, the way books gained cultural authority may or may not correspond to any overt ideological affiliation of their authors. Enlightenment books were not simply ideological expressions of a particular intelligentsia. In the case of *Telemachus*, readers and publishers actively reframed Fénelon's supposed ideological affiliation until, absurdly, the book became associated with radical Jacobinism itself. "The Enlightenment," writes book historian David Allan, "was characterized by an unending sequence of acts of creation, reception, and responding in which substantial populations of now-unknown individuals, and not just the famous thinkers and best-selling authors, were all implicated, as its meaning and significance were constantly confronted, contested, and renegotiated".[170]

Chapter 3

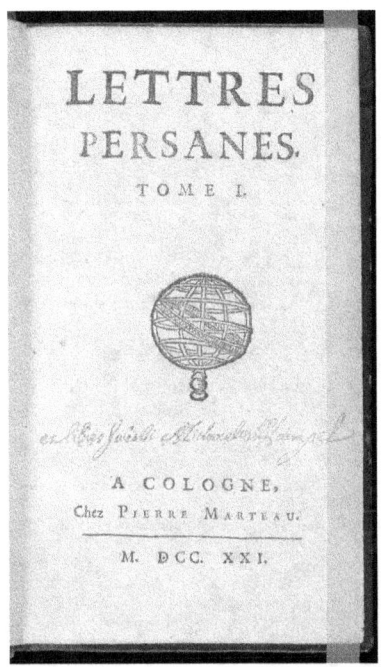

Figure 3.1 First edition title page Montesquieu's *Persian Letters*. Observant readers during the 1720s were aware that the false imprint Cologne: Pierre Marteau was code for a book that carried controversial material that was usually political, sexual, or both. Many such books were actually published in the Netherlands.

Chapter 3
Montesquieu's *Persian Letters* (1721)

Table 3.1 Eighteenth-Century Editions of *Persian Letters*

Decade	1720–9	1730–9	1740–9	1750–9	1760–9	1770–9	1780–9	1790–1800
Editions	10	14	6	16	18	12	17	21

Total Editions: 114.
Translations: Dutch, English, German, Polish, Russian.
Source: https://kates.itg.pomona.edu/books/analytics.php?type=all. Accessed March 9, 2022.

During the Academic Year 1778–9, over a dozen students at Portugal's prestigious University of Coimbra circulated among themselves a tattered copy of Montesquieu's novel *Persian Letters*. They did so secretly and at great risk because the fifty-year-old book was banned throughout Portugal and in most Catholic countries. Antônio de Morais Silva slipped it to his friend Diogo José de Morais Calado, who gave it in turn to Antônio Caetano de Freitas, and so on. The young men were studying law, medicine, philosophy, and theology, and they read French well. Most were from towns close by, but some had traveled all the way from Portuguese colonies in Brazil and Angola for their studies. *Persian Letters* was not the only book passed around by the students—books by Voltaire, Rousseau, d'Argens, and d'Holbach also circulated—but *Persian Letters* seems to have been a particular favorite. Unfortunately, we know about their reading habits only because their secret book circle was discovered by the University of Coimbra staff. University officials turned them over to the Portuguese Inquisition, who, after interrogating each student, charged them with heresy and apostasy. Caught red-handed with Montesquieu, they could not have found themselves in bigger trouble.[1]

What was especially tragic for them is that only a year or so earlier, their behavior would have been handled internally by university staff, probably resulting in little more than a warning. To be sure, Portugal had long been notorious for its religious conservatism, and even in the eighteenth century, its Inquisitorial courts were still burning heretics. Since the terrible Lisbon earthquake of 1755, the country had been in the midst of a major modernizing transformation under an extraordinary reforming prime minister, the Marquis de Pombal. Portugal's king José I let Pombal do whatever he pleased, and in effect he was the epitome of an enlightened despot. Pombal transformed industry, trade, and the economy, promoted science and learning, and tried to minimize the role of the church in political and civic affairs. He neutralized the Inquisition by transferring all of its police power to Portuguese governmental administrators, forcing the Inquistorial courts to gain permission from the government before proceeding with cases. The result was that following 1761, there was not a single auto-da-fé (public penance and execution) during Pombal's term in office. Although radical books were still banned and the book trade censored, Lisbon quickly obtained a reputation for tolerating Enlightenment ideas. "Some persons of wit have formed a small clandestine academy," wrote a French observer about Pombal's Portugal, "which furtively reads and translates our recent and most spicy works."[2]

After reforming the Inquisition, Pombal moved on to address curricular change at the University of Coimbra, effectively secularizing the institution. He substituted science, philosophy, and natural ethics for theology, and greatly expanded the mathematics and medicine faculties. The university officially shut down at the end of 1770 and reopened in 1771 on this more progressive basis. When the bishop of Coimbra opposed his reforms, Pombal threw him in jail. Pombal's de facto rule came to an end when King José died in 1777 and was succeeded by his daughter, Queen Maria I. The new monarch despised Pombal and all that he stood for, and she immediately rolled back his reforms as much as possible. This included the liberalization of the University of Coimbra, and its unfortunate students became victims of this reactionary backlash. However, the damage had already been done: as one of the students boldly told his interrogators, the problem with Pombal was that his reforms had not gone far enough.[3]

What did the *Persian Letters* mean to these students? They confessed to the inquisitors that Montesquieu's novel provided them a set of critical tools which allowed them to question Church dogma, and even the relationship between the church and the state. They found in it a compendium of insights, including questions about the Bible, the function of the Eucharist, the role of monks and nuns, and the nature of political rule. For law student Jerônimo Francisco Lobo, the novel showed him "that the Revealed Religion was a political invention of man."[4] *Persian Letters* fed Jerônimo's growing skepticism and religious liberalism. His friend Antônio Caetana agreed, telling his interrogators that *Persian Letters* led him to grasp the very basis of "natural right."[5]

In his multivolume history of the Enlightenment, Jonathan Israel argues that a radical secular and materialist ideology increasingly overcame the resistance of more conservative writers, both inside and outside of Enlightenment circles. By the late 1770s, the fall of moderates such as Turgot revealed the waning influence of reforming statesmen, leading to a resurgence of revolutionary ideology. The case of our unfortunate Coimbra students would seem to bear out Israel's controversial interpretation. Lobo's comment about revealed religion is precisely the kind of Spinozist discourse that Israel finds running throughout the Enlightenment. What is noteworthy, however, is finding *Persian Letters* among the key texts that evidently helped convert these young men to that philosophy. For Israel, Montesquieu represents the failure of the Moderate Enlightenment against its opposition, the Radical Enlightenment. Israel argues that Montesquieu was used more by conservative "anti-Philosophe" writers than radicals;

many thinkers found in Montesquieu's writing a defense of aristocratic society rather than an embrace of natural rights. However, these Coimbra students were obviously committed to the most radical Enlightenment ideas. According to the inquisitors, the students insisted during their interrogations that

> everything claimed about Hell and its punishment was no more than a fable. There was no purgatory. The soul was mortal because, lodged inside the body, it had to occupy a place, and by occupying a place it was bodily and consequently mortal. They denied the truth of the Scriptures, alleging that, in part, [holy] doctrine was aimed at keeping the people in their proper place and that some passages were mere fable, while in others it contained sinful and less licit permissible lessons. The precepts of fasting and abstinence of meat on prohibited days were unsubstantiated. The celebration of Mass was an invention aimed at making money.[6]

Historians do not usually consider *Persian Letters* as a revolutionary text along the lines of, say, the Baron d'Holbach's *Système de la nature*. Indeed, the first readers of *Persian Letters* did not appreciate its more philosophical elements. Yet among these students at the University of Coimbra, it seems to have been read in exactly that serious light. What is needed, then, is a reconsideration of *Persian Letters*' place within Enlightenment culture.[7]

Parisian Satire

In the early months of 1721, the publisher Suzanne de Caux received the manuscript of *Persian Letters*. Caux was among thousands of French Protestant refugees whose families fled religious persecution by King Louis XIV and settled in the Netherlands. After the Revocation of the Edict of Nantes in 1685, which essentially declared war on French Calvinists, 3,000 Protestants escaped from Caux's hometown of Dieppe, in the northwest corner of France. In 1703, she married Jacques Desbordes, a fellow refugee in Amsterdam, who owned a publishing and printing business. When he died in 1718, Caux took over the business, preserving it for her son, who made the firm a major publisher of Enlightenment books after Suzanne's death in 1727.

The Desbordes firm was one of hundreds of successful printers in Holland. By the second half of the seventeenth century, the Dutch had become Europe's leading printing center, the hub of a book trade industry that had grown explosively since the end of the Thirty Years War (1648) and which reached across Europe from Ireland to the Balkans. Dutch booksellers sold works in Armenian, Hungarian, Spanish, Italian, and Arabic, in addition to French, Swedish, and English. Indeed, at the time when Caux published *Persian Letters* in French, there were fourteen Jewish printers in Amsterdam alone who sold Hebrew and Yiddish books intended for readers in Eastern Europe.[8]

The Holland that the Desbordes called home was a small young republic fighting for its survival. Earlier, Holland's primary enemy had been its former rulers, the Spanish Habsburgs. When Louis XIV ascended to the French throne in 1661, France became the republic's most threatening foe. The new French king dreamt of establishing a "universal monarchy" in Europe, and he built the largest army on the continent to pursue this goal by force. Holland was one of his chief targets, and during his reign the two countries fought each other in three major wars. There is no doubt that if victorious, Louis would have forced the Dutch to give up their Calvinist faith, just as he had forced Protestants within his kingdom. Louis XIV, then, was simultaneously the greatest threat to both Dutch political independence and religious liberty.

The old Sun King finally died in 1715, at once providing Protestant Europe with opportunity and uncertainty. Would the new regency for the boy-king Louis XV liberalize France's harsh policy toward Protestants? Would it be as aggressive against its neighbors? It was in this context that Suzanne de Caux published *Persian Letters*.

In keeping with the political experiences of its patrons, the publication list of the Desbordes firm catered to relatively sophisticated Huguenot readers. Most of the books it published between 1700 and 1730 can be divided into two primary categories: First, it published an extensive list of plays and other pieces of light *belles lettres*, including the works of Cyrano de Bergerac and a French translation of Joseph Addison's famous play *Cato*. The firm's second major category was Protestant theology and history. For example, Caux published the orthodox Calvinist treatise *Les consolations de l'âme fidèle contre les frayeurs de la mort* around the same time as *Persian Letters*. This type of pietistic classic was offset in the Desbordes catalogue by anti-Catholic polemics such as the *Traité de pyrrhonisme de l'Eglise romaine*, which accused the Catholic Church of spreading errors and contradictions that led to atheism. Likewise, in 1716 Caux published a biography of Pierre Bayle (1647–1706), who was perhaps the leading Huguenot intellectual of his day living in Holland.[9]

For Caux, then, *Persian Letters* was a rallying cry against the tyranny and intolerance of the French monarchy. What Montesquieu may have had to offer about other topics, such as political theory, Muslim society, or Parisian social mores were of less interest to Caux and her market of potential readers than what the book said regarding religious toleration. Rather than treat the manuscript as a great work of fiction, Caux saw in it a biting religious polemic that would reach French-language readers through satire.

Obviously, no one living in France in 1721 had the freedom to legally publish a book critical of politics and religion, even a nobleman such as Montesquieu. While Caux had the legal right to print *Persian Letters* in Holland, she avoided doing so openly at first, choosing to publish it under the false imprint of "Cologne: Pierre Marteau." Works of light fiction were often published anonymously at the time, but this particular imprint carried significance for the knowledgeable customer. Between around 1660 and the 1730s, Amsterdam publishers designated over 100 books for this imprint, signaling subversive anti-French material usually relating to religion or politics, and sometimes spiced with erotica. Montesquieu's book mixed all three genres and discussed themes as far-ranging as suicide and incest.[10]

Almost immediately, Caux resold the rights to print the work to a fellow refugee publisher, Pierre Brunel, who produced his own version. Although this may have been a smart business decision at the time, allowing Caux to recoup most of her initial printing costs, it meant that she would have less control over further editions, and that to some extent, the two publishers would become competitors, each having the right under Dutch law to make new editions. The story of these editions, however, is complex and confusing. Without Montesquieu's approval, and for reasons that are still not clear, Caux made significant changes to her version of the second edition. Published in October 1721, Caux omitted thirteen letters and added three new ones, for a total of 140 letters instead of the 150 included in the first edition. Brunel, however, did not follow Caux's lead, and subsequent reprints and new editions of his version were simply copies of the "Pierre Marteau" first edition. Thus, between 1721 and 1754 there were two different French versions circulating throughout Europe. As for Montesquieu, only in 1754, the year before he died, did he end this confusion by producing a new corrected edition. However, after his death, publishers returned to mixing up letters more or less as they pleased.[11]

Nonetheless, the book was such an immediate success that both publishers had plenty of business and more editions followed. In 1721 alone, there were at least eight separate editions. Assuming an average print run of 1,000 copies,[12] by the end of *Persian Letter*'s first year in print, there were more than 8,000 copies of it circulating in Europe, an extraordinary number for that era. Montesquieu jotted down in his notebooks that booksellers were hustling one another for more copies of the book. The fad never really wore out. What made *Persian Letters* so popular?

Persian Letters features two travelers from Persia, Usbek and Rica, who visit Europe for the first time and settle in Paris for several years. Rica is young and impressionable. Like a college student on study abroad, he soaks up everything European, and within a short time, he is dressing in the latest French fashions. Usbek is older, wiser, and set in his ways. He is wealthy and propertied, with a harem back in Persia full of beautiful wives and resentful eunuchs. He is something of a philosopher, interested in the deepest questions of metaphysics, theology, and morals. This freethinking nature had gotten him into trouble in Persia, where his candid speech gave his political enemies an excuse to force him into exile. Rica is happy to be in France and adjusts to its manners easily, but Usbek bears the sorrow of an involuntary expatriate who longs to return home.

Much of the charm of *Persian Letters* comes from seeing French customs from the perspective of foreigners, to whom they appear bizarre and amusing. For example, Rica writes about how two individuals carefully plan in advance a salon conversation that seems witty and spontaneous.[13] The letters commenting on France are frequently interrupted by two different types of seemingly random interpolations. First, Usbek's wives and eunuchs keep writing to him about problems in the harem, and it becomes increasingly clear that he can't keep his mind off his troubled household. Second,

Usbek's friends regularly ask him questions about philosophy and morality, resulting in fascinating digressions, stories, and parables. *Persian Letters* ends with a series of letters from Usbek's household, in which it becomes clear that the wives and eunuchs are in revolt against Usbek's paternal order. The final letter describes the suicide of Roxana, Usbek's favorite wife.

Each of the 150 letters is dated according to the days and months of the Persian lunar calendar, although the year is given in the modern (European) Gregorian calendar. So, for example, the first letter is dated "the 15th of the moon of Saphar, 1711," while the final letter is dated "the 8th of the first moon of Rabia, 1720." This hybrid system, carefully developed by its author, highlights in fact an extraordinary period in French life: the transition from the monarchy of Louis XIV to the Regency of Louis XV.[14] To some extent, then, Montesquieu meant *Persian Letters* as a chronicle of France during the final years of Louis XIV and the first years of his successor, Philippe, Duc d'Orléans, who served as regent. Almost precisely in the middle of the novel, and halfway chronologically between 1711 and 1720, Usbek reports Louis XIV's death to his friend Rhedi:

> The monarch who reigned for so long is dead. Do not imagine that, here in France, this great event has prompted purely moral considerations. Everyone has thought of his own interests, and how the change may be used to his own advantage. Since the king, the great-grandson of the late monarch, is only five years old, his uncle the prince has been appointed regent of the kingdom.[15]

Early in the book, Usbek's friend Mirza asks him to explain his views regarding justice and virtue: "I have often heard you say that man was born to be virtuous, and that justice is a quality as natural to him as existence itself. Explain, I beg you, what you mean."[16] Usbek responds to Mirza's request in the following manner: "To fulfill your request, I think it best not to employ purely abstract reasoning; sometimes simply to persuade people of a truth is not sufficient. One must also make them feel it. Moral truths belong in this category."[17] Mirza expected Usbek to provide him with an abstract formal argument, something that would have been recognizable to moral philosophers such as Pufendorf or Hobbes. Instead, Usbek insists on telling a fable, because moral truths must be "felt" before they can be believed. The Troglodyte parable (which occupies several early letters) is meant to show Mirza that humans are naturally virtuous "and that justice is a quality that is as proper to them as existence." From the beginning, many readers have found the Troglodyte myth moving; as the French philosophe d'Alembert noted, it is often regarded as one of the most important sections of the book.[18] Indeed, Usbek's explanation to Mirza should be read as Montesquieu's justification of the entire novel: Unlike *The Spirit of the Laws*, which persuades the reader through rational argument, *Persian Letters* is itself a parable about the evil and abusive nature of despotic rule. Montesquieu's goal in *Persian Letters* is to move the reader to despise despotism and feel its evil nature.

The central problem in *Persian Letters* is the fate of the French monarchy. When Usbek and Rica reach Paris in 1712, "the King of France is old,"[19] and in the last years of his reign. We learn that he has pushed France toward the same Persian political system that Usbek has just fled; he "has frequently been heard to remark that of all the governments in the world, that of the Turks, or that of our august Sultan, would suit him best, so high is his opinion of the oriental political system."[20]

Montesquieu believed that Louis XIV had taken France closer to a Persian-like despotic system, but he also felt that Louis's plans were left unfulfilled at his death. In his mind, the most important question for France was whether this direction toward absolute royal authority would be hastened or altered. Would the new regency of Philippe, Duc d'Orléans (1715–23) fundamentally change the direction of French politics? In fact, Philippe's short regency did not really move France one way or the other. While there were attempts to decentralize political life through the introduction of councils, or Polysynody, the Regent held onto supreme power by insisting on personally signing every decree, just like Louis XIV.[21] However, Montesquieu's purpose in *Persian Letters* is not to analyze the Regency in any formal political sense. His purpose is rather to contrast Parisian and Persian life, and he is not as much interested in the formal rules or institutions of government as in the role they play in shaping political culture and social mores. We find ourselves laughing at the silly contradictions of the vain and superficial Parisians, but we are disturbed by the tragedy that befalls Usbek's wives and eunuchs. Montesquieu's point is not to establish equivalency between these narratives but to point out their differences.

Usbek's complicated character reflects Montesquieu's aim to portray despotism as inherently evil and unstable. To his friends and to Rica, Usbek is the epitome of an urbane, reasoned, liberal-minded person, who often is able to put himself in someone else's shoes. But regardless of his personality and inclinations, the despotic system that he represents transforms him into an abusive and sadistic tyrant at home. Even before the main plot begins, Usbek lets us know that the seraglio has become a source of anxiety, causing for him a kind of clinical depression. "I am so lacking in feeling that all desires have abandoned me. In the large seraglio where I lived, I've forestalled love, and let it destroy itself: but out of my very indifference has come a deep-seated jealousy, which devours me."[22] In Montesquieu's portrayal, the Persian seraglio is a horrible dystopia in which the man with all the power is perhaps its most unhappy character. In contrast, Parisian society doesn't look too bad; its faults seem trivial, not structural. Europeans may seem ridiculous, but they are certainly not evil, and at least they treat women like human beings.

Montesquieu's book was meant to convey to readers that despotism destroys family life, social mores, commerce, fashion, and the other delights that give European culture its energy and vibrancy. Monarchical states, Usbek tells one of his friends, "are unstable, and invariably degenerate into despotism or republicanism."[23] Montesquieu implicitly presents his reader with a choice: the French can become like the Persians or they can embrace novel forms of liberty such as religious toleration.

A month after the first publication of *Persian Letters*, its first review appeared in the *Lettres historiques*, a French-language periodical produced in Holland by none other than Suzanne de Caux, who no doubt wrote the review, or at least commissioned it.[24] Consequently, it can be read as an advertisement which also guides readers toward what were, for Caux, the novel's most important elements. The review describes Montesquieu's writing style as "lively, graceful, and natural; always in the character of the letter writer." Caux comments how Montesquieu successfully mixes this gallant style with insightful and acerbic comments on many of the most controversial religious and political issues of the day. But Caux did not focus her review on Usbek or his harem; like most reviewers and readers during the eighteenth century, she seems uninterested in the domestic story Montesquieu tells about Usbek's Persian family. Rather, her focus is on Montesquieu's mockery of the French king and the Catholic pope through the lighthearted observations of Rica. Caux was especially attracted to one of Rica's letters, which she quotes liberally in her review. "This king is a great magician," Caux quotes Rica. "He exerts his dominion over the very minds of his subjects, for he makes them think whatever he wishes: if he has one million gold pieces in his treasury, and he needs two, he has only to persuade them that one gold piece is worth two, and they believe him." The second great magician was, of course, the pope. "Sometimes he makes the king believe that three are only one, that the bread he eats is not bread, or that the wine he drinks is not wine, and countless other things of that nature."[25] And in what is apparently a kind of self-referential joke, Caux explains that given such provocative content, it is no wonder that the publisher chose to keep herself anonymous "in using" the false imprint, "à *Cologne, chez Pierre Marteau*."[26] Clearly Caux steered the reader toward viewing *Persian Letters* as controversial because of its political and religious material but also as a somewhat light and satirical work.

Writing in the *Mémoires historiques et critiques* a few months later, François Denis Camusat took Caux's bait, ignoring Usbek's tyranny and the darkness of the Persian story. Like Caux, he highlighted Montesquieu's elegant writing style and noted the witty reflections on timely religious and political subjects.[27] But Camusat thought that Montesquieu had crossed a line into offensive speech by suggesting that the pope is a kind of magician. Camusat also claimed that the book lacked originality; it was essentially an imitation of an older popular book, Marana's *L'Espion Turc* [*The Turkish Spy*],[28] which featured a fictitious Turkish ambassador at the court of Louis XIV. In the end, while Montesquieu's style gave the book merit, Camusat deemed it too dangerous in its approach and too "sophistic" in its ideas.

Camusat highlighted Letter 98, in which Usbek notes that "people here talk constantly about the Papal Bull," as an example of the book's brazen anti-Catholic views. The Bull in question, Unigenitus, attempted to suppress Jansenism, a surging heretical Catholic movement that had lured into its fold many members of the French upper class. With strong backing from Louis XIV, Unigenitus was the king's final push toward a Catholic state that tolerated no dissent. Following his death in 1715, the controversy became only more polarizing. Camusat regarded the issue as entirely too sensitive and serious for the pen of a lighthearted satirist.[29] The great playwright Pierre de Marivaux agreed with the assessment that Montesquieu had gone too far in his satire; he too failed to recognize

Persian Letters as a serious critique of despotism. Recognizing that "the author is a man full of wit," Marivaux nonetheless asserted that it was contradictory for anyone to tackle the most serious political and religious controversies of the day in a format that privileged satire, elegance, lightness, and humor. For Marivaux, *Persian Letters* was not a book to be taken seriously but a satire run amok.[30]

If these initial reviewers represented the reading public, we can see that *Persian Letters* was immediately popular because readers found it funny and well written. Perhaps sometimes Montesquieu's comedic bite risked violating the literary elite's sense of decorum. But no one in the 1720s or 1730s yet thought that the book meant anything more than great fun at the expense of church and state in a France recovering from the death of Louis XIV. Readers disagreed among themselves about whether it was respectful to treat European political and religious matters in this mocking fashion, but they nonetheless agreed that the book was primarily a satire about Paris, and that the sections on Islam and Persia were simply an exotic backdrop. Readers did not find in the letters any sort of unifying theme; they ignored plot and narrative structure, and never suspected that the author had any serious political message. To these readers, *Persian Letters* was not great literature and certainly did not qualify as philosophy. Indeed, Voltaire's comment on it is representative of most critics' initial impression: it is "a work of pleasantries, full of elements that reveal a wit more pronounced than this book."[31] While the public would soon change its perception, Voltaire would stubbornly cling to this view of *Persian Letters* out of dislike or jealousy of its author.[32]

Very few people in 1721 knew that the author of *Persian Letters* was among France's most powerful young noblemen. Charles de Secondat, Baron de Montesquieu, was born in 1689, near Bordeaux, where his father owned a large estate that made its wealth largely from its vineyards, which even then (as today) had a reputation for some of the best wine in the world. In 1715, the year of Louis XIV's death, Montesquieu increased his income even more by marrying the wealthy Jeanne de Lartigue, who secretly maintained her Protestant faith throughout her life. The following year his uncle died childless, leaving Montesquieu his baronetcy, and, more significant, the office of president of the Bordeaux Parlement, one of nine special appeals courts in the kingdom. Montesquieu also joined the Academy of Bordeaux, where he spent the next few years actively engaged in its activities, including presenting scientific papers. In short, by the time he started writing *Persian Letters* in 1717, he was a wealthy nobleman with considerable political stature, at the start of a promising intellectual career.[33]

It is no wonder, then, that Montesquieu kept *Persian Letters* a secret from practically everyone except his secretary. During the seventeenth and early eighteenth centuries, it was rare for a powerful French nobleman to openly publish books critical of political and religious life. Government policy, after all, was made by the king and members of his court, not the public. For an aristocrat to court public opinion seemed at best inappropriate, and, at worst, treasonous. This was especially true for an insider like Montesquieu, who could make his views known through the *parlements* and other standard channels of the monarchy. In choosing to have *Persian Letters* published at all, Montesquieu was incurring great personal risk.

Montesquieu was careful about how he fashioned himself as a published author. To be sure, it would have been impossible for him to print the book openly in France, even if he tried to do so anonymously—he risked arrest, prison, and even exile. At the same time, he wanted to market the book inside France. His goal was not money. Rather, his aim was to be taken seriously as a writer and thinker without jeopardizing his life or property.

As soon as Suzanne de Caux published *Persian Letters*, Montesquieu initiated an application to the French government for a *permission tacite*, allowing an imported book to be sold in Paris bookstores, perhaps paving the way eventually for a legal French edition. During the eighteenth century, the rules regarding book censorship in France were complex and convoluted. Normally, a French author was supposed to apply for a government privilege that allowed a publisher and bookseller to print and sell the book legally in France. In that case, the manuscript or galleys would be read by one of a hundred royal censors, and a recommendation would be made to the director of censorship. But what of books published in foreign lands? Obviously, foreign booksellers were under no obligation to gain the French government's permission before publishing books in their own countries. It gradually became a common practice for French authors to anonymously publish works abroad, and then ask for permission from the French government for a domestic edition, or at least to allow French booksellers to sell the imported work. This put the French state in a peculiar position: While the king's ministers did not want to cede the profitable book business to neighboring states in Flanders, Germany, England, and Holland, they felt obligated to screen publications for books dangerous to politics, morality, and religion. So, by the early eighteenth century, the government had worked out with booksellers the category of *permission tacite*, which meant that while the government was withholding the official legal status of a "privilege," it recognized the presence of the foreign book on French soil and promised not to prosecute the author or bookseller for distributing it in France. Montesquieu must have been sorely disappointed when the ministers denied the tacit permission: "Absolutely rejected," came the official response. Despite Montesquieu's status as an aristocrat—or perhaps because of it—his efforts to legalize his novel were frustrated.[34]

Here Montesquieu was involved in a delicate dance. The imprint of Pierre Marteau and the instant popularity of *Persian Letters* signaled that it was a potentially dangerous work. And yet, for the book to work to Montesquieu's advantage, he needed to find a way to domesticate it. He very much wanted to use its success to launch his career as a writer, but he could not take official responsibility for the work. Thus, a kind of standoff occurred between Montesquieu and French authorities. Montesquieu himself was never arrested or harassed. While he was not allowed to officially name himself as the author, he could informally take credit to friends and colleagues without fear of reprisal, and others were free to acknowledge him as the author. However, *Persian Letters* was never legalized during Montesquieu's lifetime. Copies were routinely seized, and booksellers throughout the country were harassed for carrying it. For example, on December 9, 1721, authorities seized fifty copies when they raided a bookshop in Rouen. Even foreign diplomats who purchased *Persian Letters* were targeted. In 1731, the Spanish ambassador to France was arrested with ten copies. Thus, while printing, buying, or selling *Persian Letters* was a crime, its author was not held culpable.[35]

Indeed, immediately following publication of *Persian Letters* in 1721, Montesquieu began spending more time in Paris, hoping to cut a figure at court among *les grands*. His biographer, Robert Shackleton, reports that Montesquieu sent Madame de Lambert supplementary Persian Letters as a way to audition for her exclusive salon. Her Tuesday gatherings brought him access to France's best-known writers, including Fontenelle, Marivaux, and Crébillon.[36]

By 1727, Montesquieu's friends nominated him to France's most prestigious intellectual institution, the French Academy. Unfortunately, here Montesquieu ran straight into problems of his own making. No one disputed his talent, social status, and high office, which made him worthy of the Academy, but *Persian Letters* had also made enemies for Montesquieu. One powerful opponent was apparently René Joseph de Tournemine, an elderly Jesuit theologian who had battled with such philosophers as Malebranche and Leibniz. Tournemine was offended by the book, especially its now-infamous Letter 22 (quoted in Caux's review), which compared both king and pope to magicians. Tournemine took his objections to Cardinal Fleury, the most important minister in the Regency government. Fleury, who was himself a member of the Academy, told colleagues that he would not approve Montesquieu's nomination unless the author disavowed authorship of the book. This indeed was a conundrum for Montesquieu, since disavowing authorship undermined the reasons why the Academy was nominating him in the first place. In the end, Montesquieu went to see Fleury himself. At that point, Fleury apparently read the book and decided that it should not hold back the nomination. Montesquieu took his seat on the Academy in January 1728.[37]

Within a year of *Persian Letters*' debut in Holland, the minor poet John Ozell produced a translation in English. He added a second edition in 1730 and a third in 1736. Right away, Ozell sensed the book was something extraordinary, among the very best books from France to appear in several years. "It is wrote [*sic*] with a strength of reasoning, a freedom of thought, and a vein of just humor."[38] This last feature, Ozell recognized, would make it especially appealing to the English, as the humor in *Persian Letters* was mostly at the expense of the French. In contrast to the initial French reviews, Ozell admired the author's abilities as a writer of fiction, specifically his attention to characterization and his success in bringing to life the personalities of Usbek and his wives. While French reviewers ignored the seraglio tale, Ozell saw that the Persian aspect of the book deserved recognition. There the author has "given us so natural an idea of the manners of the seraglio, the thoughts of women confined for the pleasures of a single man, and the notions and cast of mind of the eunuchs."[39] Ozell believed that British readers would be moved by the author's tragic tale of tyranny and abuse. Ozell's translation was quickly copied in Ireland, while a different English translation was soon printed in Scotland.[40]

Nowhere outside of France was *Persian Letters* more of a hit than in England, where some readers saw the author flattering themselves. Edmund Burke claimed that the parable of the Troglodytes was meant as "a representation of England, which [the author] calls a virtuous nation made wise by misfortune"[41] The British, evidently, identified more with the virtuous ancient Troglodytes than with their vain neighbors across the channel. Nevertheless, English readers also found in *Persian Letters* the sort of coffeehouse banter that had made Addison and Steele's recent *Spectator* such an influential journal. In both style and substance, British readers could see that *Persian Letters* was a book that could have been penned by an English writer.[42]

Persian Letters also gained influence through the countless imitators that rose in its wake. "A work which uniquely makes a mark in its field and which the public receives so favorably only encourages imitators who hope for the same success," one reviewer observed.[43] Whether it was the six-page pamphlet from a supposed Chinese diplomat visiting Paris or the six-volume account of a Jewish physician in anti-Semitic Spain, writers throughout Europe could not resist crafting variations on Montesquieu's epistolary formula. In England, Baron George Lyttelton's *Letters from a Persian in England to His Friend at Ispahan* went through almost as many editions as Montesquieu's book, and was itself translated into French. Curiously, one French reviewer thought that the English imitator suffered from a partisan spirit that was absent in the original. Although Montesquieu was forced to publish *Persian Letters* in a foreign country, this unfortunate circumstance had a silver lining: It allowed the author to exhibit "a wit free of prejudice and partisanship." Ironically, while Lyttelton was lucky enough to live "in a country where liberty itself reigns but produces such factions, it is extremely difficult to maintain a perfect neutrality."[44] Montesquieu may not have been the first to compose fictional travel letters by a foreigner writing to friends and family back home, but no one before him had provided such amusing and insightful views of European society. Imitators also recognized that Montesquieu's formula offered even more than this: The contrast between European and Oriental customs offered a space for the author to reflect on universal values.[45]

By the 1730s and 1740s, *Persian Letters* had become an immensely popular book. It had already been published in over thirty editions and had inspired numerous imitators throughout Europe. While officially anonymous, the identity of its author was by now common knowledge. Yet, popular as it was, delightful as it was to read, *Persian Letters* was recognized more for its wit than for its depth, more as satire than political theory, and more as a dig at church and state than as a serious call for reform. Montesquieu "had an early taste for a kind of bold philosophy, which he has combined with French gaiety and levity, and which has made his *Persian Letters* truly a delightful work," wrote the Marquis d'Argenson in 1736.

> But if on the one hand this book has been much admired, it has on the other been justly complained of; there are passages which a man of wit may easily conceive,

but such as a prudent man ought never to let appear in print; these passages, have, notwithstanding, established the reputation of the book and the author.[46]

For d'Argenson and many of his peers, Montesquieu was not a political theorist or a moral philosopher; he was a wit with literary talent. It was telling to whom d'Argenson compared Montesquieu. Far from writers like Descartes, Pufendorf, or Leibniz, Montesquieu reminded d'Argenson most of the elderly dean of early French Enlightenment writers, Bernard le Bovier de Fontenelle. Already sixty-four years old when *Persian Letters* appeared, Fontenelle was president of the Paris Academy of Sciences, and in that capacity, he popularized the fruits of the Scientific Revolution. Perhaps his most notable work was *Conversations on the Plurality of Worlds*, which mixes light sexual flirtation and astronomical lessons under a full moon.[47] Fontenelle was such a skillful writer that no one could tell if he was using Newtonian science as a backdrop for romance, or using the romance as a backdrop for science. For d'Argenson, and for many Enlightenment readers, *Persian Letters*, too, was filled with gallantry and elegance, but not profundity.

A Philosophical Tragedy about Despotism

This common view of *Persian Letters* changed radically in 1748, with the publication of Montesquieu's magnum opus, *The Spirit of the Laws*. The new work was very different from the earlier one. Instead of writing another epistolary novel, Montesquieu spent the better part of twenty years preparing a comprehensive treatise on political theory that featured hundreds of citations. This was obviously not the work of a philosophical lightweight but the product of a serious and ambitious thinker. It did not take long for *The Spirit of the Laws* to engender its own controversy. but that is not the focus here. For our purposes, it is enough to understand that the publication of *The Spirit of the Laws* altered forever the common understanding of *Persian Letters*. Montesquieu quickly became known as the foremost political theorist of his time, and *Persian Letters* now became seen as an early exploration of his political philosophy. While it is often the case that an author's later magnum opus results in renewed appreciation of their earlier work, in Montesquieu's case, this alteration was especially pronounced because there are so many overlapping themes between the two works. Both books are obsessed with despotism, use a comparative framework, and seek to analyze politics, civil society, and religion. Both books are concerned with universal attributes of individual human rights, and, finally, both seem to use the status of women to comment generally on the extent of human liberty. Only after *The Spirit of the Laws* did readers come to see *Persian Letters* as more than a light satire. Such a transformation in the book's reception encouraged readers such as those unfortunate students at the University of Coimbra to interpret it philosophically.

The new attitude toward *Persian Letters* is evident in the first pamphlet written specifically to attack it: Jean Baptiste Gaultier's *Les Lettres persannes, convaincues d'impiété* [*Persian Letters*, Convicted of Impiety], published in 1751, barely three years after *The Spirit of the Laws* appeared. For the first time, we find a critic bypassing the elegant style of the book and directly addressing its main ideas and themes. Unlike all reviewers before him, Gaultier saw in *Persian Letters* a firm philosophical argument that unites the many stories, characters, digressions, and social commentary. That unity is, simply put, "the principles of Spinoza."[48] For Gaultier, Montesquieu's embrace of the seventeenth-century Jewish atheist is most clearly exhibited in Usbek's separation of God from justice. Where Usbek makes declarative statements about the universality of justice, Montesquieu allows his main character to wonder aloud about the nature of God and God's existence. In Gaultier's view, Montesquieu took justice from its spiritual moorings and made it part of nature, and therefore subject to cultural relativism. By naturalizing morality, Montesquieu's "definition of justice" justified "the worst of crimes."[49] Gaultier insisted that Montesquieu must not be confused with a moderate Catholic popularizing the less offensive ideas of Descartes or Malebranche, who at least thought they were furthering the interests of Christianity. Montesquieu knew better. According to Gaultier, his intent in *Persian Letters* was to destroy any place for the sanctity of Christian truth. He was among those "atheistic philosophers"[50] who sought no reconciliation with Christianity.

Following closely on the heels of Gaultier came a similar attack from a Jansenist theologian, Gabriel Gauchat. The difference between Gaultier and Gauchat was less in ideas than format. Whereas Gaultier published a free-standing pamphlet, Gauchat's seventy-five-page broadside was produced as part of a grand project published over many years, which grew to nineteen volumes criticizing writers who spread impiety. What held Gauchat's *Lettres critiques* together was his belief that these supposed attacks upon Christianity were coming from a coordinated source, that is, from a group of "famous authors from the Republic of Letters," who were scheming with one another. Indeed, according to Gauchat, what emboldened these authors was their esprit de corps, and the sense that they were acting together in a conspiratorial fashion. At the heart of the network was the image of a new type of writer represented by Montesquieu's *Persian Letters*:

> Let us understand this essential term: nothing seems so worthy of respect as the name Philosophe. It expresses love of truth and wisdom. Nothing today is more unstable; nothing is more maligned. For a certain set of people, a Philosophe is someone who falsely and brashly judges everything from their own enlightened viewpoint, who surmounts any authority based on faith, and who rejects the most sacred truths for old prejudices. Attack these supposed learned men, that's the crucial point. They merit our serious attention.[51]

Gauchat charged that the author of *Persian Letters* always had been in league with Voltaire, Denis Diderot, Julian Offray de La Mettrie, Alexander Pope, the Marquis d'Argens, and others to defame Christianity and put a perversion of "enlightenment" in its place. Gauchat was most alarmed by their apparent intent on popularizing their ideas among an ever-larger reading public. Every minister and "even every Christian man," Gauchat proclaimed, had a duty to rise to the defense of the faith against this heinous attack. From Gauchat's perspective, *Persian Letters* was a Trojan horse for a subversive group of atheistic philosophers. As we saw with *Telemachus* in Chapter 2, *Persian Letters* became regarded as part of the Enlightenment canon only following 1748.

Gaultier's and Gauchat's attacks goaded Montesquieu to renew his involvement with *Persian Letters*. Over the years various editions and translations had been published without his permission, resulting in several mistakes and textual corruptions. Montesquieu aimed to set things straight, and so, in 1754 he prepared for publication a new edition of *Persian Letters*. Although he introduced several small changes and included eleven letters missing in many editions, the most significant addition was an introduction entitled "Some Reflections on the *Persian Letters*" that began with this sentence: "Nothing pleased the public more, in the *Persian Letters*, than to find unexpectedly a sort of novel."[52] This is a startling claim. We know from investigating the reviews that the first generation of readers mostly ignored the work as a novel. Outside England, they virtually dismissed the seraglio elements as fanciful backdrops, and they viewed Usbek as a mouthpiece for Montesquieu. There were no early reviews that tried to understand Usbek's complex and tragic personality. In short, "the public" ignored any unifying plot and saw the book as a compendium of letters. Was Montesquieu being disingenuous?

When Montesquieu wrote *Persian Letters* between 1717 and 1720, the modern novel was only just coming into being. During the next thirty years, it developed as a distinct form, culminating in the three great works of Samuel Richardson (*Pamela* [1740], *Clarissa* [1748], and *Sir Charles Grandison* [1753]).[53] Even though characterization and plot in *Persian Letters* are primitive in comparison to Richardson's novels, Montesquieu was not simply boasting when he took pride in contributing to the novel's development. In an early draft of the 1754 introduction, Montesquieu specifically referred to *Pamela* and to Françoise de Graffigny's 1747 novel *Letters of a Peruvian Woman* as prime examples of what he had aimed to achieve. In the published version, Montesquieu went on to make an even more remarkable claim about the book: "But in the letter form . . . the author allows himself the advantage of adding philosophy, politics, and ethics to the novel, and of linking it all together by a secret, and, in a sense, unrecognized chain."[54] Here Montesquieu himself claimed that the book he wrote as a young man should not be dismissed as a clever but insignificant satire. He promised something far more. First, that its comments about philosophy, politics, and religion are not meant simply to amuse but have an important point; second, that the social criticism of Parisian mores is linked with the seraglio plot into an organic whole that he terms "a secret chain." Although Montesquieu strongly wanted to reject criticism of *Persian Letters* as a work of impiety, he nevertheless strengthened Gauchat's position by asking readers to consider it as a work as serious in its own way as *The Spirit of the Laws*. Just as *Spirit* synthesized philosophy, politics, and morals, so did the earlier work, but using the new form of an epistolary novel to make his case more popular—exactly what Gauchat feared. Nearing the end of his days, Montesquieu wanted to be recognized as a philosopher and thinker who had begun his career with a daring philosophical and political novel.

In this regard, Montesquieu's death in 1755 added to his reputation as a serious writer. Eulogies and reviews of his life's work took his recent introduction as paradigmatic, and nearly everyone—friend and foe—reconceived *Persian Letters* as a precursor to *The Spirit of the Laws*. Doubtless the most influential retrospective on Montesquieu's work following his death was the "eulogy" that d'Alembert published as a preface to the fifth volume of the *Encyclopédie* in 1757. Because the *Encyclopédie* itself became such a bestseller, d'Alembert's piece was read widely throughout Europe. Soon, it became part of the standard introductory material of most editions of Montesquieu's *Oeuvres*.

D'Alembert disagreed with Voltaire's earlier view that *Persian Letters* was a slight work, imitative of other fictional travel literature popular at the time. To be sure, he admitted, there were plenty of precedents. But *Persian Letters* surpassed them all in wit, style, and substance, and only its excellence can explain its popularity. D'Alembert also admitted that for many readers the seraglio story was only a prelude to making satirical and moving social commentary on French life. And yet, the social satire of French mores, "which is lively, but without malice" is not all there is to the *Persian Letters*. D'Alembert claimed that in juxtaposing "the apologue of the Troglodytes, the description of a virtuous people," Montesquieu was advancing political theory as well. Although early French readers may have missed Montesquieu's serious message because they were laughing so hard at themselves, d'Alembert nonetheless found in *Persian Letters* "the bud of those bright ideas which have been since developed by the author in his great work." In short, like Montesquieu himself in the 1754 "Reflections," d'Alembert viewed the early work as a precursor to *The Spirit of the Laws*.[55]

D'Alembert did not mount much of a defense for Montesquieu against the charges by Gaultier and Gauchat regarding his irreligious ideas. He claimed that "foreign publishers" had added additional letters not written by Montesquieu to editions of the book, and it was the material of these ersatz letters that had most offended critics. While some publishers certainly invented their own Persian Letters, there can be no doubt that Montesquieu wrote the letters critics found most offensive, such as the one describing the king and the pope as magicians.

A more potent defense of *Persian Letters* was made in the pages of the *Journal encyclopédique*, an influential literary review edited across the French border in Liège, an independent principality of the Holy Roman Empire. There, with impunity, its extraordinary editor/publisher, Pierre Rousseau, built a press that employed over twenty-five workers, put out three periodicals, and published dozens of books. The *Journal encyclopédique* quickly became the most important organ defending the philosophes. "M. l'abbé Gauchat, in analyzing *The Spirit of the Laws*, imagines an overall plan that in no way belongs to the author," charged Pierre Rousseau.[56] While *Persian Letters* may contain the kernel of some ideas that appeared later in the great treatise, the earlier work is a romance, a tale without formal argument, Rousseau insisted. The questions that Usbek raises about Christianity were not part of some grand design of Montesquieu's, but simply an imaginative story about how a Muslim visitor might encounter Christianity. Rousseau argued that Gauchat should have known better than to find fault with an argument never intended by the book's author.

Few readers seemed to find the *Journal*'s arguments convincing. By the 1760s and 1770s, public opinion seemed to converge around the idea that while *Persian Letters* was not a formal treatise, it did share much in common with *The Spirit of the Laws*. The Enlightenment critic and playwright Charles Palissot de Montenoy was probably speaking for many readers when he wrote that "*Persian Letters* is not a work of mere pleasantries, as has been said by a celebrated writer [i.e., Voltaire]. M de Montesquieu there usually renders the most serious topics with the same depth and profundity that characterizes the immortal work *The Spirit of the Laws*."[57]

The move from seeing *Persian Letters* as a witty satire bordering on the impious to a serious work embodying—at least for some—radical philosophical values can be seen in the reactions of readers and critics to one particular letter, 74, which addresses suicide. Although the criminalization of suicide was being questioned in a number of different countries during the early eighteenth century, Montesquieu's stinging comments in Letter 74 became infamous if only for their bluntness: "In Europe the laws deal extremely harshly with those who kill themselves; suicides are, as it were, put to death a second time; they are dragged ignominiously through the streets, declared infamous, and all their goods confiscated . . . [T]hese laws are most unjust."[58] Speaking through Usbek, Montesquieu advocated not merely decriminalization, but for a society in which life belonged solely to the individual, rather than controlled by government or church. "Society is based on mutual advantage, but when I find it onerous what is to prevent me renouncing it? Life was given to me as a favour, so I may abandon it when it is one no longer." Such language shocked readers, and they wondered whether Montesquieu was speaking seriously or satirically. Either way, he was being unusually provocative. These reflections took on an extra significance because a suicide forms the climax of the novel's plot: in the final letter, Usbek's favorite wife kills herself. Her suicide is simultaneously an expression of personal liberty: "I may have lived in servitude, but I have always been free."[59] When this final letter is juxtaposed with Letter 74, it becomes clear that Montesquieu's reflections on suicide were no digression, but that they formed the core of the book's message and at least one link in his "secret chain."

An ambivalent response to Letter 74 came from the Huguenot refugee Jean Henri Samuel Formey, a leading Protestant theologian in Prussia and member of the Berlin Academy. While acknowledging the brilliance of *Persian Letters*—"the most ingenious work the century has produced"—and reprinting in its entirety Letter 74 within his own refutation, he nonetheless views the arguments of Montesquieu on suicide weak and "sophistic."[60] Although Usbek believes in God, Formey argued that Usbek did not appreciate the extent to which humans owed their lives to God and therefore could not willfully take away what is not their own. Formey also took issue with Usbek's comment that our own death would not change the universe, an implication that our lives are of no more importance than insects or inanimate objects. While Formey believed Montesquieu had gone too far, he did not associate him with any school or philosophical faction, and simply thought that his imagination led him away from the truth.

Meanwhile in England, the controversy surrounding Letter 74 rose to a fever pitch when a rumor circulated through the press that a man "had on his table the *Persian Letters* lying open at this passage, when he laid violent hands on himself." In a special introduction to the 1736 English edition, John Ozell tried feebly to dispel these concerns, arguing that Montesquieu (by this time his identity was an open secret) did not believe Usbek's position himself, and was merely using his character to engage in an abstract philosophical exercise.[61] And yet, Letter 74 continued to provoke readers well into the 1760s and 1770s. The Portuguese university students, with whom this chapter began, found the sections on suicide particularly important. Antônio Caetana informed his inquisitors "that for some time he had wondered if suicide might be a natural right, as we find that it was justified in a book entitled *Persian Letters*."[62] These young readers understood that Montesquieu meant for them to see Roxana's suicide as an act demonstrating her virtue, not her impiety.

Some critics regarded Montesquieu's position on suicide not as something singular but emblematic of the Enlightenment's radical conspiracy against Christianity. What mattered most were not Montesquieu's specific ideas (and much less their place in the plot of the novel) but rather how well such ideas fit a pattern that was designed to undermine church and state. "The authors of *Persian Letters*, [d'Holbach's]*The System of Nature*, and [Rousseau's] *New Heloise*," wrote one critic in 1773, "seem to be those who write in the strongest and most seductive style favoring suicide."[63]

Perhaps the most dramatic evidence for this new appreciation of *Persian Letters* as an important precursor to *The Spirit of the Laws* came in 1762, when the Catholic Church placed the earlier book on its Index of Forbidden Works. That is, more than forty years after its initial publication, and a decade after its condemnation of *The Spirit of the Laws*, *Persian Letters* finally made it onto this infamous list. This was a recognition not only of the place of *Persian Letters* within the corpus of Montesquieu's works but, perhaps more fundamental, of its place within the family of Enlightenment classics. *Persian Letters* originally emerged as a light political satire publicized by Huguenot expatriates in Holland. Only following the publication of *Spirit* in 1748, his death in 1755, and his posthumous association with the *Encyclopédie* was *Persian Letters* reframed as a key work of the early Enlightenment. To be sure, the book never lost its initial reputation as a touchstone for elegant wit. For example, in 1762, when Jean Jacques Rousseau was asked by a younger writer for advice on good writing, he recommended studying only the "excellent" style of *Persian Letters*.[64] By the 1760s, the book had also become worthy of serious study for its philosophical ideas. No less a figure than Cesare Beccaria (author of the best-selling *On Crimes and Punishments*) noted to friends that "the moment of my conversion to philosophy" occurred in 1761 while reading not *The Spirit of the Laws*, but *Persian Letters*.[65]

Becarria was certainly not alone. While *Persian Letters* sold extremely well between 1721 and Montesquieu's death in 1755, it sold even better after. Table 3.1 demonstrates the resilience of *Persian Letters* throughout the century. As popular as the book was in its early years, there were many more reprintings of the book even after 1755, with the number of editions rising through the century's end. By the revolutionary era, readers saw as much wisdom in *Persian Letters* as in *The Spirit of the Laws*.[66] This was the period, notes Jonathan Israel, when the "Radical Enlightenment" consolidated its gains. However, where Israel sees the leaders of the Enlightenment turning away from Montesquieu, it makes more sense to acknowledge that sympathetic readers and hostile critics together made him into an Enlightenment patriarch. By the time University of Coimbra's students were arrested for reading *Persian Letters*, the book had become an introductory textbook to Enlightenment philosophy.

Chapter 4

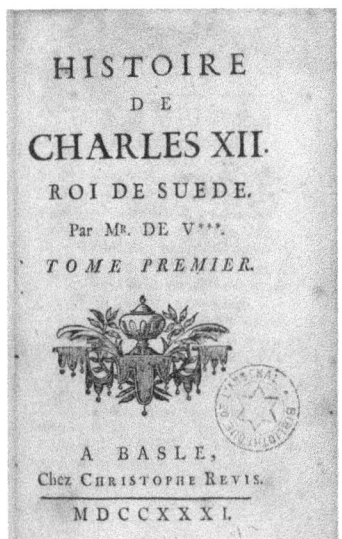

Figure 4.1 First edition title page Voltaire's *History of Charles XII*. Published only thirteen years following the death of the remarkable Swedish king, Voltaire's biography became his most popular work.

Figure 4.2 First edition title page Montesquieu's *Considerations on the Causes of the Greatness of the Romans and Their Decline.* The same publishing house that had first published *Persian Letters* also produced *Considerations*. This time, however, there was no need to develop a false imprint, since the French government allowed it to be imported so long as Montesquieu agreed to make certain changes to the manuscript.

Chapter 4
Voltaire's *History of Charles XII* (1731) and Montesquieu's *Considerations on the Causes of the Greatness of the Romans and Their Decline* (1734)

Table 4.1 Eighteenth-Century Editions of *Charles XII* and *Considerations*

Decade	1730–9	1740–9	1750–9	1760–9	1770–9	1780–9	1790–1800
Charles XII	57	14	19	18	30	20	15
Considerations	9	7	15	24	29	17	24

Total Editions *Charles XII*: 180.
Translations: Danish, Dutch, English, German, Italian, Latin, Portuguese, Russian.
Total Editions *Considerations*: 125.
Translations: Dutch, English, German, Greek, Italian, Russian, Spanish, Swedish.
Source: http://kates.itg.pomona.edu/books/analytics.php?type=all. Accessed May 14, 2022.

During the eighteenth century, Haddington was an important Scottish commercial town not far from Edinburgh. Attracting merchants, skilled artisans, and manufacturing, it boasted around 2,000 residents when, in 1730, the widow of an eminent minister donated his extensive book collection to the town. The Reverend John Gray had been a devoted collector and several of his titles went back to the fifteenth and sixteenth centuries. Unsurprisingly, the bulk of his collection consisted of theological treatises and religious pamphlets. The town accepted Mrs. Gray's donation and made the collection freely available to all Haddington residents. Though public libraries are taken for granted today, they were rare in the eighteenth century. As luck would have it, most of this library's borrowing records were preserved, giving scholars an uncommon opportunity to study eighteenth-century reading behavior.

The Gray Library became a town jewel, used throughout the century by more than 700 residents. Everyone in town was welcome, and readers included teenagers, women, artisans, and tradesmen, as well as members of the professional classes and clergy. Given the predominantly theological nature of the collection, the local clergy constituted most of its patronage during the first few years. During this time, around 80 percent of the books borrowed were religious.[1] Twenty years later, however, public usage of the library began to change, and the number of ordinary citizen borrowers increased dramatically. During the 1730s and 1740s approximately 57 percent of borrowers were professionals and clergy, while merchants, tradesmen, and artisans comprised only 36 percent. In the 1760s and 1770s, the situation reversed, as merchants, tradesmen, and artisans made up 51 percent of borrowers while professionals declined to 43 percent. This trend continued until the end of the century, by which point professionals had decreased to 33 percent of borrowers, while artisans, tradesmen, and merchants made up almost 60 percent of the library's patrons.[2]

These newer patrons were mostly uninterested in John Gray's religious books, which languished on the shelves for decades. Mirroring a trend found throughout Europe, theological tracts began to attract a smaller sector of the reading public. Instead, the reading public demanded poetry, plays, science, travel literature, geography, and, most of all, history. As the century progressed, the latter subject increasingly dominated public demand at the Gray Library, to the point that borrowers often had to wait in line for history books. According to Vivienne Dunstan, during the 1760s, seven of eleven of the library's most borrowed books concerned history; during the 1780s, this increased to eight out of ten of the most frequently checked out volumes. In fact, the majority of all books borrowed between 1790 and 1810 were history books (53 percent). Based on Dunstan's compelling findings, history was more popular than novels or any other form of literature among Haddington's borrowers.[3]

In this respect, the Gray Library seems no aberration. Gilles Eboli, for example, found similar level of interest in history in southern French book shops.[4] History became an increasingly popular subject throughout the eighteenth century, and it occupied a crucial position within Enlightenment publishing. Unfortunately, scholars undervalue the popularity of history books during the Enlightenment. Although, for example, Denis Diderot began his career translating a history of Greece and closed it by contributing over 700 pages to Raynal's monumental *History of the Two Indies*, few today would recognize Diderot as an historian. Likewise, although Hume's *History of England* was his best-selling work in the eighteenth century, he is mostly known today for his philosophical work. While the polyglot Joseph Priestley published over fifty books and pamphlets, his most popular works were two general histories.[5] In an attempt to remedy this oversight, this chapter focuses on two history books available to borrowers at the Gray Library: Voltaire's *History of Charles XII* and Montesquieu's *Considerations on the Causes of the Greatness of the Romans and Their Decline*. The enormous popular success of these two books would inspire some of the greatest historical works of the 1750s, 1760s, and 1770s, including works by David Hume, William Robertson, and Edward Gibbon.[6]

Voltaire's *Charles XII*

Charles XII became king of Sweden in 1697 at the age of fourteen and died in 1718 when he was only thirty-six. When he assumed the throne, Sweden, despite its meager resources and sparse population, was a Northern European powerhouse. As a result of political cunning and strong French financial support during the Thirty Years War, Sweden had expanded its territory to include most of Finland and much of what is today the Baltic coastal areas of Russia, Estonia, Latvia, and Lithuania as well as vital strips of territory along the southern Baltic coast between Denmark and Poland. With these Baltic lands as his base, Charles led his army southward, attacking the already weakened Polish-Lithuanian kingdom. In 1704, he overthrew his rival, the Polish king Augustus II, and replaced him with a Swedish pawn, Stanislaw. But even this monumental accomplishment was not enough for Charles, who set about planning to destroy Peter the Great's new Russian Army in order to cement Swedish control over all of Northern and Eastern Europe. If successful, Charles would have unified a greater part of Europe than any conqueror since Charlemagne. However, in 1709 at the Battle of Poltava, in what is today Ukraine, Charles's troops were defeated by the Russian Army, forcing him to seek refuge with the Ottoman sultan. After this catastrophic defeat, Augustus II quickly regained the Polish throne, and Charles never fully recovered his former power. When he finally returned to Sweden, several years later, he died from a stray bullet in a fruitless battle against the Danes. Sweden, once a major European power, would never again regain her military glory.[7]

The dramatic story of Sweden's rise and fall under Charles XII captivated eighteenth-century Europeans. It was one thing for a Louis XIV to mount wars against France's neighbors—after all, France had been a hegemonic Western European state for centuries, and its aggressive designs were taken for granted. Sweden, however, was clearly punching above its weight. While Voltaire resided in England during 1726–8, he followed discussions about Charles among his noble friends and began interviewing officers who had participated in the Battle of Poltava. By the time he returned to France in 1729, he had finished a rough draft of his biography on the Swedish king.

Given the public's intense interest in the story of Charles XII, Voltaire's book, if well written, was sure to be popular. But writing about such recent history also had its disadvantages—no matter how comprehensive the research, the facts would be vulnerable to dispute since so many participants in the story were still alive. Voltaire was one of the first major authors to chart the history of the Swedish king's reign, but the difficulty of obtaining authoritative records put him in a dangerous position.

At the time that Voltaire was preparing to publish his biography, he was already well known in the literary world. When he was only twenty-two, his first play, a reworking of Sophocles's *Oedipus*, was performed by the Comédie-Française. The play was a smash hit, and the print version went through several editions. *Brutus* became his second major hit just as he was about to publish *Charles XII*. Were that not enough, in 1728 he achieved greater fame when he reworked a 1723 epic poem into *La Henriade*, lionizing the efforts of Henry IV to put an end to the French religious wars. Published by subscription in England in a lavishly illustrated quarto edition, the poem announced the ascendency of a major French writer.

Oedipus and *Brutus* appeared openly in Paris with the endorsement of the government and Voltaire's name displayed on the title pages. The government at first also endorsed publication of *History of Charles XII*, and so with three hits under his belt, Voltaire expected to extend his literary reputation as a historian. However, to Voltaire's dismay, in January 1731, the minister in charge of book censorship suddenly revoked permission for *Charles XII*, seizing all 2,600 copies of the newly printed first edition. This reversal was driven by Louis XV's concern that the retelling of Augustus II's defeat might offend the Poles, with whom he wished to maintain a close relationship. However, Voltaire was told that if he published his book surreptitiously, the authorities would look the other way. As he would be forced to do with many of his later books, Voltaire had his work printed secretly and anonymously through a printer in Rouen, Claude François Jore (see Figure 4.1). Voltaire's name was removed from the title page, and a false city of origin and publisher were added (Basel: Christophe Revis). Voltaire arranged for Jore to print two simultaneous editions—one cheap two-volume duodecimo edition and a more substantial octavo printing. He also provided a manuscript copy to his English friends, who secretly published a separate two-volume duodecimo edition in London. In this way, Voltaire hedged his bets and ensured that Paris would have enough copies. His authorship was noted in the Parisian press, but he protested that the manuscript had been stolen from his home and published without his permission. Eventually, in 1734, the French government granted the book a *permission tacite*, which allowed it qualified circulation within the kingdom.[8]

Despite this rocky start, sales were brisk once copies began to appear at bookstalls. Following the first three editions toward the end of 1731, no fewer than sixteen editions appeared in 1732. Voltaire himself was surprised by the book's immediate success, and he regretted that he had not had more copies printed for the first Rouen printings, which he had personally financed.[9] England became an especially hot market for the book: one translation was reprinted some six times during 1732 alone, and one newspaper serialized the entire work between February 1733 and October 1734.[10] Between 1732 and 1800, new editions emerged at the astonishing rate of more than one per year. Within two years of its original publication the *History of Charles XII* was translated into Dutch, English, German, Italian, and Spanish. Before the end of the century, editions were also published in Danish, Polish, Portuguese, and Swedish. Altogether the total number of eighteenth-century editions came to 180, making *History of Charles XII* Voltaire's most popular book. Despite its poor reputation today, more editions of *Charles XII* were published in the eighteenth century than editions for *Candide*, *Philosophical Dictionary*, *Age of Louis XIV*, or even his most successful plays.[11] The popularity of Voltaire's historical work can hardly be overstated. If we accept Richard Sher's definition of a bestseller as a title produced in ten or more editions, Voltaire produced more bestsellers during the eighteenth century than any other author.[12] While today Voltaire's reputation as a historian has no doubt slipped, during the eighteenth century this biography of the great Swedish king was arguably more renowned than any of his other works. Looking at the Enlightenment as a whole, *History of Charles XII* went through more editions than any other history book, including Gibbon's *Decline and Fall of the Roman Empire* and Hume's *History of England*.

Voltaire portrayed Charles XII as a remarkable combination of virtue and hubris. He was highly disciplined and seldom overpowered by lust or greed. His conduct and way of life were widely admired, and he disciplined his troops accordingly. He could be gentle or stern, as the situation required. His moral character was above reproach. He was a model for his troops and their loyalty to him became one of his great assets. Yet despite his virtuousness, he was also hostage to a restless, unchecked ambition which eventually destroyed his empire. Besides making for a compelling story, Voltaire believed that a history of Charles XII would serve as an important lesson for contemporary monarchs.

Voltaire's book answered Fénelon's *Telemachus*, the most popular view of kingship at the time. Fénelon had argued that statecraft was noble only when it was guided by virtue and Christian values; that is, a monarch motivated only by his strict understanding of the best interests of his people. In Voltaire's telling, Charles was everything that Mentor sought in a king: young, brave, disciplined, and the epitome of moral virtue. "For where is the monarch who can say, 'I am braver and more virtuous than Charles XII; I have a more resolute spirit and a sturdier body; I have a greater understanding of warfare; I have better troops than he'?" Voltaire wrote approvingly.[13] To Voltaire and many of his contemporaries, Charles was the contemporary embodiment of Telemachus.

And yet such Christian virtue became a liability for Charles. An ancient Homeric hero seemed tragically out of place among modern statesmen. This eighteenth-century Telemachus suddenly became highly dangerous for Europe and especially for Sweden. In contrast to Fénelon's mythological world, early modern statecraft had become characterized not by the moral characteristics of a ruler, but rather by learned compromise bending toward preserving the balance of power among states. Virtue may be an asset, but only if it is moderated like all other passions. Voltaire's *History of Charles XII* was also his anti-*Telemachus*, and it became nearly as popular.

Later, in *The Spirit of the Laws*, Montesquieu would famously argue that virtue has no place in a monarchy. Voltaire did not take the argument that far. Rather, for him Charles was an outlier, like Oedipus or Brutus, and his tale a virtual Greek tragedy. Voltaire never doubted that Charles was a good man and a virtuous ruler, but his story showed that even the most virtuous statesman may be blind to his own hubris. One's ambition to perform virtuous acts can end by destroying virtue itself. Voltaire was confident that his biography would give European monarchs a lesson on the importance of keeping one's ambition in check. "There is assuredly no sovereign," he wrote, "who, on reading the life of Charles XII, must not be cured of the rage to conquer."[14]

We can see the book's early impact on readers by looking at one monthly review journal, *The Present State of the Republic of Letters*. In the January 1732 issue, the review of *History of Charles XII* was immediately preceded by a review covering Bernard Mandeville's *An Enquiry into the Origin of Honour and the Usefulness of Christianity in War*. The juxtaposition of these two book reviews was surely not coincidental. After all, as the reviewer acknowledged, Mandeville was already infamous for his *Fable of the Bees*, which denied virtue any positive role in the development of civilization. Mandeville, turning Hobbes on his head, had argued that selfishness and greed ultimately caused sociability and cooperation. *An Enquiry into the Origin of Honour* extended this argument by claiming that honor and virtue, while often used interchangeably, are in fact radically different. Notions of virtue, he argued, go back to the ancient Greek idea of putting one's community before oneself; honor however, was unknown in the ancient world. Mandeville argued that the concept of honor stemmed from the Goths' notion of "self-liking," or, in other words, of distinguishing oneself from one's community. Since such egotism underlined the warmongering quality of early modern statecraft, Mandeville provocatively claimed that while Christianity was compatible with ancient virtue, it was at odds with honor.[15]

The *Present State*'s reviewer was impressed with Mandeville's "genius and penetration," and he commended the essay to readers as an essay that "truly deserves to be thoroughly perused and meditated on."[16] And yet he noted throughout the review that Mandeville's claim, though dramatic, was hardly original. In fact, it derived from the skeptic Pierre Bayle (1647–1716), who famously argued that even virtuous actions were fundamentally driven by selfishness. Bayle had even gone so far as to speculate that a community of atheists might live more virtuously than Christians, since even good Christians were not guided by a pure, disinterested virtue. Accordingly, the reviewer noted the influence of Bayle and warned readers to be on their guard: "All the principles which the author has so freely advanced may not suit the taste of all readers in general; they will and must undoubtedly be looked upon as dangerous to society."[17]

Readers already wary of Mandeville and Bayle next met Voltaire's *Charles XII*. As with Mandeville, the review ascribed his outlook to Bayle, citing *Historical and Critical Dictionary* as an authoritative source. For this review, at least, Bayle inspired an interpretation of Charles in which he was less of an outlier than even Voltaire thought. From the start, the reviewer argued, Christian princes have behaved most unchristianly, clamoring "to deceive each other," and hoping to "become at War together."[18]

The reviewer noted that Charles was raised to be the epitome of the enlightened prince; supplementing Voltaire, the reviewer adds that Charles was tutored by the greatest political theorist of the age, Samuel von Pufendorf and that he matured quickly. Once he became a young adult, "he was the only king that had ever lived without failings," and was "liberal through a greatness of soul."[19] Despite this moral fortitude, his virtuous behavior did not lead to the outcomes predicted by Fénelon and Pufendorf. In the language of Mandeville, now explicitly used in this *Present State* review, Charles forsook virtue for honor. For example, when the residents of Riga failed to recognize him appropriately, he avenged this slight by laying siege to the town. "Thus Charles XII out of a point of Honor, undertook to [initiate] war in the eighteenth year of his age." To this reviewer, the struggle between Northern Europe's most powerful monarchs was caused not by national interest or religious ideology, but simply by what Mandeville termed self-liking (and Bayle termed amour propre): "the cause of this war was that [the residents of Riga] had not showed him all the Honor that was do [sic] him."[20] The Great Northern War was caused essentially by a personal slight. For the *Present State* reviewer, Voltaire's *Charles XII* best illustrated Mandeville's concept of honor and Bayle's dismissal of Christian virtue's role in political life.

Reviews in journals such as *The Present State of the Republic of Letters* show that, like Fénelon's *Telemachus*, Voltaire's biography was received as a serious contribution to political thought. One well-connected Lyon librarian, Claude Brossette, interpreted the book as a political lesson regarding the dangers of Louis XIV's foreign policy. Aside from the political importance of Charles XII, Brossette was also smitten with Voltaire's entertaining literary style. Shortly after the book's publication, Brossette wrote a friend to admire its "touching portraits, the lively and quick-paced narration, and all his reflections are so naturally displayed."[21] The future Swiss historian Vincenz Bernhard Tschamer likewise raved about the book to friends: "I have read the *History of Charles XII* and I can assure you that I have never read a history more interesting in terms of its story and style."[22] Lord Bolingbroke's *Craftsman* lauded it as "the best piece of modern history that has lately appeared in public."[23] Whig agreed with Tory: "I have not indeed met with any person who has read this *History*, but confessed it was with a good deal of pleasure."[24] Thirty years later opinions had not changed. While his *Philosophical Letters*, *Age of Louis XIV*, and *Essai sur les moeurs* were all highly praised, the *History of Charles XII* remained in a class by itself. "In biography, M. de Voltaire has scarce a superior. His life of Charles the XII is an admirable composition, full of that boldness and strength of coloring," noted another reviewer. "Nothing can be more lively, judicious or penetrating than his remarks; nothing more elegant than his language."[25]

By 1738, when a major collection of Voltaire's works was published in Amsterdam, critics had recognized *Charles XII* as a masterpiece. The exiled French Huguenot and future translator of David Hume's *Political Discourses*, Elézar de Mauvillon, claimed that "M. de Voltaire is without doubt one of the century's greatest geniuses who offers the most honor to France. He has written excellent works of prose. The more I read of his *History of Charles XII*, the more he seems to me [like the great Roman historian] Quintus Curtius." Mauvillon specifically praised Voltaire for avoiding the type of hagiography so common in other biographies, in which Charles XII "is raised to the status of a demi-god." Rather, in Voltaire's rendering, Charles is revealed as a man of flesh and blood whose faults competed with his virtues. Mauvillon noted that this way of approaching the monarch's character served Voltaire's overall political agenda: "This we can say with certainty: Voltaire is the enemy of tyranny and he despises all kings who turn themselves into despots." Voltaire was certainly right to use the story of Charles XII to warn against the warmongering tendencies of early modern monarchs, which usually devastates the common people on both sides of the conflict. "Let us love peace with M. de Voltaire," he exclaimed.[26]

Despite its popularity and critical praise, Voltaire's account was challenged from the start by readers, critics, and reviewers, who accused him of playing fast and loose with the facts. Readers wrote to journals complaining that they knew eyewitnesses who provided alternative accounts. As early as January 1733, *The Bee* reported that a letter had been distributed claiming Voltaire had misrepresented the burning of Altona to various journals in Amsterdam.[27] This criticism so upset Voltaire that he hurriedly affixed a special "Letter on the Fire at Altona" to his *Letters Concerning the English Nation*. A few months later, another reader claiming to be an eyewitness rebuked Voltaire in *The Bee* for getting many military facts wrong.[28] Some critics wrote straightaway to Voltaire himself. "I am enchanted by the elegance and precision of style that informs your choice of events," wrote fellow historian Valentin Philippe Bertin de Rocheret. But this compliment was only a prelude to a series of sharp criticisms that followed. For one, Rocheret disputed a letter cited by Voltaire from the deposed Polish king Augustus to his successor King Stanislaus: "Yours is better written I admit," Rocheret wrote, but the copy that he included in his packet to Voltaire was "more in keeping with historical truth."[29]

Voltaire had anticipated such negative reaction even before Jore completed the Rouen edition. He responded with a two-pronged counterattack that would serve him well for decades to come. First, he closely read every criticism, considered its merits, and made many changes and improvements to the book. Second, he surrounded the narrative history with an ever-increasing array of enhanced title pages, tables of contents, errata sheets, indexes, prefaces, forewords, discourses, letters from the author, and notices from the publisher. These *paratexts* challenged detractors and allowed him to reflect upon the historian's craft.[30] The *History of Charles XII* was published almost 150 times during the eighteenth century, and with each edition supervised by Voltaire, the work changed incrementally. Thus, the book's publication history bears witness to its development into its final form as a mature and carefully written work of history. Voltaire's paratexts were critical to reframing the book as an outstanding example of a new type of history (one soon exhibited by Montesquieu) in which analysis and criticism approached political thought. As the short forewords piled up over the decades, they came to constitute a user manual for understanding a new historical method.

Discourse on the History of Charles XII

The first paratext Voltaire developed to defend his approach was a short philosophical statement on the importance of contemporary history, the "Discourse on the History of Charles XII." Jore received the essay so late in his initial printing that the first duodecimo edition includes it as an afterword in the second volume. However, in Jore's octavo edition of the book, this essay appeared as a preface, and it retained this location in subsequent French editions and most translations. Voltaire began the discourse by observing that the last thing the public needs is another royal biography. In recent decades, the production of courtly histories and royal biographies had become such an enormous industry that no reader could possibly remain current with all the publications. As soon as a monarch died, every one of their courtiers rushed to write a memoir about them. "This frenzy to transmit pointless details to posterity," Voltaire wrote, should be resisted by the public as much as possible. He insisted that, for the most part, the lives of monarchs were no more worthy of publication than those of ordinary people. However, the story of Charles XII's struggle with his Russian rival was clearly in a different class. "I would there have most carefully refrained from adding this particular history of Charles XII . . . and his rival Peter" [the Great], Voltaire assured his readers, if they were not "by common accord the most remarkable men to have appeared in over two thousand years." He insisted that statesmen and rulers could learn much from studying the life of Charles XII, and hoped it would serve as a warning to those sovereigns who suffer from "the rage to conquer."[31]

La Motraye, *Critical and Historical Remarks on the History of Charles XII*

In 1732, a scathing 100-page review of Voltaire's newly published book was produced as a pamphlet in both English and French.[32] Its author, the French Huguenot Aubry de La Motraye, had spent several years traveling across Europe with Charles XII's entourage, and now lived in London. In 1723 he had published his own two-volume travelogue in English, followed by a French version in 1727.[33] He knew firsthand many of the stories in the *History of Charles XII* and published his review as an open letter to Voltaire, making his criticisms seem particularly confrontational. "Because I had for many years the honor of a free access to your hero," wrote La Motraye challenged, "I ought to be better informed than you." On every page of his review, he disputed one story after another, claiming that Voltaire gave the wrong dates, mistook one character for another, and invented conversations that never occurred. At the end of his review, La Motraye directly impugned Voltaire's credibility: "It is generally allowed, Sir, that your book is extraordinarily well written," he wrote sounding more like a stern schoolmaster than a colleague:

> This would be enough for a romance, 'tis said, where invention is always predominant, but not for a history where truth must reign absolute. They complain that you make Charles do and say several things which he never was seen to do, nor heard to say; that you confound and change times, places, persons, their names, characters, offices, etc.[34]

Voltaire was clearly stung by La Motraye's review, which he described to a friend as "miserable." The criticism was so severe that he had no choice but to respond.[35] Voltaire prepared an edition of *Charles XII* that included all 100 pages of La Motraye's review, but embellished his critic's work with his own stream of critical footnotes. Published the next year in 1733 in Amsterdam, its title page (itself an effective paratext that alerted readers to Voltaire's program) advertised it as a "new edition revised, corrected, and augmented by the author, with the Critical Remarks of Mr. de La Motraye and responses by Mr. de Voltaire." (Figure 4.3)[36] Following the final chapter, Voltaire used this innovative format to pull La Motraye into a pseudo-dialog with him for the benefit of entertaining the reader and defending the accuracy of his work. Like his Twenty-Fifth Letter on Pascal that completes *Philosophical Letters* (which was composed roughly at the same time), this dialogic format allowed Voltaire to ridicule La Motraye. In over sixty footnotes, Voltaire displayed the range of his wit and literary ability. Sometimes he expressed annoyance with his critic, such as asking why his adversary did not "communicate these remarks directly to M. de Voltaire instead of selling them for money to a publisher?"[37] Sometimes he blamed a typographical error on the printer and chided La Motraye for being picayune. Sometimes he simply noted that the mistake was now corrected in the most current version now before the reader. At other times, he rejected La Motraye's criticism out of hand: "This is neither reasonable nor truthful. Such stories dishonor history."[38] Most importantly, Voltaire defended himself as the superior historian: "M. de Voltaire is satisfied to write what Charles XII did; M. de La Motraye writes what Charles XII would have liked to do."[39] When they disagreed over the testimony of different eyewitness accounts, Voltaire promised to deposit his notes and source evidence in a

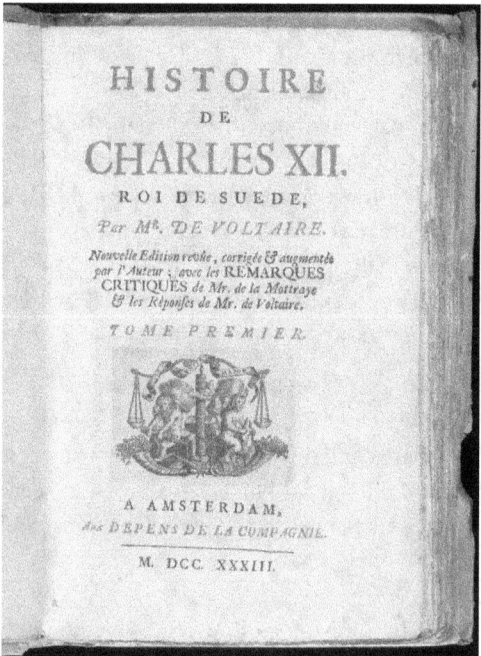

Figure 4.3 Title page of the 1733 edition of *Charles XII* with Motraye's critical remarks and Voltaire's responses. Eighteenth-century titles sometimes squeezed so many words on a page that they resembled advertisements or prologues.

public library. He fulfilled this promise in 1749 by depositing his papers for *Charles XII* in France's Bibliothèque du roi (today's Bibliothèque Nationale de France).[40] This method of responding to La Motraye only intensified the book's popularity. Between 1733 and 1748, nearly all fifteen French editions of *Charles XII* (including several editions not authorized by Voltaire) sandwiched the narrative history between the preliminary Discourse and the dialog with La Motraye's *Historical and Critical Remarks*.[41]

Voltaire's decision to publish the 1733 edition in Amsterdam reflected a shift to exert more control over the publication of his writings. In contrast to Montesquieu, who usually remained distant from his publishers, Voltaire drew ever closer to them in an effort to make them serve his burgeoning literary career. The 1730s were a remarkably prolific period for Voltaire. In addition to *Charles XII* and *Philosophical Letters*, by 1738 he had published *Zaïre* and other popular theatre pieces, controversial poetry such as *Le Mondain*, and an important work of popular science, the *Elements of the Philosophy of Newton*. Rival publishers in France and Holland were already starting to put together compilations and "complete works," beginning with a set issued by Dutch publishers in 1728, three years before Voltaire published *Charles XII*.

These unauthorized projects made Voltaire anxious. With each new unauthorized edition came mistakes and errors, and as one publisher pirated another, his words invariably became mangled. Without close attention, his writings could not be corrected from one edition to another. To some extent, this was his own fault. Voltaire constantly placed himself in editorial jeopardy because he tinkered with his works following initial publication. Every edition gave him an opportunity to revise. Voltaire also worried about the many works that were falsely attributed to him, a problem that would follow him throughout his long career. Publishers looking to produce complete works might include these misattributed works unless Voltaire intervened. Finally, Voltaire wanted the ability to exclude legitimate, but illegal, works, that if included in a collection, might place the entire publication in legal jeopardy, particularly in France. (He would soon exercise this option by excluding *Philosophical Letters* from a compilation of his works.) For all these reasons, then, he began to collaborate with publishers to produce a carefully controlled set of complete works that would standardize his writings. The improvements made to *Charles XII* occurred within this larger publishing project.[42]

Throughout the 1730s, Voltaire worked most closely with Etienne Ledet and Jacques Desbordes, two well-known Huguenots who specialized in publishing French books. Desbordes was the son of Suzanne de Caux, the original publisher of Montesquieu's *Persian Letters*. Ledet and Desbordes first published Voltaire's work by distributing unauthorized copies of his plays from 1731 to 1732, including *Brutus, Oedipus, Marianne, and L'Indiscret*. They were in the process of preparing an unauthorized edition of Charles XII when another publisher announced their own edition in a Dutch newspaper. In Holland, such an advertisement was regarded as an informal copyright to the title. So, when Ledet and Desbordes published a set of *Oeuvres de M de Voltaire* in 1732, *History of Charles XII* was the only major work excluded.[43]

It took only a few weeks for Voltaire, then living in Paris, to obtain a copy of this new collection of his works. Upset by various mistakes, typographical errors, and other imperfections, he immediately set one publisher against another. He signaled his printer in Rouen, Claude François Jore, who was about to print *Philosophical Letters*, to begin preparing a new edition of his collected works. If this move was supposed to intimidate Ledet and Desbordes, it backfired, and in 1735 they produced their own inferior version of *Philosophical Letters*. Unfortunately for Voltaire, they also purchased from the Dutch government a copyright for a fifteen-year period to produce Voltaire's complete works. This privilege was advertised publicly in June 1736. By then they had published even more of Voltaire's poetry and plays, and had also purchased the copyright to *Charles XII*. Now they could produce their own edition that would soon merge into their updated complete works. Given their clear position as his most important Dutch publisher, Voltaire was forced to deal with them directly, if he wanted control over his work.

In 1736, Voltaire took the extraordinary step of traveling to Holland and staying in the home of Etienne Ledet. There he struck a grand bargain with his host: Voltaire would give him exclusive new material in exchange for complete editorial control. Together, they would prepare updated versions of his complete works as new pieces warranted improvements. Voltaire would determine the content of each volume, when to print, how to correct for errors, and when to distribute volumes to bookstores. Voltaire also expected to collaborate on the quality of the paper, the size and type of the font, and other such issues typically left to the discretion of the publisher. While Ledet and Desbordes would be responsible for all printing costs, Voltaire insisted on the authority to make infinite corrections and delay publication until only he was ready.

This relationship between author and publisher was quite unusual. Normally, the author would receive a lump sum in return for selling the manuscript to the publisher. From that point, the manuscript belonged to the publisher, and the author lost rights over it. To be sure, publishers tried to maintain good relations with authors if only to secure their future business. However, decisions regarding reprints, format, prefatory essays, title page information, illustrations, and the like were generally thought to be the publisher's domain. Voltaire's demands marked nothing less than a revolution in author–publisher relations. This shift in power from publisher to author was less a hallmark of Enlightenment publishing and more particular to the case of Voltaire, and it became the source for endless miscommunication and trickery on both sides.[44]

Voltaire, Ledet, and Desbordes began preparation for a new edition of *Charles XII*. As Voltaire revised and improved his biography, he continued to seek out eyewitnesses, either directly through correspondence or by consulting their memoirs, including Polish Count Stanislaw Poniatowski and Johann Mathias von der Schulenburg, who served as military officers during the Great Northern War.[45] He did not simply make small editorial revisions but continued to pursue primary research and alter his work accordingly. The fruit of these long labors was first evidenced in Ledet and Desbordes's 1739 "new revised and corrected edition, with many particular and interesting changes, printed from the author's manuscript." With over fifty changes, this version constituted a considerable update. It was sold as part of a new set of Voltaire's collected works that Ledet and Desbordes had begun in 1738 and which they would continue to produce throughout the 1740s.[46]

This Ledet and Desbordes octavo edition of Voltaire's *Works* immediately became the standard for those that followed, including unauthorized printings and translations. Still, it was not good enough for Voltaire. Despite his close collaboration, he constantly expressed unhappiness over the quality of Ledet and Desbordes's publications. He demanded better. A special problem involved the premature release of the *Elements of the Philosophy of Newton*. Voltaire withheld the last section of the manuscript, but Ledet and Desbordes felt that they had invested too much capital to wait. Without telling Voltaire, they hired a mathematician to complete the final chapters, and published the book. Voltaire was furious and at one point referred to his publishers as "Dutch animals."[47] He countered by taking the entire operation away from them and turned to a Paris publisher, Laurent-François Prault. Unfortunately, Prault's 1740 and 1742 editions of *Works* exhibited their own problems, and Voltaire was forced to continue collaborating with Ledet and Desbordes until 1743, all the while covertly looking for new publishers.[48]

In 1746, a friend advised Voltaire to work with Georg Conrad Walther, a rising publisher and bookseller in Dresden, best known for procuring books for the royal library of Saxony and producing foreign-language works—he would soon publish a French translation of Henry Fielding's *Tom Jones*. Although Dresden was obviously far from Western European cities like Paris, London, and Amsterdam, its court had become a major cultural center, especially in music and bookselling. Within a few months Voltaire and Walther agreed to produce a new octavo set of *Works* in eight volumes. To protect the large capital investment required by such a large project, Walther applied for a ten-year copyright from Augustus III, elector of Saxony and king of Poland. The application was delegated to a government censor, the University of Leipzig history professor Christian Gottlieb Jöcher, who approved the project in early 1748. However, this was not enough for Walther. Given that Saxony was a member of the Holy Roman Empire, Walther also managed to secure copyright protection from the Habsburg emperor, which technically meant that only his edition could be sold legally in the Holy Roman Empire. At this point, after all, no work of Voltaire's had been condemned by the Roman Catholic Church or anywhere in the Holy Roman Empire. By September 1747, Walther was ready to print the first few volumes and publicly announced the impending publication.[49]

The 1740s witnessed the publication in French of what eventually became a four-volume memoir of Charles XII by his own military chaplain, Jöran Nordberg.[50] Voltaire assiduously mined this new source of information, and the new 1748 version of *Charles XII* published by Walther as part of his collection included at least "150 pages of additions and corrections."[51] "Voltaire invested an enormous amount of time in this edition," notes leading Voltaire scholar Nicholas Cronk.[52] The resulting edition was so different from those that came before it that Voltaire instructed Walther to drop the La Motraye afterword—those criticisms were now obsolete.

Yet the project faced other problems. As usual, Voltaire was not ready for Walther to print. He begged him to hold off, promising to purchase hundreds of sets himself so

Walther would not lose money. Additionally, Walther's public announcement triggered a hostile response from his Dutch rivals. Ledet and Desbordes (the latter died in 1742) had sold their copyright to the larger firm of Arkstée and Merkus, who continued publishing their own edition of Voltaire's *Works* after securing from Saxony the more general right to distribute books in Dutch, English, and French. In 1747 they published the seventh volume of new pieces by Voltaire and began distributing books across Europe. When they objected to Walther's new edition, Voltaire rolled up his sleeves. "The booksellers of Holland complain in vain," he wrote to Walther.

> They produced, Monsieur, a very incomplete and very incorrect edition. I suggested to them a hundred times to correct their mistakes, but they preferred to sell a badly made book rather than a good one. Your edition will be very different. You have added a lot, have made great changes, and have put everything in order. We will have volume for volume the most exemplary version. I will be very happy to please you and help you.[53]

Here Voltaire is not so much making a legal argument about legal jurisdictions, as he is asserting a dubious moral point that an author always has the right to choose a publisher for an updated version of his own books. Nowhere in eighteenth-century Europe did laws recognize such authorial sovereignty.

In January 1748, Voltaire took his campaign to the press, writing in the *Mercure de France* that "the edition of Ledet of Amsterdam and those of Arkstée and Merkus" are "replete on every page with mistakes and errors so large as to offend any reader." The Dutch publishers countered by printing a notice in *Le Vrai patriote hollandais* reminding readers that their edition had been hand-corrected by Voltaire himself while "he had been for so long lodging at Ledet's home."[54] Finally, after months of legal wrangling, the Saxon government sided with Walther and Voltaire, forbidding Arkstée and Merkus to sell their version within Saxony. Meanwhile in February 1748, Voltaire finally sent Walther "corrections and additions" for the new *History of Charles XII* that "assumes you are using the Amsterdam edition of 1739" as the base text. Despite his public declarations to the contrary, these instructions attest to Voltaire's reliance on the integrity of the 1739 edition.[55]

Voltaire promised Walther that he would pursue a marketing campaign to "discredit all the other bad editions."[56] And indeed, when Walther's eight-volume octavo edition of the *Oeuvres* finally went on sale with a print run of 1,200 copies in October 1748, Voltaire himself penned a preface that warned readers regarding other versions:

> All other editions are so badly produced leading the public to demand repeatedly a set of exemplary versions of a complete set of works. Those of Ledet and even more Arkstée and Merkus of Amsterdam, and others who copy them, raise the ire of the reader, either because of the gross typographical errors that change the meaning of words, or because of misplaced transpositions, or because of other mistakes and errors, or because of the arrogance resulting in placing a number of bad pieces that are wrongly attributed to the author.[57]

If such action was meant to silence the Dutch publishers, it was ineffective. The Dutch editions of Voltaire's works sold well enough that in 1749 Arkstée and Merkus announced the impending publication of seventh and eighth volumes. When the seventh volume appeared, Ledet shot back with his own preface that squarely refuted the Dresden accusations, referring to Walther as a con man and "Ostrogoth."[58]

Pyrrhonism in History

Per Voltaire's instructions, Walther added a short new essay to accompany the ever-present "Discourse on the History of Charles XII." The essay was initially called "Preface to This Edition of 1748," but was soon retitled in future editions "Pyrrhonism in History." In it, Voltaire developed his own approach to historical method by insisting that radical skepticism should be the lifeblood of any historian dedicated to truth-telling. Centering his theory around a concept found in Pierre Bayle's popular *Historical and Critical Dictionary*, Voltaire claimed that historians must begin their work with a proper sense of skepticism.[59] They must constantly interrogate their sources and cast aside accounts that appear "contrary to nature." Many histories, he complained, were simply bad, since their authors passed off fables and melodrama for truthful narrative. Some mistakes were due to the gullibility of certain historians; at other times, their lack of objectivity. More often than not, mistakes were the result of unreliable sources.

Voltaire, as he made clear in "Pyrrhonism in History," was aware that the story of Charles XII was a highly improbable one. Accordingly, he promised his audience that he had examined all of his sources even more carefully and critically than usual. He reminded them that his research began by interviewing reliable eyewitnesses such as Baron Earnst Friedrich von Fabrice and Robert de Villelongue, comte de la Cerda. When "wretched" critics like La Motraye indicted his account for errors, he drew upon even more eyewitnesses and compared their accounts. Unfortunately, even "these eyewitnesses did not see everything, and sometimes saw things in a false light." Eyewitness accounts must be subjected to rigorous scrutiny, but since no one can recall events with total clarity, the historian's narrative is likely to be imperfect. This acknowledgment regarding the frailty of the historical enterprise is perhaps the best reason why "that skepticism which we ought to entertain with regard to particular facts, we should likewise extend to the manners of foreign nations."[60] A few years later, when he published the article "History" in the *Encyclopédie*, Voltaire put the matter more succinctly: "History is the narration of facts presented as true, in contrast to the fable, which is the recitation of facts presented as false," but historical writing can never be completely cleansed of fable, and fables always contain a germ of history.[61]

As Voltaire was collaborating with Walther for the Dresden project, he was upset to hear of a scandalous edition of his *Oeuvres* put out by a clandestine publisher in Rouen, Robert Machuel. "This is horrible," Voltaire wrote to his niece. "And it requires the most thorough investigation and the most severe justice."⁶² Voltaire's anger came not only from the news that his work was being illegally reproduced—though this never ceased to frustrate him, it was a common problem which he dealt with throughout his career. More upsetting was that this collection included works falsely attributed to him, and, worst of all, several defamatory essays about him originally published in Holland by Arkstée and Merkus.⁶³ In short, this edition was calculated to produce short-term profits for its publisher at the expense of Voltaire's reputation. Voltaire immediately wrote to French officials demanding that they suppress the edition. Officials responded by immediately impounding all 1,200 copies—they were so successful in doing so that to this day, there does not appear an extant copy other than the first volume devoted to *La Henriade*. But Voltaire, as usual, was not content with this outcome, and looked for a way to convert a crisis into a greater opportunity. As David Smith has argued so convincingly, Voltaire soon returned secretly to Machuel, agreeing to give him material for a new edition, if he would remove all offensive material and faithfully follow Voltaire's instructions.

Anecdotes on Peter the Great

With Voltaire's secret collaboration, Machuel's new nine-volume edition was published clandestinely in 1750 with a false imprint attributed to London. The *History of Charles XII* constituted its seventh volume. Machuel followed the Dresden edition in attaching the "Discourse" and "Pyrrhonism in History," and Voltaire also instructed him to attach a twenty-page afterword titled "Anecdotes on Czar Peter the Great." This piece, which was originally published in an earlier volume of the Dresden edition, served as a commentary on the significance of the struggle between Russia and Sweden.

The "Anecdotes" reveals much about Voltaire's intellectual development. When he began writing Charles XII in the 1720s, Sweden was regarded as a more important state than Russia, a backward state, which had barely participated in European affairs before the 1730s. A mere decade later, it was clear that not only that Russia had permanently reduced Sweden to a regional power but also that Russia itself under Peter the Great had become a major European state. By the 1740s, Voltaire knew that the story of Peter the Great deserved a more thorough treatment. This brief essay on Russia was prescient: within a year of its publication in 1748, Russia became a signatory to the Peace of Aix-la-Chapelle, ending the European-wide War of the Austrian Succession and demonstrating for the first time its status as a major power. Voltaire understood that Peter was far more than simply a superb military commander who had defeated Charles at Poltava. He also built St. Petersburg, giving Russia a presence in the Baltic, and toured Western Europe extensively to learn about developments in modern industry. To Voltaire, he was a Russian version of an enlightened monarch—inferior, perhaps, to the Western version represented by Prussia's Fredrick II, but undoubtedly greater than any previous Russian czar. "The Russians ought undoubtedly to regard Peter as the greatest of men."⁶⁴

Around this time, Voltaire also learned that the political winds were changing in Paris. A new director of the book trade, Guillaume-Chrétien Lamoignon de Malesherbes, was jealous of the money Dutch publishers were able to make as a result of their relatively lax censorship laws. Although Malesherbes was no radical, he believed that a more open and commercially vibrant literary sector would strengthen the monarchy and help preserve Paris's reputation as Europe's cultural capital. In 1751, when the Paris bookseller Michel Lambert proposed the first legal French edition of Voltaire's *Oeuvres*, Malesherbes approved a *permission tacite*, allowing open circulation but without full copyright protection.[65] Voltaire, of course, began collaborating with Lambert immediately. He tried to standardize this Paris edition to align it with Rouen and Dresden, and in the case of *Charles XII*, he succeeded admirably: Lambert's edition was published in 1751 in eleven volumes, with *Charles XII* as Volume 9. The 1751 Paris edition was organized exactly like Machuel's, featuring "Pyrrhonism in History" and the "Discourse" as forewords and the "Anecdotes on Czar Peter the Great" as the afterword. Voltaire, after years of struggling with publishers, had finally succeeded in developing a standard edition of *Charles XII*.

Most authors never see one set of a complete works published. Montesquieu, for example, died before an edition of his complete works was published.[66] Yet in 1750 Voltaire was collaborating simultaneously on three separate editions of his complete works—as well as other unauthorized versions which were being published, such as the Arkstée and Merkus edition in Holland. No other eighteenth-century author garnered so many "complete" editions of his works during his lifetime. Voltaire's works, led by *Charles XII*, flooded Europe's literary marketplace in a way unlike anything else in the eighteenth century. It is noteworthy that until the late 1760s, none of these were quarto editions. Voltaire hoped to produce affordable octavos and even cheaper duodecimos to place books in the hands of every hungry reader.

Even before Lambert and Machuel came out with their editions of *Charles XII*, Voltaire was urging Walther to prepare a second Dresden edition. When it appeared in 1752, many of the paratexts changed as well. The "Anecdotes on Czar Peter" was omitted and instead, we find three additional prefatory essays joined to the "Discourse" and "Pyrrhonism": "Thoughts on Government," The Letter to Nordberg," and "The Letter to Schulenburg."

Thoughts on Government

Written during 1751 while in residence at Frederick the Great's court, "Thoughts on Government" is Voltaire's most direct attempt to link *History of Charles XII* to a political theory of European monarchy. With references to Montesquieu and Pufendorf, Voltaire noted that Charles ruled Sweden so "despotically" that its kings now had only a shadow of their former power. The appropriate check on princely ambition is "liberty," which "consists of a reliance on only the law." Here contemporary Sweden is described as a free state, along with England, Holland, Geneva, and Hamburg. Notably absent from this list was Voltaire's own country, France. Indeed, "the best form of government seems to be that where everyone of all ranks are equally protected by the laws." Perhaps because it was more an expression of political philosophy than any explanation of historical method, "Thoughts on Government" was only joined to *Charles XII* in this 1752 Dresden edition; afterward it was published in separate volumes of his complete works under the title "Thoughts on Public Administration."[67]

The Letter to Nordberg

After Jöran Nordberg published the first volume of his own *Histoire de Charles XII* in 1742, Voltaire produced a scathing sixteen-page pamphlet that first appeared in 1744. Dismissing Nordberg's account as completely unwieldy, Voltaire charged that the profusion of small unimportant details made the book tedious and almost impossible to read. He lectured Nordberg on the aims of historical writing, chiding that "a history does not consist in a recital of petty facts." The historian's duty is to help readers understand the overall significance of those facts. A good historian must understand, as Nordberg surely did not, that primary sources cannot speak for themselves. A diary, Voltaire wrote dismissively, "is no more a history than materials are a house." Worst of all, Voltaire indicted Nordberg as a biased author who had neither objectivity, nor a critical posture toward his sources. His account was irreparably harmed by his personal participation in events and his frequent editorializing. The ideal historian, according to Voltaire, should be "a man of no country and of no party," and is "never to rail and never to be tedious." Nordberg failed to meet all of these criteria.[68]

The Letter to Schulenburg

The third new essay attached to the Walther 1752 edition, the "Letter to Marshal Schulenburg, General of the Venetians," was aimed at Johann Matthias Reichsgraf von der Schulenburg (1661–1747), a former Saxon mercenary officer, who had fought against Sweden and eventually retired to Venice where he became a major art collector. Voltaire used the occasion to update and state more directly the book's historical lesson of *Charles XII*. If history is at all useful, Voltaire told Schulenburg, it is only to "point out the good and ill that kings have done to mankind." Charles had done good and ill to mankind, but his problem was that he did not know when to stop making war. If, "after having subdued Denmark, beat the Russians, deposed his enemy Augustus, and established the new king on the throne of Poland," he had ended the Great Northern War by making peace with Russian Czar Peter the Great, he could have "returned home the conqueror and peace maker of the North, and employed his attention in encouraging the arts and commerce in his country. Only then would he have been a truly great man, instead of being but a great warrior, vanquished at last by a prince whom he despised." Then, as if speaking directly to the reader, Voltaire added that he "preferred" a different sort of sovereign from either Charles or Peter. The ideal monarch is "a prince who regards humanity as the chief virtue," that is, one whose virtue would restrain him from warmongering. Such a prince who "loves peace because he loves mankind" would only go to war "through absolute necessity." In short, Voltaire preferred a king who "in one word, though a king, endeavors to act like a philosopher." Nor, he insisted, "is my hero . . . only a creature of the imagination," but a monarch who exists today. This living Telemachus was none other than Voltaire's favorite student, the young king of Prussia, Frederick II. Voltaire's portrayal of Frederick was indeed idiosyncratic. Surely all Europe knew that Frederick was no peace-loving Telemachus. Within months of taking the throne in 1740, he single-handedly sparked the War of the Austrian Succession by invading Silesia. The inclusion of this letter in the 1752 edition of *History of Charles XII* was meant to honor Voltaire's favorite king only months before their relationship soured.[69]

By the mid-1750s, Voltaire was living outside Geneva, where he finally found his most stable and cooperative publisher there in the firm of Gabriel and Philibert Cramer. Together they published several of his books, helping to distribute them across Europe at a time when Voltaire was a literary superstar. In 1756, the Cramers published his complete works in a seventeen-volume octavo edition, with the *History of Charles XII* as the sixth volume. In yet another attempt to improve the work's analytical rigor, Voltaire changed the offerings of prefatory essays. The "Thoughts on Government" was removed, and while included elsewhere in the *Oeuvres*, it was never again attached to *Charles XII*. In its place, Voltaire included two essays that were already a decade old and had previously been published separately from *Charles XII*: "Observations on History" and "New Reflections on History." Finally, for this 1756 edition, Voltaire reattached the "Anecdotes on Czar Peter the Great," but this time as a foreword. With this 1756 edition, Voltaire included a total of seven prefatory essays, allowing him to reflect extensively on his historical method.

Observations on History

First published in 1742 in a partial collection of Voltaire's works that did not include *Charles XII*,[70] "Observations on History" was an extended attack on the Abbé Rollin's *Ancient History*. First published in twelve volumes between 1730 and 1738, its volumes were the most checked out books in the Gray Library during the 1740s.[71] Voltaire's primary critique concerned Rollin's uncritical use of primary source material. Rollin, for example, accepted the Delphic oracles as if they were reliable documents. He confused ancient religion and science, and worse, he exaggerated the achievements of the ancients over the moderns. In short, he was far too partisan toward his subject. Voltaire ended his essay by pleading with the reader to ignore Rollin's empty consideration of meaningless trivia such as "the anecdotes of Cayamarrat the Persian, and of Sabaco Metrophis" in favor of more recent European topics, such as the discovery of America. As with Nordberg, Voltaire used Rollin to demonstrate the dangers of treating historical material uncritically.

New Reflections on History

During the 1740s, Voltaire worked intently on other historical research, such as *The Age of Louis XIV* and the *Essai sur les moeurs*. "New Reflections on History," initially attached to the publication of the play *Mérope* in 1744, reflected how these new projects changed his outlook as an historian. The five-page essay began with a declaration that history must follow the sciences by becoming both empirical and critically aware of the limitations imposed on it by its sources. "I doubt not but the same change which that lately happened in physics, may soon take place in the manner of writing history." This meant turning away from ancient history, given its meager and tainted primary source base. Voltaire explicitly connected this emphasis on empirical research matter with a preference for modern subject matter, since documentary evidence became so much more abundant after the invention of printing. Continuing to criticize Rollin's *Ancient History*, he compared ancient and modern history to old and new coins: Ancient coins "are deposited in the cabinets of the curious," while a modern coin "circulates the world for the use and convenience of mankind."[72]

Voltaire identified the problem facing modern historiography as deeper than the difficulty of critically examining sources. Too many historians, he charged, passed off insignificant court gossip as history. Reading the memoirs of Cardinal de Retz or Madame de Motteville may give the reader a sense of "every word of what the Queen-Mother said to M. de Jessan," but it tells us nothing important about France during this period. Voltaire argued that history should avoid pillow talk and battlefield trivia, and instead concentrate on the economy, industry, arts, crafts, and national culture. "I want to know, he explained, "what was the strength of a nation before a war, and whether that war contributed to encourage or diminish its strength." Oddly, Voltaire's growth spurt as an historian risked diminishing his earlier work. After all, the *History of Charles XII*, focusing so heavily on battle scenes, offered little sense of culture, industry, and the arts in Northern Europe. In *Charles XII*, Voltaire ignored how Charles's warmongering affected the Swedish nation, and certainly never delved deeply into the nature of the Swedish economy or arts. Voltaire's desire for a social and cultural history, however innovative, was absent in *Charles XII* and would become fully realized only in his 1751 *Age of Louis XIV*.

Let us summarize this collection of short paratext essays that surround *Charles XII* throughout its development (see Table 4.2): The first (Paris, 1730) edition, suppressed by the French government, contained neither prefatory nor afterword essays. "Discourse on the History of Charles XII" was attached to the Rouen 1731 octavo edition, first as

Table 4.2 Essays Voltaire Attached to His *History of Charles XII*

Essay Title	Date First Published	Date Attached to Charles XII
Discourse on the History of Charles XII	1731	1731
Critical Remarks of Mr. de La Motraye	1733	1733
Pyrrhonism in History	1748	1748
Anecdotes on Czar Peter the Great	1748	1750
Letter to Schulenburg	1748	1752
Letter to Nordberg	1748	1752
Thoughts on Government	1752	1752
Observations on History	1742	1756
New Reflections on History	1746	1756
The Usefulness of History	1765	1768

an afterword, and then as a preface to most later editions. Between 1733 and 1748, the annotated response to La Motraye's pamphlet served as an afterword. Voltaire dropped this piece in Walther's 1748 edition in favor of "Pyrrhonism in History." In 1750, "Anecdotes on Czar Peter the Great" was added to a Rouen edition as an afterword. The "Letter to Marshal Schulenburg" and the "Letter to Monsieur Nordberg" joined *Charles XII* in the second Walther edition of 1752. In the 1756 edition by the Cramers, "Observations on History" and "New Reflections on History" were also added, and "Anecdotes on Czar Peter the Great" was moved from a lone afterword to join the other prefaces.

The Usefulness of History

In 1768, the Cramers finally convinced the seventy-three-year-old Voltaire to allow publication of a thirty-volume quarto edition of his works, which would stand as the most exact and lavish of his lifetime. For this edition, the short, but powerful, essay "The Usefulness of History" was added, increasing the already substantial number of prefatory essays from seven to eight. These eight essays were now considered a standard part of the *History of Charles XII*. They were all included in the posthumous "Kehl" editions of 1784 and 1785, according to Voltaire's wishes. Rarely, if ever, in the history of Enlightenment publishing has there been a deeper collaboration between an author and his publishers to deepen the analytical authority of his work with introductory essays and other commentary.[73].

"The Usefulness of History," in nine short paragraphs, conveyed the importance of history to eighteenth-century Europeans. It was first published as a section of Voltaire's 1765 History article for the *Encyclopédie* and republished by the Cramers later that year in a supplemental collection of Voltaire's works. Its link with *Charles XII* is obvious from the first paragraph: "The disaster of Charles XII at Poltava should deter a general from penetrating too far into Ukraine without provisions." Throughout the piece Voltaire notes that one of the most important lessons of modern European history was that an international balance of power system could restrain would-be conquerors like Charles. "This system of balance of power was unknown to the ancients," he wrote, and it allowed modern statesmen to focus on developing "husbandry, commerce, and the sciences." To Voltaire, the careful study of modern history would show his contemporaries how to prevent civil strife and political despotism. "Abolish the study of history," he warned, "and you may again see St. Bartholomews in France and Cromwells in England."[74]

Why did Voltaire surround his narrative with so many barnacle-like small essays? Why did he feel that the "Discourse" alone was insufficient to guide readers toward an understanding of his historical framework? During the early eighteenth century, there was no convention around the proper mix of analysis and narrative in historical writing, and there was no clear division between scholarly and popular history. Voltaire himself would increasingly focus more on analysis and argument as he began to write his mature histories, such as *Age of Louis XIV* and *Essai sur les moeurs*. In this respect, the *History of Charles XII* was an early work—what Voltaire scholar J. H. Brumfitt has called "the work of an apprentice." Rather than rewrite this early work from scratch, Voltaire chose to correct its mistakes and develop his historical methodology through paratexts. This process of constant revision was a key part of Voltaire's growth into the "philosophic historian" he would eventually become. As one of Voltaire's earliest historical works, the *History of Charles XII* is at its foundation a fast-paced and entertaining narrative about the rise and fall of a military phenom, which the more mature "philosophic historian" comments on through paratexts.[75]

Montesquieu's Roman History

The contrast between Voltaire's *History of Charles XII* and Montesquieu's *Considerations on the Causes of the Greatness of the Romans and Their Decline* could not be more stark. Voltaire's focus was recent history; Montesquieu's was a well-worn ancient topic. Voltaire's approach was biographical; Montesquieu avoided focusing on great men. Voltaire's book is a fast-paced adventure story told with techniques borrowed from fiction; Montesquieu's shorter work is sober, analytical, and philosophical. Voltaire frequently revised his narrative and engaged his critics; Montesquieu made only one important revision, allowed his book to speak for itself, and never responded to critics in print. In Voltaire's book, the key turning points in the story seem almost accidental and circumstantial; in Montesquieu's telling, the fall of Rome seemed predetermined by structural causes. While Montesquieu was well aware of Voltaire's precedent,[76] he chose to write a radically different type of history.

Initially, Voltaire did not appreciate Montesquieu's innovative approach to writing history. Writing to a friend, he joked that Montesquieu's book revealed not the decadence of Rome, but rather that of its author's approach to history. Although the book "is full of hints," he wrote, "it is less a book than an ingenious table of contents written in an odd style." Nor was Voltaire alone in this reaction to *Considerations*. Many readers felt let down by Montesquieu's austere style, which some found "dry." Perhaps they expected something lighter from the author of *Persian Letters*. The legal scholars Mathieu Marais and Jean Bouhier discussed the book in letters over several weeks and reached much the same conclusion as Voltaire: "It is less the portrait that this empire deserves and more of a badly organized outline," wrote Bouhier. "The material is only sketched out."[77] Some early readers in 1734 may have wondered whether *Considerations* might be satirical, spoofing history as a genre. The Marquise du Châtelet noted that the new book did not meet the standard of its predecessor. If readers wanted a sequel to *Persian Letters*, they were sorely disappointed.[78]

Readers were surprised in part by Montesquieu's decision to eschew narrative in favor of analysis and argument, which was unusual by eighteenth-century standards. Rather than narrate the story of Rome, he focused on the underlying causes of Rome's rise and fall. Early reviewers found three central factors in Montesquieu's account explaining Rome's grandeur: first, the rise of elected consuls in place of traditional monarchs provided Rome with a crucial political innovation; second, the Romans were willing to learn from their neighbors, often absorbing the culture of those whom they conquered; and third, Rome was a society devoted to perfecting its military discipline. To some extent, Montesquieu's reasons for Rome's decline involved the reversal of these trends: Emperors replaced consuls, while tyranny and force began to characterize Rome's relations with its neighbors.[79]

From the standard accounts, readers had learned that providence had blessed Rome with prosperity, peace, and extraordinary visual and literary arts. For example, Charles Rollin's account, which in English translation was among the most popular books at Gray's Library, told essentially the same story.[80] Montesquieu, however, denied any Pax Romana and did not portray Rome as a model for statesmen to emulate. The Roman's militarism made them a constant nightmare for their neighbors; Rome, he argued, was "made for expansion" and was "a nation forever at war."[81] Moreover, the Romans largely ignored commerce, instead finding most of their wealth in plunder.[82] Unlike other historians, Montesquieu discounted Rome's cultural flowering, and instead focused his attention on the political behavior of its leaders.[83]

Although Montesquieu never mentions the Renaissance political theorist Niccolo Machiavelli, the *Considerations* can be regarded as a refutation of the central arguments in his justly famous *Discourses on Livy*, reprinted in French and other languages throughout the eighteenth century.[84] From its title alone, Jean Bouhier immediately recognized *Consideration*'s relationship to Machiavelli.[85] For Machiavelli, Rome's greatness was due to the intensity of its civic virtue, that is, of ordinary citizens' dedication toward the public good, sometimes over their private interests. Likewise, he argued that Rome's decline was caused by the corruption of this virtue. As Rome experienced success, over time Romans became soft and indulgent, leading to declining interest in public affairs. Montesquieu, however, viewed virtue more skeptically. Virtue may have been responsible for Rome's rise, but because the Romans employed virtue for militaristic ends, it carried within it the seeds of its own destruction. Montesquieu indirectly criticized Machiavelli for conflating virtue and military valor. Contrary to Machiavelli, he argued that the decline of Roman virtue was not the cause of Rome's troubles but the effect of its military aggression. Rome's constant expansion made it impossible to govern by republican principles. Only tyranny could keep the empire in line, and such violent and arbitrary policies were inherently unsustainable. In short, Roman imperialism doomed its civic virtue. In contrast to Machiavelli, who viewed Rome's early empire as the fulfillment of its republican goals, Montesquieu saw empire and republic as contradictory forms of government, a notion he would develop more formally in *The Spirit of the Laws*.[86]

Montesquieu published *Considerations* in the same way he had produced *Persian Letters*. Using the French ambassador to Holland as a mediator, he indirectly approached Jacques Desbordes, who had recently published the *History of Charles XII* and whose mother had issued *Persian Letters* a decade earlier. Unlike *Persian Letters*, which was printed in cheap duodecimo formats, the first edition of *Considerations* was produced as an octavo, signaling its more serious stature as a work of philosophical history. Although it was published anonymously, Montesquieu's authorship was again an open secret.

As he had tried (without success) when publishing *Persian Letters*, Montesquieu hoped to secure a *permission tacite,* which would have allowed the book to be imported into France from Holland. Before applying for the license, Montesquieu asked his friend and his son's former tutor, the Jesuit Père Louis Bertrand Castel, for his thoughts on corrections needed to obtain full legal status, and since Castel was in Paris, it is likely that Montesquieu used Castel as a mediator with the French censor assigned to review the book. At the time, *Persian Letters* was still outlawed in France, and Montesquieu badly wanted *Considerations* to avoid the same fate.

From the corrected version that emerged, we know that either Castel or the censor—or both—objected to about fifteen passages in the original text.[87] Some of these were minor issues of word choice, which Montesquieu was willing to give way on. For example, after a paragraph comparing the liberty of Athens, Carthage, Rome, and Italian Renaissance republics, Montesquieu noted that "the English Government is among the wisest in Europe," implying, of course, that England was wiser than France. The censor asked Montesquieu to adjust the phrase to say simply that "the English Government is wiser," implying a comparison not with France but with the ancient world.[88] A second example was Montesquieu's use of the term "despotism" to mark the "ruin" of Rome's political system. In later years, the line between monarchy and despotism would become Montesquieu's key political idea in *The Spirit of the Laws*. Here, though, Montesquieu allowed the censor to have his way, agreeing to add the qualifier "Asiatic" to "despotism," thereby removing any relevance to European politics, at least for the moment.[89] Even when Montesquieu judged the French government favorably, as when he contrasted it against Caligula's reign, the censor required him to change "as for us who" to the more clinical "as for states who."[90] Clearly, the censor wanted to ensure that readers of *Considerations* would not see any part of any political commentary on contemporary France.

Such caution also extended to France's allies. Twice in the *Considerations*, in passages that might seem rather innocuous, Montesquieu criticized Bourbon Spain, France's most consistent eighteenth-century ally. He noted that Spain was, along with Portugal, one of those countries which lived beyond their financial means, and he also compared the Spanish empire to that of the Turks and the Romans. The censor was not willing to sign off on a book which associated France's close ally either with Portugal, an English ally, or with Turkey, a Muslim foe. Again, Montesquieu willingly complied with the censor's direction and removed the references to Spain.[91]

A more substantive objection was made regarding Montesquieu's discussion of suicide among the Roman political class. Montesquieu was fascinated with understanding "this practice of committing suicide that was so common among the Romans."[92] Suicide, Montesquieu argued, allowed Roman statesmen to maintain and even increase their honor, he argued, and it was more effective than other forms of ritualized violence, such as duels. He also argued that among the Romans suicide resulted from an exaggerated form of "self-love [amour propre]," in which "a natural and obscure instinct . . . makes us love ourselves more than our very life."[93] The censor did not object to this commentary on Roman political suicide, but was displeased with Montesquieu's extension of his argument to modern statesmen. This occurred on two back-to-back pages. On page 130 of the first edition, we find this footnote: "If [English King] Charles I, if [English King] James II had belonged to a religion which would have allowed them to kill themselves, they would not have had to withstand, the one such a death, the other such a life." One page later, the chapter ends with this final paragraph: "It is certain that men have become less free, less courageous, less inclined to great enterprises, when, by this power, which they took over themselves, they could at any moment escape from all other powers."[94] Here Montesquieu went beyond describing the culture of an ancient pagan society. He indicated that Rome's values may have had relevance to the Christian culture that underpinned early modern political life in Europe. Indeed, here he criticized the Christian prohibition on suicide for worsening the political crises of Charles I and James II.

This was no small matter. Earlier we saw how the students at the University of Coimbra were moved by the argument in *Persian Letters* for decriminalizing suicide. Montesquieu would return to this topic again in *The Spirit of the Laws*. Like Voltaire, he used Christian states' criminalization of suicide to criticize Christianity's anti-liberal tendencies. Nevertheless, Montesquieu acceded to the censor's demand, agreeing to withdraw both paragraphs. This is noteworthy. Other than one or two clarifying footnotes (discussed in Chapter 9), nowhere in the long publication histories of *Persian Letters* and *The Spirit of the Laws* did Montesquieu alter his words to conform with government wishes. Indeed, with *The Spirit of the Laws*, he dug in his heels, publishing a comprehensive defense of his views instead of capitulating. Only here in *Considerations* did Montesquieu bend to the French government's wishes in order to establish legal permission for his work. Not surprisingly, of his three principal books, only *Considerations* secured legal authorization from the French government and avoided being placed on the Roman Catholic Church's Index of Forbidden Books.

Jacques Desbordes had already begun selling copies of *Considerations* before Montesquieu gave orders for him to comply with the French censor's requirements. It seems likely that Desbordes simply printed new pages for the few offending ones and patched the book back together, rather than produce an entirely new printing. Today, Desbordes's corrected version is far more common in libraries than the original edition. Figures 4.4 through 4.7 illustrate the key differences between the two printings. On page 130, the footnote about Charles I and James II has been omitted and the font on the rest of the page has been altered slightly. On page 131, the final paragraph relating suicide to liberty has been replaced by a fleuron.

The censored version of Desbordes's first edition of *Considerations* sold well enough that three bookseller/publishers in Paris combined to raise capital for a full license to print the book in France. Montesquieu again used Castel as a mediator in his discussions with the new publishers. The government approved a nine-year privilege for a Paris octavo edition that was released later in 1734, followed by a smaller duodecimo edition in 1735. Meanwhile, others began publishing unauthorized versions of the original uncensored text. Already in 1734 two cheap duodecimos emerged: one was attributed to Pierre Mortier, the Dutch publisher of Locke and Hume, and another was attributed to Desbordes. Both editions were probably produced surreptitiously in France. Then, in 1735, Desbordes issued what he called a "second edition," which restored the two suicide passages on pages

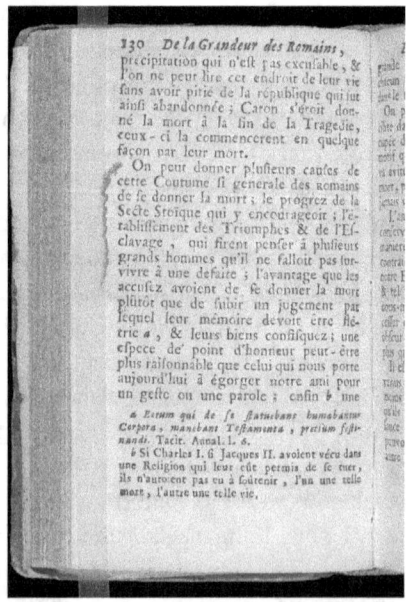

Figure 4.4 Page 130 uncensored version of Montesquieu's *Considerations*.

> 130 DE LA GRANDEUR DES ROMAINS
>
> CHAP. précipitation qui n'eſt pas excuſable,
> XII. & l'on ne peut lire cet endroit de leur
> vie ſans avoir pitié de la République
> qui fut ainſi abandonnée ; Caton s'é-
> toit donné la mort à la fin de la Tra-
> gedie, ceux-ci la commencerent en
> quelque façon par leur mort.
>   On peut donner pluſieurs cauſes
> de cette Coutume ſi générale des
> Romains de ſe donner la mort ; le
> progrès de la Secte Stoique qui y en-
> courageoit ; l'établiſſement des Triom-
> phes & de l'Eſclavage, qui firent pen-
> ſer à pluſieur grands hommes qu'il
> ne faloit pas ſurvivre à une défaite ;
> l'avantage que les accuſés avoient
> de ſe donner la mort plûtôt que de
> ſubir un jugement par lequel leur
> mémoire devoit être flétrie *, & leurs
> biens confiſqués ; une eſpece de point
> d'honneur peut-être plus raiſonna-
> ble que celui qui nous porte aujour-
> d'hui à égorger notre ami pour un
> geſte ou une parole ; enfin une gran-
> de commodité pour le Héroïsme ;
> chacun faiſant finir la piece qu'il
>
> * Eorum qui de ſe ſtatuebant humabantur
> Corpora, manebant Teſtamenta, pretium ſeſti-
> mandi Tacit. Annal. I. 6.

Figure 4.5 Page 130 censored version Montesquieu's *Considerations*. Montesquieu agreed to remove this offending footnote: "If Charles I, if James II, had belonged to a religion which allowed them to kill themselves, the one would not have had to endure such a death, the other such a life."

130 and 131 to their original state, as well as the two references to Spain, and several of the smaller alterations demanded by the censor. Unlike Voltaire, who often collaborated with publishers in pirating his own work, there is no evidence that Montesquieu cooperated with Desbordes. At the same time, no documentation shows that Montesquieu objected.[95]

Like *Persian Letters*, *Considerations* was an overnight bestseller. Despite tepid initial reviews, fourteen editions were published from 1734 to 1736 alone, in French, English, and Italian. Competition broke out between the censored and uncensored versions. Although the uncensored version had the asset of authenticity, its illegal status hindered its circulation in France. It is surprising then to find that a majority of the French-language editions published were uncensored (six editions to four editions); the four editions in England and Italian generally followed the uncensored version too. What is striking, then, is how Montesquieu's censored version—the only one authorized by Montesquieu—was unable to achieve status as the dominant version; the public preferred the uncensored version as more authentic. Reflecting this trend, in 1735 the government-approved publisher Pierre Huart produced an uncensored edition in Paris, complete with a false imprint claiming it to have been published in Amsterdam by Desbordes.

The contest between censored and uncensored versions reversed course during the 1740s, when Montesquieu authorized a new edition that would appear in association with

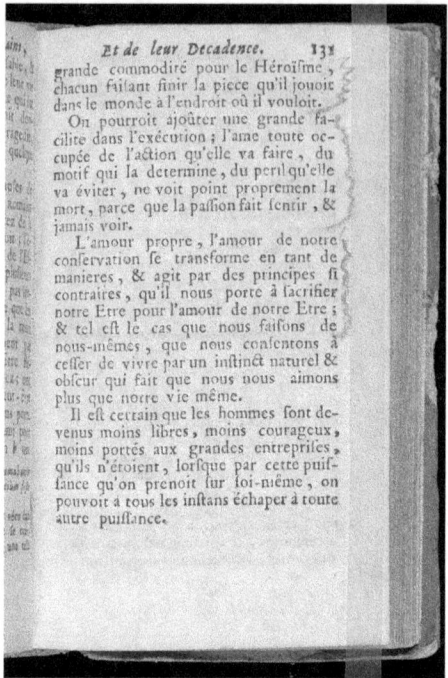

Figure 4.6 Page 131 of the uncensored Montesquieu's *Considerations*.

the launching of *The Spirit of the Laws* in 1748. While that masterpiece was produced outside of France in Geneva, the 1748 edition of *Considerations* was a fully Parisian enterprise. Produced through a collaboration of several booksellers and publishers led by Huart, it was based on the government-approved censored version printed by Huart a decade earlier. On the title page, Huart noted that this was a "new edition, reviewed, corrected, and expanded by the author." This authoritative statement, plus a fifty-page index, seems to have convinced the public of the new edition's superiority. Between 1748 and Montesquieu's death in 1755, there were six reprintings of Huart's censored 1748 version and only one new "uncensored" version—a 1755 edition covertly published in Paris by Simeon-Prosper Hardy, who snuck back in the two "suicide" sections.[96]

After Montesquieu's death in 1755, Huart began planning for a definitive edition of Montesquieu's collected works in an expensive quarto format. This collection would eventually become the standard reference for cheaper reprints and for study of Montesquieu's writings. Billed as authorized by Montesquieu before his death, this three-volume set finally appeared in 1758, but with a false title page, attributing the work to the notable Amsterdam publishing house Arkstée and Merkus. The reason for this ruse is obvious: since these collected works included *Persian Letters* and *The Spirit of the Laws*, both of which were outlawed by the French government, the set could not be legally produced or sold openly in France. The necessity of using a false attribution

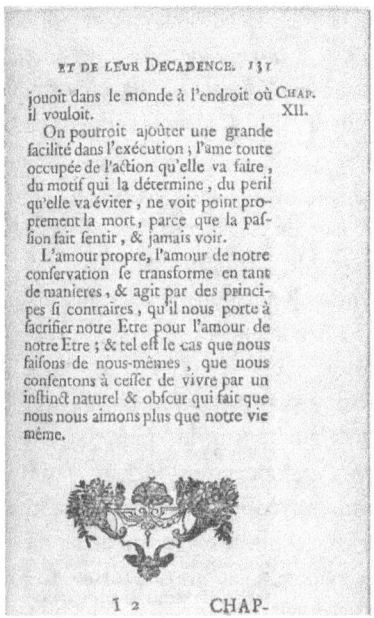

Figure 4.7 Page 131 of the censored Montesquieu's *Considerations*. Montesquieu's publisher substituted a fleuron for this offending paragraph: "It is certain that men have become less free, less courageous, less disposed to great enterprises than they were when, by means of this power which one assumed, one could at any moment escape from every other power."

also allowed the publishers to roll back the censor's work and restore *Considerations* to its original version. All subsequent eighteenth-century editions of *Considerations* would use this 1758 restored version as their template.

Over the course of the eighteenth century, *Considerations on the Greatness of the Romans and Their Decline* was an immensely popular book, moving through some 125 editions. Despite this remarkable success, its popularity was no match for Voltaire's *History of Charles XII*, which went through some 180 editions (see Table 4.1). After a surge in sales of which over fifty editions were produced during the 1730s, editions of *Charles XII* leveled off to an average of nineteen editions per decade through the rest of the century. The course of Montesquieu's *Considerations* was different. Like *Persian Letters*, the remarkable publication of *The Spirit of the Laws* in 1748 gave the already popular *Considerations* a new following and editions soared. There were twice the number of editions published in the 1750s as in the 1740s (fifteen vs. seven), and even more in the 1760s (twenty-four), until interest reached its zenith during the 1770s with almost thirty editions.

There is good reason to think that Montesquieu's book affected the course of eighteenth-century historical scholarship more than Voltaire's. *Considerations* had a direct influence on three important mid-century historians of Rome: Louis de Beaufort, Abbé Jean Paul

Bignon, and Abbé Seran de la Tour. Beaufort's important book, *A Dissertation upon the Uncertainty of the Roman History during the First Five Hundred Years*, was written with Montesquieu in mind and first published in 1738, only four years after *Considerations* appeared. Beaufort had only praise for Montesquieu's conception, and he thought Montesquieu did the best one could with the sources at hand. However, Beaufort also argued that the field needed specialists whose erudition could approach primary sources more critically. Meanwhile, Bignon and Seran de la Tour acknowledged how under the spell of "this wise and profound legislator of humanity" they were.[97] For King Frederick the Great, who jotted down many notes in the margins of his copy, the book was "the quintessence of all that the human intellect can bring forth in philosophical thought."[98]

The most consequential eighteenth-century reader of *Considerations* was Edward Gibbon. Following an unhappy year at Oxford during which Gibbon rebelled against his family by converting to Catholicism, his father sent away the fifteen-year-old to Lausanne for tutoring. There he converted back to a mild Protestantism and threw himself into reading. Voltaire moved him greatly, but he took issue with his approach to history, criticizing him for having a naïve understanding historical change and of running roughshod over the evidence. He instead turned to Montesquieu for his training as a historian. "In the hands of a Montesquieu," wrote Gibbon during this young period, "the theory of these general causes would comprise a philosophical history of man."[99] As a teenager, he returned again and again to Montesquieu, "whose energy and style and boldness of hypothesis were powerful to awaken and stimulate the genius of the age."[100] Specifically with regard to *Considerations*, no other work so inspired Gibbon's 1776 masterpiece, *The Decline and Fall of the Roman Empire*. Although in many ways surpassing its predecessor's breadth and sources, Gibbon's basic conceptualization of historical causation is borrowed from Montesquieu's *Considerations*. Robert Shackleton has demonstrated Gibbon's debt to Montesquieu by comparing an important passage in *Decline and Fall* with one from *Considerations*:

> Gibbon: "The decline of Rome was the natural and inevitable effect of immoderate greatness. Prosperity ripened the principle of decay; the causes of destruction multiplied with the extent of conquest; and, as soon as time or accident had removed the artificial supports, the stupendous fabric yielded to the pressure of its own weight. The story of its ruin is simple and obvious; and, instead of inquiring why the Roman empire was destroyed, we should rather be surprised that it had subsisted so long."[101]
>
> Montesquieu: "If the greatness of the empire ruined the republic, the greatness of the city ruined it no less . . . It is true that the laws of Rome became powerless to govern the republic. But it is a matter of common observation that good laws, which have made a small republic grow large, become a burden to it when it is enlarged . . . Rome was made for expansion, and its laws were admirable for this purpose . . . It lost its liberty because it completed the work it wrought too soon."[102]

This remarkable concordance does not reveal plagiarism or any lack of originality on Gibbon's part, but rather shows that Gibbon's edifice rested upon Montesquieu's conceptual foundation.

J. G. A. Pocock, the author of a definitive multivolume intellectual biography of Gibbon, agrees with Shackleton's view that Montesquieu was Gibbon's greatest intellectual influence. "In Montesquieu's *Considerations*," writes Pocock, Gibbon "would find a series of interpretative structures of importance to the *Decline and Fall*: an account of Roman grandeur as the product of military and civic *virtù*, and *décadence* as produced by the corruption of *virtù* under the burdens of the empire it had won." Upon returning to England, Gibbon used his Lausanne notebooks to compose his *Essay on the Study of Literature*, which was published in French in 1761, when he was barely twenty-four years old. Pocock views this minor debut as a thoroughly "Montesquieuian" work. Gibbon himself, expressing false regret when he came to writing his memoirs thirty years later, blamed it on an infatuation with Montesquieu: "How fatal has been the imitation of Montesquieu!"[103]

It is significant that Gibbon likely first read *Considerations* shortly after Montesquieu's death in 1755, when the French philosophe was being eulogized across Europe as the Newton of social studies. The teenage Gibbon knew Montesquieu not simply as a historian of Rome but also as the century's greatest political philosopher. This was true for many readers who first encountered *Considerations* after *The Spirit of the Laws* had raised Montesquieu to the unofficial post of dean of the Republic of Letters. Readers after 1748 saw in *Considerations* not merely good history but, as Gibbon noted, a "philosophical history of man." Sometimes earlier readers of *Considerations* gave it a second chance. Voltaire's encounter with *Considerations* is an excellent example of this phenomenon. We saw earlier that Voltaire read *Considerations* soon after its publication and was less than impressed by it. Over the course of the next several years, he watched it compete with his own *Charles XII*. Voltaire was never kind to those he perceived as rivals, and Montesquieu was no exception. However, when *The Spirit of the Laws* came under fire from various government and ecclesiastical officials, Voltaire, ever a critic of censorship, developed sympathy for Montesquieu. At times, this sympathy bordered on an uncharacteristically open admiration of his fellow writer.[104]

In 1750, Voltaire purchased and closely read a new edition of *Considerations* published in Lausanne by Marc Michel Bousquet. Given that Voltaire lived near Geneva at the time, it was probably easier for him to access this copy than one made in France. The Lausanne edition was an unauthorized reprinting of Huart's 1748 standard Paris edition. Although it was pirated, its octavo format, careful typography, and good paper made it equal in quality to Huart's. In the margins of his copy, Voltaire scribbled many reactions and notes. Indeed, inside this 300-page text, there are almost 100 marginal comments—more notes, in fact, than Voltaire made on his copy of *The Spirit of the Laws*. Voltaire did not simply read *Considerations*, but he used it as an opportunity to debate Montesquieu on questions of historical method, as if the two authors were engaged in conversation. In this respect, Voltaire was modeling the Enlightenment ideal of an active and critical reader, imagined by many philosophes.[105]

Voltaire's comments on *Considerations* are varied in tone, subject, and length. Most are only six or seven words. Often he responded with merely "bravo," "so true," "why not," "no," or "exaggeration." Sometimes he questioned Montesquieu's facts. After Montesquieu cited population statistics derived from supposed census records, Voltaire doubted the validity of his sources. When Montesquieu contrasted the health and vigor of Roman soldiers with that of modern French armies, Voltaire rebuked him: "That's not at all true." He criticized Montesquieu for confusing Roman mythology with historical sources, such as when discussing Sextus Tarquinius's rape of Lucretia. Sometimes Voltaire thought of examples that contradicted Montesquieu's point. For example, when Montesquieu contrasted the political deference found in monarchies with a natural tendency to despise republican statesmen, Voltaire quipped: "Not in Venice, nor in Amsterdam." On some larger points, Voltaire probed and expressed doubt. At one critical point in the book, Montesquieu compared Louis XIV unfavorably with the early Roman emperors. While the latter were admired for greatly supporting their allies, Montesquieu faulted Louis XIV for abandoning King James II during England's Glorious Revolution, thus hastening Britain's eighteenth-century rivalry with France. Voltaire, in his commentary, claimed that the French king had provided James II with 20,000 troops, and that this should have served him well enough. Considering that Voltaire was about to finish his own masterpiece, *The Age of Louis XIV*, his defense of the monarch is noteworthy. When Montesquieu contrasted the power of the centralized Roman state with the weakness of Europe's early Gothic state (implying that Rome was no model for modern European monarchies), Voltaire responded, "all this needs to be better argued, better proved." Finally, when Montesquieu noted that women in polygamous societies have less political power than in monogamous ones (a theme he had already raised in *Persian Letters*), Voltaire seemed to skirt the point by bluntly remarking, "with us women don't govern." Whatever one might say about such comments, by 1750 Voltaire had begun to take Montesquieu's Roman history seriously.[106]

While reading *Considerations* a second time, Voltaire seems to have developed a grudging respect for it. For one thing, he dramatically reversed his position on the importance of ancient history, and in fact came to see the rise and fall of Rome as history's most important subject. "The history of the Roman empire deserves the most attention because the Romans are our masters and legislators," he wrote in his "History" article for the *Encyclopédie*.[107] Of course, he would still go on to criticize Montesquieu in later writings, such as in the 1768 dialogues *The A B C*.[108] But in Voltaire's mature historical writing, it is clear that even he had learned many important ideas from Montesquieu. At one point in his 1765 *Philosophie de l'histoire*, in a chapter devoted to the ancient Romans, Voltaire described Roman virtue no longer as some idealized notion of civic humanism, but rather as the "virtue of thieves,"[109] an idea straight out of *Considerations*. Voltaire is one key example—typical in this one regard—of how after 1748 Europeans read *Considerations* differently than before, more as a work of mature political thought than as a simple history.

Chapter 5

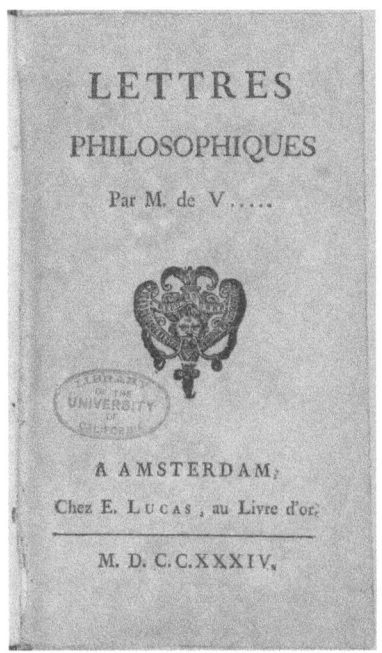

Figure 5.1 First edition title page Voltaire's *Philosophical Letters*. To outwit the censors, Voltaire supervised three simultaneous editions of *Philosophical Letters*: one from London pretending to be from Basle; one from Rouen pretending to be from Amsterdam; and one from Paris also purporting to be from Amsterdam. After 1737, there were no more independent editions of the book.

Chapter 5
Voltaire's *Philosophical Letters* (1733–4)

Table 5.1 Eighteenth-Century Editions of *Philosophical Letters* in Various Versions

Number of editions	Published title	Edition years	Language	Publication place first version
11	Letters Concerning the English Nation	1733, 1733, 1739, 1741, 1752, 1759, 1760, 1766, 1767, 1776, 1778	English	London
6	Lettres écrites de Londres	1734, 1735, 1735, 1736, 1737, 1739	French	Basle [London]
5	Lettres philosophiques	1734, 1734, 1734, 1734, 1737	French	Amsterdam [Rouen]
26	Oeuvres de M. de Voltaire	1737, 1739 (2), 1740, 1741 (2), 1742, 1743, 1746, 1748, 1750, 1751, 1752, 1756, 1757 (2), 1764 (2), 1768, 1770 (2), 1772 (2), 1775, 1784	French	Basle
2	The Works of Mr de Voltaire	1762	English	London
1	Sammlung verschiedener Briefe des Herrn von Voltaire	1747	German	Jena

Total Number of Editions: 51.
Translations: English, German.
Source: http://kates.itg.pomona.edu/books/editions.php?action=view_references&groupID=61. Accessed March 9, 2022.

At the start of the twentieth century, Gustave Lanson (1857–1934) characterized *Philosophical Letters* as "the first bomb thrown against the Old Regime."[1] Ever since, scholars have seen Voltaire's book through Lanson's colorful lens.[2] By 1906 Lanson was, after all, among the titans of French literary criticism. He would soon become director of France's most prestigious graduate centers, the Ecole Normale Supérieure, where both socialists and fascists attacked him for embodying the Third Republic's efforts at establishing what one historian has called the "Dreyfusard University," that is, a higher educational system that reflected the liberal values of secularism, individual freedom, and human rights.³ Lanson's view of *Philosophical Letters* as a weapon against the Old Regime that foreshadowed and contributed to the French Revolution was thus part of a larger project, including the reformulation of secondary and higher education curricula, to present the eighteenth-century Enlightenment as foundational to the Third Republic (1870–1940). As Lamartine did for Fénelon, Lanson's phrase implied that the ideological origins of the French Revolution began with this one book, Voltaire's *Philosophical Letters*.

However, at the time Lanson wrote his statement, *Philosophical Letters* had long been out of print; indeed, so long out of print that it had become among Voltaire's least-known books. Except for a tiny private printing of only thirty copies by the Voltaire scholar Adrien Jean Quentin Beuchot in 1818, no edition of *Philosophical Letters* appeared at all during the nineteenth century! Indeed, as this chapter will explain, no independent edition (i.e., outside of Voltaire's collected works) was printed in the French language during the second half of the eighteenth century. Moreover, it was Lanson himself who soon rectified the situation. His critical edition of *Philosophical Letters*—first published in 1909 and then reprinted in 1915, 1917, 1924, 1937, and 1964—is still considered among the best scholarly editions. It gave the book new life in Third Republic France and led to new translations in various languages during the twentieth century.⁴ *Philosophical Letters* may have become a biblical text for Third Republic France, but it is hard to see how it became weaponized for the French Revolutionaries, when that generation had little access to it. If *Philosophical Letters* was a "bomb," it was one that remained undetonated.

At the genesis of what would become *Philosophical Letters* is a curious comment in Voltaire's private notebook: "Answer to the Persian letters."⁵ If Voltaire dismissed *Persian Letters* as a lightweight effort, his *Philosophical Letters* was nonetheless an effort to surpass Montesquieu's success with a similar epistolary effort. After all, the two books have much in common in terms of format, substance, and values. Like *Persian Letters*, *Philosophical Letters* is an epistolary travel memoir by a person visiting a foreign country who writes home with his impressions. And like the 1721 novel, Voltaire's book yields comparative reflections that aim to highlight special problems in France, especially with that country's political direction. Both Montesquieu and Voltaire took a familiar popular format and infused it with serious philosophy, cloaked behind humor and satire. "Thus almost every composition is no more than an imitation. The hint of the *Persian Letters* is taken from the *Turkish Spy*," Voltaire later wrote. "The most original geniuses borrow from each other."⁶

There are, however, important differences between the two books. When Montesquieu placed two Persian travelers in Europe, he was purposely juxtaposing two cultures that saw one another as distant, exotic, and alien. Most Persians did not know much about France, and French readers knew little about the Muslim world. Voltaire worried that Montesquieu's juxtaposition exaggerated differences, even reinforcing cultural stereotypes. "Our European Travellers," he wrote in 1727, "bestow large praises upon Persians and Chinese, it being too natural to revile those who stand in competition with us, and to extol those who being far remote from us, are out of reach of envy."⁷ For Voltaire, Montesquieu's use of exoticism in *Persian Letters* clouded the clarity of his philosophical principles. Although Voltaire would write more about China and Persia later in his career, he now conceived something closer to home. By comparing not Persians and Europeans, but neighboring French and English cultures, Voltaire could move beyond satirical stereotyping to sociological analysis. His travel book would be different. By comparing societies all too familiar with one another, his practical lessons would be more sharply presented.

A second major difference between the two books is the very presence of the author. Montesquieu was a newly published author who hid behind his characters. Not only did he insist upon anonymous publication, but the book's introduction asserted that his role was merely that of an editor and translator who had been left such strange letters. The already well-known Voltaire, by contrast, makes a cameo appearance in the first pages of his own work, and it is impossible for readers to separate him from his book. His name boldly appears on the title page of the first edition, printed in English in London; later, when French editions appeared, everyone already knew who he was. Voltaire, after all, had been basking in authorial limelight from the success of his plays, poems, and *History of Charles XII*. His book is a travel memoir about himself. He really did travel from France to England, and the book originated as a sort of extended reflection on his stay there from 1726 to 1728. Some chapters may have begun as journals during his visit, even if the bulk of the manuscript was finished a few years later when he returned to France.⁸ Voltaire's portrayal of England was as real as Montesquieu's image of Persia was fictionalized.

Philosophical Letters contains twenty-five letters, which are less epistolary in the Montesquieu sense, and more polished short essays. The first seven address religion directly, as if to acknowledge that for Voltaire and his readers, organized religion forms the bedrock of any society and the first thing that an attentive traveler needs to understand about a foreign place. Curiously, though, only one of these letters concerns the Anglican Church, which was not only England's state religion but represented the faith of 85 percent of all English people. The first four letters, in fact, introduce the reader to the Quakers, and, as one early reader insightfully commented, had a satirical tone that is dropped afterward.⁹ Not only is it safe to assume that a French reader would have been unlikely to have met a Quaker before, but hardly anyone in England ever encountered Quakers, who amounted to no more than 17,000 in a population of 5 million. Why would Voltaire highlight a group that was obviously marginal to the British religious experience? Why focus on such a little-known sect? The point here is not the Quakers themselves—Voltaire largely dismisses their religious ideas—but the fact that Anglicans ignore them. The vast majority of English have no affinity whatsoever with the Quakers but leave them alone nonetheless. It is this freedom—in the case of the Quakers, the liberty to be odd—which impresses Voltaire the most. In absolutist France, of course, such minority groups were not tolerated; Quakers in France would have been arrested, expelled, or worse. No Quakers inhabited France precisely because the French authorities would not permit it.

The first seven letters, then, set up Voltaire's argument for religious pluralism, which he summarized near the end of this section in the following manner: "If one religion were allowed in England, the government would very possibly become arbitrary; if there were but two, the people would cut one another's throats; but as there are such a multitude, they all live happy and in peace."[10] Voltaire's formulation is more radical than it may appear to us. In the eighteenth century, there were no secular states in Europe; during the long period following the Peace of Westphalia (1648–1789), it was an accepted feature of the European state system that each government sponsor one form of Christianity. A country without a state church in the eighteenth century was as unthinkable as forgoing an army or fiscal bureaucracy. The issue, then, was not whether a government would retain its state church but, rather, the relationship among the state church, the sovereign government, and the religious practices of its citizens. Given that nearly all European states were monarchies, this meant that the religion of the monarch usually corresponded to the state religion. To be sure, European leaders expected kings and queens to respect local religious customs, but even the most liberal among them knew that monarchs had the power to limit the rights and activities of minority religious groups. So, for example, while Jews in Prussia were relatively well treated, Frederick the Great limited the extent to which they could worship publicly. In this sense, Voltaire in effect demanded fundamental changes to the Westphalia settlement. While he did not advocate the abolition of state religions, nor anything like the more modern notion of separation of church and state, he hoped to weaken the authority of the state religion by removing it as much as possible from the civic sphere, and thus make it more or less equal with other forms of institutionalized religion. Although Voltaire may be best known today for the catchy phrase *écrasez l'infâme* (smash infamy!), what he really wanted was for various institutionalized forms of superstition to cancel each other out, while the government looked the other way.[11]

During the seventeenth century, English kings—like their continental counterparts—rejected religious pluralism, contributing to civil war and revolution. By the time Voltaire visited England during the years when Sir Robert Walpole was prime minister, England had learned its lesson. Where Montesquieu had flirted with religious pluralism in *Persian Letters*, Voltaire comes right to the point early in *Philosophical Letters*: England's relatively weak Anglican Church and consequent religious toleration is the reason for England's newly found military strength, wealth, and confidence, and such prosperity has made its common people enjoy both personal security and, next to Holland, the highest standard of living in Europe.

After religion, Voltaire addressed English political life directly in three short, but powerful, letters that praised an essentially new form of government—limited monarchy—in which the House of Commons restrained the church and aristocracy, while the monarchy acted on behalf of the common people. Voltaire's reading of English history was odd but effective. He dismissed the Magna Carta as an aristocratic trick. For Voltaire, the nobility and clergy never attempted to restrain the king's authority for the sake of the nation, but for their own selfish interests. He called them the "villains" who "laid waste England."[12] Rather, Voltaire admired the way in which English kings used the House of Commons to roll back the gains of "the barons, the bishops, and the popes."[13] While it is a mistake to call Voltaire a democrat, his formula for positive political change involved a reforming king championing from the top the aspirations and interests of common people.[14]

Religious liberty as it emerged, then, served as the basis for political liberty. In this sense, for Voltaire the first role of any progressive statesman was to limit the power of clergymen in politics and to establish an educated elite outside the church that can combat superstition and bigotry. Voltaire devoted more than a third of the book to introducing continental readers to English scientists, philosophers, playwrights, and poets, including Shakespeare, Bacon, Newton, and Locke, contrasting them with French counterparts Pascal and Descartes. Again, Voltaire's argument was crude but effective. The English embraced their artists and scientists, turning Shakespeare into a cult figure and making Newton Master of the Mint, an important government appointment. The French cared less about Pascal, and poor Descartes wrote philosophy self-exiled in Holland, fearful of his government's long reach. Still, for a travel memoir, this much attention to intellectual elites seems odd. Voltaire ignored such topics as the character of the common people; Britain's regional differences; and its topography, music, painting, architecture, and folk crafts. He says nothing at all about the English diet. Rather, English freedom is removed from popular culture, dependent upon an engaged intelligentsia guided by literature, philosophy, and science. For Voltaire, freedom trickled down from the most educated classes to the least.

Voltaire's central message was that Europeans suffered when their educated classes came from the church and they prospered when the church was marginalized by a secular intelligentsia immersed in science and the arts. In Letter 20, among the shortest in the collection, he expressed this thesis in a novel way by considering how a contemporary English amateur poet accounted for the decline of Italy since the Renaissance. Voltaire reported on an unnamed English lord who visited Voltaire in France on his way home from Italy. Taken with his poem composed about Italy's decline, Voltaire translated it from English to French and transcribed it into his book. Even in English translations, the poem was left in Voltaire's French version and (during the eighteenth century) never rendered back into English. Although Letter 20 doesn't name the English poet, we know from Voltaire's correspondence that the visitor was Lord Hervey, who did indeed allow Voltaire to transcribe his poem during the visit and never published it himself. When Gustave Lanson hunted for Hervey's original to include in his 1909 modern critical edition, he came up empty-handed. Voltaire's French translation was all there was until Hervey's papers finally surfaced after the Second World War.[15]

Only recently, then, have we been able to read Voltaire's translation against the original by Hervey, and the comparison is instructive. Voltaire invented lines to deepen an anticlerical tone that was only hinted at in the original. For example, while Hervey includes an indirect reference to religion ("Each clown from mis'ry grows a Saint/He prays from idleness, and fasts from want"), Voltaire adds specificity:

L'extravagante Comedie	The extravagant comedy
Que souvent l'Inquisition	That the Inquisition usually
Veut qu'un nomme Religion	Calls by the name religion
Mais qu'ici nous nommons Folie	But that we call folly.[16]

Likewise, Voltaire adds stanzas about priests and the pope that were absent in Hervey, holding them responsible for Italy's poverty.

Voltaire's translation bends Hervey's original toward Voltaire's general thesis argued throughout *Philosophical Letters*: Italy's decline from its Renaissance splendor was due primarily to the Catholic Church's control over civic life. Instead of focusing on expanding trade and commerce, as Venice had done during the late medieval period, helping Italy to achieve a golden age during the fourteenth and fifteenth centuries, the church abused its power. Through oppressive institutions such as the Inquisition, priests and popes had turned on commoners with the result that eighteenth-century Italy had become an impoverished backwater. What upset Voltaire most about the situation in Italy was not only the decline of its cultural elite since the golden age of the Renaissance; here the lament is not about the decline of great art but for the grinding poverty endemic to the Italian peasantry. Indeed, it was the material lives of the common people that most interested Voltaire. The standard of success for any government was not simply whether its intellectual class produced fine art, but the extent to which such learning translated into real improvement, security, and freedom in the lives of ordinary people.

Perhaps no letter made the link between science, learning, and material improvement better than Letter 11, On Inoculation, which occupies a central place in the book, both in its positioning and in its argument. Indeed, Letter 11 contains two unique features: First, unlike the other chapters in *Philosophical Letters*, Letter 11 addressed a specific social problem ailing England at the very time of Voltaire's visit: smallpox. Second, the main protagonists in this story are women. Here Voltaire describes how England became the first European country to slow the fatality rate of smallpox through the introduction of inoculation, which occurred shortly before his own arrival. Voltaire used inoculation to highlight the ability of the English to improve themselves by attending to their own interests instead of blindly following tradition and custom.

Although smallpox's origins perhaps lay in far-away places such as Egypt and India a few thousand years earlier, the disfiguring disease reached its most deadly and dangerous levels in early modern Europe during the time that Voltaire visited England. Since 1650, over 50,000 Londoners died from recurring smallpox epidemics, the most recent in 1719. Nor did smallpox respect social class. Queen Mary succumbed in 1694, and France's Louis XV would die of smallpox in 1774. Almost as bad as death was the facial disfigurement smallpox caused. In a society where female beauty was an important consideration for marriage, surviving the disease was often a traumatic event for girls. Except perhaps for measles, anxiety surrounding smallpox was probably greater in early modern Europe than for any other disease. Perhaps this is one reason women were especially involved in attempts to eradicate smallpox.[17] As historian

Genevieve Miller noted, "the age of Reason could just as truthfully be labeled the Age of Smallpox."[18] Smallpox was an emotional issue for Voltaire, whose own experience with the illness gives Letter 11 a seriousness of purpose and rhetorical passion more intense than many of the other letters. During the final weeks of 1723, almost the very moment that inoculation was introduced in England, the twenty-nine-year-old Voltaire found himself a victim of a French smallpox epidemic that would take the lives of friends and acquaintances. For a period, he thought he would be among them. He came down with a high fever, prepared a final will, as his doctor signaled servants that Voltaire would probably die. Although he survived, it took him several months to recover. Even a year later he was still complaining to friends about his weakened condition.[19]

Voltaire's view of the illness is noteworthy. "Smallpox in itself," he wrote at the time of his illness, "unaccompanied by any complicating condition, is only a cleansing of the blood . . . It is favourable to nature, and prepares the way for vigorous health by cleansing the body of impurities." The fever further inflames the blood, increasing its volume to dangerous proportions, requiring multiple blood-lettings, which Voltaire found "indispensable." The blood-lettings were accompanied by several enemas, which Voltaire also approved. "Then strong evacuants will carry off the cause of the evil, taking with it part of the leaven of the *smallpox*, thus allowing what remains to develop more completely and preventing the *smallpox* from becoming confluent." Such purges were quickly followed by liquids. Typically these were alcoholic, including wines and brandies. But Voltaire swore off such "cordials," and credited his doctor with insisting on softer beverages. "He made me drink two hundred pints of lemonade. This procedure, which will strike you as extraordinary, was the only one that could have saved my life."[20]

Voltaire clung to his old-fashioned ideas even when challenged by friends. For example, one correspondent doubted the good effects of his enemas, and questioned how much was known about the illness even among the most famous doctors in Europe, such as Sydenham and Boerhaave, who disagreed among themselves about smallpox's etiology and remedies. This unidentified friend accused Voltaire of being led by "false prejudice."[21] Inoculation offered Voltaire a way to resist the disease without necessarily understanding its causes and nature.

Instead of focusing on a particularly visionary physician or scientists, Voltaire attributed the European discovery of inoculation to an English aristocrat, Lady Mary Wortley Montagu, "a Woman of as fine a Genius, and embu'd with as great a Strength of Mind, as any of her Sex in the British Kingdoms."[22] Montagu was herself no stranger to smallpox. While she survived her own ordeal with the illness in 1715, her brother died from it. Meanwhile her husband was elected to the House of Commons and in 1716 was appointed as England's ambassador to the Ottoman Empire. Within days of her arrival there, she learned about the Turkish custom of inoculating children with the smallpox virus taken from a scab of another person. Instantly she saw the promise this procedure held for her family, and she made arrangements to have her own son inoculated. Naturally, she also saw what inoculation could do back home in England.

"I am Patriot enough," she wrote to a friend in April 1717, "to take pains to bring this useful invention into fashion in England."[23]

Back home in 1718, Lady Montagu immediately pressed the princess of Wales, the future Queen Caroline. If the princess would successfully inoculate the royal children, it might provide the impetus for a national movement. As Voltaire noted, Princess Caroline was in her own way as extraordinary as Lady Mary Montagu. The German-raised Caroline was an advanced thinker in her own right, close with the brightest minds of Europe, such as Gottfried Willhelm Leibniz and Samuel Clarke. In Voltaire's telling, Caroline responded to the issue by acting like an experimental philosopher herself. "The Moment this Princess heard of Inoculation, she caus'd an Experiment of it to be made on four Criminals sentenc'd to die, and by that means preserv'd their Lives doubly; for she not only sav'd them from the Gallows, but by means of this artificial Small-Pox, prevented their ever having that distemper in a natural Way." This prisoner experiment took place in August 1721 and was deemed successful enough that Caroline had her own children inoculated. Voltaire believed that her example helped save countless lives: "ten thousand Children, at least, of Persons of Condition owe in this Manner their Lives to her Majesty, and to the Lady Wortley Montagu; and as many of the Fair Sex are oblig'd to them for their Beauty."[24]

Of course, as we saw in Letter 20, Voltaire couldn't resist embellishing some of these facts. He writes, for example, of the ambassador's Anglican chaplain, who beseeched Lady Mary to abandon the inoculation project since "this was an unchristian Operation, and therefore that it cou'd succeed with none but infidels."[25] While it is possible that Lady Mary said this directly to Voltaire himself, we have no evidence of any opposition from the ambassador's chaplain.

There is some debate among scholars today regarding the influence Lady Mary had on introducing inoculation into England, and some find Voltaire's presentation exaggerated.[26] Indeed, knowledge of Turkish inoculation already existed in England before Lady Mary went to the Ottoman Empire. In 1713 and 1715, the Royal Academy had published accounts of Turkish inoculation by Italian physicians who had observed it.[27] Until Lady Mary, however, this debate was academic and technical, and largely without policy implications. Only a very small circle of physicians and scientists were aware of it. In this respect, Voltaire was right to highlight Lady Mary's activities. She brought inoculation into the open and actively urged mothers to inoculate their own children. And yet, her writings and activities remained highly controversial, and inoculation did not spread as fast as Lady Mary and Voltaire had hoped. After all, inoculation (technically variolation) was still a dangerous procedure, since it involved transferring live and highly contagious smallpox pus directly from one person to another, exposing others in its path.

During the 1730s and 1740s, despite the rapid success of Voltaire's book, support for inoculation declined probably because Europe luckily avoided major epidemics. Despite the support of Princess Caroline, old attitudes persisted. "The doctrines of the Bowstring and of Inoculation in the Small Pox," announced the *Gentleman's Magazine* the same year Voltaire's letter was published, "are both of Mahometan origin and can never suit a freeborn English Constitution."[28] Only when large smallpox epidemics returned in the 1750s was there a revival of interest. Voltaire kept himself at the center of the inoculation debate by corresponding with Europe's leading physicians. After the Anglican bishop Isaac Maddox published an important sermon supporting inoculation in 1756, Voltaire quietly updated Letter 11 with a section mentioning Maddox.[29] Still, Voltaire's most important convert was the new Russian empress Catherine the Great. "He is my master. It was he—or rather his writings, which formed my mind." Following her accession to the throne in 1762, Catherine inoculated her own children and herself, and immediately wrote her "master" about it. "I have been inoculated; my son too and [Count] Orloff, and many of the courtiers, and it has been introduced into schools and hospitals. Indeed, it is becoming quite the fashion." Voltaire applauded her example: "Ah! Madame, what a lesson your imperial majesty has given to our learned professors of the Sorbonne." By 1800, two million Russians had followed her lead.[30]

Voltaire's eleventh letter is thus all the more noteworthy because it arrived on the scene well before Europeans had embraced inoculation and vaccination. New and daring procedures, it was not clear that they could be so easily transferred from one end of Europe to the other. Moreover, unlike the letters promoting Newton and Locke, here Voltaire was championing the efforts of women who were sticking their noses into the worlds of science and public health.

Nowhere does Voltaire show more clearly than Letter 11 the practicality of Enlightenment culture. In this case, English society allowed women such as Princess Caroline and Lady Mary to follow their inclinations to improve their own familial situations, that is, to follow their "maternal Tenderness and Interest."[31] Unlike France, which placed religion and other institutionalized impediments in the way of such natural interests, the English seemed to encourage innovation. After all, the French too had an ambassador in Turkey, and neither he nor his wife brought inoculation back to France. Lady Mary was an applied empiricist, not unlike Bacon, Newton, and Locke, whom Voltaire discussed in neighboring letters. Her radical approach to smallpox came from observing how ordinary Turkish mothers had treated their children.

This letter on inoculation shows that Voltaire had no narrow, esoteric view of philosophy. Letter 11 is "philosophical" only in an expansive and populist sense. Voltaire wanted to broaden the notion of philosophy by associating it with the character of British society itself. British aristocrats, particularly women, were affected by the empirical methodology of intellectuals like Newton, who, as Voltaire tells us, was treated by the English as a celebrity. Unlike France, where thinkers like Descartes were driven into exile, England openly blessed its philosophers and poets, encouraging them to engage in civic activities. "His Countrymen honour'd him in his Life-Time, and interr'd him as tho' he had been a King who had made his People happy."[32]

For Voltaire, the Enlightenment was not restricted to a highly educated elite but spilled out among a public that included anyone interested in improving the conditions of their own life. This is what Voltaire admired most among the English: their openness to change and self-improvement. Unfortunately, the rest of Europe embraced institutions far more resistant to change. "It is inadvertently affirm'd in the Christian Countries of Europe," Voltaire remarked, "that the English are Fools and Madmen."[33] Of course, Letter 11 proved the opposite: it was the French who were fools and madmen for rejecting inoculation after its benefits had become clear. The French medical community, in particular, stood against Voltaire. In 1724, for example, a Dr. Hecquet wrote that inoculation was "contrary to the views of God."[34] Because France was controlled by the Catholic Church, Voltaire worried about its future: "Perhaps our Nation will imitate, ten Years hence, this Practice of the English, if the Clergy and the Physicians will but give them Leave to do it." Meanwhile, "had Inoculation been practis'd in France, 'twould have sav'd the Lives of Thousands."[35]

From the start, Voltaire knew that he would have trouble publishing this book. If the much less direct *Persian Letters* could not find a legal way into France and Catholic Europe, what could he expect a decade later for *Philosophical Letters*? Voltaire developed a complex strategy that depended first on the notion that he was publishing an English-language book in England as a visitor to that country. "I must disguise in Paris," he wrote in 1732, "what I can say with complete openness in London."[36] Although nearly every European country had its own rules for what could and could not be published within its borders, there was nothing illegal about traveling to a foreign country, producing a manuscript in its language, and having the book published there in conformity with its laws. This made good business sense too. At the end of his long visit, Voltaire had become well known in England. By 1728, he had secured enough subscription support to publish in a lavish quarto edition his epic poem, *La Henriade*—among his sponsors was none other than Lady Mary Wortley Montagu, whom he met at that time. *La Henriade*, published in French with an English prologue and dedication, had Voltaire's name directly on the title page. It was such a success that it went through at least five more London editions in the following two decades.[37] Clearly, then, English readers were aware of Voltaire's literary reputation when his English-language *Letters Concerning the English Nation* became available at London bookstalls in August 1733 (Figure 5.2).

Due to the extraordinary research of book historian Giles Barber, who discovered its precise printing logs, we know the history of this publication better than almost any other Enlightenment work. Barber determined that it took about four months for the printers to set the type and run the presses for 2000 copies of the *Letters*. These long hours of labor constituted about half the cost of the total production; paper made up a third of the cost, with smaller amounts going out for journal notices and author or translator payments. Altogether, Barber reasoned that if the print run sold out, the publishers stood to make a profit of 156 percent![38]

It may seem obvious that once Voltaire decided to publish in London, he would also publish the book in English. However, *La Henriade* and *Charles XII* both went through French-language editions in England before the first English translation was published. During the eighteenth century, French had become so pervasive among Europe's elites that large numbers of English readers welcomed books in that language. London

Voltaire's Philosophical Letters *(1733–4)*

Figure 5.2 Title page English version *Voltaire's Letters Concerning an English Nation*. The English translation (with Voltaire's name on its title page) was actually published before any French-language edition, giving readers that sense that it was a travel memoir that Voltaire had written on his visit.

publishers routinely mounted large-scale French book productions for both domestic and export consumption.[39] Indeed, why would Voltaire go to the trouble of publishing the book first in English, when he could be assured of its London success in French?

Until recently scholars believed that *Letters* was originally an English book produced in England by a French traveler writing in English. In 1967, Harcourt Brown argued that Voltaire had written most of the letters first in English, and his article was so persuasive that in 1994 Oxford University Press produced an edition of *Letters Concerning the English Nation* based around this notion. However, in 2001, Patrick Lee convincingly showed the English edition to be a translation from the French by John Lockwood, a noted translator. Today the debate has been resolved through a compromise: Voltaire began some of the chapters in English, probably while visiting England. When he returned to France in 1729, however, he rewrote these chapters in French and added several others. The manuscript that he handed to interlocutor John Lockwood was completely in French.[40]

Voltaire, of course, wanted the book to seem as close to a genuine travel memoir as possible. The preface to the first edition, reprinted many times, claimed the book's origin as British. These letters, insisted the publishers, were written by Voltaire when he was in England, and thus, they constituted something of a journal or memoir of his visit: "Mr. de Voltaire is the author of them, they were written in London." Nor did Voltaire intend these letters for publication, they insisted. He had sent them to his friend

Nicholas Claude Theriot only as a private correspondence. Despite the dishonesty of both claims, the preface's assertions would later allow Voltaire to deny any role in the book's publication and circulation.

Even before this first English edition appeared, Voltaire sent instructions for the same printers to begin preparing an edition in French of 1,500 copies, which they started in May 1733. The timing of its publication for spring 1734 was carefully coordinated by Voltaire in conjunction with two other editions produced in France. That is, Voltaire orchestrated the publication of three simultaneous French-language editions to follow what he hoped would be the success of the English-language London edition. And his strategy paid off: *Letters Concerning the English Nation by Monsieur de Voltaire* became a blockbuster. In contrast to *Persian Letters*, which was presented to the public as an ephemeral fictional work produced in a cheap duodecimo format, Voltaire's book was produced from the start as an octavo with a full index at the end, indicating a work of some importance, worthy of reflection and study. Even before it hit London bookshelves, a Dublin publisher illicitly obtained the manuscript and immediately produced an unauthorized edition. The book's popularity was assured.

For the initial edition in France, Voltaire turned to the Rouen printer/publisher, Claude-François Jore, who had recently published editions of *La Henriade* and *Charles XII*. Jore had managed to stay on the good side of the authorities by printing liturgical work for Rouen's archbishop. But he also secretly printed licentious works with titles such as "The Fifteen Joys of Marriage" and "The Nun in Spite of Herself."[41] During the printing of *Charles XII*, Voltaire had gotten to know Jore very well by lodging in his home for several months. Knowing full well the risks involved, Voltaire offered to pay for all printing costs, leaving Jore with any profits he could make. At the same time, Voltaire went behind Jore's back, secretly planning for a separate printing of the book by the Paris printer, cousins René and François Josse, who had published Voltaire's *Brutus* in 1731. Anticipating a hostile response from the government, Voltaire instructed Josse to delay release, so that the Josse edition would appear just as the anticipated crackdown suppressed the Rouen edition. In this way, Voltaire ingeniously engineered a pirated edition of his own work as a means of outfoxing the censor.[42] Thus in April 1734, three versions in French of the book were simultaneously published in Rouen, Paris, and London, each with a false imprint: Amsterdam for Rouen, Amsterdam for Paris, and Basel for London. Within months, two more pirated versions appeared, probably from Holland. All in all, by the end of 1734, Western Europe was flooded with no fewer than seven French-language editions.

Several weeks after Jore began to typeset the book in Rouen, Voltaire made an important change that distinguished the French edition its English sibling: he added a twenty-fifth letter. This happened so late into the process that Jore had to awkwardly add the additional material. On page 288 of the Rouen edition, following Letter 24, it reads "fin," the end. But the new letter nonetheless begins on the following page, paginated as page 289. While Voltaire also sent instructions to London for its French version to include the new letter, it arrived there too late and was thus excluded from the early London editions.[43]

The addition of one more letter might not have been noticed, but this was no ordinary piece. First, it was significantly longer than any of the other twenty-four letters, constituting a third of the book; second, this letter had—at least on the surface—nothing to do with England; and third, the letter itself was not epistolary, but a dialogue with the French religious thinker Blaise Pascal (1623–62), refuting step by step the theological points spelled out in Pascal's famous work *Pensées*, first published posthumously in 1670. Given such a strange shift in genre and subject, Voltaire changed the French title from *Lettres écrites de Londres* to *Lettres philosophiques*.

Pascal's inclusion at the climax of *Philosophical Letters* demonstrates that the book was as much about France as England. But why Pascal in particular? Pascal held an extraordinary reputation during the Enlightenment, and in many ways, he haunted Voltaire and the other philosophes. Here was a theologian who could not be dismissed as superstitious. After all, for much of his career, Pascal was among France's most gifted mathematicians and inventors; he played a central role in the seventeenth-century Scientific Revolution. At age thirty-one he threw away his scientific career for a life devoted to theology after becoming reborn as an active Christian. Particularly under the influence of Saint Augustine, he and his sister became leaders of Jansenism, a movement among Catholic activists that stressed human sinfulness and Christ's grace. His *Pensées* provide a roadmap for disillusioned Christians, and they were immensely popular throughout Western Europe. Over sixty editions of the book were published during the eighteenth century.[44] Here was an adversary worthy of Voltaire's attention.

Still, why did Voltaire tack on a separate essay on Pascal at the end of a book about English thinkers? We will never know for sure, but there are hints that Voltaire left along the way. Perhaps the most important is the concept of self-interest (amour propre).[45] Throughout the twenty-four letters on England, Voltaire repeatedly showed that a society that allowed individuals to maximize their own self-interest would result in political stability, personal security, and material prosperity. But for Pascal self-interest was the root of selfishness, the basis of a Hobbesian world in which humans ruthlessly exploit one another. Here is where Voltaire aimed his rhetoric:

> It wou'd be as impossible for a society to be founded and support itself, without the principle of self-love.... 'Tis the self-love which is innate in us that aids the love of others; 'tis by our mutual wants that we are useful to the rest of mankind: 'Tis the foundation of all commerce.[46]

Without the grand example of England, Voltaire's comments on self-love might seem a technical matter of abstract thought. Letters 1–24 arm Voltaire with empirical ammunition. He is not speaking theoretically. England is a country devoted to amour propre as a governing principle, and as Voltaire shows, the result has been its rise to become France's greatest rival. In this respect, the inoculation letter is perhaps the best and most concrete example of how self-interest is both natural and a path to social improvement, and thus becomes a refutation of Pascal's Jansenism. Recalling how the British discovered inoculation by observing Turkish women inoculating their children,

Voltaire claims the universality of amour propre: It is a "cause common to all Nations, I mean maternal Tenderness and Interest."[47] Women such as Lady Montagu, who brought back to England Turkish techniques intended to help families and children, constituted Voltaire's proof against Pascal that regard for oneself and one's family is not selfish but improves the world at large. Insofar as the book's purpose is to honor principles responsible for England's success in order to critique France's degeneracy, the letter on Pascal deepens the philosophical significance of what Voltaire witnessed in England.[48]

As he helped to prepare the French-language editions for publication, Voltaire took careful steps to make sure the government would approve what he hoped would be recognized as merely a translation of a work originally published in a foreign language and in a foreign country. For several months, he circulated the manuscript to friends and government authorities to gauge the chances for legal publication. He even read some letters aloud to one of the king's ministers, the Comte de Maurepas. He also used the Abbé de Rothelin as a trusted advisor. This process gave Voltaire optimism regarding a *permission tacite* for the book. Given that his *History of Charles XII* also obtained a *permission tacite* in 1734, Voltaire's optimism was not unrealistic.[49]

Despite these preparatory moves, the publication in France of *Philosophical Letters* caused a storm of protest and controversy. One way to gauge the public's reaction is through the response of a typical reader. In 1734, the young aspiring writer and critic Parisian Jean Bernard Le Blanc (1707–81) was beginning his career. His reputation as a man of letters would take off a decade later when, interestingly, his own book on England became popular on both sides of the English Channel. Written clearly in imitation of Voltaire's, Le Blanc's book comprised ninety-two letters based on notes he had jotted down during a visit to England. He became a leading art critic and translator of David Hume into French—indeed, Hume later asked Le Blanc to give Voltaire a copy of his *History of England*. While it is understandable to assume that Le Blanc's early admiration of *Philosophical Letters* helped convert him into a philosophe, nothing could be farther from the truth.

"I have finally read Voltaire's *Philosophical Letters*," Le Blanc wrote to a friend in April 1734. "It's a different edition than the one made in England that the Minister tried to stop." From the way it was printed, he guessed that it had been produced in Paris. This itself was dangerous, and Le Blanc remarked that the printer was destined for the Bastille. "There are seven or eight letters on the English Quakers, which are hardly critical and contain things quite well written. The rest I'm less happy with, and in general, I am shocked by the contemptuous tone that reigns throughout, especially on his nation, on our government, our ministers, and above all, with such disrespect, on our [Catholic] religion." Voltaire's tone and his constant preference for all things English constitute a "horrible indecency." Voltaire's "attack" on Pascal, "the mathematician so renowned," also offended Le Blanc. While Voltaire's comparison of Descartes and Newton was better, he never stopped "attacking religion while seeming to respect it." Despite these criticisms, Le Blanc thought his correspondent would want to read the book for himself, but warned him that "the book costs six francs and is only sold under the counter and obtained with some difficulty."[50]

Many readers shared Le Blanc's reaction. As J. B. Shank has commented, "the shock of the *Lettres philosophiques* is not to be found in the philosophy it defended or the ideas it imparted per se but instead in the text's critical style; it was Voltaire's tone, his intellectual stance, and his critical voice much more than the precise ideas he defended that were truly provocative."[51] Readers inside and outside of France were mesmerized by Voltaire's prose; they hung onto his every word and loved his sense of humor. But they were outraged by his religious views and mean-spirited attitudes to clergymen. Even readers who were offended by his views, however, sought to read Voltaire because of his elegant and humorous prose. Oddly, as in the case of Le Blanc, the appreciation of Voltaire's literary talents was what made the work a public danger that required censorship. Indeed, many of the judges of the French Parlement who would soon act to burn *Philosophical Letters* owned copies in their personal libraries.[52]

Within weeks of its publication, government officials demanded the book's suppression. Because Voltaire's name appeared on the title page of the London editions, the philosophe was in danger of arrest. He pleaded his case as best he could, claiming with a straight face that he never intended to publish these letters and had not been involved in the book's publication or distribution. The book originated, Voltaire argued, as private letters written in England in English at the time of his visit, and that he had entrusted them to a friend in London, Nicholas Claude Thieriot, who had published them behind his back. The French edition, Voltaire pleaded, was obviously an unauthorized counterfeit translation. Far from violating the laws of France, Voltaire portrayed himself as the victim of literary piracy. Writing specifically to the king's eighty-year-old first minister, Cardinal Fleury, Voltaire admitted that while he was indeed the book's author, he never imagined (much less approved) of its publication. "My lord, I insist to you that I've had absolutely nothing to do with any part of this book's publication."[53]

Despite his dishonesty, Voltaire's position was not unreasonable. In France and many other Western European countries, book censorship was aimed at printers, publishers, and booksellers rather than authors. The printer/publisher, not the author, assumed legal responsibility for turning a manuscript into print. Indeed, some of Voltaire's writings that were too provocative for print circulated for many years in manuscript. Voltaire took little risk from such efforts; he was never prosecuted for his manuscripts but only for his books.[54] While there was no de jure freedom of thought in eighteenth-century France, neither was there much interest in arresting individual writers for manuscripts that never reached the printer. After all, unlike Spain, Portugal, and parts of Italy, no Inquisition operated in France; the church in France was largely subject to royal policies and procedures. What made Voltaire's work potentially illegal, and subject to both church and state prosecution, then, was not his role in writing them but his knowingly contracting with a press to turn them into books. Thus, in his letter to Fleury, Voltaire sought above all to distinguish his authorship from any participation in publication.

Voltaire's special pleading backfired. Authorities raided Jore's shop and discovered other radical works with false imprints. Jore was arrested and thrown into the Bastille. Most of Jore's print run was seized, leaving him in serious debt. Worse, the government took away his license as a publisher and bookseller. He was ruined. Meanwhile, on May 3, 1734, one of King Louis XV's most powerful ministers, the Comte de Maurepas, issued an arrest warrant, a *lettre de cachet*, for Voltaire.[55] Warned about Maurepas's order while attending a wedding in Burgundy, Voltaire quickly slipped across the border into Lorraine, an independent duchy, where he stayed for several weeks.

In a letter to the powerful minister, the Count de Maurepas, Voltaire again tried to distinguish his legal authorship of *Philosophical Letters* from its illicit publication. "I was in London six years ago when I wrote these bagatelles." Then as now, publication was the farthest thing from his mind, he asserted disingenuously. The entire affair had caused his health to deteriorate, giving him a constant dysentery that had severely weakened him. "You know that exile or imprisonment would kill me dead." Soon, he noted, he very well may be debating Pascal in person in "the other world." More significant, as a concession and compromise measure, Voltaire offered to issue a formal disavowal of the publication and to initiate a lawsuit against booksellers offering the book. Far from a provocateur, he beseeched Maurepas to see him as a victim of literary piracy.[56]

Voltaire's fate worsened in June, when the somewhat independent, often restive, judicial arm of the government, the Parlement of Paris—France's highest appellate court—intervened. On June 10, 1734, the Parlement charged that *Philosophical Letters* "inspires the most dangerous disrespect not only for religion but also for the order of civil society." Consequently, all copies confiscated thus far would be immediately "shredded and burned" in a public ceremony overseen by an official public executioner in the Parlement's courtyard. The Parlement called upon all printers, bookshops, and peddlers to immediately halt "printing, selling, peddling, or distributing in any other fashion" the book under pain of "corporeal punishment." Anyone, it pleaded, with a copy of the book should immediately turn it into appropriate court officials. The order was published by the government, and soon reprinted in the *Mercure de France*, giving the suppression unusual publicity (which only increased demand for underground copies of the book).[57]

Even by the standards of eighteenth-century France, the hostility engendered by *Philosophical Letters* was extraordinary. The Parlement's intervention was quite rare. Although in later decades the Parlement would ban four more books by Voltaire, and would launch prosecutions against other Enlightenment philosophes, during the 1730s, the court was more concerned with reining in zealous Jesuits than secular-leaning philosophes. It generally avoided becoming involved in the business of censorship. Out of some 600 books banned by the government between 1720 and 1770, the Parlement acted in less than twenty-five cases. Censoring books was even more rare for the royal Conseil d'Etat, which issued its own direct ban only a handful of times. And yet here again *Philosophical Letters* was the exception: On October 23, 1734 the Conseil d'Etat declared the book illegal and its author an outlaw.[58]

Voltaire, of course, did not simply play defense. We have already seen him orchestrating pirated editions in Paris and elsewhere. He made a trip to Amsterdam, where he negotiated a new edition with Etienne Ledet and Jacques Desbordes who had since begun specializing in the works of Voltaire. To protect himself somewhat, he had Desbordes reprint an edition of the *Lettres écrites de Londres*, albeit without the offensive anti-Pascal letter.[59] Voltaire was clearly hoping that he could wear down the government's resistance by increasing the book's popularity. His most acclaimed biographer, René Pomeau, estimates that during the 1730s at least 20,000 French-language copies circulated throughout Europe.[60] Meanwhile, *Philosophical Letters* did especially well in those parts of French-speaking Europe that were beyond the reach of French government authorities. For example, in the independent principality of Namur, in what is today southern Belgium, the book appears in a study of private eighteenth libraries more than any other work. Its owners included nobleman, professionals, clergymen, and merchants. Certainly, Pierre Rétat and Jean Sgard's team of researchers are correct in their assessment that the publication of *Philosophical Letters* was not only a milestone in the development of the Enlightenment but also constituted a turning point in the increasingly adversarial relationship between press and the French monarchy.[61]

Nonetheless, for Voltaire and his best-selling book, all his efforts yielded only a pyrrhic victory. As long as Voltaire kept trying to publish *Philosophical Letters* in France, the authorities did not back down and pursued him as an outlaw. Voltaire could keep *Philosophical Letters* in print, but only by placing himself in exile. The situation became personally untenable for him. He felt that his status as an outlaw would ruin his chances to become the dominant figure in French literature, a spot he thought he deserved. His later rise in 1745 to the honorific position of King Louis XV's Royal Historiographer, and then his election as a member to the French Academy the following year, show that his decision in 1735 to compromise with the government was the right one for him. Simply put, if Voltaire would act to curtail publication of *Philosophical Letters*, government ministers would agree to roll back his exile. In 1735 the government allowed Voltaire temporary visits to Paris.

Voltaire, of course, had no clear authority to stop European publishers from producing new editions of *Philosophical Letters*. But he could and did discourage them from doing so by making such an investment less financially rewarding. As discussed in Chapter 4, Voltaire began pitching a set of collected works to Dutch publishers Etienne Ledet and Jacques Desbordes. This meant that Ledet and Desbordes could look forward to receiving corrected versions of old material and the enticing probability of publishing new material; indeed, in 1738 they would put out the first edition of Voltaire's important book about Newton. As a requirement of the deal, however, Voltaire demanded that they halt publishing editions with the title *Philosophical Letters*.[62] As the project for a set of collected works moved closer to realization, Ledet and Desbordes eventually agreed to stop publishing separate editions of *Philosophical Letters*, either as *Lettres philosophiques* or as *Lettres écrites de Londres*, and to disperse the twenty-five letters as short individual pieces within a section of the fourth volume entitled *Mélanges de littérature et de philosophie* (Literary and Philosophical Miscellanies). In 1737, there appeared one more counterfeit edition, probably from a different Dutch or French publisher, but Voltaire's partnership with Ledet and Desbordes discouraged others from bringing new editions to the market.

The four-volume publication of *Oeuvres de M de Voltaire* in 1738–9, then, effectively prevented separate publication of *Philosophical Letters*.[63] Never again during the eighteenth century was there to be an independent publication of this incendiary book in French. This meant that the French authorities had won a large victory: if the monarchy's goal was to suppress the book's importation into France, it had succeeded. As to the many editions of Voltaire's collected works that appeared after 1739, the title *Lettres philosophiques* or *Lettres écrites de Londres* was omitted from the table of contents, although a careful reader might discern them using an index.[64] In short, the government forced Voltaire to bury his masterpiece in the untidy miscellaneous volumes of his collected works, where presumably only specialists would find them. Of all the books discussed in this study, *Philosophical Letters* was the only one successfully suppressed by the French government.

And yet, because Voltaire himself closely supervised many of the editions of his collected works, these essays continued to receive his scrutiny and that of his publishers for years to come. Here and there he made small changes to several of them, altering words and phrases, sometimes making the prose more succinct and direct. Occasionally he even added new material, such as an essay on Jonathan Swift that was inserted into the 1756 edition. The new format also allowed Voltaire to reuse old letters, such as one originally written in 1727 on decriminalizing suicide that seemed to go well with the others. In this way, the contents of *Philosophical Letters* were recycled in at least twenty-seven editions of his collected works.[65] However, this came at the cost of being able to see the twenty-five letters as a unified whole. Gradually, the letters became independent from one another and the overall integrity of the book was diluted. Following Voltaire's death in 1778, publishers dispersed the twenty-five letters into separate volumes, merging some with articles in the *Philosophical Dictionary*, while assigning others to miscellaneous literature and elsewhere.[66] When in 1789 the French Revolutionaries established press freedom, and began to publish freely the works of the Enlightenment philosophes, no French edition of *Philosophical Letters* ever appeared. While Voltaire spread ideas first articulated in *Philosophical Letters* to many other works, his book largely disappeared outside of the English reading world. Indeed, of the twelve case studies highlighted in this work, *Philosophical Letters* was the only one not published during the 1790s. While the Jacobins may have regarded Voltaire as among the revolution's patriarchs, they had forgotten this book.

The False Philosophical Letters

But there is a bit more to this story. Just as Voltaire's book was fading from the scene, another one was produced that readers might have mistaken for it, first in 1738, and then reprinted at least fourteen times in 1739, 1744, 1747, 1756, 1760, 1765, 1757, 1774, 1775 (2), and 1776 (2), 1777, and 1784.[67] The 1738 title was *Lettres de M. de V****

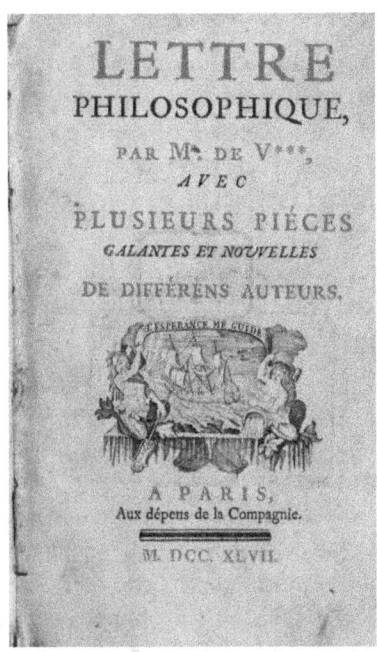

Figure 5.3 Title page from *Lettre philosophique de M. de V****... Often confused by state officials and readers as yet another edition of *Philosophical Letters*, this compilation, in fact, was filled with poetry and literary essays by other writers. Only the first piece included an early version of Voltaire's Letter on Locke. Clearly, this was meant to capitalize on European demand for *Philosophical Letters* after it had been suppressed by its author.

avec plusieurs pieces de différens auteurs. In the 1744 edition, the title changes slightly to *Lettre philosophique par M de V*** avec plusieurs pièces galantes et nouvelles de différens auteurs* [Philosophical Letter by M. de V*** With Several New and Elegant Contributions from Different Authors; see Figure 5.3]. This was an obvious attempt to lure readers who still hoped to buy copies of *Philosophical Letters* by promising them something close to the original book. Although Voltaire played no role whatsoever in the clandestine production, this knockoff was not completely fraudulent. While it included no material from the earlier book and was largely composed of unrelated poems and essays by often unknown authors, there was one gem by Voltaire that led off the volume—an essay entitled in the 1738 edition "XXVI *Lettre. Sur l'Ame*" (26th Letter On the Soul), obviously linking it as a sequel to the other twenty-five letters of the earlier volume.

Scholars now agree that this important article was not an additional twenty-sixth letter, but was an early version of Voltaire's thirteenth letter on John Locke.[68] Likely composed between 1728 and 1732, Voltaire withdrew it from *Philosophical*

Letters after showing the manuscript to his friend and critic, Abbé Rothelin, who mistakenly advised him that a revised, toned-down Locke letter would likely win a *permission tacite* from the government, allowing the work to circulate freely within France. Consequently, Voltaire's "Letter XIII On Mr Locke," first published in the 1733 English-language *Letters Concerning the English Nation*, was the revised version of this earlier and more radical letter originally intended but never published in *Philosophical Letters*.

Letter 13 on Locke and this supposed Letter 26 on the soul are similar. Their main purpose is to highlight how Locke's view of the human soul questioned the notion embraced by most Christian theology requiring a substance that was immaterial. For the followers of Descartes, since animals had no soul, they behaved according to instinct and did not have the capacity to think for themselves. Locke had wondered in print why God is prevented from enabling matter to think for itself. While he did not doubt that God was capable of creating immaterial spirit, and indeed, that God Himself was pure spirit, Locke insisted that humans might be examples of thinking matter—there really was no way for humans to determine the soul's nature. This important point called into question the distinction between humans and other animals. "We shall, perhaps, never be capable of knowing, whether a Being, purely material, thinks or not," Voltaire quotes Locke in the revised version that became Letter 13 in *Philosophical Letters*.[69] Meanwhile, the earlier version was more polemical. Instead of using Locke's voice, Voltaire appropriates Locke for his own sustained attack upon Christian dogma. The revised letter mainly uses Locke's voice by paraphrasing him in ways often light and humorous; the earlier letter is written more in Voltaire's own acerbic voice and is more directly about the soul and less about Locke.

Voltaire's earlier letter makes more explicit what is only implied in the revised version. In his *Essay*, Locke's main point had been the limitation placed on human thought given its dependence on sense experience rather than innate ideas. Locke did not so much dispute the existence of an immaterial soul so much as question how much humans could understand it. But this subtle distinction seemed to open the door to more radical doubt, even to materialism and atheism, which Voltaire's earlier essay exploits.[70] Some of the first published reviews of *Philosophical Letters* made that clear, condemning even Voltaire's revised letter, insisting that the immateriality and immortality of the soul was well beyond doubt. During the 1740s and 1750s, critics published rebuttals to both the early and revised letters, essentially conflating the two versions.[71]

Just as publishers meant to confuse *Lettre philosophique par M de V**** with *Lettres philosophiques*, so after 1738 the public confused Voltaire's two letters on Locke. When, for example, French government authorities seized copies of the former, they naturally mistook it for the latter.[72] In 1751, in its article "Ame" [Soul], the first volume of Diderot and d'Alembert's *Encyclopédie* seemed purposively to confuse the two versions of Voltaire's Locke letter.[73] When the Roman Catholic Church struck back the next year by placing *Philosophical Letters* on their Index of Forbidden Books, they surely confused it with the 1739 counterfeit, since Voltaire's book had been long out of print.[74] In this way, curiously, the reputation of *Lettres philosophiques* as a scandalous work may have continued into the second half of the eighteenth century, even though it had fallen out of print at the end of the 1730s.

Meanwhile, during the 1740s and 1750s, Voltaire never acknowledged the earlier version of the Locke letter nor allowed it to be housed within any of his collected works. Only in the 1760s, according to William H. Trapnell do we find it starting to appear in editions of the collected works.[75] In 1775, three years before his death, Voltaire directed the Geneva publishers Cramer and Baudin to publish the essay in their comprehensive edition of his collected works, under the title "Lettre philosophique sur l'âme." When following Voltaire's death, a gigantic and financially ruinous project by the playwright Pierre Caron de Beaumarchais produced a seventy-two-volume set that became the definitive edition of Voltaire's works for the next century, the original essay on Locke was reclassified as the eighth section of the article *Ame* in the well-known *Dictionnaire philosophique*.[76]

Chapter 6

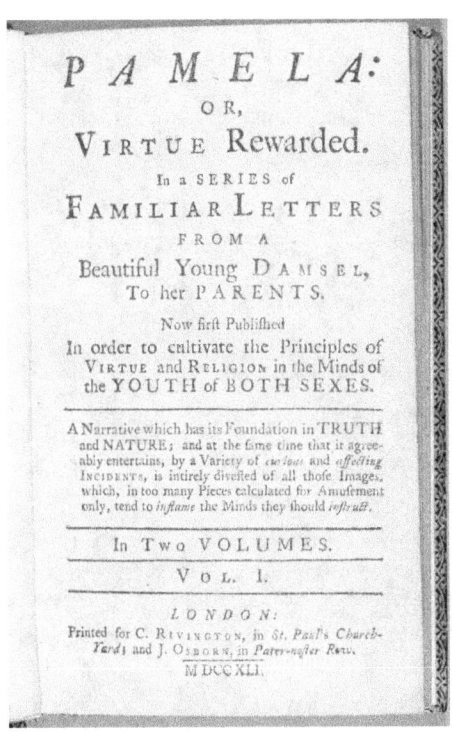

Figure 6.1 First edition title page Richardson's *Pamela*. Richardson's long title offers a justification for publishing a fictional account that some readers found too erotic, especially for younger readers.

Chapter 6
Richardson's *Pamela* (1740)

Table 6.1 Eighteenth-Century Editions of *Pamela, Clarissa,* and *Sir Charles Grandison*

Decades	1740–9	1750–9	1760–9	1770–9	1780–9	1790–1800	Total Editions
Pamela	21	5	3	6	7	8	50
Clarissa	6	11	8	3	8	18	54
Grandison	–	11	12	8	15	18	64

Translations of *Pamela*: Danish, Dutch, French, German, Italian, Russian, Spanish, Swedish.
Source: https://kates.itg.pomona.edu/books/analytics.php?type=all. Accessed March 9, 2022.

The making of *Pamela* was entirely accidental. Its creator never aspired to be the renowned author he suddenly became at age fifty-one but instead saw himself first and foremost as a printer. His identity as a tradesman never wavered; he printed all English editions of his three bestsellers, and constantly expanded his printing business with other work such as newspapers and government documents. At his death in 1761, he was among London's most successful printers.

Born in 1689, the same year as Montesquieu, Samuel Richardson was the son of a joiner, a highly skilled woodworking trade. By his own admission, young Samuel was a shy boy, who read widely and enjoyed telling imaginary stories to his friends. Family recognized his knack for letter-writing when he was a teenager. As he later told the Dutch translator of *Clarissa*, Johannes Stinstra, a few women a bit older than he began asking for his assistance in crafting letters responding to their boyfriends' overtures. Richardson complied, expanding his epistolary skills. His love for reading and his ability with words motivated him to become a printer (unlike his brother, who became a joiner like his father), and after a lengthy period as a journeyman, he finally established himself around 1713 as a master printer amid the London book world.[1]

During the eighteenth century, booksellers often also served as publishers, that is, financing a book's production by hiring the printer and purchasing the manuscript from the author. For this reason, Richardson's name rarely appeared on the title pages of the books he printed. Throughout his forty-year career, Richardson printed over 900 titles, in all genres and formats, from pocket-size novels to folio reference works aimed at connoisseurs.[2] Richardson's 1728 edition of Fénelon's *Telemachus* required twelve plates and a fold-out map.[3] As Richardson managed his close relations with London booksellers, they began to hire him to add prefaces, indexes, and other paratexts for many of the books he printed. In this way, he supplemented his printing operations with work that today we might associate with an editor. For example, in addition to printing a 1740 edition of *Aesop's Fables*, Richardson arranged its contents and even added his own material, including a substantive introduction.[4] Richardson approached his career as a craftsmen and businessman, willing to produce almost anything in print that might produce steady revenue.[5]

Richardson's work made him more sensitive than most authors to a book's materiality. He became an expert in paper quality, especially since the cost of paper made up between a third and half of a book's printing cost. He understood the trade-off between crowding letters onto a page to save money and laying out type attractively to make reading more pleasing and justify higher prices. He became an expert in design, knowing when and how to use decorative illustrations. "He acquired a substantial collection of moveable type," notes specialist Christopher Flint, including "the letters, numbers, punctuation, blanks, florets, figures, lines, rules, and ornaments that constitute the sign system upon which the book depends." Perhaps most of all, he understood that a well-designed title page could move a nonchalant customer to purchase the book. Richardson's correspondence makes clear that he thought long and hard about title pages as a key marketing strategy to attract readers. In that sense, long subtitles served as a book's advertisement, as is evident from the heavily worded and illustrated title page for *Pamela* (see Figure 5.1).[6]

Pamela, Or Virtue Rewarded; *Clarissa, or the History of a Young Lady*; and *The History of Sir Charles Grandison*, Richardson's three masterpieces, were written and published between 1740 and 1761, the final two decades of his life. Literary historians agree that together they constitute a major pillar of the emerging modern novel. Richardson painted his characters with such psychological depth that some readers experienced them as virtual friends. As Table 6.1 illustrates, each of his novels became more popular than the one before. While *Grandison* may have gone through the most editions, scholars generally cite Clarissa as his most compelling work, and the one that certainly had the most influence on Enlightenment thinkers such as Denis Diderot. Nonetheless, because the composition of *Pamela* was surprising and almost unintended and led to public arguments over the moral behavior of his eponymous protagonist, it deserves to be studied for its affect upon the social history of reading.[7]

Sometime in 1739 booksellers J. Osborn and C. Rivington asked Richardson if he might create a book for young adults that exhibited different styles of letter-writing, a skill increasingly necessary to various paths to social advancement. Harking back to his days helping the ladies, Richardson gladly accepted the task and set to work on it. While the main point of the book would be exhibiting different types and styles of letter-writing (e.g., to a parent, to a patron, to a friend), he decided that it might be fun to apply his imagination to unify the content of the letters into a single story. He tried to picture himself in the mind of a teenager, whom he named Pamela Andrews, and what might she write about as a household servant, not unlike his intended readers. At first, these were supposed to be simply exercises in model letters. But after the first few examples from Pamela to her parents, he found himself writing a story with a complicated a dramatic plot. With little planning, he furiously wrote everyday for two months between November 1739 and January 1740. In that way, *Pamela* was created more or less spontaneously by a printer who never imagined himself a novelist until the deed was done. *Pamela* was far from the project for which he was commissioned. So, shortly after his novel was published, Richardson made good on the original project, *Letters Written to and for Particular Friends, on the Most Important Occasions*, which appeared anonymously in 1741. Richardson reprinted it five times during his lifetime.[8]

After some months of rewriting and printing, including showing the manuscript to a few choice friends, Osborn and Rivington published *Pamela, or Virtue Rewarded* in November 1740. Readers entered the story at the point when the chambermaid Pamela Andrews's luck had soured. For a few years, Pamela had the good fortune to work for an aristocratic widow of a great estate, Lady B, who treated her very well. She taught Pamela the rudiments of music and sewing, and encouraged Pamela's book reading. Unfortunately, this generous mistress suddenly died, leaving her young adult son and newcomer in the House of Lords, Mr. B, in charge of the household. This new situation spelled danger for Pamela. Through letters to her parents and a private journal, we learn from Pamela that Mr. B does everything possible short of rape to seduce her. The plot revolves around her noble efforts to defend her virginity and, more impressively, her ability to convert Mr. B from a sex-hungry rake to a virtuous gentleman. Mr. B's admiration and respect for Pamela's personality and character marks the end of that process. Their marriage demonstrates both his virtue and their mutual love, and the novel concludes with Pamela emerging as a model wife and mistress of the household she first entered as a servant.

This Cinderella story is, in fact, less about Pamela Andrews than Mr. B. Although Pamela's status changes in the novel from servant to noble wife, her character remains the same: she models virtue from beginning to end. While Mr. B's status remains unchanged—he is never dislodged as master of the household—his character's transformation drives the novel's tension and plot, as Pamela continually questions whether his changes are real or just a rake's way to undermine her virtue. What caused Mr. B to grow into a gentleman? In something of a tour de force, making the epistolary form of the novel central to its plot, Richardson has Mr. B reform himself through reading Pamela's letters and journals. He secretly intercepts Pamela's letters to her parents, and there he encounters her emotions, feelings, and intent. He begins to understand, and, more important, to have empathy for her character and personality. Over several months, his lust is superseded by the recognition of her very special individuality as he grows to love the young woman he reads about in her letters. He invariably treats Pamela with more respect, despite her lowly origins.

The novel, then, is an investigation of what it means to be a gentleman. In this respect, it is worth noting that just prior to writing *Pamela*, Richardson had printed these words when producing an edition of the Roman writer Seneca: "Of the true and false Nobility ... Who then is a Nobleman, or a Gentleman? He who hath naturally a good Disposition to Virtue. This is all that is to be consider'd in the Case.... It is the Mind which makes a Man noble."[9] The novel's subtitle, "Virtue Rewarded," is usually understood from

Pamela's viewpoint—her virtue was rewarded with her new class rank—but the subtitle equally applies to Mr. B, who after becoming a gentleman is rewarded with Pamela.

Since the novel is narrated only through Pamela's letters and journals, Mr. B is, in effect, the novel's first reader. And insofar as he is also the book's ideal reader, the novel demonstrates the power of reading to improve one's character. If Mr. B himself can become a paragon of virtue through reading Pamela's letters, so can every reader of her letters. The book, then, asks readers to see a young servant girl as an autonomous human worthy of respect, and to align their behavior accordingly. In this sense, the novel conflates the reader's own moral improvement with social change. Richardson's extended title made this goal clear: "In order to cultivate the principles of virtue and religion in the minds of the youth of both sexes" (see Figure 6.1).

We should not underestimate the originality of Richardson's project. Until *Pamela*, novels were a popular, if low, form of entertainment, involving adventure stories, often in exotic lands, and usually including characters of high birth. *Pamela* goes against this grain. The plot in particular is odd for popular fiction, because in the traditional sense very little happens; that is, the characters remain in their rural English surroundings, and Pamela's letters are filled not so much with exciting adventures, but mostly with wordy reflections on daily trials, such as her efforts at sewing clothes from fabric given to her by Lady B. Thus, the book's first innovation was to forsake large-scale action in favor of dwelling instead upon Pamela's feelings and aspirations. Richardson's second innovation was perceiving the world and its power structures from the perspective of an ordinary servant. The traditional way to have told the story would have been from the perspective of the great lord, Mr. B, who managed to learn virtue from his employee. Given that the story is really about his actions, it would have been more traditional for his character to have memorialized these events, as Usbek does in *Persian Letters*. If Roxana had written most of the letters in Montesquieu's novel, her own agency would have arguably made that novel even more radical. By situating the story from Pamela's worldview, and especially within only her letters, Richardson challenged readers to care about the everyday concerns of a simple chambermaid.

Unlike today, domestic servants were ubiquitous during the eighteenth century, serving in all households except the poorest. Given the labor necessary for housecleaning, cooking, gardening, and child care, it was as difficult for working-class and middle-class families to do without them as aristocratic ones. Before the nineteenth century, working as a servant in a stranger's home was a stage in life common for young women from approximately age fifteen to around twenty-five, when first marriage typically occurred "late" in Western Europe and Britain. Such servants generally moved jobs from year to year, saving up cash toward a dowry or sending money home to their families. They constituted the largest single occupation in eighteenth-century England.[10]

From the start of the novel, Pamela's father, Goodman Andrews, worries that Mr. B's ascension to household power spells trouble for his daughter. He had good reason to be concerned. Sexual harassment was a constant problem for these young working women, who typically grew up in a village many miles from the homes where they worked. Nothing prevented masters from taking advantage of them, and throughout eighteenth-century Europe, many male householders did just that. Roughly half the servants in eighteenth-century France, according to Cissie Fairchilds, were abused by their masters. She tells the story of one Thérèse Cavaillon, who was pursued and harassed by the son of her mistress. She tried to hide in her tiny attic room, "but one day he forced his way in and raped her at knife-point."[11] If the story of Pamela Andrews seemed real and immediate to British and continental readers, it was because for them stories about the fate of servant girls were as familiar as common fairy tales. In the months preceding *Pamela*'s original publication, for example, one English newspaper, the *Universal Spectator*, told the story of the servant Honoria, favored by the lady of the house, fending off romantic advances by her son.[12]

By viewing the world through Pamela's eyes, Richardson's readers saw a vulnerable young woman with social aspirations confronted with obstacles that greatly reduced liberty and opportunity. Class, gender, and political stratification all conspired against Pamela. In lauding England as the government that best treated its ordinary people, Voltaire's *Philosophical Letters* seemed to view the situation a bit too much from the upper crust's perspective; it is instructive that his book never addresses the liberty of servants like Pamela. When viewed from her vantage point, England seemed more tyrannical than Voltaire thought.

The central question asked by Richardson in *Pamela* is the extent to which an ordinary servant girl is entitled to liberty and autonomy.[13] Does she have a right to keep her body away from the coercive designs of the male householder, or, in eighteenth-century England were such Lockean rights guaranteed only to propertied men? Pamela asks this question herself: "And pray, said I, walking on, how came I to be his Property? What Right has he in me, but such as a Thief may plead to stolen Goods?" Her rhetorical question, of course, paraphrased a well-known principle in Locke's *Second Treatise*: "Every man has a Property in his own Person. This no Body has any Right to but himself."[14] Pamela has no problem with class stratification itself; rather, it is the character of the British aristocracy that bothers her. She constantly reminds Mr. B. that his obligation as a born aristocrat is to protect rather than violate her natural right to physical autonomy: "But O Sir! My Soul is of equal Importance with the Soul of a Princess; though my Quality is inferior to that of the meanest Slave."[15]

Pamela was first published in a relatively inexpensive duodecimo format in November 1740, but in a business practice that is still with us today, Richardson stamped 1741 onto the title page to make the book appear new for as long as possible. "I can send you no news; the late singular novel is the universal, and only theme," wrote bon vivant Horace Walpole shortly after its initial publication.[16] Later novelist Clara Reeve recalled this moment in 1741 or 1742 when "the person that had not read *Pamela* was disqualified for conversation, of which it was the principal subject for a long time."[17] Almost immediately, Richardson—acting again as his own printer—began preparing for a second edition, which appeared in February 1741. *The Gentleman's Magazine* for January 1741 noted that "it being judged in Town as great a Sign of Want of Curiosity not to have read *Pamela*, as not to have seen the French and Italian Dancers."[18]

Meanwhile, 3,000 copies of a third edition sold out in two months. By the end of 1741, five authorized editions had been published. Perhaps already a total of 20,000 copies were circulating, a large number for any eighteenth-century book. In addition, there were at least two unauthorized reprints from 1741 (London and Dublin), a newspaper serialization of the novel, and an authorized French translation that was published in London intended mainly for a domestic market. The next year, Richardson printed a more lavish octavo edition that cost double the duodecimo and included over twenty-five original illustrations by noted artists Hubert Gravelot and Francis Hayman, as well as a greatly expanded table of contents that summarized each letter. Indeed, this octavo edition is the only one of his three novels for which Richardson authorized illustrations.[19] Clearly intended to be a collector's item for serious book buyers, the octavo edition sold very slowly, but it did not discourage more duodecimo editions or translations. Within five years of its original publication, the novel was translated into Danish, Dutch, German, Italian, and, most importantly, into French, probably by the well-known writer, the Abbé Prévost. The soon-to-be famous Benjamin Franklin was the first printer in colonial America to domestically produce a work of fiction when he printed *Pamela* in 1742.[20]

As the printer of his own work, Richardson was able to make changes in a way that could only be envied by other authors such as Voltaire. Richardson constantly reread his novels, looking for opportunities to improve them. Always a businessman sensitive to the marketplace, he welcomed letters from readers and closely read reviews. As he approached a new edition, he routinely made changes that responded to his readers. Usually these were small matters of wording or tone. The second edition of *Pamela*, for example, included some 841 changes. By the time he published the octavo edition in 1742, Richardson had made over 2,500 changes to *Pamela*, and he would obsessively continue to make changes to all his novels until his death in 1761. Surely no other major eighteenth-century author had such access to tinkering with the printing press as Richardson. The novelty of a printer producing his own bestseller was duly noted in this epigram that appeared in the April 1741 *Daily Advertiser* under the heading "Advice to Booksellers (After reading Pamela)":

Since Printers with such pleasing Nature write,
And since so awkwardly your Scribes indite,
Be wise in Time, and take a friendly Hint;
Let Printers write, and let your Writers print.[21]

Richardson and his bookseller partners had exclusive rights to produce Pamela in England (though not in Ireland or Scotland). But that did not stop many imitators from appropriating the name of his heroine. During the eighteenth century, copyright might exist for a particular work, but it did not extend to a brand. An author such as Eliza Haywood could title a work having nothing to do with Pamela Andrews, *Anti-Pamela*, in order to garner some popularity. At one point, Richardson counted sixteen such works appearing in London alone. *Pamela* became ripe material for dramatists who turned Richardson's novel into unauthorized plays, musicals, and operas. Already in the autumn of 1741, the famous actor David Garrick was staring in one dramatization that played for seventeen nights in London. The next year, a ballad opera was serialized in a London newspaper. There were also countless compilations and abridgements, such as the juvenile *History of Pamela, Abridged*, that, by 1771, had found its way to a Boston bookseller. Imitations and adaptations of *Pamela* appeared everywhere.[22]

Richardson took these imitations and parodies in his stride, hoping that their general effect would be to drive more sales of the novel; there is no evidence from his correspondence that he was offended by them or thought he deserved to share their revenue. Likewise, he accepted that there was little he could do the so-called pirated editions from Dublin; he recognized that it was legal for Dubliners to reprint his books without his permission.[23] It was only when other booksellers financed a sequel to the novel—*Pamela's Conduct in High Life*—that Richardson declared foul play. Through letters and advertisements in the press, Richardson asserted that no one but he, the original creator of Pamela Andrews, had the moral right to continue her story. For Richardson, sequels were distinct from adaptations and even compilations. But the producers of *Pamela's Conduct in High Life* would not back down, and their sequel appeared in May 1741, barely six months after the original *Pamela* had come off the presses. Richardson's anger led him to write his own sequel, *Pamela in Her Exalted Condition*, also published in December 1741 as the third and fourth volumes of *Pamela*. Sold always as the final pair in a four-volume set, it is generally regarded as Richardson's weakest fictional effort and rarely commented upon by readers and critics.[24]

Adaptations and dramatizations became even more popular on the continent, where thousands of Europeans turned out for the many dramatizations that took place in virtually every major European city during the mid-eighteenth century. Among the most popular were the play and opera by the Venetian dramatist Carlo Goldoni. In 1750, his own play, *Pamela nubile*, first produced in Venice, quickly became a staple of theatre companies across Europe and was immediately translated into English, French, Dutch, Danish, German, Polish, Spanish, and even Norwegian. In 1756, Goldoni rewrote the play as a libretto for possible adaptation into an opera. No fewer than three composers took him up on the idea, but the version that caught the strongest wind was *La buona figliuola*, by Niccolò Piccinni, which, from its premiere in 1760, became "one of the greatest hits of the century."[25]

It is likely that more continental Europeans saw these dramatizations than read the best-selling novel itself. If so, it is important to note that they heard a more conservative message from Goldoni and other European adaptors than they would have from Richardson. Goldoni watered down Pamela's class transgression by revealing that her ancestors were highborn aristocrats; the marriage then restores Pamela to her rightful class.[26] Nonetheless, even in Goldoni, Pamela delivers a message deeply critical of the aristocracy. "We have two things that are equal, and these are reason and honour," she tells the Mr. B character. "You will not give me to understand that you have any authority over my honour because reason teaches me that that is a treasure independent of who one is." Despite a more conventional plot, Goldoni maintained Richardson's faithfulness to Locke's principles.[27]

We first get a glimpse of the quality of public reaction to *Pamela* from Richardson's own friends. Aaron Hill read through both volumes of *Pamela* aloud to his family nearly every evening in early December 1740. In addition to his daughters and wife, there was present a small "gentle" and "gay-spirited" orphan boy adopted by the family. He demanded to be there whenever Hill read *Pamela*. After a few evenings, he "got half her sayings by heart" and spoke "in no other language but hers." But what truly "has charmed me into a certain foretaste of [Pamela's] influence, he has, at once, become fond of his books, which he could never be brought to attend to [before, so] that he may read *Pamela*, he says without stopping." Hill's reading *Pamela* aloud to his family inspired this boy to learn how to read books for himself. Hill also reported that one night when they entertained company so that the boy was not welcome, he nevertheless snuck in during the ritual *Pamela* evening reading. The "intruder, being kept out by the extent of the circle, had crept under my chair; and was sitting before me on the carpet, with his head almost touching the book, and his face bowing down toward the fire," Hill told Richardson. The boy "sat for some time in this posture, with a stillness that made us conclude him asleep; when on a sudden we heard a succession of heart-heaving sobs, which, while he strove to conceal from our notice, his little sides swelled as if they would burst, with the throbbing restraint of his sorrow." Hill concluded that the boy must be "perhaps the youngest of Pamela's converts."[28]

Such evening readings were not limited to the Hill household. *Pamela* likely reached from elite families beyond the middle class, attracting even working-class households where a parent or grandparent was literate; what Hill defined for Richardson as "a new rank of purchasers."[29] The early nineteenth-century Glasgow printer Richard Griffin looked back to his eighteenth-century childhood, fondly recalling his grandmother reading *Pamela* aloud to the working-class household during winter evenings. Griffin's grandmother was no bluestocking. Her favorite book was the Bible, and *Pamela* was the only novel Griffin observed her reading. But read it she did, following afternoon tea with an intensity and with such emotion that the experience helped determine his future reading life. "She would read aloud to the listening family, page after page, with the most supreme satisfaction," recalled Griffin decades later, "snuffing and commenting at every paragraph, and never stopping short, except when she lighted upon some thrilling passage of the bewitching author, where her voice would fail her, and her lip would quiver, and she could not go on for very fulness of heart." When Griffin woke in the morning, he was consumed with what he had heard the evening before, and would spend the day telling his friends as much of the plot as he could recall.[30]

Abigail Adams echoed Hill and Griffin's perspective regarding *Pamela* in a letter to her niece written from London during the 1780s, where her husband John was the first US ambassador there. By then, Adams had read *Clarissa* and *Grandison*, but her remarks applied "even to his *Pamela*." What made them all compelling, she thought, was their setting in "old corrupted countries" and not in a republic like the United States.

Virtue in England was under constant assault, and it took an author like Richardson to show how it was possible to navigate such adversity. Like Hill and Richardson himself, Adams believed that reading a Richardson novel was itself edifying and self-improving. "Indeed, I know not how a person can read them without being made better by them, as they dispose the mind to receive and relish every good and benevolent principle."[31]

In contrast to *Clarissa* and *Grandison*, *Pamela* was not simply popular; it was also controversial. Throughout London and soon across much of continent—in homes, schools, workshops, and coffee houses—Europeans argued over Pamela Andrews, sorting themselves into factions. "There are swarms of moral romances," wrote the Danish writer Ludwig Holberg in a 1744 book of moral essays, soon reproduced in a British newspaper. "One, of late Date, divided the World into such opposite Judgments, that some extolled it to the Stars, whilst others treated it with Contempt. Whence arose, particularly among the Ladies, two different Parties, Pamelists and Antipamelists."[32] The Pamelists defended Pamela's honor and virtue as a model to be championed and imitated. The Anti-Pamelists tended to have a much more cynical view of Pamela's motives. For them, she was a social-climbing money-hungry hypocrite who lured her young lord through erotic gestures. The Pamelist/Anti-Pamelist controversy raged throughout the 1740s and 1750s in several European countries and colonies, producing not only literary and theatrical adaptations, but even paraphernalia such as fans and illustration sets sold from stores.

In fact, given the length and range of this controversy, it is not surprising that it was as socially layered as the society around it and never about one particular issue. Gender, sexuality, and class were often conflated in efforts to forge a coherent popular morality. Many readers were put off by what they saw as Pamela's conceit, finding such amour propre inconsistent with virtue. Others found the book more romantic than instructive in virtue. One Anti-Pamelist bookseller even advertised together the pornographic *Pleasures of Conjugal Love Revealed* as "of the same Letter and Size with *Pamela*, and very proper to be bound with it."[33] Another critic charged that by exploiting the epistolary form, Richardson had taught a generation of girls how to write long letters that made much of nothing.[34] Shortly before his death, the octogenarian Charles Povey condemned the novel for inviting erotic responses and driving young people toward libertinism. "Good God! What can Youths and Virgins learn from Pamela's Letters, more than Lessons to tempt their Chastity; those Epistles are only Scenes of Immodesty, painted in Images of Virtue."[35] For these critics Richardson was not trying to apply Locke's notions to everyday situations but passing off soft erotica to young readers. By far, the most famous expression of Anti-Pamela sentiment was Henry Fielding's *Shamela* (April 1741), which imagined Pamela as a selfish brat with a huge teenage ego and an uncanny ability to make herself physically attractive to her master. For a brief moment Fielding's satire seems to have taken London by storm, as is evident from this epigram that appeared in the June 1741 *London Magazine*:

Admir'd Pamela, till Shamela shown,
Appear'd in every colour—but her own.[36]

Fielding's brilliant parody may have won respect from other literary critics at the time, but it was short-lived and not nearly as popular as the book that inspired it. *Shamela* went through only two London editions in 1741 and one Dublin reprint, but never translated into French, much less other languages. It was even excluded from the fourteen-volume collection of Fielding's works published in Geneva as well as from the twenty-three-volume set published in Paris.[37]

By 1750, *Pamela* had "met with very extra ordinary (and I think undeserved) success," reported Lady Mary Wortley Montagu, whose letters to her daughter, Lady Bute, featured a running commentary on Richardson's three novels. "It has been translated into French and into Italian; it was all the fashion at Paris and Versailles, and is still the Joy of the chambermaids of all nations." Like other readers, Montagu felt ambivalent about how Richardson's direct writing style affected her own emotions. Clearly Richardson's sentimentality made her uncomfortable; she was not quite sure what to make of it. On the one hand, she dismissed Pamela Andrews as an upstart and worried that Richardson's "mischief" undermined the clear and stable distinctions among classes, "confounding of all ranks and making a jest of order." Montagu resented the way Richardson endowed a simple domestic servant with the virtue usually reserved for a noble lady. "The heroes and heroines of the age are cobblers and kitchen wenches," she derisively remarked. But she nonetheless couldn't stop reading him. She wrote to friends that she had become addicted to his prose, which made her laugh and cry. Richardson taught the aristocratic Montagu empathy for commoners almost against her will, for which she felt a sense of guilt. "This Richardson is a strange fellow," she wrote in 1755. "I heartily despise him and eagerly read him, nay, sob over his works in the most scandalous manner." Montagu knew she was being manipulated; she realized that Richardson was "ignorant in morality," but she felt a guilty pleasure reading him nonetheless.[38] A similar reaction came from John Douglas, bishop of Salisbury, who confessed to Richardson that he could not get beyond the baliff scene in *Clarissa*. When Douglas saw that Richardson seemed offended, he explained that he could not finish the novel because his mental state had become unsteady—"he was drowned in tears, and could not trust himself with the book any longer."[39]

On the continent, Europeans first tended to treat *Pamela* as a book for women. One close observer noted if you asked Parisian women in groups of two or three, they will tell you that the "book is more perfect than the Gospels," but when you question them alone, they will confess that *Pamela* is full of faults that make it insufferably "boring."[40] Such ambivalence indicated how popular the novel was, especially among female readers: even those who found it boring felt obligated to read it. Likewise, as soon as German translations were prepared, one German periodical advised women to regard *Pamela* as required reading in the same syllabus as "a Bible, a catechism, a prayer book and hymn book, [and] a cookbook."[41]

Some conservative critics in Europe worried like Lady Montagu that *Pamela* encouraged insubordination. The Austrian professor Joseph von Sonnenfels put it this way in a weekly newspaper: "The wench falls in love with her master who is so far above her. That is just not edifying . . . . I am forever tempted to tear the whole book from that girl's hand."⁴² Meanwhile, another German writer expressed similar sentiments regarding class transgression in a 1776 play: "Your only mistake," one character tells another, "was that you did not know the world, that you did not know the governing difference between the different ranks, that you have read *Pamela*, the most dangerous book that a person of your rank can read."⁴³

A more generous, if ambivalent, response came from the twenty-year-old South Carolina plantation manager, Eliza Lucas. By May 1742, she had completed all four volumes, the last two of which had been published only months earlier. "She is a good girl and as such I love her dearly," Lucas wrote in a letter to a friend. "But I must think her very defective and even blush for her while she allows herself that disgusting liberty of praising herself, or what is very like it, repeating all the fine speeches made to her by others." Lucas found this defect inexcusable, a demonstration less of Pamela's false virtue than of her immaturity. After all, many of the compliments Pamela received come from those close to her, showing "the partiality of her friends or with a view to encourage her" to reach her aspiration toward virtue. Lucas confessed this was partially her experience as well: this "I know experimentally to be often the case." But as a judge weighing all the evidence, Lucas tried to look at the other side of the question. "But then you answer she was a young Country Girl had seen nothing of life and it was natural for her to be pleased with praise." Lucas recognized that the sheltered fifteen-year-old was out of her league, and her own insecurity made her want to take these compliments to heart. For that reason, Lucas could point out Pamela's defects, but she could hardly blame her. At the end of the day, Lucas refused to cross over to the Anti-Pamelists. "That is, I think the Author has" portrayed "one of the greatest beauties" in literature and it would not be realistic if "his Heroin no defect the character."⁴⁴

Another American woman about the same age as Eliza Lucas was equally ambivalent about *Pamela*, but for different reasons. Esther Edwards Burr (daughter of Jonathan Edwards and mother of Aaron Burr) read the novel in March and April 1755. She reacted to the plot as if her emotions were on a roller coaster. She was bitterly angry that Pamela could let herself fall in love with a man that had tried to rape her. "How could Pamela forgive Mr. B all his Devilish conduct so as to consent to marry him?" Not yet halfway through the story, Burr decided it was wrong, even misogynist, for Richardson to devise the plot in that way. "I am quite angry with Mr. Fielding," she wrote mistaking Richardson for Henry Fielding. "He has degraded our sex most horridly, to go and represent such virtue as Pamela, falling in love with Mr. B in the midst of such foul and abominable actions." But Burr soon changed her mind. She admired the marital relationship between the two protagonists, and by the end Richardson's plot had worn down her resistance. "I am highly pleased with some of Pamela's remarks on Married life, as well as her conduct in it. She was more than Woman—an Angel [e]mbodied." Finally, after finishing the novel on Friday morning, April 11, juggling the book with baby Sally on her lap, she wrote: "Well, Pamela's virtue is rewarded at last, Mr. B is [sic] become a good Man."⁴⁵

Over the course of the century, as Richardson's reputation grew with the publication of *Clarissa* (1747–8) and *Sir Charles Grandison* (1753), readers argued about the place *Pamela* deserved in Richardson's corpus. During the 1780s, poet Anna Seward became outraged when novelist Clara Reeve's self-published book about the rise of the novel declared *Pamela* Richardson's chief masterpiece. Immediately she penned an emphatic complaint for the *Gentleman's Magazine*. She refused to believe that Reeve would be "ridiculous enough to place Richardson's two immortal works, *Grandison* and *Clarissa*, below his perishable *Pamela*." Just thinking about it, Seward charged, made her almost physically ill; the words "pain as well as disgust me." At that point Seward attributed Reeve's motivation to enhancing her own importance. If *Pamela* was literature's pinnacle, then Clara Reeve's minor novel (*The Old English Baron* had just been published in 1777) might also be recognized for such genius. Finally, as if concluding her case in court, Seward mustered a closing statement: "No person endowed with any refinement of perception, any accuracy of judgment, can think *Pamela* superior to *Grandison* and *Clarissa*."[46]

Seward's perspective aside—and it has become the standard view today—in Catholic Europe it was *Pamela* and not *Clarissa* or *Grandison* that was feared by church authorities as a subversive text. Only the fear of its spreading message can explain why the Catholic Church placed *Pamela* on its Index of Forbidden Books in 1744. After all, it was only the second British piece of fiction to obtain such an "honor"—Swift's *Tale of the Tub* was placed there in 1734. The church did not want ordinary Catholics reading about a servant who used her homespun brand of lukewarm Anglicanism to challenge male aristocratic authority. What was parodied in England by Fielding as a rather silly tale was seen at least by some Catholic Church authorities as dangerous enough to warrant official suppression. The church's success in this endeavor can be seen in the novel's publication history on the continent: while produced in most Northern European languages, in Catholic Southern Europe, there were no Italian or Portuguese eighteenth-century translations of *Pamela*, and the first Spanish translation was published only in 1799. Richardson, who is today almost never regarded as any sort of political or social radical, achieved a spot on the Index several years ahead of Montesquieu, Voltaire, and Rousseau. Meanwhile, these major philosophes saw the potential of the epistolary novel for serving as social criticism, and they were determined to appropriate *Pamela* as a canonical Enlightenment book.

In 1749, less than a decade after the initial publication of Richardson's novel, Voltaire came out with *Nanine*, his own theatrical version of *Pamela*.[47] The story is very similar to Richardson's, except that the heroine is given a noble ancestry, like Goldoni's version, toning down the social message of the original. Performed sparingly until the end of the 1750s, when the Comédie-Française produced around a dozen performances, *Nanine* eventually became among Voltaire's most popular plays, with over 100 performances produced during the French Revolution. In a moment of self-referential wit, Nanine is given a novel to read—it is none other than *Pamela*—and she criticizes Richardson's progressive views as more radical than her own: "The author endeavors to prove that all mankind are brethren, born equal and on a level with each other; but it is a mere chimera. I cannot coincide with his opinion." In this weird way, Voltaire projected onto Richardson the ambitions of a progressive philosophe such as Rousseau, and by the time of the French Revolution, that's what audiences wanted to hear.

In 1750 Prussian king Frederick II invited Voltaire to live as resident philosopher at his Potsdam court outside Berlin. For years, Voltaire and the king had had a close relationship through letters, and Voltaire had helped edit Frederick's *Anti-Machiavel*. Instead of censorship and harassment, here was a European monarch welcoming advice from the philosophe. All went well for about a couple of years, and then their relationship soured. Voltaire and Frederick began to argue over Voltaire's own liberty to travel and write as he pleased, and soon the king appeared to the older Voltaire more as a despot than as a royal patron. Finally, Voltaire resigned his post at court, and headed for Paris. Frederick ordered his henchmen to detain the great philosophe in Frankfurt, where he spent a few weeks under house arrest. Voltaire finally left Prussia for Geneva in 1753.[48]

Frederick's detention of a philosopher reminded Voltaire of Mr. B's detention of Pamela at Lincolnshire, prompting him to write a memoir of the Prussian experience in the form of an epistolary novel composed of letters to his niece, Madame Denis, supposedly written earlier, when he lived in Berlin. "It's really a work in the style of *Pamela*," he wrote about his intention. But this was no ordinary version of that novel. In composing letters about the abusive treatment he had received from Frederick, Voltaire placed himself in the position of Pamela Andrews, the poor servant girl, and reimagined Frederick as having played the role of the villainous Mr. B. Voltaire's version explored the political possibilities in *Pamela*, absurdly, if insightfully, showing the emotional scars of such political and more intimate abuse. Where Richardson's *Pamela* barely scratched the service of criticizing political authority, Voltaire's *Paméla* vividly showed that too much political power in the hands of a monarch rendered personal liberty fragile. Ruled by a narcissistic young tyrant, Prussia was no England, and Voltaire's attempts to convert Frederick to Fénelonian virtue obviously failed. No wonder Voltaire never prepared this manuscript for publication. Unlike most of his other writings, Voltaire wrote *Paméla* mostly for himself, never intending to publish the "novel"; instead, he called it a book "for the nineteenth century." Nonetheless, the fact that Voltaire spent such effort composing this Pamela adaptation demonstrates just how much Richardson's novel meant to him.[49]

Jean Jacques Rousseau too used Richardson's epistolary form to further his own notions about society. Only months before publishing his two masterpieces of social theory and moral philosophy, *The Social Contract* and *Emile*, Rousseau produced his own Richardsonian epistolary novel, originally entitled *Lettres de deux amans, habitans d'une petite ville au pied des Alpes* (Letters from Two Lovers, Living in a Small Town at the Foot of the Alps), soon known throughout Europe by its subtitle, *Julie, ou la nouvelle Héloïse* (Julie or the New Héloïse). Rousseau borrowed Richardson's techniques, particularly those displayed in *Clarissa*, in such a way that readers came to feel intimate with his characters, sobbing with Julie and Saint-Preux, as they nobly tried to forge a special bond that went against corrupt social customs. As Robert Darnton has so well described, fan mail descended on Rousseau begging for more details and hoping to engage the author in discussions over the moral choices made by his characters.[50]

Twenty years after Rousseau's *New Héloïse*, a disciple published a novel that became incendiary during the years just prior to the French Revolution. Indeed, not long after publishing *Les Liaisons dangereuse*, Choderlos de Laclos became a French Revolutionary activist, where he employed Rousseau's ideas to dismantle the legal system that underlay aristocratic privilege. In his 1782 novel, Laclos used a Richardsonian approach to thoroughly discredit the French aristocracy. His debt to Richardson is made clear when a character reads *Clarissa*. Laclos took from Richardson the psychological realism made possible by the epistolary style, but he also, like Richardson, featured the letters themselves as part of the plot. Whereas Mr. B is reformed through reading Pamela's letters, the evil intent of Laclos's noble letter writers is exposed when their private correspondence is leaked to the public. Laclos reached conclusions that are nearly the opposite of Richardson's: whereas *Clarissa* and *Pamela* were written to improve the English nobility, Laclos's more cynical plot was meant to show that the aristocracy in France was beyond any possibility of reform and had lost its legitimacy to rule. Where Richardson hoped to save the aristocracy, Laclos in 1782 wanted to destroy it. Laclos demonstrated how powerful fiction can be when Richardson's epistolary format is combined with Rousseau's political radicalism.[51]

Montesquieu, Voltaire, Rousseau, and Laclos did not regard Richardson as a philosopher, nor did they see his novels as laying out even the basis for a new set of Enlightenment moral principles, as, for example, David Hume did in 1751 with his *Enquiry Concerning the Principles of Morals*, or what Adam Smith produced in 1759 with his *Theory of Moral Sentiments*. Rather, these philosophes marveled at Richardson's ability to take a low form of literature—the romance novel—and infuse it with such moral and even political intensity that a reading public became consumed with debating the story's meaning and moral consequences. Even in his *Moral Sentiments*, Smith noted that Richardson was better than philosophers like himself at conveying moral ideas.[52] Likewise, just before his death, Montesquieu recognized that what he was trying to do in 1721 was a rehearsal for what Richardson achieved in 1740.[53] But Montesquieu's characters do not achieve the psychological depth and verisimilitude of Richardson's. Indeed, it was only after Richardson, Fielding, and Sterne produced their masterpieces that *Persian Letters* acquired more respect as serious literature.

Montesquieu, Voltaire, Rousseau, and Laclos all bent their knee to Richardson. However, the philosophe who recognized the full potential of his innovations for Enlightenment literature was Denis Diderot. When Diderot began reading Richardson is unclear; but certainly, no reader ever read him more closely. After Diderot learned of Richardson's death on July 4, 1761, it took him only twenty-four hours to pen a 6,500-word eulogistic essay that he placed in the January 1762 issue of the *Journal étranger*. Reprinted in literary anthologies and attached to French editions of *Clarissa*, this emotional outburst from Diderot described in very personal terms what it was like for him to read Richardson, whose books "have been my touchstone."⁵⁴ He would walk with Richardson's characters in his head, arguing with them over the moral decisions they had made. When his lover, Sophie Volland, seemed not to appreciate the importance of a common servant's virginity, Diderot issued her a stern rebuke:

How tiny you see the subject of *Pamela*! What a pity! No, Mademoiselle, no:

Pamela is not the story of a maid harassed by a young libertine. It is the combat of virtue, religion, decency, truth, and goodness, but without strength, without protection, demeaned, if it is possible for virtue to be so, in all imaginable circumstances, by dependence, abjection and poverty, against grandeur, opulence, vice and all its infernal powers.⁵⁵

Part of Sophie's problem may have been that she read *Pamela* in French, while Diderot apparently read Richardson in the original English. "If you have only read Richardson's works in your elegant French translation, and think you know them, you are wrong."⁵⁶

Shortly before writing his essay on Richardson, Diderot composed his most Richardsonian novel, *The Nun*, distributed in limited manuscript copies until published posthumously in 1796. *The Nun* is simultaneously Pamelist and Anti-Pamelist; indeed, it dissolves differences between the two sides. Like *Pamela*, *The Nun* is an epistolary novel in the first person of an adolescent girl who is sexually abused. Like *Pamela*, *The Nun* features a pious Christian girl who appears to be the epitome of virtue and who is battling narrow social conventions in order to obtain her dignity, freedom, and autonomy. But if read slightly differently, *The Nun* is also an equally Anti-Pamelist tract as it reveals its protagonist to be anything but virtuous. She emerges as a manipulating seducer using Christianity and fake appeals to virtue only to further her own interests. *The Nun* is not a parody like *Shamela*. Its brilliance is that it can be simultaneously *Pamela* and a tragic tale much darker than *Shamela*. Diderot's short novel is an exploration of the power of the epistolary form itself, and a recognition that the point of the modern novel is to beam moral dilemmas from the story's fictional character onto the reader's own consciousness.⁵⁷

Suzanne Simonin is the name of Diderot's Pamela. She writes a letter to the Marquis de Croismare for help. He owns a chateau in Normandy and she needs to find stable employment in a safe space. Years earlier, her parents forced her into a convent, and most of the novel is Suzanne's retelling of her trials and tribulations there. Although Suzanne claims to be a pious Christian, she has no interest in being a nun, and experiences coercion and oppression everywhere. One Mother Superior treats her harshly and despotically, while another makes sexual moves on her. In her desperation for freedom, she accepts aid from a priest who helps her escape, only to be abused by him on the journey. At the end of her long letter to Croismare, she is working in a Paris laundry. Unable to support herself, she seems one step away from prostitution.

Diderot left many clues for the careful reader to perceive his double-edged approach. The key lies in the format of a long letter that instead of writing to the moment, as in *Pamela*, looks back a distance of several months. That is, when Pamela writes her letters, she describes events that occurred only moments before. But when Suzanne narrates her story for Croismare, the events she describes occurred months earlier. Suzanne tells us that when the Mother Superior made sexual advances to her, she innocently had no idea what it meant, and so she in no way can be held responsible for her actions. "She said a hundred sweet things to me and stroked me a thousand times, which made me feel rather awkward," Suzanne recalled. "But I do not know why, because I did not know what was happening and neither did she, and even now as I think back over it, what could we have possibly known?" Of course, by this time several months have passed, and she has learned that her abuser had been removed because of the homosexual affair she consummated with Suzanne, so when she writes her long letter to Croismare she certainly knows the nature of what occurred. Similarly, when Suzanne is later interrogated by a priest over the relationship, she describes it this way: "He asked me a thousand strange things which even now, as I recall them, I still do not understand."[58] In fact, the point of her interview with the priest was precisely to make her aware of what had occurred, so that "even now" she would understand. As William Edminston observed: "The narrating self often appears to be hardly more knowledgeable than the experiencing self, as though there were virtually no temporal distance between event and narration." The time difference between experiencing and narrating allows Suzanne more time for retrospection. If writing like Pamela about events that happened only moments earlier, such a naïve position might make sense, because there would have been no time for reflection. Insofar as Suzanne's narration contradicts her own retrospection, she reveals herself to be without virtue.[59] *The Nun* is among other things a novel of seduction. Suzanne asks the Marquis de Croismare for a job like Pamela's, and she is offering Croismare what Pamela did not offer to Mr. B, that is, to become his mistress.

What could have been Diderot's objective in presenting such an ambiguous and complex story? In this epistolary tale, the reader is in the position of the Marquis de Croismare; after several pages, readers naturally forget the letter is being written to another character and the author of the letter assumes the role of a meta-narrator. But letters are different from other forms of narrated stories. Every letter, after all, is a rhetorical exercise meant to impact the recipient; this was, after all, among the central messages of the Anti-Pamelists, exploited with such good humor by Fielding in *Shamela*. Suzanne is also, in effect, attempting to influence us. Novels composed of letters depend upon unreliable narrators, signaling readers to maintain a critical attitude. In this case, we must decide whether Suzanne deserves our help, our sympathy, and perhaps a job. We are not simply observers watching how other characters perform their virtue; it is also our morality that is being tested. If we succumb to Suzanne's wiles, we are no better than the debauched themselves. The modern novel for Diderot, then, was not so much a place to clinically observe moral action; rather, we are the subject of an experiment that tests our own morals. Because most readers missed Suzanne's motives, this lacuna revealed for Diderot a corruption that ran throughout society. "I have just reread at leisure these memoirs that I wrote in haste, and I have realized that, though it was utterly unintentional, I had in each line shown myself to be as unhappy as I really was, but also much nicer than I really am," Suzanne notes in a postscript at the very end of her tale. "Could it be that we believe men to be less sensitive to the depiction of our suffering than to the image of our charms, and do we hope that it is much easier to seduce them than it is to touch their hearts?"[60] *The Nun* constituted an indictment of the entire society around it, not only because Suzanne's oppression and abuse demonstrates the despotism inherent in Old Regime institutions, but also because the reader is too corrupt to know how to help Suzanne and improve her life. Here the (implied male) reader fails the test of virtue and is complicit with the patriarchal institutions harming Suzanne. While Diderot's political critique is far removed from Richardson, the narrative techniques he uses are borrowed from his reading of *Pamela* and *Clarissa*.

Richardson's literary innovations astounded Diderot. Not only was Richardson able to create characters that "make the passions speak," but by placing them in difficult moral circumstances, Richardson had created real-life situations that forced his community of readers to debate the right course of action for them. Pamela's and Clarissa's moral choices won't make as great a difference to the fate of her country, as say, those of Charles XII or Telemachus. Rather, our empathy derives from the knowledge that Pamela's and Clarissa's choices are most important only to them, and their decisions stem from their own interests. In reading Richardson's three novels, Diderot "heard the genuine language of the passions; I had seen the secret springs of self-interest and self-love [amour propre] operating in a hundred different ways."[61] When eighteenth-century readers debated whether Pamela was a hypocrite, too egotistical, ambitious, or disrespectful of authority, they drew upon their understanding of her interests and social standing. Debating Pamela Andrews with one's friends and family helped readers clarify their own moral ideas, just as they might do when reading David Hume or Adam Smith. In the hands of Richardson, Diderot argued, the novel became a forum for popularizing moral philosophy in salons, cafés, workshops, and even in the street. In this way, Diderot argued, Richardson's novels directly contributed to the maturation of the public sphere. Diderot witnessed this phenomenon himself.

> I have heard, as a consequence of their reading, the most important questions concerning morality and taste being discussed and analyzed. I have heard the conduct of characters being discussed in the way one would talk about real events; *Pamela, Clarissa, Grandison* being praised or blamed like living people whom one knew and took the greatest interest in.[62]

Diderot believed that before *Pamela* the novel was an impoverished literary form characterized by "a tissue of fantastic and frivolous events which presented a threat to the taste and morals of its readers."[63] While always remaining close to the concerns of working and middling people, Richardson raised the stature of the genre; his books have far more in common with good history than low literature.

> O Richardson! I will dare to say that the truest piece of history is full of lies, and that your novel is full of truths. History portrays a few individuals, you portray the human

race; history ascribes to a few individuals what they have neither said nor done; everything you ascribe to man he has said and done; history covers only a portion of time, a point on the surface of the globe; you have embraced all times and all places.[64]

When English travelers visited Paris and called upon Diderot, he routinely asked for news about only two British writers: the historian/philosopher David Hume and Samuel Richardson.[65]

Diderot certainly did not confuse Richardson and Hume, but he championed Richardson precisely because the novelist had broadened moral philosophy to a sector of the reading public hitherto engaged only in adventure stories. Richardson had discovered a device—the modern novel—whereby communities of ordinary readers could explore what virtue meant to them. "Richardson sows in our hearts the seeds of virtue," wrote Diderot. "We feel ourselves driven towards what is good with an enthusiasm we did not know was in us. . . . All this because we have been in contact with Richardson."[66] Richardson may not have thought of himself as a philosophe, but he nearly accomplished what the philosophes themselves sought to do, and he made his work easy for them to appropriate. Diderot's argument about the moral power of the modern novel is exactly what Anna Seward meant when she described Richardson's novels as "imaginative ethics."[67]

Diderot and the other philosophes recognized that Richardson's method facilitated moral learning among ordinary readers precisely because moral philosophy ceased to be something abstract and instead was sown into the fabric of daily life. Anne Robert Jacques Turgot, the future French controller general, understood this feature of the new novel. In the words of his friend the Marquis de Condorcet, Turgot "considered novels as being books of morality, and even (he said) the only ones in which he had ever seen morality." The new novels purposely teach us "to strengthen moral sentiments in men, and to render them more delicate and just." Diderot and his colleagues helped transform Richardson's novels into Enlightenment classics.[68]

In a brilliant essay published in 2007, the historian Lynn Hunt interprets the philosophes' appropriation of Richardson as the basis for an historical argument regarding the relationship among the rise of the modern novel, Enlightenment culture, and the invention of human rights. The key to Hunt's argument is the way in which the eighteenth-century reader gained empathy for the trials and tribulations of an ordinary domestic servant such as Pamela Andrews. When Diderot pleaded with Sophie Volland to see Pamela as something other than merely a common servant, he was, in effect, asking Sophie to move through Mr. B's cognitive process, that is, viewing Pamela from the inside as she saw her own experience. Hunt generalized on a larger scale among hundreds of elite readers during the second half of the eighteenth century, who found in Richardson's novel a means to identify with fictional characters markedly different from themselves. Such empathy allowed readers from different classes and backgrounds to place themselves in the same situations as these fictional characters. This identification itself, Hunt argued, implied some sort of equality between the reader and the character. Although Pamela is low in status, the moral decisions that guide her behavior—the way she channels her passions and aspirations—are essentially no different from anyone else, even Telemachus or King Charles XII. In 1759, Adam Smith opened his *Theory of Moral Sentiments* by observing a similar process that accounts for the presence of empathy among people who otherwise act according to their self-interest:

> Though our brother is upon the rack, as long as we ourselves are at our ease, our senses will never inform us of what he suffers. They never did, and never can, carry us beyond our own person, and it is by the imagination only that we can form any conception of what are his sensations. . . . By the imagination we place ourselves in his situation, we conceive ourselves enduring all the same torments, we enter as it were into his body, and become in some measure the same person with him.[69]

Hunt makes clear how Smith's theory was reinforced by the social phenomenon of reading and debating the epistolary novel. As we have seen with such readers as Lady Montagu, such empathy may not occur without the reader's ambivalence and resistance. Yet, as Hunt argued, through reading Richardson and other novelists, elite readers agreed however, reluctantly that everyone deserved proper dignity and autonomy. Miss Pamela Andrews was not the property of Mr. B—everyone could agree that his authority within his household was not unlimited. But what exactly were those limits? As Locke clamed, liberty began with an autonomous body, but what else did a domestic servant have the right to do? Did she have a right to write letters and mail them to her parents? Did she have any right to privacy? Readers passionately believed Pamela had a right to liberty and autonomy even if they could not define precisely what that was. In this manner, according to Hunt,

> human rights grew out of the seedbed sowed by these feelings. Human rights could only flourish when people learned to think of others as their equals, as like them in some fundamental fashion. They learned this equality, at least in part, by experiencing identification with ordinary characters who seemed dramatically present and familiar, even if ultimately fictional.[70]

Hunt gives partial credit to Richardson for "inventing human rights," and in this way, she saw *Pamela* not only as one of the great first modern novels but as itself a work adopted by philosophes and readers into the Enlightenment canon.

Chapter 7

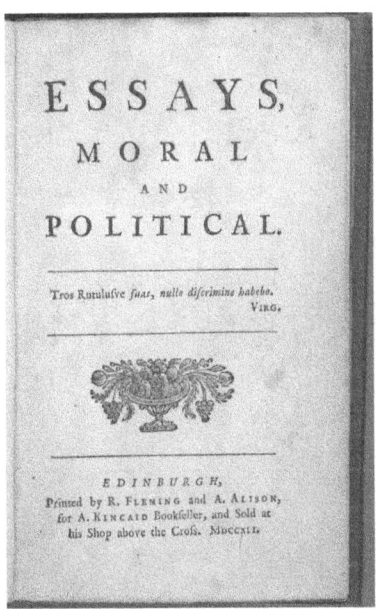

Figure 7.1 First edition title page Hume's *Essays, Moral and Political*. Constantly revised and repackaged, the title of Hume's work changed in 1758 to Essays and Treatises on Several Subjects, of which the first part was titled "Essay, Moral, Political, and Literary."

Chapter 7
Hume's *Essays, Moral and Political* (1741–2)

Table 7.1 Eighteenth-Century Editions of *Essays: Moral and Political*

Decades	1741–9	1750–9	1760–9	1770–9	1780–9	1790–1800
Editions	3	9	18	6	4	6

Total Editions: 46.
Translations: Dutch, French, German, Italian, Spanish, Swedish.
Source: https://kates.itg.pomona.edu/books/analytics.php?type=all. Accessed March 9, 2022.

> *I have never met . . . any of my friends who had travelled to England, without asking . . . "Have you seen the poet Richardson?" And after that: "Have you seen the philosopher Hume?"*[1]

Only Denis Diderot put David Hume and Samuel Richardson together on the same pedestal. Then and today, the two authors seem so different in goals, career aspirations, and genre, if not in methods, outlook, and attitudes that Diderot's comment seems amusing and odd. Indeed, of all the scholarship on the eighteenth century, to my knowledge no book or article compares these two famous contemporaneous British authors. Where Richardson was said to have "taught the passions to move at the command of reason," Hume famously claimed that "reason is and ought only to be the slave of the passions."[2] Nonetheless, Diderot perceived something central about the Enlightenment that unites these two authors. During the winter of 1741, at the very time that Richardson's *Pamela* was first catching fire, David Hume put out in Edinburgh and London a 200-page octavo entitled *Essays, Moral and Political*. Like *Pamela*, Hume's *Essays* became a bestseller first in Britain, and then eventually across Europe and in America. And indeed, like Richardson's sentimental novel, *Essays* has been reprinted regularly since that time. Within a few short years, both authors were rewarded with fame, and, perhaps more unusual during the eighteenth century, wealth from their books.

Like *Pamela*, the publication of Hume's *Essays* was somewhat accidental; Hume hurriedly improvised his way through the essays, adding additional material, and constantly tinkering and revising (and sometimes withdrawing) them until his death in 1776. Furthermore, Hume aimed his essays largely at the same readership that was engrossed with *Pamela*. While Richardson tried to raise the lowly form of the novel to something like moral philosophy, Hume tried to informalize moral philosophy in a way that was more conversational and digestible for a busy mixed-gendered public prone to distractions outside the Republic of Letters. While Richardson welcomed elite and middle-class Europeans debating at dinner parties the fate of Pamela Andrews, Hume achieved much the same thing regarding his short essays. Toward the end of the century, when a Paris bookseller announced a huge publishing project of 164 volumes featuring the most popular British authors, Richardson and Hume led the pack, each with nineteen volumes.[3]

Richardson and Hume, then, were both engaged in creating and improvising a publishing genre intended not primarily for scholars and literati, but for a broader sector of the educated public, including men and women who saw themselves as readers but not specialists. They might trek a few miles to check out Hume or Richardson from a circulating library, but they usually had no ambition to write a book of their own. They read for self-improvement and entertainment. This interaction between author and reader, as Diderot well knew from editing the great *Encyclopédie*, was the heart of the Enlightenment, representing a new dynamism between the Republic of Letters and the public sphere, and mediated by printers and booksellers. Nothing exemplified this new phenomenon better than David Hume and the response to his *Essays, Moral and Political*.

When he was in his mid-twenties, Hume traveled from Scotland to France to make his mark in philosophy, retreating to a small village on the edge of the Loire Valley, where he wrote in seclusion for two years.[4] His ambition was to write something big, bold, and controversial, in the manner of the great philosophers who had preceded him, such as Hobbes, Spinoza, Descartes, Malebranche, and especially Locke, who had upended the Republic of Letters with their own great treatises. The result was *A Treatise of Human Nature*, published in London during January 1739 (Parts I and II) and November 1740 (Part III), the same month Richardson printed *Pamela*. Today recognized as among the greatest works of modern philosophy, Hume described its reception in thoroughly disappointing terms: "It fell dead-born from the press, without reaching such distinction, as even to excite a murmur among the zealots."[5] Indeed, unlike virtually the rest of Hume's corpus, the *Treatise* was never reprinted again in his lifetime, much less translated into other languages. "The misfortune of a book," Hume wrote to the Earl of Balcarres, paraphrasing the French writer Boileau, "is not the being ill spoke of, but the not being spoken of at all."[6] Nevertheless, it would be a mistake to accept Hume's characterization that the book was a publishing failure from the start. As his biographer noted, the *Treatise* garnered its share of attention and reviews. After all, in 1740, before publication of Part III, a positive fifty-page review essay appeared in an important French journal.[7] Had the first two volumes been regarded as failures, the third would not likely have been published the following year. It may not have been a blockbuster out of the gate, but what 1,100-page philosophy book from a young twenty-eight-year-old author was popular during the eighteenth century? In its day, Hume's *Treatise* was not a failure, but, rather, his unrealistic reaction revealed its author's intense impatience and ambition.

Hume, then, did not disown the *Treatise* because it was a failure in any conventional sense; he himself chose to reject it because he recognized that its format, style, and length were off-putting to "ordinary readers."[8] He hoped that he could reach a much wider readership and become a more popular author, as Montesquieu and Voltaire were doing. Certainly he wanted respect as a philosopher; but what became more important was to garner a wide reputation as—in the jargon of the day—a Man of Letters, or what we might call today a public intellectual.[9] Sometime before the third part of the *Treatise* was published in November 1740, Hume resolved to move away from the long formal style. Instead, he embraced the short essay format made famous by Joseph Addison and Richard Steele in their *Spectator*, a daily magazine that ran in 1711–12 and then was rehabilitated briefly by Addison himself thrice weekly in 1714. These essays delivered light opinions meant to edify a general public with the goal "to enliven morality with wit, and to temper wit with morality."[10] Their 2,500-word pieces were meant for a mixed-gender public bent on self-improvement. Modern scholarship credits the *Spectator* with helping to secularize morality for an emerging Enlightenment public.[11] For his essays, Hume at first imitated Addison's style and purpose, but soon moved beyond what he perceived as Addison's superficiality and tried to infuse his own pieces with more meaty philosophical content, while always keeping the style as accessible as possible. In his *Treatise of Human Nature*, Hume used a confrontational tone, arguing with the reader about claims that the author knew would be difficult for anyone to accept. In the *Spectator*, Addison taught Hume how to use a more conversational style that treated the reader more as a friend with whom he might have an after-dinner conversation.[12] Equally important to Hume was the *Spectator*'s unprecedented publication history. No sooner had the periodical stopped its run than London publishers began converting it into a multivolume book set. In this format, Addison and Steele's essays went through at least twelve editions and two translations (French and German) by the time Hume began his essay project. Unlike his *Treatise*, Hume could see that there was a burgeoning market for this new genre.[13]

Of Essay Writing

In late 1741 the Edinburgh publisher Andrew Kincaid brought out the first volume of Hume's *Essays, Moral and Political* in an octavo format containing fifteen essays. A few months later Kincaid reprinted the first volume and produced a second volume that included twelve more essays. Among this set of twenty-seven essays, the short piece "Of Essay Writing" has special value, not only because it documents Hume's abandonment of the treatise for the essay form, but also because he used this opportunity to provide a candid assessment of his ambition to win over a new sector of the reading public. Perhaps because it is so personal, he excluded it from further editions after 1742, and consequently, it received little attention from eighteenth-century readers.

Hume began "Of Essay Writing" by noting that his intended audience was not members of the working class, who are "immersed in the animal life."[14] They are so concerned with daily survival and merely getting by, that they have no time for the leisure, reflection, and interests that the essays demand. The literate public, Hume wrote, "may be divided into the learned and conversible." By "learned," Hume meant the highly trained specialists, publishing authors, members of royal academies, and the like, who corresponded with one another within the Republic of Letters.[15] The larger group of conversibles have a disposition that makes them naturally curious and sociable, but, unlike the learned, they prefer "the easier and more gentle exercises of the understanding." These included reflections on "human affairs," the "duties of common life," and "blemishes or perfections of the particular objects that surround them." Conversibles enjoy reading, but they demand subjects that are concrete and relevant to them, and most of all, they want to talk with one another about what they have read. Conversibles may often read alone, but for the purpose of coming together in conversation, "where every one displays his Thoughts and Observations in the best Manner he is able, and mutually gives and receives information, as well as pleasure." Conversibles would work through any difficult material with friends, applying newly found principles in their lives. Knowledge is not an end to itself but a means to personal improvement and sociability.

Learned and conversibles were not new social categories for Hume; they had existed in society for a long time. In some eras, such as the Renaissance, they operated together in harmony. But during the seventeenth century, learned and conversibles moved farther apart until they became almost isolated from one another. "The separation of the learned from the conversible world," he wrote, "seems to have been the great defect of the last age, and must have had a very bad influence both on books and company." On the one hand, writers such as Hobbes, Locke, and Newton too often perfected their knowledge away from the public, in the company of only a small group of specialists; likewise, they tended to write treatises and articles in Latin featuring technical language that precluded general usage. This separation badly affected the conversible public. Instead of engaging in the writings of the learned, they were left with only "a continued series of gossiping stories and idle remarks." Without good "History, Poetry, Politics" and Philosophy to discuss, they were left with talking about the mundane scandals of the day.

Hume insisted that this gulf between intellectuals and the literate public damaged the specialists as much as the wider community of readers.

> Learning has been as great a loser by being shut up in Colleges and Cells, and secluded from the world and good company. By that means, everything of what we call Belles Lettres became totally barbarous, being cultivated by men without any taste of life or manners, and without that liberty and facility of thought and expression, which can only be acquired by conversation.

Without contact with a wider public, specialized academicians had exiled themselves from society; they may know more about a particular subject than anyone else, but they are unable to recognize its value in the world, much less communicate its significance outside of a small circle. "Even philosophy went to wrack by this moaping [sic] recluse method of study, and became as chimerical in her conclusions as she was unintelligible in her stile and manner of delivery." Aiming for Descartes and his disciples such as Malebranche, Hume added: "And indeed, what could be expected from men who never consulted experience in any of their reasonings, or who never searched for that experience, where alone it is to be found, in common life and conversation." Hume was deeply critical of thinkers who insulated themselves with private jargon. He was now determined to avoid their fate.

However, in recent years, Hume noted with optimism, philosophers had reversed their isolation, reconnecting with the public. "Men of Letters in this age have lost, in a great measure, that shyness and bashfulness of temper, which kept them at a distance from Mankind." The result was that politicians and civic leaders—"Men of the World"—"are proud of borrowing from books their most agreeable topics of conversation. 'Tis to be hoped," prayed Hume, "that this League betwixt the learned and the conversible worlds, which is so happily begun, will be still farther improved to their mutual advantage; and to that End, I know nothing more advantageous than such *Essays* as these with which I endeavor to entertain the public." Here was the context for the publication of Hume's *Essays*: to find a vehicle for the literate public to discuss philosophical ideas that originated in the Republic of Letters. And Hume made his own role and contribution very clear: "In this view, I cannot but consider myself as a kind of Resident or Ambassador from the Dominions of Learning to those of Conversation; and shall think it my constant duty to promote a good correspondence betwixt these two states, which have so great a dependence on each other." Hume, living among the learned, now promised to engage in shuttle diplomacy between the two worlds. However, it is critical to point out that he would do this only as an author of books. He never planned, for example, to undertake a series of popular lectures in Edinburgh or London, as did his close friend Adam Smith.[16] Hume's sole way of reaching the educated public was exclusively through books that would apply learned philosophy to daily issues. The public would encounter Hume only as an author.[17]

Hume's turn toward essay writing was one milestone marking the emergence of the modern intellectual, which quickly became an ideal of the Enlightenment itself, repeated in the articles "Philosopher" and "Encyclopedia" from Diderot and d'Alembert's *Encyclopédie*.[18] The goal was not simply to point philosophy in a progressive direction; books like Hume's *Essays* would connect the philosopher with the public, reorient the public away from the mundane and the bawdy to what we might today call social science and literature, and educate and entertain a new public composed of the middling classes. In Diderot's vocabulary, Hume's ambassador would hold "the power to change men's common way of thinking."[19]

"Of Essay Writing" took a final dramatic and surprising turn. The key players among the conversibles, Hume insisted, are not nobles, merchants, bankers, tradesmen, or politicians, but women. That is, women are not only part of the conversible public, they constitute its most important leadership. "Women of sense and education (for to such alone I address myself) are much better judges of all polite writing than men of the same degree of understanding." Hume himself recognized what a provocative position he had staked out. He demanded that men abandon their standard prejudices and consider female learning on its own merits. Men who discount women readers have no place among the conversible public. "Let the dread of that ridicule have no other effect, than to make them conceal their knowledge before fools, who are not worthy of it, nor of them." Hume's feminism—for that's indeed what it was—nonetheless needs to be qualified.[20] Nowhere does he mean to imply that women are equal with men; indeed, while the conversible world is mixed-sex, the learned Republic of Letters is still, in his vision, a male fraternity. Nonetheless, what Hume claimed here is that the project of enlightening the public depended on the aesthetic decisions of women, who discerned the best authors. "No polite writer," argued Hume, "pretends to venture upon the public, without the approbation of some celebrated judges of that sex." Hume understood that the reading culture around him was changing, and that women hungered to converse with men about these Addisonian essays. His remarks provided a grain of truth to the satire published in one Edinburgh periodical: "Tribes of females, deserting the card-tables, flock thither and acknowledge the superiority of philosophy."[21]

Hume's inclusion of women echoed in some of his other essays. For example, in "The Rise and Progress of the Arts and Sciences," Hume insists that material progress required better treatment of women. "Barbarous nations" systematically abused their women, "by confining them, by beating them, by selling them, by killing them." Women "among the ancients" were "considered as altogether domestic." By contrast, modern men by employing "gallantry" and polite manners include women in social company, "where the mutual endeavor to please must insensibly polish the mind." For Hume, women would staff the Enlightenment public's executive committee.[22]

This recognition of women as a significant part of civil society reflected Hume's understanding of the differences between ancient and modern society. Unlike the ancients, who had relegated women to isolation in the domestic sphere, the development of commerce in early modern Europe brought the domestic and political spheres much closer together. Given how polite conversation helped shape political discourse, it was critical that women understand the dynamics surrounding political economy and public policy. "A woman may behave herself with good manners, and have even some vivacity in her turn of wit; but where her mind is so unfurnished, 'tis impossible her conversation can afford any entertainment to men of sense and reflection."[23] It was therefore imperative that women themselves perceive how novel their role had become during the eighteenth century, and this required a good appreciation of history. "There is nothing which I would recommend more earnestly to my female readers," wrote Hume in "Of the Study of History," "than the study of history, as an occupation, of all others, the best suited both to their sex and education, much more instructive than their ordinary books of amusement."[24]

That this was a bold and controversial approach became evident when Hume dropped this essay from subsequent editions. Sometimes ridiculed for directing his comments "from the Republick of Letters to the Republic of Petticoats," Hume saw his efforts backfire. "He has incurred the displeasure of the Ladies, instead of gaining their favour," one reader insisted, advising Hume to forgo the project of reaching out to a wider public and instead establish a monkish retreat in the country "where he may pass the remainder of his days in solitude and abstruse speculations."[25] Nonetheless, Hume's early feminist attitude, however tentative and brief, was soon embraced by other major figures of the Scottish Enlightenment, whose historical sociology made the treatment and inclusion of women a kind of litmus test for recognizing a society's modernity and level of civilization. "The condition in which we find women in any country," wrote William Alexander in his influential *History of Women*, "mark out to us with the greatest precision, the exact point in the scale of civil society, to which the people of such country have arrived."[26]

Of the Liberty of the Press

Among the fifteen essays originally published in the 1741 first volume, "Of the Liberty of the Press" perhaps made the largest impact upon the public. During the 1760s, London's radical political opposition led by John Wilkes employed it when openly attacking the Bute administration. In April 1763, Wilkes published his attacks upon Lord Bute and King George III in his periodical, *The North Briton*. It was one thing to attack a king's minister, another to denigrate the king. The government shut down the paper and arrested Wilkes. Complicating matters was Wilkes's status as a member of the House of Commons. Reviewing the case, judges ruled that his parliamentary privilege protected his free speech rights. London crowds hardly had a chance to demonstrate for his victory when the House of Commons expelled him and called for an election to replace him. When Londoners re-elected Wilkes, England had a constitutional crisis on its hands over, among other things, freedom of the press. Wilkes fled to Paris, but returned to England in 1768, relaunching *The North Briton*. Its first issue contained extensive quotes from Hume's "Of the Liberty of the Press," and for the next few years, Hume's essay was reprinted and excerpted repeatedly in the radical press, despite the fact that Hume personally found the politics of Wilkes abhorrent.[27]

While Hume's essay was used in England by the popular opposition to the government, the reception was somewhat the opposite in Denmark, where progressive action by the government caused a popular reaction. On September 4, 1770, the Danish king Christian VII issued the following decree: "We have decided to permit in our kingdoms and lands in general an unlimited freedom of the press." This was the brainchild of the king's physician and soon-to-be prime minister Johann Friedrich Struensee. It was a bold move, a prime example of enlightened despotism, where reform comes from the top whether or not the country is ready for it. Voltaire applauded the effort with congratulatory writings. Not surprisingly, a pamphlet storm arose almost immediately, on a variety of topics including the abolition of feudalism, reforming banks, universities, and the status of women. Included in this sea of words were writings directly about press freedom itself. In this context, Hume's short essay was translated and published in Danish by government sympathizers to support the reforms. Unfortunately, Denmark's experiment was short-lived. In 1773, Struensee was overthrown in a coup when it was discovered that he was sleeping with the queen (who also happened to be King George III's sister). Tried and executed for treason, Struensee's press laws were dismantled, not to be reinstated until the nineteenth century.[28]

Essays, Moral and Political was no immediate bestseller, taking at least five years to sell out, but in 1748 Kincaid and Hume put out a new one-volume duodecimo edition. As would become his regular practice, Hume used the opportunity to make countless small changes, refining his language and word choices. "It is one great advantage that results from the Art of printing," wrote Hume near the end of his life, "that an Author may correct his works, as long as he lives." He also took the opportunity to add new essays and withdraw others, such as "Of Essay Writing." Indeed, the ability to make such changes in a new edition, Hume claimed, was so important for the improvement of philosophy that it was another advantage that the modern world had over the ancients.[29] Making such changes obviously required the close collaboration with the printers and publishers. Here Hume's behavior and social networks differed from his French counterparts. Where Voltaire treated his many publishers despotically, and Montesquieu hardly knew his, Hume became genuinely close to the publishers he chose. The result of such personal loyalty was decades of fruitful and remunerative work. Alexander Kincaid, after all, was a prominent Edinburgh bookseller, known to Hume before he became his publisher. As Hume's career blossomed in the 1740s, he and Kincaid partnered with another Scotsman, Andrew Millar, who had set up shop in London. From 1748 until Hume's death in 1776 all his work was published in collaboration with Millar, Kincaid, and their junior partners. Such loyalty benefited everyone. Altogether Millar paid Hume the astronomical sum of £4,000 for the *History of England*. Meanwhile, when Millar died in 1768, his own estate was worth some £60,000—by that time they both had become very rich men.[30]

"Of National Characters"

Of all Hume's essays, none was more controversial then or today as "Of National Characters," which sought to explain the essential differences between peoples. In his conversational style, Hume remarked how generalizing about other nations was ubiquitous, a daily subject of café gatherings and tea parties. Scholars corroborate that national character was among the most common discussion topics in eighteenth-century

Europe.[31] One reason for this interest was that the notion of national character addressed a central riddle that befuddled readers: if human nature is everywhere the same, what accounts for the wondrous variety of human behavior, manners, and culture? Hume set up the problem as essentially a dichotomy between cultural and environmental forces. Hume's thesis was that culture determined character far more than environmental factors. Coincidentally, this essay first appeared more or less simultaneously with Montesquieu's *The Spirit of the Laws*, which famously addressed the same subject, arguing that environmental factors such as climate and topography strongly affected culture and politics. Despite such differences in argument, Montesquieu himself championed "On National Characters," making a point to single it out for admiration in a letter he wrote to Hume.[32]

Andrew Millar first published "Of National Characters" in 1748 in a short volume entitled *Three Essays Never Before Published Which Completes the Former Edition*, quickly subsumed under the new duodecimo "third" edition of the *Essays, Moral and Political* that appeared later that year, the first edition that included Hume's name on the title page. In preparing the 1753 four-volume duodecimo set, *Essays and Treatises on Several Subjects*, Hume altered "Of National Characters" by adding an important footnote roughly halfway through the essay. Because of its shocking and controversial nature—then as now—it is worth quoting in full:

> I am apt to suspect the negroes, and in general all the other species of men (for there are four or five different kinds) to be naturally inferior to the whites. There never was a civilized nation of any other complexion than white, nor even any individual eminent either in action or speculation. No ingenious manufactures amongst them, no arts, no sciences. On the other hand, the most rude and barbarous of the whites, such as the ancient Germans, the present Tartars, have still something eminent about them, in their valour, form of government, or some other particular. Such a uniform and constant difference could not happen, in so many countries and ages, if nature had not made an original distinction betwixt these breeds of men. Not to mention our colonies, there are Negroe slaves dispersed all over Europe, of which none ever discovered any symptoms of ingenuity; tho' low people, without education, will start up amongst us, and distinguish themselves in every profession. In Jamaica indeed they talk of one negroe as a man of parts and learning; but 'tis likely he is admired for very slender accomplishments, like a parrot, who speaks a few words plainly.[33]

This quotation was regarded almost as infamous in the eighteenth century as it is today. Hume made a series of points that were manifestly racist: first, he embraced the dubious theory of polygenesis, which argued that different "breeds" of humans were created separately, thus contradicting any notion of a common human origin; second, he claimed that all other human "breeds" were inferior to whites; third, he argued that no non-white people ever excelled in the arts or sciences, that is, in producing civilization; fourth, he used colonial slavery as a demonstration that when living together Blacks could not be educated to a level near white Europeans; and finally, he dismissed one famous example of a Jamaican free Black recognized for his intellectual powers. Few statements among leading Enlightenment writers have ever been more racially charged than this one.[34]

That Montesquieu praised the 1748 version of the essay without the footnote shows how unnecessary it was for Hume to add it. The essay had not been attacked; no one had called for its removal or pointed to any special weakness. Indeed, precisely because of Montesquieu's *The Spirit of the Laws*, which by 1753 was quite well known in England because of the Thomas Nugent translation, the comparison between their differing perspectives probably helped both authors gain recognition. Moreover, the insertion of the footnote cut against the grain of Hume's overall argument regarding the predominance of moral influences upon national character. Nowhere else in the essay does Hume address whether "nature" has singled out a particular people under special circumstances. The footnote threatened to disrupt the premise of the essay, which is that nature has not predetermined the level of civilization for any people. And yet here in 1753 Hume suddenly removed Blacks from the family of humankind.

Did it make a difference that Hume's comment appeared in a footnote rather than the body of the text? Today footnotes are commonplace, even in non-scholarly books. But during the eighteenth century, authors were just beginning to make use of footnotes in a way recognizable to us. In *Essays, Moral and Political*, half the essays contain no notes at all. Of those that included footnotes, they may be divided into three types: first, documentation of a quotation. For example, in "That Politics May Be Reduced to a Science," Hume refers to the Roman writer Polybius and cites the specific source without comment in the note.[35] Such brief documentation was by far the most common type of footnote Hume produced. A second category of footnote involved commentary that was clearly too erudite for general readers, often relating to the ancient world.[36] There are approximately twenty-five such notes in the *Essays*. Finally, Hume used footnotes for commentaries (like the racist one quoted earlier) that were meant to extend or digress from a particular argument, and were intended for general readers rather than scholars. Initially rare in the essays—there are only a handful until the 1750s—they become more common later. No essay has more than one or two, except for the 1752 essay "Of the Populousness of Ancient Nations," which is replete with them. One conclusion from this survey is that in the early 1750s, Hume began to experiment with using footnotes for rhetorical commentary, and the racist one in "Of National Characters" is among them.[37]

As noted, Hume meticulously went over his essays each time they went to press; indeed, this is how Hume came to add the notorious note in the first place. Obviously, this practice also gave him opportunity to expunge, amend, or alter it. Between 1753 and his death in 1776, Hume was involved in seven new editions,[38] and each edition reproduced the notorious footnote intact. In 1768 he made a word change (from *tho'* to *though*) and in 1770 he made another word change (from *'tis* to *it is*) and moved all footnotes to endnotes. The racist footnote, in short, easily withstood the regular process of revision and reconsideration, demonstrating that Hume did not regard it as a momentary rhetorical impulse or exaggeration, but integral to the essay and reflective of his beliefs.

In 1770 one of Hume's many adversaries, the Scottish moral philosopher James Beattie, took aim at "Of National Characters." Beattie found Hume's claims of white superiority highly misguided. "These assertions are strong, but I know not whether they have anything to recommend them." For an empiricist, charged Beattied, Hume lacked evidence. For his part, Beattie claimed that 1,000 years ago Europeans looked as uncivilized as Africans do now, and within a reasonable period, Africans would certainly attain the level of the Europeans. "Civilization is the work of time. And one may as well say of an infant, that he may never become a man." Beattie went on to criticize Hume for ignoring and devaluing the great cultural artifacts made by New World peoples such as the Incas and Aztecs. They alone, Beattie charged, are proof of Hume's folly. Finally, Beattie indicted Hume for ethnocentrism, attacking him for viewing slavery only from the perspective of an arrogant European philosophe: "That every practice and sentiment is barbarous which is not according to the usages of modern Europe, seems to be a fundamental maxim with many of our critics and philosophers."[39]

Perhaps because Beattie was a fellow Scot who also published with Kincaid, Hume took umbrage at his remarks. To his friends he dismissed him as a "silly bigoted fellow."[40] But Beattie's points regarding the footnote clearly caused Hume to reconsider its content. As Hume and his publishing partners were preparing a new edition for 1777, one that would be produced posthumously months following Hume's death, he made instructions to change the start of the footnote as follows:

> I am apt to suspect the negroes ~~and in general all other species of men (for there are four or five different kinds)~~ to be naturally inferior to the whites. There ~~never~~ *scarcely ever* was a civilized nation of ~~any other~~ *that* complexion ~~than white~~, nor even any individual eminent either in action or speculation.[41]

These changes are profoundly disturbing because they reveal the extent to which Hume committed himself to racist notions even after considered reflection. Granted, here he casts aside polygenesis. It may well be true, he implicitly concedes to Beattie, that non-white civilizations flourished especially in the New World. But his judgment on Black Africans is remade with intense focus. The rest of the footnote is left unaltered. If Hume was "deeply concerned to present the best version of his thoughts to his readers," as Margaret Watkins testifies, why didn't he expunge the footnote?[42]

Between 1753 and 1777, Hume retained the mean-spirited comment at the end of the footnote regarding one well-known example of a Jamaican free Black man who had mastered Latin and learned to write poetry. This unkind remark was based on the true story of Francis Williams, the son of slaves who had been set free, and who themselves became plantation proprietors and provided their son with a decent education. When it became clear that he had an extraordinary intellect, his parents sent him to England for further education, where he acquired the celebrated reputation that made its way to Hume. After two years or so, Francis returned to Jamaica and managed his estate without fanfare. Considering his real-life accomplishment, Hume's characterization of him as a parrot lacked any confirming evidence.[43]

Much of the recent scholarship surrounding this footnote has addressed the extent to which it infected the rest of Hume's philosophy. Hume's anti-slavery position is also well known, expressed in another essay.[44] Of course, anyone can simultaneously hold racist and abolitionist views—such positions were not incompatible. It may well be true, as Frederick G. Whelan recently suggested, that "this passage is unique in Hume's writings as well as anomalous in this essay."[45] What matters more than what Hume thought or intended, however, is the effect that his footnote had upon eighteenth-century debates regarding race and slavery. Beyond doubt this footnote was used during the 1770s by activists defending slavery against the burgeoning abolitionist movement. Samuel Estwick was a Barbados plantation owner who also sat in the House of Commons from 1779 to 1795. In 1773, he published a defense of slavery, in which he quoted and commented on Hume's footnote, using it to confirm the view that Black slaves think and feel "as beasts do" because they are "incapable of moral sensations."[46] Another former Caribbean plantation owner, Richard Nisbit, echoed Estwick, quoting Hume's footnote to further a defense of slavery. Based on Hume, Nisbit concluded that Blacks "are a much inferior race of men to the whites in every respect."[47] Finally, the influential eighteenth-century historian of Jamaica, Edward Long, considered the arguments of both Hume and Beattie, deciding in favor of Hume.[48] Such print controversies occurred during Hume's lifetime, prior to the preparation of the 1777 edition, when he was still fully able to expunge the note; and yet, as we have seen, his final changes only strengthened and clarified his racism. Despite the best efforts of abolitionists, such as Granville Sharp and Benjamin Rush, to overcome the damage wrought by Hume's footnote, it helped slavery survive.[49]

A decade later, in 1786, the Austrian physician and cosmopolite, Franz Swediauer, regretted that Hume's bigoted footnote had "given occasion to some writers to quote Hume as an advocate for the slavery of the Negroes." Swediauer admired much of Hume's philosophy and for that very reason found the footnote especially troubling. He cited relevant travel literature featuring Europeans in Africa who testified to the resourcefulness, industry, and intelligence of Black Africans. If Caribbean slaves appeared dumb, it revealed nothing about their supposed nature but rather was the clear result of the "abject servility of their condition, which represses emulation, and extinguishes whatever is great and noble in the mind." Hume surely ought to have known better, for the same authors consulted by Swediauer were available to him. "These testimonials, extracted from writers who had resided on the spot," Swediauer concluded, "evidently overthrow the fallacious foundation on which Hume had hazarded his speculation."[50]

However, other Europeans were not so sure that Swediauer was correct. Hume's "Of National Characters" was first translated into French in 1764, as part of an effort by the Prussian Academy of Sciences to make Hume's pre-1752 essays and philosophical works better known in Europe. Swiss philosopher Jean Bernard Mérian, a member of the Academy, who directed its division of Belles Lettres and later became its Permanent Secretary, was lead translator for the Hume publishing project. When he came to "Of

National Characters," with its pungent footnote, Mérian not only retained Hume's full note but also added a commentary of his own: "I had the opportunity to do an experiment that confirms Mr. Hume's attitude," reported the translator. "I noticed that the young Negroes who have the most intelligence and liveliness, when applied to the arts and sciences, first make rapid progress there; but after a certain period, their ideas become confused, and every conceivable pain would be taken in vain to push them further." Thus, Mérian not only expressed support for Hume's position but also used it to justify his own position.[51] Perhaps it was Mérian's translation that Immanuel Kant had read, when he endorsed these same passages of Hume in an essay published the same year.[52] In fact, some years before, in 1757, Mérian had previewed this first translation of "Of National Characters," by placing it in one of the leading Enlightenment periodicals, the *Journal Encyclopédique*. The presentation there was somewhat different than in the later book. Hume's footnote was brought into the body of the text, where it assumed a more central place in the essay, and Mérian's short commentary was also placed directly in the essay's body, making it appear to be Hume's own words.[53]

Political Discourses

Despite the success of the *Essays* in Britain, by the early 1750s Hume's books had not yet been translated into any foreign language. He was still a provincial writer. If one hoped to cultivate a reputation across Europe, a French edition was required. Everything changed in 1752 with the publication of a new set of essays, *Political Discourses*. As Hume noted in his autobiography, *Political Discourses* was "the only work of mine that was successful on the first publication. It was well received abroad and at home."[54] Most of the twelve new essays concerned economics, exploring the appropriate role for the government to play in fostering economic prosperity. Topics included commerce, luxury, money, interest, taxes, trade, and public credit. Within a few months, a second edition appeared, and writers on the continent were at work translating it into French. These new essays were written partly under the spell of Montesquieu's *The Spirit of the Laws*. As Roger Oake demonstrated long ago, even when Hume chose to refute Montesquieu's arguments, he imitated Montesquieu's light and witty style, often borrowing wording from the French master. After 1748, Montesquieu became Hume's new Addison.[55]

"Few writers are better qualified, either to instruct or entertain their readers, than Mr. Hume," wrote William Rose in a long two-part review of *Political Discourses*, published in his brother's *Monthly Review*. Five years later, Rose was still praising Hume's essays not so much for the controversial ideas themselves but, rather, for the style which Rose found to be a model of clarity and expression.

There are but few of our modern Writers, whose works are so generally read, as those of Mr. Hume. And indeed, if we consider them in one view, as sprightly and ingenious compositions, this is not at all to be wondered at: there is a delicacy of sentiment, an original turn of thought, a perspicuity, and often an elegance of language, that cannot but recommend his writings to every Reader of taste.[56]

A year later, in 1753, Kincaid and Millar packaged Hume's writings from the preceding decade into a four-volume collected set. Volume I constituted a new "fourth" edition of *Essays, Moral and Political*. Volume II included the *Enquiry Concerning Human Understanding* (first published in 1748 as the *Philosophical Essays Concerning Human Understanding*); Volume III included the *Enquiry Concerning the Principles of Morals* (first published in 1751); and finally, Volume IV reprinted the *Political Discourses*. Together the set was entitled *Essays and Treatises on Several Subjects*. Although marketed as a set, book buyers could easily buy one volume independent from the others. Most volumes, for example, carried two title pages, one announcing the set, and another announcing the individual volume as if it were a separate publication. This process makes it difficult to chart Hume's publishing history as new and old printings became interchangeable under the umbrella of the overall set, masking themselves as new editions. Meanwhile booksellers mixed and matched as they pleased.[57]

Hume's various essays lost their autonomy over the course of the decade. In 1758, Hume, Kincaid, and Millar repackaged the set *Essays and Treatises on Several Subjects* into a one-volume larger quarto format that cost three times as much as the previous octavo, crucially changing the order of the publications so that the twelve *Political Discourses* immediately followed the other essays as Parts I and II in what was now called the *Essays, Moral, Political, and Literary*. Hume again added a few new essays, such as "Of the Standard of Taste" and "Of the Coalition of Parties." Thus, from 1758 forward the *Political Discourses*, at least in all English editions, was submerged into the more general set of essays, losing whatever separate identity it had. The *Essays, Moral, Political, and Literary* was followed by Hume's other four philosophical writings: *An Enquiry Concerning Human Understanding, An Enquiry Concerning the Principle of Morals, Natural History of Religion*, and *Dissertation on the Passions*. In this way, Hume sought to refashion himself as much as a philosopher as an essayist of belles lettres and politics. While Hume would tinker with these essays until he died, this set, including the order of the essays, remained intact, as it was reformatted into different sizes (quarto, octavo, and duodecimo) aimed at different segments of the book-buying market. Except for his equally successful multivolume *History of England*, during his lifetime Hume published nothing else after 1758 other than *Essays and Treatises on Several Subjects*.

What was possible for Hume in Great Britain was out of reach on the continent. In Richard Sher's magisterial study of Enlightenment publishing in Scotland, he reconstructs how Hume and his publishers carefully packaged his books and his reputation, creating one of Britain's most successful authors.[58] Their accomplishment was possible only because of the unique, if complex, relationship between Scotland and England. Despite the 1707 Act of Union that joined the two monarchies, Scotland and

England still retained their separate jurisdictions regarding publishing and copyright law. Yet, their political unity allowed partnerships that provided authors and publishers legal and financial stability vastly different than before 1707. Throughout Great Britain (excepting Ireland), Hume and his publishers controlled almost all aspects of his work, including printing, circulation, and royalties. On the continent, such control was difficult for any author, especially for a foreigner. Until the 1884 Berne Convention, no author anywhere could expect to manage himself internationally the way one could do at home. Hume never made a penny on any translation, nor could he approve where or when translations would appear, or in what format or packaging. For this reason, his essays have an entirely different history on the continent than in the UK. Perhaps the greatest difference, from Hume's viewpoint was that in Britain his essays and philosophical tracts were, by 1758, united into one overall work, the *Essays and Treatises on Several Subjects*, whereas on the continent his economic writings were usually published separately from his philosophical work. Where in Britain *Political Discourses* dissolved into Hume's general essays and philosophical works, in Europe they took on a life of their own as pillars of the new science of political economy. When near the start of the French Revolution, Condorcet published a twelve-volume set of political theorists most relevant to France's new patriots, he included *Political Discourses* as Hume's most seminal contribution.[59]

The Economist on the Continent

When *Political Discourses* reached France, acolytes described its author as an expert in economic affairs, almost ignoring his other work, especially his epistemology and moral philosophy. The continental framing of Hume as an economist was no accident, but the concerted effort of a progressive group of economic writers within the French government, led by its new Intendant of Trade, Jacques Claude Marie Vincent de Gournay. Hume's timely *Political Discourses* was first published between Europe's two major mid-century wars: the War of the Austrian Succession (1739–48) and the Seven Years' War (1756–63). By 1750, French officials understood that the rise of England to a world power was the partial result of its trade policies and the British government's willingness to develop its navy to protect its valuable trade routes. As Voltaire had shown in *Philosophical Letters*, where France seemed to have an economy that serviced the state and its recalcitrant nobility, the English government served the needs of its economy, improving both state and society. The stable of writers gathered around Gournay advocated similar policies for France, requiring a major overhaul of the role of commerce and business in the formation of government trade and tax policies. They thought of their goal not simply as a set of policies drafted by a political faction but as inaugurating a "science of commerce." Of all eighteenth-century thinkers, Montesquieu drew the most attention of Gournay and his writers. They saw in *The Spirit of the Laws* an argument that placed global trade in the spotlight of reforming European monarchy. "No other work did as much to place commerce at the center of enquiry," historian John Robertson has noted, "or to establish its importance in understanding human society and its betterment."[60] While Montesquieu did not think France should blindly imitate England, he nevertheless urged France to adopt liberal policies that encouraged more free trade. Such commercial policies, he believed, would help shield France from despotism. The Gournay Circle launched a print campaign for these ideas, hoping to win over other parts of the French elite and government bureaucracy. At first, the writers were blocked by conservative interests who believed such a public discussion of economic ideas dangerous to the monarchy, if not downright unpatriotic. Soon, though, the new liberal director of the book trade, Guillaume-Chrétien de Lamoignon de Malesherbes, took them under his protection and facilitated their print circulation. Hume's *Political Discourses* was adopted by the Gournay Circle to extend Montesquieu's ideas. After Montesquieu died in 1755, one Gournay writer described Hume as "alone in Europe who can replace President Montesquieu" as their lodestar.[61]

The leading writer for the Gournay Circle was François Véron Duverger de Forbonnais, whose *Elements of Commerce* (1753) became something of a manifesto for the group, outlining policies guided by more market-driven guidelines. In part a compilation of articles published in Diderot and d'Alembert's *Encyclopédie*, including the important "Commerce," *Elements of Commerce* projected a path for contemporary monarchies that differed from territorial aggrandizement. Instead of a war machine, the state was envisioned as an organization that improved its people's standard of living. "The purpose of commerce in any state is to keep the greatest possible number of men in comfortable circumstances by means of their work," Forbonnais wrote. "Agriculture and industry are the only means of subsistence; as long as they both bring advantages to those who engage in them, there will never be a lack of manpower in the state." In addition to agriculture and manufacturing, Forbonnais specifically called attention to import/export wholesalers engaged in global trade. "This profession is very essential, because it is the soul of shipping and increases the relative wealth of the state."[62]

Elements of Commerce specifically invoked Hume on the important issue of encouraging luxuries in a modern monarchy, a policy opposed by many other authors such as Fénelon and Rousseau. Throughout the eighteenth century, the debate over luxury was used as a surrogate for the more general question of commercial policy. Forbonnais quoted directly from Hume's second essay in *Political Discourses*, "Of Luxury":

> We cannot reasonably expect, that a piece of woolen cloth will be wrought to perfection in a nation, which is ignorant of astronomy, or where ethics are neglected. The spirit of the age affects all the arts; and the minds of men, being once roused from their lethargy, and put into a fermentation, turn themselves on all sides, and carry improvements into every art and science.[63]

Commerce and trade help lift a society not merely in terms of its material culture but also in terms of the fine arts and scientific innovation. During the 1760s, when Forbonnais became an editor of the *Journal d'Agriculture, du commerce, et des finances*, he supervised a 200-page analysis over five issues regarding Hume's *Political Discourses*.[64]

Within twenty years, *Elements of Commerce* was translated into German, Dutch, Swedish, Portuguese, Spanish, and Russian, usually by reformist-minded statesmen in those countries hoping to liberalize their monarchies. Indeed, so similar did the anonymous *Elements of Commerce* seem to *The Spirit of the Laws* that at least the Portuguese translator thought it had actually been penned by Montesquieu. Like Hume, Forbonnais's work was also built on Montesquieu's platform. For all three thinkers, commerce had the benefit not only of enriching citizens but also of keeping them free.[65]

A close associate of Forbonnais, and something of an expert on English political culture, Jean Bernard Le Blanc translated Hume's *Political Discourses* into French. Le Blanc's fifty-page introduction served as Hume's induction into the Gournay Circle. He associated Hume with Forbonnais, recommending *Elements of Commerce* as complementary and authoritative. Both Hume and Forbonnais, Le Blanc believed, wanted the state to tip the scales in favor of businessmen, those placed in "the third estate" who increase the state's revenue not merely for themselves but for the benefit of the "nobility who despises them." Such businessmen, noted Le Blanc, relieve the peasantry's tax burden, triggering artisanal industry that raises their wages. Only those hoping to achieve glory through war would be disappointed by the businessman's achievements. "Your *Political Discourses*," Le Blanc wrote to Hume, "are having the same effect among us as [Montesquieu's] *The Spirit of the Laws*."[66] Following Hume's essays, Le Blanc added an annotated bibliography that included other British writers translated by the Gournay Circle as well as the best French books, including of course, Forbonnais's *Elements*.[67]

Le Blanc's presentation evidently convinced the French government's royal censor, who was bewildered by a book about politics that seemed to be written without partisan ideology. Unlike others in the Gournay Circle, Hume did not seem to be a polemicist. Despite the sensitive material, the censor found no cause for alarm. He concluded by recommending that the government allow Le Blanc's translation to circulate freely in France.[68] The reviewer for the *Mercure de France* echoed the censor, noting that Hume's arguments were less powerful in themselves than the "subtlety, wit, and philosophy" displayed in them.[69]

Given the new popularity of *Political Discourses*, Le Blanc's translation had its competitors. In 1754 came another translation by the now-forgotten writer living in Leipzig, Eléazar de Mauvillon. Unlike Le Blanc's, this edition published in Amsterdam contained no unusual paratexts, and perhaps it languished for that reason. Hume much preferred Le Blanc's version. When a Dutch publisher decided to reprint the Mauvillon translation, *Political Discourses* became the overall title for a multivolume set of economic works, most of which had been not been written by Hume and had been previously published or translated by the Gournay Circle. For example, the second volume included a treatise on the Spanish economy by Forbonnais. Because Hume was often the only author named, many confused readers thought that Hume had written most of the five-volume compilation. In this way, Mauvillon's translation was strangely absorbed into the Gournay Circle. In 1767, yet a third French translation would find its way to publication. Meanwhile, German and especially Italian translations assured Hume's success in those European regions. In Italy in particular, *Political Discourses* influenced leading writers to turn their attention to political economy. Pietro Verri's *Gli elementi del commercio* (1760) owed much debt to Hume. Likewise, Antonio Genevesi, the first professor to occupy a chair in economics, acknowledged Hume as master of the genre in his *Lezioni di commercio* (1765-67).[70]

We are accustomed to regarding Adam Smith's *Wealth of Nations*, first published in 1776, the same year as Hume's death, as the start of modern economic literature and the crowning achievement of the Scottish Enlightenment. But Europeans regarded Smith's friend Hume as Britain's premier economic thinker a quarter-century before *Wealth of Nations*. During an era of intense state rivalry over trade routes and colonies, in which the relationship between military expansion and economic prosperity seemed at best complex if not confusing, European readers wanted to understand whether commerce led to pacific understanding among peoples or military confrontation between states. The almost continual warfare throughout the century between France and England seemed to signal the latter.[71]

Hume's Essays in America

We have seen that Hume's economic essays had special influence in continental Europe during the second half of the eighteenth century. A similar phenomenon occurred in the British North American colonies, where the essays were very popular, although overshadowed by the success of his *History of England* (1754–62). But the essays read in the British colonies were for the most part different than those that most impacted Europe. The Americans were less concerned with commercial policies, including technical issues surrounding public debt, money, and trade in luxuries than they were with issues regarding statecraft and the nature of political power. Unlike Europe, Hume was never published in the colonies during the eighteenth century; it was cheaper for New York and Philadelphia booksellers to import British (and later Irish) copies than lay out the expense for their own editions. Only in 1817 did a Philadelphia publisher first print a two-volume edition of the essays. Nonetheless, Hume's essays were clearly present in colonial America, as we saw earlier regarding "Of National Characters." Other essays were likewise reprinted and discussed. For example, "Of the Liberty of the Press" was reprinted in the *South-Carolina Gazette* and the *Virginia Gazette*.[72]

In 1767, Philadelphia lawyer John Dickinson employed "Of the First Principles of Government" into serving the cause of colonies against Britain in his often reprinted *Letters from a Farmer in Pennsylvania, to the Inhabitants of the British Colonies*.[73]

Ezekial Russell drew upon "That Politics May Be Reduced to a Science" to help demonstrate that the British political system no longer had any checks and balances in place.[74] James Chalmers, on the other hand, used "the profound and elegant" Hume to show that without British monarchy, the colonies would "immediately degenerate into Democracy."[75] John Adams thought that the plan for elections spelled out in Hume's "Idea of a Perfect Commonwealth" was entirely too elitist for Americans. "That of Hume is a complicated aristocracy, and would soon behave like all other aristocracies."[76]

The most dramatic story of the influence of Hume's essays in America is clearly the impact they made on James Madison and Alexander Hamilton, especially during the period leading up to the 1787 Constitutional Convention in Philadelphia, when together they composed *The Federalist Papers*. According to Garry Wills, Madison wrote with Hume's essays "open on the table beside him."[77] Madison was probably introduced to Hume years before at Princeton University, when the *Essays* were required reading for President Witherspoon's lectures. The work of Scottish Enlightenment thinkers was studied "nowhere more intensely than at Princeton."[78] Madison engaged with several of the essays, including "Of Parties in General," "Of the First Principles of Government," "Of the Independence of Parliament," and "Parties of Great Britain," all published in the original 1741 edition of *Essays, Moral and Political*.

Arguably, Madison fell more under the spell of "The Idea of a Perfect Commonwealth," first published in the 1752 *Political Discourses*, than any of Hume's other works. In the *Tenth Federalist*, it helped him sort through a fundamental problem of eighteenth-century political thought regarding the size of a republic. From Machiavelli to Montesquieu, political thinkers had reasoned that republics must be small because they depended so much upon trust between citizens, requiring an intimate sense of community, usually characterized by virtue. Such arguments, in the context of the Constitutional Convention, favored rejection of a strong federal government to keep the locus of political power with the states, as they were under the Articles of Confederation. In the final pages of "Perfect Commonwealth," however, Hume took direct aim at Montesquieu when he asserted against the French master that a republic might include large territories: "We shall conclude this subject, with observing the falsehood of common opinion, that no large state, such as France or Great Britain, could ever be modelled into a commonwealth, but that such a form of government can only take place in a city or small territory. The contrary seems probable."[79] Hume's novelty was to distinguish between the establishment of a republic and its maintenance. He admitted that throughout history there were very few instances of republics established over a large territory. But when such accidents occurred, it was actually easier to maintain political stability, because conspiracies against the government—so common in the history of Italian republican states—would be far more complicated to execute. In a city-state like Florence, for example, it was not difficult for a clan to take over the state. But in a more extensive territory, regions and cities could be set up as a check against one another's excesses. "It was Hume's next two sentences," wrote the prescient scholar Douglass Adair, "that must have electrified Madison as he read them":

> In a large government, which is modelled with masterly skill, there is compass and room enough to refine the democracy, from the lower people, who may be admitted into the first elections or first concoction of the commonwealth, to the higher magistrates, who direct all the movements. At the same time, the parts are so distant and remote, that it is very difficult, either by intrigue, prejudice, or passion, to hurry them into any measures against the public interest.[80]

In the *Tenth Federalist*, Madison rephrased Hume's insight as follows: "The question resulting is, whether small or extensive republics are most favorable to the election of proper guardians of the public weal; and it is clearly decided in favor of the latter."[81] Like Hume, Madison argued that a large republic reduces instability caused by factions and political conspiracies. "Extend the sphere and you take in a greater variety of parties and interests," he wrote. "You make it less probable that a majority of the whole will have a common motive to invade the rights of other citizens."[82] Considering the impact that *The Federalist Papers* had upon the ratification of the US Constitution, the link between Hume's *Essays* and *The Federalist Papers* may be a clear and powerful case of an Enlightenment book directly affecting large-scale political change.

Like Madison, Alexander Hamilton was equally moved by his reading of Hume's essays. We can see Hume's impact even at the start of Hamilton's own writing career. When not quite twenty-one, Hamilton defended resistance to Great Britain in a 1775 pamphlet, *The Farmer Refuted*. There we find Hamilton extensively quoting Hume from the beginning of the 1741 essay, "On the Independency of Parliament":

> "Political writers," says a celebrated author,[83] "have established it as a maxim, that, in contriving any system of government, and fixing the several checks and controls of the constitution, *every man* ought to be supposed a *knave,* and to have no other end, in all his actions, but *private interest.* By this interest we must govern him, and by means of it *make him* co-operate *to public good,* notwithstanding his insatiable avarice and ambition. Without this we shall in vain boast of the advantages of *any constitution,* and shall find, in the end, that we have no security for our liberties, and possessions except the *good-will* of our rulers—that is, we should have *no security at all.*"

"What additional force," adds Hamilton, do these observations acquire when applied to the dominion of one community over another!"[84]

Here, as Gerald Stourzh argues, is the genesis of Hamilton's political psychology, from which he never wavered. "In a way," Stourzh comments, "what follows [in Hamilton's intellectual development] consists of mere elaborations of Hume's ideas."[85] In Hume, Hamilton discovered a political philosophy based on the idea that while individual human beings were driven by passionate self-interest, politics was the art of coordinating these individuals to nevertheless honor the public good. Hamilton and

Hume rejected the common notion found in Machiavelli that republican citizenship rested upon individual virtue. Hamilton accepted Hume's perspective that citizens were naturally avaricious, craving wealth and glory, guided by what the French called amour propre. Indeed, without such passions modern commercial life was impossible. Such acceptance and recognition of human selfishness contrasted with other eighteenth-century ideologies relating republicanism with political economy, including Jeffersonian agrarians and the French followers of Mably and Rousseau.[86]

Hamilton reiterated Hume's perspective on the floor of the Constitutional Convention, held in Philadelphia between May and September 1787. On June 22, the delegates were discussing the all-important issue of how to avoid British-style parliamentary "corruption" in the new government. The notion that the House of Commons had become "corrupted" by the monarchy, that pensions and patronage jobs had violated a legislator's natural autonomy to represent his district, was among the most powerful criticisms of eighteenth-century British government. The system put in place by Robert Walpole, often described as England's first prime minister, depended upon a certain number of House of Commons leaders serving as ministers directly for the king and, therefore, having access to his purse.[87] In devising the American system, delegates hoped to correct this perceived English mistake. Madison represented a large vein of American public opinion when he told his colleagues that "no office ought to be open to a member" of Congress.[88] Drawing directly from Hume, Hamilton offered a contrary view, one more sympathetic to the British system. "We must take man as we find him, and if we expect him to serve the public [we] must interest his passions in doing so." Reliance on pure virtue was "the source of many of our errors." And then, acknowledging the debt to his Scottish mentor on the matter, he told his colleagues: "It was known that of the ablest politicians (Mr Hume) had pronounced all that influence on the side of the crown, which went under the name of corruption, an essential part of the weight which maintained the equilibrium of the Constitution." Hamilton's argument did not win the day; at the insistence of the Connecticut, Maryland, South Carolina, and Virginia delegations, the clause requiring ineligibility for legislators became part of the Constitution.[89]

Hamilton and Madison were eminently confident in their borrowings from Hume. They studied the master for guidance on style as well as on political economy. Even when they disagreed with each other, their study of Hume gave them a deep conviction of the significance of his ideas and their implications. Most readers were not so insightful about Hume's intention and struggled to figure out Hume's ideas. One such reader was James Wodrow.

When he read Hume's *Political Discourses* shortly after it was first published in 1752, Wodrow was a twenty-two-year-old graduate of the University of Glasgow, who had remained there as the college librarian until he was later ordained as a Presbyterian minister and assigned to a parish. He may have known Hume at some point, or at least knew friends of friends. "After having read such a book," wrote Wodrow to his friend Samuel Kenrick, one is "pleased and entertained (much in the same way as by a modern romance) from the propriety of the language . . . & the novelty & oddness of some of the thoughts." For a book about things that he didn't know very much about (e.g., money, commerce, public debt), Wodrow absorbed the essays as if they were a novel, enjoying Hume's wit and style. And Wodrow appreciated that while Hume's ideas may reveal complexity and irony, his prose "is very plain & popular (I mean easily understood by the people)." And yet in other ways Wodrow found the essays challenging. "But I don't know, how this Author affects a kind of unconcernedness & indifference with regard to the subjects he writes about." Hume displayed an air of objectivity and even dispassion and at times seemed "careless about the success of arguments he uses in support of any truth." Hume wrote as if the reader should not reach a firm conclusion about the subject. "His arguments & reasoning never or seldom produce any solid conviction, but leave the mind some way loose & more uncertain than when you began." Far from frustrating, however, this quality made the effort fun. "He uses an argument to establish a point then he throws out something on the other side which overturns all he said & leaves you just as you were, then he sets it up; then down with it & at the end you don't know what to think." Wodrow found Hume's style downright playful, even teasing, and he compared it to a children's game:

> Did you ever see our children throw at the Pin-Cocks. A pin for a throw at the cock there.—you missed it you Dog you—Another throw. Hollow, over he goes on his back.—Set him up again, let me have another broadside for my own cock. Hume's reasoning brings always to my mind some match of this kind.

Wodrow realized that Hume was teaching readers how to think critically by modeling his own skeptical style. In particular for Wodrow, the controversial essay "Of the Populousness of Ancient Nations" exemplified this approach. Throughout the eighteenth century, social thinkers equated population growth with prosperity, since demographic increases depended upon expanding natural resources. The inverse was also true: population decline was a sure sign of a poorly performing economy. Montesquieu was typical of thinkers who were convinced that early modern European countries were losing population and were falling far short of their ancient Greek and Roman counterparts.[90] Hume, on the other hand, challenged Montesquieu, arguing "that the World is more populous at present than it was in the flourishing ages of Greece & Rome." Wodrow ended his letter on Hume's *Essays* by giving his friend some personal advice: "There is no other copy of the book in town" because he bought the last copy in Glasgow, "so you need not pester the Booksellers with letters."[91]

Wodrow did not have Madison's or Hamilton's sophistication regarding political thought. He admitted to Kenrick that he was certainly "not qualified to give you any character of it as I have not been accustomed to think or read much upon the subjects of it." Nevertheless, he admired the book and appreciated what it did for him: without pandering or propagandizing, Hume's essays got him to think soberly about important topics central to a thriving civil society. Here was, indeed, the Enlightenment: it happened as an historical event not only when Hume wrote the *Essays*, nor even when they were published, but each time they were read and discussed between friends.

Chapter 8

Figure 8.1 First edition title page Graffigny's *Letters of a Peruvian Woman*. Little from this understated title page, published anonymously and even without proper publisher attribution, would lead one to suspect that this would become among the most popular French novels of the century.

Chapter 8
Graffigny's *Letters of a Peruvian Woman* (1747)

Table 8.1 Eighteenth-Century Editions of *Letters of a Peruvian Woman*

Decade	1747–9	1750–9	1760–9	1770–9	1780–9	1790–1800
Editions	19	8	17	14	12	25

Total Editions: 95.
Translations: English, German, Italian, Polish, Russian, Spanish.
Source: Smith, *Bibliographie des oeuvres de Mme de Graffigny*.

Near the end of 1747, *Letters of a Peruvian Woman* appeared anonymously in Paris bookstores. A small, cheaply produced epistolary novel of 337 pages modeled on *Persian Letters*, it tells the story of Zilia, a Peruvian Inca princess, who is engaged to marry Aza, the heir to the throne. She and her fiancé are seized by Spanish conquistadors, who force them onto separate boats headed for Europe. While Aza is taken to Spain, Zilia is rescued from the Spanish fleet by the French, and personally protected by Déterville, a French nobleman, who brings Zilia to his home in France. The romance that follows features Déterville falling in love with Zilia, who steadfastly maintains her fidelity to her betrothed Aza, confined in Spain. Like *Persian Letters*, the love story is punctuated by Zilia's thoughtful reflections about France. The more Zilia studies French manners and customs, the more critical of them she becomes. The plot's denouement combines love and social criticism in a surprising way: When Déterville finds Aza in Spain with a different lover, the latter renounces his engagement to Zilia, leaving her free to marry. But rather than marry the virtuous Déterville, she pledges never to marry at all, claiming that a woman's independence and autonomy in Europe are incompatible with marriage. "You imagine in vain that you might persuade my heart to take on new chains," she tells Déterville. The novel ends with Déterville and his sister helping Zilia set up her own country estate.[1]

The author of this novel was Françoise de Graffigny, a fifty-two-year-old financially strapped, if well-connected, noblewoman who late in life ran her own salon for a time in Paris. In some ways, her life was not unlike Zilia's, and the novel has several autobiographical elements. Graffigny was physically abused by her husband, who died leaving her penniless at thirty. Instead of marrying again, however, she made a life for herself as an independent—if cash-hungry—widow. At one point she was taken in by Voltaire and his partner, the Marquise du Châtelet. Perhaps it was there that she got the idea of improving upon Montesquieu's classic, since she heard it disparaged by Voltaire and his entourage.[2]

"How can someone be Persian?" Graffigny asked in the book's forward, calling attention, to the link with *Persian Letters*—even identifying in a footnote "*Persian Letters*" for those who missed the point.[3] So, it is easy to dismiss *Letters of a Peruvian Woman* as little more than another mid-century imitation of Montesquieu's great novel; "Usbek in skirts," as one nineteenth-century critic quipped, is an understandable but unfair response.[4] As Mozart was to Haydn, there was much more than imitation in Graffigny's short work. She changed enough of Montesquieu's ingredients to alter the novel's form, and the book's overt feminist perspective made it more of a response to *Persian Letters* than an imitation.

In *Persian Letters*, Montesquieu separated romance from social criticism. Save perhaps for Roxane's climatic final letter of the book, the letters authored by Usbek's Persian wives or their eunuchs drive the romantic plot, while the letters from men (mostly Usbek, Rica, and their friends) offer critical observations of European society mixed with reflections on philosophy, politics, and ethics. As posited in Chapter 3, this division allowed many contemporary readers to dismiss the seraglio scenes as simply scenery, having little to do with the satiric criticism of Parisian elites that takes up most of the book. Graffigny's originality was to integrate both features—romance and philosophy— into the plot's central story line between Zilia and Déterville. Zilia became a combination of Roxane and Usbek: a passionate woman who developed social criticism that is much deeper and more lucid than anything achieved by Déterville, the book's highly virtuous male character. Where *Persian Letters* ends with Roxane's martyrdom, *Peruvian Woman* ends with Zilia in command of her life, property, and household.

In her hunger for learning, Zilia resembles Usbek. She arrives in France already literate by Peruvian standards—she can write using *quipos*, an Inca system of textile knotting. But she longs to understand the words around her and communicate directly with the French. Everyday she studies the language, and while it is difficult, she is determined to master it. "I seek enlightenment with an urgency which quite consumes me."[5] This quest brings her to the discovery of books, which she regards as Europe's greatest and most admirable invention. "I can see that they are to the soul what the Sun is to the earth."[6] Clearly Zilia's book learning empowers and liberates; it helps navigate her new life in France. Through Zilia, Graffigny implied that education was the ultimate weapon for female improvement. When Zilia feels betrayed by Aza near the end of the novel, she turns again to books, this time less for learning than for emotional support: "I turn to books. It is difficult to read, at first, then, imperceptibly, new thoughts cloak the terrible truth hidden in the depths of my heart, and in the end bring some relief to my sorrow."[7]

Graffigny also borrowed Montesquieu's playful use of footnotes. Like today, footnotes signaled erudition and were used mainly for nonfiction genres such as history and essay writing. Montesquieu had placed eighteen footnotes in *Persian Letters*, but their function was mainly to reinforce his fictional pose as simply an editor who had inherited these exotic letters. In *Peruvian Woman*, Graffigny's fifty-five footnotes served a different function. When Zilia describes an Inca custom or institution, or uses a foreign term, Graffigny defined the word or added an historical explanation in the footnote. In this way, the story's sentimentality contrasted with the editor's erudition, reminding readers that the tale they are reading was presented by a scholarly author. Like Hume in his essays, Graffigny's persona in her notes seeks to link the intellectual Republic of Letters and a reading public hungry for good love stories. Published during the years when readers were beginning to appreciate the philosophical significance of *Persian Letters*, Graffigny hoped they would also see her novel in a similar fashion.[8]

Montesquieu compared France with Persia, a proud nation roughly equal to Europe by the standards of world history. Graffigny, by contrast, daringly contrasted France with Inca Peru, focusing on the moment when that exemplary civilization was destroyed by European invaders. Never mind that Zilia and Aza depart Peru during the sixteenth century and arrive in Europe during the eighteenth century—a point that bothered some critics but did not seem at all discomfiting to readers. Unlike Usbek, Zilia is herself a victim of European overseas violence; her reflections and criticisms are meant not simply to judge Europe by a foreigner's standard as Usbek did, but to infuse such judgments with a strong indictment of European imperialism. For literary scholar Janet Altman the novel "constitutes one of the first challenges that was delivered from within European culture to a patriarchal European ethnocentric perspective on world history."[9]

Zilia's book reading and direct observations lead her to make several sharp criticisms of French society. She wholeheartedly condemns, for example, French "prejudice" toward Peru. While claiming for themselves the "priceless spoils" found there, Europeans cannot imagine that Peruvian society has its own integrity, honor, and vibrant culture. Its strangeness seems to give Europeans permission to steal from the Peruvians rather than embrace them as honorable trading partners.[10] Graffigny's ideology here is squarely anti-imperialist, inspiring later interest in pre-Columbian South America.[11] Graffigny decried the way that Europeans dehumanized the peoples of the New World, and her Zilia reflects longing for a relationship based upon mutual reciprocity.

Graffigny went much further than Montesquieu in using the novel to question the status of European women. On the one hand, she recognized that the rules of gallantry required men to show women a certain respect and mutuality, as Montesquieu had depicted satirically in the Parisian scenes of *Persian Letters*. But Graffigny insisted that chivalry was a twisted code of honor that victimized women, who became "the principal target of the nation's customary censure."[12] At the heart of gallantry lay a pack of lies. "Sincerity has been banished from this country."[13] Men were allowed to say anything to women in order to steal their honor and reputation. Worse, men accomplished this trickery only by keeping women in a state of ignorance, treating them as trophies. "She is an ornament, there to entertain the curious; as a result, it only takes an imperious nature to combine with a taste for dissipation, and she will slip into a moral decline."[14] Graffigny found it regrettable that her fictional Zilia was by the novel's end more educated than most of her French female peers. Women were not taken seriously, Graffigny charged; they were considered by men to be toys. With no other opportunities available to them, women were forced to make the most of what they had, moving "quickly from independence to licentiousness, and soon arouse the scorn and indignation of men."[15]

Graffigny blamed French female ignorance largely on the poor system of educating girls in convents. During the eighteenth century, many elite teenage girls spent at least one year in a convent, sometimes more. "As soon as girls are of an age to receive instruction," writes Zilia, "they are shut away in a Religious House to be taught how to live in the world." Like her fellow philosophes, Graffigny was deeply suspicious of convents. The task of "enlightening" minds, she cried out in anger, "is entrusted to those for whom it might be considered a crime to have one." When Zilia is for a brief time "shut away" in a "house of virgins," she finds the nuns "are of such profound ignorance that they cannot answer my most trivial enquiry." Many of the novel's critics, including some close to Graffigny, expected Zilia to convert to Catholicism and were disappointed when she remained not only unmarried but pagan as well. In 1765, Graffigny's perceived criticism of Catholicism won the book a spot on the Catholic Church's Index of Forbidden Books (and later, in 1794, condemnation by the Spanish Inquisition).[16]

When Graffigny was ready to publish the novel in 1747, she deputized two male friends to sell the manuscript to a publisher, but they soon encountered difficulties. Given the government's old-fashioned prejudice against novels, she was unable to secure either a full or tacit *privilège*, making publication risky, subject to both government and church suppression and piracies. Because this was her first literary effort, many publishers were unwilling to take a chance. Finally, Catherine Bouchon offered her 300 livres for the manuscript, a fraction of the sum Graffigny was expecting. Still, she had little choice. Years earlier, Bouchon had taken over her husband's bookshop and publishing house upon his death, and she would expand it until her son took it over after her own death in 1753. Meanwhile, her publishing list reflected typical Enlightenment tastes. Around the time she published *Letters of a Peruvian Woman*, she also produced a mathematical treatise by Denis Diderot, a translation of Eliza Haywood's *Female Spectator*, a guidebook on winemaking, and in 1750, the first edition of Rousseau's *Discourse on the Arts and Sciences*.[17]

Letters of a Peruvian Woman was certainly not marketed as great literature. Its low status is reflected by a title page that carried no real publisher or date (see Figure 8.1). Other than the short title, the only other words on the title page are "À Peine," a word play on Paris that can mean sadness or trouble, perhaps reflecting the hard work the author put into getting it published. Despite this pedestrian start, the book sold so fast that within weeks, Bouchon reprinted it. Graffigny was upset that she could not participate in the reprint, perhaps correcting and adding material, giving her more opportunity for revenue. But Bouchon knew that the book's success left it vulnerable to piracies. Indeed, within a year at least nine more editions were produced by unauthorized printers. Even if she had made little money from her manuscript, Graffigny was assured of the book's popularity.

The early literary reviews were not only positive but surprisingly supportive of Graffigny's overt feminism. In the periodical *Observations sur la littérature moderne*, Joseph La Porte marveled at the originality of Zilia, whose character was new, he said, in European literature. He was impressed with how well the epistolary style conveyed Zilia's purity of heart, and how her understanding of French culture and society matured during the novel. He likewise admired the insightful criticisms put into the words of the Peruvian princess, especially her sense of how anxious and nervous Parisians were—always in a hurry to accomplish trivialities. Above all, he championed Zilia's sense of womanhood, applauding the full participation of women in French cultural life. "Happy the nation where women bound everywhere to obscure households, dare to flee and mix with thinkers," exclaimed La Porte. "Happy the woman who has the force of spirit to overcome the prejudices of her sex."[18] At the same time, like so many other critics and readers, La Porte did not understand why Zilia's feminist stance could not be easily accommodated into a traditional love story with a marital happy ending. La Porte regretted how Graffigny allowed the otherwise sympathetic Aza to abandon Zilia and take up with a Spanish woman. For La Porte, Aza's behavior constituted nothing less than a brazen act of "inhumanity" inconsistent with the rest of Graffigny's plot. All in all, though, La Porte recognized the book as a very important piece of literature. "One can say in general that in recent years there has not appeared any work whose style was more brilliant, feelings more tender, emotions more lively, and ideas more lucid than in this History of Zilia." For La Porte, *Letters of a Peruvian Woman* was not simply a sentimental novel, but like *Persian Letters*, it was a *"roman philosophique,"* a philosophical novel.[19]

Although Elie Catherine Fréron is sometimes portrayed as part as Anti-Enlightenment, he too responded to the book quite positively. Although he made a series of technical criticisms regarding the story's historical conflation of three centuries, Fréron admired "this ingenious work," especially for its style and characterization. He found Graffigny's Zilia a full-bodied character that inevitably affected all readers. Her "love is painted with such varied and vivid colors that even the most insensitive heart is touched."[20] However, the most interesting aspect of Fréron's long review is a five-page prologue that endorses the book's feminist agenda. Zilia's story, Fréron notes at the outset, is about the role women play within France's reading public. Women are treated as sexual objects in most countries precisely because they are kept from receiving any sort of adequate education. If their minds atrophy, it leaves only the body to appreciate. Of course, the ones "to blame" here are men, who have "condemned women to perpetual ignorance." The aim of Graffigny's book, Fréron noted, is precisely to call for an end to that patriarchy by fully welcoming women into all aspects of the Republic of Letters. "Just as we are already diminished by the attraction of the female figure, we fear the superiority of their intellectual talents." Graffigny's Zilia teaches us how to reform "our prejudices."[21]

Even reviews less effusive than La Porte's or Fréron's were respectful of the book's popularity and lauded Zilia for her learning. Pierre Clément enjoyed the book very much, but, like other critics and readers, could not leave the plot alone. Graffigny's ending was highly ambiguous; Zilia was thriving without her potential lovers. "Someone must die here," argued Clément, perhaps recalling the end of *Persian Letters*. If not Déterville and/or Aza, then Graffigny must remove Zilia herself.[22] He also felt that the integration of love and philosophy did not work well. He found Zilia's "metaphysics in love" to be "essentially cold and unnatural." Still, he also admitted that the style contained "handsome details" and "vivid images" making the book certainly worth reading. No one, it would seem, disagreed with the Abbé Antoine François Prévost's assertion that Zilia was worthy of a character in a Richardson novel—and Prévost had some authority in this remark, since he translated Richardson's *Clarissa* into French.[23]

If reviewers endorsed Graffigny's progressive views of women, it was at least partly because they recognized that she had drawn from a tradition in early modern European culture that emphasized the potential rationality of elite women. Graffigny's view of gender emancipation was highly intellectualized. Zilia's newfound solitude gives her time alone to think, read, and study. She is no Amazon: she has no interest in pursuing war like Joan of Arc; she's not interested in political power like Louis XV's mistress, Madame de Pompadour. She does not want to change the world directly; she wants to think about changing it.

This aristocratic and philosophical strain of early modern feminism harked back to seventeenth-century followers of Descartes. By signifying such a radical gap between mind and body, Descartes emphasized an older Christian view that "the mind has no sex." If the mind distinguished human nobility from other animal species, women could improve themselves by rightly having the same access to intellectual pursuits as men. This Cartesian feminism is best reflected in the thought of François Poullain de la Barre (1648–1723), whose ideas became commonplace, albeit always controversial, by the time Graffigny was an adult. Cartesian feminists saw reading, writing, and conversation as the means to self-empowerment. Among their early number was Queen Christina of Sweden, who engaged Descartes himself in a long correspondence. The famous Perpetual Secretary of the Paris Academy of Sciences, Bernard le Bovier de Fontenelle, featured a Cartesian woman in his popular dialogue, *Conversations on the Plurality of Worlds* (1686). Graffigny was neither the first nor the last Cartesian feminist thinker.[24]

Early modern Cartesian feminism was inherently elitist, making it an unlikely ancestor of modern feminist movements. Graffigny's feminism was explicitly antidemocratic, as she never suggested that all women might become like Zilia, who is envisioned, like Graffigny herself, as an exception to patriarchal rule. Rather, Graffigny's demand was that when exceptional women come along, the same opportunities given to exceptional men become available to them. Opening the doors of the Republic of Letters to meritorious women was something different and far more limited than what later suffragettes had in mind. Zilia is, after all, an aristocratic Inca princess, belonging to a caste more fortunate than most Peruvian women. Graffigny's ideology, then, amounted to an aristocratic feminism, meant to emancipate only a small segment of society's upper tier. Graffigny's feminism was developed within the social context of salonnières, bluestockings, and elite governesses: extraordinary women who had access to extraordinary resources.

What was new in Graffigny's feminism was not the call for the Republic of Letters to accommodate women, but the insistence that marriage was incompatible with such a mission.[25]

Given the initial success of *Letters of a Peruvian Woman*, sequels were quickly composed and printed. When *Suite des lettres d'une Peruvienne* (A Sequel to the Letters of a Peruvian Woman) appeared anonymously during spring 1748, Graffigny suspected the unknown author Chevalier de Mouhy had penned the sixty-page duodecimo. The sequel included added letters that did not alter the plot in a major way, but Mouhy did not leave Graffigny's ambiguous ending alone. Déterville's sister, Céline, intervened with Zilia on behalf of her brother, and by the final pages, readers discerned that Zilia's friendship with Déterville was moving toward romantic intimacy. Graffigny's initial reaction was to laugh off this silly imitation; she assumed the writing was so bad that it would be self-evident to readers that this version was counterfeit. However, a few months later the well-connected Lausanne publisher, Marc Michel Bousquet, distinguished his edition of *Peruvian Woman* by joining Mouhy's seven additional letters with Graffigny's original thirty-eight.[26] Reading both parts together made Zilia's marital renunciation one turning point in the plot rather than its climax, defusing Graffigny's message. In a forward, Bousquet led readers to believe that the sequel was written by Graffigny, and for this reason, Bousquet placed on the title page "second edition," to make it seem an authorized expansion of the original. In this format, a reader might find it difficult to discern the truth of authorship, and at least one German visitor to Paris, the Baron von Gleichen, assumed Graffigny had written the sequel.[27]

Meanwhile, London bookseller and publisher John Brindley put out the first English translation of *Letters of a Peruvian Woman*. This edition was completely faithful to Graffigny's original, save for short summaries of each letter in an expanded table of contents that signaled greater depth to the story. The summary for the final letter reads: "Declares her resolution to live free, and comforts and exhorts Deterville." Within a year the book had done well enough that Brindley prepared a new edition. However, instead of simply reprinting the first one, Brindley copied Bousquet in attaching Mouhy's sequel and calling this new version the "second edition, revised and corrected by the translator, to which is now added, the Sequel of the Peruvian Letters."[28] Consequently, English-language readers were introduced to the novel in a way that diluted Graffigny's key argument for female autonomy and led readers to think she had written all of it.

The following year, in 1749, a Dutch publisher produced a new sequel by the minor writer Ignace Hugary de Lamarche-Courmont, the *Lettres d'Aza* (Letters from Aza), in a 132-page duodecimo format. This version completely altered Graffigny's plot by returning Aza to the center of the novel and having him marry Zilia by the story's end. Popular with readers, this version alone went through at least five editions. More important, in 1751 a pirated edition printed either in Amsterdam or in Rouen (or both) featured Mouhy's sequel *and* Lamarche-Courmont's *Letters from Aza* following Graffigny's original thirty-eight letters. Reading the plot this way demoted Graffigny's message even more: after Zilia claims her autonomy (Graffigny's original) and grows closer to Déterville (Mouhy's additional seven letters), Aza's triumphal return ends with their marriage (*Letters from Aza*); in these sequels, Zilia's autonomy has been long forgotten through new tears of sentimental joy. In 1751 there were already more editions published that altered the plot by including one or both sequels than held true to Graffigny's intentions. Given the lack of international copyright, of course, Graffigny had no means to exert pressure on publishers in Switzerland, Holland, or Britain, who by the early 1750s were mainly producing these ersatz versions. For these reasons, it is hardly surprising that at least by 1751, Graffigny decided to publish a wholly revised and expanded version of her novel. Such a revision would have the obvious benefit of allowing her to sell her manuscript once again, increasing her always-fragile revenue stream. At the same time, it would supersede the various pirated editions that had appeared, rendering them obsolete, and it would allow her to make her ideas even bolder. Graffigny would follow a path forged by Voltaire, Richardson, Hume, and many other writers.[29]

Among the changes that Graffigny planned in a second edition was a new chapter devoted entirely to attaching the moral consequences of the aristocratic fashion market, weighing in on the great debate over luxury. Graffigny clarified that addiction to luxury lay at the root of France's patriarchalism, imperialism, and skewed religious values. "Their unbridled passion for luxury has corrupted their reason, their heart, and their mind." Siding with Fénelon against Hume and Montesquieu, and anticipating Rousseau's *Discourse on Inequality* (1755), Graffigny staked out an uncompromising position regarding the inequality engendered by conspicuous consumption. Luxury "has founded illusory riches on the ruins of what is essential; that it has substituted superficial politeness for good manners, and that it replaces common sense and reason with the empty brilliance of wit."[30]

As she prepared this revision project, Graffigny sought advice from her closest friends. Among them was a twenty-four-year-old writer who had just completed his first major essay on historical progress, the future intendant and French controller general, Anne Robert Jacques Turgot. Although thirty years younger than Graffigny, they became close friends during this period when Turgot, mourning the death of his father, sought consolation from the older matron. Their intimacy did not mean they saw things alike. "He surely has a lucid mind, but we rarely are of the same opinion," Graffigny wrote to a friend.[31] The most interesting aspect of Turgot's advice is how seriously he treated her ideas. He regarded the book not as a light and entertaining romance but as a serious philosophical novel filled with important thoughts on the state of French society. He believed it merited comparison with *Persian Letters*.

Of course, Turgot had his own suggestions for how to improve the book. Like so many other readers, he embraced Zilia's autonomy up to a point, but urged Graffigny to assimilate Zilia more successfully into French society, which meant, first and foremost, marriage. It was wrong, thought Turgot—who ironically stayed a bachelor all his life—for Zilia to remain independent, apart from any conjugal relationship. It was perverse for a woman to live without male companionship. After all, "it is nature that established marriage." Graffigny, he charged his good friend, was going against the "providential wisdom of the supreme being." He pleaded with her to bring Aza back from Spain and allow the couple to consummate their love in happy matrimony; in short, to incorporate the plot line sketched out by Lamarche-Courmont's *Letters from Aza*. For Turgot, conjugal fulfillment did not negate female erudition.[32]

Turgot, who would later go on to write the *Reflections on the Formation and Distribution of Wealth*, contested Graffigny's Fénelonian view of economics, expressed in her utopian rendering of Inca society, with its critique of modern luxury and inequality. Graffigny believed that Inca society's commitment to economic equality placed it on a more sustained footing than France, which teetered between boom and bust cycles. "In most houses" in France, writes Zilia in the new section, "indigence and luxury are no more than one room apart."[33] Although polite in his criticism, Turgot rejected Graffigny's basic understanding of political economy. Inequality and luxury were not problematic but necessary for the progress of society out of any primitive state. "Men are not born equal," Turgot insisted to her. They are divided by birth in countless ways, including intelligence, artistic talent, imagination, and work ethic. Being born into families, they are either plagued or blessed with the talents of their parents, and hence, their first relationships are dependent ones. Turgot believed it natural for the dependency and inequality of family relations to replicate themselves in labor. "It is more just and more useful for all that those who are deficient in mind or in good fortune should lend their strength to others who can employ them, who can, in advance, give them wages, and thus guarantee them a share of the future products." There is nothing wrong, Turgot told Graffigny, with an unequal division of labor. "Inequality will arise, and will increase, even among the most virtuous and most moral peoples." Indeed, inequality "is not an evil, it is a blessing for mankind." Anticipating Adam Smith's rejection of Rousseau's economic ideas, Turgot insisted to Graffigny that it is wrong for Zilia to favor impoverished Peru over the benefits of a modern economy like France. "To prefer the condition of the savage is a ridiculous declamation. Let [Zilia] refute it."

> Let her show that the vices which we regard as produced by civilization are the appanage of the human heart; that he who has no gold may be as avaricious as he who has it, because, in all circumstances, men have the hunger for property, the right to preserve it, the avidity which actuates them to accumulate its products.[34]

However much Turgot quibbled with Graffigny's views on inequality, he nevertheless appreciated the contribution that fiction could make to the understanding of such issues. Indeed, what is remarkable here is that Turgot related the development of the novel to the rise of political economy. Both genres presented applied moral philosophy to a readership outside the traditional Republic of Letters. Graffigny's fiction helped prepare a critical public for new ways that government might address the economy. Three decades later, when Turgot's disciple Condorcet published his eulogistic *Life of Turgot*, the role of the novel became central to understanding Turgot's thought. "M. Turgot . . . considered novels as books of morality." Indeed, Turgot had told Condorcet that novels were the "only" effective means for conveying moral ideas to a wide readership. It was in novels such as Graffigny's "that we best observe the influence of our actions upon our conduct and the happiness of those who surround us." Such happiness is, Condorcet noted, "the most important and yet the most neglected part of morality."[35]

Graffigny ignored Turgot's advice and her attack on luxury was one important element that distinguished the second version of *Letters of a Peruvian Woman* from its predecessor. In addition, she added a substantive "Historical Introduction" that meant to establish the high stage of civilization Inca society had reached at the time of the Spanish invasion. Before readers encountered Zilia's story, they learned that the backdrop for her tale was nothing less than a historical calamity. "So it was that the Peruvians became the pathetic victims of a greedy nation, having first shown them only good faith and even friendship." This introduction signaled that this new version of the novel would be even more philosophical, deepening its social criticism and presenting a stance against European imperialism unrivaled before Raynal's *History of the Two Indies* was first published in 1770. Graffigny clarified that the novel was not written from her imagination only, but rooted in eyewitness accounts, such as Garcilaso de la Vega's *Royal Commentaries of the Incas*, first published in 1609, and closely consulted by Graffigny in a 1744 French translation. "It has to be admitted," Graffigny quoted Garcilaso, that the Incas "achieved such great things, and established such a well-ordered society, that few nations can claim to have bettered them in this respect." Just as Voltaire gave his historical account of *Charles XII* greater depth by surrounding it with various historical introductions, so Graffigny bolstered her novel with this extraordinary paratext.[36]

Selling her new manuscript to a new publisher was easy compared to five years earlier. This time the well-established bookseller/publisher Nicholas Bonaventure Duchesne offered Graffigny 3,000 livres, far more than the 300 livres she had previously received from Catherine Bouchon. This was half the amount Duchesne would spend nine years later, when he purchased for "a record sum" Rousseau's huge manuscript for the four-volume philosophical treatise, *Emile*.[37] The well-connected Duchesne knew exactly what he was doing. The French book trade had liberalized in the five years between versions largely because Guillaume Chrétien Lamoignon de Malesherbes had taken over as director of the book trade in 1750. Indeed, Director Malesherbes intervened to secure an official approbation and privilège for *Letters of a Peruvian Woman*, protecting the book from easy piracy in France and providing Duchesne a guaranteed income. This more favorable climate allowed Duchesne to invest in several enhancements that would make this second version, which appeared in 1752, have the appearance of a more serious work. Expanded into two volumes, and joined with Graffigny's most successful play, *Cénie*, the work included an elaborately engraved title page (see Figure 8.2) along with fancy and detailed frontispieces for each volume that depicted scenes from the novel. These were designed by one of the premier French book illustrators, Charles Eisen, who also produced frontispieces for books by Montesquieu, Voltaire, Richardson, and Raynal.[38] In addition to a crisper and larger font, the two volumes closed with a reproduction of its legal approbation, revealing for the first time in print the name of Madame de Graffigny as the book's author.

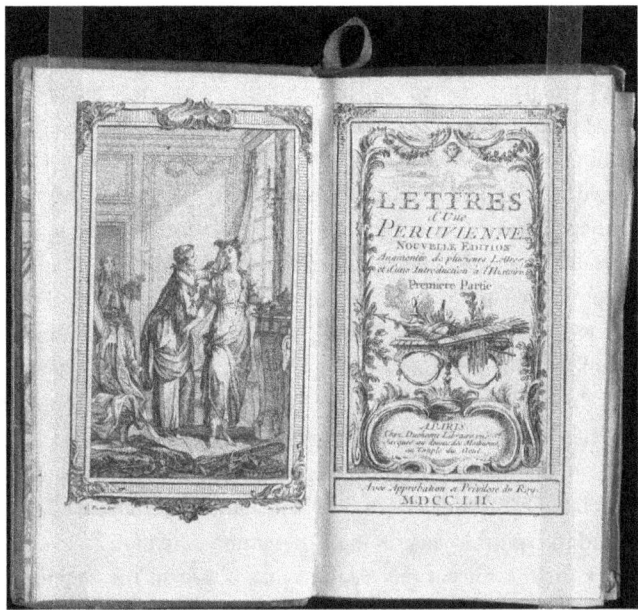

Figure 8.2 Second edition title page Graffigny's *Letters of a Peruvian Woman*, along with a frontispiece designed by Charles Eisen. This ornate title page signifies a novel of great literary quality, proud of its official "privilège" from the government. Nonetheless, it would have been impertinent for a woman author to place her name on a title page.

For evidence that contemporaries took this new version of *Letters of a Peruvian Woman* more seriously as a philosophical novel during the 1750s, we need to look no further than that centerpiece of Enlightenment publishing, Diderot and d'Alembert's *Encyclopédie*. Between 1754 and 1765, Graffigny's book was cited in six different articles (*Devoir, Divertissement, Ecriture, Larme, Quipos*, and *Religieuse* [Duty, Diversion, Writing, Teardrop, Quipos, and Nun]). Zilia herself was quoted as an authority, as if she were a real person. "Zilia was blinded by her prejudices," Louis de Jaucourt wrote in the article *Religieuse*, "but it is true that too often nuns are the victims of luxury and vanity." Elsewhere, Jaucourt treated the book more as a work of history than fiction: "this Peruvian woman full of intelligence, so well-known from her works."[39]

The 1752 Duchesne edition became the premier version, the only one authorized by Graffigny, before her death in 1758. By all accounts, it was remarkably successful. Indeed, as Table 8.1 illustrates, *Letters of a Peruvian Woman* sold consistently throughout the second half of the century. By the 1760s, the book was "in everyone's hands,"[40] and Graffigny's portrait—not Zilia's—graced the frontispiece of a 1777 edition, reflecting her status as an established author.[41] In the same decade, Graffigny became the only woman included in Gautier d'Agoty's anthology of the dozen most important figures in all of French history.[42] By 1800, over ninety editions had been published, including translations in German, Spanish, and Russian. English Showalter may well be correct when he claims that by the time of her death Graffigny had become the most famous female writer in the European world. At least one reader, William Hayley, claimed in 1785 that Graffigny's novel "is inferior, perhaps, to no performance which the literary world has received from the tender and lively imagination of woman."[43] Nor did the popularity of *Peruvian Woman* abate during the early nineteenth century. Between 1800 and 1836, twenty-six editions were published.

Suddenly, however, the well ran dry. Between 1836 and 1967, the novel was rarely published, and then only in private or very small print runs (except for Scandinavia, where it was produced in Swedish and Danish translations). By the late nineteenth century. the novel was virtually forgotten across literary Europe, and while Graffigny was recognized as a savant in her own day, twentieth-century cultural historians and philosophers, such as Gustave Lanson, Paul Hazard, and Ernst Cassirer, completely ignored *Letters of a Peruvian Woman*. Indeed, it is nowhere to be found in Peter Gay's 1960s landmark two-volume *The Enlightenment*, and, even more recently, in Jonathan Israel's epic five-volume history of the Enlightenment, the novel is mentioned on only one page. Appreciated even today mainly by specialists, *Letters of a Peruvian Woman* still has yet to find its rightful place in the Enlightenment canon.[44]

What accounts for the mysterious decline that began in the second quarter of the nineteenth century? There is no definitive answer to that question. Tastes change, of course, especially in literature and the arts. We know, for example, that the epistolary form of the novel died out at the end of the eighteenth century; the great novelists of the nineteenth century—Austen, Dickens, Balzac, Dostoyevsky—did not make much use of this format in their fiction. Still, several eighteenth-century epistolary novels continued to be published regularly during the nineteenth and twentieth centuries, including *Persian Letters* and *Pamela*. Why was *Peruvian Woman* different? Perhaps one reason is that its feminist and anti-imperialist ideology fell so much out of favor until revived by twentieth-century second-wave feminism and decolonization.[45]

The quest for gender equality does not move through history along a straight path, but lurches backward and forward from one epoch to the next. According to perceptive historians of European gender relations, such as Christine Fauré and Joan Landes, the era of the French Revolution marked a significant turning point in the status of women. When the revolution initiated modern democracy based upon popular sovereignty, it largely excluded women from political life. Where Jews won their civic rights in France during the 1790s, for example, it would take women until 1945 to secure the vote. The Napoleonic Code (1804) subordinated women in both the political and civil spheres in ways more patriarchal than the Old Regime. After the Bourbons were restored to the French throne in 1815, little sympathy emerged for a revival of elite feminism.[46]

At this point, it would seem that *Letters of a Peruvian Woman* fell into disfavor during the early nineteenth century because of a combination of factors, including female exclusion from the literary canon as well as an increasing rejection of Graffigny's elitist brand of feminism. But such a generalization would be incomplete and even misleading. In fact, *Letters of a Peruvian Woman* carried the seeds of its own demise from the start, when demand for editions that included sequels began to outweigh those authorized by the author. Graffigny's work suffered from this phenomenon.

Of all the Enlightenment bestsellers covered in this study, Graffigny's *Letters of a Peruvian Woman* has the strangest and perhaps most remarkable publication history. Altogether there were ninety-five editions published during the century. Between the publication of the second edition in 1752 and 1800 there were seventy-four editions published (including one edition produced in the Caribbean British colony Saint Christopher). Among them, only a small number of editions strictly followed the authorized 1752 version published by Duchesne; the majority of editions added material undermining the core messages of the novel, at least as intended by its author. These editions can be divided into three groups:

(1) No Sequel Editions Attached: 13 (P22A,[47] P23, P40, P42, P47, P52, P55, P60, P63, P67, P73, P75, P79). These thirteen editions were published as Graffigny wished. Five are translations, and some of the English translations track the first (1747) edition rather than the (1752) second edition. This category is clearly the smallest group.

(2) Italian Language Related Editions: 28 (P24, P28A, P32, P48, P51, P56, P57, P58, P62, P64.1, P64.2, P66.1, P66.2, P68, P70, P74, P76.1, P76.2, P77, P81, P82.1, P82.2, P82.3, P83.1, P83.2, P84.1, P84.2, P84.3). These editions were designed with foreign-language pedagogy in mind. Graffigny's novel became a vehicle for Europeans who knew French to learn Italian, and perhaps for Italians to learn French. Many of these editions were sold separately as well, to Italians, French, and others.

(3) Sequels Attached to Graffigny's Editions: 33 (P25, P26B, P27, P29A, P30, P31A, P33, P34, P35, P36A, P37, P37bis, P38, P39, P41, P42bis, P43, P44, P46, P49, P50, P53, P54, P59, P61A, P65, P69, P71, P72, P78A, P80, P 85, P86). These thirty-three editions joined one or both sequels, or invented new sequels, or as with London, 1774, altered Graffigny's original narrative. For example, the 1791 Russian translation was based on the early 1747 version, supplemented with the seven Mouhy letters and *Letters from Aza*.[48]

Despite the fact that Duchesne's 1752 edition was backed by a royal privilege, allowing for a print run perhaps two or three times greater than normal, it took several years for that edition to sell out, reflecting anemic demand for editions published without sequels.[49] Only ten or so of the seventy-four editions published between 1752 and 1800 adhered to the 1752 version in the manner intended by Graffigny. This was not the case with most novels. *Pamela*, for example, was never published jointly with *Shamela* or the other sequels or satires, even in territories outside of English legal control, such as Ireland. Montesquieu's *Persian Letters* was not produced in volumes joined with its imitators. In short, what happened to *Letters of a Peruvian Woman* was rare in the eighteenth-century publishing world.

The significance of this unusual publishing record has been poorly understood by historians and literary critics. We have seen throughout this book how paratexts affect the reader's perception of a book. For example, in Chapter 2 we saw how the various introductions to *Telemachus* reframed that novel, paving the way for its absorption into Enlightenment culture. Similarly, joining the sequels to Graffigny's original, especially without proper authorial attribution, undermined Graffigny's feminist message and social criticism. Insofar as most of these editions married off Zilia, or at least drove her in the direction of Déterville, both sequels contested Graffigny's key insights regarding female autonomy.

When we examine the English translations, it becomes even more clear that readers admired the novel more for its conventional romantic possibilities than its daring philosophical implications. In 1774 the well-established London publisher Thomas Cadell produced a two-volume new translation by a female translator named Roberts. While the first volume discarded Graffigny's historical introduction and hewed closely to the 1747 version, Roberts included a second volume that began with the seven-letter Mouhy sequel, expanding into material all her own. She revealed her motivation in a preface: "I was not indeed altogether satisfied with the conclusion, being desirous the Indian Princess should become a convert to Christianity, and that so generous a friend as Deterville might be as happy as his virtues deserved." In the telling of Miss Roberts, Zilia's religious conversion allows her to forget Aza and eventually unite with Déterville. Needless to say, this throwback to a conventional plot line would not have pleased Graffigny.[50]

Like Roberts, the Spanish translator María Romero Masegosa y Cancelada altered Graffigny's story by adding a new letter that converted Zilia to Catholicism. Some other features of the story were toned down as well, such as Graffigny's distrust of the church. And like Roberts, Romero admired Graffigny's views on female education. When, for example, Zilia writes about how her own French studies gave her a greater command of French than most uneducated French women, Romero applied the lesson in a footnote to Spanish women. In a separate footnote, Romero endorsed Graffigny's criticism of luxury and fashion: "Zilia also speaks in another section of the vast time that they waste at the dressing table. I very much desire that our dress, which is not only costly but also bothersome, be simplified; such that from here on out it will serve but for our comfort and protection." In one area, though, Romero differed from Roberts. While Romero converted Zilia to Catholicism, she left her unmarried, friends with Déterville but no more than that. Such an ending was not satisfying for at least some Spanish readers. One of them took matters into her own hands. In the National Library of Madrid there is a copy of Romero's translation whose final sentences have been changed and annotated by an emotional reader: "Zilia at long last you married your friend, good I say I am very happy, yes, very happy. Zilia [and] Déterville, Céline and her husband, Aza and his wife lived happily ever after." And then, thinking further about it, the Spanish reader scratched out "friendship," replacing it with "passion," emphasizing her wish that the two characters would become married lovers by the end of the story.[51]

Since *Letters of a Peruvian Woman* was rediscovered by scholars in the 1960s and 1970s, it has been recognized as a masterpiece of early modern feminism. Much of this evaluation still remains true. Graffigny's intentions were, within the limits of early modern aristocratic feminism, unusually progressive, especially her assertion that patriarchy rendered eighteenth-century marriage incompatible with female autonomy and authority. However, the publishing history of the novel reveals how the reading public constrained Graffigny's feminism, and in many cases directly challenged it through demanding an ending that transformed Zilia into a wife. In the end, mediated by booksellers and publishers, this Enlightenment public overcame what they saw as Graffigny's eccentricities, remaking the book from a philosophical novel into a sentimental romance, despite Graffigny's best efforts to make the book even more philosophical in the revised edition. Graffigny may have wanted an independent Zilia, but the more conservative public demanded someone who more resembled the married Pamela Andrews. If members of the reading public had preferred an unmarried Zilia, no doubt publishers would have satisfied them. Excluding Graffigny from the Enlightenment canon, then, did not wait for the nineteenth century, as scholars have previously thought, but was actively present almost from the novel's beginning. "I am highly pleased with the Peruvian Letters," proclaimed the Earl of Chesterfield to Mme de Tencin in 1748. Typical of his generation of readers in this regard, he added: "Only I wish that Zilia, justly provoked at the behavior of Aza, had married Déterville out of gratitude." Over the course of the century, publishers across Europe helped produce this outcome for Chesterfield and other readers who felt as he did.[52]

Turgot, then, was not alone in wishing Graffigny had married off Zilia. Such a reaction reveals anxiety over social issues such as fecundity and population. Montesquieu's *Persian Letters*, for example, included eleven letters fretting about Europe's declining birth rate. As Rousseau's *Emile* would soon make clear, European countries needed pro-natal policies that encouraged motherhood. Likewise, at least part of the Enlightenment's concern over convents reflected the very high rate of elite women who never married at all. These worries over the birth rate trumped Graffigny's wish for Zilia to be taken as a model for others.[53]

Cultural historians often bias their studies toward the author. The methods of Cambridge School scholarship associated with such luminaries as Quentin Skinner and J. G. A. Pocock may help reconstruct how a text was prepared and produced, but they too often minimize how a work was mediated by publishers and treated by a critical public. When we position publishers, readers, and authors in equal proximity to one another in the making and reproduction of books, a different narrative may be revealed. Graffigny's *Letters of a Peruvian Woman* shows that the emerging Enlightenment public was anything but passive. Publishers and readers, even those close to Graffigny, openly betrayed her intentions and contested her ideas, demonstrating that any history of Enlightenment Europe must regard readers and publishers as key actors who helped shape its ideas.[54]

Chapter 9

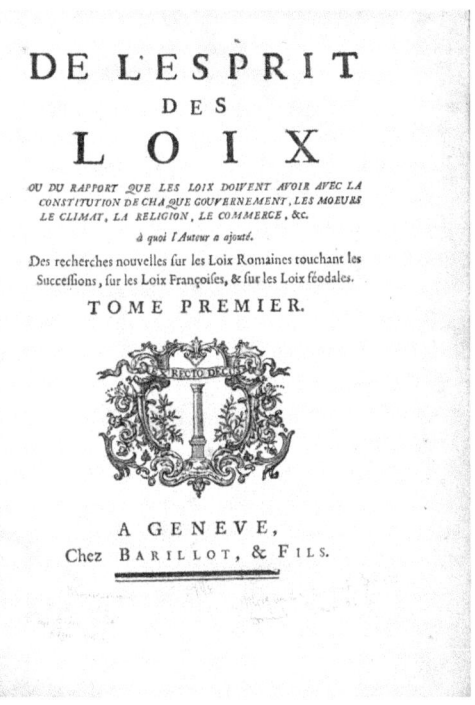

Figure 9.1 First edition title page Montesquieu's *The Spirit of the Laws*. For this expensive quarto edition, the publisher reused the same design as he had done for the recently published *Principles of Natural Law* by Jean Jacques Burlamaqui.

Chapter 9
Montesquieu's *The Spirit of the Laws* (1748)

Table 9.1 Eighteenth-Century Editions of *The Spirit of the Laws*

Decade	1748–9	1750–9	1760–9	1770–9	1780–9	1790–1800
Editions	12	18	13	26	8	20

Total Editions: 97.
Translations: Danish, Dutch, English, German, Italian, Polish, Russian.
Source: https://kates.itg.pomona.edu/books/analytics.php?type=all. accessed March 9, 2022, and Courtney, "L'Esprit des lois dans la perspective de l'histoire du livre," 65–98.

By 1747 Montesquieu was finally near completion on a large manuscript regarding comparative government, *The Spirit of the Laws*.[1] He knew that it would be virtually impossible for him to publish a work about politics freely in France, so he asked a friend to scout out whether the Desbordes firm in Amsterdam would be interested in producing his work once again. After all, Desbordes had earlier published both *Persian Letters* and his Roman history. But this time was different. In 1747 France was still fighting the long War of the Austrian Succession, and Holland was allied with Britain and Austria against France and Prussia. Given this climate, Montesquieu's efforts to publish in Amsterdam were blocked. Improvisation was required. Through a connection in Paris, Montesquieu found a Swiss diplomat, Pierre Mussard, ready to help. Mussard visited Geneva and found the firm of Barrillot & Sons eager to publish the book. They produced a mock-up of a title page for Montesquieu, indicating the quality of paper, lettering, font, and ornaments. Coincidentally, Barrillot was just then working on printing the *Principles of Natural Law* by the Genevan Jean Jacques Burlamaqui, and they simply used its design as a model for *The Spirit of the Laws*. Mussard and Montesquieu were pleased, and Barrillot was engaged to publish the work. Montesquieu would get seventy free copies but no money, and Barrillot could keep for himself any profits he could make from producing what would be an expensive book.[2]

Montesquieu's manuscript was very different from *Persian Letters* or even his Roman history. These were shorter works that were immediately accessible to a reading public. *The Spirit of the Laws*, by contrast, would be almost always published at more than 1,000 pages,[3] divided into 31 "books," each book divided into sections called "chapters." It was a large formal treatise, full of references to classical and modern sources, the culmination of a lifetime of scholarship. Aimed originally for a more narrowly erudite sector of the public than *Persian Letters*, *The Spirit of the Laws* would be first published in an expensive two-volume quarto format that appealed to serious book buyers. Montesquieu himself announced to his readers that unlike *Persian Letters*, this work was the fruit of "twenty years" labor that expressed his most mature and penetrating ideas. "Many times I began this work and many times abandoned it. . . . But when I discovered my principles, all that I had sought came to me."[4]

Transferring word to print was a huge challenge for a relatively small family publisher, especially with Montesquieu near Bordeaux, 700 kilometers from Geneva. Mussard thus brought a specialized editor into the project, a scholar in his own right, the professor Jacob Vernet, "a considerable literary and theological figure of his day, not only in Geneva and Switzerland, but throughout Europe."[5] It seemed that Montesquieu had discovered an ideal interlocutor.

Unfortunately, Vernet's work proved less than satisfactory. He turned out to be an aggressive mediator and a poor copy editor. Although Mussard had let him know the identity of the author, this did not stop his altering the text, eliminating passages, and changing the structure of the work. Montesquieu had separated groups of books into six basic parts, reflecting each section's unique theme. When Vernet cavalierly removed the parts, it made the book's structure appear less unified and more chaotic than it really was, an issue that would plague the book's reception. Even worse was Vernet's failure to fix the small but maddening typographical errors made by Barrillot's printers. To be sure, virtually all eighteenth-century books contained printing errors, commonly addressed with an errata page. But Montesquieu's book had an epidemic of such snafus. When *The Spirit of the Laws* was finally published in November 1748, Montesquieu discovered, to his horror, that there were hundreds of errors. "*The Spirit of the Laws* has been crippled at Geneva," he exclaimed to a friend.[6] Vernet blamed the publisher and Barrillot's son took responsibility. His father had died in June 1748, in the middle of printing the book, and the project overwhelmed a grieving son and son-in-law, who were left to take over the shop. Writing to Montesquieu a year later, Barrillot begged forgiveness on account of "the long illness and death of a father so loved and cherished by his son."[7]

While the author was fretting about the first edition's mistakes, the book itself was causing a sensation among its readers. Montesquieu directed an advance copy sent to Mme de Tencin, the Parisian writer opinion maker. "Philosophy, reason, humanity have been brought together to compose this work," she wrote to its author in November 1748. "Graces have taken care to adorn it with erudition."[8] A month later, another friend, the philosophe Claude Adrien Helvétius, endorsed the book as "the greatest, the most beautiful work in the world."[9] What struck these early readers, and would soon be remarked upon throughout Europe, was the combination of deep scholarship and a crisp light style that made learning agreeable; a combination of wit and useful knowledge is how the famous son of the British prime minister Horace Walpole put it:

I want to know Dr. Cocchi's & your opinion of two French books, if you have seen them. One is Montesquieu's *l'Esprit des lois*, which I think the best book that ever was written—at least I never learned half so much from all I ever read. There is as much wit as useful knowledge.[10]

Somehow Montesquieu had figured out a way to make erudite philosophy entertaining. Without pandering to a broad audience by simplifying ideas, *The Spirit of the Laws* attracted readers who were certainly educated but in no way scholarly. "The book appears to me a masterpiece of wit and philosophy," echoed socialite Mme de Geoffrin soon after it appeared.[11] Where Hume's 1739 *Treatise of Human Nature* had "fell deadborn from the press," a decade later *The Spirit of the Laws* achieved what Hume had long dreamed but thought impossible: a best-selling treatise, at once learned and readable. Hume himself appreciated its achievement, writing to Montesquieu that the book will "be esteemed by all nations and admired for all time."[12]

Meanwhile, Montesquieu drew up his own errata sheet with 200–300 corrections. Through his friend Mme de Tencin, he had 400 copies of this sheet distributed to Paris booksellers. Given the book's immediate renown, new publishers wanted in on the game. After all, Barrillot had produced a fancy two-volume quarto book priced at eighteen livres—out of reach for all but wealthy readers.[13] Normally such scholarly works took years to pay for themselves. But *The Spirit of the Laws* sold so fast that pirates were naturally interested in reproducing lavish quarto editions in lower-quality formats (octavos and duodecimos) that could be priced much cheaper. Usually the author of a successful book would be loyal to the original publisher (as Hume always was, for example), providing new "corrected" versions to that firm, so the original publisher could stay ahead of the pirates and the author recoup more revenue; indeed, normally that was the only way an author could receive further remuneration for a book. Montesquieu expected little money from his books; overseeing peasants working his vineyards of fine merlot and cabernet sauvignon grapes had made his family rich enough. So, like Voltaire but for different reasons, Montesquieu became complicit in attempts to produce counterfeit editions of his own book. When he heard from friends that a London publisher was about to print a French-language edition in London, Montesquieu instructed a friend, William Domville, to make a trip to England with a copy of the errata sheet, so that even the unauthorized version would be up-to-date.

This London edition, published by John Nourse, appeared during spring 1749 with a false title page attributed to Barrillot & Fils in Geneva that announced: "made with corrections from the author." Produced in a two-volume octavo format, it was priced at half the genuine Genevan quarto.[14] It was among several unauthorized editions sprouting up simultaneously. Already Laurent Durand (a major Paris publisher) had produced an imitation quarto edition in January 1749. In March, another copycat quarto edition, printed in Lyon, invaded the Paris market. Barrillot also reprinted his original Geneva edition with Montesquieu's corrections. Montesquieu seemed to support any and all of these publishers. He worked closely with Huart & Moreau, a Paris firm, which put out an edition in May 1749 not only "corrected by the author" but also "supplemented with a table of contents and a geographical map." Its false title page sometimes read Geneva: Barrillot & Fils and sometimes Amsterdam: Zacharie Chatelain. In any case, within a year or two more pirated reprints were copying this Huart & Moreau edition.[15] Before the book's one-year anniversary, according to the twenty-four-year-old Bordeaux lawyer and future art patron Simon Antoine Delphin de Lamothe, "eleven or twelve editions have been made. . . . It is a book that is universally valued; the most solid truths are displayed in a lively and concise style."[16]

By January 1750, only fourteen months after its initial publication, Montesquieu's frustration regarding typographical errors gave way to glee at the book's enormous popularity, as he bragged to the Duc de Nivernais that "there are twenty-two editions of my work circulating throughout Europe."[17] Even if Montesquieu slightly exaggerated, he certainly caught the prevailing winds. The explosive demand for *The Spirit of the Laws* was, in fact, only just beginning. At least fourteen more editions (six French, eight translations) were published before Montesquieu's death in 1755, when Huart & Moreau prepared a posthumous edition that would become standard.[18] Whether published separately or as the main part of collected works, *The Spirit of the Laws* remained a solid bestseller throughout the remaining years of the eighteenth century. According to best estimates, between 1748 and 1800, including translations, the book went through ninety-seven editions, with the 1770s and 1790s the leading decades.[19] Remarkably, less than a handful were abridged. In this respect, the Dutch-produced thematic compilation *Le génie de Montesquieu* proved the exception to the rule, noting in its first pages: "M. de Montesquieu is perhaps the least able of all writers to be abridged."[20] Instead, virtually all publishers made a considerable investment reprinting the entire 1,000-plus pages of Montesquieu's large treatise. This itself was very unusual during the eighteenth century. For example, Locke's *Two Treatises on Government* was usually reprinted in foreign-language editions without its *First Treatise*. In contrast, even Montesquieu's final long section on the development of feudal law, certainly the least noted and critiqued, was included everywhere.

Montesquieu's work was also widely translated, perhaps more so than any other work of political philosophy in early modern Europe. Not only was it published in at least eight languages besides French (Danish, Dutch, English, German, Italian, Latin, Polish, and Russian) during the eighteenth century, but it also went through multiple editions in most of them (only the Latin and Danish versions were not reprinted), attesting to heavy demand across Europe.

To gain some appreciation for Montesquieu's accomplishment in the world of eighteenth-century publishing, one might compare *The Spirit of the Laws* to three possible competitors. We have already seen how Barrillot had mirrored its title page with Burlamaqui's 1747 *Principles of Natural Right*. A few years later, in 1752, Barrillot published a companion book, the *Principles of Political Right*. Together these two works (often published as one book) went through many editions and had significant influence throughout Europe and especially on the American Founders. Nonetheless, there were only a total of thirty-two editions of Burlamaqui's work during the eighteenth century, translated into five foreign languages—a good run to be sure, but one far from Montesquieu's achievement. Second, John Locke published the *Two Treatises on Government* in 1690. During the 110 years between 1690 and 1800, Locke's work went through thirty-one editions, including eleven in French, one in German, and one in Italian. Indeed, Locke's *Two Treatises* was never as popular as *Essay Concerning Human Understanding,* which went through ninety-two eighteenth-century editions. Not even Montesquieu himself owned a copy of Locke's political treatise in his large library.[21] Finally, perhaps the most well-known early modern political theorist in Europe during the early modern period was Niccolo Machiavelli. Machiavelli's political works, of course, were divided between the relatively brief *Prince* and the more erudite *Discourses on the First Ten Books of Livy*. During the eighteenth century, there were eight editions published of *The Prince*, seven editions of the *Discourses*, and twenty-two editions of Machiavelli's collected works, mostly published in Italian, but translated into French, German, and Swedish. In short, while political theory as a genre was becoming more popular during the eighteenth century, no work matched the appeal of *The Spirit of the Laws*. Montesquieu's thick book was more popular than Locke, Machiavelli, or Burlamaqui, or, for that matter, Hobbes, Bolingbroke, Harrington, Spinoza, Leibnitz, Grotius, Pufendorf, or any other work of political philosophy. To suggest that *The Spirit of the Laws* was the most popular work of political thought published during the eighteenth century is even an understatement. Montesquieu's achievement was greater than that. The claim here is twofold: first, *The Spirit of the Laws* was the first erudite treatise of political thought in book history to achieve bestseller status; and second (as Chapters 10, 11, and 12 argue), this unprecedented success inaugurated an era of similarly erudite blockbusters that lasted until the 1789 outbreak of the French Revolution.

The phenomenal success of *The Spirit of the Laws* acted as a gravitational pull on Montesquieu's other published works, notably *Persian Letters*, *Considerations on the Romans*, and the attractive prose poem *Temple de Gnide*. As we see in Table 9.2, which compares Montesquieu's five publications by decade, it becomes clear that *The Spirit of the Laws* helped to make his other works even more popular. While *Persian Letters* and *Considerations* certainly did well before 1748, the table demonstrates that they reached their peak popularity during the second half of the century. As for *Temple de Gnide*, originally published in 1725, *The Spirit of the Laws* transformed it into a bestseller during the 1760s and 1770s, with a surprising eighty-three editions by 1800, which was about as many as Voltaire's *Candide*.[22]

After Montesquieu's death in 1755, his reputation as the Enlightenment's most important political philosopher solidified in a long and laudatory essay that Jean Baptiste le Rond d'Alembert appended to the fifth volume of the *Encyclopédie*, the Enlightenment's central work. Montesquieu is referenced over 500 times in the *Encyclopédie*, and he is the only writer to receive a special eulogy in its pages. D'Alembert immortalized *The Spirit of the Laws* as one of the classics of political theory and praised Montesquieu for his liberalism. D'Alembert's essay was itself republished and excerpted in various

Table 9.2 Eighteenth-Century Editions for Montesquieu's Five Most Popular Books by Decade

	Persian Letters (1721)	Temple de Gnide (1725)	Considerations on the Causes of the Greatness of the Romans and Their Decline (1734)	The Spirit of the Laws (1748)	Defense of the Spirit of the Laws (1750)	Total Montesquieu by Decade
1720–9	10	3				13
1730–9	14	2	9			25
1740–8	6	5	7	12		30
1750–9	16 (12)	16 (14)	15 (12)	18	11 (10)	67
1760–9	18 (8)	14 (7)	24 (13)	13	8 (0)	43
1770–9	12 (3)	18 (11)	29 (14)	26	6 (0)	54
1780–9	18 (9)	6 (3)	17 (6)	8	4 (0)	31
1790–1800	21 (4)	19 (13)	24 (14)	20	9 (0)	58
Total editions	115 (66)	83 (58)	125 (75)	97	38 (10)	321

Source: Kates.itg.pomona.edu/books. Accessed March 9, 2022. "Total Montesquieu by decade" has equalized books that were part of *oeuvres*. That is, if *Romans* and *The Spirit of the Laws* were both part of an *oeuvres* set, this is counted in the right column as only one publication. Numbers in parentheses represent unique titles not shared with others or in complete works to avoid duplication in totals. There were, after all, at least twenty-seven sets of Montesquieu's *oeuvres* between 1758 and 1800. See *La Notion d'oeuvres complètes*, eds. Jean Sgard and Catherine Volpilhac-Auger (Oxford: Voltaire Foundation, 1999), 52–3.

European journals and appeared often as a preface to later editions of Montesquieu's book and collected works.[23]

At once elegantly written, immense in scope, and seemingly randomly organized, *The Spirit of the Laws* discovered patterns among ancient, medieval, and modern forms of government, mainly in the West, but also in other parts of the world visited by Europeans. Montesquieu's overriding structure affirmed three basic types of government: republic, monarchy, and despotism. Within each form, Montesquieu found a psychological spring that motivated citizens: virtue in republics, honor in monarchies, and fear in despotisms. The combination of Montesquieu's graceful style, rarely seen in early modern political theory, and his mastery in finding colorful examples from throughout the historical record, helped make the work compelling and readable.

And yet, readers were confused by the book's overall argument, and critics constantly complained about Montesquieu's muddled message. Was he a closet republican who hoped to undermine monarchy with radical change? Or was he a traditionalist who hoped to domesticate absolute monarchy with the aid of a strong nobility? Readers could find points to support either perspective. All could agree that whatever his strongest political leanings, Montesquieu despised despotism, fearing that France and other European powers were headed down that path. He wanted readers to come away from his book understanding why monarchy without political limits was inherently unjust, abusive, and perverse. However, the further one proceeds through his long book, the clumsier his organization seems, until finally by Book 19, Montesquieu appears to abandon the republic/monarchy/despotism triad altogether in an innovative and imaginative, yet frustrating, analysis of England. Unquestionably Montesquieu admired England as the only government in history that had political liberty at the basis of its constitution. Montesquieu attributed this emphasis on individual freedom to a separation of powers that prevented the type of unified sovereign typically found in republics, monarchies, and despotic states alike. But England did not seem to fit Montesquieu's definition of either a republic or a monarchy. Indeed, insofar as Montesquieu regarded England as emblematic of Europe's new commercial age, he seemed to suggest that his own structure—the division of states into three categories—had itself become obsolete. Readers might be left wondering about Montesquieu's real intentions.

This chapter samples four different eighteenth-century readings of *The Spirit of the Laws* to demonstrate their variety and broad range. After reviewing the reading notes left by Louise Dupin, we compare the way church censors and political economists responded to Montesquieu's concept of honor. We then explore how republicans in the nascent United States used Montesquieu to guide them in developing the new North American republic. What is noteworthy about these various readings is how simultaneously they regarded *The Spirit of the Laws* as authoritative and canonical but also flawed and in need of correction. "Even when he is wrong," noted one commentator in 1789, Montesquieu "causes the reader to think, and shows him the road that leads to truth."[24]

Louise Dupin's Feminist Reading

Louise and Claude Dupin were one of Enlightenment France's great power couples. According to Voltaire and Rousseau, Louise was among the most glamorous women in Paris, while Claude rose (partially because of her family) to become a successful farmer-general, that is, an investor who made a fortune financing royal tax collection. During the 1730s, they used their wealth to purchase the famous Renaissance chateau of Chenonceau, still today among the most attractive sites in the Loire Valley. Both Louise and Claude read widely and deeply, and Claude published a short-lived book on trade in 1745. When in Paris, they often invited intellectual celebrities to their salon, including Voltaire and Montesquieu. Like these other philosophes, Louise made heavy use of the Bibliothèque du roi, the forerunner of today's Bibliothèque Nationale de France. She was a model savant and salon host.[25]

Sometime in 1743, Louise hired as her secretary a thirty-three-year-old recent arrival to Paris, Jean Jacques Rousseau. He had yet to publish anything, held no reputation as a writer, much less a philosophe, and was more interested in music than government. He and Louise worked on many projects, producing 3,000 manuscript pages. During the eighteenth century, a secretary might perform a variety of tasks from the mundane to the creative. Surely Rousseau was something more than a copyist, but the extent to which he became a collaborator or insightful contributor is difficult to know. This much can be said with certainty: nowhere in these manuscripts do we find any ideas resembling the mature Rousseau. If Rousseau was later influenced by his experience with the Dupins, during the late 1740s he does not seem to have shaped their feminist views very much. He likely made preparatory notes for her research, and surely they discussed ideas together; he may have guided Louise and Claude through the writings of other writers, such as Condillac and Burlamaqui. But even were this the case, Rousseau had not yet found his own voice. He was probably more Dupin's assistant than her tutor.[26]

These manuscripts were stored by Dupin's descendants until the 1950s, when they were sold to public collections around the world. Today at the University of Texas, Austin, there is one cache of papers representing a project for preparing a book that was never published entitled *Ouvrage sur les femmes* (Works on Women), a kind of feminist philosophical history of notable women from ancient times to the eighteenth century, a popular genre at that time.[27] The manuscripts are in Rousseau's clear handwriting, although it is assumed that the words were dictated to him by Louise, who seems to have been its sole author. Considering Rousseau's later notorious views of gender, this feminist tract has been of considerable interest to scholars, because it shows that Rousseau's ideas about women developed from close knowledge of early modern feminism.[28]

Louise and Claude were captivated by the publication of *The Spirit of the Laws*. Almost immediately they created a group that met regularly to study each chapter of Montesquieu's masterpiece. The club included at least four people, including their secretary Rousseau. They met so often, and their discussions were so intense, that after a while they "promised not to talk any longer among themselves, or with impartial people, about the book *The Spirit of the Laws*."[29]

This extraordinary collaboration has been known to bibliophiles since the eighteenth century because Claude Dupin published two commentaries based on their group conversations: the two-volume *Réflexions sur quelques parties d'un livre intitulé "De l'Esprit des loix,"* and a revised and expanded three-volume *Observations sur un livre intitulé: De l'Esprit des loix*. The first was published in only eight copies in 1749 and quickly withdrawn, while the second was likely published in 1751 or 1752 and withdrawn because of threatened government interference.[30] Less noticed by scholars until recently is a 350-page manuscript, purchased by the Municipal Library of Bordeaux entitled "Critique de l'Esprit des lois" (Critique of The Spirit of the Laws). Like the *Ouvrage sur les femmes*, this Bordeaux manuscript is in Rousseau's hand, but the extent to which Rousseau collaborated remains impossible to say. Eileen Hunt Botting, the most recent scholar to study these manuscripts, suggests that it should not be treated differently from the *Ouvrage sur les femmes*, since both were produced under similar circumstances. For that reason, it is reasonable to assume that Louise Dupin was its sole author, with input and assistance from Rousseau.[31]

Louise Dupin's "Critique of The Spirit of the Laws," composed during the early months of 1749, is a unique and significant historical document precisely because it allows us to track the reactions of a female reader of *The Spirit of the Laws* immediately following its first publication. Although selective, Dupin's "Critique" meticulously engages Montesquieu's ideas through a chapter-by-chapter commentary. Each section usually begins with a chapter heading from the book and a substantive quotation by Montesquieu that has been underlined to indicate its provenance. Dupin then responds to the quotation, often in conversational and informal tones. In contrast to her husband's five published tomes, Louise's analysis rarely cites the work of other philosophers. Her writing does not pretend—as his does—to be erudite or scholarly, but an intelligent and heartfelt response to Montesquieu's ideas.

The "Critique" begins with a summary of how other readers have found the book during its first months in publication. No doubt, Dupin admitted, everyone who reads it learns a great deal and profits much from its careful erudition. Nonetheless, readers "complain that this work masks any clear methodology. They say that ideas are randomly thrown together without sense or order." Dupin noted that some readers think the book lacked proper "metaphysics," while other readers appreciated its philosophical genius. As if echoing her book group, Dupin reported that readers argued over whether Montesquieu is too much a determinist regarding climate. Readers also disagreed over his writing style. Some critics believed that "the style doesn't fit the subject," while others asserted that his "ornaments" beautify the prose. At any rate, she acknowledged that everyone was reading the book because there was something here for all readers to absorb; *The Spirit of the Laws* seemed to her impossible for any serious reader to ignore.[32]

Like her husband Claude, Louise rejected Montesquieu's distinction between the nature and principle of government. Whether she and Claude did not understand

Montesquieu's innovative sociology, or whether they simply rejected Montesquieu's key notions outright, the result was resistance to those ideas that gave coherence to *The Spirit of the Laws*. Montesquieu's original tripartite division of government into republic, monarchy, and despotism meant that all other themes in the book (education, war, taxes, size, climate, etc.) were subordinated to a relativistic standard about how such themes applied to particular regimes. Dupin would have none of this relativism. All governments are inherently alike, she believed, and they should be judged by a universal standard: "Government may exhibit different forms but their nature is always the same."[33] Naturally, her resistance to Montesquieu's thoughts on the nature of government led her to oppose his innovative notion that each governmental type showed a unique principle. In Dupin's view, Montesquieu was wrong to insist that republics were guided by virtue, monarchies by honor, and despotism by fear. Each of these passions, she argued, was evident in all governments. She insisted to the contrary that any distinction between nature and principle was erroneous. The key for statesmen was to keep any government in "moderation." After all, "the principles of all governments are founded on reason."[34]

Two aspects of Montesquieu's political philosophy particularly bothered Mme Dupin. Anticipating Voltaire's later criticism, she denied any essential difference between monarchy and despotism: both regimes exhibited legitimate absolute rule by one person. Despotism was not, as Montesquieu claimed, a wholly distinct form of government, but more simply a badly run monarchy in which royal power has been abused. Second, Dupin strongly objected to Montesquieu's notion that virtue had little place in a monarchy. Embracing the more standard view of monarchy exhibited in *Telemachus*, she insisted that any well-run monarchy without virtue was "something impossible."[35]

The most interesting and original analysis that makes the "Critique" important for understanding the early reception of *The Spirit of the Laws* regards gender relations and the status of women. Louise Dupin immediately recognized that gender plays a critical role in the book, as she took copious notes and made extended reflections on this topic. Fascinated by Montesquieu's notion that the status of women across the world reflected the general level of civilization, Dupin was the earliest reader we know to perceive that Montesquieu's sociology implied a direct relationship between political regime and family life, that is, a correspondence between political and domestic authority. As he had illustrated with such brilliance in *Persian Letters*, the domestic manners between husband and wife were shaped by the political culture in which they resided. So, for example, in a despotism where fear pervaded royal courts, Montesquieu commented on how wives were often little more than slaves of their husband, with few property rights or the ability to sue on their own in a law court. Among Montesquieu's main contentions was a defense that women's liberty—their ability to control their own lives—was greatest in modern monarchies such as France. Even in republics, he argued, women were limited by conservative social mores that severely limited their role in the public sphere. In contrast to virtue and fear, honor worked best to free women from patriarchal social constraints and turn marital relations in a more egalitarian direction.

If Louise Dupin recognized Montesquieu's nascent feminism, she also strongly criticized him for not going far enough. Given that Dupin rejected any notion that despotism and republics were wholly differently from monarchies, she found Montesquieu's portrayal of women in republics and despotism more apologetic than descriptive. She was troubled by Montesquieu's acceptance that wives in such societies were normatively subordinate. Insofar as Montesquieu argued that it was natural for women to be abused in despotism, she found him complicit in the very thing he may have been attempting to criticize. Montesquieu's indirect style, his penchant for finding sociological relations, troubled Dupin because he seemed to give up on improving the lives of women who lived outside Europe, and indeed, she feared that it made European readers complacent about the status of women in their own societies.

In one remarkable commentary, Dupin responded to the short, enigmatic Book 19, Chapter 15, "Influence of Domestic Government on Political Government," in which Montesquieu makes the following claim after laying out the dismal state of women in despotic Russia: "Everything is closely linked together: the despotism of the prince is naturally united with the servitude of women; the liberty of women, with the spirit of monarchy."[36] Here is Dupin's response:

> I do not have the *esprit* to understand how the idea of a Prince who governs despotically links him with what the Author calls "the servitude of women," although the Author has already repeated it to me several times. I do not understand what advantage the freedom of women has in common with the spirit of the monarchy; this freedom seems to me to be a fact for all countries, and can only be violated by political corruption (*un vice d'administration*), which can happen anywhere and which is nowhere incompatible.[37]

For Dupin, the improvement of female status was universal, suitable for every government. No place on earth existed where the fate of women could not either improve or deteriorate. If only because despotism characterized much of the world's known governments outside of Europe, such as the Chinese, Persian, Russian, and Ottoman empires, Dupin was unwilling to accept their servile fate as predetermined. Likewise, she refused to see, as Montesquieu asserted, the relative liberty given to women under monarchy. Dupin was deeply troubled by the notion that Russian women were forever stuck in their oppression, while French women should feel grateful for their limited and fragile liberty.

Sometimes Dupin called out Montesquieu for blaming the victim of oppression and discrimination instead of criticizing the government for its discriminatory gender policies. In Book 7, Chapter 8, for example, Montesquieu explained that nearly all governments saw loose sexual behavior among women as having serious consequences, and so throughout the world "good legislators have required a certain gravity in the mores of women." Dupin rejected Montesquieu's formulation, charging him with demeaning women through a seemingly clinical tone. Montesquieu confused cause and effect, argued Dupin. Loose sexual mores among women were the result of oppressive conditions that legislation imposed on women. "This is a vice of government itself and not specifically due to women," and will only get better when government acts to improve the lot of women, such as their access to education.[38]

Dupin also worried about the way Montesquieu characterized female liberty in monarchies. For Dupin, men and women were virtually alike, with the same proclivities for good or bad morals, and with the same hunger for liberty and political power.[39] When Montesquieu quipped in Book 7, Chapter 18 that women are not naturally suited to head households or governments, Dupin challenged his empirical evidence, reminding him of the glories of ancient Egypt.[40] Extending a theme first introduced in *Persian Letters*, Montesquieu noted that the more power women obtained in monarchy, the greater they used it to attract lovers and indulge luxuries. The implications of Montesquieu's argument seemed to be that a woman's liberty came at the expense of good morals. If, as Montesquieu implied, individual liberty reduced overall virtue, what use was it? In Book 19, Chapter 12, Montesquieu made the striking, if curious, argument that in Europe female empowerment had diminished patriarchy because such women appear somewhat more masculine and men somewhat more feminine. "The two sexes spoil each other, each loses its distinctive and essential quality; arbitrariness is put into what was absolute, and manners change every day." Dupin spotted danger in this formulation:

> Philosophically speaking, I have no idea what constitutes the distinctive and essential attributes of the sexes. I believe that among mankind there are few absolutes; but if everything is arbitrary, what then? I believe that everything is continually changing; the form changes day by day. Two pages earlier the Author says that women spoil manners, [but] he says here that both sexes spoil one another. Can one call this a contradiction or indicative of a more general confusion? Men and women are made to live together, and a great deal can be done for the good of society at large with the feelings they have for one another.[41]

Dupin had cause for concern. A decade later, Rousseau himself would reconfigure this argument to blame the decline of virtue precisely on the supposed empowerment of European women. Rousseau's antifeminism would fuel a misogynist strain of democratic thought embraced by many Jacobins during the French Revolution. As Eileen Hunt Botting ironically notes, Rousseau's antifeminism had its roots not only in Louise Dupin's egalitarian feminism but also through his own close reading of *The Spirit of the Laws* with the Dupins.[42]

The Catholic Church's Reading

At the same time that the Dupin group was meeting to discuss *The Spirit of the Laws*, one of the earliest and most important reviews appeared in the April 1749 issue of the Jesuit *Mémoires de Trévoux*. Even during this very early period of the book's distribution, the review's author, the Jesuit priest Pierre Joseph Plesse, acknowledged that it was already "famous among men of letters and even well known among those incapable of understanding it." The writing style warranted praise because the book exhibited an "erudition . . . without affection or pedantry."[43] Nevertheless, Plesse criticized Montesquieu for making a series of what struck him as irreligious features. Montesquieu's liberal ideas on suicide, polygamy, and divorce; his refusal to condemn non-Christian cultures such as Japan and China; and his reluctance to endorse clerical celibacy all seemed to add up to a work inconsistent with Catholic teaching. Plesse put readers on their guard that while they might learn much from reading *The Spirit of the Laws*, they must shield themselves from Montesquieu's inconsistent piety.

Where the Jesuits merely slapped Montesquieu on the wrists, their religious rivals, the Jansenists, launched a more lethal attack on the book in their popular and influential journal, *Les Nouvelles ecclésiastiques*.[44] Jansenism in the eighteenth century was a complex and widespread movement in France that involved both religious faith and political action. Embracing a stern Augustinian form of Catholicism that emphasized human sinfulness, Jansenists demanded that the monarchy do more to guard the kingdom against immorality. This sometimes put Jansenists at odds with the royal government, and the *Nouvelles ecclésiastiques* itself was at least officially banned and forced to operate below the radar. Nonetheless, its subscribers, numbering well into the thousands, closely read its articles, and this review, written by its editor Father Jacques Fontaine de la Roche, was the most consequential evaluation of *The Spirit of Laws* published in Montesquieu's lifetime.[45]

Right away La Roche labeled *The Spirit of the Laws* a "scandalous book" and dismissed the Jesuit review as "terribly weak" and defective. The problem with *The Spirit of the Laws* lay not in its errant examples but at its very core: its conception of law was completely outside of the religious sphere. That is, Montesquieu held an entirely secular view of law that refused to acknowledge that the world is ultimately governed by God. To bring perspective, La Roche compared *The Spirit of the Laws* to the approach represented in Jean Domat's *Traité des lois* [Treatise on Law], a Jansenist work first published in the 1690s. Domat "takes Revelation for his guide," in which it is clear that "the original law" is that which "prescribes for mankind its duties towards God."[46] Religious law, then, took precedence over all other laws and was universal. By contrast, argued La Roche, *The Spirit of the Law* wholly ignored any universal commandment to love God, search for His will, and follow His commandments. Indeed, Montesquieu's project, according to La Roche, was to purposively and systematically ignore the divine edicts from revelation upon which religious law is based. This made Montesquieu no different than Deists and Atheists. "The book *The Spirit of the Laws*," charged La Roche, "is founded upon the system of natural religion," an impious system infecting European culture. One saw evidence of it in the "system of natural religion represented in [Baruch] Spinoza." *The Spirit of the Laws* belongs to this dangerous movement. "Through religious laws, God calls mankind back to his religious duties." But "the philosophes" only want duties to be applied to self-love and society: they explicitly ignore obligations to God. Despite an elegant style that made Montesquieu appear moderate and reasonable, the positions taken in his book pointed to something far more sinister: "We perceive here the author's malignity in wanting to reject the Christian religion."[47]

It is difficult to find any eighteenth-century review of Montesquieu's work more scathing than this one. And yet, La Roche did not stop there. He also objected to the way in which Montesquieu designed the principles for his tripartite division of governments. Like other readers, including Louise Dupin, La Roche criticized Montesquieu for making honor, and not virtue, the basis for monarchy. "Honor," quoted La Roche directly from *The Spirit of the Laws*, "that is, the prejudice of each person and each condition, takes the place of the political virtue of which I have spoken and represents it everywhere."[48] The nature of honor, in other words, is to regard one's own interest above everyone else's. As Montesquieu himself asserted, "ambition is pernicious in a republic. It has good effects in a monarchy."[49] La Roche pointed out that this assertation was blasphemous and abhorrent; it seemed to ground monarchies in sin. After all, European monarchies in Europe were not secular kingdoms; from England to Russia all were based upon Christianity. La Roche perceived that Montesquieu's peculiar notion of honor was incompatible with Christian values and behavior. He found it impossible to conceive of a well-functioning Christian monarchy based on Montesquieu's idea of honor. The selfish courtiers described in *The Spirit of the Laws* seem anything but Christian. How could any Christian state thrive with government leaders "devoid of virtue and full of vanity?" One might as well banish Christianity from all monarchies, La Roche sarcastically suggested.[50]

La Roche's viewpoint was informed by his deep reading of early modern Jansenist moral philosophy. What La Roche saw in Montesquieu's notion of honor was a malevolent perversion of what seventeenth-century Jansenist moral philosophers Blaise Pascal and Pierre Nicole termed amour propre. Their discovery of this selfish human psychology helped resolve a difficult conundrum: given sinfulness, in which men and women were driven by constant passions, desires, anxiety, and insecurity, how was it ever possible for European communities to build such powerful and enduring political states that gave subjects relative material wealth and security? If humans are as selfish as St Augustine claimed, how can we account for the rise of European civilization? Pierre Nicole provided the most succinct answer: "As there is hardly any action motivated by charity that would not please God, amour propre engages us to please men."[51] Amour propre made people give the impression to their neighbors that they could be trusted as good Christians, even though their hearts rendered them undeserving. Amour propre was a ruse to acquire power and wealth through seeking the approval of others. "The amour propre of other men opposes all the desires of ours," wrote Nicole. "We wish that all others should love us, obey us, and that they should be busied with the care of satisfying us."[52] In his private notebook, Montesquieu jotted down for himself how "M. Nicole has very well said that God gave amour propre to man."[53]

Pascal and Nicole certainly did not approve of amour propre; they fully condemned its inherent selfishness and the turning away from God that such masking entailed. Their arguments were meant to explain how only through God's infinite grace could sinners behave in a way that might benefit society. But soon their concepts were secularized and turned around by others.[54] Following the 1680s, honor became a synonym, a less technical term, for amour propre. We see it used that way, for example, in the influential work of Pierre Bayle. "There is among Christians a certain worldly honor that is directly contrary to the spirit of the Gospel."[55] So long as the discussion was in the hands of moral theologians, such as Pascal or Nicole or even Bayle, this understanding of honor was used for religious purposes to clarify how God's grace manifests on earth. It was Bernard Mandeville, however, the Dutch/English physician and writer, who laid the groundwork for the secularization of honor and its reboot as a political and economic concept. In his 1732 *Enquiry into the Origin of Honor*, Mandeville claimed that the roots of honor lay in amour propre, "that great value that all individuals set upon their own person." In his better-known *Fable of the Bees*, subtitled *Private Vices Public Benefits*, Mandeville fully detached honor/amour propre from its theological moorings by inverting the Jansenist formula: Instead of seeing the hand of God in the reconciliation of individual sinful acts, Mandeville argued that if actions motivated by selfishness and greed resulted in social benefit, those actions must not be sinful. Where Bayle had condemned honor, Mandeville praised it.

Condemned by the Sorbonne, placed on the Index of Forbidden Books by the Catholic Church, Mandeville's work nonetheless had a powerful impact on many eighteenth-century thinkers, none more so than Montesquieu, who cites his work twice in *The Spirit of the Laws*.[56] Specifically, Montesquieu used Mandeville's notion of honor to move amour propre from a moralistic term that addressed individual psychology to a sociological term that helped explain group behavior. Amour propre was universal and a-historical—it seemed to explain individual human behavior everywhere; honor, Montesquieu learned from Mandeville, was situated in particular societies, such as modern European monarchies, and had less relevance in other types of states. Montesquieu fully embraced Mandeville against Bayle and the Jansenists, seeing honor not simply as socially beneficial, but the crucial ingredient preventing monarchies from lurching toward despotism. While the term "amour propre" is never used in *The Spirit of the Laws* (as it had been in *Persian Letters* and *Considerations*), it is there replaced by honor, which serves as a central pillar for the entire work. Given Montesquieu's debt to Mandeville, La Roche was not mistaken, then, to see in *The Spirit of the Laws* notions dangerous to a well-ordered Christian monarchy.[57]

La Roche followed up his review by denouncing the book to the theology faculty of the University of Paris, also known as the Sorbonne. At once, it began an investigation of *The Spirit of the Laws*. Montesquieu could not ignore these developments; he knew trouble lay ahead. In February 1750, Barrillot published on his behalf a sixty-two-page response to La Roche. This *Défense de l'Esprit des lois* was perhaps Montesquieu's best-written work, despite its form as a legal brief. Little more than a long pamphlet, the *Défense* went through ten independent editions before being merged with *The Spirit of the Laws* itself and the many sets of complete works (see Table 9.2). Montesquieu devoted the most space to refuting the charge of Spinozism and Deism. He noted that no one could be both a Deist and a Spinozist, since Spinoza was perceived by friend and foe alike to be an atheist. Deism and atheism, Montesquieu reiterated, are obviously contradictory. As to Spinoza, Montesquieu argued that there was not a shred of evidence anywhere in the book to support a charge of atheism and he documented his many references to God in the book. Montesquieu insisted that everything in *The Spirit of the Laws* pointed to the fact that its author was "not only a believer but a lover of Christianity as well."[58]

La Roche responded a few weeks later by insisting, among other things, that Montesquieu had ignored his criticism about monarchies, dodging questions about the nature of honor, and the extent to which it was incompatible with monarchy. La Roche had repeatedly charged that any suggestion that honor and not virtue best characterized monarchies shifted the development of European monarchies away from any kind of Christian footing. Montesquieu seemed to have, in short, "no response" to La Roche's criticism of honor. He interpreted Montesquieu's silence on this question as an admission of guilt.[59]

At this point in the public feud, an unlikely ally came to Montesquieu's aid: In May 1750, Voltaire anonymously published his own pamphlet, *Remerciement sincère à un homme charitable* (Sincere Gratitude to a Virtuous Man), which satirically placed La Roche in a very bad light. Montesquieu and Voltaire were never close and were more rivals than allies. Voltaire, as we saw, took jabs at *Persian Letters* and *Considerations*. And while he acknowledged the enormous importance of *The Spirit of the Laws*, he also thought it was full of mistakes. Later, Voltaire—following the Dupins—argued that despotism was simply bad monarchy (i.e., royal misuse of power) and any good king must have unlimited powers to accomplish great deeds. Voltaire generally preferred to constrain the power of the church and the nobility. Nonetheless, in 1750, watching Montesquieu attacked by representatives of the Catholic Church, Voltaire felt much sympathy. Publishers sometimes responded by attaching Voltaire's piece to editions of *The Spirit of the Laws* or complete works. "This sense of common purpose, triumphing over their differences," writes Robert Shackleton, "is evidence in the best sense of the term of a party spirit."[60]

The Sorbonne investigation plodded along between 1750 and 1754. In 1752, the appropriate committee drew up two lists with thirty objections to *The Spirit of the Laws*. Given that Christianity was a universal faith, the committee argued, equally applicable to all human beings, there was concern regarding Montesquieu's apparent approval of pagan religions. For example, they were troubled by Montesquieu's reflections on the clash between Inca and Roman Catholic faiths: "And when Montezuma persisted in saying that the religion of the Spaniards was good for their country and that of Mexico for his own," Montesquieu had remarked, "he was not saying an absurd thing."[61] The professors were equally upset when Montesquieu seemed to suggest that some religions thrived in certain ecological climates, and therefore, Christianity was limited by its appeal in certain places: "In human terms, it seems that climate has prescribed limits to the Christian religion and to the Mohammedan religion."[62] This is not what the Sorbonne teachers expected to hear from France's leading political theorist. Clearly, these theologians were offended by Montesquieu's outright embrace of cultural relativism and global religious pluralism.

Montesquieu's refusal to view Christianity as a religion appropriate everywhere led him to approve certain practices elsewhere in the world that were forbidden in Catholic Europe, including polygamy, divorce, and suicide. Instead of regarding, for example, suicide as a grave moral sin, Montesquieu explored how in England it was treated as "the effect of an illness," while in ancient Rome "the act was the consequence of education" that "offered a great advantage."[63] For the Sorbonne faculty, Montesquieu's moderate and detached tone masked subversive attitudes. Montesquieu seemed to be condoning sinful practices, implicitly planting the idea that Christianity had no business rectifying such foreign customs.

The Sorbonne professors also charged that *The Spirit of the Laws* made direct attacks upon the church, specifically, making derogatory remarks about priests. Christian monks were "a nation in itself lazy."[64] Montesquieu blamed medieval church leaders for "the destruction of commerce" that was the direct result of bans against usury. He accused them of relying too much on Aristotle's *Politics*, a pagan work.[65] The Sorbonne professors often seemed most offended by even the most obscure passages. Regarding the Roman emperor Julian, Montesquieu claimed that "since him there has been no prince more worthy of governing men." But from the church's viewpoint, Julian was known first and foremost as Julian the Apostate because he had converted from Christianity to paganism. He was, in fact, the last formally pagan Roman emperor to refuse Christian conversion. Despite Montesquieu's pledge that he would never have been "an accomplice to his apostasy," the Sorbonne professors recognized that this was, in fact, the only reading of this section that made any sense.[66]

The topic of celibacy was a special area where *The Spirit of the Laws* raised the ire of the church. In one place, Montesquieu used it to warn against legislators making laws "not for what is good but for what is perfect." Trying to make men and women into angels was pointless and counterproductive. When the ancient church simply praised celibacy as an ideal, it could do little harm. But "when it was made into a law," there was no way it could be implemented and supervised without creating an oppressive and hypocritical environment. Elsewhere, Montesquieu noted that a celibate clergy only benefited the common good if it remained limited in size. "One sensed that it could become harmful in proportion as the body of the clergy became too large, and, consequently, that of the laity not large enough." Again, Montesquieu's opponents found these ideas dangerous and repellent.[67]

The Sorbonne professors naturally focused on Books 25 and 26, which were devoted to the relationship between church and state. They repudiated Montesquieu's argument that political leaders must never let the church get the upper hand in political life. Most religions, claimed Montesquieu, are "intolerant," intent on their own "propagation," which may disrupt the state's mission of peace and prosperity. "Here, therefore, is the fundamental principle for political laws in religious matters: When one is master of the state's accepting a new religion, or not accepting it, it must not be established; when it is established, it must be tolerated." This policy, of course, ruled out the most important and emphatic goal of the early modern Catholic state: to reunify Protestant states into one universal Catholic monarchy.[68]

The Sorbonne faculty's most trenchant criticism of *The Spirit of the Laws* did not concern matters that were strictly religious, anticlerical, or even toleration-related. Rather, following La Roche's review, and not unlike the Dupins, they went to the core political ideas of the book, criticizing its tripartite division of republic, monarchy, and despotism. This area of the Sorbonne's investigation was clearly its most important and consequential. Many of the faculty's criticisms cited odd examples or quirky one-liners, such as Montesquieu's quip regarding Julian the Apostate. But as Louise Dupin had noticed, the relationship between virtue and honor went deep into the book's foundation. Montesquieu might promise to omit a paragraph here or there, but he could not redefine virtue and honor without renouncing the book itself. In its report, the Sorbonne recycled the relevant part of La Roche's article, quoting the same passage beginning with the title of Book 3, Chapter 5: "That virtue is not the principle of monarchical government. . . . Thus, in well-regulated monarchies everyone will be almost a good citizen, and one will rarely find someone who is a good man; for, in order to be a good man, one must have the intention of being one." The quotation was immediately followed by this condemnation: "This proposition about monarchs and monarchies is equally injurious to the upper classes and to the people of monarchies, and seditiously reveals dishonor and ruin to the rule of monarchy."[69]

The Sorbonne faculty also took issue with Montesquieu's characterization of the nobility as lazy, mean, and lawless, forever scorning "the duties of citizens," and exploiting the weaknesses of the monarch. Honor compelled powerful men and women to act in ways that would offend any faithful Christian. Montesquieu was not saying that this was an unfortunate by-product of monarchical political life. What troubled the Sorbonne theologians was that it appeared to constitute an ideal for him. Echoing Mandeville's *Fable of the Bees*, *The Spirit of the Laws* seemed to argue that while honor may make individuals act in ways offensive to Christians, it nonetheless had "good effects" that made it "useful to the public."[70]

Montesquieu carefully wrote a long, unpublished response to the Sorbonne, claiming that their differences were fundamentally a misunderstanding. He insisted that he was a faithful Roman Catholic, with no intention other than to further the values of the church. He promised to omit phrases and sections that offended the theology faculty. For example, when the faculty objected to a remark in which he advocated allowing other peoples to worship their own gods ("But one must make divinity honored, and one must never avenge it"),[71] he promised to omit the sentence from the next edition, as well as other offending passages. Yet, here and elsewhere, these promised omissions were never carried out. He also promised to distance himself from Roman suicide by adding a note that affirmed his affiliation to Christian doctrine. However, no such note ever appeared.[72]

With regard to virtue and honor, Montesquieu insisted that the Sorbonne's objections were simply a confusion over language. By virtue, he insisted (as he had in his *Défense*) that he meant strictly political virtue and not moral virtue. "I speak here about political virtue," he wrote in a qualifying note meant to appease critics that appeared in all future editions, "which is moral virtue in the sense that it points toward the general good, very little about individual moral virtues, and not at all about that virtue which relates to revealed truths."[73] Montesquieu insisted that he was writing about political life, not morality or even organized religion, and that while his book sometimes addressed the relationship between church and state, he had no intention of commenting on moral questions per se. (Of course, such a division between politics and morality was precisely what had angered the Sorbonne professors.) As for denigrating the Christian monarchies of Europe, nothing could be further from the truth. He was, after all, a proud nobleman living and prepared to die in a Catholic monarchy. Besides, while it was clear from the book that he hated despotism, readers were divided over whether he preferred republics to monarchies or vice versa. "All Europe," he wrote in his response to the Sorbonne, "has read my book, and everyone agrees that one cannot tell whether I am inclined more for the republican type of government or for the monarchical. Indeed, it would be futile to decide, because actually both types of governments are very good."[74]

This controversy over *The Spirit of the Laws* ended in something of a stalemate. On the one hand, in November 1751, the Vatican placed the book in its Index of Prohibited Books and published its decision in March 1752.[75] But this may have been more to halt publication of a specific Italian translation than to roll back its European distribution. In fact, the Sorbonne faculty never published its own findings, and the result was that the book continued to circulate in France in a quasi-legal status. Of course, it could not be openly published in France. Nonetheless, no government or church agency in France ever officially condemned *The Spirit of the Laws*. Although several editions were printed in Paris, they included false imprints, often attributed to Barrillot in Geneva, Nourse in London, or Arkstée & Merkus in Amsterdam and Leipzig, and without Montesquieu's name on the title page during his lifetime, even though his authorship was universally recognized, published in the reviews, and fully named in the English translations. In contrast to *Persian Letters* or Voltaire's *Philosophical Letters*, for example, no publisher or book dealer was ever arrested in France for selling *The Spirit of the Laws*.

In Montesquieu's responses to his church critics, he always presented himself as a rigorous and cautious scholar, exhibiting moderation rather than provocation. Willing to defer to authorities, both ecclesiastical and political, he insisted that his books reflected a deep love of both Christianity and the French monarchy. He represented himself as misunderstood and claimed that *The Spirit of the Laws* carried no subversive messages, either explicitly or implicitly. For the most part, modern scholarship has ratified this portrait of Montesquieu as a cautious moderate, flirting with libertine ideas in his youth, and no doubt supporting the French nobility against the tendencies of the royal government to acquire unlimited powers, but nonetheless careful to avoid any confrontation or controversy that might damage his own reputation. "He was extremely anxious that his work should not be condemned," writes Robert Shackleton.[76] At the same time, readers did not err in perceiving the book's radical argument as favoring a largely secular and modern commercial monarchy.

The Economist's Reading

By embracing Mandeville's transformation of amour propre into honor, *The Spirit of the Laws* weakened links between political life and traditional morality. Like Mandeville, Montesquieu portrayed humans living in monarchies as particularly selfish, hoping to distinguish themselves from peers through wealth, power, and reputation. Unlike Jansenists, Montesquieu did not see the need for an overarching alliance between church and state to stifle those passions. Anticipating Adam Smith, and again, following the lead of Mandeville, Montesquieu recognized that honor often led people to cooperate in order to gain approval. This transition from amour propre to honor in Montesquieu's work is what led *The Spirit of the Laws* to become a foundation text in European political economy. In *Persian Letters*, Montesquieu had satirized how a nobility once steeped in military valor had become under Louis XIV experts in the arts and fashion. In *The Spirit of the Laws*, this modern transition from war to commerce in luxuries was no longer satirized but fully appreciated. In the *Defense of The Spirit of the Laws*, Montesquieu made clear his awareness regarding how honor evolved from Jansenist moral philosophy itself: "The world is very corrupt, but there are certain passions found there that are kept under great restraint by others more favored to forbid their appearance."[77]

The Jansenist attack upon Montesquieu's notion of honor was echoed by his earliest and perhaps most consequential reader, Jean Jacques Rousseau. Of course, we have already seen how Rousseau helped the Dupins digest the book during the spring of 1749. Is it merely coincidence that Rousseau made his fateful decision to write political theory only a few weeks after reading *The Spirit of the Laws*? In 1755, Rousseau's second essay, the *Discourse on the Origin of Inequality*, continued his engagement with Montesquieu's key ideas. Montesquieu's three political types were abstracted, universalized, and reshaped into a historical stage theory based around inequality. Rousseau argued that what Montesquieu perceived was only a snapshot of a society moving in time. All societies, Rousseau insisted, transformed themselves first from republics into monarchies, and then into despotisms, with each stage exhibiting increasing levels of inequality. Where Montesquieu had argued that despotism was the only inherently bad form of government, Rousseau inverted his formula, arguing that a democratic republic was the only inherently good form of government because it was the only one premised on equality. Given that very few European states were either republics or despotisms, the real debate between Montesquieu and Rousseau was over the nature of monarchy. Where Montesquieu believed that a well-ordered monarchy could exhibit high levels of freedom and prosperity, Rousseau argued that the type of monarchy imagined by Montesquieu already exhibited despotic features that were unavoidable.[78]

Rousseau largely accepted Montesquieu's presentation of republican virtue, but he rejected Montesquieu's legitimation of monarchical honor. In *Discourse on the Origin of Inequality*, he argued that honor exhibited itself in fomenting widespread inequality in which a minority of rich subjects distinguished themselves from an increasingly impoverished majority. Here Rousseau was waging a fight not only with Montesquieu, but with many readers who viewed *The Spirit of the Laws* as a founding text in modern political economy, and who defended honor's role in expanding inequality as necessary for the growth of trade and commerce that had made early modern monarchies so prosperous.

In Books 20 and 21, Montesquieu argued that commercial wealth had become such a hallmark of modern life that eighteenth-century readers could not easily accept that it had been absent among the ancients. "I know well that people, filled with two ideas, the one that commerce is the most useful thing in the world to a state," he wrote, and "that the Romans greatly encouraged and honored commerce; but the truth is that they rarely thought about it."[79] Although Montesquieu may have believed in an old-fashioned nobility that did not engage in full-time commerce, he certainly understood that such a nobility could only distinguish itself with wealth that came from a dynamic economic engine. In Michael Sonenscher's description, "the honor-based principle upon which monarchy depended for its stability implied maintaining a noncommercial, but still open, elite above a thoroughly commercial society."[80]

Honor demanded distinction and glory. If unchecked, it could produce a nobility intent upon constant war. Commerce, however, had the effect of partially domesticating the ruling class, allowing it to distinguish itself through fashion and manners rather than warfare. The result was an elite more interested in the arts and conspicuous consumption. In this way, Montesquieu suggested, commercial life in the modern period led to less war and violence. "Commerce cures destructive prejudices," he wrote. "It polishes and softens barbarous mores, as we see every day," he insisted, "and it is an almost general rule that everywhere there are gentle mores, there is commerce and that everywhere there is commerce, there are gentle mores."[81]

In a brilliant analysis published during the 1970s, the Princeton economist Albert Hirschman zeroed in on Montesquieu's insight, terming it "doux commerce" (gentle commerce), claiming that many eighteenth-century readers discovered here the genesis of modern economics, in which the market—free exchange of goods among peoples—was inherently good. Commerce softened militarism; it made room for women; it brought foreigners in contact with citizens, allowing both to compare habits and attitudes; it made the cost of war between states much higher. According to Hirschman, readers learned from *The Spirit of the Laws* that modern states distinguished themselves by their consumption habits and addiction to luxuries, that is, precisely those features decried by Rousseau in his *Discourse on Inequality*. The *Journal of Commerce* summed it up this way in 1759: "We are indebted to M. de Montesquieu hardly less for the science of commerce than we are for philosophy and letters."[82]

During the 1750s, a circle of important economic writers coalesced in France around the new French Intendant for Commerce, Vincent de Gournay. Among them was François Véron Duverger de Forbonnais, who published in 1753 a long commentary on *The Spirit of the Laws*. Often reading more like notes alongside long excerpts from the book, Forbonnais clearly championed Montesquieu's ideas on the importance of trade for contemporary monarchies. For example, explaining Montesquieu's most significant insight, he sharpens the master's words: "It is virtually a general rule that whenever there is commerce, there are sweetened mores. Trade corrupts pure mores; it softens barbaric mores; it's naturally peaceful; but if the spirit of commerce unites nations, the same cannot be said for individuals."[83] This reading aligned Montesquieu with Mandeville and against Rousseau.

Forbonnais's influential *Encyclopédie* article, "Commerce," recycled what Montesquieu had described in Books 20 and 21 of *The Spirit of the Laws* and specifically directed readers to that source. As Forbonnais put it, "A nation that does not engage in commerce to its full capacity faces a gradual commercial decline."[84] Forbonnais also repeated Montesquieu's plea that the government must "be neutral between its custom houses and its commerce and must arrange that these two things never thwart one another; then one enjoys the liberty of commerce there."[85] At the same time, Forbonnais helped to arrange for the French translation of Hume's *Political Discourses*, itself inspired by Montesquieu's new vision of political economy that identified the importance of trade in eighteenth-century political life.

This new interest in political economy stemming from *The Spirit of the Laws* also surged in Italian and German states during the 1750s. In 1754, Antonio Genovesi, who had taught metaphysics at the University of Naples since 1741, became the first occupant of a new chair in "commerce and mechanics," effectively the first professorship of economics in Europe. An admirer of the Gournay group, Genovesi was also part of a Neapolitan reading circle that met regularly to discuss and debate *The Spirit of the Laws*, an experience that led directly to the establishment of his university chair. At his death, Genovesi left a thoroughly annotated copy of *The Spirit of the Laws* that formed the basis for critical notes appended to the Italian edition published in 1777.[86] Meanwhile, in the German states, the founder of Cameralism (a theory of political economy that influenced eighteenth-century German civil servants), Johann Heinrich Gottlob Justi, constantly engaged *The Spirit of the Laws* in his own work. Both an acolyte and a critic, Justi agreed that embracing modern commerce could prevent monarchies from metastasizing into despotism, but he criticized Montesquieu for inflating the nobility's political role.[87]

The most popular expression of the new political economy came from the French writer Victor Riqueti, Marquis de Mirabeau, who in 1756 published his *L'Ami des hommes* (*The Friend of Mankind*), which went through over twenty editions in its first decade. Filled with tangents and fascinating insights, Mirabeau argued that France's declining population, rooted in a lack of investment in agriculture, was the most salient cause of its social ills.[88] Indeed, the prior publication of *The Spirit of the Laws* had first prompted this wealthy nobleman to try his hand at a similar genre of writing, and with an ample share of false modesty, he compared himself to the Bordeaux master:

> In spite of the almost infinite subdivisions which he has given to his plan, readers complain for good reason that his progress is often tangled and usually difficult to follow. We certainly have that in common, him and me. His erudition is immense and sure; mine is very limited and faulty; his style is clear, noble, pure, and trenchant; mine is unequal, without taste, neglected, often diffuse, and mixed up; his mind illuminates and awakens the reader's intellect, mine tires him and stifles him; his ideas seem the flower of ideas, and in fact are the germ, mine are singular and trivial. He was a skillful workman, and totally devoted to this kind of study and work, and by his confession he consumed ten years in that one. I am none of that.[89]

A related school of French economic writers who emerged during the 1760s, the Physiocrats, also saw themselves as building upon the ideas expressed in *The Spirit of the Laws*. Pierre Samuel du Pont de Nemour's 1768 essay, "On the Origin and Progress of a New Science," charted an intellectual genealogy of the Physiocratic school that began with Montesquieu, and led through Gournay to Quesnay and two of his collaborators: Mirabeau and Mercier de la Rivière. Du Pont highlighted as particularly influential Quesnay's articles "Farmers" and "Grain" for the 1756 volume of the *Encyclopédie*, and especially his "Tableau économique" (Economic Chart), which visually represented the Physiocratic model of agricultural productivity that was first published in various editions of Mirabeau's books. "The era of the revolution that turned our thinkers to the study of political economy goes back to M. de Montesquieu," du Pont later wrote.[90]

Church critics and political economists united in appreciating the importance of honor in Montesquieu's political thought. The Abbé de la Roche was alarmed that Montesquieu imagined that modern states could thrive without virtuous Christians at the helm of government and without Christian morality at the root of a state's mission. The political economists saw it from a wholly different perspective. They recognized in Montesquieu's notion of honor a way to explain the focus of eighteenth-century monarchy on generating trade and economic prosperity. Rousseau, ever original, built his own call for modern democracy around his criticism of *The Spirit of the Laws*. Jansenists, political economists, and Rousseau all found in *The Spirit of the Laws* a defense of modern European society that rested on a human psychology in which the infinite desires of individuals for wealth, power, and pleasure trumped displays of reason or Christian morality. Montesquieu's embrace and innovative use of Mandeville's idea of honor simultaneously repulsed Jansenists while attracting important mid-century economic writers. Meanwhile, Montesquieu tried his best in style and personal disposition to cling to a position identified with moderation. Certainly no Spinoza, his ideas spelled reformist possibilities in the eighteenth-century European world and laid the basis for commercial capitalism.[91]

An American Reading

In two separate studies scholars attempted to gauge the relative popularity and influence of various European writers upon eighteenth-century American public opinion. First, in 1976 two Berkeley historians, David Lundberg and Henry May, examined hundreds of American bookseller lists, sales brochures, and library catalogs between 1700 and 1813 for any mention of European books. Based on this database, they established a list of the 200 most popular European books in eighteenth-century America. Here *The Spirit of the Laws* was cited in 34 percent of the sources, which made it the seventh most popular European book in eighteenth-century America. Moreover, as opposed to literature, history, or epistemology, it is the first work on the list that is clearly a work of political theory. While Locke's *Essay Concerning Human Understanding* ranks first, Locke's *Two Treatises on Government* doesn't even make the top thirty—it appears in only 9 percent of these sources. In this sense, *The Spirit of the Laws* may have been four times as popular as *Two Treatises*. Indeed, Montesquieu's book was more popular than Hobbes, Sidney, or Harrington.[92]

In 1984 political scientist Donald Lutz followed up this research with a more expansive study. Gathering up 916 "political writings" published in America between 1760 and 1805, including broadsides, pamphlets, newspaper articles, and books, he developed a citation index for all political writers from Plato through Raynal. In this survey, which cites by author's name rather than book title, Montesquieu is consistently the most cited political writer in America during the second half of the eighteenth century, with 8.3 percent of the sources citing him at least once. "If there was one man read and reacted to by American political writers of all factions during all the stages of the founding era," writes Lutz, "it was probably not Locke but Montesquieu."[93]

The appeal of *The Spirit of the Laws* was not only broad in America, it was also deep. Its impact can perhaps best be seen among the principal Founders, especially during the events leading up to the ratification of the US Constitution. In 1769, shortly after beginning his political career in the Virginia House of Burgesses at the age of twenty-six, Thomas Jefferson ordered from England several books, among them Locke's *Two Treatises of Government*, Burlamaqui's *Principles of Natural and Political Right*, James Stewart's *Principles of Political Economy*, and Montesquieu's *The Spirit of the Laws*. Although *Spirit* was selling well in an English translation by Thomas Nugent, Jefferson ordered a three-volume quarto edition in the original French published by Jean Nourse, the largest London producer of books in French. If Jefferson jotted down his thoughts on reading Locke, Burlamaqui, or Stewart, they are lost. However, we know that Jefferson closely studied *The Spirit of the Laws*, making notes on all but five of its thirty-one books. He recorded these excerpts in his Commonplace Book, an informal notebook that served as a reading diary during these years. *The Spirit of the Laws* takes up more space in the Commonplace Book (twenty-eight pages) than any other political philosopher Jefferson read, attesting to its significant impact upon the young man.[94]

Unlike the political economists, Jefferson ignored the all-important Book 21 on commerce; unlike the Dupins, he ignored the discussion of polygamy in Book 15. Rather, Jefferson took extensive notes on Books II, V, and IX, where Montesquieu analyzed the role of suffrage, virtue, and equality in republics. Additionally, Jefferson was fascinated by Montesquieu's explanation of a confederate republic, an obvious model for what colonial America was becoming.

Montesquieu taught Jefferson how a state based upon popular sovereignty might be governed. By 1790, when Jefferson had become a statesman and politician, his admiration for *The Spirit of the Laws* had soured considerably. Given his practical experience in both the American and French Revolutions, he came to see Montesquieu as siding too much with an English-style monarchy rather than a regime based upon popular sovereignty. "I am glad to hear of everything which reduces that author to his just level," he later wrote to newspaper editor William Duane, "as his predilection for monarchy and English monarchy in particular, has done mischief everywhere, and here also, to a certain degree."[95]

Jefferson's lifelong rival, John Adams, also studied *The Spirit of the Laws* assiduously when he was a young man. At age twenty-four, in 1760, Adams gave the work his full attention. "I have begun to read *The Spirit of Laws*, and have resolved to read that work through in order and with attention. I have hit upon a project that will secure my attention to it, which is to write, in the margin, a sort of index to every paragraph." Although we do not have his notes, his unique method seems to have stuck. The following day he writes: "Read one hundred pages in *The Spirit of Laws*," and a week later he is still studying "diligently in *The Spirit of Laws*."[96] Many years later in 1783, when he negotiated peace in Versailles with the French and British, he found himself experiencing European nobility through Montesquieu's lens. He opened a letter to his wife Abigail by directly quoting in French a striking passage from *The Spirit of the Laws*:

> Ambition in idleness, meanness in arrogance, the desire to enrich oneself without work, aversion to truth, flattery, treachery, perfidy, the abandonment of all one's engagements, the scorn of the duties of citizens, the fear of the prince's virtue, the expectation of his weaknesses, and more than all that, the perpetual ridicule cast upon virtue, these form, I believe, the character of the greater number of courtiers, as observed in all places and at all times.

Where Montesquieu's Church critics specifically censored this entire section as false and misleading, Adams attested to its accuracy and insight to Abigail. "It is Montesquieu who draws this picture. And I think it is drawn from the Life, and is an exact resemblance." What the republican Adams had read in *The Spirit of the Laws* was exactly what he witnessed at Versailles. Baring his soul here in this letter, Adams declared that he and Abigail could never feel comfortable in the European world of noble courts. Born and bred in colonial New England, he detested Europe. "You cannot wonder then that I am weary and wish to be at home upon almost any terms. Your life would be dismal, in a high degree. You would be in an hideous solitude, among millions. None of them would be society for you that you could endure." Adams had no interest in a monarchical state energized by amour propre; he was at home only in a republic. "No," he tells Abigail, "Let us live in our own country, and in our own way. Educate our children to be good for something. Upon no consideration whatever would I have any of my children educated in Europe. In conscience I could not consent to it."[97]

By far the most dramatic and significant use of *The Spirit of the Laws* came during the 1787–8 debates over the ratification of the US Constitution. The book provided guidance for organizing the fundamental laws of the country. During the Constitutional Convention that met in Philadelphia during the summer of 1787, *The Spirit of the Laws* figured in debate roughly ten times, at least in those sessions that were privately recorded. The comments tended to cluster around Montesquieu's praise for confederated republics, and in particular, his preference for one historical example that he had found in an ancient Roman book on geography: "If one had to propose a model of a fine federal republic, I would choose the Republic of Lycia." Also known as the Lycian League, it constituted a federated group of twenty-three city-states in what is today the southwestern Anatolia (Turkish) coast. Montesquieu had discovered it in Strabo's *Geography*, published in Latin as recently as 1742. Americans in Philadelphia found in Montesquieu's use of Lycia an example they could embrace for replacing the Articles of Confederation with a much stronger central government.[98]

Following Philadelphia, the Constitution was subject to ratification in a series of state conventions held between fall 1787 and summer 1788. Each state required special elections to these conventions, and in several states, these elections required deliberative meetings on the Constitution in hundreds of towns and villages. The ratification process was among the most participatory and democratic political experiences anywhere in the eighteenth-century European world.[99] Unlike the Philadelphia Convention, which was held in secret, many of the state ratifying conventions were well covered by the press. The many letters sent to the press, of which the eighty-seven *Federalist Papers* are today justly the most famous, added spice and depth to this extraordinary national conversation regarding fundamental political institutions. Because so many documents were stored in various state and local archives, until the 1970s it was difficult to grasp a comprehensive overview of the process throughout the states. In 1976, the Wisconsin Historical Society began publishing *The Documentary History of the Ratification of the Constitution*, a daring project that grew to twenty-one volumes, now available online. These books included notes regarding speeches delivered at the conventions, newspaper articles, and letters between participants. Using the database, it is now easy to discover which political theorists drew the attention of the American political class during this seminal period. The results of that query make clear that *The Spirit of the Laws* was the book of political philosophy most often cited during the ratification process by far, with seventy-six citations, twenty-five more than the second on the list, Blackstone's *Commentaries on the Laws of England* (see Table 9.3). Others include works by Milton (32), Locke (26), Hume (22), Harrington (19) De Lolme (12), Beccaria (11), Mably (10), and Grotius (10).

Table 9.3 Most Citations Referenced from *The Documentary History of the Ratification of the Constitution*

Author	#Citations
Montesquieu	76
Blackstone	52
Sidney	41
Milton	32
Locke	26
Hume	22
Harrington	19
De Lolme	12
Beccaria	11
Mably	10
Grotius	10
Vattel	7
Hobbes	5
Pufendorf	3
Burlamaqui	3
Rousseau	2
Machiavelli	2
Bolingbroke	1

Source: *The Documentary History of the Ratification of the Constitution Digital Edition*, ed. John P. Kaminski, Gaspare J. Saladino, Richard Leffler, Charles H. Schoenleber, and Margaret A. Hogan (Charlottesville: University of Virginia Press, 2009), hereafter cited as DHRC-DE, https://rotunda.upress.virginia.edu/founders/RNCN. Accessed March 9, 2022.

Montesquieu was the key figure not only for Federalists advocating ratification, but equally for those activists critical of the new constitution, whom the Federalists labeled Anti-Federalists. Among this latter group, *The Spirit of the Laws* again was cited more than twice as often as Blackstone's *Commentaries*, and three to four times as often as Locke, Sidney, or De Lolme (see Table 9.4).[100]

Both sides—Federalists and Anti-Federalists—saw Montesquieu as the "celebrated," "great," and "learned" authority on republican governments; both thought they could use him beneficially for their own purposes. Even when they disagreed with Montesquieu on specific points or examples, they agreed with one another that *The Spirit of the Laws* was the most relevant work of political theory. In this sense, the argument over ratifying the US Constitution also became an extraordinary debate over the meaning of Montesquieu's book.

The Anti-Federalists seized on Montesquieu's rule that republics must be small. They repeatedly cited Book 8 Chapter 16: "In a large republic, the public good is sacrificed to a thousand views; it is subordinate to exceptions, and depends on accidents: in a small one, the interests of the public is [*sic*] easier perceived, better understood, and more within the reach of every citizen; abuses have a less extent, and of course are less protected."

Table 9.4 Most Cited Thinkers by Anti-Federalists

Author	Number of Citations
Montesquieu	40
Blackstone	16
Locke	12
Sidney	9
DeLolme	9
Beccaria	6
Machiavelli	5
Hume	4
Price	4
Mably	3
Milton	2
Bolingbroke	1
Grotius	1
Harrington	1
Hobbes	1
Pufendorf	1
Rousseau	1

Source: Herbert J. Storing, and Murray Dry, eds., *The Complete Anti-Federalist*, 7 vols. (Chicago: University of Chicago Press, 1981).

An influential columnist, "Cato," reprinted in several newspapers, quoted Montesquieu, noting that Athens lost its freedom precisely when it entered into a confederacy. "From this picture," Cato argued, it is clear that the "consolidation" of the thirteen states into one national government, as designed by the Constitution, would "oppress and grind you." An ally of Cato named "Brutus," echoed this sentiment, making the point that given that the population of the United States would be some three million souls, it was clearly already too large for any republic to remain free. After all, he wrote paraphrasing Montesquieu, "in a republic, the manners, sentiments, and interests of the people should be similar."[101]

Federalist writers and speakers rejected these Anti-Federalist arguments. Thomas Greenleaf, editor and publisher of the *New York Journal*, scorned the Anti-Federalists for reading Montesquieu at the expense of other theorists. Cato, for example, "totally neglected Grotius, Puffendorf, Sydney, Locke, Hume, and others equally celebrated, confining himself to one or two thread-bare quotations from Baron Montesquieu." Indeed, Greenleaf charged, "it is more than probable that [Cato] has never seen any more of Montesquieu's works than a few scraps, picked out of some late miscellaneous pieces."[102]

Americanus (pseudonym of John Stevens, Jr., a local politician from Hoboken, New Jersey) at first criticized Cato and others for drawing upon Montesquieu at all. What could "any political writer in Europe" know of the remarkable political conditions here in America? Why should the "wretched attempts that have been made in the old world to constitute Republican Governments" bear any relevance to the unique situation in which Americans find themselves? Here Americanus attacked Montesquieu as much as the

Anti-Federalists themselves. A few weeks later, Americanus tried a different argument. Instead of conceding that *The Spirit of the Laws* is an Anti-Federalist textbook, he tried to reinterpret Montesquieu for the Federalists. "Should I be able to prove that the governments of these states are founded on principles totally different from those which Montesquieu here had in view, it will then be manifest that Cato has lugged him into a controversy in which he is no ways concerned." Based on his analysis of *The Spirit of the Laws*, Americanus then argued that there was a huge chasm separating the ancient Greek and Roman republics from their modern eighteenth-century counterpart. The ancient democracies required a level of patriotic virtue and self-sacrifice that may have been necessary for security but ultimately was antithetical to individual liberty. Paraphrasing Montesquieu, Americanus argued that these ancient democracies required too much from individual citizens:

> The life of a citizen was one continued effort of self-denial and restraint. Every social passion—all the finer feelings of the heart—the tender ties of parent and child—every enjoyment, whether of sentiment or of sense—every thing in short which renders life desirable, was relinquished. . . . Magistrates were appointed for the express purpose of inspecting into the lives and conduct of every citizen—the public good superseded every consideration of a private nature—fathers condemned their own sons to the axe. Let it not be thought however that this exalted degree of patriotism—this rigid system of mortification and self-denial was the effect of choice; no! far from it! it was necessity that imposed it on them—This magnanimous people saw plainly that their safety depended upon keeping up this austerity of manners.

According to Americanus, the key difference between the ancient and modern form of republics was the development of representation. In the ancient world, every citizen was equal with everyone else, but all were expected to participate actively in political affairs. In the modern world, representation allowed citizens to specialize in certain functions over others, or to retire to one's home immersed in private affairs. This modern type of representative republicanism

> requires in the execution of it, none of those heroic virtues which we admire in the ancients, and to us are known only by story. The sacrifice of our dearest interests, self-denial, and austerity of manners, are by no means necessary. Such a Government requires nothing more of its subjects than that they should study and pursue merely their own true interest and happiness.[103]

Ultimately the discussion of the size of republics morphed into an argument regarding the wealth and inequality generated by modern representative governments. Where Americanus championed the ability of citizens to satisfy their passions through consumption, Cato praised the more frugal and egalitarian Greek and even Roman examples. "The progress of a commercial society," he remarked, "begets luxury, the parent of inequality, the foe to virtue, and the enemy to restraint."[104]

Other Federalists argued that Cato, Brutus, and Sidney were misreading Montesquieu regarding the size of republics. Rather than focus on Book 8, Chapter 16 ("It is in the nature of a republic to have only a small territory; otherwise, it can scarcely continue to exist"), one should concentrate instead on Book 9, Chapters 1 and 2, where Montesquieu argues that individual republics are too vulnerable to invasions from larger states and only a confederate republic could defend itself successfully and provide security for its citizens. Speaking in the Pennsylvania state convention, James Wilson gave his colleagues a short lesson on Montesquieu's ideas. "A very important difficulty arose from comparing the extent of the country to be governed with the kind of government which it would be proper to establish in it." Wilson then quoted *The Spirit of the Laws* directly:

> that the natural property of small states is to be governed as a republic; of middling ones, to be subject to a monarch; and of large empires, to be swayed by a despotic prince; and that the consequence is, that, in order to preserve the principles of the established government, the state must be supported in the extent it has acquired; and that the spirit of the state will alter in proportion as it extends or contracts its limits.

Wilson went on to explain that Montesquieu himself recognized the problems this posed for modern republics, and in the very next section, Book 9, offered the confederate republic as a solution: "What then was to be done? The idea of a confederate republic presented itself," Wilson continued. This kind of constitution has been thought to have "all the internal advantages of a republican, together with the external force of a monarchical government." From this study of *The Spirit of the Laws*, Wilson drew the obvious conclusion: "The *expanding* quality of such a government is peculiarly fitted for the United States, the greatest part of whose territory is yet uncultivated."[105]

It is possible, but doubtful, that Wilson was echoing what he had read in the press, rather than drawing directly on Montesquieu. On November 21, 1787, only three days before Wilson gave his speech, the ninth *Federalist* was first published in a New York newspaper. Its thirty-two-year-old author, Alexander Hamilton, had first encountered *The Spirit of the Laws* as a student in the King's College library (today Columbia University). Already in his first political pamphlet, written when he was only nineteen, he had recommended "Grotius, Pufendorf, Locke, Montesquieu, and Burlamaqui."[106]

Even though the notion of a confederate republic was worth only a small mention in Montesquieu's large book (most readers on the continent seemed to ignore it), it gave many eighteenth-century American Federalists ammunition to claim Montesquieu as one of their own. At the Philadelphia Constitutional Convention, Hamilton already let his colleagues know of his admiration for *The Spirit of the Laws*.[107] Later, in June 1788, he lectured his colleagues on Montesquieu at the New York ratifying convention. Like John Stevens, Hamilton was upset that Montesquieu had been so easily appropriated by the Anti-Federalists, and he was determined to put a stop to it. This "celebrated writer, who by being misunderstood, has been the occasion of frequent fallacies in our reasoning on political subjects."[108] *Federalist 9* was Hamilton's most brilliant attempt to set the record straight on Montesquieu.

Montesquieu's The Spirit of the Laws *(1748)*

The opponents of the PLAN proposed for the U.S. Constitution have cited and circulated the observations of Montesquieu on the necessity of a contracted territory for a republican government. But they seem not to have been apprised of the sentiments of that great man expressed in another part of his work, nor to have averted to the consequences of the principle to which they subscribe with such ready acquiescence.

In *Federalist 9*, Hamilton's first attack point against the Anti-Federalists was a devastating one: "When Montesquieu recommends a small extent for republics," he means something much smaller than any of the existing states under the Articles of Confederation. Montesquieu was addressing mainly the tiny city-states of the ancient world, or aristocratic republics like Venice or Holland. "Neither Virginia, Massachusetts, Pennsylvania, New York, North Carolina, nor Georgia can by any means be compared with the models from which he reasoned and to which the terms of his description apply." Brutus, Cato, Sidney, and the many other Anti-Federalist writers had no business citing Montesquieu's association of republics with small geographical size because the majority of states already fell outside his limits.

Although Montesquieu's republics are too small for relevance to the American situation, Hamilton argued, his positive statements regarding confederate republics had a direct bearing on current debates. "So far are the suggestions of Montesquieu from standing in opposition to a general Union of the States that he explicitly treats of a CONFEDERATE REPUBLIC as the expedient for extending the sphere of popular government and reconciling the advantages of monarchy with those of republicanism." At that point, Hamilton had reprinted verbatim into the body of the text the final six paragraphs of Book 9, Chapter 1, where Montesquieu introduced the Lycian League as a model confederate republic. "I have thought it proper to quote at length these interesting passages," comments Hamilton, "because they contain a luminous abridgment of the principal arguments in favor of the Union." In short, this section from *The Spirit of the Laws* has "an intimate connection with the more immediate design of this paper, which is to illustrate the tendency of the Union to repress domestic faction and insurrection." In the three remaining paragraphs of *Federalist 9*, Hamilton denies the Anti-Federalist distinction between a confederacy and a consolidation by noting a small, but critical, point from Montesquieu that the Lycian Common Council had the authority to appoint "all the judges and magistrates of the respective cities." In Lycia, the central government held primary political power, just as Hamilton hoped would be the case in the new United States.[109]

Another important use of *The Spirit of the Laws* by Anti-Federalists concerned the separation of powers. In Book 11, Chapter 6, Montesquieu famously explained that division of political power among three branches—legislative, executive, and judicial—was the key feature of the British constitution that resulted in political liberty. Even more than Locke, Montesquieu championed this aspect of England's political organization as uniquely modern:

> When legislative power is united with executive power in a single person or in a single body of the magistracy, there is no liberty, because one can fear that the same monarch or senate that makes tyrannical laws will execute them tyrannically.[110]

Federalists and Anti-Federalists repeatedly argued over this quotation, urging American leaders to emulate Montesquieu's insight into British constitutional arrangements.[111] But Anti-Federalist writers regarded several features of what came out of the Philadelphia Convention as violations of Montesquieu's separation principle. George Mason claimed the Senate's power to act upon Presidential ambassadorial and other appointments a clear overstepping of its legislative boundary. Others, such as Patrick Henry, George Clinton, and William Lancaster, agreed with Mason that the Constitution allowed, if not encouraged, a tyrannical alliance between the senate For exampleand presidency. Another example of this blending of the two branches was in the Office of the Vice President, who served simultaneously as President of the Senate. "The Oligarchic tendency from the combination of President, V. President, & Senate," wrote the Virginian Richard Henry Lee, "is a ruin not within legislative remedy."[112]

It was this Anti-Federalist position that James Madison addressed head-on in *Federalist 47*, entitled "The Meaning of the Maxim, which Requires a Separation of the Departments of Power, Examined and Ascertained." In this article, Madison applied Montesquieu's doctrine of the separation of power to the American context. Madison, of course, had been intimately familiar with Montesquieu since his days at the College at New Jersey (now Princeton University), where he had read *The Spirit of the Laws* for President John Witherspoon's seminal course on political thought, and he himself had referred to the book on the floor of the Philadelphia Convention. Like Jefferson, Adams, and Hamilton, Madison would never allow *The Spirit of the Laws* to become an Anti-Federalist bible.[113]

"One of the principal objections inculcated by the more respectable adversaries to the Constitution," Madison began, is the "supposed violation" of the separation of powers. The question is a significant one, he agreed. "No political truth is certainly of greater intrinsic value." Were the new federal government vulnerable to the types of violations charged by its opponents, "no further arguments would be necessary to inspire a universal reprobation." Nor did Madison object to allowing Montesquieu to umpire the question. "The oracle who is always consulted and cited on this subject is the celebrated Montesquieu. . . . Let us endeavor . . . to ascertain his meaning on this point." So, again, as with Hamilton's *Federalist 9*, the terms of the debate surrounding the US Constitution boiled down to a debate over the meaning of Montesquieu's *The Spirit of the Laws*.[114]

Madison reminded readers that while Montesquieu developed his separation of powers doctrine wholly within the context of Great Britain, it was clear to everyone that the branches of the English government were not, in fact, "separate and distinct from each other." The prime minister, for example, is the leader of the House of Commons; judges are appointed by the king; members of the House of Lords are also named by the king. This being obvious, argued Madison, Montesquieu could not possibly have meant, argued Madison, that "these departments ought to have no *partial agency* in, or no *control* over, the acts of each other." Rather, his principle was designed to prevent "the *whole* power" of one branch falling into "the same hands which possess the whole power of another" branch. For example, "if the king, who is the sole executive magistrate, had possessed also the complete legislative power," liberty would evaporate.

So, while whole power leads to tyranny, partial power acts to temper and check the arbitrary tendencies of any one branch. Here was the crux of the matter. After all, even under the Articles of Confederation, Madison reminded his reader, "there is not a single instance of a state where the legislative, judicial, and executive branches have been kept absolutely separate and distinct." Complete separation, in short, is a chimera and not at all what Montesquieu had in mind. With that, Madison devoted a paragraph each to eleven state governments (omitting Connecticut and Rhode Island), demonstrating how each allowed some partial engagement among the three branches. The Anti-Federalists, then, had fundamentally misunderstood Montesquieu's principle. Their "charge brought against the proposed Constitution of violating the sacred maxim of free government," Madison concluded, "is warranted neither by the real meaning annexed to that maxim by its author, nor by the sense in which it has been understood in America."

Scholars often describe Madison and Hamilton as "neutralizing" Montesquieu, repudiating his small-republic model.[115] But this common viewpoint errs in seeing *The Spirit of the Laws* as essentially an Anti-Federalist tract. Rather, the accomplishment of Madison, Hamilton, and their allies was not so much to repudiate Montesquieu as to move *The Spirit of the Laws* into the Federalist camp. Their method was to attack Montesquieu's small-republic theory with ideas from other parts of *The Spirit of the Laws*. Most important were the differences between modern and ancient states that Montesquieu effectively explained in his sections on Great Britain and commerce. Madison and Hamilton skillfully showed that Montesquieu viewed small republics as out of place in the eighteenth-century world.

Debates over the ratification of the US Constitution became a popular seminar held throughout the young country over the meaning of Enlightenment political theory. Sometimes minor politicians who entered the debate were cognizant of how unusual these debates may have been, and it made them self-conscious. When "An Impartial Citizen" wrote in the *Petersburg Virginia Gazette* that he feared "my frequent mention of Montesquieu, Grotius, and other writers on government" might produce accusations "of pedantry and perhaps of arrogance," he felt the need to defend himself. "The authors I have already, and hereafter intend to mention, are the most celebrated writers known to the world: their systems of jurisprudence, and their opinions are known and respected by all nations." Indeed, they should be trusted much more than the silly musings of the Constitution's opponents. After all, charged this writer, "there are more egregious errors and gross misrepresentations in that single epistle of [Richard Henry Lee's October 16, 1787 letter to Governor Edmund Randolph] than in the thirty-one books which Montesquieu wrote on the spirit of laws." And then he added for emphasis: "For the verity of my assertion, I appeal to those who have seen and read those books, and that epistle." In calling our attention to the popularity of erudite political theory, "An Impartial Citizen" demonstrated how readers like himself helped to shape the European Enlightenment.[116]

Chapter 10

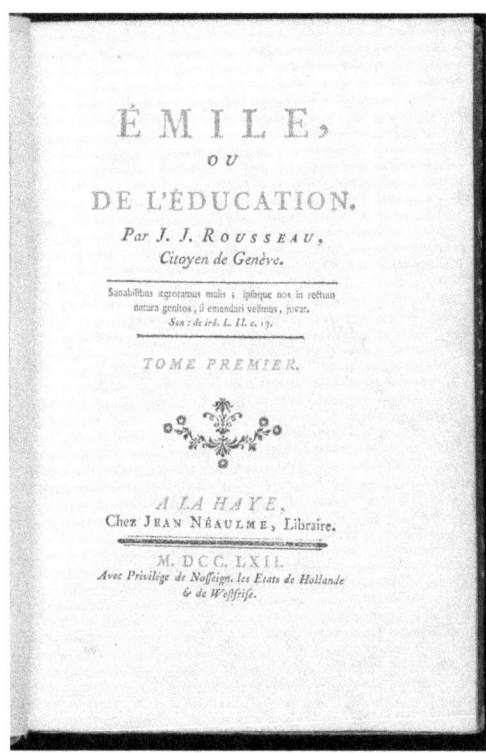

Figure 10.1 First edition title page Rousseau's *Emile*. The real publisher in Paris made a deal with Jean Néaulme in Amsterdam to take responsibility for *Emile*. This was, however, before Néaulme read the book, and so offended by its religious ideas, he immediately abandoned the project by reselling the Dutch rights to Marc Michel Rey. *Emile* was Rousseau's most controversial book.

Chapter 10
Rousseau's *Emile* (1762)

Table 10.1 Eighteenth-Century Editions of *The New Heloise*, *Social Contract*, and *Emile*

Decade	1761–9	1770–9	1780–9	1790–1800	Total
New Heloise	43	22	29	43	137
Social Contract	25	9	13	70	117
Emile	26	14	18	24	82

Translations for *The New Heloise*: English, German, Italian, Russian.
Translations for *The Social Contract*: Danish, Dutch, English, German, Italian, Polish, Spanish.
Translations for *Emile*: Danish, Dutch, English, German, Italian, Russian.
Source: https://kates.itg.pomona.edu/books/analytics.php?type=all. Accessed March 9, 2022 and Jo-Ann E. McEachern, *Bibliography of the Writings of Jean Jacques Rousseau to 1800,* 2 vols. (Oxford: Voltaire Foundation, 1989–93), and "The Bibliography of Jean-Jacques Rousseau's *Contrat social*," in *Order and Connexion: Studies in Bibliography and Book History*, ed. R. C. Alston (Woodbridge, Suffolk and Rochester: D.S. Brewer, 1997), 106–7.

During the summer of 1749, Jean Jacques Rousseau was making regular visits on foot from his home in the center of Paris (where he was secretary to Louise Dupin, who we met in Chapter 9) to the Chateau de Vincennes on the other side of a forest at the edge of the capital. One day, while skimming the *Mercure de France*, he saw a notice from the Academy of Dijon announcing its annual essay contest theme: "Has the progress of the sciences and arts tended to corrupt or purify morals?" As Rousseau began to think about the question, he was thrown into a profound existential crisis. It made him physically ill, causing nausea, and he broke down in tears in the middle of the small forest. "At the moment of that reading I saw another universe and I became another man." What he saw was a glimpse of his writing career for the next decade. All of the ideas that he would carefully build up in a series of works flooded into his head in an overwhelming fashion.[1]

In an insightful article, Paul Rahe has noted that Rousseau's epiphany came after months of closely studying Montesquieu's *The Spirit of the Laws* in the Dupin household. Rahe contends that Rousseau's ingenious response to the Dijon academy's question was framed within the context of Montesquieu's argument about the progress of civil society since antiquity. Where Montesquieu argued that the rise of the arts and sciences had led to *doux commerce*, that is, the gradual replacement of war by commerce as the governing motor of states, Rousseau from then on would counter that modern commercial society represented a corrosion of morality itself. In other words, the inspiration for Rousseau's entire project stemmed from his engagement with Montesquieu.[2]

Of all his works, *Emile, or On Education* is the most inspired by Montesquieu's *The Spirit of the Laws*. *Emile* incorporates epistemology, moral philosophy, religion, social criticism, and politics into a sustained critique of modern commercial society. Written in the format of an education manual with elements borrowed from fiction, *Emile* may be considered a novel by some readers but is Rousseau's most philosophical work. Distributed throughout the long volume are references to more than fifty classical and modern thinkers, among them Cicero, Plato, Seneca, Virgil, Herodotus, Livy, and Xenophon—plus Montaigne, Hobbes, Locke, Fénelon, Bayle, and Montesquieu himself. In that sense, *Emile* is no less scholarly than *The Spirit of the Laws* but wears its erudition even more lightly. After an introductory essay on epistemology that is largely taken from Locke's *Essay Concerning Human Understanding*, Rousseau recycled Fénelon's Telemachus/Mentor relationship through a fictional character—Emile—and a semi-fictional persona—himself as the mentor. We then move through the stages of Emile's life from infancy through adolescence, ending when the young adult finds Sophie for his wife. Judged from the reaction of church and state authorities at the time, *Emile* was also Rousseau's most radical statement. Banned throughout Europe, it changed Rousseau's life forever.

By the time *Emile* was first published in May 1762, Rousseau was fifty years old and already among the most recognized authors of the Enlightenment. His first discourse on the arts and sciences had been reprinted over a dozen times and had already been translated into English, Italian, and German. His second discourse on inequality was almost as successful. But Rousseau was not known simply as a polemicist; his range was extraordinary even for Enlightenment philosophes. In 1752 his opera, *Le Devin du Village* [the Village Soothsayer], was performed at the royal court in Fontainebleau, and by the end of the century its score had been published eight times—it is still purchased in modern recordings today.[3] During the year 1760, his career still at an early stage, five separate works of his were reprinted. Despite this success, nothing prepared the public for what was about to come. Since 1757, when Rousseau moved to a rent-free forested cottage on the estate of a wealthy nobleman in Montmorency (15 kilometers north of Paris), he worked simultaneously on three different books that were completed and published around the same time: *La Nouvelle Héloïse*, an epistolary novel in the style of Richardson, was first published in a six-volume duodecimo format in February 1761; *The Social Contract*, a 400-page political treatise in octavo format, appeared in May 1762; and one month later, *Emile*, in a four-volume octavo format. One might have thought that Rousseau was overplaying his hand by saturating the market with eleven volumes at once. And indeed, readers tended to confuse the works, if for no other reason than they purposely overlapped with one another in theme and material. For example, many of the key points of *The Social Contract* are recycled in the fifth section of *Emile*. Similarly, in *La Nouvelle*

Héloïse, the characters engage in a spirited discussion on child rearing. And yet, far from overwhelming the public, each of these works became a best-selling masterpiece in its own right, and Rousseau earned celebrity status across Europe that was nothing short of astonishing.

Rousseau's work in the 1750s was decidedly critical of European progress and, in particular, France's civilization. Even in his writing on music, Rousseau saw a France decadent and corrupt when compared with Italian states. France's reputation for art and literature veiled a cutthroat world where acting virtuously spelled disaster. The second part of his *Discourse on the Origins of Inequality* (1755) suggested that Europe was rapidly falling into an era of cruel despotic regimes, with little that anyone could do about it. This analysis was remarkably bleak. Readers impressed with Rousseau's elegance were baffled by his pessimism: Why write about something that can't be changed? The three major works of 1761–2 promised to address this central concern. Each would reimagine eighteenth-century European culture, showing that novel approaches to civil society were indeed possible. *La Nouvelle Héloïse* would demonstrate how romantic love might thrive in the modern world; *The Social Contract* reimagined the sphere of government, inspired by ancient Sparta and Rome; *Emile* showed that with a new kind of education, even modern children could be raised to become independent adults and virtuous citizens. The three books were a package showing readers how modern life could be reconceived along the lines of sincerity, equality, and virtue.[4]

Malesherbes and *La Nouvelle Heloïse*

La Nouvelle Héloïse imitates Richardson's novels in format and theme. Like Richardson, Rousseau used the form of an exchange of letters to explore the concepts of virtue and love inside and outside of marriage. Here, though, Rousseau inverts the class dynamic. Where in *Pamela* the male lover was also a nobleman, in *La Nouvelle Héoïse* Saint-Preux is a commoner. He is, in fact, tutor to the young, beautiful, and ennobled Julie d'Etanges. She is caught between her passion for Saint-Preux and her respect for her father, who has already chosen M. de Wolmar to be her spouse. As in *Pamela*, the story revolves around Julie's efforts to discipline her passion by means of her virtue.

Once Rousseau completed the long manuscript in September 1758, he immediately began discussions with Amsterdam publisher Marc Michel Rey, who in ten years had become among the largest Dutch publishers of French books. Originally from Rousseau's hometown, Geneva, Rey had moved to Amsterdam in the 1740s to start a career in publishing and bookselling. He became wealthy by marrying the daughter of one of Amsterdam's most successful publishers, Jean François Bernard, and he was able to use his father-in-law's inventory to launch his fledging business. Before long, he was publishing works by Voltaire and Diderot, as well as Rousseau's *Discourse on the Origins of Inequality*, and, more recently, his *Letter to d'Alembert on the Theatre*. By

1761, Rey was arguably the premier publisher of the French Enlightenment philosophes. Nonetheless, *La Nouvelle Héloïse* was a great challenge because of its length. He paid Rousseau 2,140 livres for the right to produce 4,000 copies of a 6-volume set.[5]

We noted earlier how Montesquieu was distant from his publishers to the point of carelessness. During the publication process, he wanted as little to do with his manuscript as possible. As with so many comparisons between these two writers, Rousseau's behavior contrasts sharply with Montesquieu's. While Rousseau sometimes worked through friends and intermediaries (usually during the earliest stages of a negotiation), he also forged a candid, intimate, and regular friendship with Rey, insisting on participating in every stage of the process. So controlling was Rousseau over the publication of his books that he gave Rey instruction on the quality of paper, the type of font chosen for text and footnotes, and the design of ornaments that graced blank pages. Rey and Rousseau even disagreed over running titles: Rey wanted to use the original title of the novel, *Letters entre deux amans* (Letters Between Two Lovers), while Rousseau insisted upon *La Nouvelle Héloïse*.[6] Rousseau's participation required that he and Rey work out a way to exchange proofs and galleys regularly and as efficiently as possible. Rousseau rejected Rey's urging that he move to Amsterdam where they could together work daily on the project over a few months. Rey had to fall back on the next best option, sending packets through the post and hoping for the best. Here Rousseau had a fascinating suggestion: if the packets traveled from Amsterdam to the offices of the French director of the book trade, Chrétien Guillaume Malesherbes, they could be shipped as diplomatic materials, avoiding the expensive postal charges. From that office, they could be forwarded to Rousseau's hut in Montmorency, again, free of charge because of Malesherbes's government position. Moreover, Rousseau and Rey intended this to be more than simply a postal arrangement. By funneling the proofs through Malesherbes, he would have the opportunity to participate himself in approving the work for publication. He was, after all, France's chief censor, managing over a hundred part-time royal censors. Rousseau knew that he needed Malesherbes's blessing if his novel was to sell freely in France. The story of the novel's publication is not simply one that took place between author and publisher, but involved a close triangular relationship from the start among Rey, Rousseau, and Malesherbes.[7]

Malesherbes was a critical figure in sorting out the complex relationship of the Enlightenment philosophes to the monarchy in mid-eighteenth-century France. A liberal friend of the philosophes, and a champion of widening press freedom, Malesherbes also embraced traditional goals of the Old Regime monarchy: first and foremost, to keep out of circulation books that attacked individuals (especially the king or queen), morality, religious institutions, and the like. After all, if Malesherbes did not keep a close watch on subversive and slanderous literature, government authority in these areas might slip out of his hands to judicial (e.g., the parlements) or religious (e.g., the Sorbonne) institutions. The best way, thought Malesherbes, toward a free press was by incremental liberalization. At the same time, he saw his role in starkly mercantilist terms: The Office of the Book Trade also served the interests of the French publishing industry, protecting it from competitors in neighboring states.[8]

Malesherbes held his office since 1750, but he nearly lost it in 1759, when the philosophe Claude Antoine Helvétius secured a privilege for the atheistic *De l'Esprit*. Almost immediately upon its publication, Malesherbes recognized his mistake, and withdrew the privilege, but it was too late. The Queen complained, the Parlement and Sorbonne intervened, and the subsequent scandal threatened not merely Malesherbes's career, but put at risk the entire project of press liberalization. From now on church and state would monitor publication more carefully.[9]

Malesherbes's intimate involvement with Rousseau's publications demonstrates that the relationship between philosophes and censorship was complex. Any simplistic view that associates the philosophes with freedom of the press and absolute monarchy with precluding press freedom is at odds with reality. Enlightenment writers, including Rousseau, expected any good government to police the press, that is, to supervise, regulate, and manage the press in such a way that writers, printers, and booksellers would all be protected. After all, the interests of writers and publishers were rarely aligned, requiring government to mediate between them. The philosophes did not expect an entirely free publishing marketplace, but rather one in which the government established a fair and liberal rulebook. Rousseau saw Malesherbes as an ally and not an obstacle.

Rey began printing *La Nouvelle Héloïse* on February 28, 1760, and continued for several months. The system for sending proofs back and forth worked surprisingly well, considering the challenges of printing technology and the postal service during the eighteenth century. Typically, typographers could set three sheets (roughly seventy-five pages) per week. It took about nine days for each packet to travel from Amsterdam to Paris, and another day for Malesherbes to convey it to Montmorency. Rousseau usually turned his corrections around within twenty-four hours, and then reversed the process to get the packet back to Rey in Amsterdam. Rey completed printing the manuscript in November. Two thousand copies were sent in three large crates from Amsterdam to Paris, where Rey had contracted with a bookseller to distribute half the print run there. Meanwhile, Rey sent 500 copies each to German and English distributors.

The German and English copies reached their destinations with no trouble. But for weeks, the three crates bound for Paris were apparently lost at sea. It took Rey several weeks to learn that the delay was due to frozen canals outside Amsterdam. The crates finally arrived in Paris in early January. By that time, however, Malesherbes had his own ideas about how Rousseau's novel should be published in France. Malesherbes sequestered the three crates in France's customs office, preventing anyone, including Rousseau, from gaining access to it. Some months earlier, Malesherbes had encouraged Paris publishers to produce their own edition of the novel, and he wanted this domestic version to come out even before Rey's edition. This development infuriated Rousseau, who complained to Malesherbes that it was unethical to place Rey in such financial jeopardy while encouraging piracy among Paris publishers. Malesherbes viewed the situation very differently and lectured Rousseau accordingly. This situation had nothing to do with book piracy, he explained. The French had every right to produce an edition for sale within the French kingdom before a foreign edition was licensed in France. Of course, during the eighteenth century there was nothing resembling international copyright. No one seriously considered foreign publishers on a level playing field with domestic ones. Malesherbes insisted that a French edition must precede Rey's imported first edition.[10]

Malesherbes also worried about the novel's content. With good reason, he was concerned about how other government authorities would respond to the book. He wanted to avoid any repetition of what happened with Helvétius's *De l'Esprit*. Consequently, he had one of his staff censors go through Rousseau's book carefully, excising its most controversial passages. From Malesherbes's viewpoint, the safest course would be to grant an official privilege for a censored French version, which would appear first, and then several weeks later allow Rey's edition to appear through the mechanism of a special license (*permission tacite*).

The French edition was produced in Paris by Etienne-Vincent Robin and Jean-Augustin Grangé. At first, they offered Rousseau 760 livres, but Malesherbes insisted this was too low for the author, and Robin and Grangé increased their offer to 1,000, which Malesherbes urged Rousseau to accept.[11] With the eventual cooperation of Rousseau and Rey, Robin and Grangé began printing their version in January 1761. When the Robin-Grangé edition was ready for publication, Rousseau received a copy and only then discovered that what was intended to be a line-by-line facsimile of Rey's edition was actually a heavily edited version; so censored, Rousseau believed, as to make the novel unintelligible in several sections. Immediately Rousseau publicly disavowed the Robin-Grangé edition and returned the promissory note for 1,000 livres.

This story explains why in France a censored and unauthorized edition of Rousseau's novel preceded the first by several weeks during the first months of 1761. It also illustrates how involved Malesherbes—the king's representative—was in Enlightenment publishing. Malesherbes came to Rousseau's aid sometimes as his agent and sometimes resembling a parole officer; the result was a close, if complicated, relationship. During the middle years of the eighteenth century, the royal government was more often a mediator of Enlightenment publishing than its adversary. In this respect, *La Nouvelle Héloïse* was as much a novel allowed by the monarchy as it was a novel against the Old Regime. Indeed, given Rousseau's own standing as a bourgeois Genevan with no direct relationship with the French kingdom, Malesherbes's efforts to allow his books to be published in Paris is striking.

The Rey and Robin-Grangé editions of *La Nouvelle Héloïse* sold out. During 1761, its first year, the book went through sixteen editions, including one German and two English translations. As Table 10.1 shows, production dipped a bit during the 1770s, but Rousseau's death in 1778 seems to have revitalized sales, as a Rousseau cult developed in the 1780s. The French Revolution gave the novel an extended life, as Rousseau's views became official government doctrine. Altogether, including translations in English and German, 137 eighteenth-century editions appeared. The novel's fame was extraordinary, and in terms of copies sold, it may have been among the century's top bestsellers.

The Social Contract

Rousseau finished *The Social Contract* at about the same time that *The New Héloïse* was published. It, too, was a direct response to Montesquieu. In both *The Spirit of the Laws* and *Persian Letters*, Montesquieu sought to demonstrate that among the variety of political states in the world, despotisms were perverse, unsustainable regimes based on human exploitation. He carefully contrasted despotism with republics and monarchies; that is, regimes that exhibited "moderation."[12] Rousseau underscored Voltaire's criticism that despotism is not a different type of government, but rather it is a monarchy gone bad. For Voltaire, a well-run monarchy uses sovereign power for the public good; a despot misuses that same authority. Rousseau twisted Voltaire's formulation by suggesting that arbitrary misuse of power was, in fact, inherent in all monarchical sovereignty. The only way for monarchs to know if their power was being used for the public good, Rousseau argued, was if, and only if, political authority emanated directly from the public. That is, while Rousseau was willing to tolerate a king or queen who administered government, he insisted that all legislative authority—law making—remain in the hands of the citizens. Sovereignty must be held and exercised by the people. Sticking to Montesquieu's tripartite framework (republic, monarchy, and despotism), this meant that monarchy moved to the other side of the fence with despotism; of the three types of government, only republics were deemed legitimate in *The Social Contract*, and within republics, only those states that gave all citizens equal legislative authority—in other words, democracies.

The Social Contract was a think piece. It was not a manual for revolution nor even a work directly aimed at the French government. Most of Rousseau's examples were from ancient Greece and Rome. Some followers of Rousseau, in fact, saw it as compatible with the eighteenth-century French monarchy.[13] Rousseau produced *The Social Contract* as a work of theory, in which concepts regarding sovereignty, legislation, administration, political justice, and elections were given new meanings.

There was no question that *The Social Contact* could not be published legally—that is, with the government's endorsement in the form of a *privilège*—in France. As with his earlier writings, such as the 1758 *Letter to d'Alembert on the Theater*, Rousseau expected that a foreign publisher would be able to obtain a *permission tacite* to allow limited circulation within France. Indeed, in February 1762, Malesherbes visited Rousseau for the second time at Montmorency, and the two men discussed strategies for publishing *The Social Contract* in this fashion. As usual, Rousseau sold the rights for a first edition for 1,000 livres to Marc Michel Rey. In March and April, Rey printed 2,500 octavo copies and 2,500 duodecimos. Meanwhile, Rey made arrangements with three prominent Paris booksellers to retail the books in Paris and made further arrangements with provincial French booksellers. After Malesherbes read an advanced copy early in May, however, he realized what a hot potato he held in his hands. He immediately issued an order banning all sales throughout France. Given the close relationship between author and chief censor, Rey and the booksellers were surprised by this sudden and grave financial setback. The *Social Contract* would not be sold freely in France until the French Revolution.

Today Rousseau's *Social Contract* is recognized as a masterpiece of Enlightenment political theory. Of all eighteenth-century works about politics, it is perhaps the most famous. Few college students major in political science without encountering it. And yet, until recently, and persisting even today, has been an almost universal belief among scholars that *The Social Contract* was one of Rousseau's least-read books until 1789, when the French Revolutionaries rescued it from near-oblivion. Instead, it is still widely believed that Rousseau was famous for his sentimental novel, his eloquent three discourses, and his pedagogical theories—but not for his formal political theory, which was passed over as too difficult for the emerging Enlightenment reading public. Abstract, theoretical, and irrelevant to the skirmishes and conflicts that marked Old Regime politics, it has been argued that *The Social Contract* was largely ignored until the new political scene that emerged in the 1790s made its notion of popular sovereignty suddenly remarkably relevant. Hence, so the conventional wisdom goes, while *The Social Contract* became gospel for Jacobin revolutionaries, it had been virtually ignored for the quarter-century prior to 1789.

This approach to Rousseau's *The Social Contract* goes back to 1910, when Daniel Mornet published one of the most influential studies of the eighteenth-century book trade in France.[14] Mornet collected 500 catalogs of private library inventories meant for sale following the owners' deaths. He discovered that while novels filled the shelves of most elite book readers, *Social Contract* appeared in only one catalog, demonstrating for Mornet its minimal impact. In contrast, *The New Héloïse* appears in 165 catalogs. Scholars have followed Mornet's lead ever since. In 1962, Joan McDonald claimed that there was only one edition of *Social Contract* published between its first edition and the French Revolution, and "therefore that there is very little evidence to support the argument that Rousseau's *Social Contract* was widely read at any time between 1762 and 1789."[15] Today's leading book historian, Robert Darnton, also endorsed Mornet's findings.[16] Only in the 1990s were reservations first expressed about Mornet's conclusions, when the editor of Rousseau's complete correspondence, Ralph Leigh, made three salient criticisms: first, Mornet's study ended around 1780, missing the rush of Rousseau publications following his death in 1778; second, Mornet excluded *The Social Contract* when it was published within a set of collected works; and third, Mornet did not take into consideration that banned books would be excluded from published library catalogs (which also may explain Montesquieu's poor showing in Mornet's study). Leigh himself discovered forty editions of *The Social Contract* published between 1762 and 1783.[17]

Based on Leigh's suggestions, scholars have radically revised the Mornet thesis. Jo-Ann McEachern, the researcher who published the definitive descriptive bibliographies of *The New Héloïse* and *Emile*, found forty-six French editions of *The Social Contract* published before the Revolution, including fourteen during 1762 alone. When combined with the explosive fifty-six editions during the revolutionary decade of the 1790s, McEachern documents 102 editions in French. Supplementing her count with translations in Danish (1), Dutch (2), German (2), English (6), Italian (4), and Spanish (1), we arrive at a total of 117 eighteenth-century editions of *The Social Contract*, fifty-one of them preceding the Revolution. Meanwhile, Berkeley historian Carla Hesse has compiled her own list that corroborates McEachern's findings. In any case, we now know that *The Social Contract* was immensely popular both before and during the French Revolution.[18]

Publishing *Emile*

Meanwhile, *Emile, or On Education*, was completed near the end of 1760. Normally Rousseau would have sent it automatically to Rey, but his friends and patrons convinced him otherwise. They had persuaded themselves that Rey had not given Rousseau enough money for *The New Héloïse* and *The Social Contract*. Rousseau, after all, had become something of a literary sensation, and any publisher would pay richly for the opportunity to publish a first edition. Rousseau acceded to this pressure, employing his close friend and patron, the powerful aristocrat Mme de Luxembourg, as an intermediary.[19] Within weeks Luxembourg had a strong offer from the well-established Paris publisher Nicolas Bonaventure Duchesne and his business partner, Pierre Guy. Duchesne and Guy promised Rousseau 6,000 livres, an extraordinary amount and well beyond anything Rey had previously paid, for the right to publish a four-volume edition. Contract negotiations turned to other matters. For example, Rousseau refused to sign one draft of the contract that required him to sit for a portrait that would grace the frontispiece of the first volume. While Rousseau wanted his name on the title page, he did not want any likeness of himself on the volume. On the other hand, he agreed to provide an index for the book, something that took him several days of work.[20]

With the contract signed in September 1761, Duchesne and Guy planned how they would publish the book in Paris. Considering Rousseau's other work, they anticipated difficulties obtaining a royal *privilège*, even from someone as tolerant as Malesherbes. Publishing in Paris might seem to some a direct attack upon France, and it could bring down the wrath of church and state. But were the book secretly printed in Paris, but appeared to be published elsewhere, it might seem less offensive and stand a greater chance of acquiring a *permission tacite*. Therefore, in November 1761, Duchesne and Guy made a deal with a prominent Dutch publisher in The Hague, Jean Néaulme, providing that Néaulme would publish his own edition that could be marketed to the Dutch and English markets. This version would be printed from proofs sent by Duchesne and Guy, making it essentially a facsimile of the now-underground Paris edition and published more or less simultaneously with that one. Just as important to Duchesne and Guy, Néaulme agreed to have his name and imprint—"A Amsterdam, Chez Jean Néaulme, Libraire"—placed on the title page of the Paris edition. When Néaulme secured his own Dutch privilege to publish the book legally in Holland, Duchesne and

Guy reproduced that privilege on their own title page. In this way, they hoped it would appear to French authorities that there was only one edition and that the books sold in Paris had been imported from Holland. Even if liberal officials such as Malesherbes knew the truth, this ruse provided a fig leaf for everyone to hide behind.[21]

Rousseau himself was torn regarding the false imprint. A false title page, especially with his own name on it, indicated that other parts of the book might be false as well. He worried it was hypocritical to present himself as honest and transparent, while sending a tricky signal from the start about the book's origins and production. But he was enough of a realist to know that *Emile* could never be published legally in Paris.

Malesherbes was intimately involved in *Emile*'s publication. In February 1762, having read proofs of the first two volumes, he visited Montmorency to ask Rousseau to make certain changes to the text. One alteration, for example, was to omit the phrase "même des Anges, s'il y en a (even the angels, if there are any of them)."[22] Rousseau showed no resistance to his request and made other changes he believed were minor. In March, Malesherbes assigned a member of his staff to personally supervise the Paris printing.

It was not until May that Néaulme first read in the third volume *Emile*'s most incendiary section, the Profession of Faith of the Savoyard Vicar, where Rousseau presented his core beliefs about religion. While Rousseau proclaimed himself a Christian, he argued that all of Christianity's key notions were derived from rational and scientific contemplation of nature rather than from revelation. This doctrine sent the Huguenot publisher Néaulme through the roof. "I must open up my heart," he wrote to Rousseau. It is one thing to publish an educational treatise that teaches respect for God, nature, mankind, and natural religion. It is quite another thing to include a polemic "using the strongest arguments against revelation" itself. The Profession of the Savoyard Vicar, pleaded Néaulme, should be published anonymously as a separate pamphlet. Otherwise, he warned, *Emile* would be designated into "the class of forbidden books," which would be devastating for both author and publisher.[23]

"I am very sorry that my profession of faith causes you distress," wrote Rousseau as soon as he received Néaulme's letter. "But I am telling you once and for all that there is no danger, no threat of violence, no power on earth that could get me to retract one syllable.... In rendering glory to God and speaking truthfully for the good of mankind, I have done my duty."[24]

Néaulme found himself in a difficult position. Offended by Rousseau's material, and worried about how Dutch authorities would react to such obvious blasphemy, he would have liked to have backed out of the entire project. But volumes 1 and 2 were already printed and he had clearly too much capital tied up with it to simply abandon the effort now. So, Néaulme quickly improvised. He revamped the title pages to suggest that the works were not his but pirated editions. Using cheap paper and only black lettering (red and black titles usually indicated a handsome Dutch-produced volume), he substituted a simple engraving for a fancy one, and used the false imprint "*A Paris, selon la copie de Paris, avec permission tacite pour le libraire*" (At Paris, based on the Paris original, with tacit permission of the bookseller). He then resold the rights to produce any reprints in Holland to Marc Michel Rey. Offended by its content, Néaulme wanted out of this project.

From its first publication, *Emile* was already an underground book for which no one took responsibility. The Duchesne edition appeared to be a Dutch import, while Néaulme's Dutch edition appeared to be a pirate of a phantom French edition. On June 1, Antoine de Sartine, the head of the Paris Police and a friend of Malesherbes, ordered Duchesne to stop selling the book. One week later the Sorbonne faculty declared it impious and dangerous. On June 9, the Parlement of Paris condemned the book for its "criminal system" and ordered its author arrested. Two days later copies of the book were ritually burned in front of the Palais de Justice. Suddenly, within days of its publication, *Emile* had brought down the wrath of the church, the judiciary, and the police upon it. Except for the case of Helvétius's *De l'Esprit*, nothing this intense had ever occurred before.

Warned by his friendly patrons, Rousseau immediately packed his bags and fled Montmorency, escaping the hands of the law only by several hours. But where could he go? Unfortunately, on June 19, the Genevan authorities banned both *Emile* and *The Social Contract*, indulging in a book-burning ceremony of their own. Under other circumstances, Rey would have welcomed Rousseau to Amsterdam, but even the tolerant Dutch turned Rousseau into an outlaw. On June 23, the Estates of Holland and West Friesland banned *Emile* and began an investigation into its Dutch publication. Néaulme told police investigators that the title page identifying him as the publisher was a false imprint, and that he had nothing to do with its publication. They chose not to pursue this septuagenarian. States across Europe refused to let the book circulate. Even Catherine the Great, who did so much to expand the book business in Russia during the 1760s, specifically banned *Emile* there, delaying any hope for a translation by a decade. Meanwhile, Rousseau finally settled in the tiny and quiet Swiss principality of Môtiers, which during the eighteenth century was governed by the accommodating Prussian King Frederick the Great. Rousseau was welcome there, at least for the moment. The residents, unaccustomed to harboring such a controversial figure in their village, would demand his expulsion in 1765.[25]

Rousseau book banning climaxed in August 1762 with the publication of a Pastoral Letter by Christophe de Beaumont, the archbishop of Paris. Ostensibly ordering a complete ban, forbidding even a private reading of *Emile*, this directive, published widely at least across Paris, was actually a long and substantive review of the book, filled with quotations and citations. Beaumont quotes Rousseau on original sin: "Let us set down, as an incontestable maxim that the first movements of nature are always right. There is no original perversity in the human heart." The archbishop responds: "From this language one does not at all recognize the doctrine of the Holy Scriptures and the Church."[26] It is hard not to sense that banning the book served to publicize Rousseau's notorious ideas more than refuting them. Moreover, ecclesiastical directives of this kind were highly unusual. Most pastoral letters addressed narrow issues of theology and observance. For example, weeks earlier Beaumont had explored whether eating eggs during Lent could be permitted; on another occasion he implored Catholics to make a special blessing for a member of the royal family who had given birth. During the archbishop's long term of office between 1747 and 1780, there were only two other instances of directives banning a particular book: one a Jansenist history of the Jews and the other Helvétius's scandalous *De l'Esprit*.[27]

The almost universal banning of *Emile* did nothing to halt its publication. Indeed, because mild censorship was a policing mechanism that tended to protect publishers with licenses and privileges, driving *Emile* underground actually stimulated piracy, incentivizing publishers everywhere to come out with their own clandestine issues, usually with false imprints attributed to "J. Néaulme, Amsterdam." Printing *Emile* became a wild free-for-all. During 1762 alone there were twenty-one French editions of *Emile*, plus translations in English and German. By the end of the century, eighty-two editions had been published, including translations in Danish, Dutch, English, German, Italian, and Russian.

Readers Respond to *Emile*

Immanuel Kant was among *Emile*'s early readers, and the work had a profoundly personal impact upon the young philosopher. The format of an adult tutor dedicated to his one student annoyed Kant as unrealistic. Rousseau nonetheless understood the moral position of the individual person within a sophisticated commercial society based upon maximizing "opulence." Kant interpreted this to mean reducing the authority of birth-ordered estates, guilds, and professional groups and recognizing the inherent equality of all individuals. Kant applied this teaching to himself. There was a time, he scribbled in notes not meant for publication, when he placed scholarship above everything else, and looked with disdain at the stupid working man. "I despised the rabble who knows nothing." Reading *Emile* corrected this personal fault. "Rousseau has set me right. This blinding prejudice vanishes, I learn to honor human beings, and I would feel by far less useful than the common laborer if I did not believe that this consideration could impart a value to all others in order to establish the rights of humanity." Kant recognized *Emile* as a major work of philosophy, not simply as an educational treatise, precisely because it argued for the dignity of every individual. He was impressed by Rousseau's "acuity of mind, a noble impetus of genius and a sensitive soul in such a high degree as has perhaps never before been possessed by a writer of any age or any people." But what most impressed Kant was not Rousseau's erudition and eloquence but rather his ability to inspire readers like himself to change the way they thought about their own life.[28]

In his well-known article, "Readers Respond to Rousseau," Robert Darnton introduced us to Jean Ranson, a Protestant silk merchant from La Rochelle, France. Ranson read Rousseau's work again and again, and read everything about his "friend" that he could get his hands on. He saw his courtship with his future wife "Miss Raboteau" through the lens of *La Nouvelle Héloïse* and a few years later, after she had given birth to his daughter, he viewed fatherhood through *Emile*: "Everything that l'Ami Jean Jacques has written about the duties of husband and wives, of mothers and fathers, has had a profound effect on me," Ranson divulged to his bookseller, "and I confess to you that it will serve me as a rule in any of those estates that I should occupy."[29]

Ranson's attachment to Rousseau may have been extreme, but his adoration was not unusual for readers during the later years of the eighteenth century. When the Princess of Württenburg gave birth to her daughter in 1763, her husband wrote to Rousseau for advice.[30] Rosalie and Marc Antoine Jullien were another couple who swore by Rousseau's methods. Per Rousseau's advice, they not only moved to a small town to avoid raising their children in the city, Rosalie also insisted on breastfeeding her babies. Marc Antoine begged friends to read Rousseau. "Read the beginning of the eighth chapter of the first book of *The Social Contract*," he implored his friend Joseph Michel Servan in 1781, "and the last paragraph of the fourth chapter of the second book." And yet it was *Emile* that was his true favorite. "Of all the books I know," he wrote, it is "the one that speaks the most powerfully to my heart." For him too, it was more than a manual for raising children. Like Kant, Marc Antoine found it "excellent for reforming men." Rousseau's readers believed he taught them how to be good in a world filled with selfishness and ignorance. "Jean Jacques alone knew how to persuade us. Sensitive hearts opened easily to the sweet warmth of his eloquence; rocks were broken under the strike of his brilliant lightning. What virtue did he omit to preach? Or what virtue did he preach without effect?"[31]

The future French Revolutionary activist Manon Roland was another reader who made Rousseau's work the centerpiece of her own intellectual and moral development, and that of her child. One evening when her husband was away and she was feeling ill, she "sat by the fireside" reading Rousseau. "*Mon ami*," she wrote her husband lovingly,

> I shall read this author all my life, and if ever we are in that position we have often amused ourselves imagining, you old and blind, and making bootlaces, while I work with the needle, it will be enough to have kept as our books the works of J. J. Reading them will make us weep delicious tears and revive feelings which will make us happy in spite of fate.

This was certainly different than the way Manon and others read Montesquieu, Voltaire, or Hume. So enamored was Roland with Rousseau that she tried in vain to meet him. During his final months, she discovered his apartment in Paris and made an attempt to secure an interview, but was rebuffed by Thérèse, Rousseau's wife.

When Roland's daughter was born, she and her husband naturally expected to raise Eudora strictly according to Rousseau. She breastfed Eudora, of course, and studied Rousseau's approach religiously. Both parents insisted on parenting directly rather than delegating such responsibilities to maids and tutors. But as Eudora turned from a toddler into a young girl, she became increasingly bored in her parent's study. After losing her temper a few times, Roland castigated herself for straying from *Emile*'s principles. "You have research to do," she reflected to her husband, "and I am happy to help you, because I am a wife as well as a mother, and was the one before the other. So let's find a way to stay at our desks, and for the child to be happy alongside us." Roland worried about how book worms like her and her husband could remain productive raising a feral Rousseauian girl like Eudora:

> in a study, between two desks, where serious work is going on in absolute silence, the child simply gets bored; especially if we forbid her to sing or babble to herself because she has no one to talk to; so we drive her into doing something to get our attention. . . . Then if there is a tantrum, we do everything to obtain silence, because without it we can't get on with our work. What makes children whine, [Rousseau] says, is the attention one pays to them . . . but if one takes no notice they soon stop, because nobody likes to go to a lot of effort for no result.
>
> People who write treatises on education never consider the scholar or any other profession; they just talk about the father and the mother; and consider them in that role, subordinating anything else to that. . . . If nature has not made her for great knowledge, don't let us force instruction on her, but educate her character, and hope the rest will come through inspiration, not compulsion.

Roland found it challenging applying Rousseau to her own life and marriage, and at times her failings filled her with doubt. Perhaps the critics were right that Rousseau's educational ideas were too speculative to put into practice. But her constant return to reading "J. J." again and again served to rejuvenate her idealism and optimism. If only she could have met Rousseau and discussed her problems with him.[32]

The English aristocrat the first Baroness Holland also raised her child, Harry, in accordance with Rousseau's guidelines, although she confessed to her sister that she cheated after hours. "At night we depart a little from Monsr. Rousseau's plan, for [Harry] reads fairy-tales and learns geography on the Beaumont wooden maps." But in the daytime, Harry "works very hard all day out of doors, which is very wholesome and . . . he eats quantities of fish, and is so happy and so pleased all day." The Baroness repeatedly told her sister to read *Emile*. "I know you'll like it."[33] Across the channel, the future revolutionary politician Honoré Gabriel Riqueti, Comte de Mirabeau, relayed the same advice to his wife: "Read his great work of art *Emile*, this admirable book full of new truths." Writing from prison, Mirabeau urged his wife in particular to give cold baths to their new daughter, as Rousseau recommends, and to read with special care the book's early sections on child development.[34]

These readers were, like Kant, inspired by Rousseau to improve their own lives and especially those of their children. Of all the many readers of Rousseau, none were more zealous or notorious than the two British friends: Richard Lovell Edgeworth and Thomas Day. The older of the pair by four years, the Irish aristocratic Edgeworth first encountered *Emile* in 1766. Married with a three-year-old son, Edgeworth was put off by the way others raised their children, even within his wealthy circles. He witnessed "obvious deficiencies and absurdities . . . in almost every family." It was not only that mothers put their infants out to wet nurses. Most parents neglected their duties, and even those who were active fathers and mothers simply replicated whatever their parents had done. Child development received little serious attention, and this state of affairs troubled Edgeworth. In reading *Emile,* he discovered a work that grounded practical advice regarding child rearing upon principles with philosophical rigor. All at once, Edgeworth decided "to make a fair trial of Rousseau's system." With his wife's grudging support, he would raise son Dick—already three years old—according to Rousseau's doctrine.

For the next five years, Edgeworth held strictly to Rousseau's regimen, often to the ridicule and satire of his friends. He dressed Dick in light comfortable clothes, even in the cold, and encouraged him to play barefoot outside in all types of weather. Dick experienced nature in all its grey English elements, and his days were unstructured. The result was a "hardy" child, who could easily tolerate many more discomforts than most six- or seven-year-olds. "Fearless of danger," he loved the outdoors and excelled at anything that involved challenging his body. As long as he could do whatever he pleased, he was "well tempered." But this came at a cost. Dick exhibited very little "deference for others." He respected neither his peers, nor adults, nor even his mother. Only his father commanded his obedience. "With me," Edgeworth later recalled, "he was always what I wish." But with others he was a wild terror.[35]

At times Edgeworth had doubts about whether he should continue raising Dick by *Emile*'s rules. But he was urged on by his friend Thomas Day, whom he had met in 1766 when the nineteen-year old was on holiday from Oxford University. Day, whose father died when he was a child, leaving a large estate from which he lived for the rest of his life, was already something of an eccentric. He spoke his mind with unusual directness and clarity and dressed completely out of fashion for the day. Edgeworth immediately got him to read Rousseau, and, like Edgeworth, it transformed Day's entire way of thinking about the world. "Were all the books in the world to be destroyed, except scientific books (which I except not to affront you) the second book I should wish to save, after the Bible, would be Rousseau's Emilius," proclaimed Day to Edgeworth. Like Kant in Königsberg and Roland in Amiens, Day absorbed *Emile* as if Rousseau were his own intimate mentor. "It is indeed a most extraordinary work—the more I read, the more I admire—Rousseau alone, with a perspicuity more than mortal, has been able at once to look through the human heart, and discover the secret sources and combinations of the passions. Every page is big with important truth." Day deeply admired Edgeworth's commitment to raising Dick according to *Emile*, and in the face of some ridicule from their other friends, particularly for following Rousseau's direction delaying reading skills, he became Dick's greatest champion. "Never trouble yourself about Dick's reading and writing; he will learn it, sooner or later, if you let him alone; and there is no danger, except that the people of Henley may call him a dunce."[36]

In 1771 Edgeworth and Day decided to take Dick on a visit to Paris to meet the famous Jean Jacques. They found his fifth-floor apartment and, unlike Manon Roland, managed to get by Thérèse for a conversation with the philosophe. Edgeworth explained the manner in which he had raised Dick, which intrigued the author. Rousseau suggested that Dick join him for his daily walk around Paris, so that he could appropriately assess the boy. Rousseau and Dick were away for two hours. When they returned, Rousseau bluntly told Edgeworth and Day that while the boy exhibited much intelligence and a fine disposition, he also had a rather obnoxious "propensity to party prejudice, which will be a great blemish in his character." Evidently whenever Dick had seen something that struck him as beautiful, he would claim it as English. "That is an English horse, or an English carriage!" Rousseau warned Edgeworth of the seriousness of such a character flaw.[37]

Dick only got worse and his jingoism was the least of it. He became impossible to control. Edgeworth blamed himself for not devoting even more time to him, but the father's lack of attentiveness does not seem to have been the problem. At any rate, when they returned to England, Edgeworth sent Dick off to a boarding school, where he grew out of his spoiled immaturity and was liked well enough by his peers. Still, he was a disappointment in the eyes of his father. He sailed the seas as young adult, settling in South Carolina where he fathered three sons and died in 1796 at the age of thirty-one. Reflecting later in his memoirs, Edgeworth admitted that Rousseau's method was not all that successful when applied to Dick—Edgeworth insisted upon blaming himself for that. "I dwell on this painful subject, to warn other parents against the errors which I committed."[38]

Thomas Day took Rousseau discipleship to an even more eccentric level. In the final book of *Emile*, Rousseau discussed the education of women, with the aim of finding Emile a suitable bride. "Woman is made specially to please man," argued Rousseau in a section that was controversial even in the eighteenth century. "If woman is made to please and to be subjected, she ought to make herself agreeable to man instead of arousing him. Her own violence is in her charms." Her education reflects this misogyny. Where Emile was raised to be active in nature, hardened by the weather, willful concerning his own desires, Sophie, as Jean Jacques named her, was raised along different principles. She stays indoors for the most part, helping her mother with sewing, cooking, and other domestic chores. "It is important that she be modest, attentive, reserved"; that is, nothing like Emile. "Dependence is a condition natural to women, and thus girls feel themselves made to obey."[39]

The eighteenth-century pioneering feminist Mary Wollstonecraft dismissed such preaching as nonsense; Manon Roland, and hundreds of other mothers (and fathers) ignored it and raised their daughters more like Emile than Sophie.[40] But Thomas Day embraced this section of Rousseau with unusual conviction. His own relationships with women were not working out as well as he might have liked—he had recently been turned down by two women, including Edgeworth's younger sister. He decided that finding the right mate was impossible, given the corrupt materialism pervasive in England. Therefore, he reasoned, if he could not find a woman like (Richardson's fictional) Pamela Andrews who would marry him, he would have to make one. He conceived a grand plan: he would adopt two orphaned girls and raise them according to Rousseau's principles. When they became adults, he would choose one of them to marry.[41]

In August 1769, Day traveled 160 miles to Shrewsbury, where only a few years before London elites had established a foundling hospital that housed and educated 350 orphans. Day chose Ann Kingston (age twelve) and Dorcas Car (age eleven). He donated £50 and was invited to join the hospital's Board of Governors. In a contract, Day accepted responsibility for the two girls, promising to obtain apprenticeships in suitable homes for them. He renamed the girls Sabrina and Lucretia. Of course, he kept his plans for marriage a secret that only his best friends knew—the girls themselves never knew there was any such scheme. He decided almost immediately to start his Emelian plan in France, and by late November the three were living under one roof in Lyon, where Day had hired suitable tutors and governesses to help him with the girls' education. There they stayed for several months, until Day realized that there was no point trying further to educate Lucretia. When they arrived back in England in the spring of 1770, Day found Lucretia an apprenticeship with a milliner and granted her a generous £400 farewell gift. With such a handsome sum, she had no trouble attracting a worthy husband, and she remained—so far as is known—stable and happy.[42] By early 1771, even with Sabrina, "Day concluded that his daring educational experiment had been a failure,"[43] and he sent her off to boarding school. Day continued to support her and in 1784 she married Day and Edgeworth's close friend, John Bicknell.

In her recent book, *How to Create the Perfect Wife*, Wendy Moore prosecutes Day for virtually kidnapping the two orphans and subjecting them to abuse even by eighteenth-century standards: "The scheme was highly unethical if not downright illegal."[44] This judgment is true but seems to miss the story's historical significance. Although this tale of two friends engaging with *Emile* was set down in more detail than most others, across England and Europe during the 1760s and 1770s adults were applying the lessons of Rousseau to children, usually their own. Both Sabrina and Lucretia, after all, faired no worse in adult life than poor Dick Edgeworth. Day's novelty lay not in domestic abuse, but rather in how far he would take the lessons from *Emile* to transform the lives of two ordinary girls as well as his own. In this respect, Day's close friend, the chemist James Keir, noted that the irony of Day's story was that he was such a better and more caring father than his idol Rousseau: "Mr. Day received two orphans under his protection, while the celebrated philosopher of Switzerland placed five of his own children in a foundling hospital at Paris."[45]

Far from renouncing *Emile* because of their parenting experiences, Day and Edgeworth followed in Rousseau's footsteps as they each developed writing careers. In 1798 Edgeworth and his daughter, Maria, published in two volumes *Practical Education*, an effort to update *Emile*'s principles on child development. The book became among England's most popular educational tracts, and was widely read in America. *Emile*'s principles are interrogated so regularly throughout the book that it is easy to see how much Richard channeled what he learned from raising Dick into his and Maria's criticism. "Rousseau advised that children should be governed solely by the necessity of circumstances," the Edgeworths wrote. "But there are *one and twenty* excellent objections to this system, the first being that it is impossible." Edgeworth knew from experience that *Emile* cannot be read uncritically. He now understood that it was foolish to imitate slavishly the way Rousseau's tutor goes about educating his ward. When Rousseau found himself with a resistant pupil, he would create elaborate schemes and fictions, often involving other adults, to get the boy to motivate himself. For one lesson, "Rousseau had prepared the neighbors on each side of the street to make proper speeches as his pupil passed by their doors." From experience Edgeworth knew how much time and effort this took away from the adult's life. No one realistically had the time necessary to devote to Rousseau's methods, even if such pedagogy turned out to be valid.[46]

Rather than dwell on his own experiences with Dick, Edgeworth at one point filters this criticism through the well-known Scottish philosopher Lord Kames, who himself wrote a commentary on Rousseau published in 1781. Kames tells the story of a friend raising his child according to principles laid down in *Emile*. One day he was playing chess with another friend, when his four-year-old son ran off with one of the chess pieces. The game now interrupted, the father turned the deed into a lesson regarding commerce. He kindly asked the son if he would exchange the piece for an apple, following Rousseau's admonition to avoid punishing children for acts defined as criminal only by adults. The son gladly complied. Soon after he had devoured the fruit, the son once again stole another piece from the board, and the scene repeated itself. "I would have such parents consider," wrote Kames, "whether they are not here misled by self-deceit." Edgeworth completely agreed with Kames. "Does it seem just that parents should become slaves to the liberties of their children?" Still, the Edgeworths nonetheless meant this criticism as a corrective, not a renunciation of *Emile*. They wanted to avoid the trap laid by other critics, who attacked Rousseau and then covertly borrowed many of his ideas. "We should not, like many who have spoken of Rousseau, steal from him after having abused him." The Edgeworths hoped to be careful students of Rousseau rather than disciples. "Whenever Rousseau is in the right, his eloquence is irresistible."[47]

Emile not only inspired many books about child development and educational approaches, it also stimulated an ocean of literature meant for children. Technically, it made no sense for a self-proclaimed follower of Rousseau to write books for children, since Rousseau believed that children should delay reading so they could experience nature directly. But no matter. Just as the most orthodox Rousseauian taught their daughters in ways Rousseau reserved only for sons, so most disciples did not follow Rousseau's rule against children reading. And in this regard, there was no greater violator than Thomas Day. During the 1780s, he published the three-volume *History of Sandford and Merton* (1783, 1786, and 1789), which remained popular in Britain for much of the nineteenth century. Tommy Merton is a spoiled rich kid whose attitudes represent everything wrong with British elite society. His friend Harry Sandford, the son of a poor, but honest, farmer, is refreshingly different. He loves the outdoors, simple food, and fun adventures. Slowly and steadily, Tommy learns from Harry how to exchange his vain, false, and feeble character for what will eventually become a strong and virtuous young man. His book made Day so famous that visitors brought their children to him for evaluation, just as he and Richard had taken Dick to see the great Jean Jacques.[48]

The reception of Rousseau's three major works reveals at least two very different dimensions. On the one hand, there was the response of states and churches, theologians and critics, who were appalled by Rousseau's religious principles, and did everything they could to suppress the work and harass its author. Advocating religious toleration was one thing; dismissing revelation as superstition was beyond the pale for both Protestant and Catholic states. If *Emile* was about education, it seemed to them the education of a republican atheist. But most readers did not see Rousseau from this vantage point. Baffled often by his "paradoxes" and "absurdities," readers nonetheless championed his "pretty thoughts" and wondered if authorities were overreacting. "His principles seems to me to be something between Arianism and Deism," the Baroness Holland wrote,

> laid down . . . but modestly and humbly, not in the least offensively I think, 'tho a vast fuss is made about it; indeed so much, I did not care to read it [i.e., The Profession of Faith of a Savoyard Vicar in Book IV of *Emile*] with the same attention I did the rest of the book, and only ran it over; but indeed by what I can judge it don't [*sic*] deserve being so violently abused.

The Baroness did not see what all the fuss was about. For her and many others, it was Rousseau's reflections on childrearing that mattered most. She urged her sister to read the book because of the elegant and compelling manner in which Rousseau put forward a new view of childhood.

It is hard to imagine *Emile* without *The Spirit of the Laws*. Large, multivolume, serious productions, both books were regarded immediately as works of philosophy that looked back to the timeless thinkers of the ancient world, the Renaissance, and the seventeenth century. And yet readers also used both books for more practical considerations, and ordinary readers quoted sections in letters to loved ones. These erudite tomes were slowly replacing religious texts as authoritative guidelines regarding how civil life should be organized. Educated readers who were non-specialists argued with their friends and families over the most philosophical books of their day. Perhaps like Darwin, Spencer, and Freud 100 years later, but quite unlike anything in the seventeenth century, Montesquieu's and Rousseau's hefty volumes became the talk of the day among a large swath of middle class and aristocratic women and men. Perhaps that's what made them so dangerous to authorities.

Chapter 11

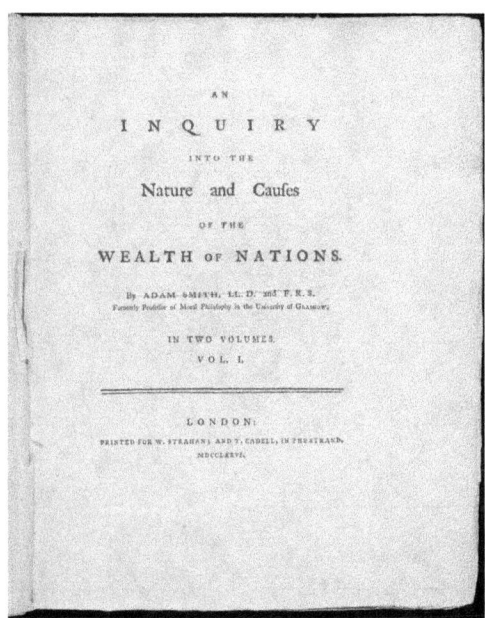

Figure 11.1 First edition title page Smith's *Wealth of Nations*. Adam Smith moved to London from Scotland in 1773 in order to closely participate in various aspects of preparing his book for publication.

Chapter 11
Smith's *Wealth of Nations* (1776)

Table 11.1 Eighteenth-Century Editions of *Wealth of Nations*

Decade	*1776–9*	*1780–9*	*1790–1800*
Editions	6	11	22

Total Editions: 39.
Translations: Danish, Dutch, French, German, Italian, Spanish, Swedish.
Source: https://kates.itg.pomona.edu/books/analytics.php?type=all. Accessed March 9, 2022.

"Montesquieu was the real French equivalent of Adam Smith," wrote John Maynard Keynes toward the end of his life. "The greatest of your economists, head and shoulders above the physiocrats in penetration, clear-headedness and good sense (which are the qualities an economist should have)."[1] This was no idle flattery of the French. During the Great Depression, around the time Keynes was composing what would become *The General Theory of Employment, Interest, and Money*, he purchased a copy of Montesquieu's *The Spirit of the Laws* and most likely read it then for the first time. Keynes's appreciation of Montesquieu was prescient; by the twentieth century Montesquieu had been all but written out of the history of economics. As we saw in Chapter 9, during the eighteenth century Montesquieu was regarded as a master of political economy, and *The Spirit of the Laws* stimulated hundreds of books meant to advance that subject. The most famous of these, of course, was Adam Smith's *An Inquiry into the Nature and Causes of the Wealth of Nations*,[2] first published in 1776, just as the popularity of *The Spirit of the Laws* was at its zenith.

Smith's *Wealth of Nations* rests upon the scaffolding built by Montesquieu. Like *The Spirit of the Laws*, *Wealth of Nations* is foremost concerned with how liberty manifests in the modern world. Like his French mentor, Smith had a keen appreciation that commerce was central to early modern monarchies in ways that were foreign to ancient states. Along with his Scottish colleagues such as David Hume, Smith agreed with Montesquieu that commerce tends to make society less prone to violence and more willing to abide by codes of manners and behavior, which, in turn, encourages autonomy and freedom. While *Wealth of Nations* charts its own independent course, Smith's arguments are inconceivable without Montesquieu's secure foundation.

Montesquieu was lionized not only by Smith, but by all leading writers of the Scottish Enlightenment. During the eighteenth century, no fewer than seven editions of *The Spirit of the Laws* were published in Scotland, a kingdom of less than 1.5 million people. What Scots appreciated most was Montesquieu's empirical bent. Smith's first biographer and successor at the University of Glasgow, Dugald Stewart, noted that European statesmen before Montesquieu acted either without any principles, or from some "vague" abstract ideas. Montesquieu reoriented political philosophy away from metaphysics and toward sociology and political economy. "Instead of bewildering himself among the erudition of scholiasts and of antiquaries, we frequently find him ... combing the casual observations of illiterate travelers and navigators into a philosophical commentary on the history of law and of manners."[3] Stewart credited Montesquieu for abandoning the search for timeless universal laws that applied everywhere, instead insisting that laws themselves are dependent upon several factors, including culture, religion, environment, history, and customs. Political theory, therefore, must be both comparative and empirical. At the very moment *Wealth of Nations* was first coming off the presses, Scot minister and professor Hugh Blair reflected on Montesquieu's influence: "Since Montesquieu's *Esprit des lois*, Europe has not received any publication which tends so much to enlarge and rectify the ideas of mankind."[4] Soon enough Blair's colleagues would see *Wealth of Nations* as the rightful successor to *The Spirit of the Laws*. "The great Montesquieu pointed out the road," wrote Smith's former student John Millar, in 1787: "He was the Lord Bacon in this branch of Philosophy. Dr. Smith is the Newton."[5]

The *Wealth of Nations'* earliest readers sometimes highlighted this new empirical direction. Complaining that political theorists in the seventeenth century (such as Hobbes, Locke, and Spinoza) were "too abstracted and speculative for present edification" after Newton, philosophers such as Montesquieu and now Smith based their arguments "more on experience and less on speculation." This new method, argued one reviewer, was much more relevant to a commercial era in which politics had become globalized and far more complex than in previous ages. This empirical method, in fact, gave "a new face to the science of politics."[6]

Some of Smith's most original and important ideas may have come from his reading of *The Spirit of the Laws*. Among these is Smith's well-known invisible hand argument, where Smith laid out how individuals are guided by their greed to nevertheless serve the public good. Compare these two sentences from the *Wealth of Nations* with Montesquieu's statement regarding honor early in *The Spirit of the Laws*:

> Smith: "By pursuing his own interest he frequently promotes that of the society more effectually than when he really intends to promote it."
> Montesquieu: "Honor makes all parts of the body politic move; its very action binds them, and each person works for the common good, believing he works for his individual interests."

As David Wootton suggests, these two statements are so close in substance and language that they, in fact, represent the same idea. Whether Smith purposely lifted Montesquieu's concept of honor for his invisible hand argument is beside the point; the alignment makes clear enough the debt he owed to the French master.[7]

Like Montesquieu, Smith wanted to write a masterpiece that was simultaneously the leading scholarly work of political economy and a treatise that would sell well and be widely read. After all, no one before Montesquieu had written a large-scale intellectual work that impressed simultaneously philosophical members of the Republic of Letters and lay readers alike. Smith's closest friend, David Hume, had tried in vain to make his *Treatise of Human Nature* (1739) this kind of book, but it failed to attract a wide readership. A decade later Montesquieu demonstrated that a work of extraordinary erudition and originality could become popular. Smith's imitation of Montesquieu, then, was not simply in terms of his methodology and ideas, nor even of his erudition, but above all was of his writerly elegance and polish. Through such clear prose, Smith hoped to attract a large section of the reading public to what was nonetheless a difficult and intimidating book. "Monsieur de Montesquieu is one of the most singular men that has ever been in the world," Adam Smith is said to have taught his students at the University of Glasgow, "for he possesses four things which are never almost united: An excellent judgment, a fine imagination, great wit, and vast erudition."[8]

However, Smith's relationship with his publishers was in sharp contrast to his mentor. As we have seen in earlier chapters, Montesquieu avoided publishers. Smith's close relationships with his publishers were nearly the opposite of Montesquieu's. In the British context of relatively strong copyright protection and less censorship, authors and publishers could carry on a more stable and open working relationship. By the 1750s, London printer/publishers would routinely make trips to Scotland to both seek partnerships with booksellers in Edinburgh and Glasgow and acquire new manuscripts from authors for publication. On one such visit, publisher Andrew Millar met Adam Smith. The result was that Millar printed and sold Smith's first book, *The Theory of Moral Sentiments* (1759), partnering with Scottish booksellers Andrew Kincaid and John Bell in Edinburgh. Soon Millar introduced Smith to his younger partner, William Strahan, who often forged a partnership with London bookseller Thomas Cadell. By the 1780s, Strahan (who took over for Millar when the latter retired) and Cadell became the most successful publishers in "London, and perhaps the world."[9]

For Smith, these relationships were more than business contacts; Strahan became a close friend. In an early letter to Strahan, Smith recommended a serious book to him, and went on at length about it.[10] Sometimes there is little difference in the correspondence between Smith and Strahan than in that between Smith and Hume. Likewise, British printer/publishers wanted their authors to regard them as more than simply businessmen unfamiliar with ideas. They hoped to be regarded as equals, with expertise in the distribution of ideas and the tastes and habits of their book-buying readers.

Smith did more than correspond with Millar, Strahan, and Cadell. After several years of working on *Wealth of Nations* in the relative isolation of Kirkcaldy (his home town, about thirty miles from Edinburgh), Smith moved to London in 1773 so that he could finish his masterpiece within close range of Strahan and Cadell. This allowed Smith to work out the book's format, design, and distribution alongside his printer/booksellers.

Although there are few documents regarding their exchanges—precisely because they were in such regular and proximity with little reason to write—Smith was able to use his time to polish his prose, making the book's final stages a collaborative effort. He returned to Scotland following the book's initial publication.

On March 9, 1776, the *Wealth of Nations* appeared in two quarto volumes of just over 500 pages each, virtually the same length and format as *The Spirit of the Laws*. Immediately it was praised for its "ingenuity, industry and utility"[11] and recognized as a work "so original in its plan, and deviating so widely in many particulars from the common track of thinking." Readers perceived that its "fundamental doctrine" revolved around the principle that "commerce should be left at perfect liberty without the interference of law."[12] "I am convinced that since Montesquieu's *Esprit des lois*," Hugh Blair wrote Smith within a month of the book's release, "Europe has not received any publication which tends so much to enlarge and rectify the ideas of mankind."[13]

Printed by Strahan and sold by Cadell from his shop on the Strand, the *Wealth of Nations*' retail price was expensive at £1.16s unbound or £2.2 already bound. Only the rich, public institutions, or circulating libraries could afford to buy a book this costly; it was well beyond the reach of even middle-class readers. For example, it would have taken a housekeeper or coachman months to earn that amount, a carpenter weeks, and a skilled engineer several days. It cost the wealthy Scottish gentleman James Boswell more than half that amount to rent an apartment in London.[14] Although we have no precise documentation, Richard Sher's best guess is that Strahan printed 750 copies of the first edition.[15] The quarto book was over twice the length of his previous one, *The Theory of Moral Sentiments*, which Strahan's predecessor, Andrew Millar, had printed in the more usual octavo format in 1759.

The cost of printing *Wealth of Nations* must have come to over £150.[16] Paper alone took up half that amount. In addition to the actual printing costs, Strahan had to calculate advertising costs (mainly notices in newspapers), which were not incidental. While keen profits could be gained from a successful quarto, the risk was substantial. Strahan and Cadell worried that *Wealth of Nations* would sell poorly, perhaps even flop, because of its length and erudition. To mitigate grave financial loss, they partnered with Smith with each side sharing the printing expenses and later sharing whatever profits emerged. In this way, Strahan and Cadell avoided buying Smith's copyright outright and having to pay him in advance of any revenue.[17]

To everyone's relief, *Wealth of Nations* sold well from the start. Cadell's bookshop attracted a steady stream of orders, and before long, author, bookseller, and printer were happy. Only a month after it appeared Strahan could declare that the book's success "had been more than I could have expected from a work that requires much thought and reflection."[18] In May, Cadell urged Strahan to print a second edition, and by the end of the year, Smith received £300 as partial payment from sales.

For the second edition, which came out two years later, similar arrangements were reached, and book historian Richard Sher estimates that Smith received something like an additional £200 from its success. Smith advised Strahan and Cadell that the second edition should be an octavo, printed in four volumes.[19] This would have made much sense and followed a usual protocol. After tapping out the smaller, but high-profit, quarto market, it was time, thought Smith, to produce a larger print run in a less expensive format that a broader group of readers could afford. In this way, *Wealth of Nations* would continue to be profitable, and it would stand a good chance of becoming truly popular. Indeed, again, this is exactly what happened to Montesquieu's *The Spirit of the Laws*, albeit without the French author's input or permission. After an initial quarto edition, the original Genevan publisher, Barillot, put out editions in both octavo and the cheaper duodecimo formats, appealing to as wide a readership as possible.

As on the continent, publishers and authors in England complained about pirated editions. We saw how *The Spirit of the Laws* was pirated countless times without regard for the author or the original publisher. However much legal copyright protected the English, illegal imports flooded in from Ireland and sometimes from Scotland. Despite the 1707 Acts of Union between England and Scotland, separate laws continued in Scotland regarding intellectual property. This explains why Strahan and Cadell invested so much time securing Scottish partners and maintaining good relations with Scottish authors, neutralizing any threat. But Ireland was a different story, as it was perfectly legal for Irish printers to publish English books for sale in Ireland without the permission of English authors or publishers. Indeed, in June 1776, barely three months after *Wealth of Nations*' original appearance in London, a group of twenty Dublin booksellers combined to reprint the book in a three-volume octavo edition with a price less than half of Strahan and Cadell's. Of course, many of these cheaper volumes were smuggled into England and sold illegally, despite the best efforts of the government's customs officials.[20]

Despite these very good reasons for publishing the second edition in a more affordable octavo format, including Smith's urging, Cadell believed that the market for expensive quartos had not, after all, been exhausted, and he convinced Strahan and Smith to go along with another expensive edition. With a somewhat smaller print run of 500 copies, the second edition was published in 1778, and although it sold steadily, it took several years to exhaust the stock. Sher estimates that Smith made £200 from this edition alone. When an octavo edition finally appeared in 1784, it was published in three volumes, stuffing more words and pages into each volume, so that its price could complete more favorably with the Irish edition. With a print run of 1,000, this third edition also included major revisions, corrections, and an index. Separately, Strahan and Cadell released an eighty-page quarto pamphlet that included the new material for earlier buyers.[21]

From this point forward, all editions printed by Strahan and Cadell were three-volume octavos. Table 11.2 illustrates the success of *Wealth of Nations* and the profits that passed to its author. Sher estimates that over his lifetime, that is, until he died in 1790, Smith received £1,500–1,800, which he estimates is worth some £100,000 today. Needless to say, this was an enormous sum for any author to make from a single title during the eighteenth century. When compared with Montesquieu, this is perhaps Smith's great difference with his mentor: As we know, Montesquieu earned no money at all from the sales of *The Spirit of the Laws*.

Table 11.2 Eighteenth-Century Editions of *Wealth of Nations* Published by Strahan and Cadell

Edition	Year	Format	Print Run	Volumes
1	1776	Quarto	750*	2
2	1778	Quarto	500	2
3	1784	Octavo	1000	3
4	1786	Octavo	1250	3
5	1789	Octavo	1500	3
6	1791	Octavo	2000	3
7	1793	Octavo	2500	3
8	1798	Octavo	2500	3
9	1799	Octavo	2500	3

Source: Sher, "Early Editions of Adam Smith's Books in Britain and Ireland," 13–26; Sher, "New Light on the Publication and Reception," 3–39.

The publication of an octavo third edition in 1784 allowed readers and reviewers to take stock of the book after eight years of publication. Before *Wealth of Nations*, wrote a reviewer for *The Scots Magazine*, there was an understanding that trade was pursued within a "hostile rivalship" that lay "in the very idea of trade." Governments had to impose their will upon markets, or resources would be lost to them. Sound policy required "casting every obstruction in the way of other trading countries." Smith's book overturned these mercantilist assumptions, allowing readers to appreciate that global trade might be carried on through collaboration and cooperation with benefits to all. States are more secure "when the trader is surrounded by opulent neighbors." Before Smith, none of this was well understood and *Wealth of Nations* constituted a successful demonstration of these new and surprising principles. Indeed, Smith's book "laid the foundations of a commercial system of policy." While Smith's notions had not yet become the political platform of any major government, his ideas nonetheless "cannot fail, in time, to subdue the narrow prejudices which have hitherto influenced the counsels of statesmen." Apparently unbeknownst to this reviewer, Smith's idea extended Montesquieu's *doux commerce* doctrine and echoed David Hume's 1758 essay, "Jealousy of Trade."[22]

There has been a tendency in Smith scholarship to think of *Wealth of Nations* as a fairly modest seller, without much influence, at least until the end of the century.[23] A glance at Tables 11.1 and 11.2 confirms that popularity as demonstrated by sales took off in the mid- to late 1780s and soared during the 1790s, the years of the French Revolution. From the third through the eighth editions, print runs in Britain were consistently increased, reflecting demand. However, as Richard Sher rightly argues, to conclude that *Wealth of Nations* was not popular during its first several years is misguided. As we have seen, by restricting publication to the quarto format, the publishers were quite consciously restricting sales to keep price levels high. Certainly there was pent-up demand and interest, but few could afford such expensive volumes.

Cadell's understanding of the market was masterful. Printing a second edition in quarto was clearly a business decision, in which publishers and author profited handsomely. Given the enormous success of *Wealth of Nations* after 1785, it is hard to imagine that it would have done any better—financially or otherwise—if the second edition had been published as an octavo, as Smith originally proposed. Altogether Smith's *Wealth of Nations* went through a startling thirty-nine editions in the twenty-four years between its initial publication in 1776 and 1800. Compared with the almost 400 editions the work went through during the nineteenth and twentieth centuries, this may seem small by comparison. However, the significance lies not in its relatively slow start, but in its sure and steady rise to fame. In contrast to Raynal's *History of the Two Indies* or even Montesquieu's *The Spirit of the Laws*, once *Wealth of Nations* became a bestseller during the 1780s, it has never ceased to be one.

Once the cheaper octavo editions made their way into bookstalls and libraries, the book acquired a more extended readership. "As our friend Adam Smith's book comes to be more generally read and known," wrote Alexander Jardine, "I think his principles must prevail . . . and it may . . . be of more service to the world than any book that has appeared since Euclid."[24] One traveler spotted an English copy on a table in the Senate chamber of Lucca, an Italian city-state.[25] One magazine thought *Wealth of Nations* the perfect curriculum, "a plan of reading," meant to allow anyone with the tools of literacy to become self-educated. No longer was a school or a tutor necessary. "Any one capable of reading may become his own preceptor."[26] Although some readers were no doubt intimated by the work's complex arguments and presentation of data, many others spent many hours extracting Smith's fine points into their own notebooks.[27] A female reader told *The Lady's Magazine* that she began each day with an hour's perusal of *Wealth of Nations*, "before my friends make their appearance."[28] One mark of the book's fame by 1788 is the medallion profile of its author's head by Josiah Wedgwood.[29]

The book's reputation extended to the young United States, where one Philadelphia resident described Smith as the "Apostle of Political Economy."[30] Thirty-one percent of American libraries from 1777 to 1813 included *Wealth of Nations*, according to the study conducted by David Lundberg and Henry May.[31] The American Founders, including Alexander Hamilton, John Adams, and James Madison, were "some of Smith's earliest readers and among the first to take him seriously in their own political lives."[32] In the year of Smith's death, 1790, when asked for book recommendations, Thomas Jefferson had placed Smith on Montesquieu's level: "In political economy, I think Smith's *Wealth of Nations* the best book extant; in the science of government, Montesquieu's *Spirit of the Laws* is generally recommended."[33]

Historians have often noted how little British commercial policy changed during the twenty-five years following 1776, and have sometimes concluded that *Wealth of Nations* had little impact.[34] However, as John E. Crowley forcefully argues, this view confuses the difference between the "genuine appreciation and understanding of Smith's thought" with the "application of it in policy." In fact, as Crowley shows in a close-up view of the

British Board of Trade, British policy planners such as Shelbourne, Sheffield, and even Pitt increasingly thought of commercial activities in "Smithian terms," even if they bent his ideas toward neo-mercantilist ends that served British interests.[35]

Between 1783 and 1800, members of the House of Commons referenced *Wealth of Nations* around forty times. While Prime Minister Pitt sometimes quoted Smith, the book became a favorite of the Whig Foxite opposition that inclined toward Smithian positions. In February 1798, while proposing a commercial treaty with Russia over the government's objections, the Foxite MP Samuel Whitbread reminded his colleagues about "a book that had been lately so ably quoted by the Chancellor of the Exchequer [i.e., William Pitt], Smith's *Wealth of Nations*. In the deep researches of that great political philosopher, he [i.e., Pitt] would find his short-sighted opinions amply discussed, and amply refuted."[36] Smith was not merely referenced; deputies sometimes opened their copy of *Wealth of Nations*, reading long passages into the record. Meanwhile, Charles James Fox himself employed Smith in urging the House of Commons to reject tax bills that unfairly discriminated against the poor in favor of a landed elite. "That author complains of the inequality with which small taxes fall on different classes of the community," Fox exhorted his colleagues in 1798. "What would he say if he were living, and should look at the inequalities of this bill?"[37]

One important event following *Wealth of Nations* was the 1786 trade pact between France and England, often called the Eden Treaty. It established a short-lived era of freer trade in which tariffs were reduced on commodities such as wine and textiles. Some supporters drew a direct link between Smith's principles and the treaty. For example, the reformer and businessman Robert Thornton told his colleagues in the House of Commons that his support for the treaty stemmed from his reading of *Wealth of Nations*.[38] And yet, some critics claimed the opposite: that the treaty did not measure up to Smith's standards. "The commercial treaty with France was indeed a measure of Mr. Pitt's, and certainly a wise and good one," wrote Anthony Robinson. "But it had been a far more noble achievement, if, instead of a commercial treaty, he had opened commerce to the world, and the world to commerce, upon the enlightened principles of Adam Smith."[39] On the French side, negotiator and economist Pierre Samuel du Pont de Nemours recognized *Wealth of Nations* as the guidebook for principles leading to the treaty. In a letter sent to Smith shortly after its passage, du Pont hoped that the Eden Treaty would lead to a new era in free trade that would quickly spread to other regions. "You have greatly accelerated this useful revolution," du Pont acknowledged to Smith.[40] Whether the Eden Treaty represented a genuine turn toward free trade or not, the debate surrounding it certainly demonstrated that *Wealth of Nations* mattered to its supporters and critics.

British readers viewed *Wealth of Nations* as much more than a free trade manual. Like *The Spirit of the Laws*, it was quickly recognized as a comprehensive historical and cultural critique of European civilization writ large. Many readers commented on Smith's devastating criticism of the clergy in Book V. In 1787, for example, in his own treatise, John Millar quoted "the ingenious and profound author of the *Inquiry into the Nature and Causes of the Wealth of Nations*": "The clergy, too, like the great barons, wished to get a better rent from their landed estates, in order to spend it, in the same manner, upon the gratification of their own private vanity and folly." Surely readers like Millar recognized that Smith had fully internalized Voltaire's own stinging attack, presented in various works, including this well-known section from *Philosophical Letters*:

> Whilst that the barons, the bishops, and the popes, all laid waste England, where all were for ruling the most numerous, the most useful, even the most virtuous, and consequently the most venerable part of mankind, consisting of those who study the laws and the sciences, of traders, of artificers, in a word, of all who were not tyrants—that is, those who are called the people: these, I say, were by them looked upon as so many animals beneath the dignity of the human species.[41]

Later, in his own *Historical View of the English Government*, Millar went on to cite more of this Voltairian-sounding Smith:

> The inferior ranks of people no longer looked upon that order, as they had done before, as the comforters of their distress, and the relievers of their indigence. On the contrary, they were provoked and disgusted by the vanity, luxury, and expense of the richer clergy, who appeared to spend upon their own pleasures what had always before been regarded as the patrimony of the poor.[42]

Several readers championed *Wealth of Nations* for attacking subsidies for clergymen through tithes. "Smith expressly said," invoked one author, "that the tithe" is found to be "a very great hindrance to improvement."[43] When Thomas Thompson and John Sheffield independently framed more comprehensive attacks, they used Smith's argument that tithes were actually "a land tax ultimately paid by the landlord" that "is always a great discouragement both to the improvements of the landlord and to the cultivation of the farmer."[44] Others went further, using Smith to condemn the church's "useless endowments" and "misapplied charities."[45] *Wealth of Nations* clearly provided ammunition to those who desired a weak church and a fundamentally secular state.

Wealth of Nations in French

Adam Smith well understood that *Wealth of Nations* could never become an Enlightenment bestseller in English alone. While the British market could certainly make him rich—as it did his friend Hume—it also limited his reputation across Europe, since few readers on the continent read English. Fame depended upon a French translation. Indeed, often books originally published in English, Italian, Dutch, or German would be translated into a third language indirectly from its French translation. The example of Cesare Beccaria's *On Crimes and Punishments* is instructive here. First published in Italian in 1764, the book did not make much impact until the Abbé Morellet produced a

French translation in 1766. It was the French Beccaria that became a bestseller, and the Swedish, German, and English translations were made from Morellet's edition. If Smith had any hope of becoming an Enlightenment author parallel to Montesquieu, Rousseau, Voltaire, Hume, and Beccaria, he knew he must secure a French translation. But how?

According to a meticulous reconstruction by Gabriel Sabbagh, the first introduction of *Wealth of Nations* to continental Europe occurred as follows:[46] In 1776, as Strahan and Cadell were about to publish Smith's work, the French controller general, Anne Robert Jacques Turgot, was embarked on a major effort to reform the French economy, known as the Six Edicts, which included deregulation of guilds and the grain trade. Turgot and Adam Smith had become friends a decade earlier when Smith was in Paris. Both were drawn to the ideas of the Physiocrats, who were among the first to preach market-driven reforms. Laissez-faire—leave it be—became their calling card, and while both Turgot and Smith had misgivings regarding key components of the Physiocratic program, they nonetheless borrowed much from Physiocracy and saw one another as ideological allies. Turgot sent Smith the minutes of the judicial hearing in which King Louis XVI ordered implementation of the Six Edicts. Meanwhile Smith sent Turgot—precisely when is not clear—an extract from the soon-to-be-published *Wealth of Nations*, from Chapter 10 of Book I, in which Smith himself advocated the deregulation of guilds.[47]

Turgot was particularly struck by Smith's argument for freeing the labor market from legal constraints, which was at the heart of the Six Edicts. He called on his friend, the Abbé André Morellet, to translate the few pages for publication, in an effort to galvanize public support for the new policies. Already known for his translation of Beccaria, Morellet was emerging as a major philosophe with particular expertise in political economy. Morellet himself had met Smith in 1766 at Helvétius's salon. Smith followed Morellet's career and owned two of his books on political economy—most likely gifts from the author.[48] Morellet immediately set to work on the extract Smith had sent to Turgot, asking the French minister to pay him for the service.[49] He also applied to the government for a *permission tacite*. This option was often given for political works generating controversy, as this pamphlet surely would do. Morellet hoped, of course, that the success of this excerpt would launch him on his way to becoming the authorized translator of the entire *Wealth of Nations*, which he and Turgot knew was about to be published. But Morellet overplayed his hand. Pursuing a *permission tacite*, rather than publishing the excerpt surreptitiously, tipped off Turgot's many opponents. Unfortunately, one of those was the king's deputy minister of justice, Miromesnil, who had the police confiscate the manuscript from Morellet's home. Although Morellet was unharmed, Turgot protested the seizure. He was overruled by Miromesnil, who insisted that one of the king's core principles was that policies up for his consideration should not become fodder for public arguments in print. The controversial excerpt was halted from publication.

Morellet finally read the first volume of the *Wealth of Nations* within weeks of its March 1776 publication, when he procured it from someone who had bought it in England. Immediately recognizing it as a masterpiece, he still hoped to be the first to translate the entire book into French. But when he approached Paris publishers, he found no interest. The vulnerability of *Wealth of Nations* to government censorship proved a huge obstacle for them. They worried about sinking so much money into the printing and marketing costs of two large volumes, only to be left with no revenue if the government suddenly declared it to be illegal. Such a thing had happened all too often in France, as with Helvétius and Rousseau. More recently, booksellers had taken a chance selling a French translation of John Dalrymple's *Memoirs of Great Britain and Ireland*. The government halted publication after the book had already been printed. Indeed, Morellet himself had been a victim of government intrusion when the controller general ordered a halt to sales of his newly published book on the grain trade. Only when Turgot took office was this ban lifted.[50] Hence, it was not government censorship per se that made publishing works like Smith so difficult, it was the instability of a system in which objections could be raised at any point from different nodes within the government. The result was a general damper on Paris publishers' desire to publish controversial works.

Thus, Morellet approached Turgot with a special request: not only should the state subsidize printing costs, but the government might publish his translation through its massive Imprimerie Royale. Strong precedence was available for this approach. The natural historian and philosophe Georges Louis LeClerc, Comte de Buffon, published his thirty-six-volume *Natural History* with the Imprimerie Royale, automatically acquiring the government's political and financial protection.[51] As Turgot wholly endorsed Smith's principles, Morellet figured that a similar sponsorship was possible. And it might have been so, had it not been that at this very moment—May 1776, two months after *Wealth of Nations* was first published in London—that King Louis XVI dismissed Turgot as minister. This ended Morellet's chance, at least in the short run, of securing government sponsorship. A French publication of *Wealth of Nations* would have to wait for a different opportunity.

Nonetheless, Morellet persevered. He decided to translate the book anyway, despite having no firm publishing commitment. He spent the next several months laboring over Smith's tomes within the lavish confines of the Archbishop Brienne's chateau in Champagne, where he had been a frequent guest. Brienne, Morellet, and Turgot had known one another since their school days at the Sorbonne; now Morellet was free to work on the Smith translation without other concerns. Unfortunately for Morellet, in 1778, the first half of another French translation was surreptitiously published in The Hague, followed in 1779 by the second half. Reviewers noted the shoddy nature of the production, produced on the fly. Printed in a cheap duodecimo format, the title page included nothing about the publisher or translator, and indeed, scholars still have not identified anyone associated with this translation. Most of Smith's many footnotes were removed, and the sections of Book V dealing with education and religious institutions were omitted. As Kenneth Carpenter observes, "there was no mediation of the text, nothing to proclaim its importance and relevance to the culture of the language of the translation."[52]

Morellet would finally complete his translation of *Wealth of Nations*, and as it circulated unpublished among friends and supporters, it attracted its own intimate kind of glory. But it would never see publication. Ironically, the failure of Morellet's translation to find a willing publisher is itself evidence of Smith's core principles in *Wealth of Nations*. There is little doubt that within a well-ordered and legal marketplace, any number of publishers would have been happy to print the manuscript. A glance at Strahan and Cadell's experience across the channel is instructive. There, copyright protection gave author and publishers a legal monopoly for fourteen years, while liberty of the press protected its free sale and distribution. This secure and stable legal environment gave British publishers the courage to risk capital for Smith's book as well as hundreds of others. French publishers, on the other hand, fearful of repeated acts of arbitrary government intervention, along with a judicial system bent to political favorites of the day, rendered the environment entirely too insecure for a publishing venture like Smith's book.

Wealth of Nations found readers in France through an odd route. In 1779, Hubert-Pascal Ameilhon, editor of the monthly economic periodical *Journal de l'agriculture, du commerce, des arts et des finances*, found himself needing more material to fill its pages. Founded a decade earlier by Samuel du Pont, the magazine began as a Physiocratic organ, but by this time had broadened its perspective in an effort to gain more readers. For almost two years, from January 1779 through December 1780, most of *Wealth of Nations* was serialized in its pages. The translator was the Abbé Jean Louis Blavet, who had previously translated Smith's *Theory of Moral Sentiments*, and who was librarian to the powerful Prince de Conti. Ameilhon found a royal censor willing to sign off on each monthly installment, and evidently publishing the book in this format did not carry the same kind of liability associated with publishing a book. It took only a few months before this translation was pirated by a Swiss publisher. In 1786, copies of the Swiss edition were reissued for sale in Paris by a bookseller there.[53]

Wealth of Nations was serialized again in 1786, this time in one of the most prestigious periodicals of the decade, the *Encyclopédie méthodique*, the successor of Diderot and d'Alembert's earlier *Encyclopédie*. Begun in 1782 by one of the largest publishers in France, Charles Joseph Panckoucke, the *méthodique* was actually a compendium of many sub-encyclopedias organized thematically. During the mid-1780s, the project attracted over 4,000 subscribers throughout Europe. Between 1784 and 1788 Panckoucke published four volumes devoted to political economy and diplomacy. About half of Blavet's 1779 translation of *Wealth of Nations* was published in Volumes 2, 3, and 4, broken up and distributed according to sub-themes, such as "colonies," "commerce," or "public debt." Clearly *Wealth of Nations* was the longest work in this series, marking its recognition as among the most significant recent work on political economy.[54] Thomas Jefferson, then minister to Versailles, most likely sent a set of the volumes to James Madison back in Virginia.[55] Despite the popularity and influence of the *Encyclopédie méthodique*, Condorcet could still complain in 1786 that *Wealth of Nations* was, "unfortunately for the happiness of mankind, hitherto too little known in Europe."[56]

By the late 1780s, the finances of the French government were in such disarray that it teetered on bankruptcy. For decades, a dysfunctional fiscal system had meant that French expenses always went beyond tax revenue, forcing the government to sell bonds on the international market. This worked well enough until France's participation in the American War of Independence (1778–83) resulted in a spike of French debt. Sometime during 1785 or 1786, the market for French bonds collapsed. Louis XVI's government had no other choice but to turn to its aristocracy to raise taxes, but of course they balked at any such policy. As the government drifted from crisis to crisis, and ministers tried various approaches, the usual restrictions on press censorship loosened, especially for works that offered advice on the fiscal situation. Given that Smith's book devoted an entire section to public debt, *Wealth of Nations* took on a special resonance during the pre-revolutionary period.

This peculiar atmosphere explains how the Paris publisher Pierre Duplain took advantage of new reforms in French publishing that sought greater copyright protection for booksellers and publishers. In 1787, Duplain secured a *permission simple* (simple permission) to publish a six-volume translation of *Wealth of Nations*. This new category of book licensing shielded *Wealth of Nations* from domestic piracies. Why Duplain printed the work in two volumes rather than six remains a mystery, and why he chose Blavet's translation over the much superior one produced by Morellet is also unclear. A reasonable speculation is that cost governed both decisions. Not only did Duplain save on paper costs, but he could pirate Blavet's translation instead of paying for Morellet's manuscript. At any rate, near the end of 1787, 1,000 copies of Duplain's edition went on sale.[57]

As the French fiscal crisis deepened into a full-scale political rebellion in 1789, interest in *Wealth of Nations* surged, and according to the authoritative book historian Kenneth Carpenter, it "became the most frequently published economic treatise of the French Revolution." With censorship eliminated, and press freedom guaranteed, Smith's books could be published anywhere in France. The Revolution put in place men who had never before served in any formal political capacity. This new generation of mainly young men were elected city mayors, regional judges, and even bishops. How would they be trained in political economy? *Wealth of Nations* became a key textbook in the education of younger patriots. For example, under the tutelage of Condorcet, himself a philosophe and revolutionary leader, a multivolume "*Bibliothèque de l'homme public* (The Public Man's Library)" began to appear in 1790. This Great Books series digested, excerpted, and summarized famous authors, not for the benefit of scholars, but so more ordinary readers might make sense of them. Volumes 1 and 2 featured Aristotle, Bodin, Machiavelli, Hume, and Locke. *Wealth of Nations* took over the second half of Volume 3 and the first half of Volume 4. Smith was followed by Plato, Thomas More, Francis Bacon, and Condorcet himself, who echoed many of Smith's ideas.[58]

At least by 1790, the year of Smith's death, the French recognized that "the excellent work of M. Smith has become a classic."[59] Another journalist judged it already "among the classical works" of political economy.[60] For French readers, comparisons with Montesquieu were natural. "Great Britain, in bringing Smith into the world, has discharged its debt toward France, which has given birth to Montesquieu," commented one reader in 1788.[61] The revolutionary writer and politician Pierre Louis Roederer noted that Smith "is to the science of public economy" what Montesquieu "is to the science of political and civil government."[62] The French Revolutionaries embraced the juxtaposition between Smith and Montesquieu. "There is no need to seek in Smith the brilliant imagination and the energetic style . . . of Montesquieu," wrote one reviewer.

> Smith is a wise and profound calculator whose only ornament is utility. Do you wish great images for your imagination, great thoughts, strong and ingenious expression that entirely sate your spirit? Close the treatise on the *Wealth of Nations* and open . . . *Spirit of the Laws*. But if you are seeking the true foundations of the prosperity of empires, if you require exact ideas on the relationship of agriculture and commerce, wages and work, on industry, banks, money, credit and all the many complicated and various elements entering into the structure of the modern state, the treatise on the *Wealth of Nations* is what is needed.[63]

Between 1790 and 1794 four French-language editions of *Wealth of Nations* were published in France, along with an English-language edition published in Basel. Clearly French Revolutionary readers saw in the book a comprehensive vision for a liberal society similar to Montesquieu's. "It is a complete system of social and political economy; here is the development and demonstration of principles that have determined the fate of nations."[64] Acknowledging its challenging length and material, reviewers warned ordinary readers to read it over and over again with immense concentration and fortitude. Were readers to put in the time and effort, reviewers promised, they would not be disappointed. As the Comte de Volney noted along with other commentators, *Wealth of Nations* had become recognized as the British version of *The Spirit of the Laws*.[65] While Smith could not match Montesquieu's polished prose and exotic digressions, *Wealth of Nations* was a much more necessary and appropriate textbook for the new revolutionary era. "No man ought to pretend to be a legislator in the present day," argued an American reader in 1800, "who is not well read in" *Wealth of Nations*. By then, of course, his advice had been heeded by at least two French controllers general (Turgot and Brienne), three British prime ministers (Townshend, North, and Shelburne), as well as many in the political elite such as Fox and Burke in England, Condorcet and Sieyes in France, as well as Hamilton, Adams, and Jefferson in the United States.[66]

On both sides of the Atlantic, *Wealth of Nations* was sometimes used to explain the origins of the French Revolution. Smith demonstrated, one pamphleteer noted, that absolute monarchy was incompatible with prosperity. Louis XIV funded wars through violating his subjects' property rights, resulting in France's economic ruin. Without political reform the nation was doomed. "The weight of debt, whose foundations were laid under Louis XIV, induced the present Revolution. That mode of government affords no sufficient security of the deposited capital," noted political observer T. F. Hill. Only a liberal monarchy whose constitution protected private property and individual liberty could thrive in the modern world. "It was left for our Adam Smith to become the oracle" who demonstrated such ideas in *Wealth of Nations*.[67]

As *Wealth of Nations* became more and more popular throughout Europe, its ideas simultaneously became associated with French Revolutionary ideology. Especially during the Revolution's early years, activists agreed that Smith's ideas resonated with the need for political reform. One Jacobin sympathizer, the Norfolk surgeon Richard Dinmore, declared Smith the "high priest of democracy."[68] Before, and indeed, after the Terror (1793–4), Smith's book was viewed largely—but certainly not exclusively—on the political left. "To see economic freedom as a component of revolutionary freedom," writes historian Emma Rothschild, "was indeed one of the distinguishing principles" of Condorcet, Sieyes, and most revolutionaries before radical Jacobins ascended to power in 1793.[69] Only Jacobins during the Terror explicitly rejected Smith. When in November 1792 the hot-headed young radical legislator Louis Antoine Saint-Just began to call for more centralized state control over the economy, he lashed out in particular at the more liberal ideas of Smith and Montesquieu, telling the National Convention that moderate deputies, such as Condorcet, "talked to you of Smith and Montesquieu. . . . But neither Smith nor Montesquieu had experience of what is happening here today."[70]

As the Terror descended upon France, Smith's reputation became entangled in the debates over the French Revolution and its implications for political reform throughout Europe. Smith's champions regarded him as "the most philosophic writer of the age."[71] There was much debate, for example, over those sections in Part Five of the *Wealth of Nations* addressing cultural institutions. Educational reformers used the book as the basis for remaking primary and higher education.[72] Similar praise was showered on Smith for advocating religious pluralism in which small and weak "independent sects" produce "a general philosophical moderation of mind."[73] On the other hand, conservative readers attacked Smith for proposing "the study of *philosophy* as an antidote to the poison of enthusiasm and superstition. . . . Is not this the very language which the French have since" devoured themselves?[74]

Some British readers seemed ready to challenge Smithian economics altogether. For example, at least one reader had no doubt that Smith's division of labor proved a sound principle for economic expansion. "But the question I wish to discuss is whether this is beneficial . . . or whether it would not be much more advantageous . . . to sell a smaller quantity of her manufactures, provided she employs more of her people in the manufacturing of them?" This critic complained that "the silk trade of Spitalfields" had recently been ruined by imported cotton.[75] For some critics, Smith had mistaken wealth for happiness. "The wealth of nations is incompatible with happiness," charged William Thomson. "No nation will ever be happy who increases trade rather than agriculture."[76] William Jones complained that the problem lay less in Smith's economic principles than in his infatuation with Voltaire.[77] Where some conservative voices damned Smith for his association with the radical democrat Tom Paine, other readers tried to take back *Wealth of Nations* from the Painite Left. "Mr Paine frequently perverts the meaning of

Mr. Adam Smith," wrote James Chalmers.[78] "Far from following the outlines of Adam Smith," added S. A. Joersson, Paine "has corrupted the principles they inculcate."[79] Finally, the more known *Wealth of Nations* became, the more it served as a target in conservative satirical poetry.[80]

When William Wilberforce introduced a bill to abolish the slave trade in 1792, he invoked the *Wealth of Nations*, while others published in magazines extractions against slavery from Smith's book.[81] After that, Smith was often cited by abolitionists to demonstrate not only the injustice of slavery but its economic inefficiency as well. Those readers who saw Smith as a progressive defender of the ordinary worker invoked his characterization of small shop owners and master artisans: "Masters are always and everywhere in a sort of tacit, but constant and uniform combination, not to raise the wages of labour above their actual rate."[82] At the end of the 1790s, radical thinker Joseph Priestley characterized the *Wealth of Nations* and Raynal's *History of the Two Indies* as the era's two most important works about politics.[83]

An important perspective was taken by feminist thinker Priscilla Wakefield, who began her 1798 *Reflections on the Present Condition of the Female* Sex with a direct critique of the *Wealth of Nations*. To be sure, she lauded Smith's defense of the working man against corrupt policies that enabled landlords and master craftsmen to conspire against them. But by his silence regarding gender, Wakefield charged, Smith had virtually excluded women from the new economy. Without acknowledging that women are systematically excluded from most crafts and occupations, Smith doomed them to continuing to exercise only their "indolent indulgence and trifling pursuits." Vocational training and all educational opportunities, she argued, should be thrown open to talent, without regard to sex.[84]

The surge in popularity of the *Wealth of Nations* during the 1790s was not confined to Britain and France but occurred throughout Europe. Translations were produced in Danish (1779), Italian (1790/1), Spanish (1792), Dutch (1796), Swedish (1800), and Russian (1802–6). But clearly the most intense interest occurred in Germany. In 1776, a translator living in London helped make Germany the first country to produce a translation. German readers had long been avid followers of the Scottish Enlightenment—works by David Hume, Lord Kames, and Adam Ferguson had all done well there, as had Smith's earlier *Theory of Moral Sentiments*.[85] Germans were primed for the book. It is likely that a copy of *Wealth of Nations* reached Immanuel Kant in Konigsberg in late 1784.[86] Nonetheless, according to economic historian Keith Tribe, it is unlikely the book made much impact before 1790.[87] In that year, the young writer and future Prussian statesman Friedrich von Gentz wrote to his friend Christian Garve that he had just finished a close rereading of *Wealth of Nations*. "I have studied Smith on national wealth for the third time with the greatest attention, and made an analysis of it to the extent of forty sheets. I recall that I have talked with you about this book occasionally, yet only incidentally," Gentz wrote. "But it seems to me you have never expressed the unrestrained praise, which I have always felt it deserves. In my opinion it is in the first place by far the most perfect work that has ever been written in any language on this subject." But even more than its innovative and profound ideas, Gentz—who had taught himself English—was impressed with its style.

> I consider it in general, in respect to method and literary art as one of the most complete and perfect books, that exist in any science. Such clarity combined with such zeal for the welfare of mankind, such an unbroken orderliness even to the smallest parts and details of such an admirable system, and such unity throughout the whole is rarely found in extremely few philosophical investigations. In respect to style I confess that I consider Smith the most perfect English prose writer; neither Hume nor Ferguson, who may most readily be compared with him, and who may excel him in single qualities, in keenness, in force, in variety, do I find, when considered from all sides, so correct and faultless.

Gentz's assessment that Garve had a poor impression of *Wealth of Nations* may have been exaggerated. Garve soon wrote to another friend that "Smith's book on national wealth I consider one of the classic works of recent times. The German translation is so wretched, that it is hardly intelligible, let alone readable." Garve acted on his words: he completed a new translation of *Wealth of Nations* that went through three editions before the decade was over.[88]

Lauderdale's Reflections

Among *Wealth of Nations*' most dedicated, critical, and unusual readers was a Scottish member of the British House of Lords, James Maitland, who succeeded his father as the eighth Earl of Lauderdale in 1789. Lauderdale was a passionate Whig supporter of the French Revolutionaries. In 1792 he made a special trip to Paris to observe the new republic for himself, and became friendly with some of its leaders, including Jacques Pierre Brissot, leader of the Girondin faction. When he returned to England he even wore Jacobin-style clothing to demonstrate his support. His economic ideas were also often radical and he spent most of his political career in parliamentary opposition. At one point he advocated replacing indirect taxes with an inheritance tax. Only in 1820, when Lauderdale was already in his sixties did he transform into a conservative Tory.

Lauderdale's copious notes on *Wealth of Nations* came to light at the end of the twentieth century.[89] They show a deep interest, almost an obsession, with Smith's ideas that were likely the product of successive rereadings and study, begun perhaps as early as the 1780s or 1790s and continuing well into the second decade of the nineteenth century. The word "notes" also doesn't capture the extent of Lauderdale's undertaking. Some of his remarks are actual annotations made on the pages of *Wealth of Nations*. Others are longer expository comments written on separate scraps of paper and stuffed into his copy of the book. Along with Lauderdale's own comments are also many excerpts from other eighteenth-century works on political economy that give a comparative framework for

Smith's own ideas. Here Lauderdale especially favored juxtaposing Smith's views with works by Turgot and the French Physiocrats. Lauderdale's copy of *Wealth of Nations* became, in fact, a kind of scrapbook, a miniature archive that he regularly visited.

The scrapbook is also a kind of genealogy project in which Lauderdale attempted to trace the lineage of Smith's ideas in early modern intellectual history. Whenever Lauderdale read an earlier book with sections related to *Wealth of Nations*, he would stuff a transcribed excerpt into Smith's book. Hume's essays are carved up in this way. Lauderdale noted that Smith's examples from the Dutch East Indies were taken from Book 20 and 21 of Montesquieu's *The Spirit of the Laws*. When Smith referred himself to "Mr. Cantillon," Lauderdale transcribed the relevant excerpt from the French version of Richard Cantillon's *Essai sur la nature du commerce en géneral*.[90]

In 1804 Lauderdale published his criticisms of *Wealth of Nations* as *An Inquiry into the Nature and Origin of Public Wealth*—the title alone reveals his debt to Smith. The book was revised in an expanded edition in 1819 and translated into French and Italian. Known only to specialists in the history of economic thought for much of the late nineteenth and early twentieth centuries, Lauderdale's work attracted new attention following the Second World War because some of his ideas seemed to anticipate the Keynesian turn. Lauderdale's book, of course, featured a polished argument in which readers benefit from his years of reflection and thought about Smith's ideas. The notes, though, are different in tone and purpose; they are livelier and filled with passion. Lauderdale struggled in his notes with Smith's ideas, questioning them, asking probing questions, and sometimes setting forth on his own way. In the notes Lauderdale treated Smith as the master artisan, allowing him to build the scaffolding of political economy. Lauderdale climbed that scaffolding and viewed vistas unseen by Smith but also realized that his own insights were dependent on the older Scot.

Lauderdale, then, accepted Smith's book as everyone's guide to political economy, and he accepted much of what was in it. The most important divergence came over Smith's labor theory of value. Near the start of the book, Smith defines labor in this light: "The real price of everything, what everything really costs to the man who wants to acquire it, is the toil and trouble of acquiring it. . . . Labour was the first price, the original purchase-money that was paid for all things."[91] Lauderdale responded: "This appears to be the great error in this part of his system." For Lauderdale, nothing—not labor, not agriculture, nor manufactured goods—has any intrinsic value. Certainly "the quantity of labor that it has cost or that it can procure no ways enter into the estimation . . . Labour itself can therefore form no real measure of value." Rather, the cost of any good is always relative to any other. Value is not a reflection of what the original item cost in terms of labor; value is instead a reflection of how badly the buyer wants the product and how much the seller is willing to part with it. "The value of labour is regulated by the same principles as the value of any other commodity."[92] Here Lauderdale preferred John Locke's formulation. He tucked into the notes this excerpt from Locke's *Considerations on Lowering the Interest* into his copy of *Wealth of Nations*: "That the Intrinsick Natural worth of any thing, consists in this, that it is apt to be serviceable to the necessities or conveniences of human life, and it is naturally more worth, as the necessity or conveniency it supplies is greater." While Lauderdale and Locke believed that an item's value was inherently relative, Smith claimed it stemmed from its labor costs.[93]

If Smith "did not understand the nature of value," Lauderdale nonetheless praised his controversial position on the relationship between master artisans and their workers. Like his colleagues in the abolitionist movement, Lauderdale also focused on Smith's passage warning that master artisans are "always and everywhere" conspiring to keep journeymen wages from rising. "The description here," Lauderdale added, "given of the relative situation of the workman and his master is perfectly just. Perhaps the description affords a pretty accurate view of the situation of the upper and lower orders in society." In *Wealth of Nations*, Lauderdale found plenty of fuel for his democratic views.[94]

Lauderdale also used the *Wealth of Nations* like a class syllabus that generates its own special assignments. When, for example, Smith argued that real wages had risen in Britain over the past century, Lauderdale formed his own project to verify the theory. Focusing as scholars do today on what might be a typical community—he chose the village of Walton just north of Liverpool—he gathered data regarding several kinds of wage labor and compared them in 1761 and 1791. So, for example, he showed that a female domestic servant made £3 for the year in 1761, but £4.10 in 1791; a thatcher made twice in 1791 what he had earned in 1761, as also was the case for a "butcher killing and cutting up a pig." Indeed, the wage prices for all occupations increased by a good deal, although not at the same rates. In this way, Lauderdale empirically verified Smith's claim that English wages had indeed risen. Nonetheless, Lauderdale also used these data to further criticize Smith, since for Lauderdale the wage increases reflected a relative rise in the value of labor versus other commodities, something outside Smith's labor theory of value.[95]

Lauderdale's notes reflect a European reader who optimistically believed that Parisian radicals would follow the insights of political economists as they built the skeleton for a new type of regime. He was far from alone. Shortly after the French Revolution began, and only weeks prior to Smith's death, the *Moniteur*, the most important Paris daily newspaper, claimed that Smith was about to publish a definitive and comprehensive analysis of *The Spirit of the Laws*. The book would be "the result of many years of reflection." Its impact would be huge: "This book will mark a watershed in the development of political philosophy." Alas, no such book ever appeared, and so far as we know, Smith never contemplated such a project. What is clear from this rumor is that such work was in great demand and would have quickly achieved the status of a blockbuster. It is too bad that Smith never planned to write it.[96]

Chapter 12

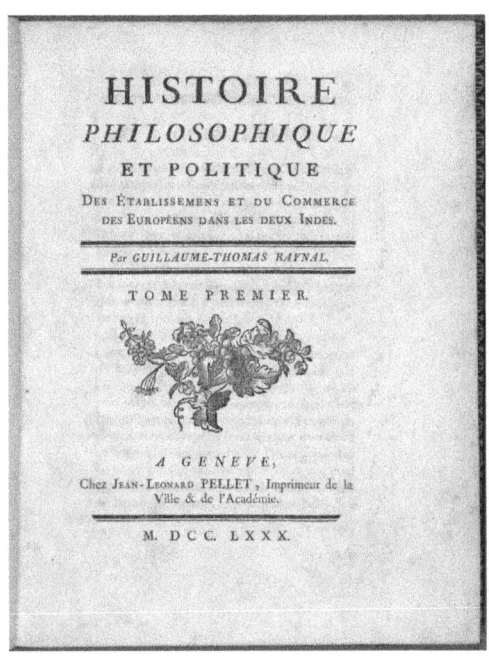

Figure 12.1 1780 edition title page Raynal's *History of the Two Indies*. The third version, first published in 1780, is the largest, most complete, and subversive.

Chapter 12
Raynal's *History of the Two Indies* (1770–80)

Table 12.1 Eighteenth-Century Editions of *History of the Two Indies*

Decade	1770–9	1780–9	1790–1800
Editions	36	17	4

Total Editions: 57.
Translations: Dutch, English, German, Italian, Spanish.
Source: https://kates.itg.pomona.edu/books/analytics.php?type=all. Accessed March 9, 2022. See also "Bibliographie sommaire des éeditions de l'Histoire des deux Indes," in Guillaume-Thomas Raynal, *Histoire philosophique et politique des établissements et du commerce des Eruopéens dans les deux Indes*, ed. Anthony Strugnell et. al. Tome 1 (Ferney-Voltaire: Centre International D'Étude du xviiie Siècle, 2010), liii–lxxx.

Table 12.2 The Three Versions of *History of the Two Indies*

Year	Place of Publication	Publisher	Number of Volumes	Approximate Number of Pages	Format
1770	Amsterdam [Paris]	Unknown	6	2,150	octavo
1774	The Hague	Gosse	7	3,300	octavo
1780	Geneva	Pellet	10 octavo 4 quarto	4,800 (octavo)	quarto and octavo

The *History of the Two Indies*[1] remains even today a long-forgotten work. After 1820, there was only a smattering of nineteenth-century editions (all in French), and strangely, no editions at all for the century between 1850 and 1950.[2] Like Graffigny's *Letters of a Peruvian Woman*, the work disappeared, even from shelves of literary scholars. Still rare today, a standard critical edition that started with two published volumes in 2010 is unlikely to be completed for several years.[3] But during the eighteenth century, it was quite a different story. From its appearance in 1772, the 3,000-page multivolume set was a runaway blockbuster. "It seems to me," remarked the Swedish ambassador to Versailles in a letter to Voltaire when the book first appeared, "that this is a work made to produce a big sensation" (Tables 12.1 and 12.2).[4]

The History of the Two Indies is an encyclopedic history of European colonialism covering virtually all parts of the world where Europeans intersected with indigenous peoples. Its volumes include eighteen "books," which, after 1774, were also subdivided into chapters. The first five books focus on European settlements in India, China, Japan, and Southeast Asia. Books 1–4 are devoted to Portuguese, Dutch, English, and French colonies, while Book 5 spills over to smaller countries, such as Denmark. Books 6–10 turn to the New World, focusing especially on Spanish settlements in Mexico, Peru, Chile, and Paraguay. Book 11, among the most famous in the entire series, narrates how Europeans came to use the coasts of Africa as global centers for purchasing slaves for their New World plantations. Books 12–14 then show in great detail the development of plantation economies, especially in the Caribbean islands, revealing how they became the crown jewels for eighteenth-century British and French empires. Books 15–18 address British and French colonies in North America.

Of course, many world histories had been published before *History of the Two Indies*, including Voltaire's deservedly famous *Essai sur les moeurs* (1756). What made *History of the Two Indies* innovative was simultaneously its global character and its focused thematic material. Here was a comparative history of European contact with native peoples. What happened when strange civilizations intersected deliberately or not with one another? The opening sentence of Book 1 set the tone for the series: "No event has been so interesting to mankind in general, and to the inhabitants of Europe in particular, as the discovery of the New World, and the passage to India by the Cape of Good Hope."[5] Repeatedly, *History of the Two Indies* stressed how European contact forged a new highly integrated global community, in which commodities and labor, as well as customs, mores, and values, traveled routinely back and forth between continents. However, Raynal told this tale in a tragic key. Over and over again, *History of the Two Indies* lamented European intercourse with non-European peoples that resulted in unprecedented levels of violence, disease, poverty, and misery inflicted by the former onto the latter. With few exceptions, *History of the Two Indies* documents the savagery of European colonists and explores how European political and religious institutions repeatedly allowed their agents to exploit indigenous peoples who obviously did not deserve such a fate. In this regard, although largely forgotten in the heyday of nineteenth-century European imperialism, Raynal's history has more recently become appreciated by postcolonial specialists as an early warning signal to Europeans about the dangers inherent in their globalist enterprise.[6]

In 1770, the Abbé Raynal, the work's primary author, was fifty-seven years old and a modestly successful figure in the French Enlightenment. Earlier in his career, he had been ordained a Jesuit and looked forward to teaching and writing religious philosophy. But literature, journalism, and political writing soon summoned him, and he left the church in his twenties. His erudite books, including histories of English and Dutch political institutions, did not reach many readers. Rather, it was his editorship of the *Mercure de France*, France's leading government-sponsored literary newspaper, that made him a regular ambassador from the Republic of Letters. While Raynal was hardly an insignificant figure, there was nothing in his background to predict that he would become an overnight sensation, elevated by contemporary public opinion to the level of a Voltaire, Montesquieu, Smith, and Rousseau.[7]

In fact, Raynal was not the singular author of the *History of the Two Indies*. He was the titular head of a stable of philosophes who contributed steadily and prodigiously to the project. The team, modeled on the success of the *Encyclopédie*, included Baron d'Holbach, Jean Joseph Pechméja, Antoine-Laurent Jussieu, Alexandre Deleyre, Jean François de Saint Lambert, and finally and, most important, Denis Diderot, the *Encyclopédie*'s general editor, who anonymously wrote hundreds of pages for Raynal's project. Despite some leaked rumors, the collective that put together *History of the Two Indies* was shrouded in secrecy until the twentieth century. During the eighteenth century, virtually everyone attributed the work to Raynal himself.[8]

Raynal's history began with a thirty-page introduction that charts the history of commerce from the ancient Phoenicians through the European Middle Ages. It opened with a dramatic prologue claiming that the discovery of the New World and the passage to India around the Cape of Good Hope caused a "revolution in commerce" that transformed politics, economics, and culture throughout "the whole world." Goods produced in the Southern Hemisphere were consumed by natives living near the Arctic Circle; people who lived in Asia helped clothe strangers living in Europe. For the first time, but not the last, human activity changed nearly everywhere. "A general intercourse of opinions, laws, customs and remedies, virtues and vices, was established among men." Raynal declared that his purpose was not simply to chart the history of this global transformation but to investigate whether it was good or bad for humankind. Will these great changes "ever add to the tranquility, the happiness, and the pleasures of mankind"? After all, commerce by its nature is supposed to benefit both producers and consumers. In this case, Raynal asked whether the commercial benefits of the era of discovery had benefited everyone or only European elites. Do the benefits of global commerce "improve our present state, or, do they only change it"? That's the key question posed by Raynal, and it is as much a philosophical as an historical one.[9]

Raynal's work was meant to test Montesquieu's thesis that global trade softens mores and reduces violence. In philosophical terms, Raynal believed that commerce in general greatly improves mankind. Not only does trade bring obvious economic benefits, but it encourages and thrives when there is at least a degree of freedom and security, usually brought about by the security of private property. Thus, Raynal associated commerce with political order and social improvement, in addition to economic gains. "Those states that have been commercial have civilized all the rest," declared Raynal, invoking Montesquieu. However, on this score European states had a mixed track record. In contrast to the Greeks and Phoenicians, the Romans insisted on despotically imposing their own style of government. Medieval Europe was no better toward commerce, establishing feudalism, a system "so fatal to mankind."[10]

Unfortunately, argued Raynal, the Portuguese kings—Europe's first colonial power—echoed these shameful Roman and medieval attitudes. Before the arrival of the

Portuguese in Persian-dominated India, Raynal found that southern Asia was filled with prosperous commercial towns, exhibiting "universal opulence, an extensive commerce, a refined luxury, politeness in the men, and gallantry in the women." But the Portuguese, led in 1507 by Afonso de Albuquerque, "began to ravage the coasts, and to plunder the towns."[11] Soon, like medieval feudal lords before him, he imposed Portuguese hegemony by ruining trade between the Indians and the Persians. Obviously, this initial direct contact between Europeans and Indians failed to improve conditions for humankind.

By 1511, Albuquerque was conquering Malacca, the port city on the coast of Malaya, ruled tyrannically by the sultan of Malacca, Malmud Syah. Albuquerque successfully took the city from the sultan and quickly established a Portuguese government for the port. Unfortunately, for most inhabitants, switching one despot for another did not improve conditions. Raynal was severe in his criticism of the Portuguese for thinking only of their short-term gain and ignoring "the rights . . . of islanders and savages." Invoking Montesquieu again, Raynal argued that the inhabitants of Malacca, like all people subjected to colonial rule, "are only to be civilized by humane treatment, by the allurements of riches or liberty, by the influence of virtue and moderation, and by a mild government."

> They must be restored to their rights or left to themselves, before we can hope to establish any intercourse with them. To attempt to reduce them by conquest, is, perhaps, the last method that should be tried, as it will only increase their abhorrence of a foreign yoke.[12]

All human beings have rights, insisted Raynal, and opening markets for commerce must respect those rights. After 100 more pages describing similar cases of terrible Portuguese colonial establishments in Asia, Raynal's passion only became more heated. "*Serve or die*, the Portuguese used to say insolently to every people they met in their rapid progress marked with blood."

> It is a grateful thing to behold the downfall of such tyranny; and a consolation to expect the punishment of those treacheries, murders, and cruelties, with which it has been preceded or followed.[13]

At the beginning of this first book, Raynal championed commerce as a force for good that increased the benefits of wealth for everyone and contributed to freedom and security. But by Book 1's end, his tone often became disgusted over the violence inflicted by the Portuguese on native peoples in Africa, the Persian Gulf, India, and Southeast Asia. Europe's first direct contact with these overseas civilizations had been disastrous from the start. Nor could it be said that the fault belonged to the native populations. In Raynal's rendering, indigenous peoples are neither noble nor passive savages, but humans whose novel cultures, religions, and social practices deserve just as much respect from the Portuguese as does Catholic Europe.

Near the end of Book 1, an interpolation by Denis Diderot added a melodramatic soliloquy to the 1780 version. Personifying an objective historian who now must come to judgment of the events that he has just narrated, he realized that he could not remain above the fray. The moral implications of what he has seen required special engagement. "Barbarous Europeans! I have often embarked with you in imagination on board the ships that were to convey you to these distant regions," he explained to ostensibly the Portuguese but really to all eighteenth-century European readers. Witnessing such despotic acts of violence caused in the writer a deep sense of alienation from Europeans. "I have withdrawn myself from you; I have thrown myself among your enemies; I have taken up arms against you, and have imbrued my hands in your blood." Until now the narrator had been writing as a European for European readers. But based on what he has just narrated, he could not continue as a European; he pledged to side with the colonized natives.

Diderot's break was significant. It immediately distinguished his work from the histories of Voltaire and Montesquieu, removing any veneer of objectivity. "I here make a solemn protestation of this," Diderot continued, "and if I have ever ceased, for one moment, considering you [Europeans] as a multitude of famished and cruel vultures, with as little principles of morality and conscience as are to be found among these rapacious birds of prey; may this work, and may my memory . . . sink into the lowest contempt." From this point forward, our historian refused to consider matters neutrally and dispassionately. The narrator promised to tell the story in a way that gave agency to colonial peoples and exhorts Europeans to change their ways.

Book 2 addressed the Dutch. In particular, it followed the establishment and development of the Dutch East India Company, which Raynal described as a "new state, erected within the state itself,"[14] that corrupted the republican nature of the fiercely independent Holland. Most of the early chapters were chronological and geographical, generally without controversy. This historical flow was interrupted at Chapter 18 by another of Diderot's anonymous contributions, this one discussing Dutch settlements at the southern tip of Africa. There the Dutch encountered a native people known as the Hottentots, who themselves already had an almost mythical reputation among travel writers and explorers. For early modern readers, the Hottentots represented humans at their most primitive, in a social state closest to other primates. Europeans considered them barely human. Modern anthropologists, who refer to these people as Khoikhoi, have shown that this reputation was very much undeserved, but it stuck well into the nineteenth century.[15]

After Raynal spent several pages introducing the Hottentots and charting their first interactions with the Dutch settlers, Diderot interrupted with this soliloquy: "But are they happy, you ask me?" His answer was unequivocal. "Are you fond of liberty? He is free. Are you desirous of health? He knows no other illness but old age. Are you delighted with virtues? He . . . is a stranger to vice." Europeans might complain about how filthy the Hottentot keeps himself, but what may be dirty on the outside is clean on the inside. "Do you think," Diderot went on, that the corruption that manifests itself in "your hatred, your perfidy, and your duplicity" is anything worse than what your senses smell as "the uncleanliness of the Hottentots"? If your design would have been to improve the life of the Hottentot, then perhaps European knowledge and manners would have served some useful purpose. But you had no such motive, he continued. "You have made a descent upon his country merely to deprive him of it. You have come near to his hut with the only view of driving him out of it.... Your only intention has been to reduce him still nearer to the condition of a brute, and to satisfy your avarice."[16]

After addressing himself to the Dutch, Diderot turned to the natives themselves:

> Fly, unhappy Hottentots, fly! And hide yourselves in the depths of the forests.... Or, if you feel yourselves animated with a sufficient share of courage, take up your axes, bend your bows, and send a shower of poisoned darts against these strangers. May there not be one of them remaining to convey to his countrymen the news of their disaster.

In direct and simple language, Diderot used the Hottentots to call for a general indigenous uprising against European colonial powers. "You must either agree with their extravagant opinions," Diderot emphatically warned the Hottentots, and thereby all natives, "or they will massacre you without mercy." In short, kill them before they kill you. "Make haste, therefore, and lay yourselves in ambush for them."[17]

Raynal, Diderot, and their associates were not primitivists; they did not argue that native peoples, particularly hunting and gathering societies, lived in a pastoral utopia free of major conflict. Rather, their claim was that Europeans were no happier than Hottentots or any other peoples, even though they were better off materially. Such economic differences, moreover, did not give Europeans any right to control or change the lives of natives, without their explicit and voluntary permission and participation. Occupying a lower stage of economic development, argued Raynal, did not disqualify any native people from exercising the same rights as Europeans.

The Dutch, then, were not so different in their treatment of indigenous peoples than the Portuguese. Both states acted despotically and dismissively, driving native peoples into forced labor, stealing their property, and upending their customs, manners, and culture. This finding surprised Raynal. After all, Portugal was an absolute monarchy supported by a Catholic Church and landed aristocracy that treated its own common people with a disrespect similar to that shown to overseas peoples. Holland was different. It was a Calvinist republic with keen respect for the civil rights and religious views of its people. How could such a free and sober people act abroad as despotically as the Portuguese? Raynal's answer was the Dutch East India Company, that "state within a state"; that is, a despotic state within a republican one. At first, the strict and virtuous Dutch controlled the company, insisting on a frugal and disciplined management. But as the company became wealthier and controlled more lands and peoples, its practices and management became more corrupt, according to Raynal. Worse, as the company began to assume a larger role in the Dutch economy, even servicing its national debt, its corruption inevitably began to pollute the very core of the Dutch republic itself, Raynal charged. The Dutch had fought to gain their independence from Spain, only to have their republican virtue undermined by the company's wealth and power. "Industrious Batavians," Diderot addressed the Dutch people, "formerly so poor, so brave, and so formidable, at present so opulent and so feeble, tremble at the idea of being again reduced to crouch under the yoke of arbitrary power. . . . It is not I who give you this caution; it is the voice of your ancestors which thus calls out to you from the bottom of their tombs."[18] In short, Diderot believed that the Dutch East India Company acted cruelly not just to colonial peoples but to the Dutch themselves. Only a popular insurrection against the company, he believed, could rectify the situation.

These anti-colonialist themes were recycled in Books 3 and 4, which traced the development of England and France in India and the East Indies. In the final chapter of Book 4, concluding the entire first section of the work, Diderot provided another dramatic twenty-page insertion establishing corrective principles for establishing colonies. "What lesson shall we have learnt from the massacre of so many Portuguese, Dutch, English, and French, unless it have taught to keep upon good terms with the natives?"[19] Mixing ideas of Montesquieu and Fénelon, Diderot urged European states to abide by a "mildness in administration; faithful observance of engagements; having goods of a better quality, and being satisfied with a moderate profit."[20] Diderot was no isolationist; he welcomed a global economy with regular and direct contact between peoples. But he felt the way in which Europeans were going about establishing a world economy was stupid in its short-sightedness, adding that universal rights to liberty and property should never be violated. Native peoples should be allowed to worship freely their own gods, and therefore, missionaries should be carefully supervised and restricted. "Will you still continue to massacre, imprison, and plunder those who have put themselves under your protection," he asked? After all, cried Diderot, "the savage, as well as the civilized man, aspires after happiness."[21]

Diderot then went on to list several other principles that could lay the groundwork for a more sustainable global economy. Growth should be measured not merely by commodities but by human capital as well: "multiply farmers, consumers, and with them every species of industry."[22] When laws are broken, European settlers should be punished more severely than natives, so that respect is gained for the Europeans by the indigenous peoples. Hard work should be followed by good fun. Be sure, Diderot advised, to "appoint some days of rest, and institute some festivals, but let them be merely of a civil nature."[23] After all, holidays make people cheerful. However, he admitted, none of these principles will prevent or even delay a great age of liberation, when colonized peoples throw off the shackles that Europeans imposed upon them.

> To what purpose is it that ye oppose a revolution, which though distant, will certainly be accomplished, notwithstanding all your efforts to prevent it? The world that you have invaded must free itself from that which you inhabit. Then the seas will only separate friends and brothers. What great calamity do ye see in this, ye unjust, cruel, and inflexible tyrants?[24]

In *The Spirit of the Laws*, Montesquieu had argued that commerce was key to a global civilizing process, softening warlike manners, and replacing violence with consumption as a critical social attribute. The description of eighteenth-century global commerce in Raynal's history seemed to contradict Montesquieu. After all, for Raynal and Diderot growth in global trade and wealth seemed to go hand in hand with militarism, slavery, piracy, and war. In *History of the Two Indies*, global commerce did not appear to be a civilizing process. And yet, Raynal admitted that even were it theoretically possible for global commerce to have beneficial effects, its current trajectory could not be reversed. Smothering commerce because Europeans have violated its natural principles would only make everything worse, increasing poverty for everyone. It was pointless, Raynal insisted, "to transform the universe into one vast monastery, and to change men into so many idle and melancholy anchorets."[25] Raynal's and Diderot's firm rejection of isolationism made their policy proscriptions, in fact, less radical than some of their more melodramatic statements may have implied. What they sought was almost an oxymoron, recently dubbed by some scholars "enlightened colonialism."[26]

Along with democratic ideals achieved through colonial revolts, Raynal advocated free trade against the mercantilist policies of European governments, echoing David Hume and the writers' circle led by French Intendant Vincent de Gournay. "Commerce is the exercise of that valuable liberty, to which nature has invited all men; which is the source of their happiness, and indeed, of their virtues."[27] Raynal argued that global commerce affected ordinary Europeans as well as the governors of the East India Company. He insisted that people everywhere have an insatiable appetite for consumer items that provide new pleasures. After tasting coffee for the first time, the Dutch cheesemaker will work harder to save up a few pennies to enjoy the coffee again. "No sooner had his industry facilitated the means of producing a subsistence, than the leisure he gained by this was employed in extending the limits of his faculties and the circle of his pleasures."[28] Consumption of new products begotten through exchange is the driving engine of economic growth in the modern world.

For Raynal, then, global commerce was thus not doomed to be only a tool of despotism and oppression but could become a direct extension of emancipation. "We may even venture to assert, that men are never so truly sensible of their freedom as they are in a commercial intercourse . . . as trade produces liberty, so it contributes to preserve it."[29] This intimate association between commerce and liberty was true both at the micro level of the individual and at the macro level of international affairs. "The refuse of all nations, mixing together during the ravages of war, are improved and polished by commerce." Raynal had not refuted Montesquieu; he had, in fact, returned to *The Spirit of the Law*'s key argument regarding *doux commerce*. Realizing the importance of economic events upon historical change, Raynal predicted how all states are becoming affected by increasing global trade.

The importation of a new commodity, the invention of some useful machine, the construction of a port, the establishment of a factory, the carrying off a branch of trade from a rival nation, will all become the transactions of the utmost importance; and the annals of nations must hereafter be written by commercial philosophers, as they were formerly by historical orators.[30]

Raynal's most passionate criticism was reserved for Spanish treatment of native New World peoples. Here was a new and especially dark chapter in European colonialism. Under Spanish rule, slaves "were indiscriminately chained together like beasts. . . . No intercourse passed between the sexes except by stealth. The men perished in the mines; and the women in the fields." Never before, not even in feudal Europe, had Europeans treated common people with such brutal disregard for life. Raynal raised the volume of the prose to its maximum level. "The whole race became extinct. Let me be allowed to pause here for a moment. My eyes overflow with tears, and I can no longer discern what I am writing."[31]

According to Raynal, this inhumane treatment of indigenous New World peoples desensitized Europeans to cruelty, a prerequisite for the slave trade, the subject of Book XI, arguably the most important section of the entire *History of the Two Indies*. After attempting to subject Native Americans to plantation slavery, European invaders imported millions of Africans to take their place. "Nothing," claimed Raynal, "is more miserable than the condition of the Negro, throughout the whole American Archipelago. . . . Deprived of every enjoyment, he is condemned to a perpetual drudgery in a burning climate, constantly under the rod of an unfeeling master." How could Europeans allow such an evil system to continue? African slaves "are tyrannized, mutilated, burnt, and put to death, and yet we listen to those accounts coolly and without emotion." How was it possible for intelligent and enlightened Europeans to devise and participate in such inhuman practices? "The torments of a people to whom we owe our luxuries, can never reach our hearts."[32]

Like *The Spirit of the Laws*, then, *History of the Two Indies* was both a reference work and something of a polemic. Encyclopedic in its scope, but intimate and accessible in its language and argumentation, it was read differently by various groups of readers. While the work was generally regarded as hostile to the church, some ministers used it to defend Christianity against other religions. William Eden employed it as a scholarly reference to establish the amount of tea consumed in Britain, while the Comte de Mirabeau soaked up its endorsement of global trade and criticisms of Spain and Portugal. The famous botanist George Louis Leclerc, Comte de Buffon relied on *Two Indies* for its geographical details regarding continents, seas, and lakes. John Curry's treatise on bleaching used the work for its expertise on China; likewise when the Reverend Singleton Harpur preached the dangers of drunkenness, he cited Raynal as an expert on Chinese opium smoking. In his magisterial *The Decline and Fall of the Roman Empire*, Edward Gibbon cited Raynal for obscure facts regarding the camphor tree. One English critic noted the "surprising circulation [of *Two Indies*] in all parts of Europe, as a companion at the idle hours of the toilet of the luxurious and ignorant." Nonetheless, he insisted the work was "a motley mixture of infidelity and credulity, of affectation, error and conceit." There was something in Raynal's work for everyone.[33]

The 1770 Version

There was no chance that a book like this could be openly published anywhere in the French kingdom. The first edition was printed in a six-volume octavo edition carrying the date 1770 and a false place of publication (Amsterdam) on the title page, without any indication of author or publisher. Likely printed in Paris with the object of distributing there, it falsely claimed a Dutch provenance as an import from Amsterdam. However, all copies of this stock seem to have languished for two years in a Paris warehouse for reasons that are still unclear.[34] *History of the Two Indies* became commercially available in the spring of 1772. During that summer Voltaire described it to Catherine the Great as a "new book."[35] One popular commentator predicted that any copies smuggled into Paris would be destroyed by the government "because of the storm" it was causing. This early reviewer was shocked that the author—identified in reviews even at this early stage as Raynal—had used the genre of an encyclopedic history as a vehicle for a polemic. "One finds opinions so forceful, bold, daring and opposing principles on which despotisms are really established, that it is difficult to imagine that anyone will tolerate its publication for very long."[36] Given the tenor of these early voices, it is clear that the gossip and well-known insider Horace Walpole was speaking for more than himself when he wrote this long colorful description in a letter from Paris to Lady Ailesbury:

> I am almost too indignant to tell you of a most amusing book in six volumes, called *Histoire philosophique et politique du commerce des deux Indes*. It tells one everything in the world, how to make conquests, invasions, blunders, settlements, bankruptcies, fortunes, etc.; tells you the natural and historical history of all nations; talks commerce, navigation, tea, coffee, china, mines, salt, spices; of the Portuguese, English, French, Dutch, Danes, Spaniards, Arabs, caravans, Persians, Indians, of Louis XIV and the King of Prussia; of La Bourdonnois, Dupleix, and Admiral Saunders; of rice and women that dance naked; of camels, ginghams and muslin; of millions and millions of livres, pounds rupees and gowries; of iron, cables, and Circassian women; of Law and the Mississippi; and against all governments and religions. This and everything else is in the two first volumes. I cannot conceive what is left for the four others. And all is so mixed, that you learn forty new trades and fifty new histories in a single chapter. There is spirit, wit, and clearness—and if there were but less avoirdupois weight in it, it would be the richest book in the world in materials—but figures to me are so many ciphers, and only put me in mind of children that say, an hundred hundred hundred millions.[37]

The government's attempts to halt the circulation of *Two Indies* only increased demand. There were four reprint editions of the six-volume set produced in 1772, and another eleven reprintings in 1773. Most appeared in octavo format, but at least seven editions were in the cheaper and smaller duodecimo format, presumably with larger print runs.

While all editions continued to identify "Amsterdam" on the title page, bibliographers have determined that these editions were printed mostly in Lyon, Rouen, Maastricht (southern Netherlands), and Liège (then an independent principality just across France's northern border in what today is Belgium). It immediately became one of Europe's best-selling books, especially during the fifteen-year period 1772–87, when this mostly eight- or ten-volume work went through more than fifty editions.[38]

In December 1772, France's royal council declared war against the *History of the Two Indies*, promising to suppress the work by preventing it from being sold or even given away. More than any other book, Chief Minister Maurepas, writing in the name of the king, proclaimed that its "bold, dangerous, and reckless" principles were "contrary to good manners and religious principles." And for good measure, Maurepas added that the work was more offensive than any other conceivable book.[39] From the government's viewpoint, *Two Indies* undermined France's fragile efforts to compete with Britain and Holland in overseas dominion; it made France and its king appear despotic and ineffective; and perhaps more lethal, it offended every Christian, whether Protestant or Catholic. Nonetheless, government intervention was largely ineffective: Far from diminishing demand for the work, criminalizing it only led the French and other Europeans to clamor for copies.

The 1774 Version

In 1774, the father and son firm of Pierre and Frederic Gosse published at The Hague an entirely overhauled seven-volume version, including many corrections and hundreds of pages of additional text, including new charts, tables, and maps. An eighth volume was also added to the project, called the *Tableau de l'Europe*, which was a thematic recapitulation of old material. In this way, owners of the 1770 version could simply purchase this single volume to keep up-to-date, rather than buy an entirely new multivolume set. Although the title pages included the real name and place of the publisher, the work was still published anonymously—Raynal's participation now an open secret. One could purchase separately an unidentified portrait of Raynal, which binders and bookstores inserted as a frontispiece. The French Lieutenant of Police Sartine ordered his chief book inspector, d'Hémery, to do whatever he could to halt its entry into France. Despite the best efforts of the government, however, publication of the 1774 version continued to surge, as the press referred to it as a "famous book."[40] Printers in Lyon, Maastricht, Geneva, Dublin, and Liège set about pirating the new version. Reprinted at least five times during 1774, it went through nine more editions before the decade was over. Among the version's new material was a chapter in the seventh volume on the raging conflict between London and its North American colonies; it became so popular that it was published as a separate pamphlet in Philadelphia and reprinted in American newspapers to aid their cause.[41]

Younger Europeans also benefited from learning about the American conflict. One such reader was twenty-two-year-old Manon Phlipon (the future Madame Roland), who read Raynal with unusual insight. As she wrote her friend Sophie Cannet, Raynal's account of the American conflict illustrated to her that traditional warfare led by a king who commands an army across borders was quickly becoming obsolete. From now on, peoples were forming their own armies to throw out their oppressors. Raynal taught Phlipon that in America "entire peoples are agitating and fighting for liberty and the public good." She regarded the British soldiers there as "slaves who fight wearing their chains, fulfilling the fantasies of their masters."[42]

While its popularity is undeniable, there must have been very few readers like Mary Urwin of Huntingdon, England, who had every word of every volume of the 1774 version read to her aloud by the poet William Cowper, even though he often had to rest his hoarse voice after an hour or so. Cowper appreciated the *History of the Two Indies* for both its erudition and its novel political viewpoint. He noted how through Raynal common "Country Folks" were exposed to fascinating areas of the world that previously had been entirely outside their domain. Likewise, Cowper admired Raynal "as a philosopher, as a writer, as a man of extraordinary intelligence. . . . He is a true patriot, but then the world is his country." Assuming Cowper's reminiscences were accurate, his experience provides another example of how *History of the Two Indies* expanded the reach of Enlightenment books among a growing reading public.

This version of *History of the Two Indies* became popular among Italian readers. During the 1770s, French versions were shared from hand to hand in Siena, Venice, Naples, and several other towns. They recognized in Raynal someone who had earned "glory through the mastery of eloquence." By the mid-1770s, Italian journals were citing the book as among the great works of the era. In 1776 and 1777 a group of Sienese intellectuals produced an Italian translation in eighteen volumes. The next year, a different abridged translation appeared in Venice, eliminating all material offensive to the Catholic Church. A year later, this sanitized edition was reprinted in Genoa.[43]

Meanwhile, the Vatican's Congregation of the Index denounced the *Two Indies*. A seasoned priest, Giuseppe Vasco, was assigned to the case, and he painstakingly prepared a dossier against the work that was heard by the Congregation in August 1774. Vasco selected 140 of the most offensive sentences, divided thematically into different folders: Against the Holy Office, Against good morals, Against Rome, Against dogmas, Favor of Toleration, Against the Crusades, Against the monarchy, Regarding the Jesuits, Calumny against the religions orders. If this history had been largely a scholarly affair, aimed solely at experts in the Republic of Letters, church and government leaders might have looked the other way. But because of its bestseller status, the book had become dangerous to both. On April 22, 1776, the Congregation announced that *History of the Two Indies* was officially included in the Index of Prohibited Books. Meanwhile, France's General Assembly of the French Clergy concurred that Raynal was "one of the most seditious authors among the modern skeptics."[44]

The 1780 Version

In 1780, a third version was published, again filled with additional material (including hundreds of new contributions from Diderot), and made especially relevant because of the American War of Independence and the ensuing conflict between Britain and France. Raynal directly supervised its publication and may have even personally received money from subscribers.[45] The first printing of this new version was produced in a lavish four-volume quarto edition by Jean Léonard Pellet, a small publisher in Geneva who specialized in anticlerical and Enlightenment tracts. "Made with great care and rare magnificence," one notice read, this expensive edition was aimed at the intelligentsia and affordable only by the very rich.[46] A group of Paris booksellers, who knew their clientele very well, financed the edition.[47] Knowing that he had a blockbuster on his hands, Pellet and his partners followed this quarto edition immediately with a more affordable 10-volume octavo edition totaling some 4,800 pages. When Geneva pastors protested its publication as offensive to morals, the Genevan city council overruled them.[48] Within weeks the Société typographique de Neuchâtel, among the most notorious pirating publishers, came out with a cheaper duodecimo edition (without most of the graphs, tables, and maps) which quickly sold out like its predecessor.[49] The octavo and duodecimo formats were endlessly pirated and reprinted, and new translations were produced in several languages, an extraordinary range for any publication. Altogether, an astounding 57 editions of the multivolume set were published between 1770 and 1800, well more than one set per year. Few erudite books of any kind were more popular during the eighteenth century than the *History of the Two Indies*.

This 1780 version was only the core of what became a virtual publishing industry, with several offshoots, abridgements, and extracts. Editions were printed in Maastricht and The Hague of "Supplements" that included only new material, so that those who had incurred already significant investments in purchasing the 1770 or 1774 versions might not need to purchase the entire set over again. Pellet published an autonomous atlas, much admired for its quality, involving a lavishly produced quarto volume of fifty engraved maps and over twenty statistical charts that fully illustrated material from the history. Sold independently, the atlas went through six editions by 1784.[50]

However popular was the multivolume set, only committed readers were willing to purchase and/or read such a large and weighty history. Many printers, editors, and hack writers saw an easy opportunity. Raynal's work was sliced and diced in a myriad of ways. One scholar has counted at least forty editions of extracts in German, Dutch, Italian, English, and French. By selecting and distilling its most radical parts and often excluding the more studious chronological histories, these compendia made the book appear even more polemical than it actually was. In 1787, one seventy-six-page compilation put selections from *History of the Two Indies* alongside Rousseau's *Discourse on Political Economy* and Montesquieu's *The Spirit of the Laws*—allotting seven pages to Montesquieu, four pages to Rousseau, and over sixty pages to Raynal. A bit later, during the lead-up to the meeting of the French Estates General in 1789, when the normal rules governing press censorship loosened, one entrepreneurial French editor reformulated *History of the Two Indies* extracts into a sixty-five-page pamphlet advising the regime how to reform itself.[51]

The 1780 version also included updated material analyzing the American War of Independence. While preparing the new edition, Raynal specifically called for leaders to send him documents, so his narrative could be accurate and authoritative. John Adams complied. "The Abby Reynel [*sic*] is writing an History of this Revolution, and is very desirous of obtaining authentic Documents," he wrote to at least one friend. "Can you help him to any?"[52] Not surprisingly, *Two Indies* sided with the Americans, although not without some criticisms of their motivation, and was generally against British policy. Soon publishers extracted this lively material and printed it as a single volume work (in both French and English versions) entitled *The Revolution of America*. Sold throughout revolutionary America from editions published in New York, Pennsylvania, Connecticut, and Massachusetts, this offshoot alone went through thirteen editions between 1781 and 1783. Among the first histories of the conflict, these excerpts became the earliest and among the most popular options for Americans to teach themselves about events that led up to their revolution. Sometimes, as in the case of James Madison, their popularity led to ordering the entire set of the *History of the Two Indies* from France.[53]

One of Raynal's sternest critics turned out to be among his closest American allies. In 1782, Thomas Paine, already famous for his popular pro-American pamphlet, *Common Sense*, published his *Letter to the Abbé Raynal*, ostensibly a scathing attack on Raynal as an historian. "Though the Abbé possesses and displays great powers of genius, and is a master of style and language, he seems not to pay equal attention to the office of an historian." In particular, Paine accused Raynal of being soft on Britain; he attacked Raynal for not indicting the English with the same passionate rhetoric that was used to denounce the slave trade and massacres of indigenous people. For Paine, what the English had done to the Americans was just as bad. "The Abbé is wrong even in the foundation of his work; that is, he has misconceived and mis-stated the causes which produced the rupture between England and her colonies."[54]

Paine's reaction may have reflected a general unhappiness with Raynal's account by the new American elite. For example, Thomas Jefferson confided to John Adams that all three versions of Raynal's work "were equally bad as to both South and North America."[55] Nonetheless, Paine's outrage was perhaps exaggerated. While Raynal may not have portrayed the British in America along the lines of the Spanish in South America, the truth is that neither did Paine. In fact, Paine and Raynal were very much on the same side; both strongly supported the American War of Independence. The differences between the two thinkers were minuscule. At the time of Paine's *Letter*, Raynal's *Revolution of America* was quickly becoming its own bestseller in North America. Paine's *Letter* was a brazen attempt to climb onto Raynal's shoulders and share some of his authorial glory. Both Raynal's extract and Paine's *Letter*, after all, were designed to rally ordinary readers to the American cause.

Paine, however, also attacked Raynal along other lines. He accused the French author of plagiarizing his early pamphlet, *Common Sense*. He even graphically compared sentences in side-by-side columns. "I observe the Abbé has made a sort of epitome of a considerable part of the pamphlet *Common Sense*, and introduced it in that form into his publication . . . without acknowledging it."[56] The charge stuck: Raynal's critics gave him the reputation of a compiler more than an original author. But Paine misunderstood the intent of the *History of the Two Indies*. Although filled with original sections and polemical insertions, it was never meant to be a wholly original work, along the lines of Edward Gibbon, David Hume, or William Robertson. Rather, Raynal and his group envisioned the *History of the Two Indies* at least partly as a great collection of information gathered from many sources. In this respect, they modeled their work somewhat on Diderot's *Encyclopédie*, which borrowed freely from many other works, and other English multivolume enterprises, such as the very popular *An Universal History, from the Earliest Account of Time, Compiled from Original Writers* (London, 1747–66) and *An Account of the European Settlements in America* (London, 1757). The uniqueness of the *History of the Two Indies* was precisely its appeal simultaneously as an encyclopedic reference work and a radical political treatise.[57]

In 1777, a young French monk named Jean Baptiste Antoine Hédouin became devoted to Raynal's cause after reading the book. He decided to make a compilation of his favorite passages and publish it secretly and anonymously in France under the title *Esprit et Génie de l'Abbé Raynal*. This time the government tracked the anthology back to its printers in Paris, and roughly shuttered the booksellers, using them as a "severe example." The author went into hiding for a few months but was otherwise left alone. A year or two after the 1780 version was published, Hédouin's compilation surfaced again, this time from publishers across the border in Switzerland.[58]

We know a great deal about the Dutch translation, thanks to the dogged research of Roberto Salverda. The ten-volume set took eight years to print (1775–83) and drew from all three French versions. Six hundred copies were printed, divided between 265 advanced subscribers (who received a 50 percent price discount) and the rest sold by eighty-five booksellers throughout the country and beyond. About one-third of the run was sold in Amsterdam. At least sixty copies were sold to residents of Dutch colonies, including Surinam and Java, demonstrating that colonialists themselves desired to read this damning history of colonialism. The subscribers represented a cross section of the Dutch elite: civic leaders, clergymen, physicians, and merchants. A large number of copies were ordered for book clubs and libraries. A decade later, the set was reprinted with a new translation based entirely on the French 1780 version.[59]

The *History of the Two Indies* inspired Russian radicals to think differently about their own government. Although already well read in Rousseau, Montesquieu, and Voltaire, it was Raynal's work that inspired the nobleman Alexander Radishchev to author *A Journey from St. Petersburg to Moscow* (1790), a scathing criticism of Catherine the Great's administration. Applying the lessons of Diderot's exhortations to support oppressed natives against the Europeans invaders, Radishchev pleaded with his countrymen to side with the serfs, championing the cause of the notorious Yemelyan Pugachev, the leader of a string of violent rebellions against the government in the 1770s. Arrested and tried for conspiring against the state, Radishchev disavowed his book, blaming everything on Raynal. "I took his passionate tone for eloquence, his bold expressions I considered to be in excellent taste, and seeing him universally read, I wanted to imitate his style," he declared at his trial. "And so I may truthfully state that Raynal's style, drawing me on from delusion to delusion, led to the completion of my insane book."[60]

The French government was increasingly frustrated by the spread of a work it had long deemed illegal for distribution. For years, its agents had tried everything they could to block the book's circulation in France. Normally, a few arrests would choke supply well enough to cause the work to become too expensive for purchase by most readers. For a few months in 1772, that tactic seemed to work. But inevitably, another new edition was printed by an unknown pirate printer, using novel supply routes into Paris. By the early 1780s, book pirates had learned how to outwit the government. According to Robert Darnton, between 1772 and 1786, no book was confiscated more by Paris customs than the *History of the Two Indies*. And yet, they captured only forty-five copies out of thousands circulating in France.[61] One exasperated Habsburg agent exclaimed that despite the work's offensive impiety, one version or another had already found its way "in every library in the world."[62]

While the 1770 and 1774 versions of the *History of the Two Indies* were published anonymously, the 1780 version was the first in which the author's name, Guillaume Thomas Raynal, was printed on the title page along with his captioned portrait serving as the frontispiece of the first volume (see Figure 12.2). While his authorship had been known for years, and some pirated editions included his portrait (without any name in the caption), the title page remained anonymous until 1780.

The inclusion of Raynal's name and named portrait ignited a scandal all its own. As long as a work was published anonymously, the responsibility for its content lay with the publishers and booksellers, who sold the book under the counter and confused officials with false publication data on the title page. Even if the author's identity was an open secret, the French government would generally not prosecute unless the name appeared on the title page. The fact that Raynal agreed to place his name on the title page and included his portrait was a slap in the face of the baroque censorship system, and it angered even liberal officials. In their eyes, it constituted a brazen act of insubordination and vanity that could not go unpunished.[63] For many critics, especially those in the church who were offended by Raynal's criticism of missionaries and his respect for indigenous pagan faiths, this feature was "the most revolting" because it demonstrated that he had lost all "decency and modesty."[64]

The government of Louis XVI now felt that it had to act with more force; at stake was not only the rickety censorship system but also the ability of the government to protect against attacks on the church. During the spring of 1781, the Parlement of Paris moved against Raynal and his history. Previously, the Parlement seldom became directly involved in prosecuting a book. In 1759 it had acted against the *Encyclopédie* and

Figure 12.2 Frontispiece of 1780 edition showing the author's portrait. This portrait of Raynal, along with his name serving as a caption, repeated on the facing title page, shocked convention everywhere, challenging statesmen to take action. As a result, Raynal was forced to flee France and remained an outlaw until the French Revolution.

Helvétius's *De l'Esprit*. In both cases, however, the authors were pretty much left alone. However, as we saw in Chapter 10, three years later the Parlement had tried to arrest Rousseau for the publication of *Emile*, and he was forced into exile, unable to return to France until 1770. Something similar now happened to Raynal. The Parlement ordered its officers "to seize upon the body of Abbé Raynal" and to "confiscate his property."[65] Instantly Raynal replaced Rousseau and Voltaire (both died in 1778) as France's number one intellectual pariah. He lost no time in fleeing France, taking refuge in the Austrian Netherlands (today Belgium). Fortunately, the reform-minded Emperor Joseph II had just ascended the Habsburg throne and allowed Raynal permanent residency there if he promised to refrain from any political and religious writings.[66]

The case against Raynal's work was brought by veteran Parlement judge Anthony Louis Séguier. Europeans followed the proceedings closely in the press, and Séguier's speech to Parlement was even published in English. His condemnation was not at all a personal attack. There was very little about Raynal the man. It was as if Raynal were merely a symbol of a larger group of philosophes. Séguier viewed the controversy as representative of a much larger culture war in which *History of the Two Indies* embodied "the spirit of philosophy, which becomes more and more the spirit of the times" against church and state. Under the pretense of championing commerce, science, and the arts, the judge argued, Raynal blatantly sought to undermine the foundations of both the French Gallican Church and the monarchy of Louis XVI. "Kings are his tyrants, and the ministers of the Church his hypocrites." Séguier insisted that the philosophes were not reformers or improvers, but bent on destroying the foundations of society, and acting arrogantly without regard for what has made Europe prosper. "O Philosophy," he cried out seemingly to the entire Enlightenment at once. "You expect to be adored as a propitious divinity upon earth! You wish to break that chain which unites the sovereign and his people." Séguier wanted everyone to know that Raynal's work was anything but a scholarly history of European settlement. Characterized by "impiety, audaciousness, irreligion, and disrespect," its goal was nothing less than the "subversion of all civil order." On Tuesday, May 29, 1782, a copy of the Pellet octavo edition of *History of the Two Indies* was torn apart and burned below the grand staircase of the Parlement's Palace of Justice by the King's Executioner.[67]

The Parlement's actions against Raynal were complemented by the results of a similar investigation by the Sorbonne faculty. In 1781 appeared a 114-page comprehensive attack upon the *History of the Two Indies*, with facing columns of French and Latin. Not surprisingly, the faculty echoed the Parlement in its overall evaluation of the work. "The pretext of a history offers an excuse for the author to exhale the poison of impiety that fills his heart."[68] This condemnation was organized around eighty-four brief quotations, arranged thematically into groups, and the groups into "articles" and "titles." The rebuttals usually followed a particular group of quotations. For example, Title 8 regards Original Sin and contains four quotations from three volumes, followed by the "censure," that is, by an analysis of its errors. Some of the topics are more overtly political than theological. For example, Article IV, Title II, the last grouping, concerns the "remedies put forth by the author regarding tyranny," and includes analyses of nine quotations. The faculty concluded by calling Raynal's work "seditious and rebellious," asserting that the only way for his ideas to gain ground would be by making himself the enemy of "the King, the fatherland, and humanity."[69]

Although these swift and forceful responses by church and state forced Raynal into exile, once again they seemed only to intensify demand for *Two Indies*. This is demonstrated by Raynal's publisher, Pellet, who in 1783 reprinted the Sorbonne's condemnation without any alteration in a volume of diverse responses to Raynal's work. In other words, Pellet most likely believed that far from hurting book sales, reprinting the condemnation itself could be used as a marketing tool to increase even further demand for the *History*. Clearly this put the government authorities in a bind. Indeed, a lesson first highlighted by Voltaire was that the government and church publicized a book by criminalizing it. Publication of state and church objections to the book served as seductive anthologies that highlighted its most offensive passages, and were quoted by the press with obvious effect.

By 1781 the *History of the Two Indies* had become recognized as among the most influential and popular works of the Enlightenment. "If there ever existed a work that had such universal praise," wrote Simon Henri Linguet in his monthly periodical, "it is the *History of the Two Indies*." This did not mean Linguet admired everything about the work. In particular, he found its radical politics obnoxious: How dare Raynal urge Black slaves to rebel against their European masters! Such childish tantrums have no place in a work of serious history, charged Linguet. Nonetheless, such sharp criticism did not stop Linguet from celebrating the work as "among the most interesting literary works of this century."[70] The same attitude was seen earlier in Grimm's *Correspondance Littéraire*: "Since *The Spirit of the Laws*, our literature has produced no greater work more deserving to be passed down to posterity as having produced our enlightenment and improvement."[71]

Readers naturally compared Raynal to other great historians of the day, such as William Robertson, whose own *History of America*, first published in 1777 was immediately translated into French. "Amongst modern writers on American affairs, the most famous and esteemed are the Abbé Raynal and Dr. Robertson," a British observer noted.[72] Another reader was unsure which was preferred, but noted that Raynal's "is in general admired, and was mentioned to me as far surpassing that of Robertson."[73] No less a historian than David Hume gave his endorsement to Raynal, whom he had met in Paris. But Hume also suspected that the *History of the Two Indies* was too large a project for any one writer. At least "the eloquence must have been borrowed," he told James Boswell. Hume speculated that Raynal must have had help from other writers; he "cannot have written that book himself."[74]

The political thinker William Godwin was another reader who preferred Raynal to Robertson. While Robertson, along with Hume and Gibbon, provided readers a sense of impartiality, Godwin admired Raynal precisely because he took the side of indigenous peoples against European colonialists, making no pretense to objectivity. The quest for impartiality "has spoiled half the well written histories in the world." How could one not judge Nero's cruelties as despicable? Instead of objectivity, Godwin argued, historians should write with engagement, from a committed sense about how to improve the world. "The first writer that has had the spirit to assert it, in its fullest extent, seems to have been the celebrated Abbé Raynal."[75]

Another innovative way that Raynal himself kept the *History of the Two Indies* in front of the public was by financing a series of essay contests through the many academic and scientific academies that had proliferated across the globe. In 1783 alone, Raynal funded essay contests in Lyon, Philadelphia, Madrid, Lisbon, London, and Calcutta on the following question: "Has the discovery of America been useful or harmful to mankind? If something positive has come from it, what are the means to conserve and increase these goods? If the discovery has created only wrongs, what are the means to remedy the situation?" This was, of course, the main question that *History of the Two Indies* itself investigated. No wonder, then, that most of the entries not only cited Raynal's work repeatedly, siding with the author that the New World discoveries resulted in more harm than good, but also offered the abolition of slavery as the one remedy immediately necessary. Each contest created its own splash. The 1783 Academy of Lyon contest generated fifty-four entries, all of them read by Raynal himself. Between

1780 and 1794, Raynal took his earnings from the book's success and funded thirty-three contests, many of them on this same topic. No other eighteenth-century author financed so many essay contests. As Jeremy Caradonna argues, by seeding the book in so many essay contests, Raynal helped popularize his Enlightenment ideas among a large group of educated people throughout Europe and its colonies.[76] As a result, Europeans acknowledged Raynal as among the greatest Enlightenment philosophes. "Bayle, Voltaire, Jean-Jacques Rousseau, Raynal," wrote one observer in 1783, "have for more than a century prepared enlightenment."[77]

Slavery and the *Two Indies*

At the same time that these academic contests were taking place, the 1780 version of *History of the Two Indies* became a foundation text for the burgeoning abolitionist movement. In 1783, the first British abolitionist association planted excerpts from *History of the Two Indies* in newspapers such as *Lloyd's Evening Post*.[78] Thomas Day (who we met in Chapter 10) used an epigraph from Raynal's work on the title page of one of his popular anti-slavery pamphlets, *Remarks on the Slave Trade*, that quoted Raynal directly. John Beatson's fiery sermons published in 1789 included excerpts from Raynal. In 1781, Anthony Benezet published in Philadelphia a short pamphlet that excerpted anti-slavery sections from *Two Indies*, hailing Raynal as "that celebrated philosopher and friend to mankind." James White invoked the "sagacious Abbé Raynal" in calling "for a specific plan for an abolition of the slave trade." William Dickson's *Letters on Slavery* quoted Raynal and Montesquieu as if they were equals. Raynal's work was not only celebrated by abolitionists, it quickly became the key authority for slave trade statistics. "The Abbé Raynal states the total importation from Africa at nine millions of slaves," noted Beilby Porteus in a sermon from 1783. When Thomas Clarkson came to publish his authoritative history of the abolitionist movement in 1808, reprinted several times during the nineteenth century, *History of the Two Indies* was featured among the abolitionist movement's founding textbooks.[79]

Ironically, the more *History of the Two Indies* became associated with the cause of abolishing slavery during the 1780s and 1790s, the further its lead author, Guillaume Thomas Raynal, tried to move away from radical politics. Perhaps Raynal had never embraced the more radical ideas of Diderot and other contributors. Samuel Romilly, for example, was one British abolitionist whose radicalism had been inspired by the *History of the Two Indies*. Excited to meet Raynal during a trip to Switzerland in 1787, he recoiled in horror over Raynal's "cold and indifferent" attitude toward the slave trade.[80] As Raynal aged into the Revolution—he turned seventy-six in 1789—his attitudes became more conservative. Siding sometimes with white colonists trying to manage the West Indian colonies, and at other times, purposively disassociating himself from French

Revolutionary republicans, Raynal became an embarrassment to the cause for which his name was associated. And yet, since his later writings were so comparatively minor, the radical brand associated with his major opus continued to shape his reputation. The public insisted on regarding him as the iconic spokesman against slavery.[81]

The reputation of *History of the Two Indies* as a key abolitionist text is nowhere better presented than in the remarkable painting by Anne Louis Girodet, *Citizen Jean-Baptiste Belley, Ex-Representative of the Colonies* (see Figure 12.3). In 1791, slaves on France's most profitable colony, Saint-Domingue, began a revolt that would last several years and eventually result in the establishment of Haiti, the first state in the Western Hemisphere created by free Blacks. In 1793, commissioners from the French National Convention tried to negotiate with the leaders of the revolt. Fearing that Saint-Domingue would fall into British or Spanish hands, the commissioners declared slavery abolished in the colony, and engineered elections for three deputies—one white, one of mixed race, and one Black—to the French National Convention. The winner of the "Black" slot was Jean-Baptiste Belley, a former slave born in Senegal, who had become a military commander in the uprising, and who had defended the commissioners against their enemies. Belley and the other deputies arrived in France in September 1793,

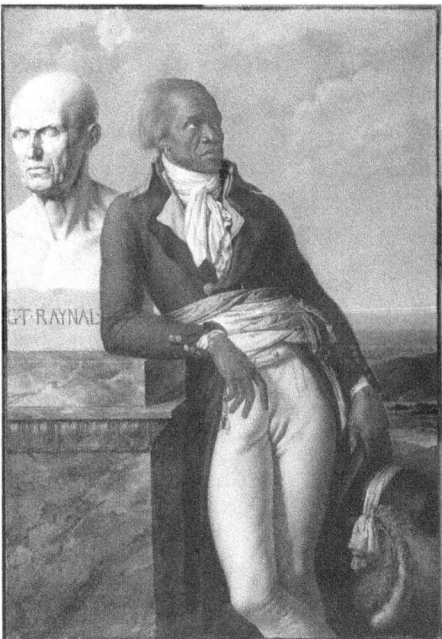

Figure 12.3 Painting: Citizen Jean-Baptiste Belley, Ex-Representative of the Colonies by Anne Louis Girodet. This painting of the first Black French legislator leaning on Raynal's bust plays on the mythology that Enlightenment ideas were responsible for slave revolts and eventually the abolition of slavery.

and were seated in the Convention on February 15, 1794, making him the first Black deputy serving in a French legislature. One day later, on February 16, 1794, the National Convention issued an historic decree abolishing slavery throughout its territories. Belley continued to represent Saint-Domingue for three years, first in the Convention and then in the Council of 500.[82]

Painted in 1797, one year after Raynal's death, and just before the retired Belley returned to Saint-Domingue, this beautiful portrait shows him in a moment of repose, leaning against a bust of Raynal. It is not the military commander portrayed here, but the student of the Enlightenment, who is leaning on Raynal's radical ideas to transform political life. His thoughtful contemplation about the public good is itself presented here as a critically important activity. For this revolutionary military leader, rational vision inspired by reading books such as Raynal's precedes and shapes action. His clothes—his outer shell—are European, in the flamboyant style of the Directory. He identifies with his Parisian peers. But inside that shell is clearly a tougher person from a different culture, symbolized by the earring, something then unfashionable in France. Indeed, the artist's interpretation of Belley may not have been exaggerated. After the diplomat Alexandre Hauterive met Belley and his Caribbean colleague, he jotted in his diary that "these two blacks have the air of good faces; the most humane character expresses itself in the dusky tone of their faces, all they have gotten from the Revolution is the confidence provided by the certainty that their color does not degrade them."[83]

This beautiful painting is a study in contrasts. The Black politician is learning against, but also turning away from, the white Enlightenment author. The painting celebrates the abolition of slavery and credits Raynal's great history with helping to end it. Here Girodet emphasizes that revolutionary change relied upon Enlightenment ideas. Although Belley's work will live forever, Raynal is dead, set in stone, and the *History of the Two Indies* can only come to life through Belley's reading, reflection, and action. In this sense, the meaning of the painting is ambiguous, if not ironic: although Belley leans upon Raynal, it is Raynal who now depends upon Belley. Books are not worth much if their ideas are not implemented by readers inspired by them. Girodet's Belley is thus more than a portrait of a man; it is a history painting commemorating the revolution's act of self-emancipation. In Belley we see the liberating future of all of France's Black population throughout its colonies.

A critic writing at the Salon of 1798, where the painting was first exhibited, quoted a woman viewer exclaiming:

> Yes, Black, but not so much a devil. Seeing him closer I find him admirable. . . . How mistaken I was. Yes, learned Girodet, this tableau pleases me! A respite from caustic humor, not a satirical feature. Never will criticism strike down your talents. Really, really, this portrait speaks.[84]

The notion that Enlightenment political thought in the form of *History of the Two Indies* inspired the abolition of slavery in Saint-Domingue became a potent myth when it was directly linked with the greatest Black leader of the Haitian Revolution, the former slave

François Dominique Toussaint Louverture. Toussaint's supposed debt to Raynal's work is chronicled in the Trinidadian author C. R. L. James's popular history of that revolution, *The Black Jacobins*, first published in 1938 and the standard work on the subject well into the 1980s. Like Girodet's Belley, James's Toussaint relies upon his reading of the *History of the Two Indies* for the inspiration to revolt. "It came into the hands of the slave most fitted to make use of it," James tells us. "Over and over again," James has Toussaint reading Book 11 regarding the evils of slavery and the Atlantic slave trade, focusing his keen attention on this dramatic 1780 Diderot interpolation from Chapter 24:

> Where is the great man, whom nature owes to her afflicted, oppressed, and tormented children? Where is he? He will undoubtedly appear, he will shew himself, he will lift up the sacred standard of liberty. This venerable signal will collect around him the companions of his misfortunes. They will rush on with more impetuosity than torrents; they will leave behind them, in all parts, indelible traces of their just resentment. Spaniards, Portuguese, English, French, Dutch, all their tyrants will become the victims of fire and sword. The plains of America will suck up with transport the blood which they have so long expected, and the bones of so many wretches, heaped upon one another, during the course of so many centuries, will bound for joy. The Old World will join its plaudits to those of the New. In all parts the name of the hero who shall have restored the rights of the human species, will be blessed; in all parts trophies will be erected to his glory. Then will the Black Code be no more; and the White Code will be a dreadful one, if the conqueror only regards the right of reprisals.[85]

It is one thing to commend Diderot for his prescient insight; it is something else to link concretely Diderot's words with Toussaint's insurrection. Like the manner in which Girodet paints Belley leaning against Raynal's bust, James insists that Toussaint's reading of Diderot's prophetic passage in *History of the Two Indies* led him directly into radicalism, rebellion, insurrection, and finally emancipation.[86]

James had borrowed Toussaint's early absorption of *History of the Two Indies* from the nineteenth-century British Unitarian minister, John Relly Beard, whose *The Life of Toussaint L'Ouverture*, was first published in 1853. Toussaint "had heard passages recited from Raynal. He procured the work," Beard claimed. "And now he found how much is involved in the simple art of reading. Toussaint could read." Beard's biography reproduced most of the famous 24th chapter of Book 11, including its call for a "great man." Beard also included an original illustration of Toussaint in his home absorbed in reading Raynal, with a quill nearby and other books in the background (see Figure 12.4). Like Girodet's Belley, there could be no missing here Toussaint's debt to Enlightenment political thought.[87]

The notion that the Haitian Revolution's core ideology stemmed from Raynal's *History of the Two Indies* had become commonplace even before Beard's biography. In Alphonse de Lamartine's 1850 play about Raynal, the myth was recycled as if common knowledge. Toussaint, wrote Lamartine in the preface to the play, "firmly believed that

Figure 12.4 Toussaint Reading the Abbé Raynal's Work. This illustration of Toussaint L'Ouverture supposedly reading Raynal's *History of Two Indies* as a young man was first published in John R. Beard, *The Life of Toussaint L'Ouverture* (London: Ingram, 1853).

he is the man announced by the Abbé Raynal who must one day arise to break the chains of the blacks."[88] When composing his influential work on the Enlightenment in 1878, John Morley took the tale for granted:

> Black Toussaint Louverture in his slave-cabin at Hayti laboriously spelled his way through its pages, and found in their story of the wrongs of his race and their passionate appeal against slavery, the first definite expression of thought which had already been dimly stirred by the brutalities that were everyday enacted under his eyes.[89]

Meanwhile, on the other side of the Atlantic, the Black writer and American college president William J. Simmons asserted the same story in a book published in 1887: "There was a French Author called Abbé Raynal, who was much opposed to slavery. One of his books fell into the hands of Toussaint and made a deep impression upon him."[90]

How true is this story? Postcolonial literary scholars and historians have questioned this story as a European fantasy meant to undermine the agency of Caribbean slaves.

After all, Raynal is not mentioned in Toussaint's published memoir,[91] and there is no direct evidence confirming his early reading of Raynal. Meanwhile, Haitians did not need the Declaration of the Rights of Man to point the way to slave rebellion; Caribbean slaves had been rebelling throughout the eighteenth century, whenever they had the chance to overcome oppressive forces. What made the Haitian situation distinctive was certainly its French Revolutionary context, but it was no prerequisite. Toussaint did not need Raynal whispering in his ear to become a rebellious leader. In this "francocentric theorizing," Louis Sala-Molins sarcastically writes, Toussaint "needed Raynal and Diderot to tell him in some big fat book to free himself before he could think of doing just that."[92]

While Sala-Molins and others are right to criticize how European writers have made use of Toussaint's reliance upon Raynal's book, there is, in fact, a reliable source text for verifying the core elements of this story. In November 1799, the semi-official newspaper of the French Revolution, the *Moniteur*, published an interview with Toussaint by a correspondent who had just returned to Paris from Saint-Domingue. There the journalist described Toussaint as a former slave with keen intelligence who taught himself to read as a boy and was always carefully observing white plantation behaviors and contradictions. From a young age Toussaint "was bewildered by just how close fatal slavery co-existed with liberty, and how a difference in skin could mark such an enormous distance between one man and another." From time to time, he would hear Raynal's book quoted among whites, which stimulated his curiosity. One day he finally procured a copy of *History of the Two Indies*. "The book kindled enthusiasm for universal emancipation." The aspect of the story that so impressed Lamartine, Beard, Simmons, and James shows up in this article: "His eye often gazed on the page where Raynal called for a liberator to rescue from Hell a large portion of humanity." When three years later the first biography of Toussaint was published in Paris, the *Moniteur*'s story of Toussaint's reading of Raynal was recycled there.[93]

Even if some parts of this account are exaggerated, there can be no doubt that Raynal's book was well known in late eighteenth-century Saint-Domingue, and may have become iconic during the insurrection. According to historian Robin Blackburn, scattered among civic building and government offices throughout the island were "busts and portraits of Raynal, who, rather than Rousseau or Condorcet, was adopted as the prophet of the new order."[94] Prominent in the libraries of wealthy plantation owners, slaves carted off *History of the Two Indies* for preservation before burning down the estates. Toussaint himself had become aware of people associating him with the savior prophesied in Book 11. For example, on April 1, 1796, the governor of the island, Etienne Laveaux, hailed Toussaint in a public ceremony as "the Black Spartacus, the leader announced by the philosopher Raynal to avenge the crimes perpetrated against his race."[95] Instead of weakening agency, Toussaint's deliberate linkage to Raynal shows how self-conscious he was to craft an image in a manner attractive to Haitians and Europeans alike.[96]

Regardless of how much *History of the Two Indies* affected Toussaint Louverture, it certainly impacted his nemesis, Napoleon Bonaparte, whose administration imprisoned

Toussaint in France, where he died in 1803, shortly after Napoleon had re-established slavery in Saint-Domingue. It is a strange dark irony that the same book that called for a new Spartacus to emancipate French slaves could impress a reader who one day would reverse such a course of history. As a teenager, the young Bonaparte was enthralled with the *History of the Two Indies*; as he himself wrote in a letter to Raynal, reading that book made him want to become an historian. He even took the liberty of attaching to the letter an essay he had written on the history of Corsica, his island homeland. "I am not yet eighteen, but I am already a writer; this is an age at which one must learn," he wrote to Raynal. In another essay written about the same time, Bonaparte exalted his favorite historian:

> Illustrious Raynal, if in the course of a life dedicated to unmasking the prejudices of the great, you have been constant and immovable in your zeal for suffering and oppressed humanity, deign today, amidst all the applause of the immense numbers who, summoned by you to liberty, duly pay homage to you, deign to smile on the efforts of a zealous disciple whose essays you have often sought to encourage. The question with which I shall concern myself is worthy of your stamp, but without having the ambition to rival your stature, I have said to myself, like Correggio: I too am a painter.

Nor would Bonaparte leave Raynal's work behind when he became a military general. In preparing for his mission to Egypt in 1798, he ordered the construction of a personal mobile library to house his favorite books, allowing him to peruse them in the far-away military campaign. Among the works in that portable library was *The Spirit of the Laws* and the *History of the Two Indies*.[97]

Notes

Introduction

1 Ernst Cassirer, *The Philosophy of the Enlightenment*, trans. Fritz C. A. Koelln and James P. Pettegrove (Princeton: Princeton University Press, 1951); Daniel Mornet, *Les Origines intellectuelles de la révolution française* (Paris: A. Colin, 1954 [1933]); Paul Hazard, *European Thought in the Eighteenth Century: From Montesquieu to Lessing*, trans. J. Lewis May (New Haven: Yale University Press, 1954); Carl Becker, *The Heavenly City of the Eighteenth-Century Philosophers* (New Haven: Yale University Press, 1932); *Carl Becker's Heavenly City Revisited*, ed. Raymond Oxley Rockwood (Ithaca: Cornell University Press, 1958).
2 "Forum: The Legacy of Alfred Cobban," *French History* 34 (2020): 512–60, especially 541–58, for the contribution by John Harvey. Cobban's most important contributions to Enlightenment scholarship were *Rousseau and the Modern State* (London: George Allen and Unwin, 1934) and *In Search of Humanity: The Role of the Enlightenment in Modern History* (London: Jonathan Cape, 1960). Cobban was the PhD advisor to my own PhD advisor, Keith Baker, who is arguably his most distinguished student in the intellectual history of the Enlightenment.
3 Peter Gay, *The Enlightenment: An Interpretation*, 2 vols. Volume One: *The Rise of Modern Paganism*. Volume Two: *The Science of Freedom* (New York: Knopf, 1966–9); *The Party of Humanity: Essays in the French Enlightenment* (New York: Knopf, 1964). Gay was influenced by Karl Mannheim, *Ideology and Utopia: An Introduction to the Sociology of Knowledge* (New York: Harcourt, Brace, 1936).
4 Peter Gay, *My German Question: Growing up in Nazi Berlin* (New Haven: Yale University Press, 1998).
5 Anthony Pagden, *The Enlightenment: And Why It Still Matters* (New York: Random House, 2013), 407. On using the Enlightenment in contemporary cultural debates, see also *What's Left of Enlightenment? A Postmodern Question*, eds. Keith Michael Baker and Peter Reill (Stanford: Stanford University Press, 2001). Another important history emphasizing literary and philosophical issues, particularly in German lands, appeared too late for my serious engagement: Ritchie Robertson, *The Enlightenment: The Pursuit of Happiness, 1680-1790* (New York: HarperCollins, 2021).
6 Steven Pinker, *Enlightenment Now: The Case for Reason, Science, Humanism, and Progress* (New York: Viking, 2018).
7 Robert Darnton, "In Search of the Enlightenment: Recent Attempts to Create a Social History of Ideas," *Journal of Modern History* 43 (1971): 113–32. For Darnton's other publications, see http://www.robertdarnton.org/publications. Accessed April 26, 2018. On Chartier and Roche see especially, Roger Chartier, *The Cultural Origins of the French Revolution*, trans. Lydia C. Cochrane (Durham: Duke University Press, 1991), and Daniel Roche, *France in the Enlightenment*, trans. Arthur Goldhammer (Cambridge, MA: Harvard University Press, 1998).

8 Robert Darnton, *The Business of Enlightenment: A Publishing History of the Encyclopédie 1775–1800* (Cambridge, MA: Harvard University Press, 1979).
9 Daniel Mornet, "Les Enseignements des bibliothêques privées (1750–1780)," *Revue d'histoire litteraire de la France* 17 (1910): 449–96.
10 Robert Darnton, *The Corpus of Clandestine Literature in France 1769–1789* (New York: Norton, 1995); *The Forbidden Best-Sellers of Pre-Revolutionary France* (New York: Norton, 1995).
11 Darnton, *Forbidden Best-Sellers of Pre-Revolutionary France*, 21.
12 Robert Darnton, *A Literary Tour de France: The World of Books on the Eve of the French Revolution* (New York: Oxford University Press, 2018), 282–3, updated on http://www.robertdarnton.org/literarytour/booksellers. Accessed September 29, 2018.
13 These points are the subject of Mark Curran, *The French Book Trade in Enlightenment Europe. 1. Selling Enlightenment* (London: Bloomsbury, 2018), and Simon Burrows, *The French Book Trade in Enlightenment Europe. 2. Enlightenment Bestsellers* (London: Bloomsbury, 2018). Darnton reviews these volumes at https://reviews.history.ac.uk/review/1355. Accessed May 20, 2021.
14 Robert Darnton, "The Case for the Enlightenment," in *George Washington's False Teeth: An Unconventional Guide to the Eighteenth Century* (New York: W.W. Norton, 2003), 3–24; Jeremy D. Popkin, "Robert Darnton's Alternative (to the) Enlightenment," in *The Darnton Debate: Books and Revolution in the Eighteenth Century*, eds. Haydn T. Mason (Oxford: Voltaire Foundation, 1998), 106–28.
15 See especially Dena Goodman, *The Republic of Letters: A Cultural History of the French Enlightenment* (Ithaca: Cornell University Press, 1994); and *Becoming a Woman in the Age of Letters* (Ithaca: Cornell University Press, 2009). Unfortunately, it is still too common to find otherwise distinguished historians banishing women from the Enlightenment. For example, Roger Emerson wrote in 2009: "The Scottish population in 1700 was about 1,100,000 and had increased to 1,600,000 by 1800. Now we can eliminate half of those people from the set of the enlightened because women played almost no roles in the Scottish Enlightenment." (Roger L. Emerson, "How Many Scots Were Enlightened?" in *Essays on David Hume, Medical Men and the Scottish Enlightenment: Industry, Knowledge and Humanity* [Farnham: Ashgate, 2008], 39.) This absurd claim ignores the work not only of recent scholars but of contemporaries as well. After all, a certain Enlightened Scot, David Hume, recognized "the Ladies" as "Sovereigns of the learned world." David Hume, "Of Essay Writing," in *Essays: Moral, Political, and Literary*, ed. Eugene F. Miller (Indianapolis: Liberty Fund, 1985), 536.
16 Franco Venturi, *Utopia and Reform in the Enlightenment* (Cambridge: Cambridge University Press, 1971), 121. For the individual titles of *Settecento Riformatore*, see John Robertson, "Franco Venturi's Enlightenment," *Past and Present* 137 (1992): 183.
17 John Robertson, *The Case for Enlightenment: Scotland and Naples, 1680–1760* (Cambridge: Cambridge University Press, 2005); *The Enlightenment: A Very Short Introduction* (Oxford: Oxford University Press, 2015), 1. Robertson's acknowledges much of his debt to (my former teacher) Franco Venturi in "Franco Venturi's Enlightenment." For a challenge to Robertson and Venturi's paradigm that highlights many Enlightenments, see J. G. A. Pocock, "Historiography and Enlightenment: A View of Their History," *Modern Intellectual History* 5/1 (2008): 83–96; and "The Re-Description of Enlightenment," *Proceedings of the British Academy* 125 (2004): 101–18.
18 Jonathan I. Israel, *Radical Enlightenment: Philosophy and the Making of Modernity 1650–1750* (Oxford: Oxford University Press, 2001); *Enlightenment Contested: Philosophy, Modernity, and the Emancipation of Man 1670–1752* (Oxford: Oxford University Press, 2006); *Democratic Enlightenment: Philosophy, Revolution, and Human Rights*

1750–1790 (Oxford: Oxford University Press, 2011); *Revolutionary Ideas: An Intellectual History of the French Revolution from The Rights of Man to Robespierre* (Princeton: Princeton University Press, 2014). These volumes are summarized in Jonathan Israel, *A Revolution of the Mind: Radical Enlightenment and the Intellectual Origins of Modern Democracy* (Princeton: Princeton University Press, 2010).

19 The Enlightenment Books Project at Pomona College: A Bibliographical Checklist of Eighteenth-Century Editions, https://kates.itg.pomona.edu/books/analytics.php?type=all. There are at least two other ongoing major digital research projects attempting to quantify Enlightenment books through other means: *MEDIATE: Understanding the Literary System of the 18th Century*, at https://mediate18.nl/?page=home, is described by its director in A. C. Montoya, "Shifting Perspectives and Moving Targets: From Conceptual Perspectives to Bits of Data in the First Year of the MEDIATE Project," in *Digitizing Enlightenment: Digital Humanities and the Transformation of Eighteenth-Century Studies*, eds. S. Burrows and G. Roe (Oxford: Voltaire Foundation, 2020), 195–218; and "Mapping Print, Charting Enlightenment: Reinterpreting Eighteenth-Century European Culture through Historical Bibliometrics and Digital, Spatial and Textual Analysis," at http://fbtee.uws.edu.au/mpce/, is a collection of databases directed by Simon Burrows and others.

20 Richard B. Sher, *The Enlightenment and the Book: Scottish Authors and Their Publishers in Eighteenth-Century Britain, Ireland, and America* (Chicago: University of Chicago Press, 2006), esp. 701.

21 Compare https://kates.itg.pomona.edu/books/analytics.php?type=all_69_89 with the list of bestsellers reproduced in Darnton, *Corpus of Clandestine Literature in France 1769–1789*, 194–5, and updated at http://www.robertdarnton.org/literarytour/booksellers. During the eighteenth century the number of editions may serve as a surrogate for popularity because—as I argue in Chapter 1—across continental Europe publishers restrained most press runs to 500–2,000 copies to protect their vulnerable inventories. Thomas Munck's important *Conflict and Enlightenment: Print and Political Culture in Europe, 1635–1795* (Cambridge: Cambridge University Press, 2019) also emphasizes publishing and anticipates several findings made in this book.

22 Roger Chartier, *The Cultural Uses of Print in Early Modern France*, trans. Lydia G. Cochrane (Princeton: Princeton University Press, 1987).

23 As discussed in Chapter 12, Diderot's secret, but extraordinary, contributions to the *History of the Two Indies* played a large role in the work's popularity.

Chapter 1

1 Moses Mendelssohn, *Jerusalem or on Religious Power and Judaism*, trans. Allen Arkush (Waltham: University Press of New England, 1983), 103–4. The following quotes also come from these pages. Italics in the original. On the wider ramifications of over-reading, see Anne C. Vila, *Suffering Scholars: Pathologies of the Intellectual in Enlightenment France* (Philadelphia: University of Pennsylvania Press, 2018).

2 Quoted in Norman Hampson, *The Enlightenment* (New York: Penguin Books, 1990), 138. David Garrioch reports that by 1780, 30 percent of Parisian wage earners owned books. "Reading in Eighteenth-Century Paris," in *The Culture of the Book: Essays from Two Hemispheres in Honour of Wallace Kirsop*, ed. David Garrioch (Melbourne: Bibliographical Society of Australia and New Zealand, 1999), 288–99.

3   Françoise de Graffigny, *Letters of a Peruvian Woman*, trans. Jonathan Mallinson (Oxford: Oxford University Press, 2009), 59.
4   Quoted in Isobel Grundy, "'Trash, Trumpery, and Idle Time': Lady Mary Wortley Montagu and Fiction," *Eighteenth-Century Fiction* 5 (1993): 294.
5   Quoted in Elizabeth L. Eisenstein, *Grub Street Abroad: Aspects of the French Cosmopolitan Press from the Age of Louis XIV to the French Revolution* (Oxford: Oxford University Press, 1992), 113.
6   Jürgen Habermas, *The Structural Transformation of the Public Sphere: An Inquiry into a Category of Bourgeois Society*, trans. Thomas Burger and Frederick Lawrence (Cambridge, MA: MIT, 1989); James Van Horn Melton, *The Rise of the Public in Enlightenment Europe* (Cambridge: Cambridge University Press, 2001), 8. Melton offers a lucid application of Habermas's theory to modern historical scholarship.
7   Habermas, *Structural Transformation of the Public Sphere*, 50, 52. See also Keith Baker, "Defining the Public Sphere in Eighteenth-Century France: Variations on a Theme by Habermas," in *Habermas and the Public Sphere*, ed. Craig Calhoun (Cambridge, MA: MIT, 1992), 181–4; William H. Sewell Jr., *Capitalism and the Emergence of Civic Equality in Eighteenth-Century France* (Chicago: University of Chicago Press, 2021), 72–86; and Stéphane Van Damme, "Farewell Habermas? Deux décennies d'études sur l'espace public," *Les Dossiers du Grihl*, http://journals.openedition.org/dossiersgrihl/682. Accessed May 3, 2021.
8   Habermas, *Structural Transformation of the Public Sphere*, 51.
9   David Allan, *A Nation of Readers: The Lending Library in Georgian England* (London: British Library, 2008); Robert Darnton, "First Steps Toward a History of Reading," *Australian Journal of French Studies* 23 (1986): 1–30.
10 Immanuel Kant, "An Answer to the Question: What is Enlightenment?" and Moses Mendelssohn, "On the Question: What is Enlightenment?" in *What is Enlightenment?*, ed. James Schmidt (Berkeley and Los Angeles: University of California Press, 1996), 53–64; James Schmidt, "What Enlightenment Was: How Moses Mendelssohn and Immanuel Kant Answered the *Berlinische Monatsschrift*," *Journal of the History of Philosophy* 30 (1992): 77–102.
11 Keith Michael Baker, "Enlightenment and the Institution of Society: Notes for a Conceptual History," in *Civil Society: History and Possibilities*, eds. Sudipta Kaviraj and Sunil Khilnani (Cambridge: Cambridge University Press, 2001), 84–104.
12 Michel Marion, *Recherches sur les bibliothèques privées à Paris au milieu du XVIIIe siècle,1750–1759* (Paris: Bibliothèque Nationale, 1978), 23; Melton, *Rise of the Public in Enlightenment Europe*, 88, drawing upon Albert Ward, *Book Production, Fiction, and the German Reading Public, 1740–1780* (Oxford: Clarendon Press, 1974), 32–3; Vivienne S. Dunstan, "Glimpses Into a Town's Reading Habits in Enlightenment Scotland: Analyzing the Borrowings of Gray Library, Haddington, 1732–1816," *Journal of the Scottish Historical Society* 26 (2006): 46. See also Mark R. M. Towsey, *Reading the Scottish Enlightenment: Books and their Readers in Provincial Scotland, 1750–1820.* (Leiden: Brill, 2010), 115. On religious books see Philippe Martin, *Une religion des livres: 1640–1850* (Paris: Cerf, 2003). For Naples, see Marcella Campanelli, "Agiographia e devozione nell'editoria napoletana del Settecento," in *Editoria e cultura a Napoli nel XVIII secolo*, ed. Anna Maria Rao (Naples: Liguori Editore, 1998), 454.
13 Lady Holland to Marchioness of Kildare, October 18, 1766, in *Correspondence of Emily, Duchess of Leinster (1731–1814)*, Vol. 1 (Dublin: Stationery Office, 1949), 471.
14 Nassy quoted in Robert Cohen, *Jews in Another Environment: Surinam in the Second Half of the Eighteenth Century* (Leiden: Brill, 1991), 113–14: "This great man [Voltaire], made

to enlighten the world, in the midst of his digressions against religions, preaching tolerance, trampling all cults under foot, conjointly took unfortunate pleasure in crushing the Jewish community and making it hideous in the eyes of the universe"; *Anticipating The Wealth of Nations: The Selected Works of Anders Chydenius (1729–1803)*, eds. Maren Jonasson and Pertti Hyttinen (London and New York: Routledge, 2012), 105, 135, 159; Elizabeth Carter to Elizabeth Vesey, January 9, 1782, at the Reading Experience Database (RED), http://www.open.ac.uk/Arts/reading/UK/search_basic_results.php?keyword=Raynal.

15 Iacob Mârza, "La Circulation de l'oeuvre de Voltaire en Transylvanie au XVIIIe siècle," *Synthesis: Bulletin du Comitée National de litterature comparée de la République Socialiste de Roumanie* 5 (1978): 149–62.
16 Quoted in Ludovica Braid, "Censure et circulation du livre en italie au xviii siècle," *Journal of Modern European History* 3 (2005): 81–2.
17 *Nova Scotia Gazette* 3 (1768–1769), Issue 133, February 16, 1769, final page (unnumbered).
18 Roger Emerson, "*Catalogus Librorum A.C.D.A.* or, The Library of Archibald Campbell, Third Duke of Argyll (1682–1761)" in *The Culture of the Book in the Scottish Enlightenment*, ed. Mark Wood (Toronto: Thomas Fisher Rare Book Library, University of Toronto, 2000), 15–17; Towsey, *Reading the Scottish Enlightenment*, 48; Patricia McCarthy, *Life in the Country House in Georgian Ireland* (New Haven: Yale University Press, 2016), 50–2; Gary Kates, *Monsieur d'Eon is a Woman: A Tale of Gender Intrigue and Sexual Masquerade* (New York: Basic Books, 1995), 150–8; Alessa Johns, *Bluestocking Feminism and British-German Cultural Transfer* (Ann Arbor: University of Michigan Press, 2014), 29–30.
19 Anne Beroujon, "Les collections privées de livres à Lyon au XVIIIe siècle," in *Mécènes et collectionneurs: Lyon et le Midi de la France*, ed. Jean-René. Gaborit (Paris: Editions du CTHS, 1999), 65–9.
20 Allan, *Nation of Readers*, 214.
21 Daniel Rosenberg, "The Library of the Disaster," *Romanic Review* 103 (2012): 317–29.
22 Quoted in Mark Towsey, "'I Can't Resist Sending You the Book': Private Libraries, Elite Women, and Shared Reading Practices in Georgian Britain," *Library and Information History* 29 (2013): 212–14.
23 Patrick Spedding, "A List of My Books: A Detailed Analysis of a 1730s Personal Library," *Script & Print* 41 (2017): 92–104.
24 Abigail Williams, *The Social Life of Books: Reading Together in the Eighteenth-Century Home* (New Haven: Yale University Press, 2017), 60–1.
25 Towsey, *Reading the Scottish Enlightenment*, 163.
26 Thomas D. Walker, "The State of Libraries in Eighteenth-Century Europe: Adalbert Blumenschein's 'Beschreibung Verschiedener Bibliotheken in Europa,'" *The Library Quarterly: Information, Community, Policy* 65 (1995): 285.
27 Quoted in Vivienne Dunstan, "Reading habits in Scotland circa 1750–1820," unpublished PhD dissertation, University of Dundee, 2010, 31. Jan Fergus, "Eighteenth-Century Readers in Provincial England: The Customers of Samuel Clay's Circulating Library and Bookshop in Warwick, 1770–1772," *PBSA* 78 (1984): 155–213.
28 David Allan, "A Reader Writes: Negotiating the *Wealth of Nations* in an Eighteenth-Century Commonplace Book," *Philological Quarterly* 81 (2002): 215.
29 *Annual Register* for 1761 as quoted in "Appendix 10: Libraries and Reading Societies," in *The Reading Nation in the Romantic Period*, ed. William St Claire (Cambridge: Cambridge University Press, 2004), 665. See also Paul Kaufman, *Libraries and Their Users: Collected Papers in Library History* (London: The Library Assn, 1969), 192–228.

30 *Lady's Magazine* (1789), quoted in Williams, *Social Life of Books*, 45.
31 Paul Benhamou, "The Reading Trade in Lyons: Cellier's Cabinet De Lecture," *Studies on Voltaire and the Eighteenth Century* 308 (1993): 305–21; "The Reading Trade in Pre-Revolutionary France," *Achttiende Eeuw: Documentatieblad Van De Werkgroep Achttiende Eeuw* 23, no. 1–2 (1991): 143–50; "The Diffusion of Forbidden Books: Four Case Studies," *SVEC* 12 (2005): 259–81; for Montpellier see Robert Darnton, *A Literary Tour De France: The World of Books on the Eve of the French Revolution* (Oxford: Oxford University Press, 2018), 136. See also Uta Janssens-Knorsch, "Commerce or Culture? The Fate of the First Circulating Library in the Netherlands," *Achttiende Eeuw: Documentatieblad Van de Werkgroep Achttiende Eeuw* 23 (1991):151–73; Mercier quoted in Carla Hesse, "Print culture in the Enlightenment," in *The Enlightenment World*, eds. M. Fitzpatrick et al. (London and New York: Routledge, 2004), 364.
32 Benhamou, "The Diffusion of Forbidden Books," 270.
33 Quoted in Ibid., 279–80 [my translation].
34 Paul Kaufman, *Borrowings from the Bristol Library, 1773–1784: A Unique Record of Reading Vogues* (Charlottesville: Bibliographic Society of the University of Virginia, 1960).
35 Mark Towsey, "First Steps in Associational Reading: Book Use and Sociability at the Wigtown Subscription Library, 1795–1799," *Papers of the Bibliographical Society of America* 103 (2009): 485; *Reading the Scottish Enlightenment*, 144.
36 Mary K. Flavell, "The Enlightened Reader and the New Industrial Towns: A Study of the Liverpool library 1758–1790," *Journal for Eighteenth-Century Studies* 8 (1985): 17–35.
37 Williams, *Social Life of Books*, 117–119.
38 Trevor Fawcett, "An Eighteenth-Century Book Club at Norwich," *The Library* 23 (1968): 47–50.
39 For one Dutch child's exposure to Enlightenment books, see Arianne Baggerman, "The Cultural Universe of a Dutch Child: Otto van Eck and His Literature," *Eighteenth-Century Studies* 31 (1997): 129–34.
40 William St Claire, *The Reading Nation in the Romantic Period* (Cambridge: Cambridge University Press, 2004), 670–71.
41 Dunstan, "Glimpses into a Town's Reading Habits in Enlightenment Scotland," 42–59.
42 John C. Crawford, "The Ideology of Mutual Improvement in Scottish Working Class Libraries," *Library History* 12 (1996): 49–61. For Dutch examples of working-class readers, see José de Kruif, "Classes of Readers: Owners of Books in 18th-Century the Hague," *Poetics* 28 (2001): 423–53.
43 Henry Brooke, *The Fool of Quality, Or, The History of Henry, Earl of Moreland*, 5 vols. (London: A. Millar, 1792).
44 Quoted in Crawford, "Ideology of Mutual Improvement in Scottish Working Class Libraries," 57–9.
45 Williams, *Social Life of Books*, 117–18.
46 Mónica Ricketts, *Who Should Rule? Men of Arms, the Republic of Letters, and the Fall of the Spanish Empire* (New York: Oxford University Press, 2017).
47 Richard van Dülmen, *The Society of the Enlightenment: The Rise of the Middle Class and Enlightenment Culture in Germany* (Cambridge: Polity Press, 1992), 88–91.
48 Dan Edelstein, *The Enlightenment: A Genealogy* (Chicago: University of Chicago Press, 2010), 73; B. M. Milstein, *Eight Eighteenth Century Reading Societies: A Sociological Contribution to the History of German Literature* (Berne: Herbert Lang, 1972).
49 Ian Jackson, "Approaches to the History of Readers and Reading in Eighteenth-Century Britain," *Historical Journal* 47 (2004): 1041–54.

50 Geneviève de Malboissière, *Lettres de Geneviève de Malboissiere à Adélaïde Méliand. Une jeune fille au xviiie siècle*, ed. Comte de Iuppé (Paris: Champion, 1925), 126. Geveviève read René Aubert de Vertot, *Histoire Des Révolutions Romaines*, 3 vols., 5th ed. (Paris: Babuty, 1753; William Robertson), *Histoire d'Écosse, sous les regnes de Marie Stuart, et de Jacques VI*, 3 vols. (Londres [Paris], n.p., 1764); Georges Louis LeClerc, Comte de Buffon, *Histoire Naturelle, générale, particulère*, 15 vols. (Paris: Imprimerie Royale, 1749–1767). Dena Goodman's masterful analysis of Geneviève de Malboissière and Manon Phlipon is a core resource for this section. See *Becoming a Woman in the Age of Letters* (Ithaca: Cornell University Press, 2009).
51 Malboissière, *Lettres de Geneviève de Malboissiere à Adélaide Méliand*, 17.
52 Joseph-Louis Ripault Desormeaux, *Histoire de la maison de Montmorenci* (Paris: Desaint et Saillant, 1764). On the general preference for reading new books, see Mark Curran, *The French Book Trade in Enlightenment Europe I: Selling Enlightenment* (London: Bloomsbury, 2018), 70–1.
53 Malboissière, *Lettres de Geneviève de Malboissiere à Adélaide Méliand*, 116.
54 Ibid., 308–9.
55 Ibid., 9.
56 Ibid., 225.
57 Denis Diderot, *Rameau's Nephew and Other Works*, trans. Jacques Barzun (Indianapolis: Hackett, 2001), 28. On Diderot's education of his daughter, see Meghan K. Roberts, *Sentimental Savants: Philosophical Families in Enlightenment France* (Chicago: University of Chicago Press, 2016), 123–5 and Leon Schwartz, *Diderot and the Jews* (Rutherford: Fairleigh Dickinson University Press, 1981), 27–8.
58 Quoted in Goodman, *Becoming a Woman in the Age of Letters*, 153–5.
59 Marie Jeanne Roland, *Lettres de Madame Roland, Tome premier, Nouvelle série 1767–1780*, ed. Claude Perroud (Paris: Imprimerie Nationale, 1913).
60 George Ridpath, *Diary of George Ridpath, Minister of Stitchel, 1755–1761*, ed. James Balfour Paul (Edinburgh: Printed at the University Press, 1922), 355.
61 Ibid., 165, 292, 296–8, 355, 361. The catalog was apparently never published, and the manuscript is apparently lost.
62 Giovanni's list of 114 books is reproduced in Lodovico Braid, *Il Commercio delle idee: editoria e circolazione del libro nella Torino del Settecento* (Firenze: Olschki, 1995), 209–19; see also Darnton, *Corpus of Clandestine Literature* and *Forbidden Best-Sellers*.
63 This section relies on Trevor G. Burnard, *Mastery, Tyranny, and Desire: Thomas Thistlewood and His Slaves in the Anglo-Jamaican World* (Chapel Hill: The University of North Carolina Press, 2004); April G. Shelford, "Pascal in Jamaica; or, The French Enlightenment in Translation," *Journal of the Western Society for French History* 36 (2008): 53–74; and more generally, James Robertson, "Eighteenth-Century Jamaica's Ambivalent Cosmopolitanism," *History* 99 (2014): 607–31. For the similar case of William Dunbar in Florida, see Bernard Bailyn, "An Enlightened Scot at Manchac," in *Voyagers to the West: A Passage in the Peopling of America on the Eve of the Revolution* (New York: Knopf, 1986), 488–92, which can be read in conjunction with Toni Morrison, "Romancing the Shadow," in *Playing in the Dark: Whiteness and the Literary Imagination* (New York: Vintage, 1992), 39–51.
64 Burnard, *Mastery, Tyranny, and Desire*, 58.
65 Nicolas de Caritat, Marquis de Condorcet, *Selected Writings*, trans. Keith Michael Baker (Indianapolis: Bobbs-Merrill, 1976), 8.
66 Burnard, *Mastery, Tyranny, and Desire*, 104 and 156–7.
67 Ibid., 104.

68 Shelford, "Pascal in Jamaica," 70–1, quoting from Rousseau, *On the Social Contract*, trans. Donald A. Cress (Indianapolis: Hackett, 2019), 10. See also F. T. H. Fletcher, "Montesquieu's Influence on Anti-Slavery Opinion in England," *Journal of Negro History* 18 (1933): 414–25.

69 Adam Hochschild, *Bury the Chains: Prophets and Rebels in the Fight to Free an Empire's Slaves* (Boston: Houghton Mifflin, 2005). Montesquieu anticipates Hannah Arendt's famous argument in *Eichmann in Jerusalem: A Report on the Banality of Evil* (New York: Penguin Classics, 2006).

70 Benedetta Craveri, *The Age of Conversation*, trans. Teresa Waugh (New York: New York Review of Books, 2005); Dena Goodman, *The Republic of Letters: A Cultural History of the French Enlightenment* (Ithaca: Cornell University Press, 1994); Kenneth Loiselle, *Brotherly Love: Freemasonry and Male Friendship in Enlightenment France* (Ithaca: Cornell University Press, 2014).

71 Eltjo Buringh and Jan Luiten Van Zanden, "Charting the 'Rise of the West': Manuscripts and Printed Books in Europe, A Long-Term Perspective from the Sixth Through Eighteenth Centuries," *Journal of Economic History* 69 (2009): 417 and 421. These figures revise the older estimate of 1.5 billion made by R. A. Houston, *Literacy in Early Modern Europe: Culture and Education 1500–1800*, 2nd ed. (Harlow: Longman, 2002), 175.

72 James Raven, "New Reading Histories, Print Culture and the Identification of Change: The Case of Eighteenth-Century England," *Social History* 23 (1998): 275.

73 Buringh and Van Zanden, "Charting the 'Rise of the West'"; James Raven, "The Importation of Books in the Eighteenth Century," in *A History of the Book in America, vol. one: The Colonial Book in the Atlantic World*, eds. Hugh Armory and David D. Hall (Cambridge: Cambridge University Press, 2000), 183–98; Thomas Munck, *Conflict and Enlightenment: Print and Political Culture in Europe, 1635–1795* (Cambridge: Cambridge University Press, 2019). 265; and Gary Marker, *Publishing, Printing, and the Origins of Intellectual Life in Russia, 1700–1800* (Princeton: Princeton University Press, 1985), 106.

74 M. Pollard, *Dublin's Trade in Books, 1550–1800.* (Oxford: Clarendon Press, 1989).

75 Graham Gargett, "List of Books Connected with the French Enlightenment, 1700–1800," in *Ireland and the French Enlightenment, 1700–1800*, eds. Graham Gargett and Geraldine Sheridan (New York: St Martin's Press, 1999), 243–84. Gargett's list omits Fénelon, but on p. 67 he nevertheless writes: "Although Fénelon's didactic novel *Télémaque* was arguably the most successful book of all in the period 1700-1800, with 18 editions so far identified (six French versions—one parallel text—and 12 translations), this achievement is easily surpassed by the sheer number of different Voltaire works and by the wide area of subjects covered."

76 Houston, *Literacy in Early Modern Europe,* 47–53, 144, 209; Melton, *Rise of the Public in Enlightenment Europe*, 82.

77 William M. Sale, *Samuel Richardson: Master Printer* (Ithaca: Cornell University Press, 1950); John Clyde Oswald, *Benjamin Franklin Printer* (New York: Doubleday, 1917); Horace Walpole was one famous exception of an author who took joy in printing his own books at his Strawberry Hill estate. See E. J. Clery, "Horace Walpole, the Strawberry Hill Press, and the Emergence of the Gothic Genre," *Ars & Humanitas: Revija Za Umetnost in Humanistiko* 4 (2010): 93–111. For one well-known case of authorial self-funding, that of Jacques Pierre Brissot, see Curran, *French Book Trade in Enlightenment Europe I*, 102–4.

78 Stephen Brown, "William Smellie and the Printer's Role in the Eighteenth-Century Edinburgh Booktrade," in *The Human Face of the Book Trade: Print Culture and its*

Creators, eds. Peter Isaac and Barry McKay (New Castle DE: Oak Knoll Press, 1999), 29–44.
79 Richard B. Sher, *The Enlightenment and the Book: Scottish Authors and their Publishers in Eighteenth-Century Britain, Ireland and America* (Chicago: University of Chicago Press, 2006), 360; Darnton, *A Literary Tour de France*, 131.
80 Maurice Cranston, *The Noble Savage: Jean-Jacques Rousseau, 1754–1762* (Chicago: University of Chicago Press, 1991), 152.
81 Roger Chartier, *The Author's Hand and the Printer's Mind: Transformations of the Written Word in Early Modern Europe*, trans. Lydia G. Cochrane (Hoboken: Wiley, 2013), 17; Chartier urges historians in particular to make more use of paratexts and criticizes some literary scholars for minimizing them. See Roger Chartier, *The Order of Books: Readers, Authors and Libraries in Europe between the Fourteenth and Eighteenth Centuries* (Stanford: Stanford University Press, 1994), 10: "Reception theorists have little regard for mediation; they ignore the publisher and the paratexts, thinking that the relationship of reception is purely between author and reader." See also Gerard Genette, *Paratexts: Thresholds of Interpretation*, trans. Jane E. Lewin (Cambridge: Cambridge University Press, 1997); Multigraph Collective, *Interacting with Print: Elements of Reading in the Era of Print Saturation* (Chicago: University of Chicago Press, 2018); Janine Barchas, *Graphic Design, Print Culture, and the Eighteenth-Century Novel* (Cambridge: Cambridge University Press, 2003).
82 Antonia Forster, "Review Journals and the Reading Public," in *Books and their Readers in Eighteenth-Century England: New Essays*, ed. Isabel Rivers (London: Continuum, 2001), 171–90; Flavell, "Enlightened Reader and the New Industrial Towns," 20.
83 Daniel Mornet, "L'intérêt historique des journaux littéraires et la diffusion du *Mercure de France*," *Bulletin de la Société d'histoire moderne* 22 (1910): 119–22.
84 Geraldine Sheridan, "Irish Literary Review Magazines and Enlightenment France: 1730–1790," in *Ireland and the French Enlightenment 1700–1800*, eds. Graham Gargett and Geraldine Sheridan (New York: St Martin's Press, 1999), 35. For Smith and Wollstonecraft, see Ryan Patrick Hanley, "Commerce and Corruption: Rousseau's Diagnosis and Adam Smith's Cure," *European Journal of Political Theory* 7 (2008): 137–58; Mitzi Myers, "Mary Wollstonecraft's Literary Reviews," in *The Cambridge Companion to Mary Wollstonecraft*, ed. Claudia L. Johnson (Cambridge: Cambridge University Press, 2002), 82–98.
85 Renato Pasta, *Editoria e cultura nel settecento* (Firenze: Olschki, 1997), 149–57; Raymond F. Birn, *Pierre Rousseau and the "philosophes" of Bouillon* (Geneva: Institute and Musée Voltaire, 1964).
86 Adrian Johns, "The Piratical Enlightenment," in *Piracy: The Intellectual Property Wars from Gutenberg to Gates* (Chicago: University of Chicago Press, 2009), 41–56. See also Siegfried Unself, *Goethe and His Publishers*, trans. Kenneth J. Northcott (Chicago: University of Chicago Press, 1996), 26, for one example where a prince encouraged publishers to reprinting the books of neighboring states.
87 Catherine Seville, *The Internationalisation of Copyright Law: Books, Buccaneers, and the Black Flag in the Nineteenth Century* (Cambridge: Cambridge University Press, 2006).
88 Defoe in 1705: "Books are printed by no body, and Wrote by every body; one Man Prints another man's Works, and calls them his own; again, another Man Prints his own, and calls them another Man's. A. is loaded with B's crimes, and B. Applauded with A.'s Virtues . . . continual Robberies, Piracies, and Invasions of Property, range among the Occupation." Quoted in Elizabeth F. Judge, "Kidnapped and Counterfeit Characters: Eighteenth-Century Fan Fiction, Copyright Law, and the Custody of Fictional Characters," in *Originality and*

Intellectual Property in the French and English Enlightenment, ed. Reginald McGinnis (New York: Routledge, 2009), 30.
89 Immanuel Kant, "On the Wrongfulness of Unauthorized Publications of Books," in *Practical Philosophy*, trans. Mary J. Gregor (Cambridge: Cambridge University Press, 1996 [1785]), 23–35.
90 René Moulinas, *L'Imprimerie, la librairie, et la presse à Avignon au xviiie siècle* (Grenoble: Presse universitaire de Grenoble, 1974); Sébastien Évrard, *Le Livre, le droit et le faux: essai sur l'édition juridique et la contrefaçon au siècle des lumières* (Paris: L'Harmattan, 2017); A. Machet, "Censure et librairie en italie au xviiie siècle," *Revue des études sud-est européennes* 10 (1972): 459–90; Daniel Droixhe, "Signatures Clandestines et autres essais sur les contrefaçons de Liège et de Maastricht au xviiie siècle," in *From Letter to Publication: Studies on Correspondence and the History of the Book; With the Besterman Lecture 2000*, ed. Anthony Strugnell (Oxford: Voltaire Foundation; 2001), 49–198. Unauthorized editions are a main focus in Curran, *French Book Trade in Enlightenment Europe I*, and Simon Burrows, *The French Book Trade in Enlightenment Europe II* (London: Bloomsbury, 2018).
91 Évrard, *Le Livre, le droit et le faux*, 45–6, 71; Gilles Barber, "Book Imports and Exports in the Eighteenth Century," in *Sale and distribution of books from 1700*, eds. R. Myers and M. Harris (Oxford: Oxford Polytechnic, 1982), xi, 77–105; Robert Shackleton, "John Nourse and the London Edition of *L'Esprit des lois*," in *Studies in the French Eighteenth Century: Presented to John Lough by Colleagues, Pupils and Friends*, eds. D. J. Mossop, G. E. Rodmell, and D. B. Wilson (Durham: University of Durham, 1978), 248–59.
92 Évrard, *Le Livre, le droit et le faux,* 14.
93 Darnton, *A Literary Tour de France,* 93–108. This situation is reminiscent of the status of Japanese or British pressing of Beatle albums during the 1960s. It may have been illegal to buy and sell them in the United States, but it was not illegal to own them.
94 *Dublin Magazine*, April 1764, quoted in Geraldine Sheridan, "Irish Periodicals and the Dissemination of French Enlightenment Writings in the Eighteenth Century," *1798: A Bicentenary Perspective*, ed. Thomas Bartlett (Dublin: Four Courts, 2003), 42. The quotation continues: "Add to this that the universality of the French language hath almost made the French citizens of the world, and put it in their power to catch the spirit, and imbibe the sentiments of the eminent men of every nation." See also Mary Helen McMurran, *The Spread of Novels: Translation and Prose Fiction in the Eighteenth Century* (Princeton: Princeton University Press, 2010); Fania Oz-Salzberger, *Translating the Enlightenment: Scottish Civic Discourse in Eighteenth-Century Germany* (Oxford: Oxford University Press, 1995); Jeffrey Freedman, *Books Without Borders in Enlightenment Europe: French Cosmopolitanism and German Literary Markets* (Philadelphia: University of Pennsylvania Press, 2012).
95 Johns, *Bluestocking Feminism and British-German Cultural Transfer*, 6; McMurran, *Spread of Novels*; Sher, *Enlightenment and the Book*, Tables 1 and 2, 613–89.
96 Johns, *Bluestocking Feminism and British-German Cultural Transfer*, 22–5.
97 Sher, *Enlightenment and the Book*, 86; Darnton, *A Literary Tour de France*, 141, quotes Mossy and mentions 1,000 copies as the average print run for the Société typographique de Neuchâtel on p. 268; for Holland see Arianne Baggerman, *Publishing Policies and Family Strategies: The Fortunes of a Dutch Publishing House in the 18th and Early 19th Centuries* (Leiden and Boston: Brill, 2013), 532, Appendix II: Average Print Runs Per Genre, 1797–1818.
98 Daniel Roche, *Les Républicains des lettres: gens de culture et lumières au xviiie siècle* (Paris: Fayard, 1988), 43.

99   David Smith, *Helvétius: A Study in Persecution* (Oxford: Oxford University Press, 1965); Raymond Birn, *Royal Censorship of Books in Eighteenth-Century France* (Stanford: Stanford University Press, 2012).
100 Robert Darnton, "The Importance of Exchanges," at Darnton's site: file:///C:/Users/gk0 04747/Downloads/Literary_Demand_Sources_And_Methods.pdf. Accessed April 30, 2018.
101 Robert Darnton, "The Life Cycle of a Book: A Publishing History of *d'Holbach's Système de la nature*," in *Publishing and Readership in Revolutionary Europe and America*, ed. Carol Armbruster (Westport: Greenwood, 1993), 16. However, Mark Curran has challenged Darnton's notion of a floating inventory of exchanged books, arguing that it was actually highly restricted to certain regions isolated from one another. See Mark Curran, "Beyond the Forbidden Best-Sellers of Pre-Revolutionary France," *The Historical Journal* 56 (2013): 89–112, esp. 105.
102 By the mid-eighteenth century, the Imprimerie Royale had become the largest printing house in Europe, with seventeen presses located on two floors of the Louvre. It contracted with exclusive Paris booksellers, who served the government in distributing its books. See Paul-Marie Ginevald, "Les Editions de *l'Histoire Naturelle*," in *Buffon 88: actes du Colloque international pour le bicentenaire de la mort de Buffon*, eds. Jean-Claude Beaune, et al. (Paris: J. Vrin, 1992), 631–7.
103 Frank A. Kafker and Jeff Loveland, "The Elusive Laurent Durand, a Leading Publisher of the French Enlightenment," in *Social History, Morellet, Social Anthropology*, ed. Jonathan Mallinson (Oxford: Voltaire Foundation, 2005), 223–58.
104 Denis Diderot, "Letter on the Book Trade," trans. Arthur Goldhammer, in *Daedalus* 131 (2002): 48–56.
105 Quoted in Robert Darnton, "The Science of Piracy: A Crucial Ingredient in Eighteenth-Century Publishing," in *History of the Book, Translation, History of Ideas, Paul et Virginie, Varia*, ed. Jonathan Mallinson (Oxford: Voltaire Foundation, 2003), 11. Curran, *French Book Trade in Enlightenment Europe I*.
106 Quoted in Nicholas Cronk, "Voltaire and Authorship," in *The Cambridge Companion to Voltaire*, ed. Nicholas Cronk (Cambridge: Cambridge University Press, 2009), 31–46, 32.
107 Robert Darnton, "The Encyclopédie Wars of Pre-Revolutionary France," *American Historical Review* 78 (1973): 1331–52.
108 *Scots Magazine* 50 (May 1788): 233.
109 Anne Goldgar, *Impolite Learning: Conduct and Community in the Republic of Letters 1680–1750* (New Haven: Yale University Press, 1995); April G. Shelford, *Transforming the Republic of Letters: Pierre-Daniel Huet and European Intellectual Life, 1650–1720* (Rochester: Boydell & Brewer, 2007).
110 *Spectator* No. 10 (March 11, 1711).
111 Richard Yeo, "John Locke and Polite Philosophy," in *The Philosopher in Early Modern Europe: The Nature of a Contested Identity*, eds. Conal Condren, Stephen Gaukroger, and Ian Hunter (Cambridge: Cambridge University Press, 2006), 254–75. The standard biography of Locke is still Maurice Cranston, *John Locke: A Biography* (London: Macmillan, 1957). See also Richard Ashcraft, *Revolutionary Politics and Locke's Two Treatises of Government* (Princeton: Princeton University Press, 1986).
112 Paul Rahe, "The Book That Never Was: Montesquieu's *Considerations on the Romans* in Historical Context," *History of Political Thought* 26 (2005): 43–89.
113 On manuscript circulation, see Harold Love, *Scribal Publication in Seventeenth-Century England* (Oxford: Oxford University Press, 1993); for a contrary approach suggesting

that manuscripts continued to be central in Enlightenment Europe, see Ira O. Wade, *The Clandestine Organization and Diffusion of Philosophical Ideas in France from 1700 to 1750* (Princeton: Princeton University Press, 1938), a view resurrected in Jonathan Israel, *Enlightenment Contested: Philosophy, Modernity, and the Emancipation of Man 1670–1752* (Oxford: Oxford University Press, 2006), 699–732.
114 Houston, *Literacy in Early Modern Europe*, 227.
115 Hume to Smith, July 28, 1759, in Ernest Campbell Mossner and Ian Simpson Ross, eds., *The Correspondence of Adam Smith*, 2nd ed. (Oxford: Clarendon Press, 1987), 33–6. See also Dennis C. Rasmussen, *The Infidel and the Professor: David Hume, Adam Smith, and the Friendship that Shaped Modern Thought* (Princeton: Princeton University Press, 2017), 104–7.
116 Frank Donoghue, *The Fame Machine: Book Reviewing and Eighteenth-Century Literary Careers* (Stanford: Stanford University Press, 1996), 2–4; Antoine de Lilti, *The Invention of Celebrity*, trans. Lynn Jeffress (London: Polity, 2017), 13, 103–4; Robert Darnton, "Rousseau Responds to Readers," in *The Great Cat Massacre and Other Episodes in French Cultural History* (New York: Random House, 1984), 215–56; Raymond Birn, *Forging Rousseau: Print, Commerce and Cultural Manipulation in the Late Enlightenment* (Oxford: Voltaire Foundation, 2001).
117 "Notice," in *The Major Political Writings of Jean-Jacques Rousseau*, trans. John T. Scott (Chicago: University of Chicago Press, 2011), 5.
118 Josiah Wedgwood, *Catalogue of Cameos, Intaglios, Medals, Bas-Reliefs, Busts, and Small Statues* (Etruria, 1787), 20, 27, 28. On Voltaire as a "wholly new type" of celebrity, see Nicholas Cronk, "Voltaire and Authorship," 31.
119 Cronk, "Voltaire and Authorship," 31–46.

Chapter 2

1 Alphonse de Lamartine, *Fénelon*, new ed. (Paris: Calmann Lévy, 1876), 72–3.
2 Jacques Le Brun describes it as clandestine in the preface to *Fénelon in the Enlightenment: Traditions, Adaptations, and Variations*, ed. Christoph Schmitt-Maass, Stefanie Stockhorst, and Doohwan Ahn (Amsterdam and New York: Rodopi, 2014), 7.
3 Frans A. Janssen, "The First Edition of Fénelon's *Les Avantures de Télémaque*," *Quaerendo* 42 (2012): 178–85.
4 Jane McCleod, "Printer Widows and the State in Eighteenth-Century France," in *Women and Work in Eighteenth-Century France*, ed. Daryl M. Hafter and Nina Kushner (Baton Rouge: Louisiana State University Press, 2015), 113–29. McCleod notes on p. 115 that women made up 16.6 percent of all printers surveyed in 1764 and 14.3 percent in 1777. See also Geraldine Sheridan, "Women in the Booktrade in Eighteenth-Century France," *Journal of Eighteenth Century Studies* 15 (1992): 51–70.
5 Gervais E. Reed, *Claude Barbin: Libraire de Paris sous le règne de Louis XIV* (Genève: Droz, 1974), especially 57.
6 François Fénelon, *Oeuvres de Fénelon*, ed. Jacques Le Brun, 2 vols. (Paris: Gallimard, 1983–1997), 2:1245.
7 Reed, *Claude Barbin*, 58.
8 Jean Baptiste Dubos to John Locke, August 29, 1699, describing one edition out of The Hague. *Electronic Enlightenment Scholarly Edition of Correspondence*, ed. Robert

McNamee et al. Vers. 3.0. University of Oxford. 2016. Web. 5 Sep. 2017 (hereafter cited as EE).

9 [P. V. Faydit], *La Télémacomanie* (Eleuterople: Pierre Philalèthe, 1700), 2, cited in Jacques Le Brun, "Les Avantures de Télémaque: destins d'un best-seller," *Littératures clasiques* 70 (2009): 135.

10 Cited in Fénelon, *Oeuvres de Fénelon*, 2:1247.

11 Ibid.

12 Richard Steele, *The Tatler*, No. 156, Thursday April 6 to Saturday April 8, 1710, in *The Lucubrations of Isaac Bickerstaff*, 4 vols. (London: H Lintot, 1754), 3:176–7.

13 EE, Elizabeth Jones to John Locke, July 16, 1701.

14 *Mercurius Politicus: Being Monthly Observations on the Affairs of Great Britain*. Vol. 2B (1717): 731–2.

15 Faydit, *La Télémacomanie*, 2; [Nicolas Gueudeville], *Critique général des aventures de Télémaque* (Cologne: Pierrre Marteau, 1700), 5.

16 EE, Jean Baptiste Dubos to John Locke, May 27, 1699.

17 Fénelon, *Oeuvres de Fénelon*, 2:1243.

18 An excerpt of the letter is reproduced in *Oeuvres*, ed. Le Brun 2:1241–2.

19 Diane Brown, "Emile's Missing Text: *Les Aventures de Télémaque*," *Symposium: A Quarterly Journal in Modern Literatures* (Spring 2009): 55; Philip Mansel, *King of the World: The Life of Louis XIV* (Chicago: University of Chicago Press, 2020), 251–2; Ryan Patrick Hanley, *The Political Philosophy of Fénelon* (Oxford: Oxford University Press, 2020), 7.

20 Paul Janet, *Fénelon: His Life and Works*, trans. Victor Leuliette (London: Pittman, 1914), 155.

21 Quoted in *Correspondance de Fénelon, Tome 9, La Condamnation des maximes des saints (3 juin 1698 – 29 mai 1699)*, ed. Jean Orcibal, Jacques Le Brun, and Irénée Noye (Geneva: Droz, 1987), 134n.

22 Fénelon, *Oeuvres de Fénelon*, 2:1248.

23 Ibid., 2:1243.

24 . The most innovative work linking Fénelon, the Quietist Affair and the Enlightenment is Charly Coleman, *The Virtues of Abandon: An Anti-Individualist History of the French Enlightenment* (Stanford: Stanford University Press, 2014), especially 64–87. See also Thomas M. Lennon, *Sacrifice and Self-Interest in Seventeenth-Century France: Quietism, Jansenism, and Cartesianism* (Leiden and Boston: Brill, 2019), especially 53–83. On the fate of the *Maxims*, see Bernward Schmidt, "The Rejected Maxim: Images of Fénelon in Rome 1699 and by Catholic Reformers c. 1800," *Fénelon in the Enlightenment*, 313–337.

25 François de Fénelon, *Telemachus, Son of Ulysses*, trans. Patrick Riley (Cambridge: Cambridge University Press, 1994), 22.

26 Volker Kapp, "Les Illustrations des éditions du *Télémaque*," in *Fénelon: Mystique et politique (1699–1999)*, eds. F. X. Cuche and Jacques Le Brun (Paris: Honoré Champion, 2004), 289–99.

27 Quoted in Coleman, *Virtues of Abandon*, 77.

28 Fénelon, *Les Avantures de Télémaque* (La Haye: Moetjens, 1701), vi, vii, xiv.

29 Ibid., xvii.

30 Fénelon to Abbé Langeron, September 18, 1701, in *Correspondance de Fénelon, Tome 11, Fénelon dans la retraite (juin 1699-décembre 1702)*. Edited by Jean Orcibal, et. al. Geneva: Droz, 1989, 143–4, 146.

31 Fénelon, *Telemachus, Son of Ulysses,* 37; Lionel Rothkrug, *Opposition to Louis XIV: The Political and Social Origins of the French Enlightenment* (Princeton: Princeton University Press, 1965), 270n.

Notes

32 *History of the Works of the Learned. Or, An Impartial Account of Books Lately Printed in all Parts of Europe with a Particular Relation of the State of Learning in Each Country* 3 (1699–1703): 603–4, reviewing *Histoire du Regne de Louis XIII*, citing *Telemachus*, trans. Riley, 60. On Whig principles, see Mark Goldie, "The English System of Liberty," in *Cambridge History of Eighteenth-Century Political Thought,* ed. Mark Goldie and Robert Wokler (Cambridge: Cambridge University Press, 2006), 40–78. Somewhat later, during the 1730s, *Telemachus* seems to have become associated with the "patriot" opposition to Walpole's administration. See in particular Max Skjönsberg, "Lord Bolingbroke's Theory of Party and Opposition," *Historical Journal* 59 (2016): 968n. See also Aris Della Fontana, "Constructing 'Englishness' and Promoting 'politeness' through a 'Francophobic' Bestseller: *Télémaque* in England (1699–1745)," *History of European Ideas* 45 (2019):1–27.
33 *History of the Works of the Learned*, 603–4.
34 Louis de Rouvroy, Duc de Saint-Simon, *Historical Memoirs of the Duc de Saint-Simon: A Shortened Version*, trans. Lucy Norton, 2 vols. (New York: McGraw Hill, 1967), 2:154.
35 Ibid., 2:156.
36 Fénelon, "Plans of Government (Tables de Chaulnes)," in *Moral and Political Writings*, ed. Ryan Patrick Hanley (Oxford: Oxford University Press, 2020), 182–210.
37 Andrew Mansfield, "The Burgundy Circle's Plans to Undermine Louis XIV's 'absolute' State through Polysynody and the High Nobility," *Intellectual History Review* 27 (2016): 1–20.
38 Quoted in Colin Jones, *The Great Nation: France from Louis XV to the Revolution* (New York: Penguin, 2002), 38.
39 Because the Archbishopric of Cambrai was an ecclesiastical principality of the Holy Roman Empire before becoming part of France, its archbishop was formally recognized as a prince of the Holy Roman Empire. On Ramsay, see Andrew Mansfield, *Ideas of Monarchical Reform: Fénelon, Jacobitism and the Political Works of the Chevalier Ramsay* (Manchester: Manchester University Press, 2015).
40 Andrew Michael Ramsay, "Discourse on Epick Poetry, Particularly on the Excellence of this Poem of *Telemachus*," in *Adventures of Telemachus*, 2nd ed., trans. John Ozell (London: Curll, 1719), xxii.
41 Ramsay, "Discourse," xxiv. Ramsay here may be thinking of *Telemachus*, trans. Riley, 147: "All mankind are but one family dispersed over the face of the whole earth. All nations are brethren, and ought to love one another as such."
42 Ramsay, "Discourse," xxiv.
43 Ramsay's "Discourse" was so integral to Telemachus that it, too, appeared in two languages in some bilingual editions. See, for example, Fénelon, *The Adventures of Telemachus . . . in French and English*, trans. Des Maizeaux (London: John Gray, 1742).
44 Caroline Winterer, *The Mirror of Antiquity: American Women and the Classical Tradition* (Ithaca: Cornell University Press, 2009), 36.
45 *The Country Magazine: or, The Gentleman and Lady's Pocket Companion,* reprinting *Craftsman* Oct. 16, 1736, no. 537.
46 James Van Horn Melton, *The Rise of the Public in Enlightenment Europe* (Cambridge: Cambridge University Press, 2001).
47 Patrick Riley, "Rousseau, Fénelon, and the Quarrel Between the Ancients and the Moderns," in *The Cambridge Companion to Rousseau*, ed. Patrick Riley (Cambridge: Cambridge University Press, 2002), 81. Riley goes on to mistakenly claim: "Louis XIV, for his part, saw nothing but the alleged 'faults' of sovereign power in *Telemachus*" (82).

48 Abbé Augustin Barruel, *Mémoires pour servir à l'histoire du Jacobinism*, 5 vols. (Hamburg: n.p., 1800), 4:126.
49 Fénelon, *Avantures de Télémaque* (La Haye: Moetjens, 1712).
50 On the importance of book formats, see Richard B. Sher, *The Enlightenment and the Book: Scottish Authors and Their Publishers in Eighteenth-Century Britain, Ireland, and America* (Chicago: The University of Chicago Press, 2006), especially 43–51.
51 David F. Foxon, *Pope and the Early Eighteenth-Century Book Trade* (Oxford: Oxford University Press, 1991).
52 *Bee, or Universal Weekly Pamphlet* 7 (1733): 188. On Picart's importance, see Lynn Hunt, Margaret Jacob, and W. W. Mijnhardt, *The Book That Changed Europe: Picart and Bernard's Religious Ceremonies of the World* (Cambridge, MA: Harvard University Press, 2010).
53 *Bibliothèque brittanique* 19 (April-May-June 1742): 67.
54 Fénelon, *Les Avantures de Télémaque* (Amsterdam: Wetstein et Smith, 1734) both in quarto and folio versions. Wetstein produced another folio edition of *Telemachus* in 1761, and one quarto published in 1773 caught the attention of writer Andre Morellet, because of its "charming illustrations." See EE, Andre Morellet to William Petter, February 25, 1773.
55 *The Present State of the Republic of Letters* 8 (1731): 460. Throughout the century, the publication of a *Telemachus* quarto brought attention. For one example, see *New Review; with Literary Curiosities, and Literary Intelligence* 3 (1783): 519: "There is to be a new [quarto] edition of Fénelon's work, by Didot [a well-known Paris publisher] containing a great number of MS. Letter, etc. [manuscript material] in the possession of the family, and a new life from memoirs furnished by it. 500 copies on fine paper, and 100 on very fine paper. The fine paper at 15 livres a volume, the superfine at 45. The number of volumes not known. The first volume is published, and to be seen at Mr. Molini's, in Woodstock Street. The others are to appear every four months." This two-volume quarto edition was indeed published by Didot in 1783.
56 "List of Books at Mount Vernon, 1764," *Founders Online,* National Archives, last modified June 29, 2017, http://founders.archives.gov/documents/Washington/02-07-02-0216. [Original source: *The Papers of George Washington*, Colonial Series, vol. 7, *January 1, 1761–June 15, 1767*, ed. W. W. Abbot and Dorothy Twohig (Charlottesville: University Press of Virginia, 1990), 343–50.]
57 It is possible that she bought the book to read to her eight-year-old daughter, also named Sarah. See Winterer, *Mirror of Antiquity*, 35.
58 For such examples, see Robert Darnton, *The Corpus of Clandestine Literature in France, 1769–1789* (New York: W. W. Norton, 1995).
59 For a different perspective on Fénelon's religious writings, see André Cherel, *Fénelon au XVIIIe siècle en France (1715–1820)* (Paris: Hachette, 1917), and Coleman, *Virtues of Abandon*.
60 *The French Book Trade in Enlightenment Europe Database, 1769–1794, downloadable edition*, http://fbtee.uws.edu.au/stn/interface/query_places.php?t=book&e=rawsales&id=spbk0002818&d1=01&m1=01&y1=1769&d2=31&m2=12&y2=1794&g=town&d=map. Accessed July 12, 2020.
61 *The Bee, Or Literary Weekly Intelligencer . . .* 14 (1793): 158–62; Jones, *Great Nation*, 27.
62 EE, Voltaire to d'Olivet, January 6, 1736.
63 *La Henriade* in *Oeuvres complètes de Voltaire*, Vol. 2, ed. Ulla Kölving et al. (Geneva: Voltaire Foundation, 1968), 336; see also EE, Voltaire to the Abbé Cideville, August 10, 1731. On Fénelon's literary influence, see Fabienne Moore, *Prose Poems of the French Enlightenment* (Burlington: Ashgate, 2009), 29–62.

64 EE, Voltaire to La Harpe, September 4, 1771.
65 EE, Voltaire to d'Argenson, May 8, 1739.
66 Voltaire and Frederick II, "Anti-Machiavel," in *The Complete Works of Voltaire Volume 19*, eds. Werner Bahner and Helga Bergmann (Oxford: Voltaire Foundation, 1996), 147. Voltaire heavily edited Frederick's manuscript, and supervised its publication.
67 "Extrait de la Nouvelle bibliothèque, ou histoire littéraire des principaux écrits qui se publient" (November 1740), reproduced in Appendix II of Ibid., 497–8. See also EE, Voltaire to Frederick, April 15, 1739; EE, Châtelet to Frederick II, December 29, 1739; EE, Voltaire to Frederick, October 13, 1740.
68 EE, Voltaire to John Hervey, 2nd Baron Hervey of Ickworth, June 1, 1740; EE, Voltaire to Philibert Charles Marie Varenne de Fénille, December 4, 1761; EE, Voltaire to Pierre Robert Le Cornier de Cideville, September 1, 1742.
69 Quoted in O*reste* in *Oeuvres complètes de Voltaire, Tome 31A, Oeuvres de 1749*, ed. David H. Jory (Oxford: Voltaire Foundation, 1992), 397.
70 EE, Voltaire to the Duc de Bouillon December 23, 1767.
71 Voltaire, *The Age of Louis XIV*, trans. Martyn P. Pollack (London: Dent, 1961), 361–2.
72 Ibid.
73 Ibid. Voltaire's estimate is accurate; our database includes thirty-three editions in English published between 1700 and 1750. See http://kates.itg.pomona.edu/books/analytics.php?type=order_quarter_english.
74 Voltaire, *Le Mondain*, ed. H. T. Mason in *Oeuvres complètes de Voltaire* 16 (Oxford: Voltaire Foundation, 2003), 302: "D'autres soupers et de nouveaux plaisirs/Or maintenant, Mentor ou Télémaque,/Vantez-nous bien votre petite Itaque."
75 *Télémaque*, ed. Le Brun, 2:59; *Telemachus*, trans. Riley, 60. Nicholas Cronk, "The Epicurean Spirit: Champagne and the Defense of Poetry in Le Mondain," *SVEC* 371 (1999): 64.
76 Quoted in Istvan Hont, "The Early Enlightenment Debate on Commerce and Luxury," *The Cambridge History of Eighteenth-Century Political Thought*, eds. Mark Goldie and Robert Wokler (Cambridge: Cambridge University Press, 2006), 413. On luxury in *Telemachus*, see also Paul Schuurman, "Fénelon on Luxury, War and Trade in the *Telemachus*," *History of European Ideas* 38 (2012): 179–99.
77 Quoted in Isaac Nakhimovsky, "The Enlightened Prince and the Future of Europe: Voltaire and Frederick the Great's Anti Machivel of 1740," in *Commerce and Peace in the Enlightenment*, eds. Bela Kapossy and Richard Whatmore (Cambridge: Cambridge University Press, 2017), 58.
78 "Sur la Télémaque," *Oeuvres complètes de Montesquieu*, ed André Masson, 3 vols. (Paris: Nagel, 1950–5), 3:707. On Montesquieu's debt to *Telemachus*, see Dena Goodman, *Criticism in Action: Enlightenment Experiments in Political Writing* (Ithaca: Cornell University Press, 1989), 7–15.
79 Montesquieu, *My Thoughts*, trans. Henry C. Clark (Indianapolis: Liberty Fund, 2012), 40 [# 115]. Late eighteenth-century readers were aware of this quotation. See "Thoughts of Montesquieu Extracted and Translated from his Manuscripts," *Morning Chronicle and London Advertiser* (London, England), Thursday, July 10, 1788 (Issue 598).
80 Ibid., 40 [# 116].
81 For one English domestic servant, Samuel Hutchins, who ordered a copy of *Telemachus* for himself, see James Raven, Helen Small, and Naomi Tadmor, eds., *The Practice and Representation of Reading in England* (Cambridge: Cambridge University Press, 1996), 203.
82 *The Complete Works of M. de Montesquieu*, 4 vols (Dublin: W. Watson, 1777), 1: xxxiii.
83 Goodman, *Criticism in Action*, 48; Elena Russo, "Virtuous Economies: Modernity and Noble Expenditure from Montesquieu to Caillois," *Historical Reflections* 25 (1999): 261–2.

84 Fénelon, *Telemachus, Son of Ulysses*, 162.
85 Montesquieu, "Sur la Télémaque," 3:707.
86 Benjamin Vaughan, *New and Old Principles of Trade Compared* (London: Johnson, 1788), vii*n*.
87 Guillaume Thomas Raynal, *Histoire philosophique et politique . . . deux indes*, 7 vols. (Amsterdam, 1774), Volume 7 *Tableau de l'Europe*, 195–6; Fénelon, *Telemachus*, trans. Riley, 148: "Happy the king, who loves his people, and is beloved by them."
88 Chesterfield to Philip Stanhope, November 28, 1752, in Lord Chesterfield, *Letters*, ed. David Roberts (Oxford: Oxford University Press, 1992), 283–4. For a modern historian with a similar perspective, see Sanford B. Kanter, "Archibishop Fénelon's Political Activity: The Focal Point of Power in Dynasticism," *French Historical Studies* 4 (1966): 320–34. A more balanced view of Fénelon's politics is Roger Mettam, *Power and Faction in Louis XIV's France* (New York: Basil Blackwell, 1988), 91–2.
89 EE, Marie Anne de Vichy-Chamrond, Marquise du Deffant to Horace Walpole, April 20, 1777.
90 Samuel S. B. Taylor, "Rousseau's Contemporary Reputation in France," *SVEC* 27 (1963): 1545–74; John N. Pappas, *Voltaire & D'Alembert* (Bloomington: Indiana University Press, 1962); Robert Darnton, *The Business of Enlightenment: A Publishing History of the Encyclopédie, 1775–1800* (Cambridge: Harvard University Press, 1979).
91 *Encyclopédie, ou dictionnaire raisonné des sciences, des arts et des métiers, etc.*, eds. Denis Diderot and Jean Le Rond d'Alembert (University of Chicago: ARTFL Encyclopédie Project, Spring 2016 Edition), Robert Morrissey and Glenn Roe, eds., http://encyclopedie.uchicago.edu/.
92 "Quietism," *Encyclopédie ou Dictionnaire raisonné des sciences, des arts et des métiers*, 26 vols. (Neufchâtel: Samuel Faulche, 1765), 13:709–10.
93 "Le Périgord," *Encyclopédie* (Neufchâtel), 12:358. Between 1699–1765, our database lists fifty-one editions in English and nine editions in Dutch.
94 "Révolte," *Encyclopédie* (Neufchâtel), 14:237, quoting *Telemachus*, trans. Riley, 184.
95 "Roi," *Encyclopédie* (Neufchâtel), 14:321, quoting *Telemachus*, trans. Riley, 60.
96 Damien Tricoire, "The Fabrication of the Philosophe: Catholicism, Court Culture, and the Origins of Enlightenment Moralism in France," *Eighteenth-Century Studies* 51 (2018): 463–4.
97 *Oeuvres complètes de M. Helvétius*, 4 vols. (London: n.p., 1777) 3:130n. The same story resurfaces in *British Critic*, 8 vols. (London: Rivington, 1793–1826), 1:50.
98 "Dialogue entre Platon et Fénelon," *Journal encyclopédique* (1773) 1:329. On p. 330, Plato continues to Fénelon: "The picture of a perfect king painted in your *Telemachus* far outweighs my judgment on my imaginary republic. Your dialogues breathe virtue, common sense, a sound criticism, and a delicate taste."
99 "Inscription pour le portrait de Fénelon," *Journal encyclopédique* (August 1789): 452–3.
100 Quoted in the *Journal encyclopédique* (1771), 7:407. This theme is emphasized in Eli Carcassonne, *Fénelon: L'homme et l'oeuvre* (Paris: Boivin, 1946), especially 158–9. Of course, Carcassonne viewed this reputation as naturally deserved, rather than an image placed upon Fénelon by the mid-century philosophes.
101 D. W. Smith, *Helvétius: A Study in Persecution* (Oxford: Clarendon Press, 1965).
102 EE, Mirabeau to Helvétius, August 11, 1758.
103 EE, Helvétius to Jean Lévesque de Burigny, end of June 1761. Another Enlightenment political philosopher heavily influenced by *Telemachus* was Isaak Iselin (1728–82), who regularly mentioned the book in his correspondence and used it as the basis for educating

his own children. See Bela Kapossy, *Iselin Contra Rousseau: Sociable Patriotism and the History of Mankind* (Basle: Schwabe, 2006), 26–7.

104 Abigail Williams, *The Social Life of Books: Reading Together in the Eighteenth-Century Home* (New Haven: Yale University Press, 2017), 81–2.

105 Benjamin Vaughan, *New and Old Principles of Trade Compared* (London: J. Johnson, 1788), viin. Vaughan's short book was translated into French in 1789. On Vaughan's place in discussions of political economy, see Richard Whatmore, "Benjamin Vaughan and the Consequences of Anonymity: An Introduction to Kenneth E. Carpenter's Benjamin Vaughan's Contributions Unveiled: A Bibliography," *History of European Ideas* 44 (2018): 292–6.

106 Henry Higgs, *Bibliography of Economics, 1751–1775* (Cambridge: Cambridge University Press, 1935); Christine Théré, "Economic Publishing and Authors," in *Studies in the History of French Political Economy: From Bodin to Walras*, ed. Gilbert Facca-Rello (London: Routledge, 1998), 1–56; *The Economic Turn: Recasting Political Economy in Enlightenment Europe*, eds. Sophus Reinert and Steven Kaplan (London: Anthem Press, 2019).

107 EE, Rousseau to Mirabeau, June 19 and 31, 1767. On Mirabeau's early reputation, see Liana Vardi, *The Physiocrats and the World of the Enlightenment* (Cambridge: Cambridge University Press, 2012), 83–112.

108 Georges Weulersse, *La Mouvement physiocratie en France (de 1756 à 1770)*, 2 vols. (Paris: Alcan, 1910), 1:53.

109 Daniel Mornet, "Les Enseignements des bibliothèques privées (1750–1780)," *Revue d'Histoire littéraire de la France* 17 (1910): 460.

110 Joseph Schumpeter, *A History of Economic Analysis* (London: Routledge, 1981), 170n.

111 Victor de Riquetti, Marquis de Mirabeau, *L'Ami des hommes, ou, Traité de la population Second partie* (Avignon, 1756), 93–4. On Physiocracy and Fénelon, see Weulersse, *Le Mouvement physiocratie en France*, 1:3–5. For another contemporary treatment of Fénelon as an expert in political economy, see Jean Jacques Lefranc de Pompignan, *Dissertation sur les biens nobles, avec des observations sur le vingtième* (n.p,: n.p., 1758), 17.

112 Michael Kwass, "Consumption and the World of Ideas: Consumer Revolution and the Moral Economy of the Marquis De Mirabeau," *Eighteenth-Century Studies* 37 (2004): 187–213, and John Shovlin, *The Political Economy of Virtue: Luxury, Patriotism, and the Origins of the French Revolution* (Ithaca: Cornell University Press, 2006), 66–7. The influence of *Telemachus* and the Physiocrats on Italian debates regarding political economy is discussed in Koen Stapelbroek, *Love, Self-Deceit, and Money: Commerce and Morality in the Early Neapolitan Enlightenment* (Toronto: University of Toronto Press, 2008), 42–4.

113 *Journal de commerce et d'agriculture*, October 1760, 148–9, quoting from *Telemachus*, trans. Riley, 300.

114 Earle E. Coleman, "Éphémérides du citoyen, 1767–1772," *The Papers of the Bibliographical Society of America* 56 (1962): 17–45.

115 "Elôges de Fénelon," *Ephemérides du citoyen, ou Bibliothèque raisonée des sciences morales et politiques* 7, Part 2, no. 4 (1771): 174–80. See also Marco Cini, "Le avventure di Telemaco di Fenelon e la cultura economica italiana (secoli XVIII-XIX)," *Il pensiero economico italiano* 25 (2017): 11–25; and François Xavier Cuche, "L'Economie du Télémaque, l'économie dans le Télémaque," *Littératures classiques* 70 (2010): 103–18.

116 See especially EE, Jean Baptiste de Gouy to Jacques-Henri Bernardin de Saint-Pierre, between 1784 and 1787, and EE, Jean Antoine Gay to Jacques-Henri Bernardin de Saint-Pierre, July 5, 1786.

117 Jones, *Great Nation*, 194.
118 Jean Jacques Rousseau, *Emile, or on Education*, trans. Allan Bloom (New York: Basic Books, 1979), 414–5.
119 EE, Marc Michel Rey to Jean Jacques Rousseau, August 17, 1761.
120 EE, Antoine Jacques Roustan to Jean Jacques Rousseau, February 19, 1761.
121 EE, Rousseau to gens de loi, October 15, 1758.
122 EE, Rousseau to Vincent Bernhard Tscharner, April 29, 1762.
123 Henri Gouhier, "Rousseau et Fénelon," *Reappraisals of Rousseau: Studies in Honour of R. A. Leigh*, eds. Simon Harvey et al. (Totowa: Barnes and Noble, 1980), 279–89; Riley, "Rousseau, Fénelon, and the Quarrel Between the Ancients and the Moderns"; Matthew D. Mendham, "Rousseau's Partial Reception of Fénelon: From the Corruptions of Luxury to the Contradictions of Society," *Fénelon in the Enlightenment*, 47–76.
124 *The Female Mentor: Or, Select Conversations* 1 (1793), v.
125 *The Trifler*, Issue 19 (1795–6), 120–1.
126 *The Lady's Magazine; Or, Entertaining Companion for the Fair Sex, Appropriated Solely to their Use and Amusement* 17 (1786): 91. This quote is taken from a serialized fiction entitled "The Mother In-Law."
127 "Letter à Louis XIV," *Oeuvres*, ed. Le Brun, 1:543–51; *Moral and Political Writings*, ed. Hanley, 108–14. It was first published in Jean Le Rond d'Alembert, *Histoire de membres de l'Académie française*, 6 vols. (Paris: Moutard, 1785), 3:351–70; EE, Voltaire to Condorcet, November 24, 1777 and January 12, 1778. See also *The York Chronicle, And Weekly Advertiser* 1772–1773, Issue 49, November 19, 1773, 386: "A discovery has lately been made at Paris of a great number of manuscript papers of St. de Fenelon, Archbishop of Cambray."
128 D'Alembert, "Elôge de Fénelon," *Oeuvres*, 4 vols. (Paris: Belin, 1821): 492–4; parts of the address were published in "Fragments de l'Elôge de Fénelon, lu par M. d'Alembert, à l'Académie Française le 17 mai 1777, en présence de l'emperor," *Journal encyclopédique* (September 1778): 495–502. See also Dennis F. Essar, "Polemical Intent and Rhetorical Style in d'Alembert's Élôges historiques," *Man and Nature* 1 (1982): 34.
129 Jean Siffrein Maury, *Elôge de . . . Fénelon* (Paris: Regnard and Demonville, 1771), 38.
130 *Journal encyclopédique* (1771), 7:400–10, especially 407n. On Fénelon's notion of the general interest, see Patrick Riley, *The General Will before Rousseau: The Transformation of the Divine into the Civic* (Princeton: Princeton University Press, 1986), 76, 185, and 206.
131 EE, Voltaire to La Harpe, September 26, 1771.
132 Jeremy L. Caradonna, *The Enlightenment in Practice: Academic Prize Contests and Intellectual Culture in France, 1670–1794* (Ithaca: Cornell University Press, 2012), 76. Although Diderot conceded eloquence in La Harpe's eulogy, he wrote friends that La Harpe did not capture Fénelon's genius. See Denis Diderot, *Correspondance, Tome XI*, ed. Georges Roth (Paris: Minuit, 1964), 182.
133 Quoted in Cherel, *Fénelon au XVIIIe siècle en France (1715–1820)*, 450.
134 [Alexandre Frédéric Jacques Masson de Pezay and Denis Diderot], *Elôge de François de Salignac de la Motte-Fénelon* (Paris: Regnard and Demonville, 1771), 21–2. For Diderot's contribution, see Chérel, *Fénelon au xviiie siècle en France (1715–1820)*, 391–3.
135 EE, Denis Diderot, "Note contre Rousseau" (March 1782).
136 [Pezay and Diderot], *Elôge de . . . Fénelon*, 22.
137 Robert Darnton, "The High Enlightenment and the Low-Life of Literature in Prerevolutionary France," *Past and Present* 51 (1971): 81–115.

138 Jacques Pierre Brissot, *New Travels in the United States of America*, 2 vols. (London: Jordan, 1794), 1:71. On Brissot, see Robert Darnton, "The Brissot Dossier," *French Historical Studies* 17 (1991): 191–205.
139 EE, Jeremy Bentham to João Baptista Felgueiras, June 5, 1821; EE, Bentham to Toribio Núñez, May 9, 1821.
140 Patrick Riley, "Fenelon's Republican Monarchism in *Telemachus*," in *Monarchisms in the Age of Enlightenment: Liberty, Patriotism, and the Common Good*, eds. Hans Blom, Luisa Simonutti and John Christian Laursen (Toronto: University of Toronto Press, 2007), 78–100. I differ with Riley insofar as I see Fénelon's republican monarchism not so much inherent in *Telemachus*, but emerging from a later Rousseauian lens.
141 EE, Garat note, September 13, 1783.
142 *Les Loisirs du Chevalier d'Eon de Beaumont,* 13 vols. (Amsterdam, 1774), 11:13.
143 Joseph Michel Servan, *Discours sur les moeurs, prononcé au Parlement de Grenoble* (Lyon: Grabit, 1769), 58–9. On Servan and Enlightenment thought, see Dena Goodman, "Michel de Servan and the Plight of Letters on the Eve of the French Revolution," *Early Modern Conceptions of Property*, eds. John Brewer and Susan Staves (London: Routledge, 1995): 339–64.
144 [Dieudonné Thiébault], *Les Adieux du duc de Bourgogne et de l'abbé de Fénelon, son précepteur* (Paris: Prault, 1788), reviewed in *Journal encyclopédique* (September 1788), 202–25.
145 Louis Sebastien Mercier, *Memoirs of the Year Two Thousand Five Hundred*, trans. W. Hooper, 2 vols. (London: G. Robinson, 1772), 2:1–34.
146 For *Belisarius*, see "Bélisaire comparé avec le Télémaque de M. de Fénelon," in *Examen du Bélisaire de M. Marmontel*, nouvel édition augmentée (Paris: Hansy le jeune, 1767), 32–6.
147 Louis Sebastien Mercier, *Fénelon à son diocese, pièce dramatique en trois actes en prose* (Paris, 1794); see also "Fénelon," in *Fragments de politique et d'histoire*, 3 vols. (Paris: Buisson, 1792), 2:269–74.
148 *Journal Encyclopédique* (January 1793), 216, reviewing Mercier's *Fragments de politique et d'histoire*.
149 Jean Henri Bernardin de Saint-Pierre, *Studies of Nature*, 5 vols., trans. Henry Hunter (London: Dilly, 1796), 1:85.
150 Ibid., 4:390.
151 Jacques-Henri Bernardin de Saint-Pierre, *Etudes de la nature* (Paris: Didot, 1848), 418.
152 Bernardin de Saint Pierre, *Studies of Nature*, 4:391–2. These stories may carry shreds of truth. See [Andrew Michael Ramsay], *The Life of François de Salignac de la Motte Fenelon, Archbishop and Duke of Cambray* (London: Vaillant, 1723), 274–9; and Janet, *Fénelon*, 241–3.
153 Ibid., 392.
154 B*** de M, *Reflections on the Causes and Probable Consequences of the Late Revolution in France* (Edinburgh: Peter Hill, and London: Cadell, 1790), 11.
155 Richard Price, *A Discourse on the Love of Our Country, Delivered on Nov. 4, 1789* (London, 1790), 14.
156 *Proceedings in the National Assembly on the Admission of Mr. William Priestley, and the Motion for his Naturalization* (London: Ridgway, 1791–1792), 13.
157 Jean Jacques de Barrett, *De la loi naturelle*, 2 vols. (Paris: Defer Demasonneuve, 1790), 143.
158 Joseph Antoine Cérutti, *Elôge funèbre de M. de Mirabeau, prononcé le 4 avril 1791* (Paris, 1791), 3.

159 Joseph Antoine Cérutti, *Idées simple et précises sur le papier monnoie, les assignats forces, et les biens ecclésiastiques* (Paris: Desenne, 1790), 70.
160 See also Jessica Goodman, *Commemorating Mirabeau: Mirabeau aux Champs Elysees and Other Texts* (Cambridge: MHRA, 2017), 155, which discusses dramatic performances along the same theme. This portrait of Fénelon walking with a folio edition of Telemachus in his arms was inspired by the statue made by Félix Lecomte in 1777 for a Versailles palace gallery of twenty-three prominent "great men." The royal factory at Sevres popularized the image by selling small porcelain figurine copies. See http://cartelfr.louvre.fr/cartelfr/visite?srv=car_not_frame&idNotice=10619&langue=fr. My thanks to Dena Goodman for leading me along this trail.
161 *Archives parlementaire*, April 18, 1793, 636; Pierre Vincent Chalvet, *Des Qualités et des devoirs des instituteurs publique* (Paris, 1793), 13.
162 *Télémaque dans l'isle de Calypso* (Paris, 1790); Mercier, *Fénelon à son diocese, pièce dramatique en trois actes en prose*; Marie Joseph Chénier, *Fénelon, ou Les Religieuses de Cambrai* (Paris: Moutard, 1793).
163 *Archives parlementaires*, October 16, 1790, 666; Fénelon, *Oeuvres*, 9 vol. (Paris: Didot, 1787–92).
164 *Fénelon à une convention française ou préliminaires à la constitution du philosophe* (Paris, 1793), 4.
165 William Godwin, *An Enquiry Concerning Political Justice, and Its Influence on General Virtue and Happiness*, 2 vols. (London: J. Johnson, 1793), 2:403n.
166 Ibid., 1:81–2. See also Graham Allen, "Godwin, Fénelon, and the Disappearing Teacher," *History of European Ideas* 33 (2007): 9–24.
167 Gary Kates, *Monsieur d'Eon is a Woman: A Tale of Political Intrigue and Sexual Masquerade* (Baltimore: Johns Hopkins University Press, 2001), 273.
168 On the unity of the European Enlightenment, see John Robertson, *The Case for the Enlightenment: Scotland and Naples, 1680–1760* (Cambridge: Cambridge University Press, 2005).
169 Jonathan Israel, *A Revolution of the Mind: Radical Enlightenment and the Intellectual Origins of Modern Democracy* (Princeton: Princeton University Press, 2010).
170 David Allan, *Making British Culture: English Readers and the Scottish Enlightenment, 1740–1830* (New York: Routledge, 2008), 239.

Chapter 3

1 Luiz Carlos Villalta, "Montesquieu's *Persian Letters* and Reading Practices in the Luso-Brazilian World (1750–1802)," in *Enlightened Reform in Southern Europe and its Atlantic Colonies, 1750–1830*, ed. Gabriel Paquette (Farnham: Ashgate, 2009), 119–44.
2 Simon Linguet quoted in Franco Venturi, *The End of the Old Regime in Europe, 1776–1789, Part 1: The Great States of the West*, trans. R. Burr Litchfield (Princeton: Princeton University Press, 1991), 206. Kenneth Maxwell, *Pombal: Paradox of the Enlightenment* (New York: Cambridge University Press, 1995).
3 Villalta, "Montesquieu's *Persian Letters* and Reading Practices," 121; Jose Ferreira Carrato, "The Enlightenment in Portugal and the Educational Reforms of the Marquis of Pombal," *Studies in Voltaire and the Eighteenth Century* 167 (1977): 359–93.
4 Quoted in Villalta, "Montesquieu's *Persian Letters* and Reading Practices," 125.
5 Ibid., 121.

6 Quoted in Ibid., 122–3.
7 For Israel's treatment of Montesquieu, see Jonathan I. Israel, *Radical Enlightenment: Philosophy and the Making of Modernity, 1650–1750* (New York: Oxford University Press, 2001), 131, 149, 154, 375, and elsewhere. Among Israel's other volumes are *Enlightenment Contested: Philosophy, Modernity, and the Emancipation of Man, 1670–1752* (New York: Oxford University Press, 2006) and *Democratic Enlightenment: Philosophy, Revolution, and Human Rights 1750–1790* (New York: Oxford University Press, 2011).
8 David W. Davies, "The Geographic Extent of the Dutch Book Trade in the Seventeenth Century," *The Library Quarterly* 22 (1952): 200–7; Jurjen Vis, "The Book Trade in the Poort," *Quaerendo* 37 (2007): 111–46; Shlomo Berger, *Producing Redemption in Amsterdam: Early Modern Yiddish Books in Paratextual Perspective* (Leiden: Brill, 2013).
9 *Les Oeuvres de Monsieur de Cyrano Bergerac*, Nouv. ed. (Amsterdam: Desbordes, 1709); Joseph Addison, *Caton: Tragédie* (Amsterdam: Desbordes, 1713); Jean LaPlacette and Nicolas Chalaire, *Traité Du Pyrrhonisme de l'Eglise Romaine* (Amsterdam: Desbordes, 1721); Charles Drelincourt, *Les Consolations de l'âme fidèle, contre les frayeurs de la mort*, nouvelle éd. (Amsterdam: Desbordes, 1714); Bernard de La Monnoye, *Histoire de Mr. Bayle et de ses ouvrages ... nouvelle ed.* (Amsterdam: Desbordes, 1716).
10 Margaret C. Jacob, "The Clandestine Universe of the Early Eighteenth Century," *Marteau Studies* (2001), http://www.pierre-marteau.com/c/jacob/clandestine.html. Accessed January 13, 2019.
11 *Oeuvres complètes de Montesquieu*, ed. Jean Ehrard, et al., 22 vols. (Oxford: Voltaire Foundation, 1998-): 1:15–44.
12 Richard B. Sher, *The Enlightenment and the Book: Scottish Authors and Their Publishers in Eighteenth-Century Britain, Ireland, and America* (Chicago: University of Chicago Press, 2006), 86.
13 Letter 52. Letter numbering follows the most recent critical edition published as the first volume of *Oeuvres complètes de Montesquieu*, ed. Jean Ehrard, et al. (Oxford: Voltaire Foundation, 1998).
14 Robert Shackleton, "The Muslim Chronology of the *Lettres persanes*," *French Studies* 7 (1954): 17–27.
15 Letter 89, the 18th of the Moon of Gemmadi 2, 1715. All English quotations come from the Margaret Mauldon translation (Oxford: Oxford World Classics, 2008).
16 Letter 10.
17 Letter 11.
18 Alessandro S. Crisafulli, "Montesquieu's Story of the Troglodytes: Its Background, Meaning, and Significance," *PMLA* 58 (1943): 372–92; Jean Le Rond d'Alembert, "An Eulogium on President Montesquieu," in *The Complete Works of Monsieur de Montesquieu*, 4 vols. (Dublin: W. Watson, 1777), 1:v.
19 Letter 35.
20 Ibid.
21 J. H. Shennan, *Philippe, Duke of Orléans: Regent of France, 1715–1723* (London: Thames and Hudson, 1979), 191.
22 Letter 6.
23 Letter 99.
24 *Lettres Historiques, contenant ce qui se passe plus important en Europe* 59 (May 1721): 546–53, reproduced in Catherine Volpilhac-Auger, ed., *Montesquieu: Mémoire de la critique* [hereafter referred to as *Montesquieu: Mémoire*] (Paris: Presses de l'Université de Paris-Sorbonne, 2003), 31–4.

25 Letter 22, cited in *Lettres historiques*, 548–9.
26 Ibid., 548.
27 *Mémoires historiques et critiques*, January 1722, 11–22, in *Montesquieu: Mémoire*, 39–44.
28 Jean Paul Marana, *L'Espion turc dans les cour des princes chrètiens*, 6 vols (Cologne, 1700).
29 Ibid. On Unigenitus, see William Doyle, *Jansenism: Catholic Resistance to Authority from the Reformation to the French Revolution* (New York: St. Martin's Press, 2000), 45–58.
30 Pierre de Marivaux, *Journaux et oeuvres diverses*. eds. Frédéric Deloffre and Michel Gilot (Paris: Garnier frères, 1969), 153–4.
31 Voltaire, "Catalogue de la plupart des écrivains français qui ont paru dans le siècle de Louis XIV," in *Oeuvres historiques*, ed. René Pomeau (Paris: Gallimard, 1957), 1187.
32 For one example, see Electronic Enlightenment (EE), Voltaire to Bernard Joseph Saurin, December 28, 1768.
33 Robert Shackleton, *Montesquieu: A Critical Biography* (Oxford: Oxford University Press, 1961), 14–26.
34 Edgar Mass, *Literatur und Zensur in der frühen Aufklärung: Produktion, Distribution und Rezeption der Lettres persanes* (Frankfurt am Main: Klostermann, 1981); Thierry Rigogne, *Between State and Market: Printing and Bookselling in Eighteenth-Century France* (Oxford: Voltaire Foundation, 2007).
35 Mass, *Literatur und Zensur in der frühen Aufklärung*, 191–3.
36 Shackleton, *Montesquieu*, 55–61.
37 Ibid., 86–7.
38 "Advertisement," *Persian Letters*, trans. Ozell, 2 vols. (London: Tonson, 1722).
39 Ibid.
40 Montesquieu, *Oeuvres Complètes*, 1:128.
41 *Annual Register* 1 (1758): 240.
42 Ursula Haskins Gonthier, *Montesquieu and England: Enlightened Exchanges, 1689–1755* (London: Pickering & Chatto, 2010), 236.
43 *Bibliothèque raisonnée des ouvrages des savans de l'Europe* (1735): 286, reviewing George Lyttelton, *Letters from a Persian in England to His Friend in Ispahan* (London: Millan, 1735).
44 Ibid., 289. See also *Le Pour et le contre* 6 (1735): 335–6.
45 Alessandro S. Crisafulli, "A Neglected English Imitation of Montesquieu's *Lettres Persanes*," *Modern Language Quarterly* 14 (1953): 209–16; W. Fairbairn, "False Attributions of the *Lettres persanes*," in *Studies in the French Eighteenth Century: Presented to John Lough by Colleagues, Pupils and Friends*, eds. D. J. Mossop, G. E. Rodmell and D. B. Wilson. Anonymous (Durham: University of Durham, 1978), 52–65; Morris Neiman, "A Hebrew Imitation of Montesquieu's *Lettres Persanes*," *Jewish Social Studies* 37, no. 2 (1975): 163–9.
46 René-Louis de Voyer, Marquis d'Argenson, *Essays, Civil, Moral, Literary and Political* (London: Logographic Press, 1789), 296.
47 Fontenelle's *Entretiens sur la pluralité des mondes* was first published in 1687 in Amsterdam and, like *Persian Letters*, became an eighteenth-century bestseller.
48 Jean Baptiste Gaultier, *Les lettres persannes, convaincues d'impiété* (1751), abridged in *Montesquieu: Mémoire,* 191.
49 Ibid., 189.
50 Ibid., 196.
51 Gabriel Gauchat, "Sur les *Lettres persannes*," *Lettres critiques, ou, Analyse et réfutation de divers écrits modernes contre la religion*, 19 vols. (Paris: Herissant, 1755–63), 2: Preface. The next two quotes are also from this source.

52 *Persian Letters*, 227–8.
53 Nancy K. Miller, *The Heroine's Text: Readings in the French and English novel, 1722–1782* (New York: Columbia University Press, 1980); Ian P. Watt, *The Rise of the Novel: Studies in Defoe, Richardson, and Fielding* (London: Chatto and Windus, 1957).
54 *Persian Letters*, 227; Montesquieu, *Oeuvres complètes* 1:567n5 for the early draft.
55 D'Alembert, "An Eulogium on President Montesquieu," 1:v–ix.
56 *Journal encyclopédique*, October 1, 1759, 80–98. See also Raymond Francis Birn, *Pierre Rousseau and the Philosophes of Bouillon* (Genève: Institut et Musée Voltaire, 1964).
57 Charles Auteur Palissot de Montenoy, *Oeuvres . . . nouvelle édition* (Paris: Plomteux, 1777), 4:241.
58 Letter 74. For the historical context surrounding efforts to decriminalize suicide, see Jeffrey R. Watt, ed., *From Sin to Insanity: Suicide in Early Modern Europe* (Ithaca: Cornell University Press, 2004); and Lester G. Crocker, "The Discussion of Suicide in the Eighteenth Century," *Journal of the History of Ideas* 13 (1952): 47–72.
59 Letter 150.
60 Jean Henri Formey, "Dissertation sur le meurtre volontaire de soi-même," in *Mélanges philosophiques*, 2 vols. (Leiden: Elie Luzac, Fils, 1754), 1:205–35.
61 *Persian Letters*, 3rd ed., trans. John Ozell (London: J. Tonson, 1736), xiii–xv.
62 Villalta, "Montesquieu's *Persian Letters* and Reading Practices," 121.
63 Jean Dumas, *Traité du suicide* (Amsterdam: D.J. Changuion, 1773), 287.
64 Rousseau to Moultou, November 25, 1762, in Jean Jacques Rousseau, *Correspondance complète*, ed. R. A. Leigh, 52 vols. (Geneva: Institut et Musée Voltaire 1965–1998),14:100–3.
65 Becarria to Morellet, January 26, 1766, in *Correspondance générale d'Helvétius*, ed. David Smith, et al., 5 vols. (Toronto: University of Toronto Press, 1981–2005), 3:252–4.
66 Paul Louis Roederer, *Oeuvres*, ed. Baron Antoine Marie Roederer, 8 vols. (Paris: Didot, 1853–9), 8:166, quoting from lectures given in 1793: "Jetez les yeux sur la peinture nécessairement fidèle d'un sérail dans les Lettres persanes. Il y a plus d'histoire dans ce morceau d'un roman que dans beaucoup d'histoires que l'Esprit des lois a extradite."

Chapter 4

1 Vivienne Dunstan, "Reading Habits in Scotland Circa 1750–1820," unpublished PhD dissertation, University of Dundee, 2010, 90.
2 Ibid., 102. See also Mark R. M. Towsey, *Reading History in Britain and America, C.1750–C.1840* (Cambridge: Cambridge University Press, 2019).
3 Ibid., 93: "Figure 6: Most frequently borrowed books at the Gray Library, decade by decade," and 104: "Table 9: Borrowings of occupational groups at the Gray Library, 1790s–1810s."
4 Gilles Éboli, *Livres et lecteurs en Provence au 18 siècle: Autour des David, imprimeurs-libraires à Aix* (Méolans-Revel: Atelier Perrousseaux, 2008), 224.
5 Ronald E. Crook, *A Bibliography of Joseph Priestley 1733–1804* (London: The Library Association, 1966).
6 The standard introduction to eighteenth-century historical writing is Karen O'Brien, *Narratives of Enlightenment: Cosmopolitan History from Voltaire to Gibbon* (Cambridge: Cambridge University Press, 1997).

7   The standard biography is R. M. Hatton, *Charles XII of Sweden* (London: Weidenfeld and Nicolson, 1968).
8   *Histoire de Charles XII*, ed. Gunnar von Proschwitz in *Les Oeuvres complètes de Voltaire* 4 (Oxford: Voltaire Foundation, 2007) [hereafter cited as *Charles XII*], 8–9, 37–42, 88–9. On the English editions, see Keith Maslen, "Some Early Editions of Voltaire Printed in London," *Library: A Magazine of Bibliography and Literature* 5 (1959): 287–93. See also Roger Pearson, *Voltaire Almighty: A Life in Pursuit of Freedom* (London: Bloomsbury, 2005), 90–1.
9   Electronic Enlightenment [hereafter cited as EE], Voltaire to Nicolas Claude Thieriot, May 26, 1732.
10 *Read's Weekly Journal or British Gazetteer*, February 1733 through October 1734. Editions printed outside of France included Voltaire's name on the title page.
11 *Histoire de Charles XII* was Voltaire's most popular book both in terms of total number of editions and by considering an annualized average of editions since first publication. See http://kates.itg.pomona.edu/books/.
12 Richard Sher, *The Enlightenment and the Book: Scottish Authors and Their Publishers in Eighteenth-Century Britain, Ireland, and America* (Chicago: University of Chicago Press, 2006), 688.
13 *Charles XII*, 153. English translations come from Voltaire, *Lion of the North: Charles XII of Sweden*, trans. M. F. O. Jenkins (Teaneck: Fairleigh Dickinson University Press, 1981), 19.
14 Ibid.
15 *The Present State of the Republic of Letters*. Mandeville's *Enquiry* is reviewed in the January 1732 issue, Article 3, 32–6, and continued in February 1732, Article 1, 93–105. For *Charles XII*, see January 1732, Article 4, 37–60, and continuing in March 1732, Article 16, 181–218. On Mandeville, see E. J. Hundert, *The Enlightenment Fable: Bernard Mandeville and the Discovery of Society* (Cambridge: Cambridge University Press, 1994).
16 Ibid., 34, 36.
17 Ibid., 36. On Mandeville and Bayle, the reviewer anticipates Lawrence Dickey, "Pride, Hypocrisy, and Civility in Mandeville's Social and Historical Theory," *Critical Review* 4 (1990): 387–431; E. D. James, "Faith, Sincerity and Morality: Mandeville and Bayle," in *Mandeville Studies: Explorations in the Art and Thought of Dr. Bernard Mandeville*, ed. Irwin Primer (The Hague: Martinus Nijhoff, 1975), 43–65.
18 Ibid, 40. Bayle's influence on Voltaire has been confirmed by H. T. Mason, *Pierre Bayle and Voltaire* (Oxford: Oxford University Press, 1963).
19 Ibid., 45, 217–18. The influence of Pufendorf on Charles is reiterated in Hatton, *Charles XII of Sweden*, 50. But there is no evidence that Pufendorf directly tutored Charles XII.
20 Ibid., 54–5. For Bayle and amour propre see Michael Locke McLendon, *The Psychology of Inequality: Rousseau's Amour-Propre* (Philadelphia: University of Pennsylvania Press, 2019), 58.
21 EE, Claude Brossette to Jean Baptiste Rousseau, May 6, 1732.
22 EE, Vincenz Bernhard Tscharner to Johann Rudolf Sinner, June 26, 1746.
23 *Craftsman*, No. 300, April 15, 1732, 74.
24 *Daily Courant*, April 20, 1732.
25 *Lloyd's Evening Post*, No. 1785, December 12, 1768.
26 Eléazar de Mauvillon, "Considérations sur quelques auteurs françois et sur M. de Voltaire en particulier," in *Lettres françoises et germaniques* (Londres: Francois Allemand, 1740), 269–307. The quotations come from 271, 281, and 285. An abridged version is reproduced

in Kees Van Strien, *Voltaire in Holland 1736–1745* (Louvain: Editions Peeters, 2011), 236–41.
27 *Letters Concerning the English Nation* (London: C. Davis and A. Lyon, 1733), 247–53.
28 *The Bee, or, Universal Weekly Pamphlet*, 9 vols (London, 1733), 1:126–7 and 5:27.
29 EE, Bertin de Rocheret to Voltaire, March 14, 1732.
30 Gérard Genette, *Paratexts: Thresholds of Interpretation*, trans. Jane E. Lewin (Cambridge: Cambridge University Press, 1997).
31 *Charles XII*, 151–6; *Lion of the North*, 17–20. On early modern attitudes to information overload, see Ann Blair, *Too Much to Know: Managing Scholarly Information Before the Modern Age* (New Haven: Yale University Press, 2011).
32 Aubry de La Motraye, *Remarques historiques & critiques sur L'Histoire de Charles XII, Roi de Suède, par M. de Voltaire* (Londres: Pierre Dunoye, 1732); *Historical and Critical Remarks on the History of Charles XII, King of Sweden, by Mr. de Voltaire* (London: T. Warner, 1732).
33 Aubry de La Motraye, *Travels through Europe, Asia, and into Part of Africa* (London: Printed for the Author, 1723); *Voyages du sr. A. de La Motraye, en Europe, Asie & Afrique* (The Hague: T. Johnson and J. van Duren, 1727).
34 La Motraye, *Historical and Critical Remarks on the History of Charles XII, King of Sweden, by Mr. de Voltaire*, 4, 6.
35 EE, Voltaire to Jean Baptiste Nicolas Formont, September 12, 1772.
36 *Charles XII*, 95–6. This edition also included the "Lettre de M. de Voltaire, écrite de Paris le 25 avril 1733," soon retitled "Lettre sur l'incendie de la ville d'Altona" and added as a final letter to Voltaire's *Letters Concerning the English Nation*.
37 *Charles XII*, 586.
38 Ibid., 590.
39 Ibid., 592.
40 Ibid., 597. A list of Voltaire's papers given to the Bibliothèque du roi is reproduced in Ibid., 616–23.
41 A list of editions during Voltaire's lifetime is well described in *Charles XII*, 85–132.
42 "Éditions collectives, 1728-1778," at https://c18.net/vo/vo_pages.php?nom=vo_oe_18_liste. Accessed March 5, 2022.
43 On Voltaire's relationship with Dutch publishers during the 1730s, I am closely relying on Van Strien, *Voltaire in Holland 1736–1745*.
44 Geoffrey Turnovsky, *The Literary Market: Author and Modernity in the Old Regime* (Philadelphia: University of Pennsylvania Press, 2010); *Voltaire et le livre*, eds. François Bessire and Françoise Tilkin (Ferney-Voltaire: Centre International D'Etude Du XVIIIe Siècle, 2009).
45 [Stanislas Poniatowski], *Remarques d'un seigneur polonois sur L'Histoire de Charles XII roi de Suede par M. de Voltaire* (La Haye: Moetjens, 1741); EE, Voltaire to Schulenburg, August 2, 1740.
46 *Charles XII*, 105.
47 EE, Voltaire to Berger, July 20, 1738.
48 Andrew Brown, "Les Editions Prault des Oeuvres de Voltaire," *Cahiers Voltaire* 10 (2011): 21–40.
49 This section closely follows Martin Fontius and David Smith, "La publication en 1748 des *Oeuvres complètes de Mr. de Voltaire* par Georg Konrad Walther, de Dresde," in *Voltaire et le livre*, 47–66. On Dresden's cultural flowering, see Janice B. Stocking, "The Court of Saxony-Dresden," in *Music at German Courts, 1715–1760: Changing Artistic Priorities*, eds. Janice B Stocking, Samantha Owens, and Barbara M. Reul (Suffolk: Boydell and Brewer, 2011), 17–50.

50 Jöran Andersson Nordberg, *Histoire de Charles XII, traduit de swédois*, 4 vols. (The Hague: Husson, 1742–8).
51 "Préface des éditeurs," in "Three Texts in Defense of the 1748 Dresden Edition," ed. Nicholas Cronk in *Oeuvres complètes de Voltaire 30C* (Oxford: Voltaire Foundation, 2004), 355.
52 "Three Texts in Defense of the 1748 Dresden Edition," 349.
53 EE, Voltaire to Walther, July 15, 1747.
54 Quoted in Fontius and Smith, "La publication en 1748 des *Oeuvres complètes de Mr. de Voltaire* par Georg Konrad Walther, de Dresde," 55–6.
55 EE, Voltaire to Walther, February 26, 1748.
56 EE, Voltaire to Walther, February 16, 1748, cited in Smith 2009.
57 "Three Texts in Defense of the 1748 Dresden Edition," 354.
58 "Avis des éditeurs," in *Oeuvres de Mr. de Voltaire, Tome 7* (Amsterdam: Ledet, 1749), 3.
59 Plinio J. Smith, "Bayle and Pyrrhonism: Antinomy, Method, and History," in *Scepticism in the Eighteenth Century: Enlightenment, Lumières, Aufklärung*, eds. Sébastien Charles and Plinio J. Smith (Dordrecht: Springer, 2013), 19–30.
60 "Pyrrhonisme de l'Histoire," *Charles XII*, 567–78. An English translation can be found in *The Works of M. de Voltaire*, ed. T. Smollett, 35 vols. (London: J. Newberry, 1762–1781), 10:49–58.
61 I have slightly changed the translation from Voltaire, [François-Marie Arouet] de. "History." *The Encyclopedia of Diderot & d'Alembert Collaborative Translation Project*, trans. Jeremy Caradonna (Ann Arbor: Michigan Publishing, University of Michigan Library, 2006). http://hdl.handle.net/2027/spo.did2222.0000.088. Accessed July 23, 2018. Originally published as "Histoire," *Encyclopédie ou Dictionnaire raisonné des sciences, des arts et des métiers,* 8:220–5 (Paris, 1765).
62 EE, Voltaire to Marie-Louise Denis, June 10, 1748. This section closely follows D. W. Smith, "Did Voltaire Collaborate in the Rouen (Machuel) 1750 edition of his *Oeuvres?*" *Journal of Eighteenth-Century Studies* 31 (2008): 571–7; "Robert Machuel, imprimeur-librarire à Rouen," *Cahiers Voltaire* 6 (2007): 35–57; and "Les relations entre Voltaire et ses libraires: Walther, Machuel, et Lambert, 1748–1752," in *Voltaire et le livre*, 37–46.
63 [Pierre-François Guyot Desfontaines], *La Voltairomanie* (London [Amsterdam], 1739).
64 "Anecdotes sur le czar Pierre le Grand," in *Les Oeuvres complètes de Voltaire, 46*, ed. Michel Mervaud (Oxford: Voltaire Foundation, 1999), 83.
65 On his attempts to reduce press censorship, see Raymond Birn, "Malesherbes and the Call for a Free Press," in *Revolution in Print: The Press in France*, eds. Robert Darnton and Daniel Roche (Berkeley: University of California Press, 1989), 50–66.
66 The first edition of Montesquieu's works, a three-volume quarto, appeared in 1758, three years after his death.
67 Voltaire, "Pensées sur l'administration Public," in *Oeuvres Complètes de Voltaire, 32A*, eds. Ahmad Gunny and David Williams (Oxford: Voltaire Foundation, 2006), 303–30. The quotations come from 318, 322.
68 Voltaire, *Lettre à Mr. Norberg, chapelain du roy de Suede Charles XII, auteur de l'Histoire de ce monarque* (Londres, 1744), reproduced in *Charles XII*, 557–66. The letter was altered and shortened when it became a preface. For an English translation, see *Works*, ed. Smollett, 10:41–8.
69 "Lettre à Monsieur le Maréchal de Schulenburg, Général des Vénitiens, 15 September 1740," in *Charles XII*, 641–7. As von Proschwitz explains, the published letter was never actually sent to Schulenburg, but was a compilation of two earlier letters. For Schulenburg's response, see 649–59. For an English translation, see *Works*, ed. Smollett,

10:35–40. On Frederick and Voltaire, see Tim Blanning, *Frederick the Great: King of Prussia* (New York: Random House, 2016), 355–61.

70 *Oeuvres mêlées de M. de Voltaire*, 5 vols. (Geneva: Bousquet, 1742), Vol. 4. Walther (1748 and 1752), Machuel (1750), and Lambert (1751) all included it in their *Works* editions, but apart from the *Charles XII* volume. It is reproduced in "Remarques sur l'histoire," ed. Myrille Méricam-Bourdet, *Oeuvres complètes de Voltaire, 28B* (Oxford: Voltaire Foundation, 2008), 143–64. For an English translation, see *Works*, ed. Smollett, 10:1–7.

71 Dunstan, "Reading Habits in Scotland Circa 1750–1820," 93.

72 Voltaire, "Nouvelle considérations sur l'histoire," in *La Mérope française: avec quelques petites pièces de littérature* (Paris: Prault, 1744), 81–6, reproduced in "Nouvelle Considérations sur l'histoire," ed. Myrtille Méricam-Bourdet, *Les Oeuvres complètes de Voltaire, 28B* (Oxford: Voltaire Foundation, 2008), 165–85. Quotes from 177 and 184. For an English translation, see *Works*, ed. Smollett, 10:8–13.

73 In *Charles XII*, 118–35, Proschwitz lists the following complete works editions by the Cramers: W56, W57G1, W57G2, 60G, W64G, 66G, W68, 70G, W71, W75G, and 76G1. On the Cramers, see Gilles Barber, "The Cramers of Geneva and their Trade in Europe between 1755 and 1766," *SVEC* 30 (1964): 377–413. On the Kehl editions of 1784 and 1785, see Gilles Barber, "The Financial History of the Kehl Voltaire," in *The Age of the Enlightenment: Studies Presented to Theodore Besterman*, eds. W. H. Barber et al. (Edinburgh: Univ. of St. Andrews, 1964), 152–70. Seven of the eight essays were attached to the English translations produced in 1761 as Volume 10 of *The Works of M. de Voltaire*, 38 vols. (London: J. Newberry) and in 1769 as Volume 1 of *The Works of Voltaire*, 2 vols. (Edinburgh: Martin and Wortherspoon).

74 Voltaire, "De l'utilité de l'histoire," in *Nouveaux mélanges philosophiques, historiques, critiques*, etc. (Geneva: Cramer, 1765); reproduced in *Les Oeuvres complètes de Voltaire 60A*, ed. Myrtille Méricam-Bourdet (Oxford: Voltaire Foundation, 2017), 447–56. For an English translation, see Voltaire, *History of Charles XII* (Edinburgh: Martin and Wortherspoon, 1769), 11–13.

75 J. H. Brumfitt, *Voltaire: Historian* (Oxford: Oxford University Press, 1958), 9.

76 Montesquieu, *My Thoughts*, trans. Henry C. Clark (Indianapolis: Liberty Fund, 2012), 201 (#641).

77 Emmanuel de Broglie, *Les Portefeuilles du president Bouhier: extraits et fragments de correspondance littéraire (1715–1746)* (Paris: Hachette, 1896), 227–8.

78 EE, Marquise du Châtelet-Lomont to Jacques François Paul Aldonce de Sade, July 15, 1734.

79 *The Present State of the Republick of Letters* 14 (July 1734): 111–16.

80 Mouza Raskolnikoff, *Histoire romaine et critique historique dans l'Europe des lumières: La naissance de l'hypercritique dans l'historiographie de la Rome antique* (Rome: Ecole Française de Rome, 1992), 501–8; Vanessa de Senarclens, *Montesquieu, Historien de Rome: Un tournant pour la réflexion sur le statut de l'histoire au xviiie siècle* (Geneva: Droz, 2003), 33–9, 152–6.

81 Charles de Secondat, Baron de Montesquieu, *Considérations sur les causes de la grandeur des Romains et de leur decadence*, eds. Françoise Weil et Cecil Courtney, in *Oeuvres complètes de Montesquieu 2* (Oxford: Voltaire Foundation, 2000) [hereafter cited as *Considérations*], 158, 94. All translations come from *Considerations on the Causes of the Greatness of the Romans and their Decline*, trans. David Lowenthal (Indianapolis: Hackett, 1965). *Considérations*, 235: "Here, in a word, is the history of the Romans. By

means of their maxims they conquered all peoples, but when they had succeeded in doing so, their republic could not endure."
82 *Considérations*, 93: "Since Rome was a city without commerce, and almost without arts, pillage was the only means individuals had of enriching themselves."
83 *Considérations,* 199: "The frightful tyranny of the emperors derived from the general spirit of the Romans." In his private notebooks, Montesquieu was even more explicit in his condemnation of Roman expansion: "If anyone doubts the misfortune a great conquest brings, he has only to read the history of the Romans. The Romans took the world away from the most flourishing condition in which it can be; they destroyed the most beautiful establishments in order to form a single one which they could not sustain; they extinguished the liberty of the universe and following that abused their own: they enfeebled the entire world, as bespoilers and bespoiled, as tyrants and as slaves." Quoted in Mark Hulliung, *Montesquieu and the Old Regime* (Berkeley and Los Angeles: University of California Press, 1976), 141. See also Jean Ehrard, "Rome enfin que je hais . . .?" in *Storia e Ragione: Le Considérations sur les causes de la grandeur des Romains et de leur décadence di Montesquieu nel 250° della pubblicazione,* ed Alberto Postigliola (Naples: Liguori Editore, 1987), 23–32.
84 See for example, *Discours politiques de Machiavel sur la I. décade de Tite Live* (Amsterdam: Pierre Mortier, 1711).
85 Broglie, *Les Portefeuilles du president Bouhier*, 227.
86 Hulliung, *Montesquieu and the Old Regime*, 142–72.
87 *Considérations*, 53–4.
88 Ibid., 152n.
89 Ibid., 157.
90 Ibid., 200.
91 Ibid., 279–80.
92 Ibid, 181.
93 Ibid, 181–2.
94 Ibid.
95 These editions and those discussed below are described in Ibid., 50–64.
96 Ibid., 64–72.
97 Raskolnikoff, *Histoire romaine et critique historique dans l'Europe des lumières,* 455–69.
98 Quoted in Thomas Chaimowicz, *Antiquity as the Source of Modernity: Freedom and Balance in the Thought of Montesquieu and Burke* (New York: Routledge, 2008), 61.
99 Edward Gibbon, "Essay on the Study of Literature," trans. Robert Mankin, *Republic of Letters* 3 (April 2014).
100 Edward Gibbon, *Memoirs of My Life*, ed. Betty Radice (Middlesex: Penguin, 1984), 99. "Gibbon," writes J. G. A. Pocock, "would have preferred one page of Montesquieu to all the historical entertainments of Voltaire." *Barbarism and Religion. Volume 1. The Enlightenments of Edward Gibbon, 1737–1764* (Cambridge: Cambridge University Press, 1999), 199. William Robertson was another historian who preferred Montesquieu to Voltaire. See Arnaldo Momigliano, "Gibbon's Contribution to Historical Method," *Historia: Zeitschrift für Alte Geschichte*, 2 (1954): 450–63
101 Edward Gibbon, *The Decline and Fall of the Roman Empire*, ed. J. B. Bury, 7 vols. (London: 1909–14), Chapter 38, 173–4; Robert Shackleton, "The Impact of French Literature on Gibbon," *Daedalus* 105 (1976), 46.
102 *Considérations*, 154, 158–9.

103 J. G. A. Pocock, *Barbarism and Religion. Volume 1. The Enlightenments of Edward Gibbon, 1737–1764* (Cambridge: Cambridge University Press, 1999), 85, 88, 139; Gibbon, *Memoirs of My Life*, 118.
104 Robert Shackleton, "Allies and Enemies: Voltaire and Montesquieu," *Essays by Diverse Hands* 39 (1977): 126–45.
105 Dena Goodman, *Criticism in Action: Enlightenment Experiments in Political Writing* (Ithaca: Cornell University Press, 1989), especially 174–85.
106 Voltaire, "Corpus des notes marginales," in *Les Oeuvres complètes de Voltaire 140B* (Oxford: Voltaire Foundation, 2012), 708–26. See also Inna Gorbatov, "From Paris to St. Petersburg: Voltaire's Library in Russia," *Libraries & the Cultural Record* 42:308–24.
107 "Histoire" in *Encyclopédie*, 223.
108 Voltaire, "L'A, B, C, dix-sept dialogues traduits de l'anglais de Monsieur Huet," in *Les Oeuvres complètes de Voltaire 65A*, eds. Roland Mortier and Christophe Paillard (Oxford: Voltaire Foundation, 2011), 169–348.
109 Voltaire, *La Philosophie de l'histoire*, ed. J. H. Brumfitt (Oxford: Voltaire Foundation, 1969), 263.

Chapter 5

1 Gustave Lanson, *Voltaire* (Paris: Hachette, 1906), 52.
2 For two examples, see Peter Gay, *Voltaire's Politics: The Poet as Realist* (Princeton: Princeton University Press, 1959), 48–65, and W. H. Barber, "Voltaire: Art, Thought, and Action," *The Modern Language Review* 88 (1993): xxvi.
3 Martha Hanna, "Laying Siege to the Sorbonne: The Action Française's Attack upon the Dreyfusard University," *Historical Reflections / Réflexions Historiques* 24 (1998): 155–77.
4 According to WorldCat, during the twentieth century *Philosophical Letters* was published for the first time in Basque, Italian, Japanese, Korean, Norwegian, Polish, Russian, and Spanish.
5 Voltaire, *Voltaire's Notebooks*, ed. Theodore Besterman, 2 vols. (Geneva: Institut et Musée Voltaire, 1952), 1:81.
6 Voltaire, *The Works of M. de Voltaire*, ed. T. Smollett (London: J. Newberry, 1762), 13:171. Voltaire added these comments to *Philosophical Letters* in 1756.
7 Voltaire, "Advertisement to the Reader," *Oeuvres de 1723–1728 II: The English Essays of 1727*, ed. David Williams (Oxford: Voltaire Foundation, 1996), 6.
8 See, for example, *Voltaire's Notebooks*, 1:31.
9 Pierre François Le Coq de Villeroy, *Réponse, ou Critique des Lettres philosophiques de Monsieur de V**** (Basle [Reims]: Chez Christophe Revis, 1735), 4. For a more general context, see Robynne Rogers Healey, *Quakerism in the Atlantic World, 1690–1830*, ed. Robynne Rogers Healey (University Park: Pennsylvania State University Press, 2021).
10 Voltaire, *Letters Concerning the English Nation*, ed. Nicholas Cronk (Oxford: Oxford University Press, 1994), 30.
11 Denis Lacorne, *The Limits of Tolerance: Enlightenment Values and Religious Fanaticism*, trans. C. Jon Delogu and Robin Emlein (New York: Columbia University Press, 2019), 31–44.
12 Voltaire, *Letters*, ed. Cronk, 38, 40.

13 Ibid.
14 Gay, *Voltaire's Politics*.
15 Voltaire, *Lettres Philosophiques*, ed. Lanson, 2: 123. For Voltaire's original transcription in English and French, see *Voltaire's Notebooks*, ed. Theodore Besterman (Geneva: Institut and Musée Voltaire, 1952), 1: 79. 118. See also John Hervey et al., *Lord Hervey and His Friends, 1726–1738: Based on Letters from Holland House, Melbury, and Ickworth*, ed. Earl of Ilchester (London: John Murray, 1950); and more recently, John Hervey, *The Collected Verse of John, Lord Hervey (1696–1743)*, ed. Bill Overton (Cambridge: Cambridge University Press, 2016), 107–19, esp. 112.
16 Voltaire, *Letters*, ed. Cronk, 99.
17 Michael Bennett, "Jenner's Ladies: Women and Vaccination against Smallpox in Early Nineteenth-Century Britain," *History* 93 (2008): 497–513.
18 Genevieve Miller, *The Adoption of Inoculation for Smallpox in England and France* (Philadelphia: University of Pennsylvania Press, 1957), 26. See also Donald R. Hopkins, *Princes and Peasants: Smallpox in History* (Chicago: University of Chicago Press, 1983).
19 Electronic Enlightenment [hereafter EE], Voltaire to Louis Nicolas Le Tonnelier de Breteuil, Baron de Preuilly, December 5, 1723; EE, Voltaire to Marguerite Madeleine Du Moutier, Marquise de Bernières, September 9, 1724.
20 EE, Voltaire to Louis Nicolas Le Tonnelier de Breteuil, Baron de Preuilly, December 5, 1723.
21 EE, [unknown] to Voltaire, c. Saturday, January 4, 1724.
22 Voltaire, *Letters*, ed. Cronk, 46.
23 Montagu to Sarah Chiswell, April 1, 1717, in Lady Mary Wortley Montagu, *Selected Letters*, ed. Isobel Grundy (London: Penguin Books, 1997), 160. On Montagu and smallpox, see Isobel Grundy, "Medical Advance and Female Fame: Inoculation and its After-Effects," *Lumen* 13 (1994): 13–42; and Diana Barnes, "The Public Life of a Woman of Wit and Quality: Lady Mary Wortley Montagu and the Vogue for Smallpox Inoculation," *Feminist Studies* 38 (2012): 330–62.
24 Voltaire, *Letters*, ed. Cronk, 46–8; B. Meli, "Caroline, Leibniz, and Clarke," *Journal of the History of Ideas* 60 (1999): 469–86; Isabel Grundy, *Lady Mary Wortley Montagu* (Oxford: Oxford University Press, 1999), 215.
25 Ibid.
26 Compare Miller, *Adoption of Inoculation for Smallpox in England and France*, 78, and Grundy, "Medical Advance and Female Fame."
27 Robert Halsband, "New Light on Lady Mary Wortley Montagu's Contribution to Inoculation," *Journal of the History of Medicine and Allied Sciences* 8(1953): 393–4.
28 Quoted in Voltaire, *Lettres Philosophques*, ed. Lanson, 1:145.
29 Roger B. Oake, "A Note on the 1752 text of *Lettres Philosophiques*," *Modern Language Notes* 58 (1943): 532–4.
30 Imma Gorbatov, *Catherine the Great and the French Philosophers of the Enlightenment: Montesquieu, Voltaire, Rousseau, Diderot and Grimm* (Bethesda: Academica Press, 2006), 66, 83–4; see also Philip H. Clendenning, "Dr. Thomas Dimsdale and Smallpox Inoculation in Russia," *Journal of the History of Medicine and Allied Sciences* 28 (1973): 109–25.
31 Voltaire, *Letters*, ed. Cronk, 44.
32 Voltaire, *Letters*, ed. Cronk, 62.
33 Ibid., 44.
34 Quoted in Voltaire, *Lettres Philosophiques*, ed. Lanson, 1:145.
35 Voltaire, *Letters*, ed. Cronk, 48.
36 Quoted in Nicholas Cronk, "Voltaire and the Uses of Censorship: The Example of the *Lettres philosophiques*," in *An American Voltaire*, eds. E. Joe Johnson and Byron R. Wells (Newcastle upon Tyne: Cambridge Scholars, 2009): 49.

37 *La Henriade de Mr de Voltaire* (London: Woodman and Lyon, 1728).
38 Giles Barber, "Les Dessous d'un livre-bombe: L'Impression de la première version des Lettres philosophiques," in *Le Livre et l'historien: études offertes en l'honneur du Professeur Henri-Jean Martin*, eds. Frédéric Barbier et al. (Geneva: Droz, 1997): 465–79.
39 Marcus Tomalin, *The French Language and British Literature, 1756–1830* (London: Routledge, 2016).
40 Harcourt Brown, "The Composition of the Letters Concerning the English Nation," in *The Age of Enlightenment: Studies Presented to Theodore Besterman*, eds. W. H. Barber et al. (Edinburgh: University of St. Andrews, 1967), 15–34; J. P. Lee, "The Unexamined Premise: Voltaire, John Lockman and the Myth of the English Letters," *Studies on Voltaire and the Eighteenth Century* 295 (2001): 240–70; Nicholas Cronk, "*The Letters Concerning the English Nation* as an English Work: Reconsidering the Harcourt Brown Thesis," in *From Letter to Publication: Studies on Correspondence and the History of the Book*, ed. A. Strugnell (Oxford: Voltaire Foundation, 2001), 226–39.
41 Albert Lantoine, *Les Lettres philosophiques de Voltaire* (Paris: SFELT, 1946), 107.
42 This complex story is reconstructed skillfully in Cronk, "Voltaire and the Uses of Censorship," 36–61.
43 *Lettres philosophiques* (Amsterdam: Chez E. Lucas, au Livre d'or [Rouen: Jore], 1734), 288. Letter 25 appeared in *Lettres écrites de Londres* (Londres, 1737). The 1741 London edition of *Letters Concerning the English Nation* was the first English-language version to include the Pascal letter, and afterward, Letter 25 was included in the Glasgow 1752 and London 1760 editions, but omitted from other editions, such as 1759, 1767, 1776, and 1778.
44 Monique Cottret, *Jansenisme et Lumières: pour un autre xviiie siècle* (Paris: Albin Michel, 1998), 25, https://kates.itg.pomona.edu/books/editions.php?action=view_references&groupID=208.
45 David Westgate, "The Augustinian Concept of Amour-Propre and Pascal's *Pensées*," *Nottingham French Studies* 10 (1971): 10–20.
46 Voltaire, *Letters*, ed. Cronk, 131.
47 Ibid., 44.
48 Roland Desné, "The Role of England in Voltaire's Polemic Against Pascal: Apropos the Twenty-Fifth Philosophical Letter," in *Eighteenth Century Studies Presented to Arthur M. Wilson*, eds. Peter Gay and John S. Dickey (Hanover: University Press of New England, 1972), 43–57.
49 This account rests upon Gustave Lanson, "L'Affaire des *Lettres philosophiques* de Voltaire," *Revue de Paris* 14 (July 1904): 367–86. See also William Hanley, "The Abbé Rothelin and the *Lettres philosophiques*," *Romance Notes* 23 (1983): 245–50. On the *permission tacite* for *Charles XII*, see *Dictionnaire général de Voltaire*, ed. Jeroom Vercruysse (Paris: Honoré Champion, 2003), 188.
50 Quoted in Hélène Monod-Cassidy, *Un voyageur-philosophe au xviiie siècle: L'Abbé Jean Bernard Le Blanc* (Cambridge, MA: Harvard University Press, 1941), 201–3.
51 J. B. Shank, *The Newton Wars and the Beginning of the French Enlightenment* (Chicago: University of Chicago Press, 2008), 31.
52 Graham Gargett, "Voltaire's '*Lettres philosophiques*' in Eighteenth-Century Ireland," *Eighteenth-Century Ireland* 14 (1999): 77–98; Gérard Laudin, "La Cohérence de l'histoire de la reception de Voltaire dans l'Allemagne des années 1760–1770," in *Voltaire et ses combats: Actes du congrés international, Oxford-Paris, 1994*, 2 vols., eds. Ulla Kölving et Christiane Mervaud (Oxford: Voltaire Foundation, 1997), 2:1435–47. On readers among the French Parlement, see Julian Swann, *Politics and the Parlement of Paris Under Louis*

XV, 1754–1774 (Cambridge: Cambridge University Press, 1995), 24. Among noteworthy readers was Prince Charles Edward Stuart, who carried a copy of *Philosophical Letters* with him during the 1745 invasion. See Jacqueline Riding, *Jacobites: A New History of the '45 Rebellion* (New York: Bloomsbury Press, 2016), 58.

53 EE, Voltaire to Cardinal Fleury, April 24, 1734.
54 Miguel Benitez, "Voltaire and Clandestine Manuscripts," in *The Cambridge Companion to Voltaire*, ed. Nicholas Cronk (Cambridge: Cambridge University Press, 2009), 65–78.
55 EE, Maurepas to the Marquis de Ferrières, May 3, 1734.
56 EE, Voltaire to Maurepas, May 24, 1734 and May 25, 1734.
57 *Arrest de la Cour du Parlement . . .* (Paris: Pierre Simon, 1734); *Mercure de France*, August 1734: 1849–50.
58 Françoise Weil, *Livres interdits, livres persecutés 1720–1770* (Oxford: Voltaire Foundation, 1999), especially 126–7; Reynald Abad, "Guillaume-François Joly de Fleury, Procureur Géneral au Parlement de Paris, face au cas Voltaire," in *Les Parlements et les lumières*, ed. Olivier Chaline (Pessac: Maison des Sciences de l'Homme d'Aquitaine, 2012), 53–72.
59 [Voltaire], *Lettres écrites de londres sur les anglois et autres sujets* (Amsterdam: Desbordes, 1735).
60 René Pomeau, *D'Arouet à Voltaire, 1694–1734* (Oxford: Voltaire Foundation, 1985), 330. Here is how one Irish *Weekly Miscellany* (November 16, 1734), 33–4, covered the scandal: "Mr. Voltaire who these seven years past, has been laboring into fame, is now in possession of a most established character in the commonwealth of learning. This rare and universal genius has had the pleasure to see all his productions greedily read, I had almost said, devoured, and himself received with great marks of distinction on the other side of the water: and since the impression of these letters here, one could hardly go into a house of any note without finding them on every gentleman's table. . . . Perhaps . . . he thinks to secure himself to a comfortable retreat in England, when his senseless affectation of libertine and irreligious principles, shall render his own country too hot for him."
61 Th. Pisvin, *La Vie intellectuelle à Namur sous le régime autrichien* (Louvain: Bureaux du recueil, Bibliothèque de l'Université, 1963), 213; Pierre Rétat and Jean Sgard, *Presse et histoire au xviiie siècle, l'année 1734* (Paris: CNRS, 1978), 139.
62 P. M. Conlon, *Voltaire's Literary Career from 1728 to 1750* (Geneva: Institute et Musée Voltaire, 1961), 78.
63 Éditions collectives, 1728-1778 available at this site: https://c18.net/vo/vo_pages.php?nom=vo_oe_18_liste. Accessed March 5, 2022.
64 See, for example, *Oeuvres de Mr. De Voltaire. Nouvelle Edition . . .* 4 vols. (Amsterdam: Aux Dépens de la Compagnie, 1741), where contents from *Philosophical Letters* appear in 3: 149–349.
65 William H. Trapnell, "Survey and Analysis of Voltaire's Collective Editions," *SVEC* 77 (1970): 103–99. For one well-known example, see *Oeuvres de M de Voltaire,* 40 vols. ([Geneva: Cramer], 1775), 33:71–175, where letters 1–24 are reproduced.
66 *Oeuvres complètes de Voltaire*, 70 vols. (Kehl: De l'imprimerie de la Societé Typographique-Littéraire, 1785–9).
67 http://kates.itg.pomona.edu/books/editions.php. Accessed March 5, 2022. See also Robert Darnton, *The Corpus of Clandestine Literature in France, 1769–1789* (New York: Norton, 1995), 100. Darnton confuses this later compilation with the original *Lettres philosophiques* in *A Literary Tour de France: The World of Books on the Eve of the French Revolution* (New York: Oxford University Press, 2018), 158, 159, 176, and 283. Simon Burrows recognizes the differences between the two versions at his website, The French Book Trade

in Enlightenment Europe, http://fbtee.uws.edu.au/stn/interface/browse.php?t=book&id=spbk0001358. Accessed July 21, 2020.
68 This section is based on Miguel Benítez, *Voltaire lit Locke: une étude de la Lettre sur l'âme* (Paris: Honoré Champion, 2019); see also Lanson, *Lettres philosophiques*, 1: 190–205; and John W. Yolton, *Locke and French Materialism* (Oxford: Clarendon Press, 1993), 38–55. See also *Lettres sur les Anglais (III)* in *Oeuvres complètes de Voltaire, Tome 6C*, eds. Antony McKenna and Gabriel Mori (Oxford: Voltaire Foundation, 2020).
69 *Letters*, ed. Cronk, 57. See John Locke, *Essay Concerning Human Understanding*, Part 4, Chapter 3, Paragraph 6, for the exact quote: "We have the ideas of matter and thinking, but possibly shall never be able to know, whether any mere material being thinks, or no; it being impossible for us, by the contemplation of our own ideas, without revelation, to discover, whether omnipotency has not given to some systems of matter fitly disposed a power to perceive and think, or else joined and fixed to matter so disposed a thinking immaterial substance: it being, in respect of our notions, not much more remote from our comprehension to conceive, that God can, if he pleases, superadd to matter a faculty of thinking, than that he should superadd to it another substance, with a faculty of thinking; since we know not wherein thinking consists, nor to what sort of substances the Almighty has been pleased to give that power, which cannot be in any created being, but merely by the good pleasure and bounty of the Creator."
70 Voltaire, of course, was not the first to see that Locke's innocent query could be used by others to make more radical arguments. Soon after its initial publication in 1690, theologians published refutations. By the time of Voltaire's visit, many of their objections and Locke's response had been incorporated into the *Essay*. For example, the 1731 edition (John Locke, *An Essay Concerning Human Understanding . . . The Tenth Edition with Large Additions*, 4 vols. [London: Arthur Bettsworth and Charles Hitch], 4:140–67) has twenty-five pages of footnotes surrounding the sentence quoted by Voltaire. See John Yolton, *Thinking Matter: Materialism in Eighteenth-Century Britain* (Minneapolis: University of Minnesota Press, 1983).
71 Yolton, *Locke and French Materialism*, 38–59.
72 Weil, *Livres interdits, livres persécutés*.
73 *Encyclopédie, ou Dictionnaire raisonné des sciences, des arts et des métiers, par une société de gens de lettres. Mis en ordre & publié par M. Diderot . . . Tome 1* (Paris: Braisson, 1751), 337–8; Nicholas Cronk, "Les *Lettres sur les Anglaise* en France au dix-huitième siècle: questions de reception et de reputation," *Revue Voltaire* 13 (2013): 153.
74 Following *Philosophical Letters*, the Index would place over thirty of Voltaire's books on its list—more than any other writer. See *Dictionnaire général de Voltaire*, 189, and J. M. De Bujanda, *Index Librorum Prohibitorum: 1600–1966* (Montréal: Médiaspaul, 2002).
75 Trapnell, "Survey and Analysis of Voltaire's Collective Editions," 140.
76 *Pièces détachées attribuées à divers hommes célèbres. Tome second* ([Geneva: Cramer and Barbin], 1775), 217–25 (Volume 39 of a 40-volume set); "Section VIII" of "Ame," *Dictionnaire philosophique* in *Oeuvres complètes de Voltaire. Tome Trente-Septième* ([Kehl]: De l'Imprimerie de la Société Littéraire de Typographique, 1784), 211–20.

Chapter 6

1 Electronic Enlightenment [hereafter EE], Richardson to Stinstra, June 2, 1763; T. C. Duncan Eaves and Ben D. Kimpel, *Samuel Richardson: A Biography* (Oxford: Clarendon Press, 1971).

2   See "Books List," in Keith Maslen, *Samuel Richardson of London, Printer: A Study of his Printing Based on Ornament Use and Business Accounts* (Otago: University of Otago, 2001), 55–160.
3   Ibid., 84.
4   *Aesop's Fables* (London: Osborn, 1740).
5   John A. Dussinger, "Fabrications from Samuel Richardson's Press," *Papers of the Bibliographical Society of America* 100 (2006): 259–79.
6   Christopher Flint, "The Material Book," in *Samuel Richardson in Context*, eds. Peter Sabor and Betty A. Schellenberg (Cambridge: Cambridge University Press, 2017), 121, and Catherine Ingrassia, "The Literary Marketplace," in the same volume.
7   Ian Watt, *The Rise of the Novel: Studies in Defoe, Richardson and Fielding* (Berkeley: University of California Press, 1957); Thomas Keymer, *Richardson's Clarissa and the Eighteenth-Century Reader* (Cambridge: Cambridge University Press, 1992).
8   Samuel Richardson, *Letters Written to and for Particular Friends, on the Most Important Occasions* (London: J. Osborn, C. Rivington, and J. Peake, 1741); Maslen, *Samuel Richardson*, 128–9.
9   Seneca, *Select Epistles on Several Moral Subjects* (London: Rivington, 1739), quoted in Samuel Richardson, *Pamela in Her Exalted Condition*, ed. Albert J. Rivero (Cambridge University Press, 2012), xlvi.
10 Bridget Hill, *Servants: English Domestics in the Eighteenth Century* (Oxford: Oxford University Press, 1996).
11 Cissie Fairchilds, "Female Sexual Attitudes and the Rise of Illegitimacy: A Case Study," *The Journal of Interdisciplinary History* 8 (1978): 639, 660.
12 Alan Dugald McKillop, *Samuel Richardson, Printer and Novelist* (Chapel Hill: University of North Carolina Press, 1936), 31.
13 This section draws on A. D. Harvey, "The Politics of Pamela," *Critical Quarterly* 61 (2019): 105–15.
14 Samuel Richardson, *Pamela*, eds. Thomas Keymer and Alice Wakely (Oxford: Oxford University Press, 2001), 126; John Locke, *Two Treatises on Government*, ed. Peter Laslett (Cambridge: Cambridge University Press, 1988), 287.
15 Richardson, *Pamela*, 158.
16 Walpole's letter is lost, but verified by Anna Seward in *Horace Walpole's Miscellaneous Correspondence*, eds. W. S. Lewis and John Riely (New Haven: Yale University Press, 1980), 29.
17 Clara Reeve, *The Progress of Romance*, 2 vols. (Colchester: W. Keymer, 1785), 1:133.
18 *The Gentleman's Magazine and Historical Chronicle* 11 (January 1741): unpaginated.
19 "Eighteenth-Century Illustrated Editions of *Pamela*," http://umich.edu/~ece/student_projects/pamela_illustrated/main.set.editions.htm.
20 This publishing history is based primarily on Thomas Keymer and Peter Sabor, *Pamela in the Marketplace: Literary Controversy and Print Culture in Eighteenth-Century Britain and Ireland* (New York: Cambridge University Press, 2005), especially Chapter 1.
21 Quoted in McKillop, *Samuel Richardson,* 44; T. C. Duncan Eaves and Ben D. Kimpel, "Richardson's Revisions of *Pamela*," *Studies in Bibliography* 20 (1967): 61–88.
22 *History of Pamela, abridged from the Works of S Richardson, Esq.* (London: F. Newbery, 1769), advertised in the *Boston Gazette and Country Journal*, June 20, 1772.
23 In 1753 Richardson famously sued Dublin publishers not for reprinting *Sir Charles Grandison*, but for stealing a manuscript copy from Richardson's office. See *The Case of Samuel Richardson, of London, Printer; with Regard to the Invasion of his Property in The*

History of Sir Charles Grandison, Before Publication, by Certain Booksellers in Dublin (London, 1753).
24 Richardson, *Pamela in Her Exalted Condition*.
25 Ted A. Emery, "Goldoni's Pamela From Play to Libretto," *Italica* 64 (1987): 576.
26 Carlo Goldini, *Pamela commedia di Carlo Goldoni Avvocato Veneziano/Pamela, a Comedy* (London: J. Nourse, 1756), Preface.
27 Quoted in Harvey, "The Politics of Pamela," 110.
28 Aaron Hill to Richardson, December 29, 1740, in *The Correspondence of Samuel Richardson*, ed. Anna Laetitia Barbauld, 6 vols. (London: R. Phillips, 1804), 1:58–61.
29 Quoted in Catherine Ingrassia, "The Literary Marketplace," in *Samuel Richardson in Context*, eds. Peter Sabor and Betty A. Schellenberg (Cambridge: Cambridge University Press, 2017), 110.
30 *Specimens of the Novelists and Romancers, with Critical and Biographical Notices of the Authors*, 2nd ed. (Glasgow: R. Griffin, 1827), 249.
31 Quoted in Kevin J. Hayes, *A Colonial Woman's Bookshelf* (Knoxville: University of Tennessee Press, 1996), 112.
32 Quoted in McKillop, *Samuel Richardson*, 101.
33 Ibid., 48.
34 Reeve, *Progress of Romance*, 137.
35 Charles Povey, *The Virgin in Eden* (London: Roberts, 1741), i.
36 Quoted in Richard Gooding, "Pamela, Shamela, and the Politics of the Pamela Vogue," *Eighteenth-Century Fiction* 7 (1995): 123.
37 [Henry Fielding], *An apology for the Life of Mrs. Shamela Andrews. In Which the Many Notorious Falshoods and Misreprsentations [sic] of a Book called Pamela, are Exposed and Refuted ; . . . By Mr. Conny Keyber* (London: A. Dodd, 1741). *Shamela* was excluded from *Oeuvres de M. Fielding*, 14 vols. (Geneva: Nouffer de Rodon, 1781–1782) and *Oeuvres complètes de M. Fielding*, 23 vols. (Paris: Perlet, 1797).
38 Lady Mary Wortley Montagu to [her daughter] Lady Bute, October 17, 1750, February 16, 1752, July 23, 1753, September 22, 1755, and October 20, 1755, in *Selected Letters*, ed. Isobel Grundy (New York: Penguin, 1997), 351, 368, 388–9, 415, 422.
39 Quoted in Sir James Prior, *Life of Edmond Malone, Editor of Shakespeare* (London: Smith, Elder, 1860), 439.
40 Salley to the Chevalier de Caylus, June 28, 1742, in *Report on the Manuscripts of the Lady Du Cane* (London: Printed for H. M. Stationery office by B. Johnson, 1905), 327.
41 Quoted in McKillop, *Samuel Richardson*, 100–1.
42 Sonnenfels quoted in Harvey, "Politics of Pamela," 108–9.
43 Ibid.
44 Eliza Lucas Pinckney to Miss Bartlett, May 2, 1742, at North American Women's Letters and Diaries at https://alexanderstreet.com/products/north-american-womens-letters-and-diaries.
45 Esther Edwards Burr, *The Journal of Esther Edwards Burr 1754–1757*, eds. Carol F. Karlsen and Laurie Crumpacker (New Haven: Yale University Press, 1984), 98–108.
46 *Gentleman's Magazine* 56, Part 1 (February 1786): 16.
47 *Nanine, comédie en trois actes, en vers de dix syllabes, donnée par l'auteur* (Paris: Le Mercier, 1749).
48 Peter Gay, *Voltaire's Politics: The Poet as Realist* (Princeton: Princeton University Press, 1959), 144–84.
49 G. J. Mallinson, "What's in a Name? Reflections on Voltaire's *Paméla*," *Eighteenth Century Fiction* 18 (2005): 157–68.

50 Robert Darnton, "Readers Respond to Rousseau: The Fabrication of Romantic Sensitivity," in *The Great Cat Massacre and Other Episodes in French Cultural History* (New York: Basic Books, 1984), 215–56.
51 Choderlos de Laclos, *Les Liaisons Dangereuses*, trans. Douglas Parmée (Oxford: Oxford University Press, 1998).
52 Adam Smith, *The Theory of Moral Sentiments*, ed. Knud Haakonssen (Cambridge: Cambridge University Press, 2004, 165).
53 Montesquieu, *My Thoughts*, trans. Henry C. Clark (Indianapolis: Liberty Fund, 2012), 627 (#2033).
54 Denis Diderot, "In Praise of Richardson," *Selected Writings on Art and Literature*, ed. Geoffrey Bremner (New York: Penguin, 1994), 92. The essay was reprinted in 1768, 1770, and published in German in 1766. See Roger Chartier, "Richardson, Diderot et la lectrice impatiente," *MLN* 114 (1999): 649.
55 Quoted in James Fowler, *Richardson and the Philosophes* (New York: Routledge, 2014), 155.
56 Diderot, "In Praise of Richardson," 88.
57 James Fowler, "*La Religieuse*: Diderot's 'Richardsonian' Novel," in *New Essays on Diderot*, ed. James Fowler (Cambridge: Cambridge University Press, 2011), 127–38.
58 Denis Diderot, *The Nun*, trans. Russell Goulbourne (Oxford: Oxford University Press, 2005), 95–6 and 128.
59 William F. Edmiston, *Hindsight and Insight: Focalization in Four Eighteenth-Century French Novels* (University Park: Penn State University Press, 1991), 127; Julie C. Hayes, "Retrospection and Contradiction in Diderot's *La Religieuse*," *Romanic Review* 77 (1986): 233–42; Walter E. Rex, Secrets from Suzanne, "The Tangled Motives of *La Religieuse*," *The Eighteenth Century* 24 (1983): 185–98; Vivienne Mylne, "What Suzanne Knew: Lesbianism and *La Religieuse*," *SVEC* 208 (1982): 167–73; Roland A. Champagne, "Words Disguising Desire: Serial Discourse and the Dual Character of Suzanne Simonin," *Kentucky Romance Quarterly* 28 (1981): 341–50.
60 Diderot, *The Nun*, 152.
61 Diderot, "In Praise of Richardson," 83.
62 Ibid., 88.
63 Ibid., 82.
64 Ibid., 90.
65 Ibid., 92.
66 Ibid., 83.
67 Seward to Mrs. Childers, December 27, 1801, in *Letters of Anna Seward Written Between the Years 1784 and 1807*, 6 vols. (Edinburgh: George Ramsay, 1811), 5:431.
68 Condorcet, *The Life of M. Turgot* (London: J. Johnson, 1787), 175.
69 Smith, *Theory of Moral Sentiments*, 11.
70 Lynn Hunt, "Torrents of Emotion: Reading Novels and Imaging Equality," in *Inventing Human Rights: A History* (New York: Norton, 2007), 58.

Chapter 7

1 Denis Diderot, "In Praise of Richardson," in *Selected Essays on Art and Literature*, ed. Geoffrey Bremner (New York: Penguin, 1994), 92.

2 James Fordyce, *Sermons to Young Women*, 9th ed., 2 vols. (London: T. Cadell and J. Dodsley, 1778), 2:147; David Hume, *A Treatise of Human Nature*, ed. L. A. Selby-Bigge (Oxford: Oxford University Press, 1888), 415.
3 Paul H. Meyer, "Hume in Eighteenth-Century France," PhD Thesis, Columbia University, 1954, 222. This project was only partially realized.
4 "My Own Life," in David Hume, *Essays Moral, Political, and Literary*, ed. Eugene F. Miller (Indianapolis: Liberty Classics, 1985) [hereafter EMPL], xxxi–xli. The standard biography of Hume is Ernest Campbell Mossner, *The Life of David Hume*, 2nd ed. (Oxford: Clarendon Press, 1980), which has been recently superseded by James Harris, *Hume: An Intellectual Biography* (Cambridge: Cambridge University Press, 2015).
5 "My Own Life," xxxiv.
6 Hume to Balcarres, in John Y. T. Greig, ed., *The Letters of David Hume* (Oxford: Clarendon Press, 1932) 1:214.
7 Mossner, *Life of David Hume*, 131–3.
8 David Hume, "Advertisement," *A Treatise of Human Nature*, Vol. III (London: Thomas Longman, 1740).
9 Voltaire, "Men of Letters," in *The Encyclopedia of Diderot & d'Alembert Collaborative Translation Project*, trans. Dena Goodman, accessed May 1, 2020, http://hdl.handle.net/2027/spo.did2222.0000.052.
10 *The Spectator*, 6th ed., 8 vols. (London: J. Tonson, 1723), 1:36 (Monday, March 12, 1711).
11 Jürgen Habermas, *The Structural Transformation of the Public Sphere: An Inquiry into a Category of Bourgeois Society*, trans. Thomas Berger (Cambridge, MA: MIT Press, 1989), 43.
12 M. A. Box, *The Suasive Art of David Hume* (Princeton: Princeton University Press, 1990), 144–5.
13 Maria Lúcia Pallares-Burke, "The *Spectator*, or the Metamorphoses of the Periodical: A Study in Cultural Translation," in *Cultural Translation in Early Modern Europe*, eds. Peter Burke and R. Po-Chia Hsia (Cambridge: Cambridge University Press, 2007), 142–60.
14 "Of Essay Writing," in EMPL 533–7. The following quotations come from this short piece.
15 Anne Goldgar, *Impolite Learning: Conduct and Community in the Republic of Letters, 1680–1750* (New Haven: Yale University Press, 1995).
16 Vivienne Brown, "The Lectures on Rhetoric and Belles Lettres," in *Adam Smith: His Life, Thought, and Legacy*, ed. Ryan Patrick Hanley (Princeton: Princeton University Press, 2016), 17–32. Public lecturing was common throughout Enlightenment Europe; see Michael R. Lynn, "The Fashion for Physics: Public Lecture Courses in Enlightenment France," *The Historian* 64 (2002): 335–50.
17 Of course, despite himself, Hume nonetheless became a celebrity and sometimes the object of public gossip. See Dena Goodman, "The Hume-Rousseau Affair: From Private 'Querelle' to Public 'procès,'" *Eighteenth-Century Studies* 25 (1991): 171–201; and Antoine Lilti, *The Invention of Celebrity*, trans. Lynne Jeffress (Oxford: Polity Press, 2017) 131.
18 Denis Diderot and César Chesneau Du Marsais, "Encyclopedia" and "Philosopher," *The Encyclopedia of Diderot & d'Alembert Collaborative Translation Project,* trans. Philip Stewart and Dena Goodman, accessed May 1, 2020, http://hdl.handle.net/2027/spo.did2222.0000.001.
19 Diderot, "Encyclopedia."
20 Dena Goodman, *The Republic of Letters: A Cultural History of the French Enlightenment* (Ithaca: Cornell University Press, 1994), 124–5; Vicki J. Sapp, "The Philosopher's Seduction: Hume and the Fair Sex," *Philosophy and Literature* 19 (1995): 1–15; Gilles

Robel, "'From the Dominions of Learning to those of Conversation': philosophie savante et philosophie populaire dans les Essais de David Hume," *RANAM* 40 (2007): 53–68.
21 *The Weekly Magazine or Edinburgh Amusement* (1774), quoted in Rosalind Carr, *Gender and Enlightenment Culture in Eighteenth-Century Scotland* (Edinburgh: Edinburgh University Press, 2014), 82.
22 EMPL, 133–4.
23 EMPL, 566. For a more general context, see Sylvana Tomaselli, "The Role of Woman in Enlightenment Conjectural Histories," in *Conceptualizing Women in Enlightenment Thought*, eds. Hans Erich Bödeker and Leiselotte Steinbrügge (Berlin: Verlag Arno Spitz GmbH, 2001).
24 EMPL, 563. For a qualified appreciation see also J. G. A. Pocock, *Barbarism and Religion. Volume Two. Narratives of Civil Government* (New York: Cambridge University Press, 1999), 180–3.
25 "Untitled Character Sketch of David Hume, 1742," *Early Responses to Hume's Life and Reputation*, 2 vols., ed. James Fieser (Bristol: Thoemmes Press, 2003), 1:5–6.
26 Quoted in Karen O'Brien, *Women and Enlightenment in Eighteenth-Century Britain* (Cambridge: Cambridge University Press, 2009), 88.
27 Ben Dew, "Waving a Mouchoir à la Wilkes: Hume, Radicalism, and *The North Briton*," *Modern Intellectual History* 6 (2009): 238.
28 John Christian Laursen, "David Hume and the Danish Debate About Freedom of the Press in the 1770s," *Journal of the History of Ideas* 59 (1998): 167–72.
29 Richard B. Sher, *The Enlightenment and the Book: Scottish Authors and Their Publishers in Eighteenth-Century Britain, Ireland, and America* (Chicago: University of Chicago Press, 2006), 50–2.
30 Ibid, 241; Hugh Amory, "Andrew Millar," Oxford Dictionary of National Biography, https://doi-org.ccl.idm.oclc.org/10.1093/ref:odnb/18714.
31 John G. Hayman, "Notions on National Characters in the Eighteenth Century," *Huntington Library Quarterly* 35 (1971): 1–17; Roberto Romani, *National Character and Public Spirit in Britain and France, 1750–1914* (Cambridge: Cambridge University Press, 2001), especially 163–70.
32 Montesquieu to Hume, May 19, 1749, *Correspondance de Montesquieu*, ed. François Gebelin, 3 vols (Paris: Champion, 1914), 2:188–9.
33 There are two versions of Hume's *Essays and Treatises on Several Subjects*, 4 vols. (Edinburgh and London: Millar, Kincaid, and Donaldson, 1753). The first version used the 1748 edition of *Essays, Moral and Political*, and so, the note did not appear there. Later that year, the publishers reset the type, issuing a new version, and the note appears there for the first time at 1:291n.
34 The literature on Hume's footnote is growing. See Richard H. Popkin, "Hume's Racism," *Philosophical Forum* 9 (1977–8): 7–78; Robert Palter, "Hume and Prejudice," *Hume Studies* 21 (1995): 3–23; John Immerwahr, "Hume's Revised Racism," *Journal of the History of Ideas* 53 (1992): 481–6; Emmanuel C. Eze, "Hume, Race, and Human Nature," *Journal of the History of Ideas* 61 (2000): 691–8; Aaron Garrett, "Hume's Revised Racism Revisited," *Hume Studies* 26 (2000): 171–77; "Hume's 'Original Difference': Race, National Character and the Human Sciences," *Eighteenth-Century Thought* 2 (2004): 127–52. For the Scottish context of Hume's racial prejudice, see Iain Whyte, "'The Upas Tree, Beneath Whose Pestiferous Shade All Intellect Languishes and All Virtue Dies': Scottish Public Perceptions of the Slave Trade and Slavery, 1756–1833," in *Recovering Scotland's Slavery Past: The Caribbean Connection*, ed. T. M. Devine (Edinburgh: Edinburgh University Press, 2015), 187–205. It is curious that more general accounts of Hume have largely ignored his racial

views. See Harris, *Hume*, and Margaret Watkins, *The Philosophical Progress of Hume's Essays* (Cambridge: Cambridge University Press, 2019). Two notable attempts to explore Hume's views on slavery are Onur Ulas Ince, "Between Commerce and Empire: David Hume, Colonial Slavery and Commercial Incivility," *History of Political Thought* 39 (2018): 107–34, and Emma Rothschild, "David Hume and the Seagods of the Atlantic," in *The Atlantic Enlightenment*, eds. Susan Manning and Francis D. Cogliano (New York: Routledge, 2008), 81–96. Perhaps the most thorough discussion of Hume's footnote is Silvia Sebastiani, *The Scottish Enlightenment: Race, Gender, and the Limits of Progress* (New York: Palgrave Macmillan, 2013), 23–43.

35 EMPL, 21.
36 For example, this is how one footnote from "Of Commerce" (EMPL, 259–60) begins: "The more ancient Romans lived in perpetual war with all their neighbors: And in old Latin, the term hostis, expressed both a stranger and an enemy. This is remarked by Cicero; but by him is ascribed to the humanity of his ancestors, who softened, as much as possible, the denomination of the enemy, by calling him by the name appellation which signified a stranger. DeOff. Lib. Ii."
37 Anthony Grafton, *The Footnote* (Cambridge, MA: Harvard University Press, 1997) is a masterful overview.
38 1758 one-volume quarto; 1760 four-volume duodecimo; 1764 two-volume octavo; 1767 two-volume octavo; 1768 two-volume quarto; 1770 four-volume octavo; and 1772 two-volume octavo.
39 James Beattie, *An Essay on the Nature and Immutability of Truth*, 2 vols. (Edinburgh: Kincaid and Bell, 1770), 1:480, 493.
40 Hume to William Strahan, October 26, 1775 in *The Letters of David Hume*, ed. J. Y. T. Greig, 2 vols (Oxford: Oxford University Press, 1932), 1:301.
41 I've reproduced the strikeouts and italics from Immerwahr, "Hume's Revised Racism," 483. See Hume, *Essays and Treatises on Several Subjects*, 4 vols (London and Edinburgh: Cadell, Donaldson, and Creech, 1777), 1:550–1 for the revised note.
42 Watkins, *Philosophical Progress of Hume's Essays*, 2.
43 Vincent Caretta, "Who Was Francis Williams?," *Early American Literature* 38 (2003): 213–37.
44 Margaret Watkins, "'A Cruel but Ancient Subjugation'? Understanding Hume's Attack on Slavery," *Hume Studies* 39 (2013): 103–21.
45 Frederick G. Whelan, "Political Science and Political Theory in Hume's Essays," in *David Hume on Morals, Politics, and Society*, eds. Angela Coventry and Andrew Valls (New Haven: Yale University Press, 2018), 294.
46 Samuel Estwick, *Considerations on the Negroe Cause*, 2nd ed. (London: Dodsley, 1773), 79n.
47 Richard Nisbet, *Slavery Not Forbidden by Scripture. Or A Defence of the West-India Planters, from the Aspersions Thrown Out against Them* (Philadelphia: [John Sparhawk], 1773), 21–2.
48 Edward Long, *History of Jamaica*, 3 vols. (London: Lowndes, 1774), 2:375.
49 Granville Sharp, *The Just Limitation of Slavery in the Laws of God* (London: B. White, 1776), 27n. For the context of these debates, see Lester B. Scherer, "A New Look at Personal Slavery Established," *William and Mary Quarterly* 30 (1973): 645–52. Hume's footnote was cited and refuted in James Ramsay, *An Essay on the Treatment and Conversion of African Slaves in the British Sugar Colonies* (London: James Phillips, 1784), 198–231.
50 Franz Swediauer, "No Original Distinction in the Intellectual Abilities of Men in Any Part of the Globe," in *Philosophical Dictionary*, 4 vols (London: Robinson, 1786), 2:165–7.

51 *Oeuvres de Mr Hume. Tome Premier. Seconde édition. Essais moraux et politiques* (Amsterdam: Schneider, 1764), 434n.
52 Immanuel Kant, *Observations on the Feeling of the Beautiful and Sublime and Other Writings*, eds. Patrick Frierson and Paul Guyer (Cambridge: Cambridge University Press, 2011), 58–9.
53 "Essai de Mr Hume célèbre auteur anglois sur la carractère des nations," in *Journal encyclopédique* 3 (May 1757): 26–51; the note and commentary appear on 40. On Mérian, see the entry in *The Cambridge History of Eighteenth-Century Philosophy*, ed. Knud Haakonssen, 2 vols. (Cambridge: Cambridge University Press, 2006), 2:1204.
54 "My Own Life," EMPL xxxvi.
55 Roger B. Oake, "Montesquieu and Hume," *Modern Language Quarterly* 2 (1941): 25–41 and 225–48.
56 [William Rose], Review of *Political Discourses*, *Monthly Review* 6 (January 1752): 19–43 and (February 1752): 81–90 reprinted in *Early Responses to Hume's Moral, Literary and Political Writings*, ed. James Fieser, 2 vols (Bristol: Thoemmes Press, 1999), 2:16 and *Monthly Review* (February 1757), cited in Mossner, *Life of David Hume*, 227.
57 The best attempt to sort this out is James Fieser, *A Bibliography of Hume's Writings and Early Responses* (Bristol: Thoemmes Press, 2003).
58 Richard Sher, *The Enlightenment and the Book: Scottish Authors and Their Publishers in Eighteenth-Century Britain, Ireland, and America* (Chicago: University of Chicago Press, 2006), especially 43–61.
59 Jean Antoine Nicolas de Caritat. Marquis de Condorcet, ed., *Bibliothèque de l'homme public ou, analyse raisonnée des principaux ouvrages françois et étrangers, sur la politique en général, la legislation, les finances, la police, l'agriculture et le commerce en particulier, et sur le droit naturel et public*, 12 vols. (Paris: Buisson, 1790), 2:3–220.
60 John Robertson, "The Enlightenment, the Public Sphere, and Political Economy," in *L'économie politique et la sphère publique dans le débat des lumières*, eds. Jesús Astigarraga and Javier Usoz (Madrid: Casa de Velázquez, 2013), 21.
61 Quoted in *The Letters of David Hume*, 2 vols, ed. J. Y. T. Greig (Oxford: Oxford University Press, 1932), 1:259n. This section relies on Loïc Charles, "French 'New Politics' and the Dissemination of David Hume's *Political Discourses* on the Continent, 1750–1770," in *David Hume's Political Economy*, eds. Carl Wennerlind and Margaret Schabas (New York: Routledge, 2008), 181–202; Antonella Alimento, "La contribution de l'école de Gournay à la naissance d'une sphère publique dans la France des années 1750–1760," in *L'économie politique et la sphère publique dans le débat des Lumières*, eds. Jesús Astigarraga et Javier Usoz (Madrid: Casa de Velázquez, 2013), 213–28; Loïc Charles and Arnaud Orain, "François Véron De Forbonnais and the Invention of Antiphysiocracy," in *The Economic Turn: Recasting Political Economy in Enlightenment Europe*, eds. Sophus Reinert and Steven Kaplan (London: Anthem Press, 2019), 139–68; Thierry Demals and Alexandra Hyard, "Forbonnais, the Two Balances and the Économistes," *The European Journal of the History of Economic Thought* 22 (2015): 445–72; Robin J. Ives, "Political Publicity and Political Economy in Eighteenth-Century France," *French History* 17 (2003): 1–18; Catherine Larrère, "Système de l'intérêt et science du commerce: François Véron de Forbonnais, lecteur de Montesquieu," in *Le Cercle de Vincent de Gournay. Savoirs économiques et pratiques administratives au milieu du XVIIIe siècle*, eds. Loïc Charles, Frédéric Lefebvre et Christine Théré (Paris: INED, 2011), 259–80; Paul Burton Cheney, "Montesquieu's Science of Commerce," in *Revolutionary Commerce: Globalization and the French Monarchy* (Cambridge, MA: Harvard University Press, 2010), 52–86; Margaret Schabas and Carl Wennerlind, *A Philosopher's Economist: Hume and the Rise of Capitalism*

Notes

(Chicago: University of Chicago Press, 2020), 222–5. I discuss Montesquieu's absorption into French political economy more in Chapter 9.
62 François Véron de Forbonnais, *Elémens de commerce*, 2nd ed., 2 vols. (Leyde and Paris: Briasson, 1754), 47 and 85.
63 Ibid., 2:300, quoting from EMPL, 270–1. In 1760, Hume changed the title from "Of Luxury" to "Of Refinements in the Arts," but eighteenth-century French editions used the older title. See also John Shovlin, "Hume's Political Discourses and the French Luxury Debate," in *David Hume's Political Economy*, eds. Carl Wennerlind and Margaret Schabas (London: Routledge, 2008), 203–22.
64 Charles, "French New Politics," 202 (note 51).
65 João Paulo Silvestre, Alina Villalva, and Esperança Cardeira, "Landmarks of Economic Terminology: The First Portuguese Translation of *Elémens du commerce*," *History of European Ideas* 40:1189–201. The entire issue of this journal is devoted to Forbonnais's book.
66 Quoted in Rudolf Mertz, "Les amitiés françaises de Hume et le movement des idées," *Revue de littérature comparée* 9 (1929): 657. On Le Blanc see George R. Havens, "The Abbé Le Blanc and English Literature." *Modern Philology* 18 (1920): 423–41.
67 David Hume, *Discours politiques*, 2 vols. trans. Le Blanc (Amsterdam and Paris: Lambert, 1754), 1: liv-lv and 2:383–417.
68 Laurence L. Bongie, "David Hume and the Official Censorship of the 'Ancien Regime'." *French Studies* 12, no. 3 (1958): 234.
69 *Mercure de France*, December 1759:102, cited in Michel Malherbe, "Hume's Reception in France," *The Reception of Hume in Europe*, ed. Peter Jones (London: Continuum, 2005), 72.
70 Hume, *Discours politiques*, 5 vols., trans. Eléazar de Mauvillon (Amsterdam: Schreuder and Mortier, 1756–1761); Paola Zanardi, "Italian Responses to David Hume," in *The Reception of Hume in Europe*, ed. Peter Jones (London: Continuum, 2005), 161–75; Till Wahnbaeck, *Luxury and Public Happiness: Political Economy In the Italian Enlightenment* (Oxford: Clarendon Press, 2004), 63–4.
71 Istvan Hont, *Jealousy of Trade: International Competition and the Nation-State in Historical Perspective* (Cambridge, MA: Harvard University Press, 2005), especially Introduction, 1–156.
72 *Hume's Reception in Early America*, ed. Mark G. Spencer, 2 vols (Bristol: Thoemmes Press, 2002), 1:27. Many of the following examples come also from Spencer.
73 John Dickinson, *Letters From a Farmer in Pennsylvania, to the Inhabitants of the British Colonies* (New York: John Holt, 1768), 97n.
74 *The Censor*, January 4, 1772.
75 James Chalmers, *Plain Truth; Addressed to the Inhabitants of America* (Philadelphia, 1776), 12. Here Chalmers focuses on, among other essays, "Of the Original Contract."
76 John Adams, "A Defense of the Constitutions of Government of the United States of America . . . (1778)," reprinted in *Hume's Reception in Early America*, 1:36.
77 Garry Wills, *Explaining America: The Federalist* (New York: Penguin, 1982), 21. Federalist 10 first appeared in the *New York Packet* on November 23, 1787.
78 Ibid., 16; Roy Branson, "James Madison and the Scottish Enlightenment," *Journal of the History of Ideas* 40 (1979): 236.
79 EMPL, 527.
80 Douglass Adair, "That Politics may be Reduced to a Science: David Hume, James Madison, and the Tenth Federalist," *Huntington Library Quarterly* 20 (1957): 351, citing EMPL, 528.
81 James Madison, Alexander Hamilton, and John Jay, *The Federalist Papers*, ed. Isaac Kramnick (New York: Penguin, 1987), 126–7.
82 Ibid.

83 Hamilton's note: Hume, Vol 1, Essay 5th.
84 Alexander Hamilton, *The Farmer Refuted* . . . (New York: Rivington, 1775), 12–13, quoting Hume, "Of the Independency of Parliament," EMPL, 42–3.
85 Gerald Stourzh, *Alexander Hamilton and the Idea of Republican Government* (Stanford: Stanford University Press, 1970), 78.
86 Drew R. McCoy, *The Elusive Republic: Political Economy in Jeffersonian America* (New York: Norton, 1980); Dennis C. Rasmussen, *The Problems and Promise of Commercial Society: Adam Smith's Response to Rousseau* (University Park: Pennsylvania State University Press, 2008).
87 The classic work is Lewis Namier, *The Structure of Politics in the Age of George III*, 2nd ed. (London: MacMillan, [1929] 1957); for the American context, Bernard Bailyn, *The Ideological Origins of the American Revolution* (Cambridge, MA: Harvard University Press, 1967).
88 Robert Yates, et al., *Secret Proceedings and Debates of the Convention Assembled at Philadelphia, in the 1787* . . . (Richmond: Curtiss, 1839), 166.
89 *The Writings of James Madison, Comprising His Public Papers and His Private Correspondence, Including Numerous Letters and Documents Now for the First Time Printed.*, ed. Gaillard Hunt, 9 vols. (New York: G.P. Putnam's Sons, 1900–1910), 3:258–9; see also Stourzh, *Alexander Hamilton*, 84–5. Hamilton's words were jotted down in Madison's journal, including the parenthetical Mr Hume.
90 David B. Young, "Libertarian Demography: Montesquieu's Essay on Depopulation in the *Lettres persanes*," *Journal of the History of Ideas* 36 (1975): 669–82.
91 James Wodrow to Samuel Kenrick, January 21, 1752, reprinted in *Early Responses to Hume's Life and Reputation*, 1:7–9.

Chapter 8

1 Françoise de Graffigny, *Letters of a Peruvian Woman*, ed. Jonathan Mallinson (Oxford: Oxford University Press, 2009), 116 (hereafter cited as *LPW*).
2 Graffigny to Devaux, [December 26, 1728] in *Correspondance de Madame de Graffigny, Tome 1, 1716–1717 juin 1739*, ed. English Showalter (Oxford: Voltaire Foundation, 1985), 247. The standard biography is English Showalter, *Françoise de Graffigny: Her Life and Works* (Oxford: Voltaire Foundation, 2004).
3 *LPW*, 3.
4 Andre Le Breton, cited in Aurora Wolfgang, "Intertextual Conversations: The Love-Letter and the Footnote in Madame De Graffigny's *Lettres d'Une Péruvienne*," *Eighteenth-Century Fiction* 10 (1997): 15.
5 *LPW*, 34.
6 Ibid., 59.
7 Ibid., 115.
8 Wolfgang, "Intertextual Conversations," 15–28.
9 Janet Gurkin Altman, "Graffigny's Epistemology and the Emergence of Third-World Ideology," in *Writing the Female Voice: Essays on Epistolary Literature*, ed. Elizabeth Goldsmith (Boston: Northeastern University Press, 1989), 175. Zilia was taken up by the early abolitionist movement in J. Jamieson, *The Sorrows of Slavery, a Poem* (London: Murray, 1789), 43.

10 *LPW*, 3.
11 Yale University's copy of a 1756 edition was previously owned by Hiram Bingham, the American adventurer who "discovered" Machu Pichu.
12 *LPW*, 96.
13 Ibid., 74.
14 Ibid., 100.
15 Ibid.
16 Ibid., 55, 98. For the general context see Mita Choudhury, *Convents and Nuns in Eighteenth-Century French Politics and Culture* (Ithaca: Cornell University Press, 2004).
17 Jo-Ann McEachern and David Smith, "Mme de Graffigny's *Lettres d'une Péruvienne*: Identifying the First Edition," *Eighteenth-Century Fiction* 9 (1996): 24.
18 [Joseph Laporte], *Observations sur la littérature moderne* (La Haye, 1749), 53–4.
19 Ibid., 33–4, 53. Twenty years later, La Porte recycled this review in an expanded version when he featured Graffigny in his *Histoire littéraire des femmes Françoises,* 5 vols. (Paris: Lacombe, 1769), 4:115–32. On the novel as philosophical, see Rachel L. Mesch, "Did Women Have an Enlightenment? Graffigny's Zilia as female 'philosophe,'" *Romanic Review* 89 (1998): 523–37.
20 [Elie Catherine Fréron], *Lettres sur quelques écrits de ce tems. Nouvelle édition. Tome premier* (Paris: Duchesne, 1752), 95.
21 Ibid., 73–4.
22 [Pierre Clément], *Les cinq années littéraires*, 4 vols (La Haye: A. de Groot, 1754), 1:21.
23 Prévost reprinted in Françoise de Graffigny, *Lettres d'une Péruvienne*, ed. Jonathan Mallinson (Oxford: Voltaire Foundation, 2002), 252–3, 277, and 289. This is the most up-to-date critical scholarly edition.
24 Londa L. Schiebinger, *The Mind Has No Sex: Women in the Origins of Modern Science* (Cambridge, MA: Harvard University Press, 1989); Erica Harth, *Cartesian Women: Versions and Subversions of Rational Discourse in the Old Regime* (Ithaca: Cornell University Press, 1992); Siep Stuurman, *François Poulain de la Barre and the Invention of Modern Equality* (Cambridge, MA: Harvard University Press, 2004).
25 Clarissa Campbell Orr, "Aristocratic Feminism, the Learned Governess, and the Republic of Letters," in *Women, Gender, and Enlightenment*, eds. Sarah Knott and Barbara Taylor (New York: Palgrave, 2005), 306–25.
26 On Bousquet see Silvia Corsini, "Vingt-cinq ans d'édition et d'imprimerie à Lausanne au siècle des Lumières: le libraire Marc-Michel Bousquet," *Revue historique vaudoise* 120 (2012): 23–53.
27 [Charles de Fieux, Chevalier de Mouhy], *Suite des lettres d'une Peruvienne* ([1748]); *Lettres d'une Peruvienne, séconde édition* (Lausanne: Bousquet, 1748). On Gleichen, see Showalter, *Françoise de Graffigny*, 264–7.
28 Unless otherwise noted, the English-language translations of *Letters of a Peruvian Woman* are included in the Eighteenth Century Collections Online (ECCO) database.
29 Geoffrey Turnovsky, *The Literary Market: Authorship and Modernity in the Old Regime* (Philadelphia: University of Pennsylvania Press, 2010), 147–83; Carla Hesse, *The Other Enlightenment: How French Women Became Modern* (Princeton: Princeton University Press, 2001), especially 60–1.
30 *LPW*, 85–6; Istvan Hont, "The Early Enlightenment Debate on Commerce and Luxury," in *The Cambridge History of Eighteenth-Century Political Thought*, eds. Mark Goldie and Robert Wokler (Cambridge: Cambridge University Press, 2006), 379–418; Christopher J. Berry, *The Idea of Luxury: A Conceptual and Historical Investigation* (Cambridge: Cambridge University Press, 1994).

31 Quoted in Vera L. Grayson, "The Genesis and Reception of Mme. de Graffigny's *Lettres d'une Péruvienne* and *Cénie*," *SVEC* 336 (1996): 31. On Turgot see R. R. Palmer, "Turgot: Paragon of the Continental Enlightenment," *Journal of Law and Economics* 19 (1776): 607–19.
32 Anne Robert Jacques Turgot, "To Madame De Graffigny," in *The Life and Writings of Turgot, Comptroller-General of France, 1774–1776*, ed. William Walker Stephens (New York: Longmans, Green, 1895 [1751]), 198–99.
33 *LPW*, 86.
34 Turgot, "To Madame De Graffigny," 195.
35 Condorcet, *Life of Turgot* (London: J. Johnson, 1787), 175. See also Emma Rothschild, *Economic Sentiments: Adam Smith, Condorcet, and the Enlightenment* (Cambridge, MA: Harvard University Press, 2001), 200.
36 *LPW*, 7, 10; Inca Garcilaso de la Vega, *Histoire des Incas, rois du Pérou*, trans. Thomas François Dalibard, 2 vols. (Paris: Prault, 1744). As Jonathan Mallinson notes (*LPW*, 147), Graffigny misattributes this last quote to Samuel Pufendorf. On anti-imperialism in general, see Sankar Muthu, *Enlightenment against Empire* (Princeton: Princeton University Press, 2003).
37 Raymond Birn, *Forging Rousseau: Print, Commerce and Cultural Manipulation in the Late Enlightenment* (Oxford: Voltaire Foundation, 2001), 30.
38 Jonathan Mallinson, "Re-présentant les Lettres d'une Péruvienne en 1752: Illustration et illusion," *Eighteenth-Century Fiction* 15 (2003): 227–39.
39 Quoted in Ibid., 298–303.
40 Joseph La Croix, *Dictionnaire historique portatif des femmes célèbres* (Paris: Cellot, 1769), 676.
41 Reproduced at Gallica, https://gallica.bnf.fr/ark:/12148/bpt6k62721455/f3.image. Accessed March 5, 2022.
42 Gautier Dagoty, *Galerie Françoise ou portraits des hommes et des femmes célèbres qui ont paru en France* (Paris: Herisant, 1770).
43 Showalter, *Françoise de Graffigny*, xv; William Hayley, *A Philosophical, Historical, and Moral Essay on Old Maids*, 3 vols (London: Cadell, 1785), 3:110.
44 Gustave Lanson, *Histoire de la littérature Française*, 5th ed. (Paris: Hachette, 1898); Paul Hazard, *European Thought in the Eighteenth Century: From Montesquieu to Lessing* (Cleveland and New York, 1963); Ernst Cassirer, *The Philosophy of the Enlightenment*, trans. Fritz C. A. Koelln and James P. Pettegrove (Princeton: Princeton University Press, 1951); Peter Gay, *The Enlightenment: An Interpretation*, 2 vols. (New York: Knopf, 1966 and 1969); Jonathan I. Israel, *Democratic Enlightenment: Philosophy, Revolution, and Human Rights, 1750–1790* (Oxford: Oxford University Press), 483.
45 Heidi Bostic, "Literary Women, Reason, and the Fiction of Enlightenment," *The French Review* 85 (2012): 1024–38.
46 Joan B. Landes, *Women and the Public Sphere in the Age of the French Revolution* (Ithaca: Cornell, 1988); Christine Fauré, *Democracy without Women: Feminism and the Rise of Individualism in France*, trans. Claudia Goodman and John Berks (Bloomington: Indiana University Press, 1991).
47 Edition designations from David Smith, *Bibliographie des Oeuvres de Mme de Graffigny, 1745–1845* (Ferney-Voltaire: Centre Internationale D'Étude de xviiie siècle, 2016).
48 Andrew Kahn, "Les lettres d'une Péruvienne et la culture du livre en Russie au dix-huitième siècle," in *Françoise de Graffigny, femme de lettres: ecriture et réception* (Oxford: Voltaire Foundation, 2004), 288–96.
49 Smith, *Bibliographie des oeuvres de Mme de Graffigny*, 106–9.

Notes

50 *The Peruvian Letters, Translated from the French. With an Additional Original Volume. By R. Roberts, Translator of Select Tales from Marmontel, Author of Sermons by a Lady, and Translator of the History of France, from the Abbé Millot*, 2 vols. (London: Cadell, 1774); [Morel de Vindé], *Suite des Lettres d'une Péruvienne* (Paris: Desenne, An VII [1797–8]). See also Marijn S. Kaplan, *Riccoboni and Brooke, Graffigny and Roberts* (London: Pickering & Chatto, 2012).
51 Quoted in Theresa Ann Smith, *The Emerging Female Citizen: Gender and Enlightenment in Spain* (Berkeley: University of California Press, 2006), 184–5, 187.
52 Chesterfield to Mme de Tencin, July 5, 1748, in *Miscellaneous Works of the Late Philip Dormer Stanhope, Earl of Chesterfield*, 2 vols (London: Dilly, 1777), 2:82–4. I have slightly altered the English translation presented here.
53 Christine Adams, "A Choice Not to Wed? Unmarried Women in Eighteenth-Century France," *Journal of Social History* 29 (1996): 883–94; Olwen Hufton, "Women Without Men: Widows and Spinsters in Britain and France in the Eighteenth Century," *Journal of Family History* 9 (1984): 355–76. For more general concerns over population see Carol Blum, *Strength in Numbers: Population, Reproduction, and Power in Eighteenth-Century France* (Baltimore: Johns Hopkins University Press, 2002).
54 The literature on the Cambridge School is immense. One important recent contribution that may stand as an introduction is J. G. A. Pocock, "A Response to Samuel James's 'J. G. A. Pocock and the Idea of the "Cambridge School" in the History of Political Thought,'" *History of European Ideas* 45 (2019): 99–103.

Chapter 9

1 The English translation of the French title, *De l'Esprit des lois* (or *loix*), often goes back and forth between *The Spirit of Laws* (see the 1750 Nugent translation) and *The Spirit of the Laws*. See Philip Stewart, "On the Nugent Translation of *L'Esprit des lois*," *History of Political Thought* 39 (2018): 83–106. Unless otherwise noted all quotations in English are from the edition translated by Anne M. Cohler, Basia Carolyn Miller and Harold Samuel Stone (Cambridge: Cambridge University Press, 1989), hereafter cited as *SL*.
2 François Gébelin, "La publication de Montesquieu's *De l'Esprit des lois*," *Révue des bibliothèques* 31 (1924): 135–58; Robert Shackleton, *Montesquieu: A Critical Biography* (Oxford: Oxford University Press, 1961), 240–3.
3 First edtion: Vol 1: [viii], XXIV, 522; Vol 2: [iv], XVI, 564.
4 *SL,* xlv.
5 Graham Gargett, *Jacob Vernet, Geneva, and the Philosophes* (Oxford: Voltaire Foundation, 1994), xii.
6 Quoted in Gébelin, "La publication de Montesquieu's *De l'Esprit des lois*," 142.
7 Barrillot Fils to Montesquieu, February 15, 1748, quoted in Gargett, *Jacob Vernet, Geneva, and the Philosophes*, 77.
8 Quoted in David Wallace Carrithers, Michael A. Mosher, and Paul Anthony Rahe, eds., *Montesquieu's Science of Politics: Essays on the Spirit of Laws* (Lanham: Rowman & Littlefield, 2001), 2.
9 Electronic Enlightenment (EE), Helvétius to Montesquieu, December 30, 1748.
10 Horace Walpole to Sir Horace Mann, January 10, 1750, in *Horace Walpole's Correspondence with Sir Horace Mann, Volume IV*, eds. W. S. Lewis, Warren Hunting Smith, and George L. Lam (New Haven: Yale University Press, 1954), 107.

11 Quoted in Janet Aldis, *Madame Geoffrin: Her Salon and Her Times* (New York: G. P. Putnam's Sons, 1905): 35 (translation altered).
12 EE, Hume to Montesquieu, April 10, 1749.
13 A rough guess is that eighteen livres in eighteenth-century England, at least, would amount to roughly 1/40 of a working man's annual income and 1/100 the annual income of someone in the middling classes. It might not be unreasonable to think of the price as something like $1,000 today. See http://www.oldbaileyonline.org/static/Coinage.jsp. Accessed March 7, 2022.
14 Robert Shackleton, "John Nourse and the London Edition of *L'Esprit des Lois*," in *Studies in the French Eighteenth Century: Presented to John Lough by Colleagues, Pupils and Friends*, eds. D. J. Mossop, G. E. Rodmell, and D. B. Wilson (Durham: University of Durham Press, 1978), 248–59.
15 Catherine Volpilhac-Auger, *Un auteur en quête d'éditeurs? Histoire éditoriale de l'oeuvre de Montesquieu (1748–1964)* (Lyon: Ens, 2012); and Cecil Patrick Courtney, "*L'Esprit des Lois* dans la perspective de l'histoire du livre (1748–1800)," in *Le Temps de Montesquieu: actes du colloque international de Genève (28–31 octobre 1998)*, eds. Michel Porret and Catherine Volpilhac-Auger (Geneva: Droz, 2002): 65–96.
16 Delphin de Lamothe to Samuel Formey, July 1, 1749, reprinted in Catherine Volpilhac-Auger, ed., *Montesquieu. Mémoire de la critique* (Paris: Presses de l'Université de Paris-Sorbonne, 2003), 119. On Lamothe, see [Charles Marionneau], *Les Vieux souvenirs de la rue Neuve à Bordeaux* (Bordeaux: Libraire Moquet, 1890); and Christine Adams, *A Taste for Comfort and Status: A Bourgeois Family in Eighteenth-Century France* (University Park: Penn State University Press, 2000), 233.
17 Montesquieu to Nivernais, January 26, 1749, quoted in Courtney, "*L'Esprit des lois* dans la perspective de l'histoire du livre," 72–3, who corrects Montesquieu's figure.
18 Courtney, "*L'Esprit des lois* dans la perspective de l'histoire du livre," 81. This edition, based on Montesquieu's final corrections, was first published in 1757, and included d'Alembert's "Elôge de Montesquieu" and "Analyse de L'Esprit des lois," both commonly found in editions afterwards. Alas, even this edition contained errors and did not always follow Montesquieu's instructions. See Charles Beyer, "Toward a Critical Edition of *l'Esprit des lois*," *Symposium* 4 (1950): 390–6; and Cecil Patrick Courtney, "Montesquieu et les imprimeurs de *l'Esprit des lois* (1748–1758)," in *L'Écrivain et l'imprimeur*, ed. Alain Riffaud (Rennes: Presses universitaires de Rennes, 2010), 193–216. A new critical edition of *The Spirit of the Laws* is scheduled to be published by Ens of Lyon as volumes 5 and 6 of *Oeuvres complètes*.
19 Editions are listed in Courtney, "*L'Esprit des lois* dans la perspective de l'histoire du livre," 78–92. I have simply counted all entries in Courtney's bibliography. See also http://kates.itg.pomona.edu/books/editions.php?action=view_references&groupID=63. Accessed March 7, 2022.
20 Alexandre Deleyre, ed., *Le génie de Montesquieu* (Amsterdam: Arkstée and Merkus, 1759), iii.
21 *Catalogue de la bibliothèque de Montesquieu à La Brède*, eds., Louis Desgraves and Catherine Volpilhac-Auger (Naples: Liguori Editore, 1999).
22 If one looks at the recent critical edition of the *Temple de Gnide* in *Oeuvres complètes de Montesquieu 8* (Oxford: Voltaire Foundation, 2003): 325–427, where it is sandwiched among many of Montesquieu's slight and ephemeral works, it is clear that today no one thinks of it as a popular literary masterpiece, as did readers during the eighteenth century. The literary genre of this prose poem is highly indebted to Fénélon's *Telemachus*, including its presentation as a kind of adaptation of ancient Greek poetry.

Notes

23 Jean le Rond D'Alembert, "Eulogy for President Montesquieu," in *Encyclopedic Liberty: Political Articles in the Dictionary of Diderot and D'Alembert*, trans. Henry C. Clark and Christine Dunn Henderson (Indianapolis: Liberty Fund, 2016), 122–38; Dan Edelstein, Robert Morissey, and Glenn Roe, "To Quote or Not to Quote: Citation Strategies in the Encyclopédie," *Journal of the History of Ideas* 74 (2013): 223–4. On his liberalism, see Thomas Pangle, *Montesquieu's Philosophy of Liberalism: A Commentary on "The Spirit of the Laws"* (Chicago: University of Chicago Press, 1973).

24 Jacques Peuchet, "Discours préliminaire," in *Encyclopédie méthodique. Jurisprudence. Tome Neuvième. La police et le municipalités* (Paris: Panckoucke, 1789), clviii.

25 J. P. Le Bouler and Catherine Lafarge, "Les emprints de Mme Dupin à la Bibliothèque du roi dans les années 1748–1750," *SVEC* 182 (1972): 107–85; Frédéric Marty, *Louise Dupin: Défendre l'égalité des sexes en 1750* (Paris: Classiques Garnier, 2021).

26 Robert Shackleton, "Montesquieu, Dupin and the Early Writings of Rousseau," in *Reappraisals of Rousseau: Studies in Honour of R. A. Leigh*, eds. Simon Harvey et al. (Totowa: Barnes & Noble, 1980), 234–49; Marty, *Louise Dupin*, 97–108. See also Rebecca Wilkin, "'Réformez vos contrats!': From the Marriage Contract to the Social Contract in Louise Dupin and Jean-Jacques Rousseau," *Early Modern French Studies* 43 (2021): 88–105.

27 Marty, *Louise Dupin*, 113–43; Joan Kelly, "Early Feminist Theory and the *Querelle des Femmes*," in *Women, History, and Theory* (Chicago: University of Chicago Press, 1984), 65–109.

28 Angela Hunter, "The Unfinished Work on Louise Marie-Madeleine Dupin's Unfinished *Ouvrage sur les femmes*," *Eighteenth-Century Studies* 43 (2009): 95–111. On Rousseau's antifeminism, see Penny A. Weiss, "Rousseau, Antifeminism, and Woman's Nature," *Political Theory* 15 (1987): 81–98.

29 Quoted from manuscript material in Eileen Hunt Botting, "The Early Rousseau's Egalitarian Feminism: A Philosophical Convergence with Madame Dupin and 'The Critique of the Spirit of the Laws,'" *History of European Ideas* 43 (2017): 1–13. The following section is based on this pathbreaking article. I am grateful to Professor Botting for sharing with me digitized copies of the "Critique de l'Esprit des lois," hereafter cited as Critique. The original manuscripts are in the Bibliothèque municipale classée de Bordeaux (MS 2111/1). See also Marty, *Louise Dupin*, 209–39.

30 Claude Dupin, *Réflexions sur quelques parties d'un livre intitulé De l'Esprit des loix*, 2 vols (Paris: Benjamin Serpentin, [1749]); *Observations sur un livre intitulé: De l'Esprit des loix, divisées en trois parties*, 3 vols (Paris). Claude Dupin also prepared revisions that remained unpublished manuscripts, according to Pauline Kra, in Columbia University's Seligman Papers in its archival collections. See https://caa.hcommons.org/deposits/item/mla:723/. Accessed July 17, 2021.

31 Botting, "The Early Rousseau's Egalitarian Feminism."
32 Critique, MS 2111_001, "Préface."
33 Critique, MS 2111_002 and 003. Section 002 is in Louise's handwriting.
34 Critique, MS 2111_002_004.
35 Ibid.
36 SL, 316.
37 Critique, MS 2111_006_011.
38 *SL*, 104; MS 2111_004_01.
39 On the early modern feminism reflected in such views, see Siep Stuurman, *François Poulain de la Barre and the Invention of Modern Equality* (Cambridge, MA: Harvard University Press, 2004); and Erica Harth, *Cartesian Women: Versions and Subversions of*

Rational Discourse in the Old Regime (Ithaca: Cornell University Press, 1992). See also Marty, *Louise Dupin*, 145–65 and 277–99.
40 *SL*, 111: "It is against reason and against nature for women to be mistresses in the house, as was established among the Egyptians, but not for them to govern an empire"; MS 2111_004-09.
41 *SL*, 314-415; MS 2111_006_09. Montesquieu's relationship to early modern feminism is a topic of scholarly debate. See, in particular, Jeannette Geffriaud Rosso, *Montesquieu et la féminité* (Pisa: Libreria Goliardica, 1977), and Diana J. Schaub, "Montesquieu on 'the Woman Problem,'" in *Rethinking the Woman Question for Liberal Democracy*, ed. Pamela Grande Jensen (Lanham: Rowman and Littlefield, 1996), 39–66.
42 Botting, "The Early Rousseau's Egalitarian Feminism." For the influence of Rousseau's antifeminism upon the French Revolutionaries, see Joan B. Landes, *Women and the Public Sphere in the Age of the French Revolution* (Cornell: Cornell University Press, 1988).
43 Reprinted in Volpilhac-Auger, *Montesquieu*, 111. See also Joan-Pau Rubiés, "The Jesuits and the Enlightenment," in *The Oxford Handbook of Jesuits*, ed. Ines G. Zupanov (Oxford: Oxford University Press, 2019), accessed through Oxford Handbooks Online on July 19, 2021.
44 *Les Nouvelles ecclésiastiques*, October 9 and 16, 1749, reprinted in Volpilhac-Auger, *Montesquieu*, 135–48.
45 For a general overview of Jansenism, see William Doyle, *Jansenism: Catholic Resistance to Authority from the Reformation to the French Revolution* (New York: St Martin's Press, 2000).
46 Ibid., 137.
47 Ibid., 138, 144.
48 *SL* 25, 26.
49 *SL* 27.
50 Volpilhac-Auger, *Montesquieu*, 140.
51 Pierre Nicole, "Of Charity and Self Love (1675)," in Bernard Mandeville, *The Fable of the Bees*, ed. E. J. Hundert (Indianapolis: Hackett Publishing Co, 1997), 5.
52 Ibid., 2.
53 Montesquieu, *My Thoughts*, trans. Henry C. Clark (Indianapolis: Liberty Fund, 2012), 635 (#2064).
54 Johan Heilbron, "French Moralists and the Anthropology of the Modern Era on the Genesis of the Notions of 'Interest' and 'Commercial Society,'" in *The Rise of the Social Sciences and the Formation of Modernity: Conceptual Change in Context, 1750–1850*, eds. Johan Heilbron, et al. (Dordrecht: Kluwer Academic Publishers, 1998), 77–106; Dale Van Kley, "Pierre Nicole, Jansenism, and the Morality of Enlightened Self-Interest," in *Anticipations of the Enlightenment in England, France, and Germany*, eds. Alan Charles Kors and Paul J. Korshin (Philadelphia: University of Pennsylvania Press, 1987), 69–85.
55 Pierre Bayle, *Various Thoughts on the Occasion of a Comet*, trans. Robert C. Bartlett (Albany: SUNY Press, 2000), 212.
56 *SL*, 97n and 312n.
57 Pierre Rétat, "De Mandeville a Montesquieu: Honneur, luxe et dépense noble dans l'Esprit des lois," *Studi Francesi* 50 (1973): 238–49; Céline Spector, "*L'Esprit des lois* de Montesquieu: une éclipse de amour-propre?," in *(Re) Lire L'Esprit des lois*, eds. Catherine Volpilhac-Auger and Luigi Delia (Paris: Éditions de la Sorbonne, 2014), 19–31.
58 *Défense de l'Esprit des lois*, ed. Pierre Rétat, in *Oeuvres completes de Montesquieu* 7 (Lyon: ENS, 2010), 77.

59 *Les Nouvelles ecclésiatiques*, April 24, 1750 and May 1, 1750, reprinted in Volpilhac-Auger, *Montesquieu*, 157–74.
60 Robert Shackleton, "When Did the French Philosophes Become a Party?" *Bulletin of the John Rylands University Library of Manchester* 60 (1977): 196. For one example of Montesquieu's works that included Voltaire's pamphlet see *Oeuvres de Monsieur de Montesquieu*, 6 vols. (Amsterdam: Arkstée and Merkus, 1773), 4:163–70. Voltaire's pamphlet is reprinted in *Oeuvres completes de Voltaire 32A*, ed. Mark Waddicor (Oxford: Voltaire Foundation, 2006), 175–208.
61 *SL*, 476. The Sorbonne's specific criticisms of passages in *The Spirit of the Laws* along with Montesquieu's responses are reprinted in *Oeuvres complètes de Montesquieu 7* (Lyon: ENS, 2010), 231–70.
62 *SL*, 478.
63 *SL*, 241–2, 607; *Oeuvres complètes*, 7:232 and 241 for the specific charges.
64 *SL*, 456.
65 Montesquieu later wrote about this criticism: "I couldn't get over my astonishment when, in reading Aristotle's *Politics*, I found all the theologians' principles on usury, word for word. I thought they had put them there. I talked about it in *The Spirit of the Laws*. But these gentlemen do not like it when their sources are revealed; their sources are unknown even to themselves, just as the source of the Nile used to be unknown. They made quite an outcry over that." Montesquieu, *My Thoughts*, ed. Henry C. Clark (Indianapolis: Liberty Classics, 2012), 646–7 (#2154).
66 *SL*, 456, 387, 466; *Oeuvres complètes*, 7:231, 235, 238–9, 242–3.
67 *SL*, 464, 483; Oeuvres complètes, 7:232 and 240.
68 *SL*, 488; Oeuvres complètes, 7:232 and 238. On the ambitions of Catholic powers, see Paul Kléber Monod, *The Power of Kings: Monarchy and Religion in Europe 1589–1715* (New Haven: Yale University Press, 1999).
69 *SL*, 25–6. The condemnation is quoted in Andrew J. Lynch, "Montesquieu and the Ecclesiastical Critics of '*L'Esprit des lois*,'" *Journal of the History of Ideas* 38 (1977): 492, whose authoritative account I'm following here.
70 *SL*, 27.
71 *SL*, 190; Oeuvres complètes, 7:238–9.
72 Charles Jacques Beyer, "Montesquieu et la censure religieuse de *l'Esprit des lois*," *Revue des sciences humaines* 70 (1953): 105–31.
73 *SL*, 25n.
74 "Réponses et explications données a la faculté de théologie sûr 17 propositions extraites de *l'Esprit des loix*, qu'elle avoit censurés," *Oeuvres complètes*, 7:256.
75 Vatican documents are reprinted in *Oeuvres complètes*, 7:165–216; Claude Lauriol, "La condemnation de *l'Esprit des lois* dans les archives de la Congrégation de l'Index," in *Montesquieu, oeuvre ouverte? (1748–1755)* (Naples: Liguori Editore, 2005), 92–102.
76 Shackleton, *Montesquieu*, 376.
77 *Défense de l'Esprit des lois*, 110–11.
78 Paul A. Rahe, "The Enlightenment Indicted: Rousseau's Response to Montesquieu," *Journal of the Historical Society* 8, no. 2 (2008): 273–302; Johnson Kent Wright, "Rousseau and Montesquieu," in *Thinking with Rousseau, from Machiavelli to Schmitt*, eds. Helena Rosenblatt and Paul Schweigert (Cambridge: Cambridge University Press, 2017), 63–91. See also Mark Hulliung, *Montesquieu and the Old Regime* (Los Angeles and Berkeley: University of California Press, 1975) for a contrasting view that sees Montesquieu's ideas as closer to Rousseau's. Some readers found Montesquieu and Rousseau perfectly compatible, Domenico Vasco, thrown into a dungeon at the

Pietmontese Castello Sabaudo di Ivrea in 1768, spent his days translating *The Spirit of the Laws* into Italian and idealizing Montesquieu's portrayal of republican virtue. See Franco Venturi, *Dalmazzo Francesco Vasco (1732–1794)* (Paris: Droz, 1940), 64–7.
79 *SL*, 382.
80 Michael Sonenscher, *Before the Deluge: Public Debt, Inequality, and the Intellectual Origins of the French Revolution* (Princeton: Princeton University Press, 2007), 105.
81 *SL*, 338.
82 "The most influential exponent of the doctrine of the doux commerce was Montesquieu." Albert Hirschman, *The Passions and the Interests: Political Arguments for Capitalism Before its Triumph* (Princeton: Princeton University Press, 1977), 60; *Journal of Commerce* quoted in Paul Cheney, *Revolutionary Commerce: Globalization and the French Monarchy* (Cambridge, MA: Harvard University Press, 2010), 51. See also, Céline Spector, *Montesquieu et l'émergence de l'économie politique* (Paris: Champion, 2006); and Catherine Larrère, "Montesquieu économiste? Une lecture paradoxale," *SVEC* 5 (2005): 243–66; Andrew Scott Bixby, *Montesquieu's Political Economy* (New York: Palgrave Macmillan, 2016). In 2011, the then French Finance Minister, Christine LaGarde (later president of the European Central Bank) echoed Hirschman on Montesquieu: "We French have known since Montesquieu that 'doux commerce' calms manners and naturally leads to attaining peace." "Déclaration de Mme Christine Lagarde, ministre de l'économie, des finances et de l'industrie, sur les relations économiques entre la France et Israël, à Paris le 7 mars 2011," https://www.vie-publique.fr/discours/181709-declaration-de-mme-christine-lagarde-ministre-de-leconomie-des-financ. Accessed June 15, 2020.
83 François Véron Duverger de Forbonnais, *Extrait du livre De L'Esprit des loix* (Amsterdam: Arkstée & Merkus, 1753), 109, commenting on *SL*, 338. Scholarship on the Gournay group has mushroomed. See in particular *Le Cercle de Vincent de Gournay: saviors économiques et pratiques administratives en France au milieu du XVIIIe siècle*, eds. Loïc Charles, Frédéric Lefebvre, and Christine Théré (Paris: Institut National d'Etudes Démographiques, 2011); Henry C. Clark, *Compass of Society: Commerce and Absolutism in Old Regime France* (Lanham: Lexington, 2007), 129–35; Robin J. Ives, "Political Publicity and Political Economy in Eighteenth-Century France," *French History* 17 (2003): 1–18.
84 François Véron de Forbonnais, "Commerce," in *The Encyclopedia of Diderot & d'Alembert Collaborative Translation Project*, trans. Nelly S. Hoyt and Thomas Cassirer (Ann Arbor: Michigan Publishing, University of Michigan Library), 2003, http://hdl.handle.net/2027/spo.did2222.0000.145. Accessed April 13, 2018. Originally published as "Commerce," *Encyclopédie ou Dictionnaire raisonné des sciences, des arts et des métiers*, 3:690–9 (Paris: Briasson, 1753).
85 Forbonnais, *Extrait du livre De L'Esprit des loix*, 116; *SL*, 346.
86 Enrico De Mas, *Montesquieu, Genovesi e la edizione italiane dello spirit delle leggi* (Florence: F. Le Monnier, 1971); Richard Bellamy, "'Da metafisico a mercatante': Antonio Genovesi and the Development of a New Language of Commerce in Eighteenth-Century Naples," in *The Languages of Political Theory in Early-Modern Europe* (Cambridge: Cambridge University Press, 1987), 277–300; Till Wahnbaeck, *Luxury and Public Happiness: Political Economy in the Italian Enlightenment* (Oxford: Oxford University Press, 2004), 59–66.
87 Adam Ulrich, *The Political Economy of J. H. G. Justi.* (Bern: Peter Lang, 2006).
88 Mirabeau was mistaken about France's so-called population decline. See Carol Blum, *Strength in Numbers: Population, Reproduction, and Power in Eighteenth-Century France* (Baltimore: Johns Hopkins University Press, 2002), 11–20, 43–4, 48–9.

89   Victor Riqueti, Marquis de Mirabeau, *L'Ami des hommes ou Traité de la population, nouvelle édition*, 6 vols. ([Avignon], 1759) 3:408–9.
90   Pierre Samuel du Pont de Nemours, "On the Origin and Progress of a New Science," in *Commerce, Culture and Liberty: Readings on Capitalism before Adam Smith*, trans. Henry C. Clark (Indianapolis: Liberty Fund, 2003), 564–97; final quotation from Cheney, *Revolutionary Commerce*, 52.
91   For a more generalized cultural history that ignores Montesquieu's contribution, see David Wootton, *Power, Pleasure, and Profit: Insatiable Appetites from Machiavelli to Madison* (Cambridge, MA: Harvard University Press, 2018).
92   David Lundberg and Henry F. May, "The Enlightened Reader in America," *American Quarterly* 28 (1976): 262–93. The books ranking above Montesquieu's were John Locke, *An Essay Concerning Human Understanding* (1690), 48 percent; David Hume, *History of England* (1753), 44 percent; Charles Rollin, *Ancient History* (1730), 41 percent; Hugh Blair, *Lectures on Rhetoric and Belles Lettres* (1783), 37 percent; Hugh Blair, *Sermons* (1777), 36 percent; Joseph Butler, *Rise and Progress of Religion in the Soul* (1745), 35 percent.
93   Donald S. Lutz, "The Relative Influence of European Writers on Late Eighteenth-Century American Political Thought," *The American Political Science Review* 78 (1984): 189–97. Both Lundberg-May and Lutz build on the older but still valuable Paul Merrill Spurlin, *Montesquieu in America, 1760–1801* (Baton Rouge: Louisiana State University Press, 1940).
94   Thomas Jefferson, *The Commonplace Book of Thomas Jefferson: A Repertory of His Ideas on Government*, ed. Gilbert Chinard (Baltimore: The Johns Hopkins Press, 1926), 33. Notes on Montesquieu are found in Articles 775–808. On the book orders see "To Thomas Jefferson from Perkins, Buchanan & Brown, October 2, 1769," in *The Papers of Thomas Jefferson, Vol. 1, 1760–1776*, ed. Julian P. Boyd (Princeton: Princeton University Press, 1950), 33–34, and available online at https://founders.archives.gov/documents/Jefferson/01-01-02-0022. Accessed March 7, 2022. Jefferson acquired *Oeuvres de Monsieur de Montesquieu*, 3 vols. (London: Nourse, 1767).
95   Thomas Jefferson to William Duane, September 16, 1810," Founders Online, National Archives, https://founders.archives.gov/documents/Jefferson/03-03-02-0052. Accessed September 29, 2019. [Original source: *The Papers of Thomas Jefferson, Retirement Series, Vol. 3, August 12, 1810 to June 17, 1811*, ed. J. Jefferson Looney (Princeton: Princeton University Press, 2006), 86–9.]; see also David Wallace Carrithers, "Montesquieu, Jefferson and the Fundamentals of Eighteenth-Century Republican Theory," *The French-American Review* 6 (1982): 160–88; and James F. Jones Jr., "Montesquieu and Jefferson Revisited: Aspects of a Legacy," *The French Review* 51 (1978): 577–85.
96   *SL* 25–6; Adams's diary entry for Thursday, June 26, 27, and July 3, 1760, *The Works of John Adams*, 10 vols. (Boston: Little, Brown, 1850–6), 2:93.
97   John Adams to Abigail Adams, February 27, 1783, Adams Family Papers: An Electronic Archive. Massachusetts Historical Society. https://www.masshist.org/digitaladams/archive/doc?id=L17830227jasecond. Accessed March 7, 2022. For the quotation itself, see *SL*, 25–6. This same excerpt became a favorite citation for the Anti-Federalists. See, for example, Cato IV (November 8, 1878, *New York Journal*), reprinted in *The Essential Federalist and Anti-Federalist Papers*, ed. David Wootton (Indianapolis: Hackett, 2003), 59–60. Adams later included a section of excerpts from *The Spirit of the Laws* in his major work of political theory, *A Defense of the Constitution of the United States of America*. See *Works* 4:423–7. Likewise, no less than Diderot cites this same quotation in the Encyclopédie article "Cour [Court]." See *The Encyclopedia of Diderot & d'Alembert*

Collaborative Translation Project (Ann Arbor: Michigan Publishing, University of Michigan Library, 2010), http://hdl.handle.net/2027/spo.did2222.0001.137. Accessed March 31, 2021. Originally published in *Encyclopédie ou Dictionnaire raisonné des sciences, des arts et des métiers*, 4:355 (Paris, 1754).

98 *SL*, 133; *The Records of the Federal Convention of 1787*, eds. Max Farrand, David Maydole Matteson, revised edition, 4 Vols. (New Haven: Yale University Press, 1966), 1:71,308,391, 485,497, 580; 2:34, 530; 3:109.

99 Pauline Maier, *Ratification: The People Debate the Constitution, 1787–1788* (New York: Simon & Schuster, 2010) does not mention Montesquieu.

100 Herbert J. Storing, and Murray Dry, eds., *The Complete Anti-Federalist*, 7 vols. (Chicago: University of Chicago Press, 1981).

101 Cato, *New York Journal*, October 25, 1787; Brutus, *New York Journal*, October 15, 1787, both online at The Documentary History of the Ratification of the Constitution, Digital Edition, https://rotunda-upress-virginia-edu.ccl.idm.oclc.org/founders/RNCN. Accessed March 7, 2022.

102 Thomas Greenleaf, *New York Journal*, December 14, 1787, available online at Ibid. Accessed March 7, 2022.

103 Americanus (John Stevens, Jr), *New York Daily Advertiser*, November 2 and 30, 1787, available online at Ibid. Accessed March 7, 2022. Americanus here anticipated notions that historians of political thought associate with Benjamin Constant, especially with his 1819 address, "The Liberty of the Ancients Compared with That of the Moderns," in *Political Writings*, ed. Biancamana Fontana (Cambridge: Cambridge University Press, 1988), 308–28.

104 Cato, *New York Journal*, November 22, 1787, available online at Ibid. Accessed March 7, 2022.

105 Version of [James] Wilson speech by Thomas Llyod, November 26, 1787, available online at Ibid. Accessed March 7, 2022.

106 *The Papers of Alexander Hamilton Digital Edition*, ed. Harold C. Syrett (Charlottesville: University of Virginia Press, Rotunda, 2011), rotunda.upress.virginia.edu/founders/ARHN-01-01-02-0057. Accessed May 16, 2014.

107 *Records of the Federal Convention of 1787*, 1:309.

108 Alexander Hamilton, New York Ratifying Convention, Remarks, June 17, 1788, available online at *Papers of Alexander Hamilton Digital Edition*. Accessed May 16, 2014.

109 James Madison, Alexander Hamilton, and John Jay, *The Federalist Papers*, ed. Isaac Kramnick (New York: Penguin Books, 1987), 118–22. See also Christopher Wolfe, "The Confederate Republic in Montesquieu," *Polity* 9 (1977): 441.

110 *SL*, 157.

111 For example, "Address and Reasons of Dissent of the Minority of the Convention of Pennsylvania, *Pennsylvania Packet and Daily Advertiser*, 18 December 1787," in *The Complete Anti Federalist*, 3: Document #11.

112 Richard Henry Lee to Samuel Adams, October 5, 1787, available online at Documentary History of the Ratification of the Constitution. Accessed March 7, 2022. See also Cecelia M. Kenyon, "Men of Little Faith: The Anti-Federalists on the Nature of Representative Government," *The William and Mary Quarterly* 12 (1955): 3–43, especially 23–4.

113 Dennis F. Thompson, "Bibliography: The Education of a Founding Father. The Reading List for John Witherspoon's Course in Political Theory, as Taken by James Madison," *Political Theory* 4 (1976): 523–9; *Records of the Federal Convention of 1787*, 2:34.

114 All citations to Federalist 47 from *Federalist Papers*, 302–8.
115 For example, Calvin H. Johnson, *Righteous Anger at Wicked States: The Meaning of the Founders' Constitution* (Cambridge: Cambridge University Press, 2005), 64–8.
116 An Impartial Citizen V, *Petersberg Virginia Gazette*, February 28, 1788, available online at Documentary History of the Ratification of the Constitution. Accessed March 7, 2022.

Chapter 10

1 Jean Jacques Rousseau, *The Confessions and Correspondence, Including the Letters to Malesherbes*, trans. Christopher Kelly (Hanover: University Press of New England, 1995), 294, 575–6.
2 Rahe, Paul A. "The Enlightenment Indicted: Rousseau's Response to Montesquieu," *Journal of the Historical Society* 8 (2008): 273–302. Helena Rosenblatt makes a similar argument in *Rousseau and Geneva: From the First Discourse to the Social Contract, 1749–1762* (New York: Cambridge University Press, 1997), 52–84.
3 discogs.com/artist/1097374-Jean-Jacques-Rousseau. Accessed July 26, 2020.
4 Arthur Melzer, *The Natural Goodness of Man: On the System of Rousseau's Thought* (Chicago: The University of Chicago Press, 1990).
5 Jo-Ann E. McEachern, *Bibliography of the Writings of Jean Jacques Rousseau to 1800. Vol 1. Julie, ou la Nouvelle Héloïse* (Oxford: Voltaire Foundation, 1993), 19. See also Raymond Birn, *Forging Rousseau: Print, Commerce and Cultural Manipulation in the Late Enlightenment* (Oxford: Voltaire Foundation, 2001). Much of this chapter rests on McEachern and Birn's careful reconstruction of Rousseau's publishing history.
6 McEachern, *Bibliography of the Writings of Jean Jacques Rousseau to 1800*, 31.
7 Best captured in Jean Jacques Rousseau and Chrétien Guillaume de Lamoignon de Malesherbes, *Correspondance*, ed. Barbara de Negroni (Paris: Flammarion, 1991).
8 Edward P. Shaw, *Problems and Policies of Malesherbes as Directeur de la Librairie in France (1750–1763)* (Albany: SUNY, 1966); Raymond Birn, "Malesherbes and the Call for a Free Press," in *Revolution in Print: The Press in France, 1775–1800*, eds. Robert Darnton and Daniel Roche (Berkeley and Los Angeles: University of California Press, 1989), 50–66.
9 D. W. Smith, *Helvétius: A Study in Persecution* (Oxford: Oxford University Press, 1965).
10 Malesherbes to Rousseau, October 29, 1760, in *Correspondance*, ed. Negroni, 71–3.
11 McEachern, *Bibliography of the Writings of Jean Jacques Rousseau to 1800*, 2:104.
12 Andrea Radasanu, "Montesquieu on Moderation, Monarchy, and Reform," *History of Political Thought* 31 (2010): 283–308; Aurelian Craiutu, *A Virtue for Courageous Minds: Moderation in French Political thought, 1748–1830* (Princeton: Princeton University Press, 2012), 40–61.
13 Keith Michael Baker, "A Classical Republican in Eighteenth-Century Bordeaux: Guillaume-Joseph Saige," in *Inventing the French Revolution* (New York: Cambridge University Press, 1990), 128–52.
14 Daniel Mornet, "Les Enseignements des bibliothèques privées (1750–1780)," *Revue d'Histoire littéraire de la France* 17 (1910): 459–96.
15 Joan McDonald, *Rousseau and the French Revolution* (London: Athone, 1962), 48.
16 Robert Darnton, *The Literary Underground of the Old Regime* (Cambridge, MA: Harvard University Press, 1982), 176–82.

17 R. A. Leigh, *Unsolved Problems in the Bibliography of Jean-Jacques Rousseau* (Cambridge: Cambridge University Press, 1990), 76.
18 Jo-Ann E. McEachern, "The Bibliography of Jean Jacques Rousseau's *Contrat Social*," in *Order and Connexion: Studies in Bibliography and Book History*, ed. R. C. Alston (Woodbridge, Suffolk: D. C. Brewer, 1997), 97–110; Carla Hesse, "A Fugitive Book," *Representations* 104 (2008): 39; "Revolutionary Rousseaus: The Story of His Editions," in *Media and Political Culture in the Eighteenth Century*, ed. Marie-Christine Skuncke (Stockholm: Kungl Vitterhets Historie och Antikvitets Akademien, 2005), 107–28.
19 Madeleine-Angélique de Neufville-Villeroy (1707–87) married Charles François Frédéric de Monmorency-Luxembourg, duc de Luxembourg (1702–64).
20 McEachern, *Bibliography of the Writings of Jean Jacques Rousseau to 1800. 2. Emile, ou de l'éducation* (Oxford: Voltaire Foundation, 1989), 36. Unless otherwise noted, details in this section regarding *Emile*'s publication come from McEachern's comprehensive introduction, as well as from Birn, *Forging Rousseau*, 32–44.
21 Duchesne and Guy also arranged for an edition to be published in Lyon by Jean Marie Bruyset.
22 McEachern, *Bibliography of the Writings of Jean Jacques Rousseau to 1800*, 1: 43
23 Electronic Enlightenment (hereafter EE), Néaulme to Rousseau, May 22, 1762.
24 EE, Rousseau to Néaulme, June 5, 1762.
25 Maurice Cranston, *The Solitary Self: Jean-Jacques Rousseau in Exile and Adversity* (Chicago: University of Chicago Press, 1997), 16–41; Thomas Barran, *Russia Reads Rousseau, 1762–1825* (Evanston: Northwestern University Press, 2002), 41–3. An abridged Russian translation of Book V was published in 1779.
26 "Pastoral Letter of His Grace the Archbishop of Paris," in Jean Jacques Rousseau, *The Collected Writings of Rousseau, Vol 9*, eds. Christopher Kelly and Eve Grace (Hanover: University Press of New England, 2001), 4.
27 *Recueil de mandemens, lettres, et instructions pastorals de Monseigneur L'Archêveque de Paris* (Paris: Simon, 1781).
28 Immanuel Kant, "Remarks in Observations on the Feeling of the Beautiful and Sublime (1764–1765)," in *Observations on the Feeling of the Beautiful and Sublime and Other Writings*, eds. Patrick Frierson and Paul Guyer (New York: Cambridge University Press, 2011), 85, 95.
29 Robert Darnton, "Readers Respond to Rousseau: The Fabrication of Romantic Sensitivity," in *The Great Cat Massacre and Other Episodes in French Cultural History* (New York: Basic Books, 1984), especially 236.
30 EE, Louis Eugene von Württemberg, duke of Württemberg to Rousseau, Tuesday, October 4, 1763.
31 Quoted in Lindsay A. H. Parker, *Writing the Revolution: A French Woman's History in Letters* (Oxford: Oxford University Press, 2013), 33–4.
32 Siân Reynolds, *Marriage and Revolution: Monsieur and Madame Roland* (Oxford: Oxford University Press, 2012), 79. See also Julia V. Douthwaite, *The Wild Girl, Natural Man, and the Monster: Dangerous Experiments in the Age of Enlightenment* (Chicago: University of Chicago Press, 2002), 134–60. On contemporary critics who viewed *Emile* as impractical, see Gilbert Py, "Rousseau et les éducateurs," *Studies in Voltaire and the Eighteenth Century* 356 (1997): 21, 35.
33 Lady Holland to Marchioness of Kildare, September 28, 1762 and August 8, 1762, in *Correspondence of Emily, Duchess of Leinster (1731–1814)*, ed. Brian FitzGerald, 3 vols. (Dublin: Stationery Office, 1949, 1957), 1:336, 343.
34 Mirabeau's letters to Sophie, quoted in Roger Barny, *Prélude idéologique à la Révolution française: Le Rousseauisme avant 1789* (Paris: Les Belles Lettres, 1985), 20.

35 *Memoirs of Richard Lovell Edgeworth, Esq.*, ed. Maria Edgeworth (London: R. Hunter, 1820), 177–9. This section is also based upon Wendy Moore, *How to Create the Perfect Wife: Britain's Most Ineligible Bachelor and His Enlightened Quest to Train the Ideal Mate* (New York: Basic Books, 2013).
36 Moore, *How to Create the Perfect Wife*, 226–7.
37 Ibid., 258–9.
38 Ibid., 274, 353.
39 Rousseau, *Emile*, 358, 361, 370.
40 Mary Seidman Trouille, *Sexual Politics in the Enlightenment: Women Writers Read Rousseau* (Albany: SUNY Press, 1997).
41 The story is brilliantly told in Moore, *How to Create the Perfect Wife*.
42 Ibid., esp. 101.
43 Ibid., 133.
44 Ibid., 53.
45 James Keir, *An Account of the Life and Writings of Thomas Day* (London: John Stockdale, 1791), 29. On this aspect of Rousseau, see Matthew David Mendham, *Hypocrisy and the Philosophical Intentions of Rousseau: The Jean-Jacques Problem* (Philadelphia: University of Pennsylvania Press, 2021), Chapter 1.
46 Maria Edgeworth and Richard Lovell Edgeworth, *Practical Education*, 2 vols (London: J. Johnson, 1798), 1:177–8.
47 Henry Home, Lord Kames, *Loose Hints Upon Education, Chiefly Concerning the Culture of the Heart* (Edinburgh: Bell and Murray, 1781), 38–9; Edgeworth and Edgeworth, *Practical Education*, 178.
48 George Warren Gignilliat, *The Author of Sandford and Merton: A Life of Thomas Day, Esq.* (New York: Columbia University Press, 1932); Sylvia W. Patterson, *Rousseau's Emile and Early Children's Literature* (Metuchen: Scarecrow Press, 1971). The visit to Day is described in *The Life, Letters and Literary Remains of Edward Bulwer, Lord Lytton* (New York: Harper, 1884), 13.

Chapter 11

1 "Preface to the French Edition," in *The Collected Writings of John Maynard Keynes, Volume 7: The General Theory*, eds. Elizabeth Johnson and Donald Moggridge (Cambridge: Cambridge University Press, 1978), xxi–xxiv.
2 I am using the one-volume edition edited by Edwin Cannan (New York: The Modern Library, 1994), hereafter cited as *WN*.
3 Dugald Stewart, "Account of the Life and Writings of Adam Smith [1794]," in *Adam Smith. Essays on Philosophical Subjects*, ed. W. P. D. Wightman and J. C. Bryce (Indianapolis: Liberty Fund, 1982), 294.
4 Cited in Henry C. Clark, "Montesquieu in Smith's Method of 'theory and history,'" *The Adam Smith Review 4* (2008): 133.
5 John Millar, *An Historical View of the English Government* (London: Strahan and Cadell, 1787), 528n. See also Richard B. Sher, "From Troglodytes to Americans: Montesquieu and the Scottish Enlightenment on Liberty, Virtue, and Commerce," in *Republicanism, Liberty, and Commercial Society, 1649–1776*, ed. David Wootton (Stanford: Stanford University Press, 1994), 368–404; Daniel Brühlmeier,

"Considération sur l'esprit de commerce et le libre marché chez Montesquieu et Adam Smith," *Revue de théologie et de philosophie* 130 (1998): 301–14; and more generally Mark Hulliung, *Enlightenment in Scotland and France: Studies in Political Thought* (London: Routledge, 2018), 22–40.

6 *The London Review of English and Foreign Literature* 3 (April 1776): 272.
7 *WN*, 485; Montesquieu, *The Spirit of the Laws*, trans. Anne M. Cohler et al. (Cambridge: Cambridge University Press, 1989), 27. David Wootton, *Power, Pleasure, and Profit: Insatiable Appetites from Machiavelli to Madison* (Cambridge, MA: Harvard University Press, 2018), 157n.
8 Cited in Clark, "Montesquieu in Smith's Method," 137. On his life see Nicholas T. Phillipson, *Adam Smith: An Enlightened Life* (New Haven: Yale University Press, 2010); on Hume and Smith see Dennis C. Rasmussen, *The Infidel and the Professor: David Hume, Adam Smith, and the Friendship That Shaped Modern Thought* (Princeton: Princeton University Press, 2017).
9 Richard B. Sher, *The Enlightenment and the Book: Scottish Authors and Their Publishers in Eighteenth-Century Britain, Ireland, and America* (Chicago: University of Chicago Press, 2006), 372.
10 Adam Smith to William Strahan, April 4, 1760, in *The Correspondence of Adam Smith*, ed. Ernst Campbell Mossner and Ian Simpson Ross (Indianapolis: Liberty Classics, 1987), 68.
11 *The London Review of English and Foreign Literature*, March 1776, 177.
12 *Monthly Review, or Literary Journal* 56 (February 1777): 117, 119.
13 *On the Wealth of Nations: Contemporary Responses to Adam Smith*, ed. Ian Simpson Ross (Bristol: Thoemmes Press, 1998), 5–6.
14 https://www.oldbaileyonline.org/static/Coinage.jsp#reading-costofliving. Accessed March 7, 2022.
15 Richard B. Sher, "New Light on the Publication and Reception of *The Wealth of Nations*," *Adam Smith Review* 1 (2004): 13.
16 I arrive at this sum by reconfiguring Strahan's reflections on publishing an octavo by Lord Kames at about the same time. See Sher, *The Enlightenment and the Book*, 345.
17 Sher, "New Light on the Publication and Reception," 5–12.
18 Quoted in Ibid., 8.
19 Adam Smith to William Strahan, November 13, 1776, in Smith, *Correspondence*, 222.
20 Richard B. Sher, "Early Editions of Adam Smith's Books in Britain and Ireland, 1759–1804," in *A Critical Bibliography of Adam Smith*, ed. Keith Tribe (London: Pickering & Chatto, 2002), 24; and more generally Sher, *The Enlightenment and the Book*, 355–6 and 445–8.
21 Adam Smith, *Additions and Corrections to the First and Second Editions of Dr. Adam Smith's Inquiry into the Nature and Causes of the Wealth of Nations* ([London]: n.p., [1784]).
22 *The Scots Magazine* 47 (March 1785): 126; Albert Hirschman, *The Passions and the Interests: Political Arguments for Capitalism Before Its Triumph* (Princeton: Princeton University Press, 1977); Istvan Hont, *Jealousy of Trade: International Competition and the Nation-State in Historical Perspective* (Cambridge, MA: Harvard University Press, 2005), 5–37.
23 Richard F. Teichgraeber, "'Less Abused Than I had Reason to Expect': The Reception of *The Wealth of Nations* in Britain, 1776–1790," *Historical Journal* 30 (1987): 337–66; Salim Rashid, "Adam Smith's Rise to Fame: A Reexamination of the Evidence," *The Eighteenth Century: Theory & Interpretation* 23 (1982): 64–85; Salim Rashid, "Charles James Fox and *The Wealth of Nations*," *History of Political Economy* 24 (1992): 493–7.

Notes

24 Alexander Jardine, *Letters from Barbary, France, Spain, Portugal, &c*, 2 vols. (London: Cadell, [1788]), 1:259–60.
25 Charles Marguerite Jean Baptiste Mercier Dupaty, *Travels Through Italy, in a Series of Letters* . . . (London: Robinson, 1788), 63–4.
26 *The Oeconomist, or, Englishman's Magazine* 2 (1799): 326–7.
27 David Allan, "A Reader Writes: Negotiating *The Wealth of Nations* in an Eighteenth-Century English Commonplace Book," *Philological Quarterly* 81 (2002): 207–33.
28 *The Lady's Magazine; or, Entertaining Companion for the Fair Sex* 28 (1797): 447.
29 Josiah Wedgwood, *Catalogue de camées, intaglios, médailles, bas-reliefs, bustes et petites statues* ([London], 1788), 102.
30 *Observations on the Commerce of Spain with Her Colonies, in Time of War* (Philadelphia: Carey, 1800), 13.
31 David Lundberg and Henry F. May, "The Enlightened Reader in America," *American Quarterly* 28 (1976): 262–93.
32 Samuel Fleischacker, "Adam Smith's Reception among the American Founders, 1776–1790." *William and Mary Quarterly* 59 (2002): 905.
33 Quoted in James F. Jones, "Montesquieu and Jefferson Revisited: Aspects of a Legacy," *The French Review* 51 (1978): 580.
34 Rashid, "Adam Smith's Rise to Fame"; Kirk Willis, "The Role in Parliament of the Economic Ideas of Adam Smith, 1776–1800," *History of Political Economy* 11 (1979): 509.
35 John E. Crowley, "Neo-Mercantilism and *The Wealth of Nations*: British Commercial Policy After the American Revolution," *Historical Journal* 33 (1990): 339–60.
36 Quoted in Willis, "The Role in Parliament of the Economic Ideas of Adam Smith," 510.
37 *Speech of the Right Honourable Charles-James Fox, in the House of Commons, on Friday, the 4th of January, 1798, on the Assessed-Tax Bill* (London: Debrett, 1798), 25; Willis, "The Role in Parliament of the Economic Ideas of Adam Smith," 513–15.
38 Willis, "The Role in Parliament of the Economic Ideas of Adam Smith," 509; *An Appeal to the Landed Interest of Great Britain, on the Operation of the Commercial Treaty with France* (London: Debrett, 1787), 8.
39 Anthony Robinson, *A Letter to the Right Hon. The Lord Mayor, on the State of the Country* (London: Hamilton, 1799), 22.
40 Robert Prasch and Thierry Warin, "'Il est encore plus important de bien faire que de bien dire' A Translation and Analysis of Dupont de Nemours' 1788 Letter to Adam Smith," *History of Economics Review* 49 (2009): 69.
41 Voltaire, *Letters Concerning the English Nation*, ed. Nicholas Cronk (Oxford: Oxford University Press, 1994), 38. At his death, one obituary noted that Smith "early became a disciple of Voltaire's in matters of religion." Cited in Emma Rothschild, *Economic Sentiments: Adam Smith, Condorcet, and the Enlightenment* (Cambridge, MA: Harvard University Press, 2001), 52.
42 Millar, *An Historical View of the English Government*, 528–9, citing *WN* 2:803–4.
43 *The Case of Tithes Truly Stated, With Some Observations on a Commutation* . . . (Canterbury: Simmons and Kirkby, 1795), 36, quoting *WN*, 420. An opposing view to Smith's is laid out in George Croft, *A Short Commentary, With Strictures, on Certain Parts of the Moral Writings of Dr. Paley* (Birmingham: Rivingtons, 1787), 144.
44 John Holroyd Sheffield, *Remarks on the Deficiency of Grain, Occasioned by the Bad Harvest of 1799*, 2 vols. (London: Debrett, 1800–1), 2:203; Thomas Thompson, *Tithes Indefensible; Or, Observations on the Origin and Effects of Tithes* (York: Wilson, 1795), 57, both citing *WN* 901.

45 *The Tocsin of Peace, in a Peal [sic] to the People, on Its Policy with France* ([London], 1794), 28. See also R. Legge Willis, *A Glimpse Through the Gloom, in a Candid Discussion of the Policy of Peace* (London: Gilley, 1794), 26.
46 Gabriel Sabbagh, "The Early Diffusion of *Wealth of Nations*, Turgot, and the Abbé Morellet: A Note," *Contributions to Political Economy* 31 (2012): 121–8.
47 Peter Groenewegen, "Turgot and Adam Smith," in *Eighteenth-Century Economics: Turgot, Beccaria and Smith and Their Contemporaries* (New York: Routledge, 2002), 363–78.
48 Richard Van den Berg and Christophe Salvat, "Scottish Subtlety: Andre Morellet's Comments on the *Wealth of Nations*," *European Journal of the History of Economic Thought* 8 (2001):149 and 179n9.
49 Carpenter, *The Dissemination of the Wealth of Nations*, xxx.
50 Christophe Salvat, "Histoire de la traduction inédite de La Richesse de nations," *Storia Del Pensiero Economico* 38 (1999): 121. Morellet's book was *Réfutation de l'ouvrage qui a pour titre Dialogues sur le commerce de bleds* (London, 1770).
51 Jacques Roger, *Buffon: A Life in Natural History*, trans. L. Pearce Williams (Ithaca: Cornell University Press, 1997), 94–5.
52 Carpenter, *The Dissemination of the Wealth of Nations*, xxxv.
53 *Recherches sur la nature et les causes de la Richesse des nations*, 6 vols. (Yverdon, 1781). See also Carpenter, *Dissemination of the Wealth of Nations*, 24–39.
54 Carpenter, *Dissemination of the Wealth of Nations*, 40–53. *Encyclopédie méthodique. Economie politique et diplomatique*, 4 vols. (Paris: Panckoucke, 1784–8). See also Robert Darnton, *The Business of Enlightenment: A Publishing History of the Encyclopédie* (Cambridge, MA: Harvard University Press, 1979), 385–481.
55 Colleen A. Sheehan, "Madison and the French Enlightenment: The Authority of Public Opinion," *The William and Mary Quarterly* 59, no. 4 (2002): 933.
56 Condorcet, *Life of M. Turgot* (London: Johnson, 1787), 73.
57 Carpenter, *Dissemination of the Wealth of Nations*, xliii; Robert L. Dawson, *The French Booktrade and the "Permission Simple" of 1777: Copyright and Public Domain* (Oxford: Voltaire Foundation, 1992), 584–5.
58 Jean Antoine Nicolas de Caritat marquis de Condorcet, ed., *Bibliothèque de l'homme public ou, analyse raisonnée des principaux ouvrages françois et étrangers, sur la politique en général, la legislation, les finances, la police, l'agriculture et le commerce en particulier, et sur le droit naturel et public*, 12 vols. (Paris: Buisson, 1790). *Wealth of Nations* summarized/excerpted in 3:108–216 and 4:3–115. See also Daniel Diatkine, "A French Reading of the 'Wealth of Nations' in 1790," in *Adam Smith: International Perspectives*, eds. Hiroshi Mizuta and Chuhei Sugiyama (New York: St. Martin's Press, 1993), 213–23.
59 *Mercure de France*, no. 31, July 31, 1790, 196.
60 *Le Spectateur national et le modérateur*, no. 160, May 9, 1791, 685–6, reproduced in Carpenter, *Dissemination of the Wealth of Nations*, 95 and 113.
61 Cited in Clark, "Montesquieu in Smith's Method," 133.
62 Cited in Gilbert Faccarello and Philippe Steiner, "The Diffusion of the Work of Adam Smith in the French Language: An Outline History," in *A Critical Bibliography of Adam Smith*, ed. Keith Tribe (London: Pickering & Chatto, 2002), 86–7.
63 *Le Spectateur national et le modérateur*, April 9, 1790, quoted with slight differences in Faccarello and Steiner, "The Diffusion of the Work of Adam Smith in the French Language," 87n.
64 *Journal général de France*, no 284, October 11, 1790, 1199; see also the *Journal de Paris*, June 4, 1790, 622: "The treatise on the Wealth of Nations is a complete system of social

economy." Both reproduced in Carpenter, *The Dissemination of the Wealth of Nations*, 98 and 94.

65 *Journal de Paris*, no 286, October 12, 88, 1221–2, reproduced in Carpenter, *The Dissemination of the Wealth of Nations*, 74.

66 Thomas Cooper, *Political Essays* (Philadelphia: Campbell, 1800), 43; Willis, "The Role in Parliament of the Economic Ideas of Adam Smith," 505–44.

67 T. F. Hill, *Observations on the Politics of France, and Their Progress since the Last Summer* (London: Hookham and Carpenter 1791), 60.

68 Richard Dinmore, *An Exposition of the Principles of the English Jacobins . . .* (Norwich: March, 1796), 20. See also *Political Dialogues, upon the Subject of Equality*, 2nd ed. (London: Ridgway, 1792), viii.

69 Emma Rothschild, "Adam Smith and Conservative Economics," *Economic History Review* 45 (1992): 74–96. On Smith's influence on Condorcet and Smith, see Emma Rothschild, *Economic Sentiments*, and William H. Sewell, Jr., *A Rhetoric of Bourgeois Revolution: The Abbé Sieyes and What Is the Third Estate?* (Durham: Duke University Press, 1994), 94–106; as well as Richard Whatmore, "Adam Smith's Role in the French Revolution," *Past and Present* 175 (2002): 65–89.

70 Quoted in Faccarello and Steiner, "The Diffusion of the Work of Adam Smith in the French Language," 88.

71 John Courtenay, *A Poetical and Philosophical Essay on the French Revolution. Addressed to the Right Hon Edmund Burke* (London: Ridgway, 1793), 33.

72 Anthony King, *Thoughts on the Expediency of Adopting a System of National Education, More Immediately Suited to the Policy of This Country . . .* (Dublin: Bonham, 1793), 103–4; Vicesimus Knox, *Liberal Education, or, a Practical Treatise on the Methods of Acquiring Useful and Polite Learning*, 2 vols., 4th ed. (London: Dilly, 1788), 2:276. See also Benjamin Heath Malkin, *Essays on Subjects Connected with Civilization* (London: Dilly, 1795), 26; Edward Miles Rudd, *The Connection between Intellectual and Moral Excellence* (Oxford: Oxford University Press, 1800), 3n.

73 Anthony Robinson, *A Short History of the Persecution of Christians, by Jews, Heathens, and Christians* (Carlisle: Jollie, 1793), 147.

74 Arthur Browne, *Miscellaneous Sketches: or, Hints for Essays*, 2 vols. (London: Robinson, 1798), 1:62. See also *The Civil and the Ecclesiastical Systems of England Defended and Fortified* (London: Longman, 1791), 109.

75 *The Commercial and Agricultural Magazine*, 6 vols (London, 1799–1802), 1:46–7.

76 William Thomson, *Letters from Scandinavia, on the Past and Present State of the Northern Nations of Europe*, 2 vols (London: Robinson, 1796), 1:361.

77 William Jones, *A Letter to John Bull, Esq. from his Second Cousin Thomas Bull, Author of the First and Second Letters to his Brother John* (London: Norman and Carpenter, 1793), 40.

78 James Chalmers, *Strictures on a Pamphlet Written by Thomas Paine, on the English System of Finance* (London: Debrett, 1796), 13.

79 S. A. Joersson, *Adam Smith, author of An Inquiry into the Wealth of Nations and Thomas Paine, Author of the Decline and Fall of the English System of Finance* (Germany [Hamburg?], 1796), 4–5.

80 Thomas James Mathias, *The Pursuits of Literature. A Satirical Poem in Four Dialogues* (Dublin: Byrne, 1799), 382: "Prove That No Doges, as Through the Streets They Range/ Give Bone for Bone in Regular Exchange," in *Miscellanies in Prose and Verse* (Edinburgh: Robertson, 1791), 25: "An art little worth is oft hardest to win/Ten workmen are paid for completing a pin."

81 *The Debate on a Motion for the Abolition of the Slave-Trade, in the House of Commons, on Monday the second of April 1792, Reported in Detail* [London, 1792], 14; "On Slavery," in *The General Magazine and Impartial Review* 66 (November 1792): 477–80.
82 *WN*, 76, cited in *A Full and Accurate Report of the Proceedings of the Petitioners Against a Bill intitled "A Bill to Prevent Unlawful Combinations of Workmen"* (London: Woodfall, 1800), 14.
83 Joseph Priestley, *Letters to the Inhabitants of Northumberland and its Neighbourhood, on Subjects Interesting to the Author*, Part II (Northumberland: Kennedy, 1799), 14.
84 Priscilla Wakefield, *Reflections on the Present Condition of the Female Sex* (London: J. Johnson, 1798), especially 1–4. See also Kathryn Sutherland, "Adam Smith's Master Narrative: Women and the *Wealth of Nations*," in *Adam Smith's Wealth of Nations: New Interdisciplinary Essays*, eds. Stephen Copley and Kathryn Sutherland (Manchester: Manchester University Press, 1995), 97–121.
85 Fania Oz-Salzberger, *Translating the Enlightenment: Scottish Civic Discourse in Eighteenth-Century Germany* (Oxford: Clarendon Press, 1995).
86 Samuel Fleischacker, "Values Behind the Market: Kant's Response to the *Wealth of Nations*," *History of Political Thought* 17 (1996): 390.
87 Keith Tribe, *Governing Economy: The Reformation of German Economic Discourse, 1750–1840* (Cambridge: Cambridge University Press, 1988), 133–48.
88 Quoted in Carl William Hasek, *The Introduction of Adam Smith's Doctrines into Germany* (New York: Columbia University Department of Political Science, 1925), 68–9.
89 *Lauderdale's Notes on Adam Smith's Wealth of Nations*, ed. Chuhei Sugiyama (Florence: Routledge, 1996).
90 *Lauderdale's Notes*, 37, 41–2, 56.
91 *WN*, 33.
92 *Lauderdale's Notes*, 16–17.
93 John Locke, *Some Considerations of the Consequences of the Lowering of Interest, and Raising the Value of Money* (London: Churchill, 1692), 65. Lauderdale's transcription is slightly different from the original: "That the intrinsic, natural worth of any thing, consists in its fitness to supply the necessities, or served the conveniences of human life; and the more necessary it is to our being, or the more it contributes to our well-being, the greater is its worth."
94 *Lauderdale's Notes*, 36, commenting on *WN*, 76.
95 *Lauderdale's Notes*, 54.
96 *Gazette National, ou, Le Moniteur universel*, no. 70, March 11, 1790, 573. See also Clark, "Montesquieu in Smith's Method," 132.

Chapter 12

1 Its full name is *Histoire philosophique et politique des établissements et du commerce des Européens dans les deux Indes* (*A Philosophical and Political History of the Settlements and Trade of the Europeans in the Two Indies*).
2 Cecil Courtney and Claudette Fortuny, "Repertoire d'ouvrages et d'articles sur Raynal (1800–2003)," *SVEC* 7 (2003): 37–113.
3 Guillaume Thomas Raynal, *Histoire philosophique et politque des établissements et du commerce des Européens dans les deux Indes. Éditions critique*, eds. Anthony Strugnell, et al. (Ferney-Voltaire: Centre International D'Etude du xviiie Siècle, 2010–) [hereafter cited as *Hp*].

4 Electronic Enlightenment (hereafter EE), Greve Gustaf Filip Creutz to Voltaire, March 13, 1772.
5 Guillaume Thomas Raynal, *A Philosophical and Political History of the Settlements and Trade of the Europeans in the East and West Indies*, trans. J. O. Justamond, 8 vols. (London: Strahan and Cadell, 1788), 1:1, hereafter cited as *History*.
6 Sankar Muthu, *Enlightenment Against Empire* (Princeton: Princeton University Press, 2003), 72–121; Sunil M. Agnani, *Hating Empire Properly: The Two Indies and the Limits of Enlightenment Anticolonialism* (New York: Fordham University Press, 2013); and Anoush Fraser Terjanian, *Commerce and Its Discontents in Eighteenth-Century French Political Thought* (Cambridge: Cambridge University Press, 2012), 74–7.
7 For comparison with Voltaire and Rousseau, see Louis Alexandre Devérité, *Recueil intéressant, sur l'affaire de la mutilation du crucifix d'Abbéville* (London, 1776), 196; John Bennett, *Divine Revelation Impartial and Universal* (London: Cadell, 1783), 36: "An Helvetius, a Voltaire, and a Raynal, whose works are now translated into most modern languages, almost universally read, and as universally admired."
8 Goggi, Gianluigi, "Quelques remarques sur la collaboration de Diderot à la première édition de l'Histoire des deux Indes," *SVEC* 286 (1991): 17–52; Muriel Brot, "La collaboration de Saint-Lambert à *l'Histoire des deux indes*: Une lettre inédite de Raynal," in *Raynal, de la polémique à l'histoire*, eds. Gilles Bancarel and Gianluigi Goggi (Oxford: Voltaire Foundation, 2000), 99–107; Yves Bénot, "Deleyre: De l'Histoire des voyages (t. XIX) à l'Histoire des deux indes," *Dix-Huitième Siècle* 25 (1993): 369–86. For one rare rumor claiming that Diderot was the work's author, see EE, Charles Gilbert Romme to M. Dubruel, November 15, 1774. Diderot's contributions have now been identified by scholars and are represented by yellow highlighting at the ARTFL database. However, because it is not possible yet to sort out the other contributions, I refer to all the passages not written by Diderot as written by Raynal.
9 *History*, 1:1–32.
10 *History*, 1:4, 27. Montesquieu is mentioned on 9. Montesquieu is also invoked at the very end of the long work (10:220): "Montesquieu wrote *The Spirit of the Laws*, and the boundaries of genius were extended."
11 *History*, 1:128.
12 *History*, 1:138–9.
13 *History*, 1:209.
14 *History*, 1:248.
15 Linda E. Merians, *Envisioning the Worst: Representations of "Hottentots" in Early-Modern England* (Newark: University of Delaware Press, 2001). Rousseau addressed the Hottentot issue in *Discourse on the Origin of Inequality*, trans. Donald A. Cress (Indianapolis: Hackett, 1992), 91–2.
16 *History*, 1:310–11.
17 *History*, 1:309–12.
18 *History*, 1:395.
19 *History*, 1:428–9.
20 *History*, 1:426.
21 *History*, 1:429.
22 Ibid.
23 *History*, 1:430.
24 *History*, 1:431.
25 *History*, 3:190.
26 Damien Tricoire, ed., *Enlightened Colonialism: Civilization Narratives and Imperial Politics in the Age of Reason* (New York: Palgrave Macmillan, 2017); Monica Michaud,

"Culture as Colonizer: Raynal's 'colonialisme éclairé' in the '*Histoire des deux Indes*,'" *French Forum* 39 (2014): 17–32.
27 *History*, 3:189.
28 *History*, 3:190. Raynal anticipated some of the findings of Jan de Vries, *The Industrious Revolution: Consumer Behavior and the Household Economy, 1650 to the Present* (Cambridge: Cambridge University Press, 2008).
29 *History*, 3:189.
30 *History*, 3:239. On the return to Montesquieu see Anthony Pagden, *Lords of All the World: Ideologies of Empire in Spain, Britain and France c.1500-c.1800* (New Haven: Yale University Press, 1995), 173–7.
31 *History*, 3:270.
32 *History*, 5:267–8.
33 Joshua Toulmin, *Dissertations on the Internal Evidences and Excellence of Christianity* (London: J. Johnson, 1785), 229; William Eden, *A Fifth Letter to the Earl of Carlisle* (London, 1780), 38; Honoré Gabriel de Riqueti, Comte de Mirabeau, *Des Lettres de cachet et des prisons d'état* (Hambourg, 1782), 72; Buffon, *Natural History*, 9 vols. (Edinburgh: Creech, 1780–1785), 9:12; John Curry, *Elements of Bleaching* (Dublin: Jones, 1779), x; Edward Gibbon, *The Decline and Fall of the Roman Empire*, 6 vols (New York: Collier, 1901), 5:278n; Singleton Harpur, *A Sermon Against the Excessive Use of Spirituous Liquors* (Dublin: William Sleater, 1788), 18; *A Letter to Dr. Price on His Additional Observations on the Nature and Value of Civil Liberty* (London: J Southern, [1777]), 15–16.
34 Guillaume Thomas Raynal, *Hp* xxxiv–xxxvii.
35 EE, Voltaire to Catherine II, September 29, 1772.
36 *Mémoires secrets pour servir à l'histoire de la république des lettres en France* 6 (May 22, 1772): 140.
37 Walpole to Lady Ailesbury, December 29, 1772, in *Horace Walpole's Correspondence with Henry Seymour Conway, Lady Ailesbury,* eds. W. S. Lewis et al. (New Haven: Yale University Press, 1974), 167–8.
38 Cecil P. Courtney, "Les Métamorphoses d'un best-seller: L'Histoire des deux indes de 1770 à 1820," in *Raynal, de la polémique à l'histoire*, eds. Gilles Bancarel and Gianluigi Goggi (Oxford, England: Voltaire Foundation, 2000), 115; Raynal, *Hp*, Liv–lix.
39 *Arrest du Conseil d'Etat du Roi, qui supprime un imprimé ayant pour titre: Histoire philosophique et politique des établissemens et du commerce des Européens dans les deux indes. du 19 Décembre 1772* (Paris: De l'Imprimerie royale, 1772).
40 *Mémoires secrets*, August 10, 1775, ed. Christopher Cave (Paris: Honoré Champion, 2010), 4:949.
41 *The Sentiments of a Foreigner on the Disputes of Great Britain with America* (Philadelphia: James Humphreys, [1775]); Paul Benhamou, "La Diffusion de l'Histoire des deux indes en Amérique (1770–1820)," in *Raynal, de la polémique à l'histoire*, eds. Gilles Bancarel and Gianluigi Goggi (Oxford: Voltaire Foundation, 2000), 301–12.
42 Manon Phlipon to Sophie Cannet, January 23, 1776, in *Lettres inédites de Mlle Phlipon, Mme Roland, adressées aux Demoiselles Cannet, de 1772 á 1780*, ed. Guillaume Joseph Auguste Breuil, 2 vols. (Paris: Coquebert, 1841), 1:267–68.
43 EE, William Cowper to Joseph Hill, May 7, 1778. Girolamo Imbruglia, "Les Premières lectures italiennes de *l'Histoire philosophique et politique des deux Indes*: Entre Raynal et Robertson," *Studies on Voltaire and the Eighteenth Century* 286 (1991): 235–51, esp. 237.

Notes

44. Girolamo Imbruglia, "Reflected Images: The *Histoire des deux indes* and the Censorship of the Roman Congregation of the Index," in *Voltaire Raynal Rousseau . . .*, ed. Anthony Strugnell (Oxford: Voltaire Foundation, 2003), 184.
45. *Memoirs of the Life and Peregrinations of the Florentine Philip Mazzei 1730–1816*, trans. Howard R. Marraro (New York: Columbia University Press, 1942), 295: "he was in search of subscribers to pay a louis in advance and a half louis on receipt of the work. I subscribed, paid the louis to the man himself, and left it to a friend of mine to receive the work and pay the half louis."
46. *Mémoires secrets* 15:232 (July 1, 1780).
47. Gianluigi Goggi, "Les Contrats pour la troisième édition de *l'Histoire des deux Indes*," *Dix-Huitieme Siecle* 16 (1984): 261–77.
48. C. P. Courtney, "Literary History and Book History: The Approach to an Eighteenth-Century Best-Seller: Raynal's *Histoire des deux indes*," in *The Culture of the Book: Essays from Two Hemispheres in Honour of Wallace Kirsop* (Melbourne: Bibliographical Society of Australia and New Zealand, 1999), 305.
49. Claudette Fortuny, "La troisième édition de l'Histoire des deux indes et ses contrefaçons: Les contributions de Genève et Neuchâtel," *SVEC* 12 (2001): 269–98. On the STN, see FBTEE: The French Book Trade in Enlightenment Europe, where *History of the Two Indies* ranks third in terms of copies produced (6236) and twelfth in terms of copies sold (3694) at http://fbtee.uws.edu.au/stn/interface/rank.php?t=book&n=10&e=supply&d1=01&m1=01&y1=1769&d2=31&m2=12&y2=1794&g=everywhere&d=table. Accessed July 21, 2021.
50. Maps and charts have been faithfully reprinted in a new facsimile edition, *Tableaux, atlas et cartes de l'Histoire philosophique et politique des établissements et du commerce des Européens dans les deux indes*, ed. Andrew Brown (Ferney-Voltaire: Centre International D'Etude du XVIIIe Siècle, 2010).
51. *Les trois philosophes sur la nature de la monarchie* (London, 1787); Guibert, *L'Abbé Raynal aux Etats généraux* (Marseille, 1789) is discussed in Hans-Jürgen Lüsebrink, "L'Histoire des deux indes et ses extraits: Un mode de dispersion textuelle au XVIII e siècle," *Littérature* 69 (1988): 28–41. See also Courtney, "Les Métamorphoses d'un best-seller," 119.
52. John Adams to Thomas Cushing, July 25, 1779, Founders Online https://founders.archives.gov/documents/Adams/06-06-02-0244. Accessed March 8, 2022.
53. Colleen A. Sheehan, "Madison and the French Enlightenment: The Authority of Public Opinion," *The William and Mary Quarterly* 59 (2002): 933.
54. Thomas Paine, "Letter to the Abbé Raynal," in *The Complete Writings of Thomas Paine*, ed. Philip S. Foner, 2 vols (New York: Citadel, 1945), 1:215, 221–2.
55. Thomas Jefferson to John Adams, August 27, 1786, at Founders Online https://founders.archives.gov/documents/Jefferson/01-10-02-0222. Accessed March 8, 2022.
56. Ibid, 251.
57. C. P. Courtney, "L'Art de la compilation de l'Histoire des deux indes," *SVEC* 333 (1995): 307–23.
58. *Mémoires secrets* 10:152 (June 16, 1777).
59. Reinier Salverda, "Raynal and Holland: Raynal's *Histoire des deux Indes* and Dutch Colonialism in the Age of Enlightenment," in *Raynal's Histoire des deux Indes: Colonialism, Networks, and Global Exchange*, eds. Cecil Courtney and Jenny Mandar (Oxford: Voltaire Foundation, 2015), 217–34.
60. Quoted in Allen McConnell, "Abbé Raynal and a Russian Philosophe," *Jahrbücher für Geschichte Osteuropas, Neue Folge* 12 (1965): 499. I have slightly modernized the translation for clarity.

61 Robert Darnton, *The Corpus of Clandestine Literature in France 1769–1789* (New York: Norton, 1995), 89, 258. See also 194, where *History of the Two Indies* occupies the fifth spot on Darnton's list of the most demanded forbidden books of the era, based on orders from the Société Typographique de Neuchâtel.
62 Cited in Anatole Feugère, *Un précurseur de la Révolution: L'Abbé Raynal (1713–1796). Documents Inédits* (Geneva: Slatkine, 1970 [1922]), 146; François Pidanzat de Mairobert, *Journal historique de la révolution*, 7 vols (London, 1775), 3:125–6 (22 mai 1772).
63 *Correspondence secrète, politique, et littéraire*, 18 vols. (London, 1787) 11:278 (May 25, 1781). Dispatch from Paris.
64 "Remonstrances du clergé à Louis XVI, en 1780, sur les dangers de la religion et du clergé," quoted in Feugère, *Un précurseur de la Révolution*, 281–2.
65 *The Speech of Anthony Louis Séguier in the Parlement of Paris* (London: P. McQueen, 1781), 37–8.
66 Jeroom Vercruysse, "Les impressions clandestines Bruxelloises de l'Abbé Raynal (1781)," *SVEC* 12 (2000): 145.
67 *The Speech of Anthony Louis Séguier,* 23–4, 31, 34; *Arrest de la Cour de Parlement, qui condamné un imprimé . . . par Guillaume-Thomas Raynal* (Paris: Simon, 1781).
68 *Determinatio Sacrae Facultatis Parisiensis in Librum Cui Titulus . . . Par Guillaume-Thomas Raynal* (Paris: Clousier, 1781), vi. The corresponding French title is *Censure de la Faculté de Théologie de Paris contre un livre . . .*
69 *Determinatio Sacrae Facultatis Parisiensis in Librum Cui Titulus . . . Par Guillaume-Thomas Raynal*, 112 and 114.
70 *Annales Politiques*, June 15, 1781, 399–400.
71 *Correspondence Littéraire*, July 1774, 10:454–5, cited in William R. Womack, "Eighteenth-Century Themes in the *Histoire philosophique et politique des deux Indes* of Guillaume Raynal," *SVEC* 96 (1972): 133.
72 Francisco Javier Clavijero, *The History of Mexico*, trans. Charles Cullen, 2 vols. (London, 1787), 1:xxxv–xxxvi.
73 "Remarkable Extracts from the Works of Abbé Raynal," *The Gentleman's Magazine* (July 1781): 315–16.
74 EE, James Boswell to William Johnston Temple, June 18, 1775.
75 William Godwin, *The History of the Life of William Pitt, Earl of Chatham* (London: Kearsley, 1783), xiii. For a similar sentiment, see the *European Magazine, and London Review*, 86 vols. (London, 1782–1826), 6:185 for September 1784: "[Raynal's] writings are of a particular class, being a mixture of history and philosophy, blending and supporting each other in a manner than renders him original in this sort of composition. I recommend him to your most attentive perusal. His head and his heart seem of the purest and sublimest frame. No writer appears more sincerely zealous for the common happiness of society; none more determined to promote it by the uniform tenour of all his writings."
76 Jeremy L. Caradonna, *The Enlightenment in Practice: Academic Prize Contests and Intellectual Culture in France, 1670–1794* (Ithaca: Cornell University Press, 2012), 156–9, 233–5.
77 *Lettres historiques, politiques et critiques sure les évenements, que se sont passés depuis 1778 jusqu'à present . . .* 18 vols. (London: De l'Imprimerie d'un ministre disgracie, 1788), 12:35 (Mars 29, 1783).
78 Judith Jennings, *The Business of Abolishing the British Slave Trade* (London: Frank Cass, 1997), 24–5.
79 Thomas Day, *Fragment of an Original Letter on the Slavery of the Negroes, Written in the Year 1776* (London: Stockdale, 1784); Africanus, *Remarks on the Slave Trade, and*

the *Slavery of the Negroes* (London: Phillips, 1788), 28; John Beatson, *Compassion the Duty and Dignity of Man* (Hull: G. Prince, 1789), 60 and 64; Anthony Benezet, *Short Observations on Slavery, Introductory to Some Extracts from the Writing of the Abbé Raynal on That Important Subject* [Philadelphia: Crukshank, 1781], 7; [James White], *Hints for a Specific Plan for an Abolition of the Slave Trade, and for Relief of the Negroes in the British West Indies* (London: Debbrett, 1788), 14; William Dickson, *Letters on Slavery* (London: Phillips, 1789), x; Beilby Porteus, *A Sermon Preached Before the Incorporated Society for the Propagation of the Gospel in Foreign Parts* (London: Harrison and Brooke, 1783), 33; Thomas Clarkson, *The History of the Rise, Progress, & Accomplishment of the Abolition of the African Slave-Trade by the British Parliament*, 2 vols. (London: Longman, 1808) 1:88.

80 *Memoirs of the Life of Sir Samuel Romilly*, 2 vols, 3rd ed. (London: John Murray, 1841), 1:88.

81 Jonathan Israel, *Revolutionary Ideas: An Intellectual History of the French Revolution From The Rights of Man to Robespierre* (Princeton: Princeton University Press, 2014), 158–9.

82 Jeremy D. Popkin, *You Are All Free: The Haitian Revolution and the Abolition of Slavery* (New York: Cambridge University Press, 2010), 201–2, 320–1; Laurent Dubois, *Avengers of the New World: The Story of the Haitian Revolution* (Cambridge, MA: Harvard University Press, 2004), 285.

83 Cited in Popkin, *You Are All Free*, 322; see also Helen D. Weston, "Representing the Right to Represent: The 'Portrait of Citizen Belley, Ex-Representative of the Colonies' by A.-L. Girodet," *RES: Anthropology and Aesthetics* 26 (1994): 83–99. On Belley's earring, see Sylvia Musto, "Portraiture, Revolutionary Identity and Subjugation: Anne-Louis Girodet's Citizen Belley," *RACAR: revue d'art canadienne/Canadian Art Review* 60 (1993): 66. On the bust itself see Guilhem Scherf, "Un buste de l'Abbé Raynal à l'Académie de Lyon," *Bulletin des musées et monuments Lyonnais* 1 (1988): 10–19.

84 Quoted in Darcy Grimaldo Grigsby, *Extremities: Painting Empire in Post-Revolutionary France* (London: Yale University Press, 2002), 56.

85 *History*, 5:309–10. For the original, see Raynal, *Hp,* 3:204–5.

86 C. R. L. James, *The Black Jacobins: Toussaint Louverture and the San Domingo Revolution* (New York: Vintage, 1963), 25. James changes "great man" to "courageous chief." On James and his approach, see Paul B. Miller, *Elusive Origins: The Enlightenment in the Modern Caribbean Historical Imagination* (Charlottesville: University of Virginia Press, 2010), 177.

87 John Relly Beard, *The Life of Toussaint L'Ouverture, the Negro Patriot of Hayti* (London: Ingram, Cooke, 1853), 23–30, 90. The illustration appears after page 30. The book was immediately translated into Dutch and reprinted in Boston in 1863. More recently, a popular reprint edition was published by the Negro Universities Press in 1970 and a scholarly edition by the University of North Carolina Press in 2012.

88 Alphonse de Lamartine, *Toussaint Louverture* (Paris: Michel Lévy, 1850), xcii–xviii. See also E. Freeman, "From Raynal's new Spartacus to Lamartine's Toussaint Louverture: A Myth of the Black Soul in Rebellion," *Myths and its Making in the French Theatre: Studies Presented to W. D Howarth*, eds. E. Freeman et al. (Cambridge: Cambridge University Press, 1988), 138.

89 John Morley, *Diderot and the Encyclopedists*, 2 vols. (London: Chapman and Hall, 1884), 1:377.

90 William J. Simmons, *Men of Mark: Eminent, Progressive and Rising* (Cleveland: Rewell, 1887), 938.

91 *The Memoir of Toussaint Louverture*, trans. Philippe R. Girard (Oxford: Oxford University Press, 2014).

92 Louis Sala-Molins, *Dark Side of the Light: Slavery and the French Enlightenment*, trans. John Conteh-Morgan (Minneapolis: University of Minnesota Press, 2006), 123–4. See also Srinivas Aravamudan, *Tropicopolitans: Colonialism and Agency, 1688–1804* (Durham: Duke University Press, 1999), 300–15; Michel-Rolph T. Rouillot, *Silencing the Past: Power and the Production of History* (Boston: Beacon Press, 2015), 82–5; Alyssa Goldstein Sepinwall, *Slave Revolt on Screen: The Haitian Revolution in Film and Video Games* (Jackson: University Press of Mississippi, 2021), 39–40.
93 *Réimpression de l'ancien Moniteur*, 32 vols. (Paris: Bureau Central, 1840–1845), 29:585bis (January 9, 1799); Charles Cousin d'Avallon, *Histoire de Toussaint l'Ouverture* (Paris: Pillot, 1802), 37n: "Toussaint-Louverture étoit devenu le partisan le plus déclaré de Raynal; l'ouvrage de ce philosophe étoit devenu pour ainsi dire son bréiaire. Il croyoit y lire sa destinée dans les chapitres qui traitoient de l'indépendance probable des colonies du Nouveau-Monde; il en recommandait vivement la lecture. L'histoire de Raynal, le chapelet et le rosaire étoient le talisman en vertu duquel il agissoit sur les esprits foibles et superstitieux, pour les associer aux projets de son ambition." See also Sudhir Hazareesingh, *Black Spartacus: The Epic Life of Toussaint Louverture* (New York: Farrar, Straus, and Giroux, 2021), 30, 32.
94 Robin Blackburn, *The Overthrow of Colonial Slavery, 1776–1848* (London: Verso, 1988), 243.
95 Hazareesingh, *Black Spartacus*, 46, 99,100. The term "Spartacus" appears only in the second version of *History of the Two Indies*, published between 1774 and 1780 ("Où est-il ce Spartacus nouveau"), which was omitted in Diderot's more lengthy 1780 exhortation. See Raynal, *Histoire des deux indes*, in ARTFL, http://artflsrv02.uchicago.edu.ccl.idm.oclc.org/philologic4/raynal/query?report=concordance&method=proxy&q=spartacus&start=0&end=0. Accessed February 20, 2021. Beard refers to a new Spartacus in *Life of Toussaint L'Ouverture*, 90.
96 On this theme see especially David A. Bell, *Men on Horseback: The Power of Charisma in the Age of Revolution* (New York: Farrar, Straus and Giroux, 2021).
97 Quoted in Andy Martin, *Napoleon the Novelist* (Cambridge: Polity, 2000), 12, 17–18, 61; Andrew Roberts, *Napoleon: A Life* (New York: Viking, 2014), 31.

Bibliography of Works Cited

Primary Sources: Unpublished

Dupin, Louise. Critique de l'Esprit des lois. Bibliothèque municipale classée de Bordeaux (MS 2111).
Kra, Pauline. Seligman Papers, Columbia University. See https://caa.hcommons.org/deposits/item/mla:723/ (accessed July 17, 2021).

Primary Sources – Books

Adams, John. *The Works of John Adams*. 10 vols. Boston: Little, Brown, 1850–1856.
Addison, Joseph and Richard Steele. *The Spectator*. 6th ed. 8 vols. London: J. Tonson, 1723.
d'Alembert, Jean Le Rond. "An Eulogium on President Montesquieu." In *The Complete Works of Monsieur de Montesquieu*. 4 vols, i–xxxv. Dublin: W. Watson, 1777.
d'Alembert, Jean le Rond. "Eulogy for President Montesquieu." In *Encyclopedic Liberty: Political Articles in the Dictionary of Diderot and D'Alembert*. Translated by Henry C. Clark and Christine Dunn Henderson, 122–38. Indianapolis: Liberty Fund, 2016.
d'Alembert, Jean Le Rond. *Histoire de membres de l'Académie française*. 6 vols. Paris: Moutard, 1785.
d'Alembert, Jean Le Rond. "Elôge de Fénelon." In *Oeuvres*. 4 vols, 492–4. Paris: Belin, 1821.
Arrest de la Cour du Parlement […]. Paris: Pierre Simon, 1734.
B*** de M. *Reflections on the Causes and Probable Consequences of the Late Revolution in France*. Edinburgh: Peter Hill; London: Cadell, 1790.
Barrett, Jean Jacques de. *De la loi naturelle*. 2 vols. Paris: Defer Demasonneuve, 1790.
Barruel, Abbé Augustin. *Mémoires pour servir à l'histoire du Jacobinism*. 5 vols. Hamburg, 1800.
Bayle, Pierre. *Various Thoughts on the Occasion of a Comet*. Translated by Robert C. Bartlett. Albany: SUNY Press, 2000.
Beattie, James. *An Essay on the Nature and Immutability of Truth*. 2 vols. Edinburgh: Kincaid and Bell, 1770.
Beaumont, Christophe de. "Pastoral Letter of His Grace the Archbishop of Paris" In Jean Jacques Rousseau, *The Collected Writings of Rousseau*, Vol 9, translated by Christopher Kelly, 1–17. Hanover: University Press of New England, 2001.
Beaumont, Christophe de. *Recueil de mandemens, lettres, et instructions pastorals de Monseigneur L'Archêveque de Paris*. Paris: Simon, 1781.
Bernardin de Saint Pierre, Jacques-Henri. *Etudes de la Nature*. Paris: Didot, 1848.
Bernardin de Saint-Pierre, Jacques-Henri. *Studies of Nature*. 5 vols. Translated by Henry Hunter. London: Dilly, 1796.
Bibliothèque de l'homme public ou, analyse raisonnée des principaux ouvrages françois et étrangers, sur la politique en général, la legislation, les finances, la police, l'agriculture et le

commerce en particulier, et sur le droit naturel et public. Edited by Jean Antoine Nicolas de Caritat, Marquis de Condorcet. 12 vols. Paris: Buisson, 1790.
Brissot, Jacques Pierre. *New Travels in the United States of America*. 2 vols. London: Jordan, 1794.
Brooke, Henry. *The Fool of Quality, Or, The History of Henry, Earl of Moreland*. 5 vols. London: A. Millar, 1792.
Burr, Esther Edwards. *The Journal of Esther Edwards Burr 1754-1757*. Edited by Carol F. Karlsen and Laurie Crumpacker. New Haven: Yale University Press, 1984.
The Case of Samuel Richardson, of London, Printer; with Regard to the Invasion of his Property in The History of Sir Charles Grandison, Before Publication, by Certain Booksellers in Dublin. London, 1753.
Cérutti, Joseph Antoine. *Elôge funèbre de M. de Mirabeau, prononcé le 4 avril 1791*. Paris, 1791.
Cérutti, Joseph Antoine. *Idées simple et précises sur le papier monnoie, les assignats forces, et les biens ecclésiastiques*. Paris: Desenne, 1790.
Chalmers, James. *Plain Truth; Addressed to the Inhabitants of America*. Philadelphia, 1776.
Chalvet, Pierre Vincent. *Des Qualités et des devoirs des instituteurs publique*. Paris, 1793.
Chénier, Marie Joseph. *Fénelon, ou Les Religieuses de Cambrai*. Paris: Moutard, 1793.
Chesterfield, Philip Stanhope, Earl of. *Letters*. Edited by David Roberts. Oxford: Oxford University Press, 1992.
Chesterfield, Philip Stanhope, Earl of. *Miscellaneous Works of the Late Philip Dormer Stanhope, Earl of Chesterfield*. 2 vols. London: Dilly, 1777.
Chydenius, Anders. *Anticipating The Wealth of Nations: The Selected Works of Anders Chydenius (1729–1803)*. Edited by Maren Jonasson and Pertti Hyttinen. London and New York: Routledge, 2012.
[Clément, Pierre]. *Les cinq années littéraires*. 4 vols. La Haye: A. de Groot, 1754.
The Complete Anti-Federalist. 7 vols. Edited by Herbert J. Storing and Murray Dry. Chicago: University of Chicago Press, 1981.
Condorcet, Nicolas de Caritat, Marquis de. *The Life of M. Turgot*. London: J. Johnson, 1787.
Condorcet, Nicolas de Caritat, Marquis de. *Selected Writings*. Translated by Keith Michael Baker. Indianapolis: Bobbs-Merrill, 1976.
Dagoty, Gautier. *Galerie Françoise ou portraits des hommes et des femmes célèbres qui ont paru en France*. Paris: Herisant, 1770.
Deleyre, Alexandre, ed. *Le génie de Montesquieu*. Amsterdam: Arkstée and Merkus, 1759.
[Desfontaines, Pierre François]. *La Voltairomanie*. London [Amsterdam], 1739.
Dickinson, John. *Letters From a Farmer in Pennsylvania, to the Inhabitants of the British Colonies*. New York: John Holt, 1768.
Diderot, Denis. *Correspondance*. Tome XI. Edited by Georges Roth. Paris: Minuit, 1964.
Diderot, Denis. "Letter on the Book Trade." Translated by Arthur Goldhammer. *Daedalus* 131 (2002): 48–56.
Diderot, Denis. *The Nun*. Translated by Russell Goulbourne. Oxford: Oxford University Press, 2005.
Diderot, Denis. "In Praise of Richardson." In *Selected Writings on Art and Literature*. Translated by Geoffrey Bremner. New York: Penguin, 1994.
Diderot, Denis. *Rameau's Nephew and Other Works*. Translated by Jacques Barzun. Indianapolis: Hackett, 2001.
Diderot, Denis and Jean Le Rond d'Alembert, eds. *Encyclopédie ou Dictionnaire raisonné des sciences, des arts et des métiers*. 26 vols. Neufchâtel: Samuel Faulche, 1765.
Dupin, Claude. *Observations sur un livre intitulé: De l'Esprit des loix, divisées en trois parties*. 3 vols. [Paris, 1751].

Dupin, Claude. *Réflexions sur quelques parties d'un livre intitulé De l'Esprit des loix*. 2 vols. Paris: Benjamin Serpentin, [1749].

Du Pont de Nemours, Pierre Samuel. "On the Origin and Progress of a New Science." In *Commerce, Culture and Liberty: Readings on Capitalism Before Adam Smith*. Translated by Henry C. Clark, 564–97. Indianapolis: Liberty Fund, 2003.

Early Responses to Hume's Life and Reputation. 2 vols. Edited by James Fieser. Bristol: Thoemmes Press, 2003.

Early Responses to Hume's Moral, Literary and Political Writings. Edited by James Fieser. 2 vols. Bristol: Thoemmes Press, 1999.

Edgeworth, Richard Lovell. *Memoirs*. Edited by Maria Edgeworth. London: R. Hunter, 1820.

Edgeworth, Maria and Richard Lovell Edgeworth. *Practical Education*. 2 vols. London: J. Johnson, 1798.

d'Eon, Charles Geneviève, Chevalier. *Les Loisirs du Chevalier d'Eon de Beaumont*. 13 Vols. Amsterdam, 1774.

Estwick, Samuel. *Considerations on the Negroe Cause*. 2nd ed. London: Dodsley, 1773.

Examen du Bélisaire de M. Marmontel, nouvel édition augmentée. Paris: Hansy le jeune, 1767.

[Faydit, Pierre Valentin]. *La Télémacomanie*. Eleuterople: Pierre Philalèthe, 1700.

Fénelon à une convention française ou préliminaires à la constitution du philosophe. Paris, 1793.

Fénelon, François. *The Adventures of Telemachus...in French and English*. Translated by Pierre Des Maizeaux. London: John Gray, 1742.

Fénelon, François. *Correspondance de Fénelon. Tome 9. La Condamnation des maximes des saints, 3 juin 1698 – 29 mai 1699*. Edited by Jean Orcibal, Jacques Le Brun, and Irénée. Geneva: Droz, 1987.

Fénelon, François. *Correspondance de Fénelon*. Tome 11. *décembre Fénelon dans la retraite, juin 1699-décembre 1702*, edited by Jean Orcibal, Jacques Le Brun, and Irénée Noye. Geneva: Droz, 1989.

Fénelon, François. *Les Avantures de Télémaque*. La Haye: Moetjens, 1701.

Fénelon, François. *Moral and Political Writings*. Translated by Ryan Patrick Hanley. Oxford: Oxford University Press, 2020.

Fénelon, François. *Oeuvres de Fénelon*. Edited by Jacques Le Brun. 2 vols. Paris: Gallimard, 1983–1997.

Fénelon, François. *Telemachus, Son of Ulysses*. Translated by Patrick Riley. Cambridge: Cambridge University Press, 1994.

Fielding, Henry. *An Apology for the Life of Mrs. Shamela Andrews. In Which the Many Notorious Falshoods and Misreprsentations [sic] of a Book Called Pamela, are Exposed and Refuted.... By Mr. Conny Keyber*. London: A. Dodd, 1741.

Forbonnais, François Véron de. "Commerce." In *The Encyclopedia of Diderot & d'Alembert Collaborative Translation Project*. Translated by Nelly S. Hoyt and Thomas Cassirer. Ann Arbor: Michigan Publishing, University of Michigan Library, 2003. http://hdl.handle.net/2027/spo.did2222.0000.145 (accessed April 13, 2018).

Forbonnais, François Véron de. "Commerce." In *Encyclopédie ou Dictionnaire raisonné des sciences, des arts et des métiers*, 690–9. Tome 3. Paris: Briasson, 1753.

Forbonnais, François Véron de. *Elémens de commerce*. 2nd ed. 2 vols. Leyde and Paris: Briasson, 1754.

Forbonnais, François Véron Duverger de. *Extrait du livre De L'Esprit des loix*. Amsterdam: Arkstée & Merkus, 1753.

Fordyce, James. *Sermons to Young Women*. 9th ed. 2 vols. London: T. Cadell and J. Dodsley, 1778.

Fréron, Elie Catherine. *Lettres sur quelques ecrits de ce tems. Nouvelle édition. Tome premier*. Paris: Duchesne, 1752.

Garcilaso de la Vega, Inca. *Histoire des Incas, rois du Pérou*. Translated by Thomas François Dalibard. 2 vols. Paris: Prault, 1744.
Gibbon, Edward. *The Decline and Fall of the Roman Empire*. 7 vols. Edited by J. B. Bury. London: Methuen, 1909–1914.
Gibbon, Edward. "Essay on the Study of Literature." Translated by Robert Mankin. *Republic of Letters* 3/3 (April 2014).
Gibbon, Edward. *Memoirs of My Life*. Edited by Betty Radice. Middlesex: Penguin, 1984.
Godwin, William. *An Enquiry Concerning Political Justice, and Its Influence on General Virtue and Happiness*. 2 vols. London: J. Johnson, 1793.
Godwin, William. *The History of the Life of William Pitt, Earl of Chatham*. London: Kearsley, 1783.
Goldini, Carlo. *Pamela commedia di Carlo Goldoni Avvocato Veneziano/Pamela, a Comedy*. London: J. Nourse, 1756.
Graffigny, Françoise de. *Correspondance de Madame de Graffigny, Tome 1, 1716–17 juin 1739*. Edited by English Showalter. Oxford: Voltaire Foundation, 1985.
Graffigny, Françoise de. *Letters of a Peruvian Woman*. Translated by Jonathan Mallinson. Oxford: Oxford University Press, [1747] 2009.
Graffigny, Françoise de. *Lettres d'une Péruvienne*. Edited by Jonathan Mallinson. Oxford: Voltaire Foundation, 2002.
Gueudeville, Nicolas. *Critique général des aventures de Télémaque*. Cologne: Pierre Marteau, 1700.
Hamilton, Alexander. *The Farmer Refuted*. New York: Rivington, 1775.
Hamilton, Alexander, John Jay, and James Madison. *The Federalist Papers*. Edited by Isaac Kramnick. New York: Penguin, 1987.
Hayley, William. *A Philosophical, Historical, and Moral Essay on Old Maids*. 3 vols. London: Cadell, 1785.
Helvétius, Claude Adrien. *Oeuvres complètes*. 4 vols. London, 1777.
Hervey, John. *The Collected Verse of John, Lord Hervey (1696–1743)*. Edited by Bill Overton. Cambridge: Cambridge University Press, 2016.
Hervey, John, et al. *Lord Hervey and his Friends, 1726–38: Based on Letters from Holland House, Melbury, and Ickworth*. Edited by Earl of Ilchester. London: John Murray, 1950.
Home, Henry, Lord Kames. *Loose Hints Upon Education, Chiefly Concerning the Culture of the Heart*. Edinburgh: Bell and Murray, 1781).
Hume, David. *A Treatise of Human Nature*. Edited by L. A. Selby-Bigge. Oxford: Oxford University Press, 1888.
Hume, David. "Advertisement." *A Treatise of Human Nature*. Vol. III. London: Thomas Longman, 1740.
Hume, David. *Discours politiques*. 2 vols. Translated by Jean Bernard, Abbé Le Blanc. Amsterdam; Paris: Lambert, 1754.
Hume, David. *Essays: Moral, Political, and Literary*, Edited by Eugene F. Miller. Indianapolis: Liberty Fund, 1985.
Hume, David. *The Letters of David Hume*. Edited by John Y. T. Greig. Oxford: Clarendon Press, 1932.
Hume, David. "My Own Life." In *Essays Moral, Political, and Literary*, edited by Eugene F. Miller, xxxi–xlii. Indianapolis: Liberty Classics, 1985.
Hume, David et al. *Discours politiques*. 5 vols. Translated by Eléazar de Mauvillon Amsterdam: Schreuder and Mortier, 1756–1761.
Hume's Reception in Early America. Edited by Mark G. Spencer. 2 vols. Bristol: Thoemmes Press, 2002.
Jamieson, J. *The Sorrows of Slavery, a Poem*. London: Murray, 1789.

Jefferson, Thomas. *The Commonplace Book of Thomas Jefferson: A Repertory of His Ideas on Government*. Edited by Gilbert Chinard. Baltimore: The Johns Hopkins Press, 1926.

Jefferson, Thomas. *The Papers of Thomas Jefferson, Vol. 1, 1760–1776*. Edited by Julian P. Boyd. Princeton: Princeton University Press, 1950.

Jefferson, Thomas. *The Papers of Thomas Jefferson, Retirement Series, vol. 3, 12 August 1810 to 17 June 1811*. Edited by J. Jefferson Looney. Princeton: Princeton University Press, 2006.

Journal encyclopédique ou universel. Edited by Pierre Rousseau. Bouillon, 1760–1793.

Kant, Immanuel. "An Answer to the Question: What is Enlightenment?" In *What Is Enlightenment?* edited by James Schmidt, 53–64. Berkeley and Los Angeles: University of California Press, 1996.

Kant, Immanuel. *Observations on the Feeling of the Beautiful and Sublime and Other Writings*. Edited by Patrick Frierson and Paul Guyer. Cambridge: Cambridge University Press, 2011.

Kant, Immanuel. "On the Wrongfulness of Unauthorized Publications of Books." In *Practical Philosophy*. Translated by Mary J. Gregor, 23–35. Cambridge: Cambridge University Press, [1785] 1996.

Keir, James. *An Account of the Life and Writings of Thomas Day*. London: John Stockdale, 1791.

Laclos, Choderlos de. *Les Liaisons Dangereuses*. Translated by Douglas Parmée. Oxford: Oxford University Press, 1998.

La Croix, Joseph. *Dictionnaire historique portatif des femmes célèbres*. Paris: Cellot, 1769.

La Motraye, Aubry de. *Historical and Critical Remarks on the History of Charles XII, King of Sweden, by Mr. de Voltaire*. London: T. Warner, 1732.

La Motraye, Aubry de. *Remarques historiques & critiques sur L'Histoire de Charles XII, Roi de Suède, par M. de Voltaire*. Londres: Pierre Dunoye, 1732.

La Motraye, Aubry de. *Travels through Europe, Asia, and into Part of Africa*. London: Printed for the Author, 1723.

La Motraye, Aubry de. *Voyages du sr. A. de La Motraye, en Europe, Asie & Afrique*. The Hague: T. Johnson and J. van Duren, 1727.

Laporte, Joseph. *Histoire littéraire des femmes Françoises*. 5 vols. Paris: Lacombe, 1769.

Laporte, Joseph. *Observations sur la littérature moderne*. La Haye, 1749.

Leinster. Duchess of. *Correspondence of Emily, Duchess of Leinster (1731–1814)*. Edited by Brian FitzGerald. 3 vols. Dublin: Stationery Office, 1949, 1957.

Locke, John. *An Essay Concerning Human Understanding...The Tenth Edition with Large Additions*. 4 vols. London: Arthur Bettsworth and Charles Hitch, 1731.

Locke, John. *Some Considerations of the Consequences of the Lowering of Interest, and Raising the Value of Money*. London: Churchill, 1692.

Locke, John. *Two Treatises on Government*. Edited by Peter Laslett. Cambridge: Cambridge University Press, 1988.

Long, Edward. *History of Jamaica*. 3 vols. London: Lowndes, 1774.

Lytton, Edward Bulwer. *The Life, Letters and Literary Remains of Edward Bulwer, Lord Lytton*. New York: Harper, 1884.

Madison, James. *The Writings of James Madison*. Edited by Gaillard Hunt. 9 vols. New York: G.P. Putnam's Sons, 1900–1910.

Malboissière, Geneviève de. *Lettres de Geneviève de Malboissière à AdélaïdeMéliand. Une jeune fille au xviii siècle*. Edited by Comte de Luppé. Paris: Champion, 1925.

Malesherbes, Chrétien Guillaume de Lamoignon de. *Correspondance*, ed. Barbara de Negroni (Paris: Flammarion, 1991).

Marana, Jean Paul. *L'Espion turc dans les cour des princes chrétiens*. 6 vols. Cologne, 1700.

Marivaux, Pierre de. *Journaux et oeuvres diverses*. Edited by Frédéric Deloffre and Michel Gilot. Paris: Garnier frères, 1969.

Maury, Jean Siffrein. *Elôge de...Fénelon*. Paris: Regnard and Demonville, 1771.

Mauvillon, Eléazar de. "Considérations sur quelques auteurs français et sur M. de Voltaire en particulier." In *Lettres françoises et germaniques*. Londres: Francois Allemand, 1740.

Mendelssohn, Moses. *Jerusalem or on Religious Power and Judaism*. Translated by Allen Arkush. Waltham: University Press of New England, [1783] 1983.

Mercier, Louis Sebastien. "Fénelon." In *Fragments de politique et d'histoire*. 3 vols., 2:269–74. Paris: Buisson, 1792.

Mercier, Louis Sebastien. *Fénelon à son diocese, pièce dramatique en trois actes en prose*. Paris, 1794.

Mercier, Louis Sebastien. *Memoirs of the Year Two Thousand Five Hundred*. Translated by W. Hooper. 2 vols. London: G. Robinson, 1772.

Mirabeau, Victor de Riqueti, Marquis de. *l'Ami des hommes ou Traité de la population, nouvelle edition*. 6 vols. [Avignon], 1759.

Mirabeau, Victor de Riquetti, Marquis de. *L'ami des hommes, ou, Traité de la population. Second partie*. Avignon, 1756.

Montagu, Lady Mary Wortley. *Selected Letters*. Edited by Isobel Grundy. London: Penguin Books, 1997.

Montesquieu, Charles de Secondat, Baron de. "Censure romaine 1750–1752." Edited by Pierre Rétat. *Oeuvres complètes de Montesquieu 7*, 165–216. Lyon: EMS, 2010.

Montesquieu, Charles de Secondat, Baron de. *The Complete Works of M. de Montesquieu*. 4 vols. Dublin: W. Watson, 1777.

Montesquieu, Charles de Secondat, Baron de. *Considerations on the Causes of the Greatness of the Romans and Their Decline*. Translated by David Lowenthal. Indianapolis: Hackett, 1965.

Montesquieu, Charles de Secondat, Baron de. *Considérations sur les causes de la grandeur des Romains et de leur decadence*. Edited by Françoise Weil et Cecil Courtney. In *Oeuvres complètes de Montesquieu 2*. Oxford: Voltaire Foundation, 2000.

Montesquieu, Charles de Secondat, Baron de. *Correspondance de Montesquieu*. Edited by François Gebelin. 3 vols. Paris: Champion, 1914.

Montesquieu, Charles de Secondat, Baron de. *Défense de l'Esprit des lois*. Edited by Pierre Rétat. In *Oeuvres complètes de Montesquieu 7*, 71–113. Lyon: ENS, 2010.

Montesquieu, Charles de Secondat, Baron de. *My Thoughts*. Translated by Henry C Clark. Indianapolis: Liberty Fund, 2012.

Montesquieu, Charles de Secondat, Baron de. *Oeuvres complètes*. 22 vols. Edited by Jean Ehrard, et al. Oxford: Voltaire Foundation; Lyon: EMS, 1998-.

Montesquieu, Charles de Secondat, Baron de. *Persian Letters*. Translated by Margaret Mauldon. Oxford: Oxford World Classics, 2008.

Montesquieu, Charles de Secondat, Baron de. *The Spirit of the Laws*. Edited by Anne M. Cohler, Basia Carolyn Miller, and Harold Samuel Stone. Cambridge: Cambridge University Press, 1989.

Montesquieu, Charles de Secondat, Baron de. "Sur la Télémaque." In *Oeuvres complètes*. Edited by André Masson. 3 vols. Paris: Nagel, 1950–1955.

Montesquieu, Charles de Secondat, Baron de. *Temple de Gnide*. In *Oeuvres complètes de Montesquieu 8*, 325–427. Oxford: Voltaire Foundation, 2003.

Mouhy, Charles de Fieux, Chevalier de. *Suite des lettres d'une Peruvienne*. [1748].

Nicole, Pierre. "Of Charity and Self Love (1675)." In Bernard Mandeville. *The Fable of the Bees*, Edited by E. J. Hundert, 1–8. Indianapolis: Hackett Publishing Co, 1997.

Nisbet, Richard. *Slavery Not Forbidden by Scripture. Or A Defence of the West-India Planters, from the Aspersions Thrown Out Against Them*. Philadelphia: [John Sparhawk], 1773.

Nordberg, Jöran Andersson. *Histoire de Charles XII, traduit de swédois*. 4 vols. The Hague: Husson, 1742–1748.

Peuchet, Jacques. "Discours préliminaire." In *Encyclopédie méthodique. Jurisprudence. Tome neuvième. La police et le municipalités*, i–clx. Paris: Panckoucke, 1789.

Pezay, Alexandre Frédéric Jacques Masson de and Denis Diderot. *Elôge de François de Salignac de la Motte-Fénelon*. Paris: Regnard and Demonville, 1771.

Pompignan, Jean Jacques Lefranc de. *Dissertation sur les biens nobles, avec des observations sur le vingtième*. 1758.

Poniatowski, Stanislas. *Remarques d'un seigneur polonois sur l'Histoire de Charles XII roi de Suede par M. de Voltaire*. The Hague: Moetjens, 1741.

Povey, Charles. *The Virgin in Eden*. London: Roberts, 1741.

Price, Richard. *A Discourse on the Love of Our Country, Delivered on Nov. 4, 1789*. London, 1790.

Proceedings in the National Assembly on the Admission of Mr. William Priestley, and the Motion for his Naturalization. London: Ridgway, 1791–1792.

Ramsay, Andrew Michael. "Discourse on Epick Poetry, Particularly on the Excellence of this Poem of Telemachus." In *Adventures of Telemachus*. 2nd ed. Translated by John Ozell, i–xlviii. London: Curll, 1719.

Ramsay, Andrew Michael. *The Life of François de Salignac de la Motte Fenelon, Archbishop and Duke of Cambray*. London: Vaillant, 1723.

Ramsay, James. *An Essay on the Treatment and Conversion of African Slaves in the British Sugar Colonies*. London: James Phillips, 1784.

Raynal, Guillaume Thomas. *Histoire philosophique et politique...deux indes*. 7 vols. Amsterdam, 1774.

Raynal, Guillaume Thomas. *Histoire philosophique et politique des établissements et du commerce des Européens dans les deux Indes*. 6 vols. ([Paris]: n.p., 1770).

Raynal, Guillaume Thomas. *Histoire philosophique et politique des établissements et du commerce des Européens dans les deux Indes*. 4 vols. (Geneva: Pellet, 1780).

Raynal, Guillaume Thomas. *Histoire philosophique et politique des établissements et du commerce des Européens dans les deux Indes*. 10 vols. (Geneva: Pellet, 1780).

Raynal, Guillaume Thomas. *Histoire philosophique et politque des établissements et du commerce des Européens dans les deux Indes. Èditions critique*, eds. Anthony Strugnell, et al. (Ferney-Voltaire: Centre International D'Etude du xviiie Siècle, 2010–).

Reeve, Clara. *The Progress of Romance*. 2 vols. Colchester: W. Keymer, 1785.

"Réponses et Explications données a la faculté de théologie sûr 17 propositions extraites de *l'Esprit des loix*, qu'elle avoit censures." In *Oeuvres complètes de Montesquieu 7*. Edited by Catherine Volpilhac-Auger and Pierre Rétat, 241–56. Lyon: EMS, 2010.

Report on the Manuscripts of the Lady Du Cane. London: Printed for H. M. Stationery office by B. Johnson, 1905.

Richardson, Samuel. *The Correspondence of Samuel Richardson*. Edited by Anna Laetitia Barbauld. 6 vols. London: R. Phillips, 1804.

Richardson, Samuel. *Letters Written to and for Particular Friends, on the Most Important Occasions*. London: J. Osborn, C. Rivington, and J. Peake, 1741.

Richardson, Samuel. *Pamela in Her Exalted Condition*. Edited by Albert J. Rivero. Cambridge: Cambridge University Press, 2012.

Richardson, Samuel. *Pamela, or Virtue Rewarded*. Edited by Thomas Keymer and Alice Wakely. Oxford: Oxford University Press, 2001.

Ridpath, George. *Diary of George Ridpath, Minister of Stitchel, 1755–1761*. Edited by James Balfour Paul. Edinburgh: Printed at the University Press, 1922.

Roland, Marie Jeanne. *Lettres de Madame Roland, Tome premier, Nouvelle série 1767–1780*. Edited by Claude Perroud. Paris: Imprimerie Nationale, 1913.

Rousseau, Jean Jacques. *Emile, or On Education*. Translated by Allan Bloom. New York: Basic Books, 1979.

Rousseau, Jean Jacques. *Émile, ou De l'éducation*, 4 vols. (Amsterdam [Paris]: Jean Néaulme [Duchesne and Guy], 1762)

Rousseau, Jean Jacques. *The Confessions and Correspondence, Including the Letters to Malesherbes*. Translated by Christopher Kelly. Hanover: University Press of New England, 1995.

Rousseau, Jean Jacques. *The Major Political Writings of Jean-Jacques Rousseau*. Translated by John T. Scott. Chicago: University of Chicago Press, 2011.

Saint-Simon, Louis de Rouvroy, Duc de. *Historical Memoirs of the Duc de Saint-Simon: A Shortened Version*. Translated by Lucy Norton. 2 vols. New York: McGraw Hill, 1967.

Secret Proceedings and Debates of the Convention Assembled at Philadelphia. Edited by Robert Yates, et al. Richmond: Curtiss, 1839.

Seneca. *Select Epistles on Several Moral Subjects*. London: Rivington, 1739.

Servan, Joseph Michel. *Discours sur les moeurs, prononcé au Parlement de Grenoble*. Lyon: Grabit, 1769.

Seward, Anna. *Letters of Anna Seward Written Between the Years 1784 and 1807*. 6 vols. Edinburgh: George Ramsay, 1811.

Sharp, Granville. *The Just Limitation of Slavery in the Laws of God*. London: B. White, 1776.

Smith, Adam. *The Correspondence of Adam Smith*. 2nd ed. Edited by Ernest Campbell Mossner and Ian Simpson Ross. Oxford: Clarendon Press, 1987.

Smith, Adam. *The Theory of Moral Sentiments*. Edited by Knud Haakonssen. Cambridge: Cambridge University Press, 2004.

Smith, Adam. *An Inquiry into the Nature and Causes of the Wealth of Nations*. 2 vols. London: W. Strahan and T. Cahill, 1776.

Smith, Adam. *An Inquiry into the Nature and Causes of the Wealth of Nations*. Edited by Edwin Cannan. New York: The Modern Library, 1994.

Specimens of the Novelists and Romancers, with Critical and Biographical Notices of the Authors. 2nd ed. Glasgow: R. Griffin, 1827.

Steele, Richard. *The Lucubrations of Isaac Bickerstaff*. 4 vols. London: Lintot, 1754.

Swediauer, Franz. "No Original Distinction in the Intellectual Abilities of Men in Any Part of the Globe." In *Philosophical Dictionary*. 4 vols., 2:165–7. London: Robinson, 1786.

Télémaque dans l'isle de Calypso. Paris, 1790.

Thiébault, Dieudonné. *Les Adieux du duc de Bourgogne et de l'abbé de Fénelon, son précepteur*. Paris: Prault, 1788.

Turgot, Anne Robert Jacques. "To Madame De Graffigny." In *The Life and Writings of Turgot, Comptroller-General of France, 1774–6*. Edited by William Walker Stephens, 198–9. New York: Longmans, Green, 1895 [1751].

Vaughan, Benjamin. *New and Old Principles of Trade Compared*. London: Johnson, 1788.

Villeroy, Pierre François Le Coq de. *Réponse, ou Critique des Lettres philosophiques de Monsieur de V****. Basle [Reims]: Chez Christophe Revis, 1735.

Voltaire. "Advertisement to the Reader." In *Oeuvres de 1723–1728 II: The English Essays of 1727*, edited by David Williams. Oxford: Voltaire Foundation, 1996.

Voltaire. *The Age of Louis XIV*. Translated by Martyn P. Pollack. London: Dent, 1961.

Voltaire. "Anecdotes sur le czar Pierre le Grand." In *Les Oeuvres complètes de Voltaire, 46*. Edited by Michel Mervaud, 51–84. Oxford: Voltaire Foundation, 1999.

Voltaire. "Avis des éditeurs." In *Oeuvres de Mr. de Voltaire*. Tome 7. Amsterdam: Ledet, 1749.

Voltaire. "Corpus des notes marginals." In *Les Oeuvres complètes de Voltaire 140B*, edited by Natalia Elaguina, et al., 708–76. Oxford: Voltaire Foundation, 2012.

Voltaire. "De l'utilité de l'histoire." In *Les Oeuvres completes de Voltaire 60A*, edited by Myrtille Méricam-Bourdet, 447–56. Oxford: Voltaire Foundation, 2017.

Voltaire. "De l'utilité de l'histoire." In *Nouveaux mélanges philosophiques, historiques, critiques*, etc. Geneva: Cramer, 1765.

Voltaire. *Histoire de Charles XII*. Edited by Gunnar von Proschwitz. In *Les Oeuvres complètes de Voltaire 4*. Oxford: Voltaire Foundation, 2007.

Voltaire. "L'A, B, C, dix-sept dialogues traduits de l'anglais de Monsieur Huet." In *Les Oeuvres complètes de Voltaire 65A*, edited by Roland Mortier and Christophe Paillard, 169–348. Oxford: Voltaire Foundation, 2011.

Voltaire. *La Henriade*. In *Oeuvres complètes de Voltaire*. Vol. 2. Edited by Ulla Kölving et al. Geneva: Voltaire Foundation, 1968.

Voltaire. *La Philosophie de l'histoire*. Edited by J. H. Brumfitt. Oxford: Voltaire Foundation, 1969.

Voltaire. *Le Mondain*. In *Oeuvres complètes de Voltaire*. Vol. 16. Edited by H. T. Mason. Oxford: Voltaire Foundation, 2003.

Voltaire. *Letters Concerning the English Nation*. London: C. Davis and A. Lyon, 1733.

Voltaire. *Letters Concerning the English Nation*. Edited by Nicholas Cronk. Oxford: Oxford University Press, 1994.

Voltaire. *Lettre à Mr. Norberg, chapelain du roy de Suede Charles XII, auteur de l'Histoire de ce monarque*. Londres, 1744.

Voltaire. *Lettres philosophiques. Édition critique*. Edited by Gustave Lanson, 2 vols. Paris: Hachette, 1909.

Voltaire. *Lettres sur les Anglais (III) in Oeuvres complètes de Voltaire, Tome 6C*. Edited by Antony McKenna and Gabriel Mori. Oxford: Voltaire Foundation, 2020.

Voltaire. *Lion of the North: Charles XII of Sweden*. Translated by M. F. O. Jenkins. Teaneck: Fairleigh Dickinson University Press, 1981.

Voltaire. *Nanine, comédie en trois actes, en vers de dix syllabes, donnée par l'auteur*. Paris: Le Mercier, 1749.

Voltaire. "Nouvelle considérations sur l'histoire." In *La Mérope française: avec quelques petites pièces de littérature*, 81–6. Paris: Prault, 1744.

Voltaire. "Nouvelle Considérations sur l'histoire." In *Les Oeuvres complètes de Voltaire, 28B*, edited by Myrtille Méricam-Bourdet, 165–85. Oxford: Voltaire Foundation, 2008.

Voltaire. *Oeuvres complètes de Voltaire*. 70 vols. Kehl: De l'imprimerie de la Sociétè Typographique-Littéraire, 1785–1789.

Voltaire. *Oeuvres de Mr. De Voltaire. Nouvelle édition*. 4 vols. Amsterdam: Aux Dépens de la Compagnie, 1741.

Voltaire. *Oreste*. In *Oeuvres complètes de Voltaire. Oeuvres de 1749*. Vol. 31A. Edited by David H. Jory. Oxford: Voltaire Foundation, 1992.

Voltaire. "Pensées sur l'administration public." In *Oeuvres complètes de Voltaire, 32A*, edited by Ahmad Gunny and David Williams, 303–30. Oxford: Voltaire Foundation, 2006.

Voltaire. "Préface des éditeurs." In "Three Texts in Defense of the 1748 Dresden Edition." In *Oeuvres complètes de Voltaire 30C*, edited by Nicholas Cronk. Oxford: Voltaire Foundation, 2004.

Voltaire. "Remarques sur l'histoire." In *Oeuvres complètes de Voltaire, 28B*, edited by Myrille Méricam-Bourdet, 143–64. Oxford: Voltaire Foundation, 2008.

Voltaire. *Remerciement sincère à un homme charitable*. Edition by Mark Waddicor. In *Oeuvres complètes de Voltaire 32A*, 175–208. Oxford: Voltaire Foundation, 2006.

Voltaire. *Voltaire's Notebooks*. Edited by Theodore Besterman. 2 vols. Geneva: Institut et Musée Voltaire, 1952.

Voltaire. *The Works of M. de Voltaire*. Edited by T. Smollett. 35 vols. London: J. Newberry, 1762–1781.

Voltaire. *The Works of Voltaire*. 2 vols. Edinburgh: Martin, 1769.

Voltaire and Frederick II. "Anti-Machiavel." In *Oeuvres complètes de Voltaire*. Edited by Werner Bahner and Helga Bergmann. Vol. 19. Oxford: Voltaire Foundation, 1996.
Walpole, Horace. *Horace Walpole's Correspondence with Sir Horace Mann, Volume IV*. Edited by W. S. Lewis, Warren Hunting Smith, and George L. Lam. New Haven: Yale University Press, 1954.
Walpole, Horace. *Miscellaneous Correspondence*. Edited by W. S. Lewis and John Riely. New Haven: Yale University Press, 1980.
Wedgwood, Josiah. *Catalogue of Cameos, Intaglios, Medals, Bas-Reliefs, Busts, and Small Statues*. Etruria,1787.

Secondary Sources

Abad, Reynald. "Guillaume-François Joly de Fleury, Procureur Géneral au Parlement de Paris, face au cas Voltaire." In *Les Parlements et l.es lumières*, edited by Olivier Chaline, 53–72. Pessac: Maison des Sciences de l'Homme d'Aquitaine, 2012.
Adair, Douglass. "That Politics may be Reduced to a Science: David Hume, James Madison, and the Tenth Federalist." *Huntington Library Quarterly* 20 (1957): 343–60.
Adams, Christine. "A Choice Not to Wed? Unmarried Women in Eighteenth-Century France." *Journal of Social History* 29 (1996): 883–94.
Adams, Christine. *A Taste for Comfort and Status: A Bourgeois Family in Eighteenth-Century France*. University Park: Penn State University Press, 2000.
Aldis, Janet. *Madame Geoffrin: Her Salon and Her Times*. New York: G. P. Putnam's Sons, 1905.
Alimento, Antonella. "La contribution de l'école de Gournay à la naissance d'une sphère publique dans la France des années 1750–1760." In *L'économie politique et la sphère publique dans le débat des Lumières*, edited by Jesús Astigarraga et Javier Usoz, 213–28. Madrid: Casa de Velázquez, 2013.
Allan, David. *A Nation of Readers: The Lending Library in Georgian England*. London: British Library, 2008.
Allan, David. "A Reader Writes: Negotiating the Wealth of Nations in an Eighteenth-Century Commonplace Book." *Philological Quarterly* 81 (2002): 207–33.
Allan, David. *Making British Culture: English Readers and the Scottish Enlightenment, 1740–1830*. New York: Routledge, 2008.
Allen, Graham. "Godwin, Fénelon, and the Disappearing Teacher." *History of European Ideas* 33 (2007): 9–24.
Altman, Janet Gurkin. "Graffigny's Epistemology and the Emergence of Third-World Ideology." In *Writing the Female Voice: Essays on Epistolary Literature*, edited by Elizabeth Goldsmith. Boston: Northeastern University Press, 1989.
Amory, Hugh. "Andrew Millar." *Oxford Dictionary of National Biography*, https://doi-org.ccl.idm.oclc.org/10.1093/ref:odnb/18714.
Arendt, Hannah. *Eichmann in Jerusalem: A Report on the Banality of Evil*. New York: Penguin Classics, 2006.
Ashcraft, Richard. *Revolutionary Politics and Locke's Two Treatises of Government*. Princeton: Princeton University Press, 1986.
Baggerman, Arianne. "The Cultural Universe of a Dutch Child: Otto van Eck and His Literature." *Eighteenth-Century Studies* 31 (1997): 129–34.
Baggerman, Arianne. *Publishing Policies and Family Strategies: The Fortunes of a Dutch Publishing House in the 18th and Early 19th Centuries*. Leiden and Boston: Brill, 2013.

Bailyn, Bernard. "An Enlightened Scot at Manchac." In *Voyagers to the West: A Passage in the Peopling of America on the Eve of the Revolution*, 488–92. New York: Knopf, 1986.

Bailyn, Bernard. *The Ideological Origins of the American Revolution*. Cambridge, MA: Harvard University Press, 1967.

Baker, Keith Michael. "A Classical Republican in Eighteenth-Century Bordeaux: Guillaume-Joseph Saige." In *Inventing the French Revolution, 128–52*. New York: Cambridge University Press, 1990.

Baker, Keith Michael. "Defining the Public Sphere in Eighteenth-Century France: Variations on a Theme by Habermas." In *Habermas and the Public Sphere*, edited by Craig Calhoun, 181–211. Cambridge, MA: MIT, 1992.

Baker, Keith Michael. "Enlightenment and the Institution of Society: Notes for a Conceptual History." In *Civil Society: History and Possibilities*, edited by Sudipta Kaviraj and Sunil Khilnani, 84–104. Cambridge: Cambridge University Press, 2001.

Baker, Keith Michael and Peter Reill, eds. *What's Left of Enlightenment? A Postmodern Question*. Stanford: Stanford University Press, 2001.

Barber, Gilles. "Book Imports and Exports in the Eighteenth Century." In *Sale and Distribution of Books from 1700*, edited by R. Myers and M. Harris, 77–105. Oxford: Oxford Polytechnic, 1982.

Barber, Gilles. "The Cramers of Geneva and their Trade in Europe between 1755 and 1766." *Studies in Voltaire and the Eighteenth Century* 30 (1964): 377–413.

Barber, Gilles. "The Financial History of the Kehl Voltaire." In *The Age of the Enlightenment: Studies Presented to Theodore Besterman*, edited by W. H. Barber, et al., 152–70. Edinburgh: Univ. of St. Andrews, 1964.

Barber, Gilles. "Les Dessous d'un livre-bombe: L'Impression de la première version des *Lettres philosophiques*." In *Le Livre et l'historien: études offertes en l'honneur du Professeur Henri-Jean Martin*, edited by Frédéric Barbier, et al., 465–79. Geneva: Droz, 1997.

Barber, W. H. "Voltaire: Art, Thought, and Action." *The Modern Language Review* 88 (1993): xxv–xxxvi.

Barchas, Janine. *Graphic Design, Print Culture, and the Eighteenth-Century Novel*. Cambridge: Cambridge University Press, 2003.

Barnes, Diana. "The Public Life of a Woman of Wit and Quality: Lady Mary Wortley Montagu and the Vogue for Smallpox Inoculation." *Feminist Studies* 38 (2012): 330–62.

Barny, Roger. *Prélude idéologique à la Révolution française: Le Rousseauisme avant 1789*. Paris: Les Belles Lettres, 1985.

Barran, Thomas. *Russia Reads Rousseau, 1762–1825*. Evanston: Northwestern University Press, 2002.

Becker, Carl. *The Heavenly City of the Eighteenth-Century Philosophers*. New Haven: Yale University Press, 1932.

Bellamy, Richard. "'Da metafisico a mercatante': Antonio Genovesi and the development of a new language of commerce in eighteenth-century Naples." In *The Languages of Political Theory in Early-Modern Europe*, edited by Anthony Pagden, 277–300. Cambridge: Cambridge University Press, 1987.

Benhamou, Paul. "The Diffusion of Forbidden Books: Four Case Studies." *Studies on Voltaire and the Eighteenth Century* 12 (2005): 259–81.

Benhamou, Paul. "The Reading Trade in Lyons: Cellier's Cabinet De Lecture." *Studies on Voltaire and the Eighteenth Century* 308 (1993): 305–21

Benhamou, Paul. "The Reading Trade in Pre-Revolutionary France." *Achttiende Eeuw: Documentatieblad Van De Werkgroep Achttiende Eeuw* 23, no. 1–2 (1991): 143–50.

Benitez, Miguel. "Voltaire and Clandestine Manuscripts." In *The Cambridge Companion to Voltaire*, edited by Nicholas Cronk, 65–78. Cambridge: Cambridge University Press, 2009.

Benítez, Miguel. *Voltaire lit Locke: une étude de la Lettre sur l'âme*. Paris: Honoré Champion, 2019.
Bennett, Michael. "Jenner's Ladies: Women and Vaccination against Smallpox in Early Nineteenth-Century Britain." *History* 93 (2008): 497–513.
Berger, Shlomo. *Producing Redemption in Amsterdam: Early Modern Yiddish Books in Paratextual Perspective*. Leiden: Brill, 2013.
Beroujon, Anne. "Les collections privées de livres à Lyon au XVIIIe siècle." In *Mécènes et collectionneurs: Lyon et le Midi de la France*, edited by Jean-René Gaborit, 63–77. Paris: Editions du CTHS, 1999.
Berry, Christopher J. *The Idea of Luxury: A Conceptual and Historical Investigation*. Cambridge: Cambridge University Press, 1994.
Bessire, François and Françoise Tilkin, eds. *Voltaire et le livre*. Ferney-Voltaire: Centre International D'Etude Du XVIIIe Siècle, 2009.
Beyer, Charles. "Toward a Critical Edition of *l'Esprit des lois*." *Symposium* 4 (1950): 390–6.
Beyer, Charles Jacques. "Montesquieu et la censure religieuse de *l'Esprit des lois*." *Revue des sciences humaines* 70 (1953): 105–31.
Birn, Raymond. *Forging Rousseau: Print, Commerce and Cultural Manipulation in the Late Enlightenment*. Oxford: Voltaire Foundation, 2001.
Birn, Raymond. "Malesherbes and the Call for a Free Press." In *Revolution in Print: The Press in France*, edited by Robert Darnton and Daniel Roche. Berkeley: University of California Press, 1989.
Birn, Raymond. *Pierre Rousseau and the "philosophes" of Bouillon*. Geneva: Institute and Musée Voltaire, 1964.
Birn, Raymond. *Royal Censorship of Books in Eighteenth-Century France*. Stanford: Stanford University Press, 2012.
Bixby, Andrew Scott. *Montesquieu's Political Economy*. New York: Palgrave Macmillan, 2016.
Blair, Ann. *Too Much to Know: Managing Scholarly Information Before the Modern Age*. New Haven: Yale University Press, 2011.
Blanning, Tim. *Frederick the Great: King of Prussia*. New York: Random House, 2016.
Blum, Carol. *Strength in Numbers: Population, Reproduction, and Power in Eighteenth-Century France*. Baltimore: Johns Hopkins University Press, 2002.
Bongie, Laurence L. "David Hume and the Official Censorship of the 'Ancien Regime'." *French Studies* 12 (1958): 234–46.
Bostic, Heidi. "Literary Women, Reason, and the Fiction of Enlightenment." *The French Review* 85 (2012): 1024–38.
Botting, Eileen Hunt. "The Early Rousseau's Egalitarian Feminism: A Philosophical Convergence with Madame Dupin and 'The Critique of the Spirit of the Laws.'" *History of European Ideas* 43 (2017): 1–13.
Box, M. A. *The Suasive Art of David Hume*. Princeton: Princeton University Press, 1990.
Braid, Ludovica. "Censure et circulation du livre en italie au xviii siècle." *Journal of Modern European History* 3 (2005): 81–99.
Braid, Ludovica. *Il Commercio delle idee: editoria e circolazione del libro nella Torino del Settecento*. Firenze: Olschki, 1995.
Branson, Roy. "James Madison and the Scottish Enlightenment." *Journal of the History of Ideas* 40 (1979): 235–50.
Broglie, Emmanuel de. *Les Portefeuilles du president Bouhier: extraits et fragments de correspondence littéraire (1715–1746)*. Paris: Hachette, 1896.
Brown, Andrew. "Les Editions Prault des *Oeuvres* de Voltaire." *Cahiers Voltaire* 10 (2011): 21–40.

Brown, Diane. "Emile's Missing Text: *Les Aventures de Télémaque.*" *Symposium: A Quarterly Journal in Modern Literatures* (Spring 2009): 51–71.
Brown, Harcourt. "The Composition of the Letters Concerning the English Nation." In *The Age of Enlightenment: Studies Presented to Theodore Besterman*, edited by W. H. Barber, et al., 15–34. Edinburgh: University of St. Andrews, 1967.
Brown, Stephen. "William Smellie and the Printer's Role in the Eighteenth-Century Edinburgh Booktrade." In *The Human Face of the Book Trade: Print Culture and Its Creators*, edited by Peter Isaac and Barry McKay, 29–44. New Castle: Oak Knoll Press, 1999.
Brown, Vivienne. "The Lectures on Rhetoric and Belles Lettres." In *Adam Smith: His Life, Thought, and Legacy*, edited by Ryan Patrick Hanley, 17–32. Princeton: Princeton University Press, 2016.
Brumfitt, J. H. *Voltaire: Historian.* Oxford: Oxford University Press, 1958.
Buringh, Eltjo and Jan Luiten Van Zanden. "Charting the 'Rise of the West:' Manuscripts and Printed Books in Europe, A Long-Term Perspective from the Sixth Through Eighteenth Centuries." *Journal of Economic History* 69 (2009): 409–55.
Burnard, Trevor G. *Mastery, Tyranny, and Desire: Thomas Thistlewood and His Slaves in the Anglo-Jamaican World.* Chapel Hill: The University of North Carolina Press, 2004.
Burrows, Simon. *The French Book Trade in Enlightenment Europe. 2. Enlightenment Bestsellers.* London: Bloomsbury, 2018.
The Cambridge History of Eighteenth-Century Philosophy. Edited by Knud Haakonssen. 2 vols. Cambridge: Cambridge University Press, 2006.
Campanelli, Marcella. "Agiographia e devozione nell'editoria napoletana del Settecento." In *Editoria e cultura a Napoli nel XVIII secolo*, 447–75. Naples: Liguori Editore, 1998.
Caradonna, Jeremy L. *The Enlightenment in Practice: Academic Prize Contests and Intellectual Culture in France, 1670–1794.* Ithaca: Cornell University Press, 2012.
Carcassonne, Eli. *Fénelon: L'homme et l'oeuvre.* Paris: Boivin, 1946.
Caretta, Vincent. "Who Was Francis Williams?" *Early American Literature* 38 (2003): 213–37.
Carr, Rosalind. *Gender and Enlightenment Culture in Eighteenth-Century Scotland.* Edinburgh: Edinburgh University Press, 2014.
Carrato, Jose Ferreira. "The Enlightenment in Portugal and the Educational Reforms of the Marquis of Pombal." *Studies in Voltaire and the Eighteenth Century* 167 (1977): 359–93.
Carrithers, David Wallace. "Montesquieu, Jefferson and the Fundamentals of Eighteenth-Century Republican Theory." *The French-American Review* 6 (1982): 160–88.
Carrithers, David Wallace, Michael A. Mosher, and Paul Anthony Rahe, eds. *Montesquieu's Science of Politics: Essays on the Spirit of Laws.* Lanham: Rowman & Littlefield, 2001.
Cassirer, Ernst. *The Philosophy of the Enlightenment.* Translated by Fritz C. A. Koelln and James P. Pettegrove. Princeton: Princeton University Press, 1951.
Catalogue de la bibliothèque de Montesquieu à La Brède. Edited by Louis Desgraves and Catherine Volpilhac-Auger. Naples: Liguori Editore, 1999.
Chaimowicz, Thomas. *Antiquity as the Source of Modernity: Freedom and Balance in the Thought of Montesquieu and Burke.* New York: Routledge, 2008.
Champagne, Roland A. "Words Disguising Desire: Serial Discourse and the Dual Character of Suzanne Simonin." *Kentucky Romance Quarterly* 28 (1981): 341–50.
Charles, Loïc. "French 'New Politics' and the Dissemination of David Hume's *Political Discourses* on the Continent, 1750–70." In *David Hume's Political Economy*, edited by Carl Wennerlind and Margaret Schabas, 181–202. New York: Routledge, 2008.
Charles, Loïc, Frédéric Lefebvre, and Christine Théré, eds. *Le Cercle de Vincent de Gournay: saviors économiques et pratiques administratives en France au milieu du XVIIIe siècle.* Paris: Institut National d'Etudes Démographiques, 2011.

Charles, Loïc and Arnaud Orain. "François Véron De Forbonnais and the Invention of Antiphysiocracy." In *The Economic Turn: Recasting Political Economy in Enlightenment Europe*, edited by Sophus Reinert and Steven Kaplan, 139–68. London: Anthem Press, 2019.

Chartier, Roger. *The Author's Hand and the Printer's Mind: Transformations of the Written Word in Early Modern Europe*. Translated by Lydia G. Cochrane. Hoboken: Wiley, 2013.

Chartier, Roger. *The Cultural Origins of the French Revolution*. Translated by Lydia G. Cochrane. Durham: Duke University Press, 1991.

Chartier, Roger. *The Cultural Uses of Print in Early Modern France*. Translated by Lydia G. Cochrane. Princeton: Princeton University Press, 1987.

Chartier, Roger. *The Order of Books: Readers, Authors and Libraries in Europe Between the Fourteenth and Eighteenth Centuries*. Translated by Lydia G. Cochrane. Stanford: Stanford University Press, 1994.

Chartier, Roger. "Richardson, Diderot et la lectrice impatiente." *MLN* 114 (1999): 647–66.

Cheney, Paul. *Revolutionary Commerce: Globalization and the French Monarchy*. Cambridge, MA: Harvard University Press, 2010.

Cherel, André. *Fénelon au XVIIIe siècle en France (1715–1820)*. Paris: Hachette, 1917.

Choudhury, Mita. *Convents and Nuns in Eighteenth-Century French Politics and Culture*. Ithaca: Cornell University Press, 2004.

Cini, Marco. "Le avventure di Telemaco di Fenelon e la cultura economica italiana (secoli XVIII-XIX)." *Il pensiero economico italiano* 25 (2017): 11–25.

Clark, Henry C. *Compass of Society: Commerce and Absolutism in Old Regime France*. Lanham: Lexington, 2007.

Clendenning, Philip H. "Dr. Thomas Dimsdale and Smallpox Inoculation in Russia." *Journal of the History of Medicine and Allied Sciences* 28 (1973): 109–25.

Clery, E. J. "Horace Walpole, the Strawberry Hill Press, and the Emergence of the Gothic Genre." *Ars & Humanitas: Revija Za Umetnost in Humanistiko* 4 (2010): 93–111.

Cobban, Alfred. *In Search of Humanity: The Role of the Enlightenment in Modern History*. London: Jonathan Cape, 1960.

Cobban, Alfred. *Rousseau and the Modern State*. London: George Allen and Unwin, 1934.

Cohen, Robert. *Jews in Another Environment: Surinam in the Second Half of the Eighteenth Century*. Leiden: Brill, 1991.

Coleman, Charly. *The Virtues of Abandon: An Anti-Individualist History of the French Enlightenment*. Stanford: Stanford University Press, 2014.

Coleman, Earle E. "Éphémérides du citoyen, 1767–1772." *The Papers of the Bibliographical Society of America* 56 (1962): 17–45.

Conlon, P. M. *Voltaire's Literary Career from 1728 to 1750*. Geneva: Institute et Musée Voltaire, 1961.

Corsini, Silvia. "Vingt-cinq ans d'édition et d'imprimerie à Lausanne au siècle des Lumières: le libraire Marc-Michel Bousquet." *Revue historique vaudoise* 120 (2012): 23–53.

Cottret, Monique. *Jansenisme et Lumières: pour un autre xviiie siècle*. Paris: Albin Michel, 1998.

Courtney, Cecil Patrick. "L'Esprit des lois dans la perspective de l'histoire du livre (1748–1800)." In *Le Temps de Montesquieu: Actes du college international de Genève (28–31 octobre 1998)*, edited by Michel Porret and Catherine Volpilhac-Auger, 65–98. Geneva: Droz. 2002.

Courtney, Cecil Patrick. "Montesquieu et les imprimeurs de *l'Esprit des lois* (1748–1758)." In *L'Écrivain et l'imprimeur*. Edited by Alain Riffaud, 193–216. Rennes: Presses universitaires de Rennes, 2010.

Craiutu, Aurelian. *A Virtue for Courageous Minds: Moderation in French Political thought, 1748–1830* (Princeton: Princeton University Press, 2012.

Cranston, Maurice. *John Locke: A Biography*. London: Macmillan, 1957.
Cranston, Maurice. *The Noble Savage: Jean-Jacques Rousseau, 1754–1762*. Chicago: University of Chicago Press, 1991.
Cranston, Maurice. *The Solitary Self: Jean-Jacques Rousseau in Exile and Adversity*. Chicago: University of Chicago Press, 1997.
Craveri, Benedetta. *The Age of Conversation*. Translated by Teresa Waugh. New York: New York Review of Books, 2005.
Crawford, John C. "The Ideology of Mutual Improvement in Scottish Working Class Libraries." *Library History* 12 (1996): 49–61.
Crisafulli, Alessandro S. "Montesquieu's Story of the Troglodytes: Its Background, Meaning, and Significance." *PMLA* 58 (1943): 372–92.
Cronk, Nicholas. "The Epicurean Spirit: Champagne and the Defense of Poetry in Le Mondain." *Studies in Voltaire and the Eighteenth Century* 371 (1999): 53–80.
Cronk, Nicholas. "Les *Lettres sur les Anglaise* en France au dix-huitième siècle: questions de reception et de reputation." *Revue Voltaire* 13 (2013): 141–58.
Cronk, Nicholas. "The Letters Concerning the English Nation as an English Work: Reconsidering the Harcourt Brown Thesis." In *From Letter to Publication: Studies on Correspondence and the History of the Book*, edited by A. Strugnell, 226–39. Oxford: Voltaire Foundation, 2001.
Cronk, Nicholas. "Voltaire and Authorship." In *The Cambridge Companion to Voltaire*. Edited by Nicholas Cronk, 31–46. Cambridge: Cambridge University Press, 2009.
Cronk, Nicholas. "Voltaire and the Uses of Censorship: The Example of the *Lettres philosophiques*." In *An American Voltaire*, edited by E. Joe Johnson and Byron R. Wells, 36–61. Newcastle upon Tyne: Cambridge Scholars, 2009.
Crook, Ronald E. *A Bibliography of Joseph Priestley 1733–1804*. London: The Library Association, 1966.
Cuche, François Xavier. "L'Economie du Télémaque, l'économie dans le Télémaque." *Littératures classiques* 70 (2010): 103–18.
Curran, Mark. *The French Book Trade in Enlightenment Europe. 1. Selling Enlightenment*. London: Bloomsbury, 2018.
Curran, Mark. "Beyond the Forbidden Best-Sellers of Pre-Revolutionary France." *The Historical Journal* 56 (2013): 89–112.
Darnton, Robert. *A Literary Tour de France: The World of Books on the Eve of the French Revolution*. New York: Oxford University Press, 2018.
Darnton, Robert. "The Brissot Dossier." *French Historical Studies* 17 (1991): 191–205.
Darnton, Robert. *The Business of Enlightenment: A Publishing History of the Encyclopédie 1775–1800*. Cambridge, MA: Harvard University Press, 1979.
Darnton, Robert. "The Case for the Enlightenment." In *George Washington's False Teeth: An Unconventional Guide to the Eighteenth Century*, 3–24. New York: W.W. Norton, 2003.
Darnton, Robert. *The Corpus of Clandestine Literature in France 1769–1789*. New York: Norton, 1995.
Darnton, Robert. "The Encyclopédie Wars of Pre-Revolutionary France." *American Historical Review* 78 (1973): 1331–52.
Darnton, Robert. "First Steps Toward a History of Reading." *Australian Journal of French Studies* 23 (1986): 1–30.
Darnton, Robert. *The Forbidden Best-Sellers of Pre-Revolutionary France*. New York: Norton, 1995.
Darnton, Robert. "The High Enlightenment and the Low-Life of Literature in Prerevolutionary France." *Past and Present* 51 (1971): 81–115.
Darnton, Robert. "In Search of the Enlightenment: Recent Attempts to Create a Social History of Ideas." *Journal of Modern History* 43 (1971): 113–32.

Darnton, Robert. "The Life Cycle of a Book: A Publishing History of d'Holbach's *Système de la nature*." In *Publishing and Readership in Revolutionary Europe and America*, edited by Carol Armbruster, 15–43. Westport: Greenwood, 1993.

Darnton, Robert. *The Literary Underground of the Old Regime*. Cambridge, MA: Harvard University Press, 1982.

Darnton, Robert. Review of *The French Book Trade in Enlightenment Europe, 1769–1794* (review no. 1355), https://reviews.history.ac.uk/review/1355 (accessed May 20, 2021).

Darnton, Robert. "Rousseau Responds to Readers." In *The Great Cat Massacre and Other Episodes in French Cultural History*, 215–56. New York: Random House, 1984.

Darnton, Robert. "The Science of Piracy: A Crucial Ingredient in Eighteenth-Century Publishing." In *History of the Book, Translation, History of Ideas, Paul et Virginie, Varia*, edited by Jonathan Mallinson, 3–29. Oxford: Voltaire Foundation, 2003.

Davies, David W. "The Geographic Extent of the Dutch Book Trade in the Seventeenth Century." *The Library Quarterly* 22 (1952): 200–7.

De Bujanda, J. M. *Index Librorum Prohibitorum:1600–1966*. Montréal: Médiaspaul, 2002.

De Mas, Enrico. *Montesquieu, Genovesi e la edizione italiane dello spirit delle leggi*. Florence: F. Le Monnier, 1971.

Demals, Thierry and Alexandra Hyard. "Forbonnais, the Two Balances and the Économistes." *The European Journal of the History of Economic Thought* 22 (2015): 445–72.

Desné, Roland. "The Role of England in Voltaire's Polemic Against Pascal: Apropos the Twenty-Fifth Philosophical Letter." In *Eighteenth Century Studies Presented to Arthur M. Wilson*, edited by Peter Gay and John S. Dickey, 43–57. Hanover: University Press of New England, 1972.

Dew, Ben. "Waving a Mouchoir à la Wilkes: Hume, Radicalism, and *The North Briton*." *Modern Intellectual History* 6 (2009): 235–60.

Dickey, Lawrence. "Pride, Hypocrisy, and Civility in Mandeville's Social and Historical Theory." *Critical Review* 4 (1990): 387–431.

Dictionnaire général de Voltaire. Edited by Jeroom Vercruysse. Paris: Honoré Champion, 2003.

Donoghue, Frank. *The Fame Machine: Book Reviewing and Eighteenth-Century Literary Careers*. Stanford: Stanford University Press, 1996.

Douthwaite, Julia V. *The Wild Girl, Natural Man, and the Monster: Dangerous Experiments in the Age of Enlightenment*. Chicago: University of Chicago Press, 2002.

Doyle, William. *Jansenism: Catholic Resistance to Authority from the Reformation to the French Revolution*. New York: St. Martin's Press, 2000.

Droixhe, Daniel. "Signatures Clandestines et autres essais sur les contrefaçons de Liège et de Maastricht au XVIIIe siècle." In *From Letter to Publication: Studies on Correspondence and the History of the Book*, edited by Anthony Strugnell, 49–198. Oxford: Voltaire Foundation; 2001.

Dülmen, Richard van. *The Society of the Enlightenment: The Rise of the Middle Class and Enlightenment Culture in Germany*. Cambridge: Polity Press, 1992.

Dunstan, Vivienne S. "Glimpses Into a Town's Reading Habits in Enlightenment Scotland: Analyzing the Borrowings of Gray Library, Haddington, 1732–1816." *Journal of the Scottish Historical Society* 26 (2006): 42–59.

Dunstan, Vivienne S. "Reading habits in Scotland circa 1750–1820." PhD dissertation, University of Dundee, 2010.

Dussinger, John A. "Fabrications from Samuel Richardson's Press." *Papers of the Bibliographical Society of America* 100 (2006): 259–79.

Eaves, T. C. Duncan and Ben D. Kimpel. "Richardson's Revisions of *Pamela*." *Studies in Bibliography* 20 (1967): 61–88.

Eaves, T. C. Duncan and Ben D. Kimpel. *Samuel Richardson: A Biography*. Oxford: Clarendon Press, 1971.
Éboli, Gilles. *Livres et lecteurs en Provence au xviiie siècle: Autour des David, imprimeurs-libraires à Aix*. Méolans-Revel: Atelier Perrousseaux, 2008.
Edelstein, Dan. *The Enlightenment: A Genealogy*. Chicago: University of Chicago Press, 2010.
Edelstein, Dan, Robert Morissey, and Glenn Roe. "To Quote or Not to Quote: Citation Strategies in the Encyclopédie." *Journal of the History of Ideas* 74 (2013): 213–36.
Edmiston, William F. *Hindsight and Insight: Focalization in Four Eighteenth-Century French Novels*. University Park: Penn State University Press, 1991.
Ehrard, Jean. "Rome enfin que je hais…?" In *Storia e ragione: Le Considérations sur les causes de la grandeur des Romains et de leur décadence di Montesquieu nel 250° della pubblicazione*, edited by Alberto Postigliola, 23–32. Naples: Liguori Editore, 1987.
Eisenstein, Elizabeth L. *Grub Street Abroad: Aspects of the French Cosmopolitan Press from the Age of Louis XIV to the French Revolution*. Oxford: Oxford University Press, 1992.
Emerson, Roger L.. "Catalogus Librorum A.C.D.A. or, The Library of Archibald Campbell, Third Duke of Argyll (1682–1761)." In *The Culture of the Book in the Scottish Enlightenment*, edited by Paul Wood, 15–17. Toronto: Thomas Fisher Rare Book Library, University of Toronto, 2000.
Emerson, Roger L. "How Many Scots Were Enlightened?" In *Essays on David Hume, Medical Men and the Scottish Enlightenment: Industry, Knowledge and Humanity*, 39–48. Farnham: Ashgate, 2008.
Emery, Ted A. "Goldoni's Pamela From Play to Libretto." *Italica* 64 (1987): 572–82.
Essar, Dennis F. "Polemical Intent and Rhetorical Style in d'Alembert's Élôges historiques." *Man and Nature* 1 (1982): 31–9.
Évrard, Sébastien. *Le Livre, le droit et le faux: essai sur l'édition juridique et la contrefaçon au siècle des lumières*. Paris: L'Harmattan, 2017.
Eze, Emmanuel C. "Hume, Race, and Human Nature." *Journal of the History of Ideas* 61 (2000): 691–8.
Fairchilds, Cissie. "Female Sexual Attitudes and the Rise of Illegitimacy: A Case Study." *The Journal of Interdisciplinary History* 8 (1978): 627–67.
Fauré, Christine. *Democracy Without Women: Feminism and the Rise of Individualism in France*. Translated by Claudia Goodman and John Berks. Bloomington: Indiana University Press, 1991.
Fawcett, Trevor. "An Eighteenth-Century Book Club at Norwich." *The Library* 23 (1968): 47–50.
Fergus, Jan. "Eighteenth-Century Readers in Provincial England: The Customers of Samuel Clay's Circulating Library and Bookshop in Warwick, 1770–72." *PBSA* 78 (1984): 155–213.
Fieser, James. *A Bibliography of Hume's Writings and Early Responses* Bristol: Thoemmes Press, 2003.
Flavell, Mary K. "The Enlightened Reader and the New Industrial Towns: A study of the Liverpool library 1758–1790." *Journal for Eighteenth-Century Studies* 8 (1985): 17–35.
Fletcher, F. T. H. "Montesquieu's Influence on Anti-Slavery Opinion in England." *Journal of Negro History* 18 (1933): 414–25.
Flint, Christopher. "The Material Book." In *Samuel Richardson in Context*, edited by Peter Sabor and Betty A. Schellenberg. Cambridge: Cambridge University Press, 2017.
Fontana, Aris Della. "Constructing 'Englishness' and promoting 'politeness' through a 'Francophobic' bestseller: Télémaque in England (1699–1745)." *History of European Ideas* 45 (2019): 1–27.

Fontius, Martin and David Smith. "La publication en 1748 des *Oeuvres complètes de Mr. de Voltaire* par Georg Konrad Walther, de Dresde." In *Voltaire et le livre*, 47–66. Ferney-Voltaire: Centre International D'Etude Du XVIIIe Siècle, 2009.

Forster, Antonia. "Review Journals and the Reading Public." In *Books and their Readers in Eighteenth-Century England: New Essays*, edited by Isabel Rivers, 171–90. London: Continuum, 2001.

"Forum: The Legacy of Alfred Cobban." *French History* 34 (2020): 512–60.

Fowler, James. "La Religieuse: Diderot's 'Richardsonian' Novel." In *New Essays on Diderot*, edited by James Fowler, 127–38. Cambridge: Cambridge University Press, 2011.

Fowler, James. *Richardson and the Philosophes*. New York: Routledge, 2014.

Foxon, David F. *Pope and the Early Eighteenth-Century Book Trade*. Oxford: Oxford University Press, 1991.

Freedman, Jeffrey. *Books without Borders in Enlightenment Europe: French Cosmopolitanism and German Literary Markets*. Philadelphia: University of Pennsylvania Press, 2012.

Gargett, Graham. "Voltaire's '*Lettres philosophiques*' in Eighteenth-Century Ireland." *Eighteenth-Century Ireland* 14 (1999): 77–98.

Gargett, Graham. *Jacob Vernet, Geneva, and the Philosophes*. Oxford: Voltaire Foundation, 1994.

Gargett, Graham and Geraldine Sheridan, eds. *Ireland and the French Enlightenment, 1700–1800*. New York: St Martin's Press, 1999.

Garrett, Aaron. "Hume's Revised Racism Revisited." *Hume Studies* 26 (2000): 171–7.

Garrett, Aaron. "Hume's 'Original Difference': Race, National Character and the Human Sciences." *Eighteenth-Century Thought* 2 (2004): 127–52.

Garrioch, David. "Reading in Eighteenth-Century Paris." In *The Culture of the Book: Essays from Two Hemispheres in Honour of Wallace Kirsop*, 288–99. Melbourne: Bibliographical Society of Australia and New Zealand, 1999.

Gay, Peter. *The Enlightenment: An Interpretation. Volume 1: The Rise of Modern Paganism. Volume Two: The Science of Freedom*. 2 vols. New York: Knopf, 1966–1969.

Gay, Peter. *My German Question: Growing up in Nazi Berlin*. New Haven: Yale University Press, 1998.

Gay, Peter. *The Party of Humanity: Essays in the French Enlightenment*. New York: Knopf, 1964.

Gay, Peter. *Voltaire's Politics: The Poet as Realist*. Princeton: Princeton University Press, 1959.

Gébelin, François. "La publication de Montesquieu's *De l'Esprit des lois*." *Révue des bibliothèques* 31 (1924): 135–58.

Genette, Gerard. *Paratexts: Thresholds of Interpretation*. Translated by Jane E. Lewin. Cambridge: Cambridge University Press, 1997.

Gignilliat, George Warren. *The Author of Sandford and Merton: A Life of Thomas Day, Esq*. New York: Columbia University Press, 1932.

Grinevald, Paul-Marie. "Les éditions de *l'Histoire naturelle*." In *Buffon 88: actes du Colloque international pour le bicentenaire de la mort de Buffon*, edited by Jean-Claude Beaune, et al., 631–7. Paris: J. Vrin, 1992.

Goldgar, Anne. *Impolite Learning: Conduct and Community in the Republic of Letters 1680–1750*. New Haven: Yale University Press, 1995.

Goldie, Mark. "The English System of Liberty." In *The Cambridge History of Eighteenth-Century Political Thought*, edited by Mark Goldie and Robert Wokler, 40–78. Cambridge: Cambridge University Press, 2006.

Gooding, Richard. "Pamela, Shamela, and the Politics of the Pamela Vogue." *Eighteenth-Century Fiction* 7 (1995): 109–30.

Goodman, Dena. *Becoming a Woman in the Age of Letters*. Ithaca: Cornell University Press, 2009.

Goodman, Dena. *Criticism in Action: Enlightenment Experiments in Political Writing*. Ithaca: Cornell University Press, 1989.

Goodman, Dena. "The Hume-Rousseau Affair: From Private 'Querelle' to Public 'procès.'" *Eighteenth-Century Studies* 25 (1991): 171–201.

Goodman, Dena. "Michel de Servan and the Plight of Letters on the Eve of the French Revolution." In *Early Modern Conceptions of Property*, edited by John Brewer and Susan Staves, 339–64. London: Routledge, 1995.

Goodman, Dena. *The Republic of Letters: A Cultural History of the French Enlightenment*. Ithaca: Cornell University Press, 1994.

Goodman, Jessica. *Commemorating Mirabeau: Mirabeau aux Champs Elysees and Other Texts*. Cambridge: MHRA, 2017.

Gorbatov, Inna. *Catherine the Great and the French Philosophers of the Enlightenment: Montesquieu, Voltaire, Rousseau, Diderot and Grimm*. Bethesda: Academica Press, 2006.

Gorbatov, Inna. "From Paris to St. Petersburg: Voltaire's Library in Russia." *Libraries & the Cultural Record* 42 (2007): 308–24.

Gouhier, Henri. "Rousseau et Fénelon." In *Reappraisals of Rousseau: Studies in Honour of R. A. Leigh*, edited by Simon Harvey et al., 277–89. Totowa: Barnes and Noble, 1980.

Grafton, Anthony. *The Footnote*. Cambridge, MA: Harvard University Press, 1997.

Grayson, Vera L. "The Genesis and Reception of Mme. de Graffigny's *Lettres d'une Péruvienne* and *Cénie*." *Studies in Voltaire and the Eighteenth Century* 336 (1996): 1–152.

Grundy, Isobel. *Lady Mary Wortley Montagu*. Oxford: Oxford University Press, 1999.

Grundy, Isobel. "Medical Advance and Female Fame: Inoculation and Its After-Effects." *Lumen* 13 (1994): 13–42.

Grundy, Isobel. "'Trash, Trumpery, and Idle Time:' Lady Mary Wortley Montagu and Fiction." *Eighteenth-Century Fiction* 5 (1993): 293–310.

Habermas, Jürgen. *The Structural Transformation of the Public Sphere: An Inquiry into a Category of Bourgeois Society*. Translated by Thomas Burger and Frederick Lawrence. Cambridge, MA: MIT, 1989.

Halsband, Robert. "New Light on Lady Mary Wortley Montagu's Contribution to Inoculation." *Journal of the History of Medicine and Allied Sciences* 8 (1953): 393–4.

Hampson, Norman. *The Enlightenment*. New York: Penguin Books, 1990.

Hanley, Ryan Patrick. "Commerce and Corruption: Rousseau's Diagnosis and Adam Smith's Cure." *European Journal of Political Theory* 7 (2008): 137–58.

Hanley, Ryan Patrick. *The Political Philosophy of Fénelon*. Oxford: Oxford University Press, 2020.

Hanley, William. "The Abbé Rothelin and the *Lettres philosophiques*." *Romance Notes* 23 (1983): 245–50.

Hanna, Martha. "Laying Siege to the Sorbonne: The Action Française's Attack upon the Dreyfusard University." *Historical Reflections / Réflexions Historiques* 24 (1998): 155–77.

Harris, James. *Hume: An Intellectual Biography*. Cambridge: Cambridge University Press, 2015.

Harth, Erica. *Cartesian Women: Versions and Subversions of Rational Discourse in the Old Regime*. Ithaca: Cornell University Press, 1992.

Harvey, A. D. "The Politics of Pamela." *Critical Quarterly* 61 (2019): 105–15.

Hatton, R. M. *Charles XII of Sweden*. London: Weidenfeld and Nicolson, 1968.

Havens, George R. "The Abbé Le Blanc and English Literature." *Modern Philology* 18 (1920): 423–41.

Hayes, Julie C. "Retrospection and Contradiction in Diderot's *La Religieuse*." *Romanic Review* 77 (1986): 233–42.

Hayes, Kevin J. *A Colonial Woman's Bookshelf*. Knoxville: University of Tennessee Press, 1996.
Hayman, John G. "Notions on National Characters in the Eighteenth Century." *Huntington Library Quarterly* 35 (1971): 1–17.
Hazard, Paul. *European Thought in the Eighteenth Century: From Montesquieu to Lessing*. Translated by J. Lewis May. New Haven: Yale University Press, 1954.
Healey, Robynne Rogers, ed. *Quakerism in the Atlantic World, 1690–1830*. University Park: Pennsylvania State University Press, 2021.
Heilbron, Johan. "French Moralists and the Anthropology of the Modern Era on the Genesis of the Notions of 'Interest' and 'Commercial Society.'" In *The Rise of the Social Sciences and the Formation of Modernity: Conceptual Change in Context, 1750–1850*, edited by Johan Heilbron, et al., 77–106. Dordrecht: Kluwer Academic Publishers, 1998.
Hesse, Carla. *The Other Enlightenment: How French Women Became Modern*. Princeton: Princeton University Press, 2001.
Hesse, Carla. "A Fugitive Book." *Representations* 104 (2008): 39.
Hesse, Carla. "Revolutionary Rousseaus: The Story of His Editions." In *Media and Political Culture in the Eighteenth Century*, ed. Marie-Christine Skuncke, 107–28. Stockholm: Kungl Vitterhets Historie och Antikvitets Akademien, 20.
Hesse, Carla. "Print Culture in the Enlightenment." In *The Enlightenment World*, edited by Martin Fitzpatrick, 366–80. London and New York: Routledge, 2004.
Higgs, Henry. *Bibliography of Economics, 1751–1775*. Cambridge: Cambridge University Press, 1935.
Hill, Bridget. *Servants: English Domestics in the Eighteenth Century*. Oxford: Oxford University Press, 1996.
Hirschman, Albert. *The Passions and the Interests: Political Arguments for Capitalism Before its Triumph*. Princeton: Princeton University Press, 1977.
Hochschild, Adam. *Bury the Chains: Prophets and Rebels in the Fight to Free an Empire's Slaves*. Boston: Houghton Mifflin, 2005.
Hont, Istvan. "The Early Enlightenment Debate on Commerce and Luxury." In *The Cambridge History of Eighteenth-Century Political Thought*, edited by Mark Goldie and Robert Wokler, 379–418. Cambridge: Cambridge University Press, 2006.
Hopkins, Donald R. *Princes and Peasants: Smallpox in History*. Chicago: University of Chicago Press, 1983.
Houston, R. A. *Literacy in Early Modern Europe: Culture and Education 1500-1800*. 2nd ed. Harlow: Longman, 2002.
Hufton, Olwen. "Women Without Men: Widows and Spinsters in Britain and France in the Eighteenth Century." *Journal of Family History* 9 (1984): 355–76.
Hulliung, Mark. *Enlightenment in Scotland and France: Studies in Political Thought*. London: Routledge, 2018.
Hulliung, Mark. *Montesquieu and the Old Regime*. Berkeley and Los Angeles: University of California Press, 1976.
Hundert, E. J. *The Enlightenment Fable: Bernard Mandeville and the Discovery of Society*. Cambridge: Cambridge University Press, 1994.
Hunt, Lynn. "Torrents of Emotion: Reading Novels and Imaging Equality." In *Inventing Human Rights: A History*, 35–69. New York: Norton, 2007.
Hunt, Lynn, Margaret Jacob, and W. W. Mijnhardt. *The Book That Changed Europe: Picart and Bernard's Religious Ceremonies of the World*. Cambridge, MA: Harvard University Press, 2010.
Hunter, Angela. "The Unfinished Work on Louise Marie-Madeleine Dupin's Unfinished *Ouvrage sur les femmes*." *Eighteenth-Century Studies* 43 (2009): 95–111.
Immerwahr, John. "Hume's Revised Racism." *Journal of the History of Ideas* 53 (1992): 481–6.

Ince, Onur Ulas. "Between Commerce and Empire: David Hume, Colonial Slavery and Commercial Incivility." *History of Political Thought* 39 (2018): 107–34.

Ingrassia, Catherine. "The Literary Marketplace." In *Samuel Richardson in Context*, edited by Peter Sabor and Betty A. Schellenberg, 100–7. Cambridge: Cambridge University Press, 2017.

Israel, Jonathan I. *A Revolution of the Mind: Radical Enlightenment and the Intellectual Origins of Modern Democracy*. Princeton: Princeton University Press, 2010.

Israel, Jonathan I. *Democratic Enlightenment: Philosophy, Revolution, and Human Rights 1750–1790*. New York: Oxford University Press, 2011.

Israel, Jonathan I. *Enlightenment Contested: Philosophy, Modernity, and the Emancipation of Man, 1670–1752*. New York: Oxford University Press, 2006.

Israel, Jonathan I. *Radical Enlightenment: Philosophy and the Making of Modernity, 1650–1750*. New York: Oxford University Press, 2001.

Ives, Robin J. "Political Publicity and Political Economy in Eighteenth-Century France." *French History* 17 (2003): 1–18.

Jackson, Ian. "Approaches to the History of Readers and Reading in Eighteenth-Century Britain." *Historical Journal* 47 (2004): 1041–54.

Jacob, Margaret C. "The Clandestine Universe of the Early Eighteenth Century." *Marteau Studies* (2001), http://www.pierre-marteau.com/c/jacob/clandestine.html (accessed January 13, 2019).

James, E. D. "Faith, Sincerity and Morality: Mandeville and Bayle." In *Mandeville Studies: Explorations in the Art and Thought of Dr. Bernard Mandeville*, edited by Irwin Primer. The Hague: Martinus Nijhoff, 1975.

Janet, Paul. *Fénelon: His Life and Works*. Translated by Victor Leuliette. London: Pittman, 1914.

Janssen, Frans A. "The First Edition of Fénelon's *Les avantures de Télémaque*." *Quaerendo* 42 (2012): 178–85.

Janssens-Knorsch, Uta. "Commerce or Culture? The Fate of the First Circulating Library in the Netherlands." *Achttiende Eeuw: Documentatieblad van de Werkgroep Achttiende Eeuw* 23 (1991): 151–73.

Johns, Adrian. *Piracy: The Intellectual Property Wars from Gutenberg to Gates*. Chicago: University of Chicago Press, 2009.

Johns, Alessa. *Bluestocking Feminism and British-German Cultural Transfer*. Ann Arbor: University of Michigan Press, 2014.

Jones, Colin. *The Great Nation: France from Louis XV to the Revolution*. New York: Penguin, 2002.

Jones, Jr. James F. "Montesquieu and Jefferson Revisited: Aspects of a Legacy." *The French Review* 51 (1978): 577–85.

Judge, Elizabeth F. "Kidnapped and Counterfeit Characters: Eighteenth-Century Fan Fiction, Copyright Law, and the Custody of Fictional Characters." In *Originality and Intellectual Property in the French and English Enlightenment*, edited by Reginald McGinnis, 22–68. New York: Routledge, 2009.

Kafker, Frank A. and Jeff Loveland. "The Elusive Laurent Durand, a Leading Publisher of the French Enlightenment." In *Social History, Morellet, Social Anthropology*, edited by Jonathan Mallinson, 223–58. Oxford: Voltaire Foundation, 2005.

Kahn, Andrew. "Les lettres d'une Péruvienne et la culture du livre en Russie au dix-huitième siècle." In *Françoise de Graffigny, femme de lettres: ecriture et reception*, edited by Jonathan Mallinson, 288–96. Oxford: Voltaire Foundation, 2004.

Kanter, Sanford B. "Archibishop Fénelon's Political Activity: The Focal Point of Power in Dynasticism." *French Historical Studies* 4 (1966): 320–34.

Kaplan, Marijn S. *Riccoboni and Brooke, Graffigny and Roberts*. London: Pickering & Chatto, 2012.

Kapossy, Bela. *Iselin Contra Rousseau: Sociable Patriotism and the History of Mankind.* Basle: Schwabe, 2006.
Kapp, Volker. "Les Illustrations des éditions du Télémaque." In *Fénelon: Mystique et politique (1699–1999)*, edited by F. X. Cuche and Jacques Le Brun, 289–99. Paris: Honoré Champion, 2004.
Kates, Gary. *Monsieur d'Eon Is a Woman: A Tale of Political Intrigue and Sexual Masquerade.* Baltimore: Johns Hopkins University Press, 2001.
Kaufman, Paul. *Borrowings from the Bristol Library, 1773–1784: A Unique Record of Reading Vogues.* Charlottesville: Bibliographic Society of the University of Virginia, 1960.
Kaufman, Paul. *Libraries and Their Users: Collected Papers in Library History.* London: The Library Assn, 1969.
Kelly, Joan. "Early Feminist Theory and the *Querelle des Femmes*." In *Women, History, and Theory*, 65–109. Chicago: University of Chicago Press, 1984.
Keymer, Thomas and Peter Sabor. *Pamela in the Marketplace: Literary Controversy and Print Culture in Eighteenth-Century Britain and Ireland.* New York: Cambridge University Press, 2005.
Kruif, José de. "Classes of Readers: Owners of Books in 18th-Century The Hague." *Poetics* 28 (2001): 423–53.
Kwass, Michael. "Consumption and the World of Ideas: Consumer Revolution and the Moral Economy of the Marquis De Mirabeau." *Eighteenth-Century Studies* 37 (2004): 187–213.
La Notion d'oeuvres complètes, edited by Jean Sgard and Catherine Volpilhac-Auger. Oxford: Voltaire Foundation, 1999.
Lacorne, Denis. *The Limits of Tolerance: Enlightenment Values and Religious Fanaticism.* Translated by C. Jon Delogu and Robin Emlein. New York: Columbia University Press, 2019.
Lamartine, Alphonse de . *Fénelon.* New ed. Paris: Calmann Lévy, 1876.
Landes, Joan B. *Women and the Public Sphere in the Age of the French Revolution.* Ithaca: Cornell, 1988.
Lanson, Gustave. "L'Affaire des *Lettres philosophiques* de Voltaire." *Revue de Paris* 14 (July 1904): 367–86.
Lanson, Gustave. *Histoire de la littérature Française*, 5th ed. Paris: Hachette, 1898.
Lanson, Gustave. *Voltaire.* Paris: Hachette, 1906.
Lantoine, Albert. *Les Lettres philosophiques de Voltaire.* Paris: SFELT, 1946.
Larrère, Catherine. "Montesquieu économiste? Une lecture paradoxale." *SVEC* 5 (2005): 243–66.
Larrère, Catherine. "Système de l'intérêt et science du commerce: François Véron de Forbonnais, lecteur de Montesquieu." In *Le cercle de Vincent de Gournay. Savoirs économiques et pratiques administratives au milieu du XVIIIe siècle*, edited by Loïc Charles, Frédéric Lefebvre, and Christine Théré, 259–80. Paris: INED, 2011.
Laudin, Gérard. "La Cohérence de l'histoire de la réception de Voltaire dans l'Allemagne des années 1760–1770." In *Voltaire et ses combats: Actes du congrès international, Oxford-Paris, 1994*, edited by Ulla Kölving et Christiane Mervaud, 2 vols, 1435–1447. Oxford: Voltaire Foundation, 1997.
Lauriol, Claude. "La condemnation de *l'Esprit des lois* dans les archives de la Congrégation de l'Index." In *Montesquieu, oeuvre ouverte? (1748–1755)*, edited by Catherine Larrère, 92–102. Naples: Liguori Editore, 2005.
Laursen, John Christian. "David Hume and the Danish Debate About Freedom of the Press in the 1770s." *Journal of the History of Ideas* 59 (1998): 167–72.
Le Bouler, J. P. and Catherine Lafarge. "Les emprints de Mme Dupin à la Bibliothèque du roi dans les années 1748–1750." *Studies in Voltaire and the Eighteenth Century* 182 (1972): 107–85.
Le Brun, Jacques. "Les Avantures de Télémaque: destins d'un best-seller." *Littératures Clasiques* 70 (2009): 133–46.

Le Brun, Jacques. "Preface." In *Fénelon in the Enlightenment: Traditions, Adaptations, and Variations*, edited by Christoph Schmitt-Maass, Stefanie Stockhorst, and Doohwan Ahn, 7–12. New York: Rodopi, 2014.

Lee, J. P. "The Unexamined Premise: Voltaire, John Lockman and the Myth of the English Letters." *Studies in Voltaire and the Eighteenth Century* 295 (2001): 240–70.

Leigh, R. A. *Unsolved Problems in the Bibliography of Jean-Jacques Rousseau*. Cambridge: Cambridge University Press, 1990.

Lennon, Thomas M. *Sacrifice and Self-Interest in Seventeenth-Century France: Quietism, Jansenism, and Cartesianism*. Leiden and Boston: Brill, 2019.

Lilti, Antoine de. *The Invention of Celebrity*. Translated by Lynn Jeffress. London: Polity, 2017.

Loiselle, Kenneth. *Brotherly Love: Freemasonry and Male Friendship in Enlightenment France*. Ithaca: Cornell University Press, 2014.

Love, Harold. *Scribal Publication in Seventeenth-Century England*. Oxford: Oxford University Press, 1993.

Lundberg, David and Henry F. May. "The Enlightened Reader in America." *American Quarterly* 28 (1976): 262–93.

Lutz, Donald S. "The Relative Influence of European Writers on Late Eighteenth-Century American Political Thought." *The American Political Science Review* 78 (1984): 189–97.

Lynch, Andrew J. "Montesquieu and the Ecclesiastical Critics of '*L'Esprit des lois*'." *Journal of the History of Ideas* 38 (1977): 487–500.

Lynn, Michael R. "The Fashion for Physics: Public Lecture Courses in Enlightenment France." *The Historian* 64 (2002): 335–50.

Machet, A. "Censure et librairie en italie au xviiie siècle." *Revue des études sud-est européennes* 10 (1972): 459–90.

Malherbe, Michel. "Hume's reception in France." In *The Reception of Hume in Europe*, edited by Peter Jones, 43–97. London: Continuum, 2005.

Mallinson, G. J. "What's in a Name? Reflections on Voltaire's *Paméla*." *Eighteenth Century Fiction* 18 (2005): 157–68.

Mallinson, Jonathan. "Re-présentant les Lettres d'une Péruvienne en 1752: Illustration et illusion." *Eighteenth-Century Fiction* 15 (2003): 227–39.

Mannheim, Karl. *Ideology and Utopia: An Introduction to the Sociology of Knowledge*. Translated by Louis Wirth and Edward Shills. New York: Harcourt, Brace, 1936.

Mansel, Philip. *King of the World: The Life of Louis XIV*. Chicago: University of Chicago Press, 2020.

Mansfield, Andrew. "The Burgundy Circle's Plans to Undermine Louis XIV's 'absolute' State through Polysynody and the High Nobility." *Intellectual History Review* 27 (2016): 1–20.

Mansfield, Andrew. *Ideas of Monarchical Reform: Fénelon, Jacobitism and the Political Works of the Chevalier Ramsay*. Manchester: Manchester University Press, 2015.

Marion, Michel. *Recherches sur les bibliothèques privées à Paris au milieu du XVIIIe siècle, 1750–1759*. Paris: Bibliothèque Nationale, 1978.

[Marionneau, Charles]. *Les Vieux souvenirs de la rue Neuve à Bordeaux*. Bordeaux: Libraire Moquet, 1890.

Marker, Gary. *Publishing, Printing, and the Origins of Intellectual Life in Russia, 1700–1800*. Princeton: Princeton University Press, 1985.

Martin, Philippe. *Une religion des livres: 1640–1850*. Paris: Cerf, 2003.

Marty, Frédéric. *Louise Dupin, defendre l'égalité des sexes en 1750*. Paris: Classiques Garnier, 2021.

Mârza, Iacob. "La Circulation de l'oeuvre de Voltaire en Transylvanie au xviiie siècle." *Synthesis: Bulletin du Comiteé National de litterature comparée de la République Socialiste de Roumanie* 5 (1978): 149–62.

Maslen, Keith. *Samuel Richardson of London, Printer: A Study of his Printing Based on Ornament Use and Business Accounts*. Otago: University of Otago, 2001.
Maslen, Keith. "Some Early Editions of Voltaire Printed in London." *Library: A Magazine of Bibliography and Literature* 5 (1959): 287–93.
Mason, H. T. *Pierre Bayle and Voltaire*. Oxford: Oxford University Press, 1963.
Maxwell, Kenneth. *Pombal: Paradox of the Enlightenment*. New York: Cambridge University Press, 1995.
McCarthy, Patricia. *Life in the Country House in Georgian Ireland*. New Haven: Yale University Press, 2016.
McCleod, Jane. "Printer Widows and the State in Eighteenth-Century France." In *Women and Work in Eighteenth-Century France*, edited by Daryl M. Hafter and Nina Kushner, 113–29. Baton Rouge: Louisiana State University Press, 2015.
McCoy, Drew R. *The Elusive Republic: Political Economy in Jeffersonian America*. New York: Norton, 1980.
McDonald, Joan. *Rousseau and the French Revolution*. London: Athone, 1962.
McEachern, Jo-Ann and David Smith. "Mme de Graffigny's *Lettres d'une Péruvienne*: Identifying the First Edition." *Eighteenth-Century Fiction* 9 (1996): 21–35.
McEachern, Jo-Ann E. "The Bibliography of Jean Jacques Rousseau's Contrat Social." In *Order and Connextion: Studies in Bibliography and Book History*, ed. R. C. Alston, 97–110. Woodbridge, Suffolk: D. C. Brewer, 1997.
McEachern, Jo-ann E. *Bibliography of the Writings of Jean Jacques Rousseau to 1800. Vol 1. Julie, ou la Nouvelle Héloïse* (Oxford: Voltaire Foundation, 1993).
McEachern, Jo-Ann E. *Bibliography of the Writings of Jean Jacques Rousseau to 1800. Vol 2. Emile, ou De l'éducation* (Oxford: Voltaire Foundation, 1989).
McKillop, Alan Dugald. *Samuel Richardson, Printer and Novelist*. Chapel Hill: University of North Carolina Press, 1936.
McLendon, Michael Locke. *The Psychology of Inequality: Rousseau's Amour-Propre*. Philadelphia: University of Pennsylvania Press, 2019.
McMurran, Mary Helen. *The Spread of Novels: Translation and Prose Fiction in the Eighteenth Century*. Princeton: Princeton University Press, 2010.
Meli, B. "Caroline, Leibniz, and Clarke." *Journal of the History of Ideas* 60 (1999): 469–86.
Melton, James Van Horn. *The Rise of the Public in Enlightenment Europe*. Cambridge: Cambridge University Press, 2001.
Melzer, Arthur. *The Natural Goodness of Man: On the System of Rousseau's Thought* (Chicago: The University of Chicago Press, 1990).
Mendham, Matthew D. "Rousseau's Partial Reception of Fénelon: From the Corruptions of Luxury to the Contradictions of Society." In *Fénelon in the Enlightenment: Traditions, Adaptations, and Variations*, edited by Christoph Schmitt-Maass, Stefanie Stockhorst, and Doohwan Ahn, 47–76. New York: Rodopi, 2014.
Mendham, Matthew David. *Hypocrisy and the Philosophical Intentions of Rousseau: The Jean-Jacques Problem*. Philadelphia: University of Pennsylvania Press, 2021.
Mertz, Rudolf. "Les amitiés françaises de Hume et le movement des idées." *Revue de littérature comparée* 9 (1929): 44–713.
Mesch, Rachel L. "Did Women Have an Enlightenment? Graffigny's Zilia as female 'philosophe'." *Romanic Review* 89 (1998): 523–37.
Mettam, Roger. *Power and Faction in Louis XIV's France*. New York: Basil Blackwell, 1988.
Meyer, Paul H. "Hume in Eighteenth-Century France." Ph.D. Thesis. Columbia University, 1954.
Miller, Genevieve. *The Adoption of Inoculation for Smallpox in England and France*. Philadelphia: University of Pennsylvania Press, 1957.

Milstein, B. M. *Eight Eighteenth Century Reading Societies: A Sociological Contribution to the History of German Literature*. Berne: Herbert Lang, 1972.

Momigliano, Arnaldo. "Gibbon's Contribution to Historical Method." *Historia: Zeitschrift für Alte Geschichte* 2 (1954): 450–63.

Monod, Paul Kléber. *The Power of Kings: Monarchy and Religion in Europe 1589–1715*. New Haven: Yale University Press, 1999.

Monod-Cassidy, Hélène. *Un voyageur-philosophe au xviiie siècle: L'Abbé Jean Bernard Le Blanc*. Cambridge, MA: Harvard University Press, 1941.

Montoya, A. C. "Shifting Perspectives and Moving Targets: From Conceptual Perspectives to Bits of Data in the First Year of the MEDIATE project." In *Digitizing Enlightenment: Digital Humanities and the Transformation of Eighteenth-Century Studies*, edited by S. Burrows and G. Roe, 195–218. Oxford: Voltaire Foundation, 2020.

Moore, Fabienne. *Prose Poems of the French Enlightenment*. Burlington: Ashgate, 2009.

Moore, Wendy. *How to Create the Perfect Wife: Britain's Most Ineligible Bachelor and His Enlightened Quest to Train the Ideal Mate*. New York: Basic Books, 2013.

Mornet, Daniel. "Les Enseignements des bibliothèques privées (1750–1780)." *Revue d'histoire littéraire de la France* 17 (1910): 449–96.

Mornet, Daniel. *Les Origines intellectuelles de la révolution française*. Paris: A. Colin, 1954 [1933].

Mornet, Daniel. "L'intérêt historique des journaux littéraires et la diffusion du Mercure de France." *Bulletin de la Société d'histoire moderne* 22 (1910): 119–22.

Morrison, Toni. "Romancing the Shadow." In *Playing in the Dark: Whiteness and the Literary Imagination*, 39–51. New York: Vintage, 1992.

Mossner, Earnest Campbell. *The Life of David Hume*. 2nd ed. Oxford: Clarendon Press, 1980.

Moulinas, René. *L'Imprimerie, la librairie, et la presse à Avignon au xviiie siècle*. Grenoble: Presse universitaire de Grenoble, 1974.

Multigraph Collective. *Interacting with Print: Elements of Reading in the Era of Print Saturation*. Chicago: University of Chicago Press, 2018.

Munck, Thomas. *Conflict and Enlightenment: Print and Political Culture in Europe, 1635–1795*. Cambridge: Cambridge University Press, 2019.

Muthu, Sankar. *Enlightenment against Empire*. Princeton: Princeton University Press, 2003.

Myers, Mitzi. "Mary Wollstonecraft's Literary Reviews." In *The Cambridge Companion to Mary Wollstonecraft*, edited by Claudia L. Johnson, 82–98. Cambridge: Cambridge University Press, 2002.

Mylne, Vivienne. "What Suzanne Knew: Lesbianism and *La Religieuse*." *Studies in Voltaire and the Eighteenth Century* 208 (1982): 167–73.

Namier, Lewis. *The Structure of Politics in the Age of George III*. 2nd ed. London: MacMillan, [1929] 1957.

Nakhimovsky, Isaac. "The Enlightened Prince and the Future of Europe: Voltaire and Frederick the Great's *Anti Machivel* of 1740." In *Commerce and Peace in the Enlightenment*, edited by Bela Kapossy and Richard Whatmore, 44–77. Cambridge: Cambridge University Press, 2017.

Oake, Roger B. "A Note on the 1752 text of *Lettres philosophiques*." *Modern Language Notes* 58 (1943): 532–4.

Oake, Roger B. "Montesquieu and Hume." *Modern Language Quarterly* 2 (1941): 25–41 and 225–48.

O'Brien, Karen. *Narratives of Enlightenment: Cosmopolitan History from Voltaire to Gibbon*. Cambridge: Cambridge University Press, 1997.

O'Brien, Karen. *Women and Enlightenment in Eighteenth-Century Britain*. Cambridge: Cambridge University Press, 2009.

Orr, Clarissa Campbell. "Aristocratic Feminism, the Learned Governess, and the Republic of Letters." In *Women, Gender, and Enlightenment*, edited by Sarah Knott and Barbara Taylor, 306–25. New York: Palgrave, 2005.

Oswald, John Clyde. *Benjamin Franklin Printer*. New York: Doubleday, 1917.

Oz-Salzberger, Fania. *Translating the Enlightenment: Scottish Civic Discourse in Eighteenth-Century Germany*. Oxford: Oxford University Press, 1995.

Pagden, Anthony. *The Enlightenment: And Why It Still Matters*. New York: Random House, 2013.

Pallares-Burke, Maria Lúcia. "The *Spectator*, or the Metamorphoses of the Periodical: A Study in Cultural Translation." In *Cultural Translation in Early Modern Europe*, edited by Peter Burke and R. Po-Chia Hsia, 142–60. Cambridge: Cambridge University Press, 2007.

Palmer, R. R. "Turgot: Paragon of the Continental Enlightenment." *Journal of Law and Economics* 19 (1776): 607–19.

Palter, Robert. "Hume and Prejudice." *Hume Studies* 21 (1995): 3–23.

Pangle, Thomas. *Montesquieu's Philosophy of Liberalism: A Commentary on "The Spirit of the Laws."* Chicago: University of Chicago Press, 1973.

Pappas, John N. *Voltaire & D'Alembert*. Bloomington: Indiana University Press, 1962.

Parker, Lindsay A. H. *Writing the Revolution: A French Woman's History in Letters*. Oxford: Oxford University Press, 2013.

Pasta, Renato. *Editoria e cultura nel settecento*. Firenze: Olschki, 1997.

Patterson, Sylvia W. *Rousseau's Emile and Early Children's Literature*. Metuchen: Scarecrow Press, 1971.

Pearson, Roger. *Voltaire Almighty: A Life in Pursuit of Freedom*. London: Bloomsbury, 2005.

Pinker, Steven. *Enlightenment Now: The Case for Reason, Science, Humanism, and Progress*. New York: Viking, 2018.

Pisvin, Th. *La Vie intellectuelle à Namur sous le régime autrichien*. Louvain: Bureaux du recueil, Bibliothèque de l'Université, 1963.

Pocock, J. G. A. "A Response to Samuel James's 'J. G. A. Pocock and the Idea of the "Cambridge School" in the History of Political Thought.'" *History of European Ideas* 45 (2019): 99–103.

Pocock, J. G. A. *Barbarism and Religion. Volume 1. The Enlightenments of Edward Gibbon, 1737–1764*. Cambridge: Cambridge University Press, 1999.

Pocock, J. G. A. *Barbarism and Religion. Volume 2. Narratives of Civil Government*. New York: Cambridge University Press, 1999.

Pocock, J. G. A. "Historiography and Enlightenment: A View of Their History." *Modern Intellectual History* 5/1 (2008): 83–96.

Pocock, J. G. A. "The Re-Description of Enlightenment." *Proceedings of the British Academy* 125 (2004): 101–18.

Pollard, M. *Dublin's Trade in Books, 1550–1800*. Oxford: Clarendon Press, 1989.

Pomeau, René. *D'Arouet à Voltaire, 1694–1734*. Oxford: Voltaire Foundation, 1985.

Popkin, Jeremy D. "Robert Darnton's Alternative (to the) Enlightenment." In *The Darnton Debate: Books and Revolution in the Eighteenth Century*, edited by Haydn T. Mason, 106–28. Oxford: Voltaire Foundation, 1998.

Popkin, Richard H. "Hume's Racism." *Philosophical Forum* 9 (1977–1978): 7–78.

Prior, Sir James. *Life of Edmond Malone, Editor of Shakespeare*. London: Smith, Elder, 1860.

Py, Gilbert. *Rousseau et les éducateurs: étude sur la fortune des idées pédagogiques de Jean-Jacques Rousseau en France et en Europe au XVIIIe siècle. Studies in Voltaire and the Eighteenth Century* 356. Oxford: Voltaire Foundation, 1997.

Radasanu, Andrea. "Montesquieu on Moderation, Monarchy, and Reform." *History of Political Thought* 31 (2010): 283–308.

Rahe, Paul A. "The Book that Never Was: Montesquieu's Considerations on the Romans in Historical Context." *History of Political Thought* 26 (2005): 43–89.

Rahe, Paul A. "The Enlightenment Indicted: Rousseau's Response to Montesquieu." *Journal of the Historical Society* 8 (2008): 273–302.

Raskolnikoff, Mouza. *Histoire romaine et critique historique dans l'Europe des lumières: La naissance de l'hypercritique dans l'historiographie de la Rome antique*. Rome: Ecole Française de Rome, 1992.

Rasmussen, Dennis C. *The Infidel and the Professor: David Hume, Adam Smith, and the Friendship that Shaped Modern Thought*. Princeton: Princeton University Press, 2017.

Rasmussen, Dennis C. *The Problems and Promise of Commercial Society: Adam Smith's Response to Rousseau*. University Park: Pennsylvania State University Press, 2008.

Raven, James. "The Importation of Books in the Eighteenth Century." In *A History of the Book in America, vol. One: The Colonial Book in the Atlantic World*, edited by Hugh Amory and David D. Hall, 183–98. Cambridge: Cambridge University Press, 2000.

Raven, James. "New Reading Histories, Print Culture and the Identification of Change: The Case of Eighteenth-Century England." *Social History* 23 (1998): 268–87.

Raven, James, Helen Small, and Naomi Tadmor, eds. *The Practice and Representation of Reading in England*. Cambridge: Cambridge University Press, 1996.

Reed, Gervais E. *Claude Barbin: Libraire de Paris sous le règne de Louis XIV*. Genève: Droz, 1974.

Reinert, Sophus and Steven Kaplan, eds. *The Economic Turn: Recasting Political Economy in Enlightenment Europe*. London: Anthem Press, 2019.

Rétat, Pierre. "De Mandeville a Montesquieu: Honneur, luxe et dépense noble dans l'Esprit des lois." *Studi Francesi* 50 (1973): 238–49.

Rétat, Pierre and Jean Sgard, eds. *Presse et histoire au xviiie siècle, l'année 1734*. Paris: CNRS, 1978.

Rex, Walter E. "Secrets from Suzanne: The Tangled Motives of *La Religieuse*." *The Eighteenth Century* 24 (1983): 185–98.

Reynolds, Siân. *Marriage and Revolution: Monsieur and Madame Roland*. Oxford: Oxford University Press, 2012.

Ricketts, Mónica. *Who Should Rule? Men of Arms, the Republic of Letters, and the Fall of the Spanish Empire*. New York: Oxford University Press, 2017.

Riding, Jacqueline. *Jacobites: A New History of the '45 Rebellion*. New York: Bloomsbury Press, 2016.

Riley, Patrick. "Fenelon's Republican Monarchism in *Telemachus*." In *Monarchisms in the Age of Enlightenment: Liberty, Patriotism, and the Common Good*, edited by Hans Blom, Luisa Simonutti and John Christian Laursen, 78–100. Toronto: University of Toronto Press, 2007.

Riley, Patrick. *The General Will Before Rousseau: The Transformation of the Divine into the Civic*. Princeton: Princeton University Press, 1986.

Riley, Patrick. "Rousseau, Fénelon, and the Quarrel Between the Ancients and the Moderns." In *The Cambridge Companion to Rousseau*, edited by Patrick Riley, 78–93. Cambridge: Cambridge University Press, 2002.

Roberts, Meghan K. *Sentimental Savants: Philosophical Families in Enlightenment France*. Chicago: University of Chicago Press, 2016.

Robertson, James. "Eighteenth-Century Jamaica's Ambivalent Cosmopolitanism." *History* 99 (2014): 607–31.

Robertson, John. *The Case for Enlightenment: Scotland and Naples, 1680–1760*. Cambridge: Cambridge University Press, 2005.

Robertson, John. *The Enlightenment: A Very Short Introduction*. Oxford: Oxford University Press, 2015.

Robertson, John. "The Enlightenment, the Public Sphere, and Political Economy." In *L'économie politique et la sphère publique dans le débat des lumières*, edited by Jesús Astigarraga and Javier Usoz, 9–32. Madrid: Casa de Velázquez, 2013.

Robertson, John. "Franco Venturi's Enlightenment." *Past & Present* 137/1 (1992): 183–206.

Robel, Gilles. "'From the Dominions of Learning to those of Conversation': philosophie savante et philosophie populaire dans les Essais de David Hume." *RANAM* 40 (2007): 53–68.

Robertson, Ritchie. *The Enlightenment: The Pursuit of Happiness, 1680–1790*. New York: HarperCollins, 2021.

Roche, Daniel. *France in the Enlightenment*. Translated by Arthur Goldhammer. Cambridge, MA: Harvard University Press, 1998.

Roche, Daniel. *Les Républicains des lettres: gens de culture et lumières au xviiie siècle*. Paris: Fayard, 1988.

Rockwood, Raymond Oxley, ed. *Carl Becker's Heavenly City Revisited*. Ithaca: Cornell University Press, 1958.

Romani, Roberto. *National Character and Public Spirit in Britain and France, 1750–1914*. Cambridge: Cambridge University Press, 2001.

Rosenberg, Daniel. "The Library of the Disaster." *Romanic Review* 103 (2012): 317–29.

Rosenblatt, Helena. *Rousseau and Geneva: From the First Discourse to the Social Contract, 1749–1762* (New York: Cambridge University Press, 1997).

Rosso, Jeannette Geffriaud. *Montesquieu et la féminité*. Pisa: Libreria Goliardica, 1977.

Rothkrug, Lionel. *Opposition to Louis XIV: The Political and Social Origins of the French Enlightenment*. Princeton: Princeton University Press, 1965.

Rothschild, Emma. "David Hume and the Seagods of the Atlantic." In *The Atlantic Enlightenment*, edited by Susan Manning and Francis D. Cogliano, 81–96. New York: Routledge, 2008.

Rothschild, Emma. *Economic Sentiments: Adam Smith, Condorcet, and the Enlightenment*. Cambridge, MA: Harvard University Press, 2001.

Rubiés, Joan-Pau. "The Jesuits and the Enlightenment." In *The Oxford Handbook of Jesuits*, edited by Ines G. Zupanov. Oxford: Oxford University Press, 2019. Available online at Oxford Handbooks Online. Accessed March 9, 2022.

Russo, Elena. "Virtuous Economies: Modernity and Noble Expenditure from Montesquieu to Caillois." *Historical Reflections* 25 (1999): 251–78.

Sale, William M. *Samuel Richardson: Master Printer*. Ithaca: Cornell University Press, 1950.

Sapp, Vicki J. "The Philosopher's Seduction: Hume and the Fair Sex." *Philosophy and Literature* 19 (1995): 1–15.

Schabas, Margaret and Carl Wennerlind. *A Philosopher's Economist: Hume and the Rise of Capitalism*. Chicago: University of Chicago Press, 2020.

Schaub, Diana J. "Montesquieu on 'the Woman Problem.'" In *Rethinking the Woman Question for Liberal Democracy*, edited by Pamela Grande Jensen, 39–66. Lanham: Rowman and Littlefield, 1996.

Scherer, Lester B. "A New Look at Personal Slavery Established." *William and Mary Quarterly* 30 (1973): 645–52.

Schiebinger, Londa L. *The Mind Has No Sex: Women in the Origins of Modern Science*. Cambridge, MA: Harvard University Press, 1989.

Schmidt, Bernward. "The Rejected Maxim: Images of Fénelon in Rome 1699 and by Catholic Reformers c. 1800." In *Fénelon in the Enlightenment: Traditions, Adaptations, and Variations*, edited by Christoph Schmitt-Maass, Stefanie Stockhorst, and Doohwan Ahn, 313–37. New York: Rodopi, 2014.

Schmidt, James. "What Enlightenment Was: How Moses Mendelssohn and Immanuel Kant Answered the Berlinische Monatsschrift." *Journal of the History of Philosophy* 30 (1992): 77–102.

Schmitt-Maass, Christoph. *Fénelon in the Enlightenment: Traditions, Adaptations, and Variations*. Edited by Christoph Schmitt-Maass, Stefanie Stockhorst, and Doohwan Ahn. New York: Rodopi, 2014.

Schumpeter, Joseph. *A History of Economic Analysis*. London: Routledge, 1981.

Schuurman, Paul. "Fénelon on Luxury, War and Trade in the *Telemachus*." *History of European Ideas* 38 (2012): 179–99.

Schwartz, Leon. *Diderot and the Jews*. Rutherford: Fairleigh Dickinson University Press, 1981.

Sebastiani, Sylvia. *The Scottish Enlightenment: Race, Gender, and the Limits of Progress*. New York: Palgrave Macmillan, 2013.

Senarclens, Vanessa de. *Montesquieu. Historien de Rome: Un tournant pour la réflexion sur le statut de l'histoire au xviiie siècle*. Geneva: Droz, 2003.

Seville, Catherine. *The Internationalisation of Copyright Law: Books, Buccaneers, and the Black Flag in the Nineteenth Century*. Cambridge: Cambridge University Press, 2006.

Sewell, William H. *Capitalism and the Emergence of Civic Equality in Eighteenth-Century France*. Chicago: University of Chicago Press, 2021.

Shackleton, Robert. "Allies and Enemies: Voltaire and Montesquieu." *Essays by Diverse Hands* 39 (1977): 126–45.

Shackleton, Robert. "John Nourse and the London Edition of *L'Esprit des lois*." In *Studies in the French Eighteenth Century: Presented to John Lough by Colleagues, Pupils and Friends*, edited by D. J. Mossop, G. E. Rodmell, and D. B. Wilson, 248–59. Durham: University of Durham, 1978.

Shackleton, Robert. *Montesquieu: A Critical Biography*. Oxford: Oxford University Press, 1961.

Shackleton, Robert. "Montesquieu, Dupin and the Early Writings of Rousseau." In *Reappraisals of Rousseau: Studies in Honour of R. A. Leigh*, edited by Simon Harvey et al., 234–49. Totowa: Barnes & Noble, 1980.

Shackleton, Robert. "The Muslim Chronology of the *Lettres persanes*." *French Studies* 7 (1954): 17–27.

Shackleton, Robert. "When did the French Philosophes Become a Party?" *Bulletin of the John Rylands University Library of Manchester* 60 (1977): 181–99.

Shank, J. B. *The Newton Wars and the Beginning of the French Enlightenment*. Chicago: University of Chicago Press, 2008.

Shaw, Edward P. *Problems and Policies of Malesherbes as Directeur de la Librairie in France (1750–1763)*. Albany: SUNY, 1966.

Shelford, April G. "Pascal in Jamaica; or, The French Enlightenment in Translation." *Journal of the Western Society for French History* 36 (2008): 53–74.

Shelford, April G. *Transforming the Republic of Letters: Pierre-Daniel Huet and European Intellectual Life, 1650–1720*. Rochester: Boydell & Brewer, 2007.

Shennan, J. H. *Philippe, Duke of Orléans: Regent of France, 1715–1723*. London: Thames and Hudson, 1979.

Sher, Richard B. *The Enlightenment and the Book: Scottish Authors and Their Publishers in Eighteenth-Century Britain, Ireland, and America*. Chicago: University of Chicago Press, 2006.

Sher, Richard B. "*New Light on the Publication and Reception of The Wealth of Nations*". *Adam Smith Review* 1 (2004): 3–29.

Sheridan, Geraldine. "Irish Literary Review Magazines and Enlightenment France: 1730–1790." In *Ireland and the French Enlightenment 1700–1800*, edited by Graham Gargett and Geraldine Sheridan, 28–51. New York: St Martin's Press, 1999.

Sheridan, Geraldine. "Irish Periodicals and the Dissemination of French Enlightenment Writings in the Eighteenth Century." In *1798: A Bicentenary Perspective*, edited by Thomas Bartlett, 28–51. Dublin: Four Courts, 2003.

Sheridan, Geraldine. "Women in the Booktrade in Eighteenth-Century France." *Journal of Eighteenth Century Studies* 15 (1992): 51–70.
Shovlin, John. "Hume's Political Discourses and the French Luxury Debate." In *David Hume's Political Economy*, edited by Carl Wennerlind and Margaret Schabas, 203–22. London: Routledge, 2008.
Shovlin, John. *The Political Economy of Virtue: Luxury, Patriotism, and the Origins of the French Revolution*. Ithaca: Cornell University Press, 2006.
Showalter, English. *Françoise de Graffigny: Her Life and Works*. Oxford: Voltaire Foundation, 2004.
Silvestre, João Paulo, Alina Villalva, and Esperança Cardeira. "Landmarks of Economic Terminology: The First Portuguese Translation of *Elémens du commerce*." *History of European Ideas* 40 (2014): 1189–201.
Skjönsberg, Max. "Lord Bolingbroke's Theory of Party and Opposition." *Historical Journal* 59 (2016): 947–73.
Smith, David W. *Bibliographie des Oeuvres de Mme de Graffigny, 1745–1845*. Ferney-Voltaire: Centre Internationale D'Étude de xviiie siècle, 2016.
Smith, David W. "Did Voltaire Collaborate in the Rouen (Machuel) 1750 edition of his Oeuvres?" *Journal of Eighteenth-Century Studies* 31 (2008): 571–7.
Smith, David W. *Helvétius: A Study in Persecution*. Oxford: Oxford University Press, 1965.
Smith, David W. "Les relations entre Voltaire et ses libraires: Walther, Machuel, et Lambert, 1748–1752." In *Voltaire et l.e livre*, 37–46. Ferney-Voltaire: Centre International D'Etude Du XVIIIe Siècle, 2009.
Smith, David W. "Robert Machuel, imprimeur-librarire à Rouen." *Cahiers Voltaire* 6 (2007): 35–57.
Smith, Plinio J. "Bayle and Pyrrhonism: Antinomy, Method, and History." In *Scepticism in the Eighteenth Century: Enlightenment, Lumières, Aufklärung*, edited by Sébastien Charles and Plinio J. Smith, 19–30. Dordrecht: Springer, 2013.
Smith, Theresa Ann. *The Emerging Female Citizen: Gender and Enlightenment in Spain*. Berkeley: University of California Press, 2006.
Sonenscher, Michael. *Before the Deluge: Public Debt, Inequality, and the Intellectual Origins of the French Revolution*. Princeton: Princeton University Press, 2007.
Spector, Céline. "L'Esprit des lois de Montesquieu: une éclipse de amour-propre?" In *(Re) Lire L'Esprit des lois*, edited by Catherine Volpilhac-Auger and Luigi Delia, 19–31. Paris: Éditions de la Sorbonne, 2014.
Spector, Céline. *Montesquieu et l'émergence de l'économie politique*. Paris: Champion, 2006.
Spedding, Patrick. "A List of My Books: A Detailed Analysis of a 1730s Personal Library." *Script & Print* 41 (2017): 92–104.
Spurlin, Paul Merrill. *Montesquieu in America, 1760–1801*. Baton Rouge: Louisiana State University Press, 1940.
Stapelbroek, Koen. *Love, Self-Deceit, and Money: Commerce and Morality in the Early Neapolitan Enlightenment*. Toronto: University of Toronto Press, 2008.
St Claire, William. *The Reading Nation in the Romantic Period*. Cambridge: Cambridge University Press, 2004.
Stewart, Philip. "On the Nugent Translation of *L'Esprit des lois*." *History of Political Thought* 39 (2018): 83–106.
Stocking, Janice B. "The Court of Saxony-Dresden." In *Music at German Courts, 1715–1760: Changing Artistic Priorities*, edited by Janice B Stocking, Samantha Owens, and Barbara M. Reul, 17–50. Suffolk: Boydell and Brewer, 2011.
Stourzh, Gerald. *Alexander Hamilton and the Idea of Republican Government*. Stanford: Stanford University Press, 1970.
Strien, Kees van. *Voltaire in Holland 1736–1745*. Louvain: Editions Peeters, 2011.

Stuurman, Siep. *François Poulain de la Barre and the Invention of Modern Equality*. Cambridge, MA: Harvard University Press, 2004.

Swann, Julian. *Politics and the Parlement of Paris Under Louis XV, 1754–1774*. Cambridge: Cambridge University Press, 1995.

Taylor, Samuel S. B. "Rousseau's Contemporary Reputation in France." *Studies in Voltaire and the Eighteenth Century* 27 (1963): 1545–74.

Théré, Christine. "Economic Publishing and Authors." In *Studies in the History of French Political Economy: From Bodin to Walras*, edited by Gilbert Facca-Rello, 1–56. London: Routledge, 1998.

Tomalin, Marcus. *The French Language and British Literature, 1756–1830*. London: Routledge, 2016.

Tomaselli, Sylvana. "The Role of Woman in Enlightenment Conjectural Histories." In *Conceptualizing Women in Enlightenment Thought*, edited by Hans Erich Bödeker and Leiselotte Steinbrügge, 7–22. Berlin: Verlag Arno Spitz GmbH, 2001.

Towsey, Mark R. M. "First Steps in Associational Reading: Book Use and Sociability at the Wigtown Subscription Library, 1795–9." *Papers of the Bibliographical Society of America* 103 (2009): 455–95.

Towsey, Mark R. M. "'I Can't Resist Sending You the Book:' Private Libraries, Elite Women, and Shared Reading Practices in Georgian Britain." *Library and Information History* 29 (2013): 210–22.

Towsey, Mark R. M. *Reading History in Britain and America, C.1750 - C.1840*. Cambridge: Cambridge University Press, 2019.

Towsey, Mark R. M. *Reading the Scottish Enlightenment: Books and their Readers in Provincial Scotland, 1750–1820*. Leiden: Brill, 2010.

Trapnell, William H. "Survey and Analysis of Voltaire's Collective Editions." *SVEC* 77 (1970): 103–99.

Tricoire, Damien. "The Fabrication of the Philosophe: Catholicism, Court Culture, and the Origins of Enlightenment Moralism in France." *Eighteenth-Century Studies* 51 (2018): 463–4.

Trouille, Mary Seidman. *Sexual Politics in the Enlightenment: Women Writers Read Rousseau*. Albany: SUNY Press, 1997.

Turnovsky, Geoffrey. *The Literary Market: Author and Modernity in the Old Regime*. Philadelphia: University of Pennsylvania Press, 2010.

Ulrich, Adam. *The Political Economy of J.H.G. Justi*. Bern: Peter Lang, 2006.

Unself, Siegfried. *Goethe and His Publishers*. Translated by Kenneth J. Northcott. Chicago: University of Chicago Press, 1996.

Van Damme, Stéphane. "Farewell Habermas? Deux décennies d'études sur l'espace public." *Les Dossiers du Grihl*, http://journals.openedition.org/dossiersgrihl/682 (accessed May 3, 2021).

Van Kley, Dale. "Pierre Nicole, Jansenism, and the Morality of Enlightened Self-Interest." In *Anticipations of the Enlightenment in England, France, and Germany*, edited by Alan Charles Kors and Paul J. Korshin, 69–85. Philadelphia: University of Pennsylvania Press, 1987.

Vardi, Liana. *The Physiocrats and the World of the Enlightenment*. Cambridge: Cambridge University Press, 2012.

Venturi, Franco. *Dalmazzo Francesco Vasco (1732–1794)*. Paris: Droz, 1940.

Venturi, Franco. *The End of the Old Regime in Europe, 1776–1789. Part 1. The Great States of the West*. Translated by R. Burr Litchfield. Princeton: Princeton University Press, 1991.

Venturi, Franco. *Utopia and Reform in the Enlightenment*. Cambridge: Cambridge University Press, 1971.

Vila, Anne C. *Suffering Scholars: Pathologies of the Intellectual in Enlightenment France*. Philadelphia: University of Pennsylvania Press, 2018.

Villalta, Luiz Carlos. "Montesquieu's Persian Letters and Reading Practices in the Luso-Brazilian World (1750–1802)." In *Enlightened Reform in Southern Europe and its Atlantic Colonies, 1750–1830*, edited by Gabriel Paquette, 119–44. Farnham: Ashgate, 2009.

Vis, Jurjen. "The Book Trade in the Poort." *Quaerendo* 37 (2007): 111–46.

Volpilhac-Auger, Catherine, ed. *Montesquieu: Mémoire de la critique*. Paris: Presses de l'Université de Paris-Sorbonne, 2003.

Volpilhac-Auger, Catherine. *Un auteur en quête d'éditeurs? Histoire éditoriale de l'oeuvre de Montesquieu (1748–1964)*. Lyon: Ens, 2012.

Wade, Ira O. *The Clandestine Organization and Diffusion of Philosophical Ideas in France from 1700 to 1750*. Princeton: Princeton University Press, 1938.

Wahnbaeck, Till. *Luxury and Public Happiness: Political Economy in the Italian Enlightenment*. Oxford: Clarendon Press, 2004.

Walker, Thomas D. "The State of Libraries in Eighteenth-Century Europe: Adalbert Blumenschein's 'Beschreibung Verschiedener Bibliotheken in Europa.'" *The Library Quarterly: Information, Community, Policy* 65 (1995): 269–294.

Ward, Albert. *Book Production, Fiction, and the German Reading Public, 1740–1780*. Oxford: Clarendon Press, 1974.

Watkins, Margaret. "'A Cruel but Ancient Subjugation'? Understanding Hume's Attack on Slavery." *Hume Studies* 39 (2013): 103–21.

Watkins, Margaret. *The Philosophical Progress of Hume's Essays*. Cambridge: Cambridge University Press, 2019.

Watt, Ian. *The Rise of the Novel: Studies in Defoe, Richardson and Fielding*. Berkeley: University of California Press, 1957.

Weil, Françoise. *Livres interdits, livres persecutés 1720-1770*. Oxford: Voltaire Foundation, 1999.

Weiss, Penny A. "Rousseau, Antifeminism, and Woman's Nature." *Political Theory* 15 (1987): 81–98.

Westgate, David. "The Augustinian Concept of Amour-Propre and Pascal's *Pensées*." *Nottingham French Studies* 10 (1971): 10–20.

Weulersse, Georges. *La Mouvement physiocratie en France (de 1756 à 1770)*. 2 vols. Paris: Alcan, 1910.

Whatmore, Richard. "Benjamin Vaughan and the Consequences of Anonymity: An Introduction to Kenneth E. Carpenter's Benjamin Vaughan's Contributions Unveiled: A Bibliography." *History of European Ideas* 44 (2018): 292–6.

Whelan, Frederick G. "Political Science and Political Theory in Hume's Essays." In *David Hume on Morals, Politics, and Society*, edited by Angela Coventry and Andrew Valls. New Haven: Yale University Press, 2018.

Whyte, Iain. "'The Upas Tree, Beneath Whose Pestiferous Shade All Intellect Languishes and All Virtue Dies': Scottish Public Perceptions of the Slave Trade and Slavery, 1756–1833." In *Recovering Scotland's Slavery Past: The Caribbean Connection*, edited by T. M. Devine, 187–205. Edinburgh: Edinburgh University Press, 2015.

Williams, Abigail. *The Social Life of Books: Reading Together in the Eighteenth-Century Home*. New Haven: Yale University Press, 2017.

Wills, Garry. *Explaining America: The Federalist*. New York: Penguin, 1982.

Winterer, Caroline. *The Mirror of Antiquity: American Women and the Classical Tradition*. Ithaca: Cornell University Press, 2009.

Wolfgang, Aurora. "Intertextual Conversations: The Love-Letter and the Footnote in Madame De Graffigny's *Lettres d'Une Péruvienne*." *Eighteenth-Century Fiction* 10 (1997): 15–28.

Wootton, David. *Power, Pleasure, and Profit: Insatiable Appetites from Machiavelli to Madison*. Cambridge, MA: Harvard University Press, 2018.

Wright, Johnson Kent. "Rousseau and Montesquieu." In *Thinking with Rousseau, from Machiavelli to Schmitt*, edited by Helena Rosenblatt and Paul Schweigert, 63–91. Cambridge: Cambridge University Press, 2017.
Yeo, Richard. "John Locke and Polite Philosophy." In *The Philosopher in Early Modern Europe: The Nature of a Contested Identity*, edited by Conal Condren, Stephen Gaukroger, and Ian Hunter, 254–75. Cambridge: Cambridge University Press, 2006.
Yolton, John. *Locke and French Materialism*. Oxford: Clarendon Press, 1993.
Yolton, John. *Thinking Matter: Materialism in Eighteenth-Century Britain*. Minneapolis: University of Minnesota Press, 1983.
Young, David B. "Libertarian Demography: Montesquieu's Essay on Depopulation in the *Lettres persanes*." *Journal of the History of Ideas* 36 (1975): 669–82.
Zanardi, Paola. "Italian Responses to David Hume." In *The Reception of Hume in Europe*, edited by in Peter Jones, 161–75. London: Continuum, 2005.

Electronic Resources

Adams Family Papers: An Electronic Archive. Massachusetts Historical Society, http://www.masshist.org/digitaladams.
ARTFL Archives Parlementaires, https://artfl-project.uchicago.edu/node/148.
ARTFL Encyclopédie Project, Edited by Robert Morrissey and Glenn Roe, Spring 2016 Edition, http://encyclopedie.uchicago.edu/.
Burrows, Simon. The French Book Trade in Enlightenment Europe, https://frenchbooktrade.wordpress.com/.
Centre International d'étude du xviiie siècle. c18.net, https://c18.net/vo/vo_pages.php?nom=vo_oe_18_liste.
Darnton, Robert. Publications, http://www.robertdarnton.org/publications.
The Documentary History of the Ratification of the Constitution Digital Edition. Edited by John P. Kaminski, Gaspare J. Saladino, Richard Leffler, Charles H. Schoenleber, and Margaret A. Hogan. Charlottesville: University of Virginia Press, 2009. https://rotunda.upress.virginia.edu/founders/RNCN.
Eighteenth Century Collections Online (ECCO), https://www.gale.com/primary-sources/eighteenth-century-collections-online.
"Eighteenth-Century Illustrated Editions of *Pamela*," http://umich.edu/~ece/student_projects/pamela_illustrated/main.set.editions.htm.
Eighteenth-Century Journals, https://www.18thcjournals.amdigital.co.uk/.
Electronic Enlightenment Scholarly Edition of Correspondence, Edited by Robert McNamee et al. Vers. 3.0. University of Oxford. 2016.
The Encyclopedia of Diderot & d'Alembert Collaborative Translation Project. Ann Arbor: Michigan Publishing, University of Michigan Library, 2006.
Founders Online, https://founders.archives.gov/.
Kates, Gary. The Enlightenment Book Project at Pomona College, https://kates.itg.pomona.edu/books/analytics.php?type=all.
Montoya, A. C. MEDIATE, https://mediate18.nl/?page=home.
North American Women's Letters and Diaries, https://alexanderstreet.com/products/north-american-womens-letters-and-diaries.
The Reading Experience Database (RED), 1450–1945, http://www.open.ac.uk/Arts/RED/index.html.
Sevres Factory Porcelain, http://cartelfr.louvre.fr/cartelfr/visite?srv=car_not_frame&idNotice=10619&langue=fr.

Index

Note: *Italicized* and **bold** page numbers refer to figures and tables. Page numbers followed by "n" refer to notes.

A B C, The (Voltaire)   130
absolutism   49, 51, 68
Academy of Bordeaux   85
Academy of Dijon   28, 257
Academy of Lyon   319
Account of the European Settlements in America, An   315
Act of Union, 1707   192
Adair, Douglass   198
Adamoli, Pierre   14
Adams, John   197, 245, 292, 314
Addison, Joseph   15, 39, 191
   Cato   80
   Spectator   36–7, 88, 181
Adventures of Telemachus (Fénelon)   4, 6, 24, 32, 37, *41*, 43–73, 103, 105, 157, 216, 373 n.22
   Book V   58, 61
   Book XIII (today's Book XI)   61
   eighteenth-century editions of   **43**
   Enlightenment absorption   56–62
   First Edition Title Page   *47*
   Kingdom of Salente in   63
   Moetjens's 1701 edition   47–50, *47*
   Ramsay's 1717 "first edition"   51–6
   as serious political thought   52
Aesop's Fables (Richardson)   158
"Age of Conversation"   26
Age of Louis XIV, The (Voltaire)   58, 61, 69, 105, 118, 120
Albuquerque, Afonso de   304
d'Alembert, Jean Le Rond   60, 66, 82
   Encyclopédie   3, 14, 30, 35, 60, 92, 152, 180, 183, 194, 213, 225, 242, 243, 290, 303, 315, 316
Alexander, William
   History of Women   185
Allan, David   14–15

"Enlightenment, The"   73
Almanach Royal   14
Ameilhon, Hubert-Pascal   290
American Revolution   245
Americanus   248–9, 379 n.103
American War of Independence (1778–83)   291, 313, 314
amour propre   48, 104, 123, 145, 146, 165, 173, 199, 234, 235, 240, 246, 351 n.20
Analytical Review   30
Ancient History (Rollin)   118
Annual Register   16
Anti-Federalists   247–53, **248**
Anti-Machiavel (Frederick II)   57, 58, 169
anti-Semitism   13
Arabian Nights   32
Archbishopric of Cambrai   340 n.39
d'Argens, Marquis   77, 90
d'Argenson, Marquis   88–9
   Considérations sur le gouvernement ancien et présent de la France   57
Arianism   275
Aristotle
   Politics   376 n.65
Arkstée & Merkus   239
Articles of Confederation   197, 246, 253
atheism   3, 5, 80, 152, 236
Atticus   13–14, 24
Augustus II   102, 106
Austria   26
   War of the Spanish Succession (1701–14) and   50
authors/authorship   36–40, 87, 102, 122, 147, 148, 209, 239, 316
Ayr Library Society   18

Bacon, Lord   280
Barber, Giles   142

Index

Barbin, Claude   43, 44
Barre, François Poullain de la   208
Barrett, Jean Jacques de   70
Barrillot & Fils   28, 221–5, 235, 239, 283
Battle of Poltava   101
Battyani, Ignatius   13
Bayle, Pierre   37, 39, 44, 80, 104, 235, 258
   Historical and Critical Dictionary   113
   Nouvelles de la République des Lettres   36, 38
Beard, John R.
   Life of Toussaint L'Ouverture, The   323, *324*, 392 n.87
Beatson, John   320
Beaufort, Louis de   127
   Dissertation upon the Uncertainty of the Roman History during the First Five Hundred Years, A   128
Beaumarchais, Pierre Caron de   153
Beaumont, Christophe de   67, 267
Beauvilliers, Paul de   50
Beccaria, Cesare
   On Crimes and Punishments   32, 94, 287
Becker, Carl
   Heavenly City of the Eighteenth-Century Philosophers, The   1
Bee, The   106
Belisarius (Marmontel)   69
Bell, John   281
belles lettres   20
Belley, Jean Baptiste   321–3, *321*
Benezet, Anthony   320
Bentham, Jeremy   67
Berlinische Monatsschrift   11
Bernard, Jean François   259
Bernardin de Saint-Pierre, Jacques-Henri   69–70
   Studies of Nature   69
Berne Convention (1884)   30, 193
Beroujon, Anne   14
Beuchot, Adrien Jean Quentin   134
Bibliothèque de l'homme public (The Public Man's Library) (Condorcet)   291
Bignon, Abbé Jean Paul   127–8
Blackburn, Robin   325
Black Jacobins, The (James)   323
Blackstone, William
   Commentaries on the Laws of England   246, 247

Blair, Hugh   280, 282
Blavet, Abbé Jean Louis   290, 291
Blumenschein, Adalbert   15–16
Bodleian Library   38
Bolingbroke, Lord   225
   Craftsman   105
Bomare, Valmont
   Dictionnaire raisonné universel d'histoire naturelle   20
Bonaparte, Napoleon   325–6
booksellers   26–36
Bordeaux Academy   37
Bossuet, Bishop   46, 48, 49, 60, 62, 67, 68
   Politics Drawn from the Very Words of Holy Scripture   54
Boswell, James   319
Botting, Eileen Hunt   232
Bouchon, Catherine   206, 212
Bouhier, Jean   121
Bourgogne, Duc de   50, 57, 58
Bousquet, Marc Michel   129, 209
Braid, Lodovica   23
Brienne, Archbishop   289, 292
Brindley, John   209
Brissot, Jacques Pierre   67, 295
Bristol Library   17
Brossette, Claude   105
Brown, Harcourt   143
Brumfitt, J. H.   120
Brunel, Pierre   81
Brutus (Voltaire)   101, 103, 109, 144
Buffon, Georges Louis Le Clerc, Comte de   22, 28, 34, 67, 309
   Natural History   20, 21, 289
Burgundy Circle   50
Buringh, Eltjo   26–7
Burke, Edmund   88, 292
Burlamaqui, Jean Jacques   228
   Principles of Natural and Political Right   244
   Principles of Natural and Politic Law, The   21
   Principles of Natural Law   221, 224
   Principles of Political Right   224
Burnard, Trevor   24–5
Burr, Esther Edwards   167
Burrows, Simon   56
Business of Enlightenment (Darnton)   3
Bute, Lord   185

Cadell, Thomas   29, 216, 281–3, **284**, 285, 288
Caetana, Antônio   78, 94
Calado, Diogo José de Morais   77
Cameralism   242
Camusat, François Denis   84
Canapé couleur de feu   23
Candide (Voltaire)   22, 56, 225
Cannet, Sophie   312
Cantillon, Richard
   Essai sur la nature du commerce en géneral   296
Caradonna, Jeremy   320
Caroline Fox, 1st Baronness Holland   12–13
Carpenter, Kenneth   289, 291
Cassirer, Ernst   1, 5, 214
Castel, Père Louis Bertrand   122
Catherine the Great   141, 267, 310, 315
Catholic Church   33, 80, 111, 142, 236, 312
   control over civic life   138
   Index of Forbidden Works/Index of Forbidden Books   94, 124, 152, 168, 206, 235
   Spirit of the Laws, The, reading of   232–40, 257, 275
Catholicism   128, 206
Cato (Addison)   80
Caux, Suzanne de   29, 79–81, 84, 86, 87, 109
   Les consolations de l'âme fidèle contre les frayeurs de la mort   80
celibacy   233, 237
Cellier, Pierre   16
Cénie (Graffigny)   212
censorship   13, 34, 35, 62, 115, 129, 148, 169, 268, 281, 316
   book   33, 86, 102, 147
   government   33, 289
   and philosophes, relationship between   261
   press   291, 314
Cérutti, Joseph   70
Chalmers, James   197, 294
Chamroud, Marie Anne de Vichy, Marquise du Deffand   60
Chartier, Roger   2, 6, 29
Chatelain, Zacharie   55, 224
Châtelet, Marquise du   121, 204
Chesterfield, Lord   60
Chevreuse, Duc de   50
Chevrier, Jean François   17
Child, Josiah   24

Christianity   49, 90, 93, 94, 104, 123, 136, 171, 216, 234, 236, 237, 239, 266, 309
   anti-liberal tendencies   123
Christopher, Saint   214
church–state relationship   237–8, 240
Chydenius, Anders   13
Cicero   258
circulation libraries   16–18, 32
Citizen Jean-Baptiste Belley, Ex-Representative of the Colonies (Girodet)   321
Clarissa (Richardson)   22, 23, 32, 56, 91, 157, 164–6, 168–71, 173, 208
   eighteenth-century editions of   **157**
Clarke, Samuel   140
Clarkson, Thomas   320
Clément, Pierre   207–8
Cobban, Alfred   1, 4
Cochart, Marie   43, 44
Colbert, Jean Baptiste   63
Comédie-Française   101, 168
Commentaries on the Laws of England (Blackstone)   246, 247
Common Sense (Paine)   314, 315
Condillac, Étienne Bonnot de   228
Condorcet, Marquis de   60, 66, 174, 290, 292, 293, 325
   Bibliothèque de l'homme public (The Public Man's Library)   291
   Life of Turgot   211–12
Conseil d'Etat (Royal Council)   33, 148
Considerations on Lowering the Interest (Locke)   296
Considerations on the Causes of the Greatness of the Romans and Their Decline (Montesquieu)   37, *97*, *99–131*, 225, **226**, 235, 236, 355 n.83
   eighteenth-century editions of   **99, 226**
Constant, Benjamin   379 n.103
Conversations on the Plurality of Worlds (Fontenelle)   89
Corpus of Clandestine Literature in France 1769–1789, The (Darntin)   3
Cowper, William   312
Craftsman (Bolingbroke)   105
Critical and Historical Remarks on the History of Charles XII (La Motraye)   107–13, *109*
Critical Review   29
"Critique de l'Esprit des lois" (Critique of The Spirit of the Laws) (Dupin)   229, 230

Index

Croismare, Marquis de   172
Cronk, Nicholas   58, 111
Crowley, John E.   285–6
cruel persecution   49
Curran, Mark   35
Curry, John   309

Daily Advertiser   162
Dalrymple, John
   Memoirs of Great Britain and Ireland   289
Darnton, Robert   2, 4, 6, 23, 34, 35, 39–40, 67, 264, 316
   Business of Enlightenment   3
   Corpus of Clandestine Literature in France 1769–1789, The   3
   Forbidden Best-Sellers of Pre-Revolutionary France, The   3
   Literary Tour de France, A   3
   "Readers Respond to Rousseau"   268
D'Arouet à Voltaire (Pomeau)   359 n.60
David, Jacques-Louis   7
Day, Thomas   270–5
   History of Sandford and Merton   274
Declaration of the Rights of Man   325
Decline and Fall of the Roman Empire, The (Gibbon)   102, 128, 309
de Conti, Prince   290
Défense de l'Esprit des lois   235, 239
Defense of the Spirit of the Laws (Montesquieu)   **226**, 240
Defoe, Daniel   31
   Moll Flanders   23
Deism   236
de la Landelle, Jean Baptiste   48
de la Motte-Guyon, Jeanne-Marie Bouvier   48
De l'Esprit (Helvétius)   23, 33, 62, 261, 262, 267, 268, 317
Deleyre, Alexandre   303
Denis, Madame   169
Desbordes, Jacques   79, 80, 109–12, 124–5, 148, 149, 221
Descartes, René   68, 69, 137, 146, 152, 183, 208
Desormeaux, Joseph-Louis Ripault
   Histoire de la Maison de Montmorenci   21
despotism   53, 61, 82, 83, 85, 122, 173, 194, 227, 230, 231, 235, 236, 238–40, 242, 263, 308, 310
   enlightened   185

   ministerial   71
   philosophical tragedy about   89–95
   political   120
Dickinson, John
   Letters from a Farmer in Pennsylvania, to the Inhabitants of the British Colonies   196
Dickson, William
   Letters on Slavery   320
Dictionnaire philosophique (Voltaire)
   Ame   153
Dictionnaire raisonné universel d'histoire naturelle (Bomare)   20
Diderot, Denis   5, 6, 14, 18, 21, 22, 33–5, 54, 67, 90, 100, 170, 172–4, 179, 206, 303–7, 313, 320, 323–5
   Encyclopédie   3, 14, 30, 35, 60, 92, 152, 180, 183, 194, 213, 242, 290, 303, 315, 316
   Natural Son   20
   Nun, The   171, 173
   Pensées sur l'interpretation de la nature   23
Didot   56, 341 n.55
Dinmore, Richard   293
"Discourse on Epic Poetry and of the Excellence of the Poem of Telemachus, A" (Ramsay)   51, 52
Discourse on Political Economy (Rousseau)   313
"Discourse on the Arts and Sciences" (Rousseau)   28, 206
Discourse on the Origins of Inequality (Rousseau)   30, 34, 210, 240–2, 259
Discourses on Livy (Machiavelli)   121
Discourses on the First Ten Books of Livy (Machiavelli)   225
Dissertation upon the Uncertainty of the Roman History during the First Five Hundred Years, A (Beaufort)   128
division of labor   211, 293
Documentary History of the Ratification of the Constitution, The (Wisconsin Historical Society)   246, **247**
Domat, Jean
   Traité des lois [Treatise on Law]   233
Domville, William   223
Donoghue, Frank   39
Don Quixote   32
Douglas, John   165
doux commerce   241, 257, 284, 308

430

Dreyfusard University   133
Duane, William   245
Dublin Magazine   30
Dubos, Abbé   45
Duchesne, Nicolas Bonaventure   212, 214, 265
Duke of Argyll   14
Dunstan, Vivienne   100
Dupin, Claude   228, 236, 238, 240
  Observations sur un livre intitulé: De l'Esprit des loix   229
  Réflexions sur quelques parties d'un livre intitulé "De l'Esprit des loix"   229
Dupin, Louise   236, 238, 240, 257
  "Critique de l'Esprit des lois" (Critique of The Spirit of the Laws)   229, 230
  feminist reading   228–32
  Ouvrage sur les femmes (Works on Women)   228
Dupin, Mme   230
Duplain, Pierre   291
Du Pont de Nemour, Pierre Samuel   286, 290
  "On the Origin and Progress of a New Science"   243
du Pont de Nemours, Pierre Samuel   286, 290
Durand, Laurent   34, 223
Dutch East India Company   305–7

Eastern Europe   101
  Hebrew and Yiddish books   79
  literacy   27, 28
Eboli, Gilles   100
Ecole Normale Supérieure   133
Edelstein, Dan   19
Eden, William   309
Eden Treaty   286
Edgeworth, Maria
  Practical Education   273–4
Edgeworth, Richard Lovell   270–4
Edinburgh Review   30
Edminston, William   172
Eisen, Charles   212
Elements of Commerce (Forbonnais)   194, 195
Elements of the Philosophy of Newton (Voltaire)   108, 111
Emile (Rousseau)   24, 26, 36, 64, 65, 169, 212, 217, *255*, 257–75, 317
  eighteenth-century editions of   **257**
  "Profession of Faith of the Savoyard Vicar"   25, 30, 266

  publishing   265–8
  readers respond to   268–75
Encyclopédie   3, 14, 30, 35, 60, 61, 92, 152, 180, 183, 194, 213, 225, 243, 290, 303, 315, 316
  "Commerce"   242
  "Farmers"   243
  "Grain"   243
  "History"   113, 130
Encyclopédie méthodique   290
England   26
  Acts of Union (1707)   283
  British Board of Trade   286
  Glorious Revolution of 1689   46, 70, 130
  literacy   27
  printers   26
  Quietism in   51
  Telemachus in   49
  translation   32
  War of the Spanish Succession (1701–14) and   50
Enlightenment   1–6
  absorption   56–62
  claims of   4–5
  Enlightenment Now (Pinker)   2
  European   32, 34, 68
  French   4, 27, 260
  and French Revolution   4
  as historical event   2
  of individual *vs.* emergence of an enlightened public   11
  political theory   6, 61, 62, 72, 253, 264
  Radical   78, 79, 95
  reading public   9–40
  Scottish   28, 196, 279
Enlightenment and the Book, The (Sher)   32
Enlightenment: And Why It Still Matters, The (Pagden)   1–2
Enlightenment: An Interpretation, The (Gay)   214
Enlightenment Books Project   329 n.19
Enquiry Concerning Human Understanding, An Enquiry Concerning the Principle of Morals, Natural History of Religion, and *Dissertation on the Passions, An* (Hume)   192
Enquiry Concerning Political Justice (Godwin)   72
Enquiry Concerning the Principles of Morals (Hume)   170

Index

Enquiry into the Origin of Honour and the Usefulness of Christianity in War, An (Mandeville)   103, 235
d'Eon, Chevalière   14, 68
Ephemérides du citoyen   63
Esprit et Génie de l'Abbé Raynal (Hédouin)   315
Essai sur la nature du commerce en géneral (Cantillon)   296
Essai sur les moeurs (Voltaire)   105, 120, 302
Essay (Locke)   152
Essay Concerning Human Understanding (Locke)   38, 225, 244, 258, 360 n.69
Essay on the Study of Literature (Gibbon)   129
Essays, Moral, Political, and Literary (Hume)   3, 17–18, 21, 24, 39, *177*, 179–200
   eighteenth-century editions of   **179**
   Enquiry Concerning Human Understanding   192
   Enquiry Concerning the Principles of Morals   192
   "Of the Coalition of Parties"   192
   "Of the Standard of Taste"   192
   Philosophical Essays Concerning Human Understanding   192
Essays and Treatises on Several Subjects (Hume)   187, 192, 193
Estwick, Samuel   190
d'Etanges, Julie   259
Europe
   Enlightenment   32, 34, 67
   literacy   30

Fable of the Bees (Mandeville)   103, 235, 238
Farmer Refuted, The (Hamilton)   198
Fauré, Christine   214
Federalist Papers, The   197, 198, 246
Female Mentor, The   65
Female Spectator (Haywood)   206
feminism
   antifeminism   232
   egalitarian   232
   overt   207
Fénelon, François   14, 22, 27, 104, 258, 307
   Adventures of Telemachus   37, *41*, 43–73, 103, 105, 157, 216, 373 n.22
   death of   50
   as enlightened economist   62–5
   as late dauphin's preceptor   52
   Maxims of the Saints Explained   46, 55, 60
   model of kingship   53
   model philosophe   64–7
   Quietism   46–8, 50, 51, 54, 58, 61, 62, 73
   religious dissent   48, 50
   religious leader (the Archbishop of Cambrai)   52, 73
   revolutionary philosophe   67–73
   as statesman   51
   Telemachus   4, 6, 24, 32
Fénelon, Marquis de   51, 54
Ferguson, Adam   294
Fergusson, Betsy   53
feudalism   4
Fielding, Henry   14
   Shamela   165–6, 172, 215
   Tom Jones   111
Filmer, Robert   36
Finland   27
Fleury, Cardinal   87, 147
Flint, Christopher   158
Fontanel, Abraham   16
Fontenelle, Bernard le Bovier de
   Conversations on the Plurality of Worlds   89, 208
Forbidden Best-Sellers of Pre-Revolutionary France, The (Darnton)   3
Forbonnais, François Véron Duverger de   4, 194–5, 242
   Elements of Commerce   194, 195
Formey, Jean Henri Samuel   93, 94
Fox, Charles James   286, 292
France   26
   Declaration of the Rights of Man and Citizen   *71*
   Enlightenment in   4, 27, 260
   French Academy   24, 38, 66, 87, 149
   French National Convention   321
   Imprimerie Royale   34
   literacy   27–8
   literary market   31
   Mercure de France   29, 148, 195, 257, 302
   monarchical constitution   3
   Paris Parlement   33, 148, 267, 316
   political theory   53
   translation   32
Franklin, Benjamin   28
   Library Company   17
Frederick II   23, 57, 58, 115, 117, 267

Anti-Machiavel 169
Freitas, Antônio Caetano de 77
French Gallican Church 318
French Revolution 56, 69–73, *71*, 168, 170, 193, 214, 225, 232, 245, 262, 264, 284, 291–3, 297, *317*, 325
  Enlightenment and 4, 31
Fréron, Elie Catherine 207

Gabrielli, Giovanni Maria 45
Galanteries d'une religieuse 23
Gallican Church 50
Garat, Dominique Joseph 68
Gargett, Graham 27
Garrick, David 163
Garve, Christian 294, 295
Gauchat, Gabriel 90–2
  Lettres critiques 90
Gaultier, Jean Baptiste 92
  Les Lettres persannes, convaincues d'impiété 90
Gay, Peter 2, 3, 5
  Enlightenment, The 214
  Party of Humanity 1
Gee, Joshua 24
Genovesi, Antonio 4, 242
Gentleman's Magazine 141, 161, 168
Gentz, Friedrich von 294–5
Geography (Strabo) 246
Germany 26
Gibbon, Edward 29, 100, 315
  Decline and Fall of the Roman Empire, The 102, 128, 309
  Essay on the Study of Literature 129
Giovanni, Ignazio di 23, 26
Girodet, Anne Louis 322, 323
  Citizen Jean-Baptiste Belley, Ex-Representative of the Colonies 321
Gli elementi del commercio (Verri) 196
Glorious Revolution of 1689 50, 70, 130
Godwin, William 319
  Enquiry Concerning Political Justice 72
Goldgar, Anne 36
Goldoni, Carlo 163–4, 168
  Pamela nubile 163
Goodman, Dena 4
Gosse, Henri-Albert 23
Gosse, Jean 23

Gournay, Jacques Claude Marie Vincent de 193, 242
Gournay Circle 194–6
government
  nature and principle of 229–30
  types of 227, 238, 263
Graffigny, Françoise de 3, 10, 18, 33, 54
  Cénie 212
  Letters of a Peruvian Woman 4, 27, 91, *201*, 203–17, *213*, 301
  Peruvian Letters 56
  Reflections on the Formation and Distribution of Wealth 211
  Suite des lettres d'une Peruvienne (A Sequel to the Letters of a Peruvian Woman) 209
Grangé, Jean-Augustin 262
Gray, John 99, 100
Gray Library 12, 17, 18, 99–100, 121
Great Britain, *see* England
Great Depression 279
Great Northern War 104–5, 110, 116
Greenleaf, Thomas 248
Griffin, Richard 164
Grimm's *Correspondance Littéraire* 319
Grotius, Hugo 6, 32, 36, 52, 253
Gutenberg, Johannes
  printing press 10
Guy, Pierre 265, 266
Guy of Warwick 32

Habermas, Jürgen 10–11
  reading public, notion of 11
  Structural Transformation of the Public Sphere, The 10
Halifax
  Atticus 24
Hamilton, Alexander 197–9, 253, 292
  Farmer Refuted, The 198
Hardy, Simeon-Prosper 126
Harpur, Singleton 309
Hauterive, Alexandre 322
Haywood, Eliza 162
  Female Spectator 206
Hazard, Paul 1, 5, 214
Heavenly City of the Eighteenth-Century Philosophers, The (Becker) 1
Hédouin, Jean Baptiste Antoine
  Esprit et Génie de l'Abbé Raynal 315

Index

Helvétius, Claude Adrien 22, 40, 56, 60, 222, 289
   De l'Esprit 23, 33, 62, 261, 262, 267, 268, 317
   On the Mind 69
Henri IV 38
Henry, Patrick 252
Herodotus 20, 258
Hervey, Lord 137
Hill, Aaron 164, 165
Hill, T. F. 293
Hirsching, Friedrich Karl Gottlob 15
Hirschman, Albert 241
Histoire de la Maison de Montmorenci (Desormeaux) 21
Histoire du dom B..., portier des Chartreux 23
Histoire philosophique et politique du commerce des deux Indes (Raynal) 310
Historical and Critical Dictionary (Bayle) 104, 113
Historical View of the English Government (Millar) 287
History of America (Robertson) 24
History of Charles XII (Voltaire) 13, *97*, 99–**131**, 135
   "Anecdotes on Czar Peter the Great" 114–15, 119
   "Discourse on the History of Charles XII" 106–7, 113, 115, 118–19
   eighteenth-century editions of **99**
   "Letter to Nordberg, The" 116, 119
   "Letter to Schulenburg, The" 116–17
   "New Reflections on History" 118–19
   "Observations on History" 117–19
   "Pyrrhonism in History" 113–15, 119
   "Thoughts on Government" 115–17, 119
   "Usefulness of History, The" 119–20
History of England (Hume) 22, 24, 100, 102, 186, 192, 196
History of Pamela, Abridged 163
History of Peter the Great (Voltaire) 22
History of Sandford and Merton (Day) 274
History of the Two Indies (Raynal) 13, 15–17, 22, 24, 29, 36, 100, 212, 285, 294, *299*, 301–26, *321*, *324*
   1770 version 310–11
   1774 version 311–12
   1780 version 313–20, *317*
   eighteenth-century editions of **301**
   slavery and 320–6, *321–6*
   versions of **301**
History of Women (Alexander) 185
Hobbes, Thomas 6, 36, 37, 52, 82, 104, 225, 258
d'Holbach, Baron 20, 22, 77, 303
   Système de la nature 79
   System of Nature, The 94
Holberg, Ludwig 165
Holland
   Telemachus in 50
   War of the Spanish Succession (1701–14) and 50
Homer 46
   Iliad 44, 55
   Odyssey 44, 51
honor 104, 227, 230, 240, 241, 243
Horace 20
How to Create the Perfect Wife (Moore) 273
Huart & Moreau 223–4
Huart, Pierre 125, 126, 129
Huguenot, French 31, 94
human capital 307
Hume, David 14, 19, 28, 29, 36, 37, 54, 56, 58, 63, 146, 173, 174, 205, 269, 279, 287, 294, 315, 319
   death of 186, 189
   Dissertation on the Passions 19
   as economist on the continent 193–6
   Enquiry Concerning Human Understanding 192
   Enquiry Concerning the Principles of Morals, An 19, 170
   Essays, Moral, Political, and Literary 3, 17–18, 21, 24, 39, *177*, **179**, 179–200
   Essays and Treatises on Several Subjects 187, 192, 193
   essays in America 196–200
   feminism 184
   History of England 22, 24, 100, 102, 186, 192, 196
   "Idea of a Perfect Commonwealth" 197
   "Jealousy of Trade" 284
   Natural History of Religion 19
   "Of Essay Writing" 181–6
   "Of National Characters" 186–91, 196
   "Of Parties in General" 197
   "Of the First Principles of Government" 196, 197

"Of the Independence of Parliament"   197
"Of the Liberty of the Press"   185–6, 196
"Of the Populousness of Ancient
    Nations"   188, 200
"Of the Study of History"   184
"On the Independency of Parliament"   198
"Parties of Great Britain"   197
"Perfect Commonwealth"   197
Political Discourses   105, 191–7, 199, 242
"The Rise and Progress of the Arts and
    Sciences"   184
Treatise of Human Nature, A   39, 180, 181,
    223, 281
Hunt, Lynn   174, 175

"Idea of a Perfect Commonwealth"
    (Hume)   197
Il Caffè   13
Iliad (Homer)   44, 55
"Impartial Citizen, An"   253
imperialism   210
    European   205, 212, 302
    Roman   122
    Western   2
Imprimerie Royale   34, 289, 337 n.102
Index of Forbidden Works/Index of Forbidden
    Books/Index of Prohibited Books   94, 124,
    152, 168, 206, 235, 312
inequality   58, 210, 211, 240, 241, 249, 258,
    286
*Inquiry into the Nature and Causes of the Wealth
    of Nations* (Smith)   286
*Inquiry into the Nature and Origin of Public
    Wealth, An* (Lauderdale)   296
Intrigues Monastiques   23
Ireland book trade   27
Iselin, Isaak   343–4 n.103
Israel, Jonathan   4, 5, 78
Italy   26

Jackson, Ralph   62
Jacques, Jean   40
James, C. R. L.   325
    Black Jacobins, The   323
James, Elizabeth   45
Jansenism   84, 145, 233
Jardine, Alexander   285
Jaucourt, Louis de
    Religieuse   213

"Revolt"   61
"Jealousy of Trade" (Hume)   284
Jefferson, Thomas   244, 245, 290, 292, 314
Jerusalem (Mendelssohn)   9
Jöcher, Christian Gottlieb   111
Joersson, S. A.   294
Johns, Alissa   32
Jones, Colin   57
Jore, Claude François   102, 110, 144, 147
José I   77, 78
Josse, François   144
Josse, René   144
*Journal d'Agriculture, du commerce, et des
    finances*   195
Journal de commerce et d'agriculture   63
*Journal de l'agriculture, du commerce, des arts
    et des finances*   290
Journal encyclopédique   30, 61, 66, 68, 92, 191
Journal étranger   170
Journal of Commerce   242
Journey from St. Petersburg to Moscow, A
    (Radishchev)   315–16
Julian the Apostate   236, 238
Jullien, Marc Antoine   269
Jullien, Rosalie   269
Jussieu, Antoine-Laurent   303
Justi, Johann Heinrich Gottlob   242

Kames, Lord   274, 294
Kant, Immanuel   31, 191, 268–71, 294
    Enlightenment of individual *vs.* emergence of
        an enlightened public   11–12
    on reading public   12
Keir, James   273
Kenrick, Samuel   199, 200
Keynes, John Maynard
    *General Theory of Employment, Interest, and
        Money, The*   279
Kincaid, Alexander   186, 281
Kincaid, Andrew   181, 186, 189, 192
King Charles XII   38
King George III   185
kingship   53
King Stanislaus   106
labor theory of value   296, 297
La buona figliuola (Piccinni)   163
Laclos, Choderlos de
    Les Liaisons dangereuse   170
Lady Bute   166

435

Index

Lady Mary Wortley Montagu 10, 21, 139, 142, 146, 166, 175
Lady's Magazine, The 16, 65, 285
La Harpe, Jean François de 66
La Henriade (Voltaire) 57, 101, 114, 142, 144
Lamarche-Courmont, Ignace Hugary de
 Lettres d'Aza (Letters from Aza) 209–11
Lamartine, Alphonse de 43, 325
Lambert, Jean François de Saint 303
Lambert, Madame de 87
Lambert, Michel 115
La Mettrie, Julian Offray de 23, 90
L'Ami des hommes (*Friend of Mankind*)
 (Riqueti) 62, 242–3
Lamothe, Simon Antoine Delphin de 224
La Motraye, Aubry de 119
 Critical and Historical Remarks on the History of Charles XII 107–13, *109*
Landes, Joan 214
La Nouvelle Héloïse (Rousseau) 64, 258–62, 268
Lanson, Gustave 133–4, 214
La Porte, Joseph
 Observations sur la littérature moderne 207
La Pucelle (Voltaire) 23
La Roche, Jacques Fontaine de 233–6, 238
Lartigue, Jeanne de 85
Lauderdale 387 n.93
 Inquiry into the Nature and Origin of Public Wealth, An 296
 reflections on *The Wealth of Nations* 295–7
Laveaux, Etienne 325
Laws (Plato) 22
Leadhills Mining Society 18
Le Blanc, Jean Bernard 146, 195
Ledet, Etienne 109–13, 148, 149
Lee, Patrick 143
Lee, Richard Henry 253
Le Gallois, Pierre
 Traité des plus belles bibliothèques de l'Europe [Treatise on the Most Beautiful European Libraries] 15
Le génie de Montesquieu (Montesquieu) 224
Le Gras, Marie-Madeleine 55
Leibniz, Gottfried Willhelm 6, 37, 87, 140, 225
Leigh, Ralph 264

Leipzig Book Fair 12
Le Mondain (Voltaire) 58, 108
Les consolations de l'âme fidèle contre les frayeurs de la mort (Caux) 80
Les Lettres persannes, convaincues d'impiété (Gaultier) 90
Les Liaisons dangereuse (Laclos) 170
Les Nouvelles ecclésiastiques 233
L'Espion Turc (Marana) 84
Letter on Toleration (Locke) 38
 "Historical Introduction" 212
Letters Concerning the English Nation (Voltaire) 106, 142
 "Letter XIII On Mr Locke" 152
Letters Concerning the English Nation by Monsieur de Voltaire 144
Lettres entre deux amans (Letters Between Two Lovers) (Rousseau) 260
Letters from a Persian in England to His Friend at Ispahan (Lyttelton) 88
Letters of a Peruvian Woman (Graffigny) 4, 27, 91, *201*, 203–17, *213*, 301
 eighteenth-century editions of **203**
Letters on Slavery (Dickson) 320
Letter to d'Alembert on the Theatre (Rousseau) 259
Letter to the Abbé Raynal (Paine) 314
"Letter XIII On Mr Locke" (Voltaire) 152
Lettre philosophique de M. de V*** 150–2, *151*
Lettres critiques (Gauchat) 90
Lettres d'Aza (Letters from Aza) 209–11
Lettres écrites de Londres 150
Lettres historiques 83–4
Lettres philosophiques 150, 153
Le Vrai patriote hollandais 112
Life of Toussaint L'Ouverture, The (Beard) 323, *324*, 392 n.87
Life of Turgot (Condorcet) 211–12
Lilti, Antoine 39
L'Indiscret (Voltaire) 109
Linguet, Simon Henri 318–19
Lisbon earthquake of 1755 77
literacy, growth of 27–8
Literary Tour de France, A (Darnton) 3
Liverpool
 Liverpool Library Selection Committee 18
 subscription library 17
Lloyd's Evening Post 320

436

Lobo, Jerônimo Francisco 78
Locke, John 37–8, 45, 69, 141, 153, 251, 258
  Considerations on Lowering the Interest 296
  Essay 152
  Essay Concerning Human Understanding 38, 225, 244, 258, 360 n.69
  Letter on Toleration 38
  Second Treatise 161
  Some Thoughts on Education 24
  Two Treatises of Government 37, 38, 224, 225, 244
Lockwood, John 143
London Magazine 165
Long, Edward 190
Louis XIV 45, 46, 49–51, 53, 54, 58, 60, 61, 63, 66, 68, 69, 73, 80, 82–4, 101, 102, 130, 292
  absolutism 51
  Burgundy Circles reforms 51
  death of 82, 85
  Quietist Affair 51
  regency 51
  Revocation of the Edict of Nantes (1685) 23, 60, 79
  special advisory councils (Polysynody) 50
Louis XV 52, 57, 67, 80, 102, 148, 149
  death of 138
  regency 51, 54, 82
Louis XVI 288, 289, 291, 316, 318
Love, James
  "The Pantheon of Taste" 16
Lucas, Eliza 167
Lundberg, David 244
Lutz, Donald 244
Luxembourg, Mme de 265
luxury 58, 211, 213, 241
Luynes, Charles Honoré d'Albert de 50
Luzac, Elie 31
Lycian League 246, 251
Lyttelton, Baron George
  Letters from a Persian in England to His Friend at Ispahan 88

McDonald, Joan 264
McEachern, Jo-Ann 264–5
Machiavelli, Niccolò 6, 199
  Discourses on Livy 121
  Discourses on the First Ten Books of Livy 225
  Prince, The 52, 53, 57, 69, 225
Machuel, Robert 113–15
McMurran, Mary Helen 32
Madame Duron 7
Madison, James 197–9, 252, 253, 290
Magna Carta 136
Mairobert, Pidansat de 6
Maitland, James 295
Malboissière, Geneviève Randon de 20–2, 26
  "Of the Rise and Progress of the Arts and Sciences" 20
Malebranche, Nicolas 87
Malesherbes, Guillaume-Chrétien Lamoignon de 34, 115, 194, 212, 259–62, 266
Mandeville, Bernard 58, 63
  Enquiry into the Origin of Honour and the Usefulness of Christianity in War, An 103, 235
  Fable of the Bees 103–4, 235, 238
  Modest Defense of Publick Stews 23
  Private Vices Public Benefits 235
Marana, Jean Paul
  L'Espion Turc 84
Marianne (Voltaire) 109
Marivaux, Pierre de 84–5
Marmontel, Jean-François
  Belisarius 69
Marraro, Howard R.
  Memoirs of the Life and Peregrinations of the Florentine Philip Mazzei 1730–1816 390 n.45
Marteau, Pierre 86
Mary, Queen 138
Masegosa y Cancelada, María Romero 216
Mason, George 252
materialism 152, 272
Maurepas, Comte de 146, 148
Maury, Abbé 66
Mauvillon, Eléazar de 195, 196
Maxims of the Saints Explained (Fénelon) 46, 55, 60
May, Henry 244
MEDIATE: Understanding the Literary System of the 18th Century 329 n.19
meditation
  emotional 48
  solitary 48

Index

Mélanges de littérature et de philosophie (Literary and Philosophical Miscellanies) 149
Méliand, Adélaïde 20
Mémoires de Trévoux 233
Mémoires historiques et critiques 84
Memoirs of Great Britain and Ireland (Dalrymple) 289
Memoirs of the Life and Peregrinations of the Florentine Philip Mazzei 1730–1816 (Marraro) 390 n.45
Mendelssohn, Moses 9–11, 14, 24
  Jerusalem 9
Mercier, Louis Sebastien 68, 69
  Tableau de Paris 16
Mercure de France 29, 112, 148, 195, 257, 302
Mérian, Jean Bernard 190–1
Mérope (Voltaire) 118
Merton, Tommy 274
Millar, Andrew 186, 192
  Historical View of the English Government 287
Millar, John
  Inquiry into the Nature and Causes of the Wealth of Nations 286–7
  Observations on the Distinction of Ranks 18–19
Miller, Genevieve 139
Mirabeau, Honoré Gabriel 71
  death of 71
Mirabeau, Marquis de 56, 60, 62
  Théorie des impôts 23
Modest Defense of Publick Stews (Mandeville) 23
Moetjens, Adrian 44, *47*, 54
  Telemachus (1971 edition) 47–51, *47*
Moll Flanders (Defoe) 23
Monarchy 227, 238, 263
  female liberty in 232
  French 239
Moniteur 297, 325
Montaigne, Michel de 258
Montenoy, Charles Palissot de 93
Montesquieu 5, 18, 19, 23, 24, 27, 33, 39, 40, 54, 56, 60, 63, 64, 70, *71*, 157, 170, 181, 194, 200, 204, 205, 212, 258, 269, 292, 303, 305, 307
  A B C, The 130

  Considerations on the Causes of the Greatness of the Romans and Their Decline 37, *97*, 99–*131*, 225, **226**, 235, 236, 355 n.83
  death of 95, 126, 194, 224
  Defense of the Spirit of the Laws **226**, 240
  doux commerce 241, 257, 284, 308
  Le génie de Montesquieu 224
  "Our European Travellers" 134–5
  Persian Letters 4, 6, 22, 25–6, 29, 34–5, 37, 38, 56, 59, *75*, 77–95, **77**, *97*, 121–3, 125, 126, 130, 142, 204, 215, 221, 222, 225, **226**, 230, 232, 235, 236, 239, 240, 263
  Réflexions sur la monarchie universelle en Europe 38
  refusal to view Christianity as a religion 237
  Roman history 120–30
  Spirit of the Laws, The 3, 11, 17, 21, 24, 25, 27, 28, 31, 35, 36, 56, 59, 67, 68, 82, 89–95, 103, 122, 123, 126, 127, 129, 187, 188, 191, 193–5, *219*, 221–53, **226**, 275, 279, 282, 283, 285, 292, 296, 309, 313, 326, 376 n.65
  Temple de Gnide 225, **226**
  Thérèse Philosophe 6
  Troglodyte, parable of 59
Monthly Review 29, 191
Moore, Wendy
  How to Create the Perfect Wife 273
Morellet, Abbé André 32, 287–90
Morelly, Etienne Gabriel 22
Morlet, Claude 16
Morley, John 324
Mornet, Daniel 1, 3, 5
Mortier, Pierre 123
Mossy, Jean 33
Motteville, Madame de 118
Moureau, François 35
Municipal Library of Bordeaux 229
Mussard, Pierre 221, 222
mysticism 66
  Christian 48
  Quietist 48
  religious 49, 50

Napoleonic Code (1804) 214
Nassy, David 13

National Library of Madrid 216
Natural History (Buffon) 20, 21
Natural History (LeClerc) 289
Natural Son (Diderot) 20
Néaulme, Jean 265–7
Netherlands, the 26
New Hélöise (Rousseau) 23, 69, 170, 264, 265
  eighteenth-century editions of **257**
News of the Republic of Letters 44
Ngram, Google 39
Nicole, Pierre 234–5
Nisbit, Richard 190
Nivernais, Duc de 224
Nordberg, Jöran 111
North, Lord 292
North Briton, The 185
Northwest Europe
  literacy 27
Norway 27
Nourse, John 223, 239, 244
Nouvelle Heloïse (Rousseau) 94
Nouvelles de la République des Lettres (Bayle) 36, 38
Nova Scotia Gazette 14
Nugent, Thomas 31, 188, 244
Nun, The (Diderot) 171, 173

Observations on the Distinction of Ranks (Millar) 18–19
Observations sur la littérature moderne (La Porte) 207
Observations sur un livre intitulé: De l'Esprit des loix (Dupin) 229
Odyssey (Homer) 44, 51
Oedipus (Sophocles) 101
Oedipus (Voltaire) 38, 103, 109
Oeuvres (Voltaire) 112, 113, 115
Oeuvres de M de Voltaire 109, 150
"Of Commerce" 366 n.36
"Of Essay Writing" (Hume) 181–6
Office of the Book Trade 260
Office of the Vice President 252
"Of National Characters" (Hume) 186–91, 196
"Of Parties in General" (Hume) 197
"Of the First Principles of Government" (Hume) 196, 197
"Of the Independence of Parliament" (Hume) 197

"Of the Liberty of the Press" (Hume) 185–6, 196
"Of the Populousness of Ancient Nations" (Hume) 188, 200
"Of the Rise and Progress of the Arts and Sciences" (Malboissière) 20
"Of the Study of History" (Hume) 184
Old English Baron, The (Reeve) 168
On Crimes and Punishments (Beccaria) 32, 94, 287
"On the Independency of Parliament" (Hume) 198
On the Mind (Helvétius) 69
"On the Origin and Progress of a New Science" (Du Pont de Nemour) 243
"O Philosophy" (Séguier) 318
d'Orléans, Duc 45, 51, 82, 83
Osborn, J. 158, 159
Ottoman Empire 139, 140
"Our European Travellers" (Montesquieu) 134–5
Ouvrage sur les femmes (Works on Women) (Dupin) 228, 229
Oxford University Press 143
Ozell, John 87–8, 94

paganism 1, 237
Pagden, Anthony
  Enlightenment, The: And Why It Still Matters 1–2
Paine, Thomas
  Common Sense 314, 315
  Letter to the Abbé Raynal 314
Pamela (Richardson) 11, 91, *155*, 157–75, 179, 180, 215, 259
  eighteenth-century editions of **157**
  Pamela in Her Exalted Condition 163
  Pamela's Conduct in High Life 163
Pamela nubile (Goldoni) 163
Papal Bull 84
paratext 29, 52, 106–7, 115, 118, 120, 157, 195, 212, 215–16, 335 n.81
Parisian satire 79–89
"Parties of Great Britain" (Hume) 197
Party of Humanity 1
Pascal, Blaise 137, 145, 146, 234–5
  Pensées 145
patriarchalism 210
Peace of Aix-la-Chapelle 114

Peace of Westphalia   136
Pechméja, Jean Joseph   303
Pellet, Jean Léonard   313, 318
Pensées (Pascal)   145
Pensées sur l'interpretation de la nature (Diderot)   23
"Perfect Commonwealth" (Hume)   197
permission tacite   86, 102, 115, 122, 146, 152, 262, 263, 265, 288
Perrault, Charles   44
Persian Letters (Montesquieu)   4, 6, 22, 25–6, 29, 34–5, 37, 38, 56, 59, *75*, 77–95, *97*, 121–3, 125, 126, 130, 142, 203, 204, 215, 221, 222, 225, 230, 235, 236, 239, 240, 263
  eighteenth-century editions of   **77, 226**
  female liberty in monarchies   232
  suicide, decriminalizing   123
Peruvian Letters (Graffigny)   56
Petersburg Virginia Gazette   253
Peter the Great   101, 107
Pezay, Marquis of   67
Philadelphia Convention   246, 250, 252
Philosophical Dictionary (Voltaire)   12–13, 150
Philosophical Letters (Voltaire)   38, 105, 108–10, *131*, 133–53, 239, 287, 356 n.4
  eighteenth-century editions of   **133**
  false   150–3
  Letter 11   138, 139, 141, 142
  Letter 13   152
  Letter 24   144
  Letters 1–24   145
Philosophie de l'histoire   130
Phlipon, Manon   21–2, 26, 312
Physiocracy   62, 243, 288
Piccinni, Niccolò
  La buona figliuola   163
Pierre and Frederic Gosse   311
piracy   31–3, 291
Pitt, William   286
Plato   244, 258
  Laws   22
Pleasures of Conjugal Love Revealed   165
Plesse, Pierre Joseph   233
Pocock, J. G. A.   129, 217
Poland   27
Political Discourses (Hume)   105, 191–7, 199, 242
political economy   63

Politics (Aristotle)   376 n.65
Politics Drawn from the Very Words of Holy Scripture (Bossuet)   54
Pollard, Mary   27
Polysynody   51
Pombal, Marquis de   77–8
Pomeau, René
  D'Arouet à Voltaire   359 n.60
Pompadour, Madame de   208
Poniatowski, Stanislaw   110
Pope, Alexander   55, 90
Popple, William   38
Porteus, Beilby   320
Portugal   27
Portuguese Inquisition   77, 78
Powder Literary Society   18
Practical Education (Maria)   273–4
Prault, Laurent-François   111
Present State of the Republic of Letters, The   103–5
Prévost, Abbé Antoine François   208
Price, Richard   70
Priestley, Joseph   100, 294
Prince, The (Machiavelli)   53, 57, 69, 225
Principles of Natural and Political Right (Burlamaqui)   244
Principles of Natural and Politic Law, The (Burlamaqui)   21
Principles of Natural Law (Burlamaqui)   221, 224
Principles of Political Economy (Stewart)   244
Principles of Political Right (Burlamaqui)   224
printers   26–36
Private Vices Public Benefits (Mandeville)   235
Protestantism   128
Prussia   56
  literacy   28
Prussian Academy of Sciences   190
publishers   26–36
Pufendorf, Samuel von   6, 52, 82, 104, 225
Pugachev, Yemelyan   316

Quakers   135, 146
Queen Caroline   140
Quesnay, François   62
  "Tableau économique" (Economic Chart)   243
Quietism   46, 48, 50, 51, 54, 58, 61, 62, 73
Quietist Affair   51

Index

Radical Enlightenment   78, 79, 95
radical Jacobinism   18, 73
Radishchev, Alexander
  Journey from St. Petersburg to Moscow,
    A   315–16
Rahe, Paul   257
Ramsay, Andrew Michael   51, 59
Ramsay, David   15
  "Discourse on Epic Poetry"   52
  "Discourse on Epic Poetry and of the
    Excellence of the Poem of Telemachus,
    A"   51
  Telemachus (1717 "first edition")   51–6
Randolph, Edmund   253
Ranson, Jean   268, 269
Raynal, Abbé   5, 6, 18, 19, 27, 33, 40, 57, 60,
    244
  Histoire philosophique et politique du
    commerce des deux Indes   310
  History of the Two Indies   13, 15–17, 22, 24,
    29, 36, 100, 212, 285, 294, *299*, 301–26,
    301, *317*, *321*, *324*
Raynal, Guillaume Thomas   316, 320
"Readers Respond to Rousseau" (Darnton)   268
reading public   9–40
Real Sociedad Economica   19
Réaumur, René Antoine Ferchault de   34
Reeve, Clara   161
  Old English Baron, The   168
Reflections on the Formation and Distribution of
    Wealth (Graffigny)   211
Reflections on the Present Condition of the
    Female Sex (Wakefield)   294
Réflexions sur la monarchie universelle en
    Europe (Montesquieu)   38
Réflexions sur quelques parties d'un livre
    intitulé "De l'Esprit des loix" (Dupin)   229
Religieuse (Jaucourt)   213
religious liberty   80, 137
religious pluralism   136, 237, 293
Remarks on the Slave Trade   320
Remerciement sincère à un homme charitable
    (Sincere Gratitude to a Virtuous Man)
    (Voltaire)   236
representative republicanism   249
Republic of Letters   9, 13, 29, 36–9, 54, 90,
    180, 181, 184, 205, 207, 208, 211, 281, 302,
    312
republics   227, 230, 238, 240, 263

  ancient and modern form of   249
  confederate   251
Rétat, Pierre   149
Retz, Cardinal de   118
"Revolt" (Jaucourt)   61
Revolution of America, The   314
Rey, Marc Michel   29, 34, 64, 259–65, 267
Ricardo, David   16
Richardson, Samuel   3, 14, 18, 28, 212
  Aesop's Fables   158
  Clarissa   22, 23, 32, 56, 91, *157*, **157**,
    164–6, 168–71, 173, 208
  Letters Written to and for Particular Friends,
    on the Most Important Occasions   159
  Pamela   11, 91, *155*, 157–75, **157**, 179, 180,
    215, 259
  Sir Charles Grandison   91, **157**, 164, 165,
    168
Richelieu, Cardinal   60
Riddell, Robert   19
Ridpath, George   22–3, 26
Riley, Patrick   54
Riqueti, Honoré Gabriel, Comte de
  Mirabeau   270
Riqueti, Victor, Marquis de Mirabeau
  L'Ami des hommes (*Friend of*
    Mankind)   242–3
"Rise and Progress of the Arts and Sciences,
    The" (Hume)   184
Rivington, C.   158, 159
Robertson, John   194, 319
  claims of Enlightenment   4–5
  History of America   24
Robertson, William   29, 100, 315
  Roman Revolutions   20
Robin, Etienne-Vincent   262
Robinson, Anthony   286
Robinson Crusoe   21, 64
Roche, Daniel   2
Rocheret, Valentin Philippe Bertin de   105
Roederer, Pierre Louis   292
Roland, Manon   269–70
Rollin, Charles
  Ancient History   118
Roman Revolutions (Robertson)   20
Romilly, Samuel   320
Rose, Elizabeth, Lady of Kilravock   15
Rose, William   191–2
Rothelin, Abbé   152

441

Rothkrug, Lionel 49
Rousseau, Jean Jacques 5, 16–19, 22, 24, 27, 29, 33, 36, 39–40, 54, 56, 57, 60, 62, 69, 77, 228, 241, 289, 325
   antifeminism 232
   death of 262, 264
   Discourse on Inequality 210
   Discourse on Political Economy 313
   "Discourse on the Arts and Sciences" 28, 206
   Discourse on the Origins of Inequality 30, 34, 240–2, 259
   Emile 24–6, 30, 36, 64, 169, 212, 217, *255*, 257–75, **257**, 317
   La Nouvelle Héloïse 64, 258–62, 268
   Le Devin du Village [the Village Soothsayer] 258
   Letters entre deux amans (Letters Between Two Lovers) 260
   Letter to d'Alembert on the Theatre 259
   Lettres de deux amans, habitans d'une petite ville au pied des Alpes (Letters from Two Lovers, Living in a Small Town at the Foot of the Alps) 169
   New Hélöise 23, 69, 94, 170, **257**, 264, 265
   radical political theories 68
   Social Contract, The 3, 6, 25, 72, 169, **257**, 258, 259, 263–5, 267, 269
Rousseau, Pierre 31
Roustan, Antoine Jacques 64
Royal Commentaries of the Inca (Vega) 212
Rush, Benjamin 190
Russell, Ezekial 197
Russia 27

Sabbagh, Gabriel 288
Saint-Aignan, Duc de 50
St Augustine 234
Saint-Domingue 321, 322, 325, 326
Saint-Just, Louis Antoine 293
Saint-Rémy, Abbé de 48–51
Saint-Simon, Duc de 50
Sala-Molins, Louis 325
Salverda, Roberto 315
Sandford, Harry 274
Sandy, George 18
Sartine, Antoine de 34
Saurin, Bernard-Joseph 26

Schumpeter, Joseph 63
Scientific Revolution 89, 145
Scotland 30
   Acts of Union (1707) 283
   Enlightenment 196, 279
   literacy 27
Scots Magazine, The 28, 36
Secondat, Charles de, Baron de Montesquieu 85
Second World War 1, 296
Séguier, Anthony Louis 317–18
   "O Philosophy" 318
self-interest 145
self-liking 104
Seneca 258
Seran de la Tour, Abbé 128
Servan, Michel de 68
Settecento Riformatore (Venturi) 4
Seward, Anna 174
Sgard, Jean 149
Shackleton, Robert 87, 129, 236, 240
Shamela (Fielding) 165–6, 172, 215
Shank, J. B. 147
Sharp, Granville 190
Shelburne, Lord 292
Shelford, April 36
Sher, Richard 5, 102, 192, 282, 284
   Enlightenment and the Book, The 32
Sieyes, Abbé 292, 293
Silva, Antônio de Morais 77
Simmons, William J. 324
Simonin, Suzanne 171–3
Sir Charles Grandison (Richardson) 91, 164, 165, 168
   eighteenth-century editions of **157**
Skinner, Quentin 217
slavery, and *History of the Two Indies* 320–6, *321–6*
smallpox 138, 139, 141
Smellie, William 28
Smith, Adam 5, 6, 14, 15, 18, 19, 28–30, 35, 55, 173, 240
   death of 291
   labor theory of value 296, 297
   Theory of Moral Sentiments 22, 39, 170, 175, 282, 290, 294
   Wealth of Nations, The 3, 16, 24, 35, 36, 63, 196, *277*, 279–97, **279**, **284**
Smith, David 114

Social Contract, The (Rousseau) 3, 60, 72, 169, 258, 259, 263–5, 267, 269
  eighteenth-century editions of **257**
  "On Slavery" 25
Société typographique de Neuchâtel (StN) 3–4, 35, 56, 313
Some Thoughts on Education (Locke) 24
Sonenscher, Michael 241
Sophocles
  Oedipus 101
South-Carolina Gazette 196
Southern Europe
  literacy 27
sovereignty 30
Spain 27
Spanish Inquisition 206
special advisory councils 51
Spectator (Addison and Steele) 36–7, 181
Spinoza, Baruch 5, 37, 225, 236, 243
Spinozism 236
Spirit of the Laws, The (Montesquieu) 3, 11, 17, 21, 24, 25, 27, 28, 31, 35, 56, 59, 67–9, 82, 89–95, 103, 122, 123, 126, 127, 129, 187, 188, 191, 193–5, *219*, 221–53, 279–80, 282, 283, 285, 292, 296, 309, 313, 326, 376 n.65
  American reading 244–53, **247**, **248**
  Catholic Church's reading 232–40
  economist's reading 240–3
  eighteenth-century editions of **221**, **226**
Steele, Richard 39, 44
  Spectator 37, 181
Stevens, John 250
Stewart, Dugald 280
Stewart, James
  Principles of Political Economy 244
StN, *see* Société typographique de Neufchâtel
Stourzh, Gerald 198
Strabo
  Geography 246
Strahan, William 29, 281–3, **284**, 288, 290
Structural Transformation of the Public Sphere, The (Habermas) 10
Struensee, Johann Friedrich 185
Studies of Nature (Bernardin de Saint-Pierre) 69
subscription library 17–19
Suite des lettres d'une Peruvienne (A Sequel to the Letters of a Peruvian Woman) (Graffigny) 209

Suite du quatrième livre de "l'Odyssée" d'Homère, ou les Avantures de Télémaque, fils d'Ulysse (*Continuation of the Fourth Book of Homer's Odyssey, or, The Adventures of Telemachus, Son of Ulysses*) 44
Sweden 27
Swediauer, Franz 190
Swift, Jonathan 150
  Tale of the Tub 168
Switzerland 27
Syah, Malmud 304
Système de la nature (d'Holbach) 79, 94
System of Nature, The (d'Holbach) 94

Tableau de l'Europe 311
Tableau de Paris (Mercier) 16
Table de Chaulnes 51
Tale of the Tub (Swift) 168
Télémaque 60
Temple de Gnide (Montesquieu) 225, **226**
Tencin, Mme de 223
Tenth Federalist 197, 198
Théorie des impôts (Mirabeau) 23
Theory of Moral Sentiments (Smith) 22, 39, 170, 175, 281, 290, 294
Thérèse Philosophe 6
Thieriot, Nicholas Claude 144, 147
Third Republic 133, 134
Thirty Years War (1648) 79, 101
Thistlewood, Thomas 23–6
Thompson, Thomas 15, 287
Three Essays Never Before Published Which Completes the Former Edition
  "Of National Characters" 187
Tom Jones (Fielding) 111
Tournemine, René-Joseph de 87
Townshend, Thomas 292
Traité de pyrrhonisme de l'Eglise romaine 80
Traité des lois [Treatise on Law] (Domat) 233
Traité des plus belles bibliothèques de l'Europe [Treatise on the Most Beautiful European Libraries] (Le Gallois) 15
translation 32
Trapnell, William H. 153
Treatise of Human Nature, A (Hume) 39, 180, 181, 223, 281
Tribe, Keith 294
Troglodytes 88, 92
Tschamer, Vincenz Bernhard 105

Index

Turgot, Anne Robert Jacques 210, 288, 289, 292
Turkish Spy 134
Two Treatises of Government (Locke) 37, 38, 224, 225, 244

Universal History, from the Earliest Account of Time, Compiled from Original Writers, An 315
Universal Spectator 161
Urwin, Mary 312
US Constitution 198, 244, 246, 253
"Usefulness of History, The" (Voltaire) 119–20

Vandenhoeck, Abraham 32
Vandenhoeck, Anna 32
Van Zanden, Jan Luiten 26–7
Vasco, Giuseppe 312
Vaughan, Benjamin 50, 62, 344 n.105
Vega, Garcilaso de la
  Royal Commentaries of the Inca 212
Venturi, Franco 5, 328 n.17
  Settecento Riformatore 4
Vernet, Jacob 222
Verri, Pietro 13
  Gli elementi del commercio 196
Vesey, Elizabeth 13
Victor de Riqueti, Marquis de Mirabeau
  L'Ami des hommes 62
Vie voluptueuses des capuchi 23
Villelongue, Robert de 113
Vincennes, Chateau de 257
Virgil 46, 258
Virginia Gazette 196
virtue 23–5, 52–4, 57–8, 61, 66, 82, 94, 103–4, 117, 121–2, 130, 159–60, 165–7, 171–4, 199, 227, 230, 232, 234, 238–9, 259
Volney, Comte de 292
Voltaire 3, 5, 15–19, 23, 24, 26, 27, 33, 35–7, 39, 40, 54, 56–61, 63, 66, 67, 69, 70, *71*, 77, 85, 90, 93, 169, 170, 181, 186, 204, 212, 230, 263, 269, 301, 305, 310, 318, 360 n.70
  Age of Louis XIV, The 58, 61, 69, 105, 118, 120
  Anti-Machiavel 57
  anti-Semitism 13
  Brutus 101, 103, 109, 144
  Candide 22, 31, 56, 225
  death of 150

Dictionnaire philosophique 153
Elements of the Philosophy of Newton 108, 111
Essai sur les moeurs 105, 120, 302
History of Charles XII 13, *97*, 99–**131**, 135
History of Peter the Great 22
La Henriade 57, 101, 114, 142
La Pucelle 23
Le Mondain 58, 108
Letters Concerning an English Nation 142, 143, *143*
Letters Concerning the English Nation 106
"Letter XIII On Mr Locke" 152
L'Indiscret 109
Marianne 109
Mérope 118
Oedipus 38, 103, 109
Oeuvres 112, 113, 115
Philosophical Dictionary 12–13, 150
Philosophical Letters 38, 105, 108, 109, *131*, 133–53, 239, 287, 356 n.4
Remerciement sincère à un homme charitable (Sincere Gratitude to a Virtuous Man) 236
Works 111, 112
"XXVI *Lettre. Sur l'Ame*" (26th Letter On the Soul) 151
Zaïre 108
von der Schulenburg, Johann Matthias Reichsgraf 110, 116
von Fabrice, Baron Earnst Friedrich 113

Wakefield, Priscilla
  Reflections on the Present Condition of the Female Sex 294
Walpole, Horace 310
Walpole, Sir Robert 136, 199, 222–3
Walther, Georg Conrad 111–13
  "Letter to Marshal Schulenburg, General of the Venetians" 116
War of the Austrian Succession 221
War of the Spanish Succession (1701–14) 50, 58, 69
Washington, George 55
Watkins, Margaret 189
Watson, Robert 15
Wealth of Nations, The (Smith) 3, 16, 24, 36, 63, 196, *277*, 279–97

eighteenth-century editions of **279**, **284**
  in French 287–95
  Lauderdale's reflections 295–7
Wedgwood, Josiah 40
Weekly Miscellany 359 n.60
Whelan, Frederick G. 190
Whitbread, Samuel 286
White, Miss Hannah 15
Whole Duty of Man, The 62
Wilberforce, William 294
Wills, Garry 197
Wilson, James 250
Wisconsin Historical Society

Documentary History of the Ratification of the Constitution, The 246, **247**
Wodrow, James 199–200
Wollstonecraft, Mary 30, 73, 272
Wootton, David 280
Works (Voltaire) 111, 112
WorldCat 356 n.4
World Trade Organization 30

Xenophon 258
"XXVI *Lettre. Sur l'Ame*" (26th Letter On the Soul) (Voltaire) 151

Zaïre (Voltaire) 108

www.ingramcontent.com/pod-product-compliance
Lightning Source LLC
Chambersburg PA
CBHW051802230426
43672CB00012B/2604